# HITLER`S
## Bandit Hunters

**Related Titles from Potomac Books**

*The Forgotten Soldier*
By Guy Sajer

*Insurgency and Terrorism:*
*From Revolution to Apocalypse*, 2nd edition
By Bard O'Neill

*Hitler's Ambivalent Attaché:*
*Lt. Gen. Friedrich Von Boetticher in America, 1933–1941*
By Alfred M. Beck

*Tannenburg*
By Dennis Showalter

*Guderian: Panzer Pioneer or Myth Maker*
By Russell Hart

An AUSA Book

# HITLER`S
## Bandit Hunters

The SS and the Nazi Occupation of Europe

# Philip W. Blood

Potomac Books, Inc.
Washington, D.C.

C1

**Library of Congress Cataloging-in-Publication Data**
Copyright© 2006 by Potomac Books, Inc.

Blood, Philip W., 1957–
  Hitler's bandit hunters : the SS and the Nazi occupation of Europe / Philip W. Blood.—1st ed.
    p. cm.
  Includes bibliographical references and index.
  ISBN 1-59797-021-2 (alk. paper)
  1. World War, 1939–1945—Occupied territories. 2. World War, 1939–1945—Destruction and pillage—Europe. 3. Internal security—Europe—History—20th century. 4. Waffen-SS. I. Title.
  D802.A2B66 2006
  940.54'1343—dc22

                    2005032891

ISBN-10 1-59797-021-2
ISBN-13 978-1-59797-021-1


Printed in Canada on acid-free paper that meets the American National Standards Institute Z39-48 Standard.

Potomac Books, Inc.
22841 Quicksilver Drive
Dulles, Virginia 20166

First Edition

10 9 8 7 6 5 4 3 2 1

D
802.A2
B66
2006

*Geh nicht nach Norden, und hüte dich*
*Vor jenem König in Thule,*
*Hüt dich vor Gendarmen und Polizei,*
*Vor der ganzen historischen Schule.*

*Don't go North and beware*
*of the king in Thule,*
*Beware of gendarme and police*
*of the historic school.*

From the poem "Deutschland: Ein Wintermärchen"
by Heinrich Heine (1844)
in *Atta Troll: Ein Sommernachtstraum,*
*Deutschland: Ein Wintermärchen.*

# CONTENTS

# FOREWORD

This book does not make for comfortable reading. It is a meticulous examination of *Bandenbekämpfung,* a term that has much broader and more pervasive meaning than simply "antipartisan warfare" and that characterized the German approach to security in occupied areas during the Second World War. Philip Blood demonstrates that the concept predated this conflict and actually stretched into Germany's colonial past and its conduct in France in the Franco–Prussian War of 1870–71. Indeed, by its conception of "bandits" as microbes hostile to the very existence of the body politic, its roots go deeper, to the Thirty Years' War or even to the Roman Empire. But on September 16, 1941, a decree under Keitel's signature established Bandenbekämpfung as the strategic doctrine behind the Germanization of Europe. It affirmed that immediate and drastic action was imperative at the first sign of trouble, and the death penalty was to be used lavishly as a reprisal: this was how "great peoples restored order." The implementation of this doctrine was eventually to become the responsibility of an SS officer who occasionally changed his name but is best known as Erich von dem Bach-Zelewski. He had served as an infantry officer in the First World War and by 1942 was the higher SS and police leader in the region of Russia-Centre. In August 1942, he became inspector of Bandenbekämpfung for the entire eastern area and was speedily appointed "plenipotentiary" that autumn, representing Himmler in all relevant matters and providing a key link between the SS and the Wehrmacht. But, in a way so typical of the rival fiefdoms that characterized the Nazi state, there were numerous squabbles and overlaps, and Bach-Zelewski's appointment in mid-1943 as *Chef der Bandenkampfverbände*, responsible, as he put it "for all partisan reports for the whole of Europe," was intended to produce overall coherence.

Philip Blood describes *Bandenbekampfverbände* as "an exceptional form of information warfare and the driving force of an asset-stripping strategy that encompassed extermination and enslavement." The details of the process and the troops involved, including formations that combined SS Police with Waffen-SS units, a variety of non-German units, and even the Dirlewanger brigade recruited from criminals serving prison sentences, are carefully cataloged. For instance, in 1943, Operation "Nasses Dreiek" ("Wet Triangle") near Kiev, involved an ad hoc battle group supported by river police, a Luftwaffe signals regiment, pro-German Cossacks, and Hungarian supporting troops, with support from dive-bombers, which attacked a village "to cleanse it of enemies and return to its legal standing." Although 843 "bandits" were killed and another 205 summarily executed, only ten rifles were recovered. The operation's commander explained that this was because the bandits either buried their weapons or dropped them in swamps, but it is hard not to discern the wholesale brutality that characterized such operations. In another case, a Luftwaffe noncommissioned officer reported that "we had orders to kill all persons over five years of age." In contrast, Operation "Wehrwolf," which used Germans, Russians, Italians, Ukrainians, Poles, and Hungarians against a well-organized force under Major General Kovpak in 1943, saw substantial casualties on both sides.

Philip Blood uses abundant documentary and oral evidence to take us beyond the verdict of Christopher Browning's ground-breaking *Ordinary Men,* his study of Reserve Police Battalion 101 in Poland, by examining the policy and structure that enabled ordinary men to do such extraordinarily dreadful things. Both historians observe the phenomenon, which still gives us pause for thought: men capable of carrying out deeds that might make us doubt our common humanity were themselves subject to the whole gamut of human emotions. Finally, Dr. Blood concludes by warning us that the events that he describes may not simply be confined to history, for he suggests that in the post-September 11 world "the impulses to turn to Bandenbekämpfung still resonate."

RICHARD HOLMES
JANUARY 2006

# PREFACE

This book is the offspring of doctoral and post-doctoral research started in November 1997. Following a brief survey of literature and broad discussions with Professor Richard Holmes, I decided to focus my research on the Nazi implementation of Bandenbekämpfung—"the combating of bandits"—in the period 1942–45. In keeping with most students, I raised a suitably vague and general question to get the process under way: Why did the Nazis discard the term "antipartisan warfare" (*Partisanenbekämpfung*) and adopt Bandenbekämpfung, if the words meant the same thing? The original plan called for a typical analysis of the origins, formulation, and implementation of Bandenbekämpfung. I thought this analysis might extend the existing historiography by only a small step, but all the same, it would fulfil the requirements of a doctorate. In the immortal words of Robert Burns, "the best-laid plans of mice and men often go awry," and so they proved. Early in the research process, it was apparent that Bandenbekämpfung was a highly complex subject. It was not a simple case of antipartisan warfare dressed up in Nazified language but rather a completely different approach to the administration of security, opening up a new perspective on Nazism. Instead of pinpointing the origins of Bandenbekämpfung in the recent past, it appears that generations of German soldiers acquired their blueprints from antiquity. The formulation of Bandenbekämpfung into an operational concept was complex with several stages of development. It was no surprise, therefore, when the implementation was neither confined to a single theater of operations nor directed toward one enemy. Right up until the very end, the character and shape of Bandenbekämpfung proved very illusive, and the subject is far from being closed with this book.

Nazi Bandenbekämpfung was not Partisanenbekämpfung as it is so often assumed. After the war, it was convenient for allied war crimes prosecutors to adopt simple translations in the proceedings. The German defendants trying to avoid responsibility for war crimes preferred sweeping translations. Thus Bandenbekämpfung was officially treated as Partisanenbekämpfung. The first impression one should take from this is that words, translations, and interpretations play a significant part in history. Many German words do not translate well into English or lose their power when translated; Bandenbekämpfung is one such example. It was derived from two words: *Banden*, which means criminal bands(s) or gang(s), and *Bekämpfung*, to combat or to fight. The members of such bands or gangs are called bandits (*Banditen*) or gangsters, and collectively they conducted banditry or gangsterism. In effect the compound form of *Banden* and *Bekämpfung* meant combating banditry or gangsterism to its absolute eradication or extermination. The subtlety of this wordplay lies in its influence on the interpretation of legality and illegality in combatant classification. The tradition of the partisan, under German military law and in the general professionalization of warfare, was a legally recognized combatant function. The bandit or gangster has always been treated as an outcast and a criminal. Therefore, the implementation of Bandenbekämpfung was first concerned with the reclassification of certain enemy combatants and second, with their extermination.

Nazification was the final stage of a long process of militarization of Bandenbekämpfung. During and after the Thirty Years' War, Bandenbekämpfung was practiced to eradicate roaming bands and organized by local communities. Prior to the Napoleonic age, Bandenbekämpfung was a purely civilian law and order issue. The first cases of the modern militarized form of Bandenbekämpfung, adopting small unit tactics to restore order, was introduced by the French gendarmerie during the occupation of the Rhineland, in the effort to combat banditry. German states adopted Bandenbekämpfung methods as a matter of course, especially in 1848 to counter revolution. During the Franco–Prussian War (1870–71), German troops resorted to Bandenbekämpfung as a means to eradicate French resistance (the *francs-tireurs*) but mostly to combat random acts of French armed civil disobedience against the occupation. During this campaign, the German army began the process of institutionalizing and internalizing a broad security apparatus. The Etappen, originally concerned with rear-area support functions in the Prussian army, was transformed after 1872. The purpose of this security establishment was to support the army at the front while securing its rear. Between 1871 and 1919, with a burgeoning security establishment, the German army collected together practices that can be loosely termed security warfare (refer to chapter 1). Operationally, this form of warfare embraced colonization, occupation, pacification, and intervention, of which Bandenbekämpfung was one facet.

# Race, Space, and War

All said and done, Bandenbekämpfung was only a tool of the state. The reason it was adopted and adapted by the state is an altogether different issue. The race for space and space for race, purified by a perpetual state of war—these fundamental abstractions represented Hitler's ideological trinity, from which he never wavered. For public consumption, he dressed them up with political slogans for a greater German empire, the purity of the Aryan race, and short wars of revenge and retribution. Hitler's ambition was to bequeath German "living space" (*Lebensraum*), a concept not conjured up by him and incorrectly assumed to mean only the acquisition of territory. Hitler's Lebensraum was about German existence, in its broadest meaning, in a Germanic world. There had been other versions. Woodruff Smith argued that Lebensraum was a product of nineteenth-century agrarian-based anti-industrialism.[1] During World War I, according to Fritz Fischer, Lebensraum came to shape Germany's long-term occupation ambitions.[2] After 1918, Germany's grand exponent of Lebensraum, Karl Haushofer, a retired army general and professor at Munich University, was a prolific scholar who advocated the science of space (*Raumwissenschaft*) or geo-political studies.[3] Ian Kershaw thought Hitler met Haushofer, through Rudolf Hess, before 1922.[4] Whatever the circumstances, by the time *Mein Kampf* was published, Hitler's spatial politics were cast in stone along with his racism. Hitler wrote, "When we speak of new territory in Europe today we must principally think of Russia and the Border States subject to her." His scheme was not confined to land; Hitler's expansion envisaged racial cleansing. He synthesized his idea for space in the East with a parody of Karl Marx's "Jewish question" prophesying, "The end of the Jewish domination in Russia will also be the end of Russia as a state." From the outset, Hitler's grandiose ambitions demanded a foundation of destruction. His vision became Germany's fate: "We are chosen by Destiny to be the witnesses of a catastrophe which will afford the strongest confirmation of the nationalist theory of race."[5]

Bandenbekämpfung, in the context of race, space, and war, had a longer pedigree than Lebensraum. By the time Hitler's protégé, Heinrich Himmler, proposed it, it had undergone numerous makeovers. Before World War II, the history of banditry in Germany was presumed to have been the residue of the apocalyptic Thirty Years' War. Bandits in bands, deserters and stragglers from the war, ravaged German towns and countryside.[6] The paranoia of that time still resonates deep within the German consciousness today. According to Uwe Danker, it was in the interests of the state and church to depict banditry as a threat to society. The church and state complex denounced criminal banditry as the vile act of immoral and ungodly men and outlawed bandits as robbers and murderers.[7] From the outset of state-sponsored education, banditry was portrayed as the antithesis of an ordered society of lawfulness. Criminal banditry, however, was not the only form of banditry rooted in the consciousness of pre-1939 German society. Political banditry, defined in antiquity as an early form of terrorism or guerrilla warfare, was passed down through the Bible and ancient texts. Banditry or brigandage was as an endemic problem for ancient Rome. Classically educated Germans were tutored against the evils of political banditry and its social consequences. For generations of Germans, Bandenbekämpfung came to mean the restoration of law and order. Himmler was not, therefore, the first to exploit security for political ends.

In the latter half of the nineteenth century, Friedrich Nietzsche warned Prussia against the manipulation of history and the emulation of the past. His words proved prophetic. The distortion of history played its part in German security culture. When Victor Klemperer accused Hitler's "Jewish war" of lacking any familiarity with Flavius Josephus's book, he overlooked the classically educated Himmler.[8] Gebhardt Himmler, Heinrich's father, was a classical scholar and court teacher.[9] He read excerpts of Josephus's classical text to young Himmler, and there is every reason to believe this subject was discussed in the Himmler home, especially once the new translation by Dr. Heinrich Clementz was published in 1900.[10] In the "Jewish war" of antiquity, Roman soldiers "admired the nobility" of the mass suicide of Jews at Masada. By stark contrast, in Hitler's Jewish war, the SS showed only contempt and loathing for its Jewish victims. Hitler drew parallels with ancient Rome in his table talk. He once explained to Himmler that Rome paid for its mastery in blood and the employment of mercenaries.[11] Martin Van Creveld noted that underpinning the Roman system was the principle of *lex talionis*, making the punishment fit the crime, a law for retaliation. The Romans exploited the law to suit their purposes.[12] The Germans, in the name of Roman law, did much the same, and Himmler applied a form of lex talionis through so-called revenge actions (*Vergeltungs-massnahmen*). Himmler understood the meaning of Josephus and the dire implications for Germany if Hitler's war against the Jews failed. After the war, in a state of utter collapse, one leading Nazi reflected in his Nuremberg cell that the collapse of Germany was synonymous with the fall of Carthage. In 1945, he was presumably alluding to the surrounding piles of rubble.[13] These classical influences were instrumental in shaping the character of Bandenbekämpfung.

Gradually, the militarization of Bandenbekämpfung branched off into the dimension of political-security. The Etappen was expected to improve rear-area functions, but in doing so, it became an occupation administration, a security establishment, and a network for colonization. In 1872, the first colonies administered by the Etappen were Alsace and Lorraine. Germany's brief but violent soirée with colonialism saw the adaptation of Bandenbekämpfung to colonial warfare through the Etappen. Germany used colonial conflict as a dress rehearsal for European war. In the process, Bandenbekämpfung became an extension of offensive operations as Germany perfected its security warfare concept. This kind of warfare percolated colonial policing, military tactics, and economic warfare. By 1912, security measures had internalized the practice of enslavement and extermination of occupied populations. During World War I, Bandenbekämpfung was further adapted to compensate for the various security demands of different theaters of war. By 1918, Bandenbekämpfung entered the German military lexicon alongside "small war" (*kleine Krieg*), "partisan warfare" (*Partisanenkrieg*), "irregular warfare" (*Freischärlerkampf*), and "people's war" (*Volkskrieg*). This transformation of Bandenbekämpfung can be traced by comparing the 1908 and the 1929 editions of Brockhaus.[14] Thus, by 1930, Bandenbekämpfung was already a powerful political weapon.

The struggle between Bandenbekämpfung and Partisanenbekämpfung began long before the Nazis. Before the 1880s, a long-cherished doctine of the professional soldier was the practice of Napoleonic-style small war. This was fundamentally Partisanenbekämpfung and gradually lost ground in the concentrated drive to build a machinelike conscript army led by an autonomous elitist officer corps. By 1900, the Imperial German Army had one measure that was the catchall for all circumstances, known as the *Cannae* principle. The Germans took Hannibal's victory over the Roman army as the blueprint for their strategic, operational, and tactical war making. The colonial wars from 1900 to 1912 saw the demise of kleine Krieg in favor of the universal practice of Cannae for all operations. In German military terminology, therefore, the last vestiges of Partisanenbekämpfung were subsumed into security warfare before the Battle of the Waterberg (1904). All subsequent military security operations were waged as a desperate struggle against banditry. In 1919, the German army waged unrestricted Bandenbekämpfung in German streets against German communists, thereby removing any pretense at combating criminal banditry.

In a world that placed great store on the classification of opponents, Bandenbekämpfung had significant ideological clout. In 1941, the German army adopted Partisanenbekämpfung to regulate the cold-blooded killing of guerrillas, Red Army commissars, Jews, and stragglers. The army treated Soviet prisoners of war in the same manner as Herero tribesmen had thirty-six years before. Terror as a deterrent failed, and in Hitler's mind, Partisanenbekämpfung fudged the issue; Hitler demanded the treatment of the Soviet Union as a "Jewish-Bolshevik bandit state" and a doctrine to see it through. He passed the job to Himmler. Once in command, Himmler immediately adopted Bandenbekämpfung. In his crusade against Bolshevism, he encouraged the scourge of banditry to biblical proportions and treated captives and innocents alike in ways more in keeping with the Romans. Under Himmler's leadership, Bandenbekämpfung reengineered security warfare to enhance the SS leadership in its attempts to install Lebensraum. Typically, political justification for this policy was attributed to the racial and political banditry of Hitler's opponents. Hitler declared all Soviet and Yugoslavian partisans "Jewish-

Bolshevik bandits." Not content with denigrating the East, he labeled all Anglo-American Special Forces gangsters and denigrated Winston Churchill as the gangster-godfather of liberal democracy. Criminalizing all resistors placed captives outside the minimal protection of the existing laws of war. The disposition of German retribution catapulted the world into an abyss of horror and despair that has never really gone away. By 1944, Bandenbekämpfung doctrine was not only applied on all fronts but also represented a Nazi response to the laws and customs of war.

## Conventions and Structure

Please note that there is a bibliographical review at the end of this book that refers to some of the literature on this topic. In case readers have read or intend to read my PhD thesis, it is necessary to offer some explanation regarding its differences with this book.[15] The overall Luftwaffe content is reduced and the security battalion case study removed in preparation for another book. The large content on the German army has been greatly reduced. The chapter and content associated with Kurt Daluege, the chief of the German uniformed police, was removed and published as a chapter of a book on European policing.[16] Replacing this content is a greater focus on Himmler and his lieutenants, in particular Erich von dem Bach-Zelewski. The chapters on Poland and Western Europe are post-doctoral extensions of the original research. The aim here has been to create an in-depth study of Bandenbekämpfung from its origins to its domination by the SS.

The research for this book was concerned with upholding the accepted conventions of terms and phraseology. This was not straightforward. If this had been a study of social banditry, there would be little problem in using the word "bandit." However, this book falls within the parameters of research into the Third Reich and Nazi genocide. The Nazis ensured that "bandit" was at the receiving end of virulent politicization. Since the war, scholars have generally adopted the stance that all "bandits" were partisans, primarily because they fought to resist and destroy Nazism. To delve into the conundrum of whether all "bandits" were partisans or all partisans bandits somewhat panders to Nazi rhetoric. To answer the question what is or was a partisan further complicates matters. The literal definition of the partisan is a soldier fighting on the flank or adjunct of the main army, dressed in uniform, serving under a military code, and operating under superior orders. Not all partisans could meet this definition, while many bandits were the personification of military bearing. What then of the terrorist, brigand, guerrilla, resistor, social bandit, *Freikorps*, freedom fighter, spy, or scout, who do not necessarily fit into this discussion?, it might be asked. Argument inevitably turns on the eye of the beholder: one man's terrorist is another's freedom fighter. The problem here is that the Nazis also randomly categorized innocent civilians as bandits or Jews, usually to kill them. There has to be some latitude, albeit cautious, in the use of words without breaching political etiquette. The solution adopted here places a word with Nazi connotations within quotes or leaves it in the German original, for example "bandit" or Banden. Henceforth, through these forms readers are alerted to the contextual usage of words.

Another sensitive issue among scholars concerns the use of SS ranks and titles. Readers might be surprised to find that German titles, especially those of the SS, are kept in their original form, whereas the German armed forces are cited in their English equivalent. There is a practical reason for this. From the standpoint of order, with so many different rank titles across a plethora of organizations, it seemed important to distinguish the SS. The SS organization was judged criminal in 1946, but since then, scholars have tended to refer to them as "SS-Generals," "SS-Colonels," or "SS-Majors." This has aided the social rehabilitation of former SS men; for example, the gravestones of former senior SS officers have "General a.d." (general officer in retirement) engraved beneath their name. This suggests they had been a general officer in life. Yet the SS ranks were purely political and symbolic of the faith the Nazis had in the "leadership principle" (*Führerprinzip*). The translation into "group-leader" or "storm-leader," so brazenly political (rank equivalencies are in tabulated form in appendix 2), has no military comparison with a general or a major.

During the war, the SS adopted the term Waffen-SS, denoting armed-SS, and by 1944, most SS personnel came under this branch of the service. The SS hierarchy hoped that by adopting the Waffen-SS ranks they could circumvent the onset of allied war crimes. Some authors have unwisely assumed that this differentiated the SS between soldiers with a purely military role and the political soldiers. In the same remit, across all the years of research, no examples were found of SS officers refusing to participate in crimes. Likewise, no evidence was found of a refusal to carry out criminal orders, or for that matter expressing the wish to care for the helpless. The SS officers discussed here did not decline medals or baubles for mass slaughter. In fact they embellished their performance in security reports for material rewards. When the war was over and members of the SS faced judgment, this odious group of men proved both dishonest and cowardly in the denial of their deeds. This book, therefore, does not rehabilitate criminals and sets out to place the SS ranks and recipients within their criminal structures.

This book is divided into three parts. Part 1 traces the origins and development of Bandenbekämpfung in terms of security warfare. The purpose behind this first section is to explain how a minor function turned into a dominating policy. Part 2 examines Nazi Bandenbekämpfung in detail, principally from the viewpoint of the Soviet Union, focusing on organization, doctrine, terrain control, and operations. Examining Bandenbekämpfung by its salient points exposes the flaws in its doctrinal formulation while explaining its apparent high performance. Part 3 examines its climactic decline. The application of

Bandenbekämpfung in Poland, Yugoslavia, Italy, and France highlights how far the practice became the universal doctrine of German occupation. The contrast between the demands of the conventional military equation of troops, terrain, and tactics set against the flexibility and simplicity of Banden-bekämpfung made its application universal. In the final chapter, attention turns to the war crimes process, explaining the problem of eradicating such an insidious concept as Bandenbekämpfung and the origins of denial common to revisionist circles.

# ACKNOWLEDGMENTS

This book was completed in several phases and across many years. The only constant has been the generosity of people. Professor Richard Holmes, PhD supervisor, mentor, and friend, shaped the first phase of the project. His team—Professor Chris Bellamy, Peter Caddick-Adams, Steph Muir, and his wife, Lizzie Holmes—have encouraged and supported me through the research, the examination, and beyond. This phase concluded with the viva conducted by Keith Simpson, member of Parliament and erstwhile scholar of German counterinsurgency methods. The germ of the idea for this book came from discussions with members of the Polish Liberation Institute in London. Dr. Jürgen Zimmerer introduced me to the fundamentals of German colonial history and its influence in shaping security thinking. In 1998, I was fortunate to discuss the question of training with the late Professor Wilhem Deist; he advised scrutinizing the training methods of the SS and Wehrmacht. During the brief existence of the Anglo-German study group, in London 1997–98, I struck up what has proved to be a long-lasting friendship with Dr. Bernd Lemke, a military historian at the MGFA. Immeasurable help and advice has come from Professor Stig Förster, Dr. Jan-Bart Gewalt, Professor Brian Bond, and Professor M. R. D. Foot, Dr. Gerhard Wiechmann, and Emeritus Professor Martin Edmonds.

Archivists I have since discovered to my cost come and go, but a precious few ensured that the research went relatively smoothly. Stephen Walton of the Imperial War Museum advised me on the German sources very early on. Herr Dilgard the former director of Bundesarchiv Zentralnachweisstelle in Aachen-Kornelimünster, his deputy Herr Meentz, and Herr Genter, responsible for handling the Wehrmacht personnel files, worked hard to ensure my visits were successful. A particular thanks should go to the unsung heroines of the military archive in Freiburg, Frau Noske and Frau Weibl. Niels Cordes, his wife, Virginia, "Sunshine," and "Lucky" deserve a special mention for opening their home to me during a particularly difficult period of transition. During my visits to the National Archives at Columbia Park, Niels; Robin Cookson, an archivist; and Jim Kelling, responsible for the microfilm room, offered regular advice that improved my research. The librarians of the Rheinisch-Westfälische Technische Hochschule (RWTH-Aachen) deserve thanks for locating works through the German academic library service.

I would like to thank the following for allowing me to present my research: the Weiner Library for a work-in-progress paper; the interdisciplinary seminar of the RWTH-Aachen, German security methods (2000); the Institute of Historical Research (University of London), hosting the 2000 Anglo-American *War and Peace* conference, a paper on Bandenbekämpfung; the Florida Conference of Historians (2003); and the Open University for a paper and subsequent publication as a chapter on policing. I should like to mention my former colleagues, Professor Paul Thomes, Christoph Rass, Marc Engels, and students from the Institute of Economic and Social History at the RWTH-Aachen, who endeavored to help me settle into German society while I was completing my PhD. I have profound gratitude for Dr. Roy Douglas, Surrey University History circle, for his patience and encouragement in the early days. I would also like to mention Stefan Pehker and Toshiba International for their technical support and generosity over recent years.

The future beckons and some special people have helped bring about the completion of this book. Bettina Wunderling gave expert advice on translations, grammar, and vocabulary. Lt. Col. Roger Cirillo (retired) of the Association of the U.S. Army has become a dear friend and colleague. His confidence in this project eased the transfer from thesis to book and his sponsorship for the forthcoming *Wehrmacht at War* series. Rick Russell and the team at Potomac Books have enabled the smooth transfer of my thesis into book form. Special thanks are deserved for Dr. Nick Terry, a close friend and the technical adviser of both the PhD thesis and this book. His research will change our opinion of German arms. Dr. Declan O'Reilly has regularly advised and confided his thoughts on my work with his scholarly criticism.

Finally, I wish to mention my family and friends. My parents, Pamela and Peter Blood, who have always encouraged and supported me. My extended family include Manny, Maria, Ricky, and Lenny, Mike and Chris Buckley, Gary Ward and Christina, Ian and Alison, sadly now departed, Ron and Mitzi Orner, Tim and Manass Wells, and, my godchildren, Charlie, James, and Emma.

# BIBLIOGRAPHIC ABBREVIATIONS

There is a full glossary of relevant German and Bandenbekämpfung terms in appendix 1.

**BA:** Bundesarchiv, Berlin (Lichterfelde).

**BA-K:** Bundesarchiv (Koblenz).

**BA-MA:** Bundesarchiv Militärarchiv (Freiburg).

**BA-ZNS:** Bundesarchiv-Zentralnachweisstelle (Aachen).

**BDC:** Berlin Document Centre, collection of pre-war crimes trial files.

**BZ-IMT:** refers to NARA, RG238, T1270-1, Bach-Zelewski interrogations for the IMT.

**BZ-USMT:** refers to NARA, RG238, M1019-4, Bach-Zelewski interrogations on behalf of USMT.

**CMH:** Center for Military History, U.S. Army (Pennsylvania).

**DDKH:** Der Dienstkalender Heinrich Himmlers 1941/42, Forschungsstelle für Zeitgeschichte in Hamburg (Hamburg, 1999). Heinrich Himmler's appointments diary.

**DDst:** Deutsche Dienststelle (Berlin), muster rolls for the Wehrmacht and SS.

**FMS:** U.S. Army Historical Branch, Foreign Military Studies (German army).

**IMT:** International Military Tribunal, Nuremberg, documents and evidence, 1945–1946.

**IWM:** Imperial War Museum (London).

**JNSV:** Justiz und NS-Verbrechen, German Trial Judgements (1945–99), found at http://www1.jur.uva.nl

**NARA:** National Archive, Washington D.C., College Park Annex.

**NCA:**      Nazi Conspiracy and Aggression, vols. 1–8, Supps. A and B. Office of U.S. Chief of Counsel for Prosecution of Axis Criminality, Government Printing Office (Washington 1946–48).

**PRO:**      Public Record Office, London (National Archives), series designations—HW, HS, WO and FO.

**RUSI:**      Royal United Services Institute (London).

***Table Talk:*** a record of Hitler's comments published as Hugh Trevor-Roper, intro., *Hitler's Table Talk, 1941–1944: His Private Conversations* (London: Phoenix, 1953).

**TVDB:**      BA R20/45b war diary of SS-*Obergruppenführer* Erich von dem Bach-Zelewski.

**USHMM:**      U.S. Holocaust Memorial and Museum.

**USMT:**      U.S. military tribunals (1946–49), cases 1–12, cited as follows:

     **USMT-11:**    USA vs. Ernst von Weiszäcker et al., known as the Ministries case 11.

     **USMT-12:**    USA vs. Wilhem Leeb et al., High Command case 12.

     **USMT-4:**    USA vs Oswald Pohl (SS-WVHA), known as the Pohl case 4;

     **USMT-7:**    USA vs. Wilhelm List et al., known as the Hostages case 7;

     **USMT-9:**    USA vs. Otto Ohlendorf et al., known as the Einsatzgruppen case 9.

**Wiener:**      Wiener Library and archives (London).

# PART ONE

## ORIGINS AND IMPLEMENTATION

# 1
# SECURITY WARFARE

**M**ilitary politics troubled the world in 1919. Military interventions, from Ireland to India, stretched British security capabilities. The U.S. armed forces were involved in "sphere of influence" actions in Panama, Honduras, Haiti, and the Dominican Republic. The *Entente Cordiale* had seen fit to intervene in Russia, as their former ally descended into revolution and civil war; allied troops were still there in 1919. Together with France and Belgium, Britain and America deployed occupation troops in the Rhineland, the symbol of Germany's military-industrial complex. In April 1919, two events occurred that have cast a long, dark shadow over the history of civil-military relations. At Amritsar, in India, British troops massacred nearly four hundred men, women, and children; a further fifteen hundred were injured. In Munich, troops from the former Imperial Army and Freikorps encircled the city on April 27. Their mission, sanctioned by the Weimar government, was to eradicate the Munich Soviet republic (*Räterepublik*); cleansing the city of left-wing "dirt and filth" was completed by May 1, 1919. Amritsar contributed to the end of British rule in India. Munich was an object lesson in German military security capabilities. From the perspective of this book, Munich proved to be the more profound event. German soldiers had the opportunity to carry out their long desired and planned-for intervention into German politics, set aside in 1914. The application of full-scale professional violence against civilians and poorly trained militia failed to disturb a world reeling from the consequences of total war. Munich was the culmination of trials and errors in German military security methods, percolating down since 1814, and was evidence that the army had perfected its capacity for police actions.

Between the occupation of the Rhineland by Prussia in 1814 and by the allied powers in 1919, Germany developed extraordinary military capability, which has been attributed to rapid industrialization, extension of bureaucracy into military organization, and the rise of a professional army. With these developments, Munich marked a watershed in military culture that has largely gone unnoticed, occurring when it did as the army was reduced in size and authority. Weimar placed security on the political agenda and looked to a professional police force as a cure-all. Long before Munich, the army was the "pillar" of the German nation, and national security the remit of the Great General Staff of the Imperial Army. A doctrine of military security had developed from theories of war and military establishment. The origins of all modern military security began with the bureaucratization of baggage trains as permanent corps of security and supply, new formations added to the army's traditional order of battle. The very emphasis of security changed from a dull backwater duty into an essential component of the offensive. Victory and occupation forced the army into contending with military government and policing. A tide of security expertise washed through the army officer corps and transformed it into a fully fledged operational responsibility with the potential to become a generalissimo. This flowering of the security concept within the realm of German military science, however, was not the corollary of a specific school of security, but only the residue from an army deliberately expending considerable state resources on studying, planning, and preparing for aggressive war. Consequently, Germany scaled the heights of Harold Lasswell's "garrison-state and security determined by the specialists of violence."[1]

Munich had been on the receiving end of a security action then known as Bandenbekämpfung. The operation was praised in right-wing and military circles as a resounding political and military success. Operationally, Munich demonstrated that professional soldiers and militia volunteers could work together toward a common mission irrespective of different service backgrounds. Munich proved that ad hoc and scratch units with a minimum of training could be turned into effective combat groups under firm and determined leadership. This presented commanders in the field with greater flexibility in preparing a concerted plan of action, while using resourceful officers to bring these groups into the combat area, with minimal confusion. Approaching the target area from the north, south, east, and west, the combat groups had successfully brought about the complete encirclement of the city. They then systematically exterminated "the enemy," on that occasion, communists. This lesson had a profound effect on German security culture.

## Doctrine

Armed intervention had long been a feature of German political history, the most noteworthy examples being von Schill and the attempted storm of Westphalia (1807); the Freikorps and the Landwehr, raised to ward off French retribution at Prussian defection in Russia (1813); and the pacification of the 1848 revolution.[2] In 1912, the Great General Staff carried out a feasibility study into the possibility of intervention in towns threatened by armed insurgents.[3] The demands made by the army on society for men and resources were, according to Alfred Vagts, inexorably leading toward revolution.[4] The Zabern incident of 1913 was an indication of the attitudes that prevailed between the army and society. A lieutenant insulted the people of Alsace; this triggered public outrage. The commanding officer stood by the lieutenant as a matter of honor, declared martial law, and arrested civilians who jeered the army.[5] European war in 1914 dampened the friction between the army and society.[6]

From 1815, the study of warfare flourished, especially among the armies of Europe. Antoine-Henri Jomini took Napoleon's legacy and rooted it into the texts of military science.[7] Jomini's presence with the "master" was long enough to establish his credentials as a scholarly pretender to Napoleon's interpretation of warfare. Jomini's *Summary of the Art of War* (1837) had such a profound impact on the study of warfare, as Michael Howard observed, that his principles were institutionalized into the armed forces of Europe with the growing expectancy of a general European war.[8] The thrust of Jomini's ideas lay with the offensive through the concentration of superior force at a decisive point in battle. He ruled that success was assured when an army secured its own lines of operations (*lignes d'opérations*).[9] Under Jomini's influence, Prussian officers serving in the rear areas became as mindful of the enemy as their comrades in the front line were. The baggage train became a mobile barracks and depot; and advances in railway engineering hastened the transformation, which in turn led the railway to become integrated into the field security functions. Jomini's teachings were used to champion a distinct Prussian–German way of warfare that became the mantra for every efficient officer.[10] He declared that the aggressive prosecution of war, fully secured in the field, was a winning strategy.

Oberstleutnant Albrecht von Boguslawski, inspired by Jomini, tried to proliferate the military scientist's ideas of operational technique. In 1881, Boguslawski published a series of lectures titled *Der kleine Krieg (The Small War)*.[11] This book described the tactical procedures for the conduct of both partisan and antipartisan warfare. In the final chapter, the book addressed the problem of training and explained that adequate training was fundamental to achieving success. Intensified training correspondingly raised the level of expertise, providing the ambitious commander with alternative ploys such as night operations. A subsequent review by a British military journal included the partial translation of *Der kleine Krieg* into *Partisan Warfare*.[12] Boguslawski's reviewer was impressed by the function of partisan warfare, which included gathering enemy intelligence, preventing a surprise attack, keeping the enemy occupied with tactical movements, and harassing the enemy without becoming compromised. The continued resistance against invaders by civilians struck the reviewer into commenting,

[W]e must imagine an invader to have occupied one or more provinces, making it incumbent on the defender not only to threaten
his flanks and rear to the utmost, but also to make the public at
home and abroad believe that the provinces in question are not
really subdued. Such acts must often, in order to gain the end in
view, be combined with armed resistance on the part of the civil
population. [13]

The British review mildly rebuked Boguslawski for not defining his terms
of reference. Definition and classification was already commonplace in international military scholarship. It was germane to the general acceptance of a
codification and legislation for the conduct of war. Boguslawski avoided clas-
sifications of combatants and even included guerrilla-style operations in his
examples. This went against Francis (Franz) Lieber's principles of classification for belligerents and nonbelligerents. Lieber was a Prussian immigrant in
America and a professor of law at Columbia University. During the American
Civil War, he had answered legal questions over the standing of "guerrilla
parties" that had become the accepted terms of reference for small-war combatants.[14] Lieber strongly approved of partisan warfare as legally acceptable
but in equal measure disapproved of guerrillas in any form. He labeled guerrillas self-constituted bands of armed men conducting irregular war. In Lieber's
opinion, guerrillas relied on the dynamics of the band, lacking regular status
or permanent standing, and consequently, they were outlaws—bandits. The
explanation of Lieber's attitude stems from his experience of soldiering in the
Prussian Freikorps during 1813–14. Guerrilla war bore too striking a resemblance to the stereotypical banditry from the Thirty Years' War of Lieber's
Prussian middle-class schooling. The tenets of Lieber's ideas remain strong
today, but we should be mindful of his background and the prejudices underpinning his judgments.[15]

The Prussian regulations for the code of conduct in war were revised in
1856 and still in force when the *War Book* (*Kriegsbrauch im Landkriege*) was
introduced in 1902. These revised regulations followed after a long series of
vicious parliamentary squabbles between the military and the antimilitarist
lobbies.[16] During the Franco–Prussian War and the subsequent occupation
of France, Germany proved capable of applying a strict legal code in its military administration. Even in the 1940s, this occupation was regarded as legally sound and relatively properly administered.[17] However, Lieber's fundamental belief in the professional soldier's code of honor as the means of
applied self-regulation was at odds with changing developments in warfare
and the incremental effects of colonialism. The international attempts to
impose humanitarian controls in war that led to The Hague and Geneva conventions (1899 and 1907) were the products of Lieber's thinking. Lieber and
humanitarianism, however, were both made redundant when the 1902 German

*War Book* stated, "What is permissible includes every means of war without which the object of the war cannot be obtained; what is reprehensible on the other hand includes every act of violence and destruction, which is not demanded by the object of war."[18] Laws and wars were turning into conflicts of interpretation, judged by the victor.

In February 1871, a senior British officer was so appalled by Germany's war making against France that he wrote to *The Times* arguing that the aggression should no longer be tolerated. The article particularly identified the institution of terror used by the Germans on the grounds of security and therefore "military necessity." The Germans used the system of "cantonment," billeting soldiers and animals with civilians. Added to this, they ruthlessly enforced hard fighting on the French and imposed a strict regime of occupation. The collapse of the French army did not lead to the collapse of France. An upsurge of the People's War led by civilian militias known as francs-tireurs ("free-shooters," in German *Freischärler*) caused the Germans large-scale organizational problems and legal headaches in trying to impose their rule. The campaign against the francs-tireurs had a lasting impact on the German way of war. The Great General Staff declared that all Freischärler were guerrillas and irregulars, and thus illegal. A franc-tireur who survived beyond the immediate moment of capture, which was far from certain, faced court-martial and a minimum prison term of ten years' hard labor.[19] The collective view of German war making, then and now, was the tendency toward the overreliance on fear as a deterrent, without compensating for the countervailing response of desperation.[20]

In the 1890s, the social benefits of education and a rising tide of nationalistic jingoism coincided in the popularization of the military through literature. The public gorged on cheap and cheerful stories of war and adventure. This literature dispensed with legal precaution regarding the treatment of irregulars, foreign civilians, or the realities of war. The twenty-fifth anniversary of the Franco–Prussian War inspired a proliferation of celebratory books or *Festschriften*.[21] One such Festschrift, by Professor Theodor Lindner, University of Halle, typically was embossed with Iron Crosses and Germanic eagles and proclaimed German mastery in war.[22] To determine his argument for balance and accuracy, Lindner included examples of German soldiers' less-than-honorable behavior. In many respects, this distinguished Lindner from court historians of the time. Lindner exposed two security issues. The first was guerrilla warfare during occupation. By 1873, the army had dispensed with the threat of the francs-tireurs through careful handling of the occupation. When Lindner published his book, however, the franc-tireur had become a virulent form of state-encouraged fanaticism and a social outlaw symbolic of France. The term *Franktireur* represented an extreme form of guerrilla in German military terminology.

Explaining the nature of this fanaticism, Lindner described an incident reputed to have taken place on September 9, 1870, when francs-tireurs blew up the town arsenal of Laon. Forty men were killed, and many local inhabitants, including the commander of a Prussian cavalry division, were wounded.[23] Lindner judged the indiscriminate violence as immoral and completely unethical. He then broached the subject of civil-military relations in occupied France in general and Alsace-Lorraine, where the civilian population proved largely hostile toward Germans, in particular. The French civilians took potshots at the soldiers attributing them the status of barbarians (*Barbaren*). Lindner upheld German honor, justifying German actions under the most trying circumstances. Most significant, he praised the troops for remaining true to their "soldiers' code," labeled the French as underhanded, questioning their national ability to comprehend modern warfare, and concluded that the Germans were superior warriors.[24] Mark Stoneman has explained that the ill-treatment meted out by soldiers of the Bavarian army against French civilians earned them lasting international notoriety. He concluded that the veterans' subsequent justifications for their actions were based on a combination of excuses, including military necessity, pride in their army, and social Darwinism.[25]

Lindner's second issue concerned the behavior of the soldiers and the problem of supply. Even with the system of cantonment, German soldiers plundered shoes and boots from French citizens, even stripping them in the streets. The real problem was the failure of the regular supply channels, but Lindner could not admit this. He chose to excuse outright theft of underwear on the grounds that the troops wished to remain "human." Food shortages that led the troops to pillage "empty" houses were declared acceptable because the homeowners had fled. Likewise, he condemned "sneaky" French attempts to hide away food but condoned the "cleverer" German ability to root out the goods. Lindner explained that the troops resorted to stripping "wet" walls, digging up "foul smelling dung heaps," and bayoneting recently planted herb gardens to find buried food and wine.[26] Lindner adopted wit and humor to explain away the widespread theft of chickens. The chickens, he wrote, overcome by the disgrace of national defeat, chose to commit suicide. They hurled themselves under the wheels of passing Prussian army carts or jumped into soldiers' cooking pots. The climax of his tale was a cockerel, the symbol of France, which "followed the call to arms and vigorously attacked a group of German soldiers."[27] Lindner explained that once the occupation was established, the army resolved its supply problem by imposing taxes—collected through the military administration—on French communities and using this money to pay French farmers to deliver cattle and food.[28]

In 1891, Alfred von Schlieffen, a Prussian of the old school and a disciple of Jomini, became the chief of the Great General Staff. Schlieffen invigorated the German officer corps with the challenge to reach the fame of generalissimo or *Feldherr*. In rising to the level of senior command or great generalship

(*Feldherrnkunst*), the professional officer was expected to live the dictum that for every problem, there was a military solution. The implications of such ideas, drummed into every soldier, forged a peculiar mindset. Schlieffen also had the measure of great leadership in which a commander not only defeated enemies but annihilated them.[29] This annihilation became the only acceptable measure of success in war. Schlieffen set out to transform the conscript Imperial German Army into a machine employed to fulfill the offensive spirit. In so doing, he offered ambitious officers rapid advancement but the side effect was a system imbued with internal competition, career jealousy, and bureaucratic inertia. Since the end of the First World War, Schlieffen's life has been subject to considerable interpretation.[30] Gunther Rothenberg argued that Schlieffen instilled the economy of effort, maneuver, and the concentration of force into all levels of the army. An observation made in 1952 of the German high command concluded that Schlieffen's ideas "permeated the German officer corps even to the lower ranks."[31] Recently, Robert Foley suggested that "Schlieffen the man" became "Schlieffen the idea" within the German army.[32]

Schlieffen became obsessive in solving Germany's self-imposed strategic dilemma of war on two fronts and against overwhelming forces. He believed the solution lay in the precedents of Hannibal's victory over the Romans at the Battle of Cannae (216 BC). After a series of spectacular military achievements, Hannibal set his numerically inferior forces to encircle a Roman army. The audacity of Hannibal's victory exploited the terrain and his opponents' way of warfare so completely that the Romans were completely destroyed. Schlieffen studied the battle and found strategic solutions that suited him. He likened himself to Hannibal laboring at the head of a federated army of military establishments (the Prussians, the Bavarians, and the other Germanic states). He also assumed that Germany's principal opponents (France and Russia) were nations that had overcome military tribalism, fielding homogeneous forces under unified command. Schlieffen concluded that Cannae proved Clausewitz and Napoleon wrong: smaller forces could encircle larger opponents. However, in establishing Cannae's credentials, Schlieffen smoothed over uncomfortable but salient points. Hannibal was, by the prevailing standards of the German officer corps, a maverick. Schlieffen demanded that his officer corps follow his orders to the letter. The battle, although an overwhelming victory, was not exploited by Hannibal and proved his undoing, because it reinforced the Roman determination to destroy him. Irrespective of this, Schlieffen ensured Cannae became the dogma behind all aggressive German army operations.

In theory, Schlieffen sought to make the army flexible in responding to all situations.[33] In practice, the enlargement of the army from 400,000 in 1870 to 864,000 by 1913 forced him to simplify tactics and standardize operations. The principles of Cannae were reduced to enveloping attack (*umfassender Angriff*), encirclement (*Einkesselung*), encircling maneuvers (*Einkreisungsmanöver*), and encircling pursuit (*überholende Verfolgung*). These were exhaustively trained for and rehearsed by the army. Schlieffen's solution was a cyclical process of standardized basic training, war planning, mobilization rehearsals, and large-scale military exercises, implemented with every new intake of conscripts. This tortuous cycle of inducting recruits and transforming them into the cogs of a military machine was seen as instilling discipline and building military efficiency. This turned the army into either the manipulative agent of socialization described by Volker Berghan[34] or the seal of the national spirit professed by veterans.[35] The twelve-week basic training program culminated in massive exercises held on expansive troop training grounds. On these mock battlefields, troops were honed to perform the maneuvers of encirclement and envelopment, the reinforcement ad nauseam of Cannae, which was expected to help establish a doctrine of aggressive warfare and the coup de grace in security actions.[36]

## The Institutions

In the eighty years after the demise of Napoleon, most armies of Europe responded to the socioeconomic challenges of the nineteenth century through technocratic professionalism. In Prussia, professionalism came from a process of regimented schooling, conscription, and training in the military academies. In time, the professionalization of the officer corps, the regimented bureaucratization of the state, and the influx of military officials defined the German military establishment over society; Christopher Dandeker has called this the militarization of government.[37] The armies of Germany had been active in financing and planning the development of the states. The Prussian army endorsed the construction of state railways during the 1840s and established strong links with banks and business. When Schlieffen became chief of the Great General Staff in 1891, the full potential for a unified Imperial German Army had still to be realized. He recognized that troops could neither march to the beat of different drums nor perform the precious Cannae, unless welded into a clockwork-like army. Historians have focused on the social consequences of latent civilian militarism. The paradox of deep-seated anxieties and fears about the military came from within a society deeply dependant on the protection of the army and its regulation of law and order. The consequences of Schlieffen's efforts were seen in 1914. The Imperial German Army entered the war on a sounder operational footing than any other army, but its rapid collapse in November 1918 indicated the underlying frailties of a militarized society.

One Prussian tradition, after 1813, was to assign older reservists to security duties. The Landwehr, a territorial militia, was the backbone of homeland defense. Although formed from reservists, the Landwehr was responsible for securing Germany's conquests and military occupation. In the early days of the Prussian annexation of the Rhineland, Landwehr regiments were garrisoned in every town and city. In 1822, the 25th Duke of Wellington Landwehr Regiment had three battalions of infantry. The regiment was raised from men over twenty-four years old and was mustered from within the area of Aachen, Jülich, and Düren.[38] The total manpower was 8,113, with the main fighting complement listed as 56 officers, 333 noncommissioned officers, and 5,859 troopers; the rest was made up of 1,848 elderly war reservists, 73 bandsmen, and 3 surgeons. Michael Howard regarded the Landwehr as critical to Prussian security operations during the Franco–Prussian War with a total deployment in excess of 110,000 men.[39] Its duties ranged from guarding railway lines and strong points to taking hostages and committing reprisals to when called on, detering franc-tireur activity. During the war, the Landwehr received frontline troops, especially the cavalry, bolstering their aggressive operational mobility.

The German military rear-area system was called the Etappen. The term originated from the French *étape,* meaning stages, and referred to the army's lines of communication. The Etappen were the responsibility of the quarter-master-general (*Generalquartiermeister*) within the Great General Staff (*grosser Generalstab*). In time, the Etappen grew into a larger and more complex organization than the fighting (teeth) arms. Its mission was to support and supply offensive operations from the rear area and into the combat zone. In practice, this usually meant plundering the land as offensive operations ground forward. Its secondary mission, growing in greater importance over time, involved countering incursions by partisans or guerrillas and preventing disruption of the rear area. Operationally, the Etappen expanded and contracted, rather like an accordian, to given circumstances. At its greatest extension, the system controlled the corridors between the army's bases in Germany and the front lines. The Etappen were erected on a cadre of professional soldiers, reservists, and civilian experts and tradesmen. They carried out a broad range of tasks including taking prisoners of war, policing, controlling civilians, and administering the occupation. When the war ended, the Etappen were reduced as an unnecessary financial burden on the state. In response to supply problems during the wars of 1866 and 1867 and the insecurity caused by francs-tireurs in 1870–71, the system was reformed and regulated under the 1872 Etappen regulations.[40]

After 1872, this system became a fixture of the permanent military establishment. The publication of its ordinances immediately attracted British attention.[41] The British noticed that responsibility for the Etappen remained within the decision-making circle of the quartermaster-general of the army. The senior field officer was the general inspector rear area of the army (*Generaletappeninspektionen der Armee*), who administered the operational functions and later joined with the inspector general of communications (*Generalinspekteur des Etappen- und Eisenbahnwesens*). To sustain the mission demanded by the new instructions, the Etappen received specialists from all branches and services of the army. The new guidelines also reflected advancing railway engineering and the growing dependency of the army on railways. Reflecting this new requirement, the army introduced the post of chief of the field railway (*Chef des Feldeisenbahnwesens*). Military traffic managers joined the Etappen to prevent bottlenecks in transportation and to maintain the flow of traffic along roads and railways. A railway protection regiment was raised with railway reservists; this led eventually to the military railway corps (*Feldeisenbahnkorps*). In theory, local military commands (*Etappenkommandantur*) were placed in railway junctions and towns. During occupation, they ruled local civilians by distributing work and food and imposing social control. In the surrounding hamlets and villages, a district commander (*Ortskommandantur*) extended this system of control. The priority task was protection, and to this end the flow of replacements could be interrupted in an emergency, forming troop-cadres (*Stammtruppe*) for security duties. Local rear-area departments (*Etappenhauptorte*) and roving special military courts (*Sondergerichte*) supervised military justice.[42]

Political considerations dictated whether the occupation system took the form of a general government or a military government. The former was staffed by civilians and administered by the army; the latter was a military state. According to Michael Rowe, the Prussian army in the Rhineland (1814) formed a working relationship between local collaboration and military administration.[43] In 1870–71, this same army, with Prussian state assistance, knitted together a highly profitable and financially rewarding occupation of France. The Prussian government, through the secondment of senior public servants, tax and finance specialists, and sociopolitical experts from universities, assisted the army. Public servants or civilian commissioners, working with French mayors and local councilors, handled the civil functions of occupied France.[44] German army civil-military relations policy for occupation in 1873 had crafted a subtle form of control. The complete Etappen function reflected Germany's central position in Europe and thus threatened Russia and France. The British army review of the regulations concluded that no organization comparable to the Etappen existed within the armies of Europe. They were particularly struck with authority handed to the Etappen commanders, "great powers of organisation" arranged around "three perceptions": first, providing necessities for the army in the field; second, "calming the temper of the local population"; and last, preventing enemy infiltration. The British were also interested in what they termed the duties of the communications officer during an occupation. This involved installing civil government, establishing collaboration with the indigenous population, and turning "the resources of the country to the best account for the benefit of the army."

The final pieces in the organizational development of the German military security establishment were the field police and military intelligence. In August 1866, Bismarck promoted Baron Wilhelm Stieber as director of the

Prussian State Ministry and charged him to erect a central intelligence bureau (*zentrale Nachrichtenbüro*) for political security and intelligence.[45] The first secret field police (*Geheime Feldpolizei*), known as the GFP, began with fifty conscripted police officers.[46] Its mission was to safeguard the senior commanders and staff officers of the high command. In 1870–71, Stieber became the chief of Field Police under the Great General Staff and commanded thirty-one administrators (*Polizeibeamten*) and 157 field officers.[47] The military police (*Feldgendarmerie*) usually came from the cavalry and served with each army corps. The normal command was a cavalry captain (*Rittmeister*), two noncommissioned officers (*Wachtmeister*), and sixty military police (*Feldgendarmen*). For civil-military relations purposes during an occupation, they joined local commands and worked alongside the beat police (*Landespolizei*). Policing the occupation of France (1871–73) involved cadres of constables, collaborators, prefects, mayors, and the men from the Etappenkommandanten. In Lorraine, the chief of the local rural police (*Landgendarmeriekommando*) came from the Berlin police. In Rheims, the Germans employed collaborators to raise a local protection militia (*Schutzmänner*), used to counter the roving bands of francs-tireurs and bandits. In the 1880s, the introduction of passports and controls, primarily to administer the annexation of Alsace-Lorraine, led to the founding of the Border Police (*Grenzschutzpolizei*), attached to the GFP. By 1914, the GFP was the central secret police agency for the army, commanded by Major und Polizei-Rat Bauer, under Oberst Nicolai. During the Great War, members of the GFP were granted the right to wear either uniforms or civilian clothing, depending on their duties.

In 1884, Major von Lettow-Vorbeck became director of military intelligence and counterintelligence for the Imperial German Army.[48] Between 1900 and 1917, the intelligence services underwent a series of changes. Initially, their functions were to monitor foreign press and propaganda, censor mail, operate the border police, recruit spies, and conduct counter-espionage. After the Russo–Japanese War, reforms were introduced, and in 1906, the intelligence and security police agencies were reorganized. Developments continued to separate military intelligence from counterintelligence. In 1910, Department IIIb, the German army Abwehr was formed to handle foreign military intelligence, and in the spirit of the times, the navy established its own Abwehr branch. In 1913, IIIb came under Oberst Walter Nicolai, aged thirty-nine, chief of military intelligence of the German Supreme Command (*Chef des Nachrichtendienstes der obersten Heeresleitung*). Nicolai scored several successes revealing spies and traitors. He believed an iron curtain (*eiserner Vorhang*) had descended around Germany and her allies prior to the war, leaving only Switzerland as a small window to the outside world and thus restricting intelligence operations. The occupation and annexation of Alsace-Lorraine was soon regarded as a springboard for French espionage by the

German army. Rightly or wrongly, German perceptions fixated on French revanchism, and these perceptions became connected with a deeply held suspicion of Britain.[49] In 1917, the army finally decided to separate counterintelligence from foreign military intelligence. The intelligence section within IIIb became the Foreign Armies Section (*Fremde Heeresabteilung*). Therefore, by 1917, military policing, counterintelligence, and military intelligence were three distinct branches of the army.

## Rehearsals for War

Between 1870 and 1912, security warfare became an integral part of the German way of war. A supremo of security was not elected during the Franco–Prussian War. The only Feldherr was Field Marshal Helmuth von Moltke. The francs-tireurs were a serious security problem for only a brief time. The military governments, the extent of the Etappen, and the number of security operations did not fall to a single commanding officer of an occupation security army. Security was a common responsibility accepted as a regular military routine. The rise of security warfare and the first dubious contests of its Feldherr followed the institutional changes of 1872 and surfaced within Germany's colonial conflicts. When Schlieffen became chief of the general staff in 1891, he inherited a military and national political disaster. In July, the governor of German East Africa (Tanzania) ordered Emil von Zelewski, the commander of the local militia (*Schutztruppen*), to quell an uprising of the Wehehe tribe, in the south of the country.[50] Zelewski led a force of fourteen "European" officers and men with 362 locally recruited Schutztruppen through the bush and mountain range. They came under repeated hit-and-run attacks, primarily because their marching order lacked discipline. On August 17, one of the German officers took a shot at an eagle flying overhead. This precipitated the Wehehe's signal for attack. The ensuing Battle of Rugaro turned into Germany's Little Big Horn, and Zelewski, like George Armstrong Custer, suffered the ignominy of defeat, by a band of tribesmen. In the ensuing chaos, the Schutztruppen fled, and a sixteen-year-old boy speared Zelewski to death. Only three Europeans survived, and 250 out of 320 Askaris were killed. News of the debacle, according to Jan-Bart Gewalt, arrived in Berlin by telegram announcing that Zelewski's corps had been "shattered" (*aufgerieben*).[51] Erick Mann thought much of what was later written about Emil von Zelewski absolved him. However, consciousness of the disaster became deeply rooted in the consciousness of German officer corps.[52]

This inauspicious beginning spurred Schlieffen to institute performance standards for all aspects of operations. It is often assumed that colonial wars played no part in European warfare and that Schlieffen was not involved in these operations, but this was not the case. He ensured that military expeditions were fully planned, organized, and commanded by professional officers.

He also observed colonial conflicts as putative testing grounds for his operational ideas. Fate, however, interrupted his plans with the first major international incident. The Boxer Rebellion (1900) might have served his purpose had Kaiser Wilhelm II not intervened. The kaiser agreed to send a military expedition to join the great powers under the command of Field Marshal Count Alfred von Waldersee, a notorious political intriguer and racist.[53] The expedition embarked on July 27, 1900, under the kaiser's orders to neither show mercy nor take prisoners.[54] Encirclement failed in China. A youthful Leutnant Franz Ritter von Epp of the Ninth Bavarian Infantry Regiment volunteered for the China expedition in the hope of achieving the cherished opportunity of a baptism of fire. In April 1901, Epp took part in an operation near the Great Wall of China. Although the security operation was sanctioned by the great powers commission, the tactical details were left to the Germans. The German commander, not surprisingly, opted for encirclement, which he attempted twice against both the left and right flanks of the Boxer force, reputed to be more than one thousand soldiers strong. The Germans managed to kill two hundred, while the rest escaped. The failure of the first attempt at encirclement was blamed on the poor geographical position; the second remains less clear, although almost certainly it reflected a tactical failure by the Germans.[55]

Pursuit and Bandenbekämpfung also failed in China. On March 19, 1901, Epp's company received word of the murder of two German soldiers. That afternoon, Epp's 6th Company received orders to conduct a search for the men. In the dusk, they conducted a house-to-house search and interrogated the locals looking for the two men. Epp had detailed collection carts and coffins for the bodies prior to setting off, certain that the men were dead. During the search, there was obviously some kind of incident, although not clarified, but that evening the Germans camped outside the village. They had set the village on fire and held thirty Chinese as prisoners. One prisoner apparently choked through the night, without relief, the consequences of a chest wound. They found no trace of the missing soldiers except for their guns, which been thrown down a well.[56] After arriving in China, the German troops participated in more than fifty operations. Years later, the fighting in the rebellion was recorded in the German infantry handbook as operations against Chinese "bandits" (Banden).[57] The German performance in China came under severe political scrutiny from the Social Democratic Party. On January 11, 1902, August Bebel, the leader of the SPD, accused the army of excesses based on the evidence received from soldiers' letters. One soldier told his parents that when the Chinese refused to give up food, he "hit them on the skulls" with a lance, and when several tried to protect themselves, he ran them through. The Germans invoked penalties on villages that did not conform to their rule; fines were as high as 30,000 Marks. Epp returned to Germany and reflected on the wider implications of the campaign. He thought Bebel's accusations exaggerated or invented and believed the army had behaved bravely and humanely. Epp did agree that the drinking and general unruly behavior of the troops remained a problem in China.

In 1904, thirteen years after the Zelewski debacle, Schlieffen had another opportunity to fully rehearse his concept of war under hostile fire conditions. In German Southwest Africa (Namibia), the Herero tribes were challenging the German's right to rule them. With a population estimated at eighty thousand, they represented more than a few unruly clans waging a bush war (*Buschkrieg*). Schlieffen prepared a full-scale operational plan and recommended Lothar von Trotha to command the expedition. Trotha's chief of staff was Oberstleu-tnant Charles de Beaulieu from the Army General Staff. Among the line officers were Franz Ritter von Epp and Paul von Lettow-Vorbeck. The German plan called for a series of oblique maneuvers by the troops, coordinated through the Etappen, to pressure the Herero into congregating in one place. The coup de main, an encirclement of the Herero, would lead to their annihilation through superior tactics and systematic killing. The Herero gathered at the Waterberg in August 1904, and Trotha sensed this was his opportunity to strike. After the battle, Trotha wrote, "My initial plan for the operation, which I always adhered to, was to encircle the masses of Herero at Waterberg, and to annihilate these masses with a simultaneous blow." He expected to "establish various stations to hunt down and disarm the splinter groups who escaped, later to lay hands on the captains by putting prize money on their heads and finally to sentence them to death."[58] A *Festschrift* published by approval of the German War Ministry (*Kriegsministerium*) confirmed the plan for battlefield decapitation and extermination.[59]

Although technically outnumbered, the German order of battle included artillery and heavy machine guns, field telecommunications, and exploitation of the railway network. The central command (*Etappenkommandantur Swakopmund*) controlled the main supply depots, as well as the flow of reserves and replacements, and managed all communications (transport and telecommunications). From the central hub, each Ortskommandantur was placed in a strategic position and guarded by a ring of guard posts. Linking these outposts was the militarized railway system with station commanders (*Bahnhofskommandantur*) and the railway troops (*Eisenbahntruppen*), erecting an internal security web across Namibia. The military railroad increased the army's response to Herero incursions. Landwehr troops posted to the Etappen and railway installations erected defensive positions, armed strongpoints (*Stützpunkte*), with machine-gun posts and trench lines.[60]

Contradictory accounts of the battle that followed exist. Helmut Bley argued that the Herero broke out of the encirclement.[61] Horst Drechsler believed Trotha deliberately deployed troops in such a way as to leave an opening. A gap filled by a small force under Major von der Heyde was to hold its position, while the stronger pressing force under Oberst Deimling was to force the Herero, during the melee, to break out, but only into the wastelands of the Omaheke Desert (referred to as the Sandveld).[62] Tilman Dedering suggested that poor coordination and planning allowed the Herero to break out and escape. Dedering also explained that subsequent justifications by Trotha and his staff only confused the outcome further.[63] Epp happened to serve at the Waterberg in his second colonial campaign, and Epp's version is the tacit acceptance of failure. After Trotha issued the orders on August 4, Epp noticed that there were large gaps between the encircling forces. One group, under Deimling, was slow to arrive at its designated position and was last in line. The fighting opened at 6:30 a.m., when Epp's troops entered the fighting zone. Another unit from Epp's group came on the receiving end of a surprise and concerted Herero counter-attack. At 8:00 a.m., the Herero attacked the left flank, and only with machine guns could the Germans hold them off. Another counter-attack at 9:30 a.m. forced Epp to deploy his artillery. A strong attack at 12:30 p.m. forced Epp to keep firing while on the move. After an hour, the fighting gave way to a pursuit that lasted until 3:15 p.m., when the Germans, without explanation, marched back to their encampments. Epp recorded that, after the battle, until August 16, his unit spent time in the "noble" soldierly task of cattle rustling.[64]

The escape of the Herero and their continuing acts of insurgency led the Germans to introduce Bandenbekämpfung operations. Kurd Schwabe described several such operations, and one example is especially revealing. During the occupation of Namibia in 1905, Etappen troops attempted to destroy Andreas, a Herero guerrilla leader (*Bandenführer*), and his followers. On May 12, a detachment from an Etappen company located and attacked the guerrillas by a river. After five hours of hard fighting on difficult ground, the Herero leader escaped with the loss of twenty men. The Germans had no idea of the actual size of his force. The German casualties included one officer, two troopers, and three members of the Schutztruppen. The Germans divided into two troops; one followed Andreas, while the other returned to the nearest Etappen base to report the incident. Raising a general alarm, two more detachments set off in pursuit of Andreas. One detachment came from an Etappen company; the other included ninety volunteers armed with an artillery piece and led by an Oberleutnant of the reserve.[65] On May 26, Andreas fled toward the British border and was intercepted. The next day, as the Germans tried to prevent him crossing into British territory, Andreas changed direction and joined up with the Herero leader Hendrik Witbooi and remained inside Namibia.

On June 7, Andreas turned up again to rustle cattle from a German farmer and attracted the attention of three patrols, each led by an officer. They decided on immediate action and attacked Andreas, who once again disappeared. The following day, Andreas was located again and one hundred riflemen attacked his position. On the morning of June 9, the Germans attacked, and during a three-hour clash of arms, they killed Andreas's son and fourteen other Herero, capturing 250 cattle and various booty. German casualties included one officer killed and another wounded. Andreas fled initially along the river, and then moved into the mountains, losing the trailing Germans. German reserve companies moved into the area and conducted a cleansing (*Säuberung*) operation, rounding up non-combatants and placing them in labor camps.[66] Andreas, like the proverbial bad penny, reappeared in September 1905, this time joined by a band of "Hottentots" (*Hottentottenbanden*). The Germans located his position within a mountain range. They conducted a six-hour climb to inflict a five-hour skirmish on the guerrillas. The Germans recorded more than eighty Hottentots dead from a band estimated at three hundred; a further twenty Herero were confirmed killed. The German casualties were two troopers killed and ten wounded, and again they rounded up cattle.[67] Andreas escaped, outrunning the Germans to reach the British border, but was arrested by the local police. Schwabe reported that 107 Herero were captured, of whom forty-five were men with twenty-eight rifles between them.[68] Referring to the latter part of the conflict, the 1913 infantry handbook recorded that in July 1905, Hendrik Witbooi had faced a concentric attack (*konzentrischen Vormarsch*) and had only escaped in "small groups of bandits" (*kleine Banden*).[69]

The sting was in the tail. Trotha failed with Cannae, which cost the German government the deployment of sixteen thousand soldiers on long-term overseas service. In 1907, the Germans formed a police zone in Namibia as the means toward the permanent protection of the colonists.[70] The zone operated 113 police stations with approximately seven men per post. A police troop of 60 senior NCOs, 320 NCOs, 60 constables, and 330 native police functioned as a rapid reaction force to quell serious outbreaks of trouble. The numbers indicate a deterrent policing screen to discourage the native population from resistance.[71] Even with the German military railway serving as an iron noose around the country, preventing further uprisings, the patrols did not cause large-scale killing. In fact, the Germans had proved largely inept in both leadership and general operational capability. Schlieffen's ideas had not defeated Herero ingenuity. The real cause of the killing lay in the occupation measures. Jürgen Zimmerer's research of the German administration highlighted the mass deaths caused by slave labor and a deliberate policy of starvation. Zimmerer has identified the army's experimentation with social controls and their devastating consequences on colonized communities.[72]

The transition of the war from a military campaign into a full-scale security operation coincided with the deterioration in the treatment of the Herero. They went from classification as valiant foes to objects for extermination. On the grounds that they had committed brutalities, Trotha had ordered the Herero to leave Namibia.[73] The extermination of the Herero was only partly attributable to full-blown military or Bandenbekämpfung operations. The German military occupation lasted from 1904 until 1912. The ethnic cleansing of the Herero people led to a population reduction from eighty thousand in 1904 to twenty thousand by 1912.[74] The scale of killing was new, but the extreme behavior was not, as the China expedition bears out. The political reverberations and criticism of the army's performance again seeped into German society. At a time of great power rivalry and following the kaiser's criticism of British behavior during the Boer War, Trotha's failure became the army's national embarrassment. Schlieffen ensured that Trotha never served in the field again, and he died in retirement in 1920.[75] Throughout 1905, Schlieffen had to defend himself against accusations that he had harmed the good name of the army.[76] Perhaps this political criticism, more than his fall from a horse, eventually led to his retirement in 1906. Epp's fundamental criticism of the army reflected Schlieffen's drive for professionalism: "If we want to make serious military progress, we must do this through the education of the people. . . . The soldier class must become a fundamental element and pillar of the nation."[77]

## The First World War

Two recent and original pieces of research into the German armed forces during the First World War have refocused our attention on the army's performance and repositioned perceptions of its underlying motivations. John Horne and Alan Kramer conducted an exhaustive study of the 1914 atrocities committed by the army in Belgium and France.[78] Vejas Gabriel Liulevicius examined the "Ober Ost" (*Oberbefehlshaber Ost)* and found a military government that aspired to utopian idealism.[79] Together, their work provides a framework for a brief but structured analysis of German military security in the First World War. An analysis of the troops, the Etappen, and the occupation highlights the continuous swing away from offensive military operations and toward the expansion of the rear area as the basis of the German war effort. Within this enlargement of security, Bandenbekämpfung played a small but significant part in the war. In the stages, Germany's war depended on the success of the rigid application of Schlieffen's (modified) plan. The massive Cannae of the Western allied forces was meticulously planned, with offensive operations running to a forty-two-day schedule. The army initially sliced through Belgium, supported by the home depots and the mobile Etappen that relentlessly pushed troops and replacements to the front. By August, however, the scale of operations and the unexpected resistance from the Allies kept stalling the German progress, and the logistics system backed up as railheads were unable to distribute supplies fast enough. The Russian invasion of eastern Germany caused apprehension. Eventually, a Cannae victory was scored at Tannenberg, but it was in the wrong place at the wrong time. The long road of failures since 1891 was, in the light of Germany's military record, consistent. The general staff descended into a strategic depression and was unable to cast off the inertia until 1918.

There is every reason to assume that Schlieffen analyzed Trotha's failure, and there is also every reason to believe he was unable to accept that Cannae hamstrung the army with an impossible tactical task. After Schlieffen retired, the general staff looked to Clausewitz for solutions to make the plan work, including reducing friction in operations and increasing the impact of the surprise essential in gaining superiority over a larger opponent.[80] Between August and October 1914, the army deliberately killed sixty-five hundred French and Belgian civilians. Horne and Kramer wrote that these acts were isolated to the deliberate killing of civilians, plundering, and causing widespread destruction.[81] Horne and Kramer proposed reasons for the killing, including the presence of colonial officers, the franc-tireur paranoia that gripped the popular press, and the speed in which orders were issued to punish civilians for a host of crimes. Had the army ordered a "shoot first and ask questions afterward" policy? Were the soldiers "trigger-happy" troopers? Did they believe in the franc-tireur myth? And how many of the million who invaded Belgium pulled the trigger on defenseless civilians?

The potential of a franc-tireur threat held implications for Schlieffen's plan and a two-front war. The rapid drain on reserves could not afford the luxury of an 1870–71 style security campaign. The Landwehr of 1914–18 played a central part in offensive operations. Landwehr regiments organized as divisions and brigades and participated in major battles. One frontline infantry regiment, six Landwehr regiments, and four Landsturm regiments successfully carried out the Battle of Nowogeorgiewsk (1915) northwest of Warsaw.[82] An indication of the change can be found in the record of the 6th Landwehr Infantry Regiment, which served all four years on the Eastern Front. Initially deployed on August 28, 1914, this regiment was formed from three battalions with a single machine-gun company. More than 1,550 officers and men were killed while serving with the regiment, and collectively they tell an interesting story. From the large numbers of casualties suffered in 1914, the majority came from the former German towns of Glogau and Fraustadt in Upper Silesia, reflecting the three battalion depots. By the end of the war, the casualties were men drawn from across Germany.[83] During the war, regiments were swallowed up not by the Etappe, but to fill gaps in the front. Not for the first or the last time, German security troops were posted to frontline duties in times of emergency. By 1917, in the east, these units were integrated into an occupation organization. The 9th Etappen Inspectorate of the 8th Army, for example, contained the 45th Reserve Field Artillery Regiment, 8th Cavalry Division, 1st Cavalry Division, 19th Landwehr Division, and the 7th Mobile Railway Command for railhead duties.[84]

The Etappen grew into an enormous establishment in an effort to support the army, exploit the occupation, and impose social control. In the west, the Etappen evolved a static structure with an offensive capability to exploit breakthroughs. The Mobile Etappen were also used to erect a defensive line prior to a retreat.[85] On the Western Front, the frontline trenches and the Etappen caused the overlapping of layers of military establishment, which in turn led to a melting pot of front and rear echelons.[86] The range of humanity that was capable of passing through the Etappen charged with overseeing a particular area was colossal. There was the clockwork movement of fighting units back and forth to the front, the arrival of replacements, the care system for casualties, the movement of prisoners of war, the collection of forced labor, and the ubiquitous army of entertainers, including publicans, actors, musicians, and prostitutes. The relations between the controllers and the interlopers led to difficulties and, in Richard Holmes's opinion, caused the vehement cultural distinction between "front and rear" and the adoption of the invective "rear-area swine" (*Etappenschweine*).[87] This situation was common to soldiers of all armies, but in the German army, the Etappen represented more than the extension of authority and jurisdiction: it was the regulator of a military society. Ernst Jünger left an impression of one Etappen commander: "One Captain of Horse dubbed himself the King of Quéant, and made his appearance every night at our round table, where he was greeted by upraised right hands and a thunderous 'Long Live the King!'"[88]

The introduction of integrated operational intelligence, counterintelligence, policing with secured perimeters and guard networks, and border controls began to take shape in German security policy. When Maj. Gen. Fritz Gempp, of German military intelligence, recorded the outbreak of irregular fighting (*Freischärlerkampf*) in Antwerp, on September 29, 1914, there was no such system of security in place.[89] Gradually a system developed that included an industry of occupation bureaucracy, with everything from identity cards, transit papers, rationing systems, population censuses, the recording of inhabitants of individual buildings, and the regulation of schools and businesses. In the west, there were celebrated espionage cases. From the post-war writing of Gottfried Benn, the famous German poet, we have an account of Edith Cavell's execution in 1915. Benn served in the German occupation of Brussels as the army's senior medical officer. He had the duty of attending the execution and later wrote an account of what happened. Benn's skills articulated a snapshot of the German occupation; collection-detention camps for deported French and Belgian females, prior to being assigned for hard labor (Cavell was briefly imprisoned in one such camp), were located in the Aachen area.[90] The railway line between Brussels and Aachen, operated by the Etappen military railroad, a journey today of less than two hours, was constructed and paid for with loans from the Bank of Brussels in the 1840s. By September 1916, this railway was working flat-out and the camps were bursting to cope with Ludendorff's order to extradite twelve thousand Belgians into forced labor; by October his weekly demand was twenty thousand.[91] German methods were driven toward absolute security and massive economic exploitation. These drives required the disposal of large numbers of civilians through collaboration.[92] From the few documents that have survived, it is possible to piece together a snapshot of occupation, as French and the Belgian civilians were held hostage to their very existence.[93]

The German occupation of Northern France led to the organization of six districts with headquarters in Valenciennes, Laon, Cambrai, Vouziers, Charleville, and Vervin. Helen McPhail found that the army controlling the sector determined the regulation of occupation. The system depended on the active collaboration of town and village mayors to regulate the civilian population.[94] On the Eastern Front, there were shifting priorities with the experience of victory and annexation of formerly Russian territory. Liulevicius thought that in the Ober Ost the Germans displayed a form of rule that encompassed both bureaucracy and technology, reaching a peak of professional occupation.[95] He argued that the occupation authorities espoused a military utopia that came to underpin Nazi ideology and war making. This is a credible assumption, but as always in German history, there remain those loose strands that indicate the potential for other influences and direction. In the central area of the Eastern Front, the German army entered Warsaw on August 4, 1915, and Field Marshal Falkenhayn immediately established a general government under General von Beseler.[96] Records from the Warsaw general government survive and indicate that it was a complex organization with an in-depth security network of guard posts and strongpoints strung across the city.[97] German civilians attached to the Etappen in the east included university professors, architects, accountants, doctors, hunters, foresters, and significant numbers of public servants. The depth of planning, infrastructure rebuilding, introducing an education system, and distributing publications, however, was not evidence of "enlightened" occupation. Evidently, innocent care facilities arranged for the benefit the troops were also amenable for terrorizing civilians.

Gempp's description of the security problem on the Eastern Front as "ruthless struggle" showed that pacification was in reality the application of terror to galvanize the population into accepting German rule.[98] Bandenbekämpfung operations, according to Gempp, were instituted to combat a deliberate Russian policy of leaving troops behind to raise chaos within the German rear areas.[99] Gempp wanted the masses of Russian stragglers to be processed quickly and ruthlessly. He felt it was necessary to have captured Russians placed in work battalions and detailed to projects for the German war economy. The vast numbers of Russian prisoners, he complained, were in wide-open areas unguarded and thus granted the opportunity to escape and join the guerrilla bands or become "bandits." The problem of the large open spaces on the Eastern Front diminished attempts to reach a state of total security. Military intelligence relied heavily on deserters, prisoners of war, and local civilians for information. Gempp alleged that the Jewish community furnished numbers of spies and agents to assist him. He regarded them as his best source of intelligence. In 1915, Gempp noticed that the Russians were making special efforts to scout and conduct reconnaissance behind German lines.[100] Therefore, he believed Russian deserters no longer brought reliable information; in other words, they were actively practicing disinformation on the Germans. In other sectors, the Russians were disrupting lines of communications and destroying munitions. In commenting on a message from November 21, 1915, Gempp noted that during a partisan operation the partisans had donned Austrian uniforms.[101]

Liulevicius confirmed Gempp's commentary. He referred to the case of Gen. Rochus Schmidt, a former member of the East African "colonial forces" who commanded the gendarmerie in the Ober Ost. His duties included crushing armed resistance and banditry. By 1917, the bands had grown immeasurably because of the impact of German measures imposed on the native populations. A cycle of violence developed as Germans forced natives to inform on the bands, or suffer punishment, while the bandits in turn began to kill German soldiers rather than restrict themselves to looting. The problem grew so large that the German authorities resolved to introduce passive measures of clearing away the ground of obvious places of ambush, traveling in convoys, and suspending all movement at night.[102] During 1915 in Cracow, the army erected delousing camps to cleanse soldier's uniforms of lice. It soon became accepted practice to delouse local Jews because of their inherent "dirtiness," an early harbinger of Nazi crimes.[103] Liulevicius found evidence of similar facilities in the Ober Ost. Delousing stations were used as part of a public health system that employed special plague troops to locate sick people and quarantine them.

In September 1916, leading members of the German security network in the east sat down to discuss whether they should continue with the existing arrangements or introduce a new security system.[104] The commander of all eastern security, according to Gempp, was concerned at the threat to the railways and communications from "banditry," although this was neither fully explained nor articulated. The regional security officers (Kowno, Mitau, Schaulen, and Tilsit) joined representatives from 10th and 8th armies to discuss these problems. A new system meant erecting large physical structures, fences, stockades, and garrisons with control posts. They decided to introduce a security force—the Secret Rear-Area Police (*Geheime Etappenpolizei*)—to conduct a system of passes administered by military bureaucrats (*Militärverwaltungsbeamte*). Field police director Oberstleutnant Toussaint complained at having to supply large numbers of passes at great cost, as well as having to handle the perpetual Bandenbekämpfung problem caused by escaping Russian prisoners of war.[105] Not for the first time, military security suffered because of financial budgetary constraints or manpower shortfalls. Ironically, the public servants carried on, expanding their bureaucratic demands, effectively firmly rooting their status. In the same time frame, a secret police report from August to October 1916 identified as operations to counteract the Russian intelligence service itemized the results: August, 117 arrested and 38 found guilty; September, 118 arrested and 39 found guilty; October, 98 arrested and 21 found guilty. Those found guilty were executed; the rest were released.[106]

In the final stages of the war, the Germans, fixated with control, turned to absolute security on the grounds of military necessity. The Gempp files reflect the security fears that continued to grow stronger among members of the high command.[107] The Dutch–Belgian border was an acute problem for the Germans, as it was notoriously difficult to police. It was an escape route for Belgian men avoiding enforced labor, spies and saboteurs, and increasingly would-be German deserters. The army wanted to cage in its soldiers and the population and so erected a long electric fence, closing the border permanently.[108] The electricity was supplied from Aachen's suburban tramway, an AC supply, with large generating facilities. The fence was more than 180 kilometers long, and there is still evidence of it today. German border guards were ordered to shoot on sight anyone who survived the fence.[109] By 1917, security and labor had become the army's primary concern. An order from 1917 conscripting labor for the mines stipulated that all persons, without exception, aged fifteen to sixty, had to be registered (*Erfassung*) by labor offices (*Arbeitsämter*). They were categorized by expertise for mine work or other employment. The officials kept lists of availability for work and recorded shifts. The order concluded, "The Etappen-Kommandanturen are to place a 1.5 kilometer security zone around the local community."[110]

In France between February and March 1917, Ludendorff unleashed Operation "Alberich," as the German army conducted a controlled withdrawal of its front line; they "resettled" 126,000 French civilians. The level of plundering, already high, increased as nine hundred trainloads of French booty were transported to Germany. Troop vigilance was only a small part of a larger scheme to ensure complete military security. By 1918, the doctrines of security and occupation had the added impetus of cross-fertilization of methods from the different theaters of war. On February 25, 1918, the German 50th (Reserve) Division had been transferred from the Eastern Front to France. The divisional intelligence officer reminded all officers and men of the need to check on civilian infiltration into military zones. Three weeks earlier, on February 4, 1918, the same division posted rules for the implementation of cavalry patrols. The patrols had parallel authority with the gendarmerie and placed under the command of the divisional security officer. The patrol members wore distinctive collar emblems and carried divisional instructions of their authority. Prior to a patrol, the designated security officer briefed the troops of specific field activities and provided details for their routes. The patrols were conducted in the early hours of the evening or at dawn. Their task was to arrest spies air-landed into the area, destroy reconnaissance balloons, collect up all enemy propaganda leaflets, and kill all carrier pigeons. Civilians detected outside their village limits had to be in possession of valid documentation. All persons were searched for food or letters.[111] The Etappen and the occupation had become the principle forms of regulating the German way of war, the tail in effect wagged the dog, and within this emerging scenario lay Bandenbekämpfung.

## Urban Warriors

In November 1918, Germany tumbled into revolution. After forty-eight years of autocracy and militarism culminating with Ludendorff's military dictatorship, the SPD, the long-standing political opponent of the army, took power. The repercussions of defeat and change were not long in surfacing. An eruption of demobilized troops, rampant influenza, food shortages partly because of the ongoing allied naval blockade, the arrival of allied occupation armies enforcing the separation of disputed lands, and widespread industrial redundancy pushed Germany to the verge of anarchy. The political ramifications led to rival crowds of marchers on the streets carrying banners in nationalist, socialist, and republican colors, displaying their refusal to be counted as the foot soldiers of democracy. Revolutionaries raised armed militias who were volunteers from the soldiers' and workers' councils, many of whom were former soldiers. The militias sometimes were bolstered by a cadre of "experts" from Russia. The right wing, opponents to everything but themselves, called on German patriotic sentiment to make a stand against the left. Political authority—whether nationalist, revolutionary, or republican—was imposed by the persuasiveness of the gun. Soldiers faced former soldiers, left-wing activists faced right-wing activists, while civilians tried to dodge the bullets. With anarchy running the streets, the government turned toward a paramilitary solution. Those first years of Weimar, hamstrung by fumbling internal security policy, left a mark of insecurity.

The old order was quick to make a political stand. Ludendorff had fled Germany in November 1918, hoping to avoid allied war crimes jurisdiction. He returned from his self-imposed exile disguised as "Mr. New-man" (Herr Neumann). He quickly passed the blame for the failure of the army to win its long rehearsed and prepared-for war on the "stab-in-the-back" and the plague of "Jewish-Bolshevism."[112] In the absence of leadership from its former commanders, the inner professionalism of the army wavered. The old Imperial Army, even under Schlieffen's unified and rigid system, was beset with cliques. The Prussians, Bavarians, Kolonialmensch, technocrats, staff officers, daredevil cavalrymen, and the poor bloody infantry all came home expecting recognition from an ambivalent society. The end of the Kaiserreich finally destroyed the rigid professionalism of Schlieffen's uniform military code. So when prominent heroes of the war such as Epp and Lettow-Vorbeck came home, they received sharply divergent welcomes. Although they appeared to share a common colonial past, their respective wartime experiences divided them.

Lettow-Vorbeck had spent the whole war in East Africa fighting a partisan campaign. He personified the concept of small war that Boguslawski had championed. The Feldherr of partisan warfare came home to Germany with the mission to project his military achievements as a romantic image of war. This bore little comparison with the general picture of trench fighting that millions of German men had experienced. He duly arrived in Germany in February 1919, having missed the momentous events of November 1918, and the first operations of the Freikorps. Undaunted, in March 1919, the newly promoted general of infantry paraded the European contingent of his "army" along the Unter den Linden in Berlin. This dreamlike final victory parade, by an "undefeated" German army, attracted the attention of the Berlin crowds as they flocked to a spectacle last seen in 1914. However, this kind of fame was fleeting, the relic of a rapidly dwindling past, and recognizing this, Lettow-Vorbeck turned to publication.

The first set of memoirs, suitably titled *Heia Safari!* (1919), contained the drama of arrogant self-promotion. Lettow-Vorbeck painted his "small war" across the larger canvas of the Great War.[113] This modern professional soldier had waged a successful campaign, and he conspired to profit from it. Irrespective of this, the contents make an interesting analysis since his partisan campaign was the very antithesis of Bandenbekämpfung. In his memoirs, Lettow-Vorbeck played down his prior colonial experiences in China and Namibia, referring to the latter as a Buschkrieg, in other words, a police action. This was a deliberate act of disassociation from past colonial failures in order to glorify his successes. To emphasize his argument, he stressed Emil von Zelewski's debacle thirty years earlier, calling it a major military blunder. He cited Zelewski as the model example of how things can go wrong in operations. This commentary is a brief window into the army's mindset and further illustrates both the magnitude of Zelewski's defeat and its impression on the military culture.[114]

Lettow-Vorbeck had detractors of his fame, namely Heinrich von Schnee, the last German East African governor. Schnee's bitterness toward Lettow-Vorbeck came from the firm opinion that his "glorious" campaign was simply unnecessary under the prevailing colonial agreements between the great powers.[115] Setting Schnee's criticisms aside, in 1919, Lettow-Vorbeck took command of a Freikorps formation, the Freiwillige Division v. Lettow-Vorbeck, and then led pacification operations in Hamburg. On May 15, 1920, the partisan leader supported the Kapp putsch, yet he proved ill-suited at conducting small war within the fatherland. In 1926, he attempted to remodel himself with a second set of memoirs. More charitable this time to Trotha, he mentioned serving on his staff, but his distance from the colonies was ever more pronounced.[116] He entered politics and the *Reichstag*, proving his political naiveté by proposing a ban on the SS and SA in 1930, at the height of the political violence at the end of the Weimar Republic.

Epp was a professional soldier and a member of the secret Thule Society in Munich. His war included the horror of Verdun, commanding a regiment of the Alpenkorps, and serving as the kaiser's fire-brigade in hot spots in southern Europe. In October 1918, he returned to Germany by conducting a fighting withdrawal from Serbia. His former regimental adjutant, Adolf von Bomhard, later published the regiment's history.[117] In 1919, Epp was unable to even reside safely in Munich. The Red Republic under Kurt Eisner and the members of the secret Thule Society were locked in a microcosm of class war, ferociously slaughtering each other.[118] The Thule–Gesellschaft membership held a common belief in the sacred destiny of the Germanic soul, which they thought flowed from an Aryan community that had populated the icy wastes long before civilization. Imbued with this belief in the sanctity of Germany and her greater destiny, the members participated in illegal political acts and carried out assassinations or sectarian killings. For a brief period, the Thule Society collected together the right-wing elites and would-be political activists including Epp, Ernst Röhm, Bomhard, Ludendorff, Adolf Hitler, Rudolf Hess, and Heinrich Himmler. Against this background, Epp's Freikorps prepared for the battle of Munich.

The Nazi chronicler of the "battle" of Munich, Frederick von Oertzen, happened to be a veteran of the Waterberg, having commanded the ill-fated Deimling detachment's artillery batteries. With this bitter experience behind him, he praised Epp for his determination and the plan that called for a march on the city in a highly coordinated and crushing encirclement. Epp ordered the piecemeal extermination without escape of the members and supporters of the republic, the embodiment of the Waterberg plan.[119] His chronicler, Oertzen, recorded the sentiment of Freikorps orders, "the destruction of the . . . bandits" (*die Vernichtung der Banden*), a form common to all three epochs of Bandenbekämpfung.[120] He praised Epp and his men as the epitome of professionalism because they did not need to be told what to do, nor did they require special coaching. After a brief, but formal, parade in Ulm, the detachments marched into the battle lines (*Kampffront*) in Munich. Josef Krumbach, Epp's official Nazi biographer, memorialized the battle of Munich for leading Germany away from the dirt and filth (*Schmutz und der Fäulnis*) of the "red" period (*Rätezeit*). Krumbach explained that few officers studied their enemy as thoroughly as Epp did. His military logic was simple: the Soviet of Marxists and Jews were a plague led by the "eastern Jew" (*Ostjude*) Dr. Levine and had illegally occupied Munich. Under these circumstances, Bolshevik Jews, in Epp's opinion, deserved little better than the Herero.[121]

The Nazis mythologized Munich as an example of national heroism and self-sacrifice. While this later contributed to the burgeoning dogma of military politics, in the short term, Epp participated in other calculated acts. He imposed law and order on Munich but without permanent military government. He later went to the Ruhr and did much the same. His "achievement," the product of his professionalism, was depicted as transcending both the Kaiserreich and Weimar, making him a true servant to the nation. It was inverted glory. Munich granted Epp national prominence, the status of Feldherr, and subsequent promotion to general. Unlike Lettow-Vorbeck, he embellished his experiences in China and Namibia. This did not tarnish his political or military career. Unlike Trotha and Lettow-Vorbeck, Epp made Cannae work. As a "cleansing action" (*Säuberungsaktion*), with after-action executions, Epp had applied Bandenbekämpfung to restore order within a sharply focused military landscape. The suppression of the Räterepublik, through initiative and police action atrocities, was Epp's adaptation of Schlieffen security methods for the post-Schlieffen world.

# 2
# THE NEW ORDER

W hither Germany? In the twenty years between 1919 and 1939, German national security experienced several makeovers. The shift in the balances of governing elites, from army and monarchy, to politicians and police, finally resting with dictatorship, placed security at the forefront of political agendas. In the chaotic early years of Weimar, the widespread application of Banden-bekämpfung swiftly imposed law and order, but for a nation in political flux, it was a temporary expedient. Once the atmosphere calmed, the enormity of national security came to rest on two issues. The first concerned the external forces manipulating German society; the second involved the appropriate level of internal security. The army, which had been aloof to civilian society during the Kaiserreich, began to concentrate on questions of civil-military relations during times of war and occupation. The Weimar police, albeit a professionalized force, maintained law and order while laying down the foundations for a national security state. When public opinion polarized, democratic and extremist parties alike tried to make political capital by exploiting fears of inadequate law and order and institutionalized the concept of guardianship policing. By 1933, all the structural elements were in place for Hitler to erect a national security state.

The loss of lands under the provisions of the Treaty of Versailles accentuated German national uncertainty and insecurity over territory. The concept of "living space" (Lebensraum) became a popular political theme. This geopolitical picture of Germany's international status and the long-term perspective of national survival was shared across class and party boundaries. Long before 1914, the opinion that great nations had plentiful land for population growth and were rich in raw materials for industrial development had taken hold. The book *People without Land* (*Volk ohne Raum*), which popularized the word Lebensraum, was in fact a work of fiction, but it nonetheless created a national political slogan.[1] Karl Haushofer had a more significant influence on Hitler. His voluminous works included an in-depth study of the Pacific Ocean, an examination of the movement of indigenous populations. His work leaned toward anthropology, and he dismissed Darwin as a mere sociologist trained in the natural sciences. He also published a short pamphlet on Lord Kitchener, which examined him in the context of a supreme empire builder.[2] Today, Haushofer's work retains some interest for the scholar, but at the time, it made an important contribution in the political debates over land and self-determination in Weimar Germany. In the Rhineland, where suspicions of French schemes for separation were rife, the reading materials for schools, apprentice and training colleges (*Berufschulen*), universities and state academies were filled with questions of land.[3] Weimar did not neutralize this sub-liminal nationalistic agenda, which served to politicize several generations of young Germans. The land question also absorbed the hangover from the period of international rivalry before 1914. In particular, Anglo-German rivalry was turned into land benchmarking; the British Empire with its small population set against the landless German masses.[4]

The question of race became a central political question after 1918. In 1919, Britain sponsored a commission to investigate allegations of brutality in Namibia was under German rule. Germans criticized the British commission not because they were embarrassed of their ill-treatment of the Herero but because they assumed that Britain coveted the colony.[5] Another race issue became a political crisis, inflaming German public attitudes toward the French. The French had detailed black soldiers from its colonial regiments to occupation duties of the Ruhr in 1923. It became known as the "black disgrace" (*schwarze Schmach*) and proved to extremists groups that there were votes in harnessing race and security.[6] The commander of the U.S. occupation forces recorded in his diary that French methods had set Germans on the road to revenge.[7] The Nazis turned Ludendorff's "stab-in-the-back" myth and the Freikorps sentiment of combating Jewish-Bolshevism into effective slogans that amplified these questions of race and space. By the mid-1930s, the Jews took the brunt of hostile racism that blamed them both for the corruption of capitalism and as the agents of Bolshevism. These contradictions appealed to a large cross-section of the German populace who preferred ideological slogans that amplified Germany's plight rather than commonsense policies to alleviate the national predicament.

Herein lay the path to the Holocaust and the origins of Hitler's empire building. In power, Hitler manufactured struggles between institutions and individuals to erect a national security state. All sides in the territorial debate craved revenge on France and Poland, but only hard-liners comprehended the meaning of Lebensraum for Jews and Slavs. The early Nazi banner of guardianship and "blood and soil" (*Blut und Boden*) policies called for the forcible acquisition of territory and the purification of race. However, few in 1936 recognized the subtle transfer from community guardianship policing to the administration of state security. With the onset of war, the priority was for the prevention of another "stab-in-the-back." The euphoria of conquests turned caution into aggression. Hitler unleashed his ultimate drive for Lebensraum.

## The Marriage of Militarism and Guardianship

During the interwar years, the armed forces went through a process of change. The old "state within a state" was reduced and reconfigured. The Great General Staff, in the guise of the Heeresleitung and the Truppenamt, was reduced to the minimum but retained its essential functions. The key task it set itself was evaluating the First World War, a memorial exercise to Schlieffen's principles. Publicly, this evaluation covered the origins and causes as well as the strategic and tactical progress of the war during the many campaigns and battles. Less publicly, the army conducted in-depth research into non-military factors such as industry and mobilization, military technology, and foreign armies study. The other tasks involved organization, training, and regulations formulation.[8] The first military objective of the Reichswehr involved securing the eastern frontiers against Polish incursions. The army manipulated the threat to border security (*Grenzschutz*) in ways that resembled the global powers' maneuvers during the Cold War. Open conflict broke out in Silesia in 1919 and lasted until 1921. The army exploited the presence of a military dictatorship in Poland as grounds for a reorganization of the Grenzschutz. The Cold War conditions returned on the German–Polish border but an unofficial shooting war continued beyond the Silesian plebiscite until 1930. The militarization of politics extended the pernicious form of militarism of the Kaiserreich Weimar. This process began in 1916 when Ludendorff became supreme commander of the German war effort and passed his responsibilities to General Groener. Ludendorff was an expert of Etappen administration and the politics of occupation in the east. In 1918, he assisted in the birth of the Weimar republic, while protecting the interests of the army. Gradually, military-led coup d'etats came to blight Weimar. Kapp, Buchrucker, and Munich were not the wildcat coup d'etats of a banana republic. Even a mature democracy would struggle to maintain its cohesion under such attacks. Weimar's progress was crippled from within. The public desire for stability was answered when Field Marshal Paul von Hindenburg assumed the presidency in 1926, and the coup d'etats subsided as the officer corps was reminded of its to higher authority.[9] The end of putschism enabled the army to undertake in-depth foreign military studies. In 1929, Hauptmann Walter Warlimont traveled to America to learn about industrial production and mobilization.[10] In later years, Warlimont confided to his interrogators that the army's priority under Weimar was "maintaining the military spirit of the German people."[11]

Findings from the study of the war were adopted into training and planning. Schlieffen had tried to perfect the supreme military mechanism by rigid professionalization. The war had proved that the drive for perfection was impossible and "that politics pervades all military operations and [has] unremitting influence over them."[12] The army regarded Schlieffen's doctrines as tactical masterpieces but shelved his strategic outlook. In 1924, Maj. Hermann Geyer, one of Ludendorff's most capable staff officers, published an article on the future of Cannae in war. Geyer had joined the army under Schlieffen and served with Ludendorff's staff during the capture of Liège in 1914. In 1916, he published the German infantry combat guidelines, and from 1919, he served in the Reichswehr. His article addressed the broad question of Germany's preparations for war and its lack of technical ability as compared with the Allies. He was dismissive of the value of colonial warfare in modern European war and critical of the overemphasis on Cannae in training before the war. He found no congruency between the overtraining and the absence of Cannae during the war. Geyer praised Hindenburg for the Battle of Tannenberg, the only example of a Cannae in the war. He cautioned his readers to recognize the real failings, namely the inadequate technical ability of the German officers. He was critical of the growing tendency toward specialization and the rise in overorganization. Geyer believed these factors prevented officers from applying initiative and taking risks. He believed officers were not prepared to take the risk of gaps in their lines to attempt Cannae. They feared an enemy infiltration. This, he argued, had turned officers into "straight-rule strategists" (*Linealstrategie*) who had forgotten that

> Striving for the greatest possible victory, the victory *a la Cannae*, in the strategy of extermination was prospective, but more risky. Attack and defense, advance and retreat, economical and excessive use of force needs to be balanced carefully, according to time, place and scale. It was the military mistake of the world war that we did not follow this path, as Schlieffen had taught us.[13]

The army also conducted research into occupation. A lecture by Oberleutnant von Ziehlberg delivered May 1930 typified the scrutiny into civil-military issues. His theme examined the extent of the damage caused to civilians and livestock in East Prussia, from the Russian invasion of 1914–15. The Russians inflicted 1,620 deaths and 433 injuries and "evacuated" 5,419 men, 2,587 women, and 2,719 children into their rear areas. The total number of refugees who tried to escape was 870,000, of whom 400,000 crossed the River Vistula. In the subsequent invasion, preplanned German transport evacuated 175,000 civilians west. Ziehlberg recorded that the invasions cost large numbers of livestock including 600,000 horses, 1,400,000 cattle, 200,000 pigs, 50,000 sheep, and 10,000 goats. Destruction of the infrastructure affected thirty-five towns: 3,400 buildings were destroyed, 1,900 villages attacked, and

27,000 homes lost. In four days (March 18–21, 1915), the Memel area suffered intense damage. Losses included the forcible evacuation of 458 men, women, and children by the Russians. The total cost of destruction and plundering was estimated at RM 5 million. The lecture was not intended for public consumption, drew conclusions from Ludendorff and Geyer, and was a portent for the future.[14]

One particular problem for the army in the 1920s was finding a working alternative to the intricacies of the Etappen system. The Imperial Army system relied on reservists and Landwehr, which was undermined by the by Versailles limitations on length of service and manpower. The Reichswehr was forced to dispense with the traditional system of reserves. This further restrained strategic thinking toward a single offensive, reduced to the single knockout blow, but left the ongoing problem of security. One solution was the "Black Army" (*Schwarze Reichswehr*). Oberst Fedor von Bock, chief of staff of Wehrkreis III, ordered Maj. Bruno Buchrucker to build a reserve disguised as work teams (*Arbeitskommando*). The system rapidly mobilized more than eighty thousand men. Recruitment exploited the old *Krümper* system devised by Scharnhorst to expand or contract the army. As an army reserve, they expected reinforcement with cadres of regular troops. The scheme concentrated on discipline and training. When Bock ordered the scheme closed, Buchrucker and Hauptmann Walter Stennes attempted a putsch in September 1923. The army arrested its rebellious officers, cashiered them, and had them imprisoned. Buchrucker received a ten-year sentence for high treason, served two, and joined the Nazis. Stennes was cashiered and also joined the Nazis.[15]

A unique feature of Weimar society was the coexistence of republican democracy and militarized politics. The allied control commission had forced Germany to dismantle its military power base and monitored Weimar's efforts to solve the question of national security with a seemingly ineffective army.[16] Weimar introduced a catchall federal constitution and raised a professional police force, but the states retained their uniform regulations and codes. Weimar police authority came under Article 7 of the constitution, which listed fourteen categories of law and order. The application for greater police powers, including the maintenance of public order, came from statutory instruments addressed under Article 9. The most controversial Article 48 granted the government the authority to suspend civil rights fundamental to the constitution in times of emergency and to employ the armed force to restore order.[17] In convoluted form, Article 48 legitimized the Freikorps experience.[18] A major weakness of Weimar, in this context, concerned the manner in which the new republic coupled with the remains of the former system. Individual German *Länder* (states), in common with other federal systems of government, retained their legislative rights over law and order. This legal belt and braces was more a hangover from 1871 than the establishment of a sinister police state. The notion of the *Rechtsstaat*, a state contrived in pure law, had taken hold in Germany long before the Weimar constitution. The old regulations had proved their value in the immediate aftermath of war. Border cities like Aachen overwhelmed by war, occupation, and social collapse, resorted to Prussian ordinances from 1851 as their only legal remedy for the restoration of order.[19] According to Otto Loening, Weimar had introduced a police force on democratic principles but attempted to overcome its opponents, including the German Länder, by relying on secret political policing, methods incompatible with democracy.[20]

The former military caste returned to the state under Weimar as police officers and public servants. The character of the uniformed police inclined toward internal security rather than simple beat policing. Policing within Germany consumed a broad interpretation of regulation and supervisory functions in the service of the state. It was a by-product of internal security. Richard Evans' essay on the historical development of German policing, a compact survey of the period from 1800 to 1945, viewed this period as one of increased policing without a proportional reduction in crime. The contrasts in the development were profound but led to bureaucratization. French influence on German policing included the introduction of the gendarmerie in 1812, effectively containing the roving bands of robbers. Wilhelm Stieber's undoubted performance on behalf of securing the Great General Staff was not matched in his handling of domestic policing. His underhand methods, including bribery, deception, and fraud, caused widespread corruption to develop within the Prussian police. Long after Stieber's death in 1882, the German press continued to refer to political policing as *Stieberschen Art*.[21] The gradual militarization of the police, so often used to explain away its inherent brutality, was an expression of Germany's internal regulation through the dictatorship by state bureaucracy service and its inherent self-protectionism. Retiring professional soldiers then, like German public servants today, were a protected occupation with the right to permanent employment. Former army NCOs took up police employment on retirement, becoming military bureaucrats (*Militäranwärter*) within the national civilian administration.[22]

According to Richard Bessel, the Weimar police were "modern and democratic," in contrast with the militarized police and "bureaucratic-soldier" of the Kaiserreich.[23] Weimar followed the conventional path toward police professionalization through recruitment, training, and technology. The deployment of a professional police force depended on significant numbers of trained troopers and officers, although neither existed in 1920. The lack of available and untainted manpower was, in one form or another, a critical factor in policing until 1945. Attracted to the police as uniform body, former Kaiserreich police officers, veteran soldiers, and Freikorps bonded to form an inner "old school." The Prussian Schutzpolizei, what Evans called a republican guard, had to contend with the ongoing pressure from within its ranks to adopt militaristic tendencies. Bessel thought the recruitment of younger men in the final years of Weimar gave a fleeting glimpse of what might have been. He identified the police relationship with new technology and confidence in comprehensive training programs. The utilization of motor vehicles and advanced telecommunications indicated a corporate inclination for specialization. Police training schools and academies, including the School of Technology and Communications, trained cadets in a range of advanced skills and techniques.[24]

Weimar politicians, like politicians the world over, brandished slogans to encourage public acceptance of their protégés. The police force was not an exception when it was called the "guardian of public order and security, servant of the general public in selfless, devoted activity."[25] Carl Severing's catchphrase, "The Police—Your Friend and Helper," the official police motto, was, by today's standards, a soundbite without substance. Legal scholars like Otto Loening were sceptical of these slogans. Loening believed they were poorly conceived, lacked authority, and were without adequate definition under the law.[26] He accepted that the constitution granted the police the right to conduct interrogations and place listening devices for the sake of law and order. He, however, was not distracted by what he thought was thinly veiled politicking. He concentrated on the issue of ill-defined ordinances within police regulations that circumvented the constitution. Loening pointed out the growing inconsistency between federal and state policing. The police stood between soldiers and civilians and found solace in their exclusivity. Entrenched social distinctions between the police and the civilian world in Weimar came to resemble the distinction between soldiers and civilians in the Kaiserreich. Effectively, civil-police relations had superseded civil-military relations during the interwar years.

While police regulators and practitioners made uneasy bedfellows, Weimar society began to distill alternative forms of organized protection, more appropriately labeled guardianship. In terms of total policing, the federal and state police left a discernible vacuum that unsettled the public. Weimar was committed to national policing while the states were concerned with preventing anarchy on the streets. Under these circumstances, the middle class (*Mittelstand*) believed they went unpoliced. The rise of community self-policing and self-protection schemes reflected this perception. The political challenge of communal guardians undermined the case for professional policing. James Diehl has argued that the rise of radical militarized politics in Europe proved that Germany was not the only country affected by paramilitarism. However, Diehl suggests that when the "respectable" middle classes endorsed the civic guards (*Einwohnerwehre*), Germany became the exception.[27] Diehl explained that this was the by-product of Bismarck's power politics, rooted in the hearts and minds of law-abiding citizens' fear of enemies of the state (*Reichsfeinde*). The Kapp putsch was, in Diehl's opinion, the catalyst for the growth in civic guards. In Munich, Epp raised the civic guards and the Technical Emergency Police (*Technische Nothilfe*), abbreviated as TN) to secure public utilities.[28] Armed bands (*Wehrbände*) and the political combat leagues (*politische Kampfbünde*) sustained militarism in German politics. In the first months of Hitler's rule, volunteers to the Aachen police included members of the *Deutschenationalen Kampfringes*.[29] These volunteers were mostly war veterans, patriots, and middle-class professionals including foresters and influential businessmen.[30] They also aspired to professionalism through regular training.[31]

A bridge between the military and social militarism was established between the army and public associations. One such association was the League of Front-Soldiers, known as the Steel Helmets (*Stahlhelm*), founded by veterans of the Great War, in December 1918. Their initial intention was to keep alive the spirit of comradeship, born in the trenches, in common with a host of similar organizations around the world. The greeting of its members, "hail the front" (*frontheil*), symbolized the merger of trench culture and paramilitarism. While the Stahlhelm conducted obvious military activities, including weapons training and full-scale exercises, it also waged a hostile political campaign for a return to the pre-1914 order. The Stahlhelm administered a welfare campaign of social help for the poorer communities and charitable activities that included winter-help schemes. They were reasonably successful in proving an acceptable face to militarism under Weimar.[32] There was a flood of political party protection squads. They were essential for protecting officials and ensuring the party message was delivered without interference. The Nazis raised two guard formations: the SA (*Sturmabteilung*) and the Protection Squad (*Schutzstaffel–SS*). The SS was initially formed as small elite to protect Hitler.[33] Their growth in power and influence was because of Hitler. In *Mein Kampf,* Hitler thought the SA would become the highly trained champions of national socialism, the devoted soldiers of the Nazi *Weltanschauung*. However, the unruly behavior of the SA, especially toward elements within the party, including himself, led Hitler to abandon the SS as a personal bodyguard.

In 1929, Hitler promoted Heinrich Himmler to Reichsführer-SS with the mandate to increase the post's political authority and influence. Himmler arranged the central office of the SS and, in 1931, opened two branches that addressed questions of security and race. The Security Service (*Sicherheitsdienst–SD*), under Reinhard Heydrich, was an internal security bureau that monitored society and the party. The other was the SS Race and Settlement Office (*Rasse- und Siedlungshauptamt, RuSHA*), which, under Richard Darré, codified Blut und Boden ideas into SS dogma. [34] In the early years, the SS leadership embedded its harsh discipline and blind obedience to Hitler that remained until May 1945.[35] The end of freebooting paramilitarism coincided with the destruction of Ernst Röhm and the emasculation of the SA. The culling of Nazi comrades by the SS in June 1934, during the "night of the long knives," was inevitable. The end of paramilitarism was confirmed in July 1934 when Hitler declared, "I elevate [the SS] to the status of an independent organisation within the NSDAP subordinate to the supreme SS leader. The Chief of Staff and the Reichsführer-SS are both invested with the Party rank of Reichsleiter."[36]

In 1935, Kurt Daluege, later the chief of the Order Police (*Chef der Ordnungspolizei*), mimicked Carl Severing when he asked the question, "What are the police for?" He believed that if the police were to meet the National Socialist mission then they should aspire to become soldiers of the community (*Gemeindesoldat*).[37] Erich Ludendorff also made an encore appearance at this time. In the chaos after 1918, he had brought together a disparate group of individuals that subsequently became the backbone of the Nazi Party. Epp, Hitler, Röhm, Hess, and Ludendorff shared a vision of the pure Germanic (Aryan) society, a militarized community, regimented, racist, rich in territories and raw materials, led by a man of vision.[38] The Nazi mindset believed in Ludendorff for his near victory in 1918, the "stab-in-the-back" slogan, and his support for Hitler during the failed Munich putsch (1923). His book *Der totale Krieg* (1935) was published in the same year Hitler introduced the Nuremberg race laws and conscription, the key foundations of the racist militarized society.[39] In Wilhelm Deist's opinion, Ludendorff had drafted the blueprint for the Nazi concept of warfare. A vision of power lay at the heart of Ludendorff's total war. This was a vision of conflict and struggle as the permanent way of life. Interpretations of Ludendorff's "total war" have played down the experiences that underpinned his theories. The "Ober Ost" and his supreme command had scaled the heights of the purely militarized society, alien to civilian social norms.[40] Ludendorff's model for the militarized national community founded the Nazi concept of a national community (*Volksgemeinschaft*) and met Daluege's ideas of a community soldier. He recommended the application of sweeping preventative measures to suppress "disgruntled" groups in times of war and their classification as enemies of the state.[41] Ludendorff answered Daluege's question by encapsulating the role of a militarized police within the dogma of race and space.

In June 1936, Heinrich Himmler became chief of the SS (*Reichsführer-SS und Chef der Deutschen Polizei*), marking the next stage in the radicalization of security. The merger of the SS and police signaled the rise of a national police force following the road of national security. Himmler's experience of political soldiering, policing, and Nazi administrative politics was not the only reason Hitler chose him to become the supreme police officer. The exponent of guardianship policing, Himmler propagandized this mission as "inner security, the inner protection of the National Socialist people." As he argued, "From the traditional concept of Police has arisen the new concept of a protective Corps of the German people. And just as the old idea was typically personified in the bailiff, the new idea also demands a new man." Thus, he wrote, "The police again was carried into the midst of the people as an important member for the protection and defense of the community."[42] Himmler's legendary administrative skills, education and career, classical upbringing, degree in agricultural economics, and even his grasp of the principles of modern business, especially the concepts of profit and loss and the cost-benefit method of German bureaucracy, served as the guidelines for the SS corporation. From a bureaucratic standpoint, the merger of the SS and police simplified the regulation of doctrines. The administration of the Nuremberg race laws became a state code. In the codified nation, police officers and civilians alike could practice unrestricted institutional racism without telegraphing as publicly or overtly racist.

The elevation of his two lieutenants—Reinhard Heydrich as chief of the Security Police and Daluege as chief of the Order Police—amplified Hitler's faith in Himmler as his highly motivated protégé.[43] This triumvirate reinforced the competence of SS-Police leadership and proved highly productive.[44] There were practicalities to this arrangement. Before his death, Röhm proposed creating a Nazi army by absorbing the Reichswehr into the SA and creating an armed state protection corps (*Staatsschutzkorps*) responsible for internal and external security. Hermann Göring proposed the transformation of the federated police forces into a centralized police army. Himmler's plan involved centralizing all internal security assets into a single corporation led by the SS. Himmler's triumph was the catalyst to all the ideas and the radical compromise for Nazi security.

This "new man" was mentally energetic and craved to follow in the footsteps of men such as Hitler and Ludendorff. He came from a family dominated by the father, a senior school official who taught the classics. Alfred Andersch did not write of Himmler's father in glowing terms. He described him as a member of the Bavarian People's Party, a conservative to the core (*Schwarz bis in die Knochen*), who was known for being a "rear-area stallion" (*Etappenhengst*) and a fervent Catholic, but most notably a non-racist. Andersch portrayed the youthful Himmler as a fine young man, denied the chance of becoming a soldier, who moved in the correct circles of Hitler's followers and the "Ludendorff people."[45] Fascinated by Germanic myths and mythology, Himmler grasped Hitler's one-thousand-year Reich and, through Nazi symbiotic cultism, was able to flaunt his interests. His SS uniform collar patches combined the oak leaves of Germanic culture with the Roman laurel-leaf crown symbolizing the fusion of German mythology with ancient Rome. In climbing the greasy pole of Nazi politics, Himmler had self-styled his SS as Hitler's Wagnerian Praetorian Guard.[46] As Hitler's most trusted soldier, Himmler was bent on imposing the lessons from the past as the benefactors to the Nazi future. "We are not wiser than the men of two thousand years ago," he said. "Persians, Greeks, Romans and Prussians all had their guards. The guards of the new Germany will be the SS."[47]

## Political Prominence

Erich Julius Eberhard von Zelewski was born in March 1899 in Lauenberg, a small Pomeranian town in West Prussia. His rise to prominence was rapid and unsurprising. Although the son of a Junker family, he grew up poverty stricken. His father, Otto Johannes von Zelewski, was born in 1859. He undertook a range of jobs, including in civil service and agriculture, and died on April 17, 1911, in Dortmund while working as an insurance clerk. His mother, Eveline Schimanski, was born in Thorn in April 1862 or 1864. His parents married in Lauenberg in June 1890. The family reputation was also blighted: his father's brother was the ill-fated Emil von Zelewski who brought disgrace to the nation. Young Erich lived to restore the family honor. He spent his formative years under the guidance of his uncle, Oskar von Zelewski, who became his stepfather and was killed in action on the Eastern Front in 1915. Oskar was twenty-five years old and Erich just sixteen. Like his stepfather, Erich joined the army and, in November 1914, had the status of the youngest recruit of the war.[48] His first posting was to the 3rd West Prussian Infantry-Regiment Nr.129 (*Neustettin*). While serving with this regiment, he was awarded the Iron Cross (Second Class), and he received his first wound in 1915 and then earned a battlefield commission in 1916. The psychological effects of his wounding and extreme pain haunted him for the rest of his life. As Leutnant von Zelewski, he was posted to the Grenadier Regiment König Friederich Wilhelm (1st Silesian) Nr.10 based in Schweidnitz. This elite regiment had served in China during the Boxer Rebellion and fostered a close relationship with both Trotha and Lettow-Vorbeck. The regiment prided itself on a reputation for passing on its military skills and expertise from one generation of officers to the next. Leutnant von Zelewski found a home freely mingling with other Junker vons, including Manteuffel, Lüttwitz, Blankensee, Kleist, Bonin, and Bülow. [49] In July 1918, he was awarded the Cross of Honor (*Ehrenkreuz*) for his war service and then the Iron Cross (First Class). Leutnant von Zelewski ended the war as a young, battle-scared hero.

In November 1918, following the kaiser's abdication, Germany descended into revolution. During the ensuing chaos, Leutnant von Zelewski took his first political steps. His 1944 SS curriculum vitae (*Lebenslauf*) notes that in 1919 he joined the monarchist and right-wing German National People's Party (DNVP). His military career appeared safe in July 1919, although the regiment lost its monarchical status and became the 11th Infantry Regiment. It became part of Reichswehr Brigade 6 (formerly the 11th Infantry Division), within military district (Wehrkreis) III, and retained its home depot in Schweidnitz. From 1919 to 1924, the regiment was committed to German–Polish border duties. Leutnant von Zelewski made a memorable impression on Kurt von Bülow, his battalion commander, as a trustworthy (*Vertrauensmann*) officer revealing qualities of leadership and bravery. He led an aggressive reconnaissance, was wounded in the arm, and, in another incident, led a squad in the arrest of a doctor and his daughter working for the Polish authorities.[50] The young Leutnant received a new batch of medals for bravery, including the "Silesian Eagle" (*Schlesischer Adler* I and II), the "Protection of Silesia Medal," and the courage award (*Tapferkeitsabzeichen*). It was significant that the awards came from fighting against Polish nationalism. His SS files also list service with the former 4th Foot Guards, which was later renumbered to "29." In 1947, he alleged that, at the time of the Kapp putsch (1920), he was serving as the ordnance officer for the 29th Infantry Regiment of the Reichswehr based in Berlin-Moabit.[51] Both regiments came under Wehrkreis III, and for a war-commissioned officer without a specific base, his postings were common. The reasons for his departure from the army remain obscure. Under interrogation in 1946, he blamed his sisters for marrying Jews and destroying his reputation. He also suggested he became a battalion commander in the Black Reichswehr under Buchrucker. Given his proximity to the events, he was probably granted a battalion posting to soften the impact of his eventual demobilization and was released after the putsch.[52] In the mid-1930s, he briefly returned to the army, reactivating his reserve status with the 8th Infantry Regiment (Schweidnitz), and was promoted to Hauptmann. On October 23, 1925, the young Zelewski changed his name by legal decree from the justice ministry to include "von dem Bach."[53] Years later, he wrote to Himmler referring to Bülow's book. He failed to explain why the author referred to Leutnant von Zelewski in the narrative but listed "von dem Bach-Zelewski" in the index.[54] His military career had closed at the age of twenty-five; yet he had taken on a new identity and delved into politics.

Bach-Zelewski married Ruth Apfeld in September 1921, and together they had six children. Ruth's family came from Ratibor, which in 1921 lay close to the Polish and Czechoslovakian borders. Bach-Zelewski showed in his diary their devotion to one another: he called her *Mutti* (as in mother), and she referred to him as *Vati* (father). They owned a farm near Dühringshof near Frankfurt on the Oder, and later he set up home in Breslau.[55] Between 1924 and 1930, he became involved in local farming association politics, building a reputation for soldiering and farming that would place him at the forefront of Himmler's Blut und Boden warriors. In 1930, he joined the Allgemeine-SS and came under Daluege's command in the Frankfurt/Oder area. Daluege thought very highly of him, probably because they had both been youthful volunteers in the Great War. The SS records indicate that Daluege assessed Bach-Zelewski as "true and honest, starkly impulsive, in many cases unrestrained, uncontrolled recklessness (*hemmungslos*). Promotion is recommended if he controls his impulsiveness."[56] Bach-Zelewski's transfer of loyalty to Daluege proved immediately valuable in the attempted internal coup by the Berlin SA in April 1931. Walter Stennes and Bruno Buchrucker had become members of the SA. True to form, they attempted to inspire a revolt in Berlin against Hitler. Intervention by Daluege, assisted by Bach-Zelewski, tipped off Hitler, and the coup was crushed. Afterward, Hitler wrote to Daluege a letter of thanks that included the words "my honor is loyalty" (*Meine Ehre heist Treue*), which Himmler had etched into the blade of all SS ceremonial daggers.

In the 1930s, senior SS officers were required to prove their racial ancestry. Bach-Zelewski wrote to the SS Race and Resettlement Office in December 1935 explaining that he had not been able to retrieve the appropriate documentation from Poland. He alleged that proof of his wife's Aryan ancestry was in her brother's possession, the police chief of Neisse-Schlesien (Poland). Bach-Zelewski promised to make every effort to retrieve the documents. On January 11, 1937, however, the SS Race and Resettlement Officer of Breslau declared that the Poles had frustrated their efforts. The SS, in the 1930s, also institutionalized proselytism as religion and paganism existed in a permanent state of flux. Bach-Zelewski changed religion from Catholic to Evangelist in 1933 and then to "believer in a higher form of life" (*gottgläubig*) in 1938, further evidence of his immersion into SS orthodoxy.[57] In 1935, Himmler accepted one of Bach-Zelewski's children as a godson (*Patenkind*), in his ever-growing list of politicized godchildren.[58] The bond between Himmler and Bach-Zelewski thrived during the war.

Bach-Zelewski began his SS career of political killing in 1930 with the murder of three communists. On July 2, 1934, he ordered his subordinates, SS driver Paul Zummach and SS-Hauptsturmführer Reinhardt, to kill Anton Freiherr von Hohberg und Buchwald in Eylau in East Prussia. In 1935, he was chief of SS and security police in Königsberg. He very quickly came to blows with Gauleiter Koch over a series of matters, including, most significantly, who controlled Königsberg.[59] In August, Hjalmar Schacht, in his role as president of the Reichsbank and economics minister, attended the Königsberg eastern conference (*Ostmesse*) to present the keynote speech on the consequences of Nazi economic policies. Schacht was critical of the growing attacks on Jews. He said they were detrimental to the performance of the economy and weakened Germany's currency trade balances with foreign countries. Bach-Zelewski was incensed. He shouted at Schacht, calling him a traitor to the German people, while declaring that the Jews would pay for their crimes. He ordered the SS and police to leave the conference in a deliberate show of blatant anti-Semitism.[60] Koch took exception to Bach-Zelewski's behavior and reported him to Goebbels and Himmler. Attending the conference were representatives from the army and the navy who witnessed the incident and reported it to their respective commanding officers. Both officers condoned Bach-Zelewski's behavior, placing on the record that he was a fine comrade and correct, endorsing the professionalism of his actions against Schacht.[61]

## Conflicting Ideologies

The old idiom, absence makes the heart grow fonder, described Weimar's relationship with Germany's former colonies. Instead of fading away, interest in the colonies continued to flourish. This resilience was a boon and a burden for politicians. The Weimar constitution made provision for the colonies, although these had been sequestrated by the Versailles Treaty, and the German colonial administration remained in service. Trade schools (*Berufschulen*) continued to train recruits for overseas service during the interwar years. A typical case was that of a former sergeant of the Tanganyika *Schutztruppen* who was able to send his son to colonial university because the costs were paid by the Foreign Office.[62] The Minister of Interior and Education even opened a new colonial school for women (*Koloniale Frauenschule*) in 1926.[63] Ideologically, Hitler thought the colonial issue was dead, superseded by his concept of Lebensraum. His brand of Lebensraum (and there were others) was not only geo-political in concept but also racial and militaristic in its dimensions.[64] Yet until 1938, Nazi policy appeared to endorse the claim for the return of the colonies. Hitler declared, "The German Lebensraum is too small without a colonial addition to guarantee an undisturbed sure and constant food supply for our people." Even in 1941, a Nazi publication declared, "We demand land and territory [colonies] for the sustenance of our people, and colonisation for our surplus population."[65] Was it a decoy for his real intentions? Did Hitler manufacture an internal struggle between the followers of traditional colonialism against the believers in Lebensraum fundamentalism? There are indications that Hitler used this ideological battle as a yardstick of loyalty within his inner circle.

The leading exponent of the old colonialism was Franz Ritter von Epp. The doyen of the extreme right, the Feldherr of Munich, had sealed a special relationship with Hitler. Epp also maintained strong links with the army and, after 1919, joined the governing elites of Munich. He was the Nazis' secret benefactor and, through his undoubted political authority in southern Germany, became their Trojan horse and protector.[66] In 1927, his defection from the Bavarian People's Party to the Nazis was hailed as a measure of their political maturity. Once in the party, Epp patronized the colonial question, the Nazi motor corps (*Nationalsozialistisches Kraftfahrkorps*), and the SA; he was after all a close associate of Röhm.[67] Once Hitler came to power, Epp became a Nazi director (*Reichsleiter der NSDAP*) and governor of Bavaria (*Reichsstatthalter für Bayern*). His first cabinet included Himmler, Röhm, and Hans Frank, the Nazi legal expert. He promoted Himmler and Heydrich to responsibility for security policing. Epp's political tentacles reached beyond the senior Nazis to include middle-ranking officers from the SS-Police and Wehrmacht. In 1934, Epp's influence over Hitler was broken when he tried to grant Röhm an honorable court-martial. Adding weight to Hitler's suspicions, Epp's personal clique included many homosexuals, including a disgraced senior SA officer, Edmund Heines.[68]

Before 1938, Hitler was unable to remove Epp either by force, as in the case of Röhm, or through political deception. Within colonial circles, the

Munich "victory" was heralded as a vindication of their fighting ability and comradeship. This had spurred many to join the party, and Peter Merkel believed this colonial contingent brought a swashbuckling adventurism. The colonialists were vehemently anti-French, anti-British, and imbued with hatred for Weimar.[69] In 1927, Epp gave his first official speech on the colonial question at a party rally for former colonial veterans in Königsberg. Two years later, he hosted the twenty-fifth anniversary commemorations of the war against the Herero. In 1933, he hosted several colonial conferences, including the Marine- und Kolonialkriege Verbände annual gathering. A year later, Hitler promoted him as Nazi Party colonial policy director (*Kolonialleiter der NSDAP*). This led to a new department created from the amalgamation of the Colonial Department of the Foreign Office with the planning and press offices of the Ministry of Economics, and the *Kolonialreferat* of the army.[70] Epp's job entailed raising the political temperature of the colonial debate. In parallel with these developments, the former colonial association (*Kolonialgesellschaft*) was renamed the *Reichskolonialbund*, known as the RKB, and in 1936, Epp became its national leader (*Bundesführer*). In 1934, the membership of the RKB stood at forty thousand; by October 1936, it had increased to two hundred thousand, and it reached its ceiling of one million in 1938. This proved Epp's power of persuasion and was the reason Hitler could not easily dispense with his services in the 1930s.

Since 1935, Nazi Germany and Fascist Italy had worked to find common ground in forging a power block at the heart of Europe. Epp's Nazi biographer contextualized this relationship by suggesting an international Fascist debate over colonies was opened on October 1, 1935, the day when Italy invaded Abyssinia (Ethiopia). Mussolini announced that the invasion was revenge for Italy's defeat at Adowa (1896) and the first steps in becoming a world power. Typical of the sentiments at the time, Mussolini declared a "modern" Roman Empire. From the ensuing international crisis, Epp tried to raise his political influence to the world stage.[71] In 1936, Italian–German military assistance for Franco tipped the balance in the Spanish Civil War and led to wider cooperation between the two powers. By the end of 1936, Italy and Germany were signatories to the Anti-Comintern Pact and had firmly established the "Pact of Steel," the Axis.[72] Cooperation between the Axis powers went beyond the political-strategic level. German police officers were encouraged to take secondment in Abyssinia (Ethiopia) through the Italian colonial administration. There they gained experience in broad range of colonial security.[73] Jakob Sporrenberg, a senior SD officer, later confessed under interrogation that the two police forces shared intelligence.[74] In 1942, U.S. Army intelligence circles observed that Daluege had been actively infiltrating the Italian police with German personnel for years.[75]

In May 1937, Düsseldorf hosted one of the largest colonial rallies in what proved to be a significant event. The rally was timed to coincide with

Whit-weekend (*Pfingsten*), an important holiday in the Rhineland calendar, ensuring maximum attendance with the minimum impact on industrial output.[76] It was a critical time for Hitler; aligning domestic, foreign, and military policy toward warlike goals had caused grumbling. The Rhineland, Germany's military industrial complex, was the largest support base for Epp and the colonial question. In 1919, Epp had contributed in "saving" the Ruhr from Bolshevik revolution, and certain industrialists' and workers' associations welcomed him. The industrialists of the Rhineland were fully committed to returning the colonies as exclusive markets for their goods. The RKB membership therefore increased dramatically among industrialists.[77] There was also growing uncertainty over the direction of Hitler's economic policy and in particular the Four Year Plan.[78] Epp began the speeches by congratulating the support for the RKB through the Düsseldorf branch of the part, calling it the "pacemaker of the colonial idea" and the "patent maker of the colonial schools." He then led his audience through the familiar narratives of a Volk ohne Raum. Most important, Epp soothed concerns over the Four Year Plan by indicating that it was a temporary scheme and that, in the long term, the colonies would return. He announced that the conference demonstrated that "people and leader" were firmly committed to their return. While Epp's words calmed his audience, Hitler's absence was thunderous.[79]

A few days after the rally, Major der Schutzpolizei Kummetz presented Daluege with a report.[80] The report detailed the proportions of membership to the RKB within the police precincts of the Rhineland. The figures showed that in Düsseldorf of 1,136 police, 90 percent were members of the RKB; in Duisburg, 59 percent of 670 police; in Essen, 73 percent of 1,091; in Wuppertal, 98 percent of 1,079; and in Oberhausen, 100 percent of 572 police.[81] The Düsseldorf chief of police had explained to Kummetz the growing interest in colonial political training. The promotion of the RKB, within the police and state bureaucracy, had raised calls for expert seminars and lectures. Kummetz confirmed that there had been total adherence with the order by Rudolf Hess to support the colonial debate through the RKB. He noted that, although it had been held on a workers' holiday, ten thousand people had attended the rally.[82] Thus, when Epp gave his final speech of 1937 at the Sportspalast in Berlin, the impression given was of a regime endorsing traditional colonialism. Indeed, prior to the rally, Hitler had written to Epp calling for continuing pressure over the return of the colonies to be sustained into the new year.[83] If it was a smoke screen for foreign policy initiatives, its deception worked. Epp interpreted the request as the signal for a new impetus behind his colonial policy. Externally, Epp had attracted attention for the cause, and in Britain, there was growing support for a return of the colonies.

By 1938, Epp's standing had reached its peak. The SS putsch against the SA in 1934 was followed by Göring's intrigues against Schacht. Hitler introduced the Nuremberg race laws and conscription in 1935 and embarked on the remilitarization of the Rhineland (1936). In 1937, he set down his guidelines for war recorded in the Hossbach memo. Finally, the Blomberg-Fritsch crisis removed the armed forces as a potential political threat to Hitler and shook the foundations of Epp's spiritual pillar, the army. In March 1938, he accepted an invitation from Air Marshal Balbo of the Italian Air Force and the governor general of Libya to attend a gathering at the Fascist Institute of Italian-Africa (*Istituto Fascista dell' Africa Italiana*). In attendance were senior delegates from Mussolini's regime, including members of the Ministry of Italian Africa and the Italian armed forces. The Anschluss with Austria took the world's attention away from the meeting. Then, twenty years after his victory in Munich, Epp was a bystander as Germany and Italy cajoled the Entente Cordiale into relinquishing control of Czechoslovakia without a fight. Britain and France offered Hitler a return of the colonies—the alternative to his ambitions for Czechoslovakia—but he declined.[84] Meanwhile, Nazi economic measures ruptured Epp's influence on the economy and big business. In November 1938, after the "Night of Broken Glass" (*Reichskristallnacht*),[85] industry received a major investment boost. Aside from the violent attacks on Jewish property, the chambers of commerce initiated the "Aryanization" of business. German business received an artificial "investment" boost of cash and balance sheet assets. This bought off the last commercial opposition to Hitler.[86] Elsewhere, the culmination of these events signaled to Winston Churchill that a regime change in Germany was the only answer to Hitler.

Epp's political standing declined from 1939. In January, Himmler wrote to Martin Bormann on the political value of colonial schooling and training. He wished to halt general training for the leadership corps, accepting in principle that it was necessary for Germany to gain raw materials but claiming this could continue for Nazi officials, administrators, and soldiers. However, he believed it was no longer appropriate for the police to attend general colonial training schemes. He confirmed that "real experience" in colonial policing was being gained elsewhere. He had decided to stop colonial schooling for the SS, Hitler Youth, and the SA.[87] By design, Himmler had outmaneuvered Epp and snubbed Hess. The relations between Mussolini and Hitler had brought about Austria and Czechoslovakia, which were mainstream Lebensraum projects. The Rome–Berlin Axis divided Europe, in Fascist terms, on a north-south latitude, erecting a central power block, granting Hitler the opportunity to pursue Lebensraum goals without fear of the southern flank. The path seemed set for Lebensraum building through war, but then the impact of revenge came to play its part.

## Revenge, Lebensraum, and Mechanized Cannae

In September 1939, Hitler unleashed Germany's mechanized armies in a surprise attack on Poland (Operation "Tannenberg"), announcing that it was the supreme act of revenge for Versailles. The military operations in Poland concluded with total victory through the skilled coordination of armored and air warfare. A second act of revenge, against France, orchestrated rapid victory through surprise and large-scale encirclement. These successes of mechanized Cannae, since known as *Blitzkrieg*, reconfirmed the army's faith in Schlieffen's operational legacy. Rapid success, however, concealed the glaring absence of coherent security warfare preparations. In 1914, the Etappen quickly expanded from its peacetime cadre into operational status. German reservists and civilian specialists began operating a fully functional rear-area system almost in step with the attacks at the front. The offensive failed, but the Etappen continued to operate, in some respects with over-efficiency. This situation was reversed in 1939–40. The dual impact of Versailles, which removed the reserves, compounded with Hitler's rapid rearmament and mobilization program, had not provided the army with a viable alternative to the Etappen. The Nazi focus on the motorization of the armed forces had failed to complement similar attention to the railways and left the quartermaster functions unevenly dispersed among the operational and rear-area troops. The offensives in 1939–40 granted the armed forces the advantage of exploiting internal lines, surprise, and airpower.[88] Rapid victory had also denied the countries attacked sufficient time to coordinate a national uprising, and so resistance was sporadic and localized. Thus, by the standards of past security warfare, German military power in 1939–40 was like that of 1870–71, fielding a dynamic offensive army but lacking both a contingency plan for security and a dedicated force of occupation troops.

In the past, the German response was to strengthen internal security and depend on the army. A similar pattern emerged on September 1, when Hitler announced to the Reichstag that "a November 1918 shall never occur again in German history."[89] It was an indication of new moves in security. On September 3, he granted Himmler authority over law and order and the right to employ "all means" as required.[90] That same day, Heydrich issued a policy document titled "Basic Principles for Maintaining Internal Security during the War." An addendum of September 20 brought Germany under martial law, targeting saboteurs, suspicious persons, communists, and defeatists, all to "be eliminated through ruthless action." Seven days later, the Reich Main Security Office (*Reichssicherheitshauptamt,* RSHA) was formed; this constituted the first phase in turning the SS into Germany's national security corporation.[91] In September 1940, Rudolf Querner, the chief of Order Police in Hamburg, hosted an official visit from leading Spanish police officials. In his presentation, Querner highlighted the contribution of the police to the German war effort. He began by describing how the Order Police was organized and militarized under the guiding leadership of Daluege. Its tasks included the confiscation of civilian arms, oil field protection, population registration, and protection of the German administration in occupied countries.[92]

In fact, SS-Police tasks included duties common to both the German homeland and the occupation zones. They included countering espionage, sabotage, and corruption; the investigation of violations of orders, acts against state property, and carelessness or even treason; and the hunting down of deserters and escaped prisoners of war; as well as the escort of dignitaries, or advising industrial concerns on policing. The criminal police duties included the investigation of incidents of violence; prevention of black markets, illegal trading by soldiers; investigation of military suicides, fire arms misuse, and detection of illegal radios and transmitters. Specific security routines included guarding installations, securing local population registers, investigations of the population, supervising deportation and plunder transports, checking hotels, and validating identification papers. The police also took control of photography shops, registered carrier pigeon owners, supervised brothels and soldiers' bars, safeguarded telecommunication cables, secured quarters for staff, managed traffic control, and maintained military order.[93]

Querner mentioned certain organizational developments introduced before the war. In August 1938, Hitler fused the functions of the SS and police.[94] The year before, Himmler established the regional field command of the Higher SS and Police Leader (*Höhere SS- und Polizeiführer,* HSSPF). Its important functions were to centralize control and to extend SS central leadership expertise in the field. The HSSPF led coordinated and controlled SS-Police units. As Ruth Bettina Birn has noted, through the HSSPF, Himmler was able to maintain a tight grip on the implementation of policy.[95] Another key development, mentioned Querner, was the impact of Daluege's leadership. Daluege was driven toward militarizing the Order Police. He had also handed Bomhard, his chief of staff, the job of organizing the main office (*Hauptamt Ordnungspolizei*) as a headquarters. Bomhard had the expertise to carry out this task and ensure that the police continued to function as a state bureaucracy. Bomhard, a police-soldier, like many of the senior officers of the Order Police, retained his relationship with Epp. In 1919, Bomhard joined the Bavarian Landespolizei, and in 1934, he joined Daluege's staff in Berlin. From 1936, Bomhard became the quintessential legislative bureaucrat the Order Police depended on to ensure the Ministry of Interior endorsed regulations.[96]

Querner referred to Poland but avoided any references to Lebensraum or Germanizationization. Upon the cessation of hostilities, Hitler passed control of the occupation to Nazi civil authorities. "The armed forces should welcome the opportunity of avoiding having to deal with administrative questions in Poland," he explained to Keitel. "On principle there cannot be two administrations."[97] The Nazis immediately began a process of Germanization. To eliminate Polish nationality and culture, the SS began carrying out killing actions and introduced resettlement programs. The situation worsened through random acts of violence, carried out by soldiers and SS troops alike, excused by the authorities on the grounds of revenge.[98] The rapid military defeat of Poland had not crushed the will to resist, which proliferated contempt for the Poles in all German circles. The SS received a request from state foresters (*Reichsforstamt*) to assist in the combating of "bandits" in the Polish forests.[99] The "bandits" included German army deserters, escaped Polish POWs, and genuine outlaws who had troubled the Polish police long before the war.[100] The forests proved to be a hurdle for the SS-Police as serious attacks increased. Himmler attempted to flush out the "bandits" by sending teams of gendarmerie, and Wheeler believed they proved highly capable in their work.[101] From his regular visits to Krüger, Daluege recognized the gendarme's free-ranging capability proved far superior to his Schutzpolizei battalions, cocooned in barracks and dependent on trucks for mobility. The gendarmerie, trained to function individually or in small groups, was able to counter the "bandits." Although Daluege recognized the usefulness of the gendarmerie, he elected not to increase their numbers. For Himmler, Daluege, and Heydrich, Poland was an opportunity to experiment with occupation security in a hostile and volatile environment. The volatility came from within the Nazi administration; Hans Frank and Himmler were at loggerheads over raising self-defense militia. Himmler took this as a direct challenge to his authority.[102]

Himmler set SS-Obergruppenführer Friedrich-Wilhelm Krüger, HSSPF in the General Government, against Frank. Krüger was a tough veteran of the First World War and the Freikorps but a trusted lieutenant. He was wholeheartedly committed to implementing Lebensraum. The SS-Police under Krüger, assisted by his neighboring HSSPFs, planned an extensive settlement program. One neighboring colleague was Bach-Zelewski, HSSPF Southeast (Breslau). The defeat of Poland involved the annexation of Polish territory, and so his command territory extended into southwest Poland.[103] Krüger and Bach-Zelewski were part of a team of seven SS officers who planned the transfer of Jews into ghettos, the permanent removal of "antisocials," and the preparation of evacuated areas for an influx of ethnic Germans from Russia in an operation called the *Saybuscher Aktion*. The British intercepted a message on September 25, 1940, reporting one of these transports: The Migration Centre in Litzmannstadt reports to Berlin that a transport train (called "Cholm Action Train") had departed for Lublin with 512 Poles and twenty-six children under the age of two.[104] This program contributed to the training of SS-Police personnel in large-scale population transfers.

For a short period from October 1939, Bach-Zelewski was the deputy commissioner for the strengthening of Germandom (*Reichskommissar für die Festigung des Deutschen Volkstums*, RKFDV).[105] In April 1939, he undertook a university lectureship (*Lehrauftrag*) in religious science for the department of theology under Professor Wendel, a specialist of the Old Testament.[106] Since 1934, Bach-Zelewski had made numerous complaints to Himmler about the Jews of Poland. He described Danzig as "full of Jews" (*verjudet*) in 1935 and complained to Wolff in 1940 about Frank's intervention over preventing the imprisonment of the Jews of Silesia. Bach-Zelewski believed they should have been in concentration camps, wearing armbands with the Star of David and breaking stone in the quarries.[107] In December 1939, Adolf Eichmann informed him that cooperation between his office and the RSHA was virtually perfect. In January 1940, Bach-Zelewski sent his representatives to a conference with Heydrich on the evacuation process. Promoting himself while treating human beings like cattle became his trademark. From mid-1940, he was busily engaged in forcibly deporting Poles from Zywiec in Poland while personally welcoming eighteen trainloads (17,500) of ethnic Germans from the Posen resettlement center.[108] He visited Auschwitz with Rudolf Höss in 1940 and instructed the appropriate rules for shooting prisoners in reprisal for escapes. The rapid defeat of France and Germany's domination of continental Europe led Bach-Zelewski to make another change of name. In November 1940, the Breslau Justice Ministry department confirmed the official removal of the "Zelewski" part of his name.[109] For the rest of the war, he lived as Erich von dem Bach. This did not prevent him from passing evidence to Himmler over his ancestral connection to Johannes von dem Bach-Zelewski, the last knight commander of the Teutonic Order of Knights in Marienburg.[110]

The experience gained in Poland by the SS forced another confrontation between Epp and Himmler. It was triggered by Heydrich, who extracted from Epp the plan for the administration of the colonial office. This proposed five departments, one dedicated to policing. Epp expected each colony to be self-sufficient in the administration of law and order; with a colonial commissioner, aided by an SS representative. Acting on this information, Himmler concluded it was another plot, like Frank's, to challenge his authority in control of the police. He tackled the question of colonial police guidelines through Daluege. In July 1940, Daluege sent instructions to Bomhard indicating that the differences between Epp and the SS had widened. Daluege explained that Himmler was prepared to acknowledge Epp's seniority for the colonies but not for colonial policing. He insisted that policing for the colonial office must conform to that for the General Government, with an HSSPF under his direct control. Defeating Epp in SS plans was one thing, explaining them to him was obviously a daunting prospect. Timidity in the face of the party godfather led Himmler to order Karl Wolff, Epp's former political adjutant, to explain to Epp policing for colonial office, while Daluege, equally timid, delegated Bomhard to explain the Order Police role in the scheme.[111] Thus, the final triumph of Lebensraum in police policy matters became complicated again following the German victory in the west.

Querner referred to operations but chose to ignore the less savory aspects of SS behavior. The SS-Police performance in the western campaign ranged between capability and atrocity. The performance of the newly raised Waffen-SS Polizei-Division, under SS-Gruppenführer und Generalleutnant der Polizei Pfeffer-Wildenbruch, embellished his reputation as the "top-soldier" of the Order Police. Other Waffen-SS formations played a minor part in the campaign, and two committed separate acts of slaughter against British prisoners of war (Le Paradis and Wormhoudt). The Order Police played a significant part in organizing the traffic system behind the armored thrusts of the army. Their mission involved locating favorable routes to maintain a steady flow of supplies and reinforcements; the NSKK assisted in handling the motor transportation pools. The police raised a rapid reaction force with a fire-defense-police (*Feuerschutzpolizei*) regiment, six traffic platoons, two traffic sections, and five radio detection detachments for technical emergencies such as city fires and for maintaining public utilities during the occupation. The radio detection teams worked to intercept propaganda and allied signals traffic.[112] However, most significant after the campaign, Germany found itself in control of French, Dutch, and Belgium colonies.

Himmler was forced to recognize the need for a colonial police department, not just for German and captured colonies, but within the breadth of SS-Police functions. Daluege initiated the regulation for a colonial service in June 1940. Bomhard drafted the regulations and, in July, issued the first instructions for police serving in the colonial department.[113] On October 31, Daluege released further instructions for all senior SS-Police officers announcing the opening of a colonial police department.[114] These instructions covered the basic details of service, including assignment periods, regulations, and codes of practice.[115] In December, announcements were made for courses for district inspectors (*Revierbezirksoffiziere*) with the upper age limit of forty-eight. The Rhineland police presidents of Düsseldorf and Bochum were the first to send lists of potential candidates to Krakow, a collection center for the colonial service. The British assessed the required medical fitness for service in the tropics as measured by productive potential.[116]

Hitler initiated the second phase in the development of the SS as a national security corporation and confirming their responsibility for Lebensraum policing. In August 1940, he assigned them the role of "state protection corps" (Staatsschutzkorps). The "Statement on the Future Armed State Police" was intended to clarify the status of the Wehrmacht and the Waffen-SS. The statement formed the ideological direction for the Staatsschutzkorps. Hitler began by soothing the army: "Never again must the German Wehrmacht, now based on universal military service, be required to use its weapons against its own fellow-countrymen in times of internal crisis. . . . In future the Wehrmacht is solely and only to be used against the Reich's external enemies." The power of the Waffen-SS, he added, would not grow beyond 5 to 10 percent of the Wehrmacht. Hitler explained its mission in the context of Lebensraum. "In its final form the Greater German Reich will include within its frontiers peoples who will not necessarily in all cases be well disposed towards the Reich." Beyond the "borders of the old Reich," he concluded, "it will be necessary to create a state protection corps capable, whatever the situation, of representing and enforcing the authority of the Reich in the interior of the country concerned." This Staatsschutzkorps was expected to carry out its duties with "men of the best German blood," able to "resist subversive influences in times of crisis," and with the "authority to carry out their duties as state police."[117] Scholars have argued without definite conclusion the impact of the Staatsschutzkorps announcement. They have generally focused on what this decision led to, emphasizing either the political-racial solution to commit extermination, or the formation of a radical political soldiery operating beyond the boundaries of traditional military and police forces.[118] Hitler's Staatsschutzkorps decision was in fact the conclusion of the long struggle between the supporters of colonialism and his followers of Lebensraum. The status of the SS-Police within Nazi ambitions was finalized.

In the accelerating momentum of preparations for the invasion of Russia, the SS-Police expanded its corporate size and functions. The Waffen-SS increased the size of its militarized formations.[119] The Order Police took the significant step of raising a colonial police department. In January 1941, Daluege presented his annual senior commander's report to his IdOs.[120] He announced the promotion of Pfeffer-Wildenbruch as inspector of the colonial police. Pfeffer-Wildenbruch's tasks included the improvement of infantry training within the colonial police service and the extension of the foreign languages program.[121] Daluege visited the Berlin Colonial School and was pleasantly surprised to find six hundred colonial officers and fifteen hundred officials (Polizeibeamten) undergoing training.[122] He maintained that this training was turning them into the best-qualified troops so they would not be an embarrassment as compared to troops from other colonial powers.[123] On March 6, the colonial police department joined the central office of the Order Police (*Kolonialpolizeiamt im Hauptamt Ordnungspolizei*), regulated through the Ministry of the Interior. Ministerial staffs conducted the department's public administration while senior police staff administered its operations.[124] These developments progressed in line with Ludendorff's maxims of preparing for total war, they complemented Hitler's Lebensraum ambitions, and Himmler began to administer the Staatsschutzkorps within the national security ethos. As Leonie Wheeler correctly concluded, the SS and Police had become more "sophisticated than that of its prewar counterpart."[125]

## Himmler's Praetorian

Operation "Babarossa," the codename for the attack on Soviet Russia on June 22, 1941, was the catalyst for all subsequent SS-Police operations during the war. The campaign for Lebensraum was two-sided: the racial-ideological war against Jewish-Bolshevism hand in hand with the military conquest of Soviet Russian territory.[126] To fully participate in the invasion, the SS introduced command components that became its standard operating procedure: policymaking and implementation; centralized command, communication, and control; and micromanagement of limited human resources. Hitler's instructions for the attack on Russia were handed to Generalmajor Walter Warlimont of the Armed Forces High Command (*Oberkommando der Wehrmacht*, OKW) for drafting them as military regulation, later known as the "Barbarossa directives." The SS-Police and Wehrmacht singled out Jews, Soviet officials, and Red Army political commissars for execution under the auspices of the "Commissar Order" and other directives.[127] These "criminal orders" were a license to kill, although not the great departure from German military traditions often professed by veterans and scholars.[128] The directives, including the often-quoted Heydrich–Wagner settlement, included an agreement between Warlimont and Himmler made in March 1941. This agreement confirmed the frontiers of field security for both the army and SS. Behind the front lines, in the rear areas, senior SS officers and army intelligence officers were expected to share intelligence and orders for the roundup and killing of political opponents. This was a preemptive security strike intended to eradicate all racial and ideological resistance before political opponents could rally a counter-reaction. In theory, based on experience in Poland, this would bring about unhindered Lebensraum.[129]

The SS applied its peculiar structures of command, communication, and control methods to the invasion. Leadership was highly visible in SS-Police culture. Predictably, Himmler draped himself in the mantle of *strategos* and carried on like a civil-military leader of antiquity. In the early part of the campaign, he visited armies, the SS-Police, and civilian administrators and was one of the few Nazi leaders to have a grasp on the overall campaign. He formed several command facilities. The first was a motor cavalcade codenamed "Wagenkolonne-RFSS"; the other, his special train *Heinrich*, was equipped as a communications center and was stabled close by Hitler's headquarters at Rastenburg. Himmler dispatched a team of liaison officers into the field, personal representatives who freely entered SS-Police field command posts to monitor, measure, and report performances.[130] Daluege lifted the marshal's baton in the vain hope of becoming Feldherr, but this ambition outweighed his physical endurance. He also raised a command convoy codenamed "Wagenkolonne Daluege" and tramped around the rear areas inspecting "his" troops and overseeing killing actions.[131] The convoy was slow and costly in fuel but carried a technically advanced radio-wireless capability.[132] The field command system was based on Himmler's trusted HSSPF structure. The leading personalities and their eventual commands were SS-Obergruppenführer Hans Prützmann (HSSPF Russia-South) in Kiev, SS-Obergruppenführer Erich von dem Bach-Zelewski (HSSPF Russia-Centre) in Minsk, and SS-Obergruppenführer Friedrich Jeckeln as (HSSPF Russia-South) in Riga.

Owing to prejudices dating from the First World War, Hitler forced the army to replace the Etappen concept, which introduced complex structural formulae for rear-area armies instead. There was an integration of static rear-area units alongside the mobile and semimobile formations, purposely designed to meet the expectations in Russia. The leading personality among the security formations was the commander of the Rear Area Army of Army Group Centre, General of Infantry Max von Schenckendorff. He came to dominate the initial phases of Germany's response to the Soviet partisan movement. Bach-Zelewski's HSSPF initially came under the command of Schenckendorff. There is evidence to suggest that Bach-Zelewski had served under Schenckendorff at the end of the First World War.[133] This was not the only coincidence. The Army Group commander was Field Marshal Fedor von Bock, the former chief of staff of Wehrkreis III. Bock was responsible for crushing the Buchrucker putsch, while the 29th Infantry Regiment came under his Wehrkreis responsibility. This ménage à trois indicates deliberate selection; these forces were meant to work together in an area designated for mass extermination and exploitation.

In preparation for the invasion, in May 1941, Himmler established the Command Staff of the Reichsführer-SS (*Kommandostab Reichsführer-SS*, KSRFSS).[134] He realized that the scale of tasks and diversity of his troops required a central command. Diagram I (p. 307) shows a chart illustrating the different branches of this organization. Yehoshua Büchler was one of the first scholars to recognize the lynchpin role of the KSRFSS and its influence in the killing operations in 1941.[135] However, the functions of the KSRFSS were more complex than simply recording killing. The KSRFSS served as the model command for the Staatsschutzkorps concept. The primary task of the KSRFSS was to facilitate and support rapid decision making. Its routines involved monitoring the progress of all SS operations. This gave the SS a distinct advantage over the army in communications where conditions in Russia forced long lead times on decision making. Its war diary records a steady routine of collected information on security operations, killing actions, and the regular visits by dignitaries.[136] Another of its tasks was regulation through preventing the dilettantes within the SS from derailing corporate progress. To this end, the senior staffs of KSRFSS were proven staff officers. The chief of staff, Kurt Knoblauch, was a deputy to Theodor Eicke, commander of the SS-*Totenkopfverbände*, and was noted for his obtuse behavior.[137] Ernst Rode, the senior Order Police officer in the KSRFSS, served as chief of operations (designated Ia) and was experienced in coping with Daluege's prickly character. The significance of the KSRFSS, therefore, was not conducting killing actions, but keeping the SS-Police establishment functioning, mindful of Clausewitz's warnings of reducing friction in operations.

The overall complement of the KSRFSS was approximately eighteen thousand troops. The principle combat formations within its remit were two SS-Infantry brigades and one SS-Cavalry brigade. It also carried support units such as the Waffen-SS geological detachment. Later in the campaign, significant numbers of foreign volunteers from various western European countries joined these troops. The Waffen-SS component, largely reservists and only basic-trained recruits, was the backbone of the fighting formations. The three brigades were coordinated within a pooling arrangement to provide the maximum support for the three HSSPF. In effect, although under the direct control of KSRFSS, they were "loaned out" to reinforce HSSPF forces during specific actions. Each HSSPF commanded a dedicated police regiment of three battalions per regiment with mobility provided by motor vehicle sections from the NSKK. Detachments of Technische Nothilfe assigned to each regiment provided the HSSPF public works expertise. Thus, from the onset of the campaign, there was a large civilian component attached to SS-Police operations. [138]

Once the invasion was in progress, plans and policies rapidly became redundant as the conditions fluctuated. Within weeks of the campaign, Hitler provided another example of his First World War consciousness. During a heated moment caused by Stalin's declaration of a general guerrilla uprising, Hitler invoked memories of the franc-tireur complex of 1914. "This partisan war," he declared, "has some advantage for us; it enables us to eradicate everyone who opposes us." Ignoring the fact that he had unleashed a surprise attack of Russia, Hitler suggested they cloak their territorial ambitions and appear as the guardians of the Russian people. "We shall emphasise again," he added, "that we were forced to occupy, administer, and secure a certain area; it was in the interest of the inhabitants." Hitler wanted to disguise his real intentions: "Nobody shall be able to recognise that it initiates a final settlement. This need not prevent our taking all necessary measure— shooting, resettling, etc.—and we shall take them." In an absurd remark, totally out of proportion with the program of mass killing and slaughter already in progress, Hitler said, "We do not want to make people into enemies prematurely and unnecessarily."[139] Typically for Nazi polycracy, Hitler ranted while the army struggled to find a suitable answer to the Soviet partisans. It wrestled over directives and guidelines, even tampering with the soldiers' conduct. Characteristically, the army concentrated its efforts on controlling ground and targeting strong-arm blows against all incursions. On October 25, the Wehrmacht released its last major regulatory guidelines for combating partisans in the east. They proved ineffectual and took until November for Otto Winkelmann to relay them as binding on police troops.[140]

The decision to absorb Slav collaborators into the police was part of the calculated plan to raise a colonial police department within the SS-Police. The hurdle to raising Slav collaborationist manpower might appear to have been Hitler himself following one of his racist outbursts during the July 16 meeting:

> We must never permit anybody but the Germans to carry arms! [translator's italics] This is especially important; even when it seems easier at first to enlist the armed support of foreign subjugated nations, it is wrong to do so. In the end this will prove to be to our disadvantage unconditionally and unavoidably. Only the

German may carry arms, not the Slav, not the Czech, not the Cossack nor the Ukrainian![141]

However, within days Himmler and his cohorts had moved in an opposite
direction. There is evidence indicating that the army was at least thinking
about the colonial situation in the late 1930s:

> The Schutztruppe had 260 Germans and 2,470 coloureds. In sup-
> port there was a Polizeitruppe of 55 Whites and 2,140 coloureds.
> The proportion of coloureds and military protection troops
> [Schutztruppen] is in strong relation to the proportion to the popu-
> lation. The proportions in [Southwest Africa] were different where
> there were no coloured in the Schutztruppe whereas in the
> Polizeitruppe the coloureds represented 40% of all operatives.[142]

Himmler moved first and announced, on July 25, 1941, the formations of Russian collaboration police forces, the *Schutzmannschaft* (Schuma).[143] These
Schuma formations were organized under the inspector of Colonial Police. On
November 4, 1941, the Schuma formations received official regulation through
the Reich Ministry of Interior and were granted legal status as a regular branch
within the police.[144] This decision came after the Nazis had implemented a
policy of killing millions of Soviet prisoners of war and citizens. Martin Dean
found that the first duty of the Schuma was to man small outposts (*Einzeldienst*) erected by the gendarmerie, connecting towns and districts to a network of security.[145] British intelligence made an early assessment of the Schuma:

> [Police] units formed of local inhabitants are being enlisted in the
> central sector. But a good many difficulties are arising in the pro-
> cess: officers to take charge of the units cannot be released; and
> while questions of provisioning and pay are settled, that of their
> uniform and footwear is not. Russian uniform is ruled out as im-
> possible, besides being difficult to procure. The units have been
> waiting "for weeks."[146]

By December 1941, Georg Jedicke (BdO Ostland) could write to the Hauptamt
Ordnungspolizei with precise muster numbers for Schuma battalions. He suggested 140 men per company, with three companies per battalion, and a battalion staff of forty. The desired strength for each battalion was expected to total
seven hundred, and only under special circumstances or for local reasons
were the numbers to drop below seven hundred.[147]

The language and terminology of the campaign was old and included
many terms used against the Herero and in previous actions. No SS leader
appears to have thought about the subject of secure communiqués prior to

the campaign. The explicit nature of the language sprinkled throughout police signals included combating partisans (Partisanenbekämpfung), cleansing (*Säuberung*), and destruction (*Vernichtung*) consistent with operational terminology adopted from earlier conflicts.[148] Victor Klemperer noted that, since his days in the Ober Ost, new words, such as "liquidated" (*liquidiert*), "executed" (*exekutiert*), and "shot" (*erschossen*), had been added to the Nazi lexicon to reflect the semi-automation of actions.[149] This can be seen from messages in August 1941 that referred to combating "bandits" (Banden), the killing of 3,274 partisans (Partisanen) and Jews and 260 irregulars (Freischärler). The executions were attributed to the Police Battalion 309. In a message from August 24, references were made to the presence of "bandits," irregulars, and parachutists, which resulted in the shooting of 70 Jews, 294 Jews, 61 Jews and 113 Jews, and 65 Bolshevik-Jews, respectively. These killings concluded a series of tasks, designated a cleansing action (Säuberungsaktion), commonly used in Namibia.[150]

Eventually it dawned on Daluege that someone other than the SS might be listening, and he warned against the use of overly explicit reporting:

> The danger of decipherment by the enemy of wireless messages is great. For this reason, only such matters can be transmitted by wireless as can be considered open . . . , confidential or secret; but not information, which is containing State Secrets, calls for especially secret treatment. Into this category fall exact figures of executions (these are to be sent by courier post).[151]

The British tracked the change in transmissions language. "The effect of this was that situation reports from September 14 onward contained the enigmatic phrase 'action according to the usage of war' under the heading which had formerly contained the figures of executions."[152] By December, others were discussing the effects of the killings on the progress of the war. General Thomas, chief of the Economics and Armaments Office within OKW, received a report from his representative in the Ukraine. The report explained that the killing of the Jews took place publicly. Men of the Ukrainian militia and German army volunteers participated in the mass killing of more than one hundred and fifty thousand men, women, and children. The report summarized the effect of the killings. There had been a partial extermination of "superfluous eaters," liquidation of those most hateful toward the Germans, removal of badly needed tradespeople, negative effects on foreign policy, and undermining of troop morale. The report also noted a "brutalising effect on the formations which carry out the executions—regular police—[Order Police]."[153] Thus, camouflaging the evidence after its release and undermining the morale of the troops were only two of the strategic lapses in planning.[154]

The greatest strategic errors made by the SS-Police planners had been to place too much faith on the Wehrmacht and to assume it would be a short, successful campaign. There was little provision if the Soviet Union continued to fight. There were no instructions of how to respond to a complete breakdown in the infrastructure resulting from Red Army scorched-earth methods. The planners overlooked the problem of the weather and failed to prepare a contingency plan that addressed simple human requirements. As early as August 1941, the Police Regiment Centre received orders to take up positions east of Slutsk in Belorussia, and remain there for seven days. Being out of action exposed the regiment's weakness of the relatively simple task of collecting their fuel ration. Because of rules and regulations, the SS ration system procured and collected on an individual unit basis, rather than by convoy, from supply dumps. Release of the regiment's fuel reserves could only be granted in times of combat. Further, the poor condition of the roads forced light loading procedures for vehicles and increased the number of trips to collect reserves and supplies, causing serious wear and tear. This Catch-22 situation caused unit deterioration. These problems were aggravated as regimental staff vehicles suffered breakdowns and were unable to receive maintenance or replacement.[155]

With the onset of severe weather, conditions deteriorated further. "We're slowly sinking in mud," Hermann Fegelein, the commander of the SS-Cavalry Brigade, cabled a friend in Berlin on September 4. "Be a good fellow and release two tractor-cars for the Brigade. You'll really be doing us a good turn." The British collected evidence of a virtual collapse of all SS-Police transportation. "The badness of the roads is the Leitmotiv of these decodes." The road conditions led to a shortage of drivers exhausted from battling against the severe conditions.[156] The strains on the system grounded courier flights, while trains departing east from Warsaw were limited to sixty per day. Men on leave, about to go on leave, or waiting for mail from home were stuck, and this further undermined morale.[157] The calls for warm clothing became frantic as the troops began to freeze.[158] The complications associated with disease took their toll. Medical officers requisitioned inoculations for Typhus and paratyphus, and in particular they requested cholera serum.[159] In July, all SS depots were ordered to carry stocks of mineral water. The SS had not addressed the question of drinking water and had failed to deploy distillation facilities. Himmler's adjutant urgently requested a courier flight to bring as much bottled water as possible to the KSRFSS. At the same time, the SS authorities in Riga requisitioned thirty thousand bottles of mineral water for the Polizei Division. In September, the Waffen-SS geological detachment was ordered to locate fresh-water sources. Fresh water had become so critical that trainloads of water traveled under convoy and special guard.[160]

During "Barbarossa," Bach-Zelewski behaved like the champion of all the Nazi rhetoric and dogma that punctuated the SS cult. He was a driven man motivated to exterminate Jews and Communists in the name of Lebensraum.

Jeckeln and Prützmann were able to construct significant SS empires in their respective zones, but Bach-Zelewski's command was ruptured by the intensity of fighting on the central front. To comprehend the extent of Bach-Zelewski's performance in "Barbarossa" involves recognizing that he was not only an SS officer under orders but also someone desperate to restore his family honor after Zelewski's African debacle. The significant period of Bach-Zelewski's criminal actions was between July and October 1941. In that time, he traveled extensively, and his diary's itinerary matches the progress of mass slaughter. In July, he was in Bialystok, Warsaw, Grodno, and the Pripyat marshes, each scenes of terrible slaughter.[161] In August, his travels included Baranovichi, Minsk, Breslau, Turov, Starye Dorogi, Pinsk, Biaełowieźa, Mogilev, and Starobin, an area of fifteen hundred thousand miles and all significant scenes of mass killing. In September, he traveled another thousand miles but, in October, confined himself to Vitebsk and Mogilev. His first communiqués on arrival at killing sites incorporated population demographics. "Baranowicze: roughly thirty-five thousand people; of these roughly seventeen thousand Jews, nine thousand Russians and nine thousand Poles."[162] In one signal, he placed a claim on his killing score: "Thus the figure in my area now exceeds the thirty thousand mark." British intelligence judged,

> The tone of this message suggests that the word has gone out that a definite decrease in the total population of Russia would be welcome in high quarters and that the leaders of the three sectors stand somewhat in competition with each other as to their "scores."[163]

If a competition existed between the HSSPFs, then Bach-Zelewski was determined to win. On August 18, he requested the use of the mobile gassing units.[164] That same month, he met with Daluege to discuss further actions. On September 1, together they observed the killing of nine hundred Jews from Minsk.

On July 20, Himmler issued a bizarre set of orders. He ordered the SS-Cavalry Brigade to drive Jews into the Pripyat marshes and swampland to drown.[165] This derivation of Trotha's plan of mass extermination replaced the desert with the watery wastes and included the ultimate madness of calling on Zelewski's nephew to atone for the past debacle with a successful killing spree. Bach-Zelewski's diary only recorded that he led the 1st and 2nd SS-Cavalry Regiments into combing through (*Durchkämmung*) the Pripyat marshes.[166] However, a captured report from 2nd SS-Cavalry Regiment stated, "We drove women and children into the marshes, but this did not yield the desired result, as the marshes were not deep enough to drown them. In most places the water was not more than three feet deep."[167] On August 1, the 2nd SS-Cavalry Regiment received a message from Himmler instructing them to reinstate the practice of shooting Jewish women.[168] We can only speculate what inspired Himmler and Bach-Zelewski to contemplate such a plan. In October, he entered Mogilev to kill another 2,208 Jews.

In September 1941, Schenckendorff approved a list of medals for SS and police troops under his command. Since the opening of the campaign, Bach-Zelewski had been forming a clique (*Klüngel*) of men who would remain close to him throughout the war. Included on the list were Pail, Lombard, Montua, Fegelein, Diekmann, Magill, and Charpentier (the son of a former regimental commander).[169] In October, Bach-Zelewski's health began to deteriorate, and this was directly attributable to the lack of fresh water. It was probably during the swamp operations that he contracted his intestinal problems. The British noticed that his pleas for fresh water became desperate. "Demand for space on the plane is very heavy, and even so high an official [as Bach-Zelewski] is unable to get bottles of his favorite vintage sent to him by this means."[170] To compensate for his failing health, he turned to addictive drugs to reduce his sensitivity to pain and need for fresh water.

Bach-Zelewski claimed an unusual relationship with the army. He came under the command of the Rear Area Army Centre and partly under Himmler. Schenckendorff was well aware of Bach-Zelewski's political tasks of population control and mass executions. When the security situation deteriorated, Bach-Zelewski tended to side with Schenckendorff in moving police troops forward to support the army. The peak of their cooperation culminated in an antipartisan field course (*Bekämpfung von Partisanen*) in September 1941 (further discussed in chapter 5).[171] Bach-Zelewski's participation in the conventional warfare of the campaign alongside the army proved his ability in tactical operations. A Russian cavalry division broke into the rear area of Army Group Centre but was halted and destroyed by Bach-Zelewski.[172] He was a practitioner of encirclement as one signal confirmed:

> 1st Regiment has formed a ring ("Kessel") north and north-east of Lake Sporowskie to tackle troops reported there. Up to August 3, 1941 the SS cavalry Brigade has "liquidated 3,274 partisans and Jewish Bolsheviks." Their own losses nil.[173]

In the process of a cleaning up exercise, another signal reported that

> Police Battalion 306 shot 260 guerrilla fighters. Russian cavalry north of the railway is ringed in and faces destruction; south of the railway they appear to have crossed the [River] Petsch after continual sniping matches with the army and SS.[174]

On August 3, 1941, Bock passed on his personal congratulations for the defeat of the breakthrough. Bach-Zelewski immediately wired Himmler and

Daluege boasting of this recognition of his military prowess.[175] On August 8, Bach-Zelewski made his way to Borisov with the SS-Cavalry Brigade and joined the army's 162nd Infantry Division to combat further Red Army intrusions. The 252nd Infantry Division and Police Regiment Centre combined their efforts to destroy a breakthrough of the 12th Russian Infantry Division.[176] Two weeks later, Bach-Zelewski received a letter of thanks from the commander of the 252nd Infantry Division, praising the cooperation between the "SS-Polizeiverbände" and the army.[177]

In mid-November 1941, at the height of the Germany's las-gasp drive on Moscow, the Russians began desperate counter-attacks and incursions. This was the clinching moment of the first year. Hitler ordered more encirclements of the Red Army, but the German armored thrusts gradually wore down, hindered by poor weather, lack of reserves, and the deteriorating maintenance system. On December 3, the British intercepted the first message saying that the lead formations were considering forming a defensive line. The British intercepted another signal on December 7, confirming that the police had advised retreat. The many different parts of the German armed forces on the central front seemed incapable of making joined up decisions. The SS-Police continued to conduct antipartisan operations, while their battalions gradually plugged the front lines. By mid-December 1941, ad hoc units littered the Russian landscape like little islands, forming the German front lines.

Red Army counter-attacks continued through December; one had the objective of encircling the German armored forces around Smolensk. The chaos on December 27 was such that Bach-Zelewski thought it had parallels to the failure of the Ludendorff offensives in 1918.[178] Bock, in his last days as army group commander, requested police battalions to plug gaps in the line. Police Battalion 307, under the temporary command of Hauptmann Binz, and Police Battalion 131, under Major Orth, deployed to contrasting fortunes. The Soviets landed six thousand paratroops and air-landing forces on the airfield southeast of Viazma. Police Battalion 307 assisted in fending off this attack and made a significant contribution in saving the situation. Bach-Zelewski recommended that the commander receive the Knight's Cross (*Ritterkreuz*) and added to the report that Binz had ridden on a tank shouting, "Look here you swine, you can't shoot German police."[179] The contrast with Police Battalion 131 was dramatic. The British decoded a signal stating that the battalion had collapsed in the face of strong Red Army offensives during the battle of Kaluga. A situation report to Himmler stated, "The battalion failed completely, officers and men alike; would not attack and gradually crumbled to pieces." A subsequent report that the battalion had failed explained that the commander (Major Orth) and the battalion doctor (Dr. Rotlauf) had suffered "heart failure" (*Herzkollaps*) and fled in the medical vehicle homeward. They had taken all the battalion's medical supplies with them.[180]

The pressure caused by the collapse placed strains on the relationship between Bach-Zelewski and Daluege. On December 16, Bach-Zelewski sent a message to Daluege to the effect that he had lost all available battalions to Bock and urgently requested the availability of Police Battalion *Minsk* to continue operations in the army rear areas. On January 6, 1942, Bach-Zelewski sent a message to Himmler announcing, "My power for taking decisive action nullified," and charged Daluege with failing to appreciate the conditions at the front. He accused Daluege of allowing Police Regiment Centre to be sent to the front and complained that his "judgement about weapons, equipment, winter-clothing is inaccurate, since that of the Army is much worse. We are called into action in gaps where there simply is no army." Bach-Zelewski began to heap scorn on Daluege: "He sends a long and ridiculous message. . . . The fundamental and spontaneous use of the police battalions is only possible under the listed agreements, or you consciously lose the best military and personnel characteristics of the police like combating partisans' expertise."[181] He ranted on: "So the front can collapse, the 'Hunnish Horde' can flood the homeland so long as the police are kept safe for Germany's sake." In Bach-Zelewski's opinion, such "nonsense" was worthless after experiencing the chaos of the frontline situation.[182] Conversely, Daluege's fears contained an ounce of logic; he was well aware of the police troops' limitations in training and wished to preserve them for the longer war. Daluege realized that if the army could not cope with the situation, then it was beyond the police to improve Germany's fortunes.

The failure of the German army at the gates of Moscow shattered Nazi hopes of quick Lebensraum. Bach-Zelewski's diary confirmed that his grasp of impending disaster came from a situation meeting with the new commander-in-chief of Army Group Centre, Field Marshal von Kluge. The field marshal confessed that the army was close to total collapse, generals and colonels had fled or taken leave, and junior staff officers took command of shattered divisions.[183] The front barely held, but the attrition on German forces caused a permanent loss of the best troops. The calamity continued unabated. On January 10, 1942, Bach-Zelewski received confirmation from Himmler that he was responsible for plugging the gaps and saving the situation, and five days later, he faced the burden of evacuating two hundred wounded police troopers and soldiers. The army group failed to respond to his pleas for help, so he adapted Himmler's Junkers Ju52 airplane to ferry the men to an emergency field hospital in Minsk.[184]

The final tally of losses in senior German personnel was high. Bock stepped down on grounds of ill health. In 1924, Maj. Hermann Geyer had questioned the relevance of Cannae dogma for the future German army. In January 1942, he was an unemployed general, his campaign report accusing Cannae of failing the army. His words were lost on an army desperately trying to hold together the Eastern Front.[185] Among Bach-Zelewski's clique, there also were casualties. The commander of SS-Infantry Brigade, SS-Brigadeführer

Hermann, was killed in action during heavy fighting in Orel area in December. Oberst Montua, the commander of Police Regiment Centre, was ordered to Germany to become an SS officer and instructor. Even his fighting favorite, Binz, was wounded in combat. After rescuing the troops from capture or death, Bach-Zelewski was relieved and ordered to attend the SS hospital in Berlin. His campaign was temporarily over, but Emil von Zelewski's nephew had restored the family honor and carved a reputation for dogged determination in combat. His leadership in killing operations and administering population control elevated him as Himmler's praetorian. In January 1942, a confirmed drug addict, he faced a difficult future. In terms of security policy, Hitler was mired in ambiguity. In July 1941, Stalin's declaration of a partisan uprising offered an excuse for mass extermination. This had increased the level of killing but had not pacified Russia. The longer the Soviet Union resisted the Germans, the greater the delay in imposing Lebensraum. In addition to the problems of overefficiency and effectiveness of the economy, calls for rationalization and radical organization echoed through the regime. In terms of Lebensraum, Hitler had reached a crossroads. He could no longer tolerate the existence of Jews, even in ghettos, and abhorred the presumed heroism of the Soviet partisan. In 1942, German security policy was redrafted to meet his ambitions.

# 3
# HITLER'S BANDENBEKÄMPFUNG DIRECTIVE

The redirection of security warfare, from a function controlled by the army toward a policy serving Lebensraum and led by the SS, became apparent in the latter half of "Barbarossa." On September 16, 1941, Field Marshal Keitel issued an order-decree concerning the increase in communist-inspired insurrection within German occupied countries. The words were Keitel's but their inspiration was Hitler. Keitel attributed the increase to the invasion of Soviet Russia and the actions of a "mass movement centrally directed by Moscow." Consequently, he expected "nationalist and other circles" to take advantage of the situation. The existing security measures, he added, had proved inadequate, and the only remedy was spontaneous action, through drastic means, bringing about the rapid destruction of this movement. Keitel justified his orders on historical grounds. What was about to be introduced was how "great peoples restored order." The general direction of his new order came in five parts. First, the German armed forces were to infer that every case of "bandit war" (*Bandenkrieg*) was communist-inspired, irrespective of the facts. Second, the armed forces were to take immediate and drastic action at the first indication of trouble. In reprisal, the death penalty was to be used, with fifty to one hundred hostages deemed the appropriate number because "life was valueless in these territories." The selected method of execution was not elaborated but was supposed to heighten the deterrent effect. Third, the political relationship with the country concerned had no bearing on the conduct of reprisals. To calm the fears of the indigenous populace, Keitel ordered appropriate propaganda explaining the greater good that resulted from eradicating communist "bandits." Fourth, collaborator units were regarded as unsuited to the task and incapable of reaching the "acts of violence" necessary for reprisals and had to be handled cautiously. Finally, if court-martial proceedings were necessary, the death penalty was the only acceptable sentence. In a veiled reference to Britain, Keitel ordered the death penalty for all captives of foreign armed forces. This decree marked the turning point in Hitler's war of security, when Bandenbekämpfung became the strategic doctrine behind the Germanization of Europe.[1]

From the outset, the Second World War involved guerrillas, fifth columnists, the bombing of cities, and the abuse of civilians. Governments excused this war in a third dimension as acceptable practices on military, political, and even moral grounds. In 1942, the effectiveness of covert and partisan warfare was still largely a hit-or-miss affair. The first phase of the Soviet partisan campaign had not achieved appreciable results. In Yugoslavia, the two politically polarized resistance movements were more likely to attack one another than the Germans. The British adopted a broad aggressive strategy that included covert warfare in a desperate attempt to stir resistance against Nazi occupation. The Nazis countered, swatting the hoped-for resistance swarm before it had even taken wing. They countered Churchill's efforts with an effective propaganda campaign, stirring up considerable public hostility in Europe toward Britain.[2] Widespread collaboration with Nazism, even participation in ethnic cleansing, indicated Hitler's upper hand.[3]

Allied insurgency was not the only challenge facing the SS. The scale of Germany's security commitments were enormous. In 1942, it could take three days to travel from one end of occupied territory to the other, even by airplane. The occupation counted more than thirty main languages, hundreds of dialects, and several alphabets. The total territory crossed numerous time zones, climatic conditions, and major geographical features, from undulating steppes to long coastlines with rich farmlands merging into rugged mountain ranges, swamplands, and icy wastes. Man-made obstacles included virulent diseases (in particular typhus, cholera, and tuberculosis), disjointed railway gauges, and every conceivable road construction. The occupation absorbed political administrations, religions, cultural differences. Communities included tiny hamlets of isolated illiterate peasants to the highly sophisticated capital cities of Europe. The accounted population was in excess of three hundred million including Germany. To meet these challenges, Himmler had to exploit all his ability to rally an effective security policy.

The rapid increase in territory placed severe strains on the SS-Police organization struggling to adjust to the constant challenges of war. The winter battles of 1941–42 exposed weaknesses and caused shudders from overstretched resources to ripple throughout the organization. Reinhard Heydrich was not complacent; he understood the implications of Churchill's drip-drip strategy and Stalin's war of attrition. In the summer of 1941, Heydrich's commitment increased when he received the order to prepare the ground for the final solution of European Jewry. Plans and initial killing experiments had been tested through the summer and autumn of 1941, and on December 18,

Himmler's appointment book carried the cryptic note, "Jewish question / to be exterminated as partisans." Eventually, bringing the leading bureaucrats of the regime into concordance at the Wannsee conference (January 20, 1942), Heydrich succeeded in introducing the industrialized mass extermination of the Jews. Given the multiplying problems of limited resources and the polycratic nature of the regime, the SS had little choice but to organize the mass extermination of both racial and political enemies of the state under a series of coordinated programs. The SS plans forced Himmler to reorganize the SS-Police. Meanwhile, Hitler shifted the initiative toward southern Russia in an effort to seize and secure the rich ore and oil fields of the Caucasus. In May 1942, Hitler was on the verge of realizing his vision of Lebensraum, with the end of European Jewry and confirmation of German mastery in Europe: Bandenbekämpfung.

## Europe Ablaze

Britain troubled Hitler. His strategy to bring Britain quickly to heel involved, terrorizing the population through indiscriminate bombing, threatening starvation, and promising invasion. The German air force (Luftwaffe) attempted to destroy the Royal Air Force (RAF), during the Battle of Britain, while it also conducted widespread indiscriminate bombing of cities and ports. The bombing of London on August 25, 1940, albeit accidental, triggered a retaliation air raid.[4] The German navy (Kriegsmarine) opened a blockade to starve Britain into submission. These naval operations included laying mines in international shipping lanes, raiding convoys, and engaging in intensive submarine warfare. The threatened invasion of Gibraltar exposed the frailty of British lifelines to the east. On February 6, 1941, Hitler introduced Directive 23, the "Directions for Operations against the English War Economy" (*Richtlinien für die Kriegführung gegen die englische Wehrwirtschaft*), which concentrated on the destruction of British shipping.[5] The acquisition of colonies through his victories in Europe allowed Hitler the opportunity to pursue counterclandestine operations against British colonies and threaten its oil supplies. The German–Italian commission to Syria wished to stimulate an uprising against British interests in Iraq. Hitler issued Directive 30, *Unterstützung des Irak*, dispatching a military mission and aid to Rashid Ali, the leader of rebellion in Iraq. The military mission was codenamed Sonderstab-F, under General Felmy, and the German volunteers wore tropical uniforms with Iraqi insignia. It was a supreme failure.[6]

The British reaction to Hitler escalated. Williamson Murray has argued that Britain erected an effective strategic planning system of committees fully integrated into an intelligence network.[7] Churchill applied the breadth of his experience and leadership behind a broad strategy. The fundamental strategic direction was political, to undermine Nazi rule and force regime change. The British had no compunction about turning to covert warfare. In 1938, a British Foreign Office report of the Italian occupation of Abyssinia identified fifty-six thousand Italian troops, sixty thousand indigenous troops, and ninety-five thousand white laborers. In response to the potential threat posed to her colonial interests, Britain planned covert operations against the Italian occupation.[8] Between 1940 and 1943, the British main effort was clandestine operations, strategic bombing of German cities, and military operations in the Mediterranean region. A significant part of Churchill's operations in the early days of the war was inspired by the Ministry of Economic Warfare, the Combined Operations Executive, the RAF, and the intelligence services. The British held a strategic advantage in intelligence, having broken German police and "Ultra" signals codes and used her remaining open embassies and consuls as an intelligence collection network.[9] In 1940, Churchill endorsed the Special Operations Executive (SOE), responsible for acts of sabotage and espionage against targets in occupied Europe.[10] He also agreed to forming commando units wearing full military uniform, carried into combat by the Royal Navy and carrying out "hit-and-run" raids against German installations along the European coastline.[11] A shock wave of raids in Norway and France culminated in the attack against St. Nazaire (March 27–28, 1942) that closed the harbor facilities. The RAF assisted clandestine operations by ferrying SOE agents into and out of occupied Europe. In February 1942, RAF Bomber Command joined the offensive for regime change by striving to break the morale of the German public.

The German answer to Britain was to solicit mass collaboration across Europe. Marshal Pétain encouraged the French to volunteer; in Belgium, Leon Degrelle raised a unit of Catholic Walloon volunteers; and Dutch SS units participated in Operation "Barbarossa." From 1940, Czechoslovakia came sharply into focus for both Germany and Britain. Intelligence gathered by either side indicated that adopting less stringent measures in Czechoslovakia had reaped benefits for the Nazis.[12] Heydrich exploited this to marginalize the Czech resistance movement into irrelevance. In the winter of 1941, Prime Minister Benes of the Czechoslovakian government in exile encouraged opposition in Czechoslovakia when he announced in the British press that the German army at the gates of Moscow was on the point of collapse on the Eastern Front.[13] At the same time, Heydrich's strategy of combining counterintelligence with counter-espionage was taking its toll on British covert strategy. It was in an atmosphere of despondency that Benes approached Churchill for assistance and approval to assassinate Heydrich. He received a positive reception.[14] Preparations for Operation "Anthropoid," the assassination of Heydrich, began in December 1941. Several Czech SOE teams parachuted into Czechoslovakia to destroy strategic targets and prepare the ground for the assassination team.[15]

From the German viewpoint, the sequence of events that led to Heydrich's death began on May 2, 1942. Himmler and Heydrich discussed allied covert operations and the recent discovery of a weapons cache in Czechoslovakia.[16]

Three days later, Himmler took part in discussions concerning the training of police officers. To counter covert forces, the Order Police received training in the use of flare pistols, hand grenades, and other countermeasures. On May 16 and 23, the subject of "English" sabotage equipment was again on the agenda for a meeting between Himmler and Heydrich.[17] On the morning of May 27, Himmler began his usual routine with a telephone call with Kurt Daluege at 10:30. They discussed antipartisan warfare (Partisanenbekämpfung) and other SS matters. Then, at 11:30 a.m., Himmler received a call from SS-Obergruppenführer Karl Frank, the Nazi state secretary in Prague, informing him of the assassination attempt on Heydrich by Czechoslovakian partisans.[18] Himmler told Frank to relay the details to Hitler, personally. He ordered Wolff to organize immediate travel arrangements for Professor Gebhardt, the leading SS physician, to attend Heydrich. Afterward, Himmler lunched with Hitler whereupon they discussed a series of issues including a proposal for sending Bach-Zelewski to eradicate all Czech resistance. Himmler persuaded him otherwise, suggesting that Bach-Zelewski's work in Russia was far too valuable.[19] By coincidence, that evening the RAF carried out its first "1,000 bomber" raid against Cologne. Leaflets dropped by the RAF following the raid announced the opening of a new form of bomber offensive. Unlike previous raids, the bombing was concentrated into ninety-eight minutes and claimed four hundred dead and five thousand injured and left forty-five thousand homeless. The German air raid services were useless in the face of the storm as flak artillery expended their ammunition supply, and for a brief period, the city faced anarchy. In response, on May 31, the Luftwaffe retaliated against Canterbury, the *Berliner Morgenpost* recorded, adding that it was revenge for Heydrich.[20] A few days later, Heydrich died.

The fear of assassination kept the security troops assigned to protect Hitler and the inner circle in a constant state of readiness. The Nazis went to extraordinary lengths to minimize their exposure to assassination, but still it became a major feature of the war.[21] Hitler actually had little sympathy for Heydrich's acts of bravado and called him "stupid and idiotic" for exposing himself to danger. He tightened the security procedures for senior officers and officials, demanding eradication of all "foreign rabble" from the occupation zones as a prerequisite to guaranteeing German safety.[22] During Heydrich's funeral orations, Daluege announced that the British and Americans were guilty of murder. Daluege warned of retribution, and this was relayed across Europe.[23] Hitler called for collective punishment (*Kollektivmassnahmen*) as reprisal and revenge. Immediate punishment fell on four villages—Lidice, Le•áky, Svermovo, and Javøièko. The SS-Police led by Daluege and Karl Frank killed the adults, packed the children off to concentration camps, and killed family pets in their kennels.[24] The Nazi propaganda service produced a documentary of the destruction, a visual record of the procedures, which the police incorporated into their training schedules. In Mogilev, fifty Jews were

executed by members of the HSSPF Russia-Centre for their collective responsibility in killing Heydrich.[25]

Assassination, or decapitation, as modern covert parlance calls it, has
changed the course of history. Shooting, bombs, and kidnapping became
norms in the occupation theaters. The question of assassination, irrespective
of target, however, raises certain moral and ethical questions. Rab Bennett
explored these dilemmas in Heydrich's case. In Bennett's opinion, the decision to kill Heydrich factored in the expectation of grievous German reprisals.
He termed this an "artificial stimulation" of resistance by forcing the Germans
to commit atrocities, which would lead to an upsurge in resistance and establish a cycle of violence. He understood this contributed to undermining Nazi
rule and authority, but the views of many former SOE agents inclined toward
doubts over the value of the mission. On the accumulated evidence, Bennett
concluded that there was no satisfactory reason for the assassination.[26] The
cycle of violence was already in play long before Heydrich's death. The manner of his death gave the Nazis another excuse to adopt more severe measures
because their opponents deliberately breached the laws of war. The interpretation of the war was left for the victor.

## The Return of Erich von dem Bach

In May 1942, Bach-Zelewski (Erich von dem Bach) returned to duty as
HSSPF Russia-Centre. His illness has been the subject of some controversy
among scholars, and given his prominence to Bandenbekämpfung, it is important to gauge his state of health in 1942. An indication of his poor state of
mind prior to hospitalization can be found in his diary, "Dr. Sachs . . . to my
great relief, I received a small box of strong poison. [I was] concerned with
being captured, like my 1915 wounding and unable to kill myself."[27] Seventeen days later, he sent a signal to his SS surgeon, Dr. Grawitz, that under the
orders of Himmler he would be arriving in Berlin the next day for an operation
on his intestines.[28] A series of stories developed after the war that he suffered
from a nervous breakdown or required a varix operation for a dilated vein.[29]
According to the diary, he was absent from duty between January 29 and
April 30, 1942.[30] During this period, his medical attention was neither straightforward nor trouble-free. On March 4, Dr. Grawitz provided Himmler with a
detailed report of his condition. Grawitz explained that the patient was given
more opium during his surgery for hemorrhoids. The post-operative conditions had helped the healing process but Bach-Zelewski's inactivity had led
to a thickening of his stools. This forced the medical staff to clear them manu-
ally, and his extreme sensitivity to pain caused them to administer ether as a
further anesthetic.[31]

The delicate issue of drug abuse placed Grawitz and Himmler in an
awkward position. Grawitz assured Himmler that the patient was on the way to
recovery but it would take time before he was fit for work. The crucial part of

Grawitz's letter referred to Bach-Zelewski's state of mind. Grawitz explained that Bach-Zelewski was in a state of severe nervous exhaustion caused by arriving straight from the Eastern Front. This psychological trauma was awkward: "He is suffering particularly from hallucinations connected with the shootings of Jews, which he himself carried out, and with other grievous experiences in the East."[32] Grawitz assured Himmler that the patient would soon undertake convalescent leave. To assist the process, Grawitz allowed Bach-Zelewski's wife (Mutti) to assist in his nursing. At no point was there any indication that Bach-Zelewski was repentent or suffering from pangs of guilt for the crimes committed in Russia. Within a few days, Bach-Zelewski registered a complaint through Himmler's personal adjutant, Wolff, against the medical staff and the hospital. The problem again turned on the use of narcotics in his treatment. On March 6, Grawitz again wrote to Himmler describing Bach-Zelewski's condition of blocked bowels and the removal of stools through surgery. Three days later, Himmler received another letter outlining the patient's difficulty with an acute sensitivity to pain.[33] The doctor (probably Professor Umber, the SS psychiatrist) indicated that the patient was suffering from a nervous condition but concluded with the ill-considered phrase, ". . . he wants to serve his dear Reichsführer very soon." This combination of drugs, sensitivity to pain, and nervous condition did not portray the *Übermensch* of Himmler's praetorian. Himmler's response was predictable.

Himmler fired a full salvo at the medical staff, questioning the ability of the doctors while reiterating his concern over the patient.[34] He referred to prior correspondence concerning Wolff's visit. He pointed out that the patient was anesthetized at 10:00 a.m., but when Wolff arrived (6:00 p.m.), Bach-Zelewski was still under the influence of drugs. Himmler refuted the medical staff's allegation that Bach-Zelewski's complaint was the product of his self-induced drugs. He accused Grawitz of failing to explain the full extent of the patient's medical condition from the beginning. In consequence, he intended to "counter objectivity with objectivity." Himmler pointed out that if Bach-Zelewski were dependent on certain drugs, they would have to bring him down, causing further difficulties. "I form a picture from out of the Bach-Zelewski case of the sins you commit on our poor little man in this hospital," he concluded. "If the SS-Obergruppenführer is so badly treated psychologically what can ordinary people expect?"[35] Hallucinations aside, Bach-Zelewski's pride was hurt; he was disgusted with his ailment and the disgrace at being unable to continue his duties. His susceptibility to imputations about his family reputation only disturbed him further. On March 31, he wrote to Himmler about both his treatment and state of mind, complaining about the severe stomach cramps caused by his poor medical attention. He accused Professor Umber of casting aspersions against his character. He decried his treatment as leading him to quiet death (*Strohtod*), which denied him the honor of a soldier's death.[36] Bach-Zelewski accepted his medical condition regarding difficult bowel movements but begged Himmler, as one old fighter (*alter Kämpfer*) to another, to be allowed to return to duty. Himmler agreed but only after four extra weeks of recuperation.[37]

Bach-Zelewski returned to duty on May 1, 1942, fully fit and psychologically prepared for the rigors of the campaign. He wrote to his wife on May 7, describing his impressions. Traveling east by car, his first stop was to meet SS-Brigadeführer Fromm (SSPF Bialystok). He then drove on to Baranowicze but was disappointed at what he found there and blamed the situation on SS-Brigadeführer Carl Zenner, the SSPF Weissruthenien (White Russia), for allowing the Nazi civilian administration "to walk all over" him. Ordered to Russia in the summer of 1941, Zenner had carved a spectacularly dubious career. Before the war, while serving with the Aachen police, he had led illegal "Jew hunts" across the Dutch border. He rather laconically noted that "laziness in the east led to primitiveness." He moved on to Bobruisk and visited the SS training complexes under construction. From there he flew by "stork" airplane to Mogilev, flying over burning partisan villages, the sight of which gave him the "itchy finger" for action.[38]

The welcoming party in Mogilev included Carl Graf von Pückler-Burghaus (Bach-Zelewski's stand-in) and Oberst Walter Schimana, commander of the gendarmerie. There was a Russian guard of honor and a Ukrainian band adding a touch of pomp to his arrival ceremony. His first impression on arrival was described with a pathos—destroyed wooden housing contrasted with the fully functional library—that completed the sentimentality of his return to duty. That evening Bach-Zelewski and his officers stayed up until the early hours drinking alcohol. Pückler surprised him by drinking wine, schnapps, and a bottle of vodka, which he had been saving, and then made matters worse by staggering into Bach-Zelewski's bedroom. Bach-Zelewski depicted Pückler as the embodiment of the proud paper warrior. In the three months as substitute HSSPF, he had apparently not bothered to visit the troops. The next day, Bach-Zelewski began a schedule of visits to all his commanders and troops. On May 6, he flew to meet Schenckendorff at his headquarters in Smolensk and discovered yet more truths about Pückler. The army considered him egotistical, criticized his refusal to cooperate in operations, and thought his concentration on police matters was only to gain promotion kudos. The latest partisan drive threatened supply lines, and so Bach-Zelewski quashed all Pückler's orders and immediately sent the police units forward to Smolensk. He issued a command decree that "the life of milk and honey" (*Schlaraffenleben*) was over and that all seriousness had returned to their lives.[39]

## Planning Bandenbekämpfung

Some weeks prior to Bach-Zelewski's return to duty, the army's influential senior officer of security warfare Gen. Max von Schenckendorff protested that he no longer had the resources to continue operations against Soviet partisans. On March 1, 1942, Schenckendorff vented his fears in a situation report titled, "Proposals for the Liquidation of the Partisans."[40] He wished to strike a balance of effort concentrating on the occupied population as the source of exploitation and plunder, while using collaborators in operations against the partisans. The report combined military efficiency and economic expediency and conformed to the German military tradition of simply employing Russians to defeat the partisans. Hitler obviously thought the time had come for change. In May, Schenckendorff again attempted to garner a response for resources and reassert military authority for security, but the report was far too pessimistic. "No longer in control of the situation," he complained, "everything built up over the last few months had been destroyed." [41] Schenckendorff represented tradition; his methods could be traced back to Boguslawski's teachings, while Hitler's appreciation of the situation differed completely. He interpreted demands for troops as a sign of weakness and a lack of will. Since the failure of the army at Moscow, he was not prepared to accept advice on strategy or occupation policy. From his perspective, the rising tide of lawlessness and insurgencies had culminated with Heydrich's death. Hitler demanded action, not words.

Himmler was well positioned to exploit events. He was determined to take control of all operational security. A few days after the conference of July 16, 1941, referred to in chapter 2, Himmler ordered the KSRFSS to evaluate the Soviet partisan. Hannes Heer has mentioned the circulation of an SS-Einsatzgruppen report on recommendations for handling the partisans. The report, primarily based on the partisans' manual, included an analysis of its general principles and of partisan tactics, in particular their focus on destruction of communications (*Verkehrswege und der Verbindungen*), plundering and destruction of supply depots, and surprise attacks on German soldiers. The SD-Einsatzgruppen field studies and reports allowed Himmler to issue SS-Directive 42 on November 18, 1941. Heer identified this as the first realistic appraisal of the partisan.[42] On the strength of received wisdom, Himmler extended the Gestapo "trusty" system to increase surveillance and raise the quality of intelligence in Russia. He began to draw the conclusion that eliminating the partisans through extermination was preferable to the army's approach of controlling ground and conducting formal operations. The Einsatzgruppen began to adopt a higher profile in security actions against partisans as their reports confirmed a renewed campaign. The onset of spring and milder weather saw renewed partisan attacks directed against the symbols of German rule and military authority. For a brief period, however, the SS-SD-Police organization proved effective in countering deep-ranging partisan incursions. The political implication was that the weakened SS-Polizeiverbände had countered the partisans without Schenckendorff's bluff and bluster.[43]

Hannes Heer thought Keitel's announcement in July requesting Himmler to form a unified command to combat the partisans originated from a report issued by OKW on May 26 or a civilian administration report from June 17, 1942.[44] The details appear to indicate other possibilities. On June 6, 1942, Himmler held the first in a series of conferences and planning meetings with senior officers from the east. There seems to be no record of this meeting other than an entry in Himmler's appointments diary. Given usual SS practice, Himmler was almost certainly building a planning team to concentrate on internal security matters, especially since the removal of Heydrich. Seven days later, Himmler received a report from Carl Zenner titled *Partisanen-bekämpfung*. The report was supposed to recommend and ingratiate Zenner to Himmler, but its implications ran deep, far beyond his personal remit.[45] The report typically summarized straightforward issues and concluded with a clearly identifiable cure-all as preached by the SS planning cult. Zenner opened by advising that "partisan bands" were deployed in specific districts (*ortsgebundene Partisanen*) and received regular resupply by the Soviet air force. Soviets were in regular contact with Moscow and had welded the myriad of small bands of the region into a common military purpose. He concluded his report by reiterating the scale of the partisan problem that was terrorizing and bullying the populace. He inferred doubt and concern over the capability of the army and police to guarantee German protection. The partisans endangered food supplies with their attacks on large farmsteads, and their presence in the forests threatened the woodland industry. In one of his few positive comments, Zenner noted, "At the moment of combating the partisans, there is comradely co-operation between the security forces and the army."

Irrespective of the direction of the report, the body of analysis contained implications that Himmler embraced. Zenner was confident that his position enabled him to interpret the partisan mission. They had three identifiable tasks. The first was to disrupt railway traffic with mines or by removing track and set roadblocks along the three categories of German military highways (*Rollbahn*). The second involved ambushes, using machine pistols and machine guns, against single vehicles or unprotected truck convoys. The third exploited the psychological impact of their presence within communities and the specter of Stalin's wrath and retribution. This deepened the sense of isolation and stirred an atmosphere of insecurity among the collaboration police, Schuma guard posts, and depots. There were cases of partisans shooting members of the Schuma or killing their families. Stalin had sanctioned the assassination of mayors and inhabitants who collaborated. Zenner put forward the prospect of wholesale disruption within the German civilian administrations (Rayon).

The foremost territorial problem facing the SS, according to the Zenner report, was contending with the inhospitable Russian forests. He suggested clearing trees and brush up to three hundred meters on either side of roads and railways to neutralize the potential for ambush. The political challenge of the partisans could be found in the casualties they had caused: May 1942—four gendarmes and twenty-three Schutzmänner killed in action, nine Schuma cold-bloodedly executed, twenty wounded and two were still missing.[46] The casualties in June indicated a trend. An ambush by partisans armed with machine guns and mortars attacked the police station in Naliboki, a town west of Minsk. The Schuma trapped inside the building suffered fourteen killed, eight missing, and only three escaped. The next day, a police officer with a senior NCO and a driver were killed in an ambush on the military highway. These incidents proved to Zenner that a determined challenge to German authority was being orchestrated. He assumed that the partisans were operating in small groups and as part of several larger bands. They were mobile, were familiar with the terrain, and had secured bases deep within the forests. The partisans practiced a "quiet" routine when German troops were in close proximity to the encampments. Zenner suggested that the most successful bands included professional soldiers carrying out military objectives. Not surprisingly, Zenner blamed Jewish partisans for plundering but judged all the partisans without exception to be well-armed.

The report's proposals for combating (Bekämpfung) the bands were delivered in section six. Zenner recommended the further extension of the network of trusties (Vetrauensmänner). This was apparently difficult because the indigenous populations of his multi-ethnic region were reluctant to collaborate. His security department had addressed this problem through a smaller network of collaborators. He also proposed raising the alertness and response level of the police. To counter the initiative of surprise held by the partisans, Zenner thought increased preparedness and heightened mobility was the answer. He recommended, given the scale and the distances involved, strengthening the motorized contingents in the police with armored scout cars and armored personnel carriers. The pursuit troops also required ample supplies to hunt down the partisans until they killed the last one. He proposed the formation of combat groups (Kampfgruppen), stationed within cities and well prepared with contingency plans for pacification actions. To support these forces, he argued that it was essential to use airplanes in a close liaison role.

Zenner's report had varying degrees of reasoned solutions, especially in the proposals to improve the troops and resources available. The reason for this was the German reliance on collaborators. Zenner's forces numbered a handful of Latvian and Lithuanian Schuma battalions and four platoons of motorized gendarmerie. He expected several more Lithuanian Schuma battalions, a signals intelligence detachment, and another motorized gendarmerie platoon to arrive soon. He projected as an immediate solution that fifteen battalions might restore order, with each battalion assigned to patrol an area of approximately seven thousand square meters. This was only achievable if the army also shared the security burden and protected the supply routes. His radical proposal recommended bringing forward troops still in training, police reservists, depots, and units under construction into the security zone. He explained that deploying these troops in Byelorussia would increase the overall presence of German authority. This offered the added bonus of improving the quality of training and increased the pool of available units for counter-operations.[47] Zenner went on to describe the poor condition of the Schuma and their equipment. Few possessed boots, there was no leather for repairs to those with boots, and there were no bootmakers. The Schutzmänner on guard posts (Einzeldienst) duties worked barefoot. Zenner blamed the clothing and equipment problems on management without specific explanation. There were too few weapons in comparison with the partisan's supplies. The signals functions were inadequate. He requested portable wireless radios and a signals support vehicle for each battalion. This communications issue had become critical since the partisans had cut the telephone cables. At that time, the Germans found it virtually impossible to pass on orders. His final comment was bleak, that even with nearly eighty Schuma battalions, this was but "a drop on a hot stone" (*ein Tropfen auf dem heissem Stein*).

Zenner's report almost certainly embarrassed Jeckeln and Bach-Zelewski, not in content but in the manner of its release to Himmler, their superior officer, constituting a break in protocol.[48] Nevertheless, Himmler decided to test Zenner's proposals in both Russia and in the HSSPF Alpenland covering Carinthia (Oberkrain) and Styria (Untersteiermark). This region had suffered from continuing partisan problems since mid-1941. The British had first intercepted signals in August 1941, confirming serious fighting in the area of Veldes (Slovenia). The German Police Battalion 181 had come under serious attack.[49] The district army commander, General Bader, had countered Tito's partisans with six divisions and very nearly caught them in encirclement. This was the first of several near misses when the Germans nearly destroyed Tito.[50] Himmler's order, on June 25, 1942, called for the application of Bandenbekämpfung. The HSSPF Alpenland, SS-Gruppenführer und Generalleutnant der Polizei Erwin Rösener, was a well-known workaholic but had not recorded any particular expertise in combating partisans. Daluege received instructions from Himmler to provide Rösener with the assistance and support sufficient to cover operations for four weeks. The central command of the Waffen-SS (*SS-Führungshauptamt*) supplied heavy weapons, in particular rifle grenades, mortars, flamethrowers, and mountain field guns. Daluege also assigned several gendarmerie detachments. The Security Police and SD were ordered to deploy a reinforced Einsatzgruppen to cleanse the area. Local army reserve units were requested to assist in the operations but not at the expense of their training schedule. Significantly, Himmler ordered all German men in the region between seventeen and fifty-five to take up arms.[51]

Beside the order, Himmler issued specific guidelines for operations against "partisans" and other "bandits." They stipulated that the security police should conduct a reconnaissance of the region and make an intelligence assessment to locate the bands' leaders. He ordered the task force to encircle, blockade, and clear the area in coordination with the *Landesschützen*, reserve police troops and army reserve. The security police were to assault the heart of the "bandits" and decapitate their leaders. The escaping "bandits," dissipated and splintered in combat, were to be killed in flight and the escapees to be pursued, hunted down, and executed. The decision to impose punishment (*Strafaktion*) against villages guilty of supporting the "bandits" was passed on to the field commanders. Their job was to segregate the "bandit"-supporting villagers from the rest of the population or community. All men of guilty families and their immediate family circle (*Sippe*) were brought under an automatic death penalty. All the women were sent to concentration camps and their children were deported to Austria for racial examination and adoption. The SS confiscated households as property of the state. The purpose of the operation, according to Himmler, was to liberate the friendly from the unfriendly. For this action, he ordered the troops to conduct themselves appropriately in great expectation for their success even in the difficult mountainous region.[52]

Between June 13 and July 9, Bach-Zelewski was heavily committed in joint SS and Wehrmacht security operations. On June 17, he met Oskar Dirlewanger and the commanders of the Police Battalions 51 and 122. He awarded Iron Crosses to Oberst Worms and Oberst Schimana on June 25. He wrote in his diary of his suspicion of the reliability of the Russian auxiliary police of the Ordnungsdienst (OD). Three days later, the partisans shot a member of a collaborator family during a wave of incidents in the Mogilev area. During an operation on July 5, the OD was excluded and the SS surprised fifty-four partisans and shot them. This confirmed Bach-Zelewski's opinion of the unreliability of the OD.[53] On July 9, Himmler held a senior command conference. Those attending included Daluege, Bomhard, three eastern HSSPFs (Krüger from Poland, Bach-Zelewski, and Prützmann), and two SSPF officers, Zenner and Odilo Globocnik from Lublin. Heinrich Müller (chief of the Gestapo), Bruno Streckenbach (RSHA), and Dr. Erhard Schöngarth (BdS Kraków), the former SD-Einsatzgruppen field commander, represented the SD and Gestapo.[54] From the SS field branches came Kurt Knoblauch, the chief of staff of the KSRFSS; SS-Brigadeführer Willi Bittrich, the newly promoted commander of the SS-Cavalry Division; and police generals Herbert Becker (BdO General Government) and Georg Jedicke (BdO Ostland), one of Daluege's senior officers. Hannes Heer suggests that during this meeting Himmler announced his intention of taking control of all Nazi field security.[55] On July 27, Himmler's appointments diary referred to Bandenbekämpfung for the first time, although it was not yet official policy, indicating that the planning phase had ended.[56] In correspondence with Himmler, Daluege asked who was going to be responsible for this new policy and received the curt reply "me personally" (*ich persönlich*). Himmler explained that, in practice, the HSSPF would take charge locally and field commanders were responsible for combat. Given that, Daluege was asking these questions, having attended the meeting of July 9, suggests that the conference was predominately ideological in content and not about implementation.[57]

In the period prior to the introduction of Bandenbekämpfung, Himmler concentrated on outlawing partisans as "bandits." He took on the demeanor of the high priest of Bandenbekämpfung. Himmler challenged the use of such "heroic" terms as partisan, guerrilla, and freedom fighter as inappropriate descriptions of the Jewish-Bolshevik "evil" of terrorists, "bandits," and outlaws. He understood that it was necessary to prevent the emergence of a heroic "bandit" figure. In a file memo titled, "Thoughts on the Word 'Partisan,'" Himmler complained about the deliberate corruption of the word "partisan" by the Soviets. "In the concept of the partisan, Bolshevism tries to promote banditry to a national status," he explained apropos this new mission of selective attrition. "We have challenged this newly coined status by the Jewish-Bolshevik sub-humans [*Untermensch*], and have fought to remove the 'bandits' from within the population."[58] From July 31, he waged a vigorous paper war over correct terminology; the word "partisan" was no longer acceptable; it was superseded by "bandit," franc-tireur, or outlaw.[59] This was justified because the Soviets had adopted the term "partisan" to disguise their criminal activities in a "Bolshevik plot conceived by a Jewish propaganda swindle." Himmler added, "bandits who fire their underhand shots, and commit their acts of sabotage as snipers, franc-tireurs and highway-robbers [*Strassenräuber*] then flee, hoping to very often encumber the innocent inhabitants of the country, will be held responsible for their deeds."[60]

On August 12, Himmler issued an SS order that explained on "psychological grounds" why the word "partisan" was no longer acceptable. He reiterated the opinion that Bolshevism had corrupted the original term and that in future correspondence only "Banditen" or "Frank-Tireur" was acceptable. Himmler stressed the importance of differentiating between the "quiet people" and the snipers (*Heckenschützen*) and of deterring the "quiet people" from siding with the "bandits."[61] The description of "bandits" in field reports, however, remained inconsistent. To counter Soviet propaganda and partisan incursions, and endorse the righteousness of his strategy, Himmler ordered a propaganda campaign to begin leafleting the inhabitants of Russian villages. The leaflets warned the largely peasant populations that Moscow's use of the term "partisan" was neither heroic nor patriotic. The message warned that German soldiers would shoot anyone who supported the "bandits" or allowed them into their homes. In a letter to the SS-propaganda unit, Himmler expected reports of actions to reflect accurately the facts through official terminology (i.e., *Banden, Banditen-Bekämpfung,* or *Franktireur-Bekämpfung*).[62] From then on, the SS internal publicity unit, the SS-Standarte "Kurt Eggers," standardized this terminology in all its newsprint and publications.[63] William Combs, however, found that the coverage of Bandenbekämpfung in the SS corporate self-promotional publication, *Das Schwarze Korps*, was sporadic and limited to fewer than a dozen examples of "bandit" hunts.[64]

## Directive 46

Until August 1942, issuing regulations for the combating of partisans was largely a hit-and-miss affair between OKW and the Army High Command (*Oberkommando des Heeres,* OKH), with the occasional interference from Hitler in July and September 1941. Since the introduction of the "Barbarossa" directives, the armed forces had fumbled with security regulations. This reflected the difficulty of gauging the scale of the resistance that Stalin had initiated in July 1941 and its growing sophistication. In response to the intensified partisan activity, OKH distributed Field Marshal Brauchitsch's guidelines of October 25. They codified existing German practices and began a process of building a common doctrine for all forces committed to security. These guidelines were oriented toward prescribing operations by scale and planning and by encouraging initiative and aggression. Brauchitsch's initiative was proactive and biased toward the German tradition of responding aggressively toward incursions.[65] When Schenckendorff tried to raise awareness of the security problem, he was attempting to contain it within this existing doctrine. Himmler's Bandenbekämpfung took a fundamentally different direction in the first instance by accepting that Lebensraum had happened. The criminalization of the partisan was the first step in interpreting the laws of conquest rather than war. When OKW issued Führer Directive No. 46, "Instructions for Intensified Action against Banditry in the East" (*Richtlinien für die verstärkte Bekämpfung des Bandenunwesens im Osten*), in August 1942, it confirmed that Germany would treat the conquered lands as Germanized.[66]

To the untutored, the plethora of Führer orders (*Führerbefehl*) and Führer directives (*Führerweisungen*) can befuddle the mind. Wrapped together in the concept of the Führer principle (*Führerprinzip*), they formed a peculiar triangulated equation of decision making. The Führer, or leader principle, was in theory a strict centralizing and hierarchical methodology but in practice the excuse that allowed those approved worthy to manipulate Nazi and military power. What Kershaw described as "working towards the Führer" involved a complex cycle of encouraging initiative and constructing regulatory devices to promote a climate for further motivating initiative.[67] Hugh Trevor-Roper and Walter Hubatsch agreed that the "order" and the "directive" were both binding but that in the directive, the manner of execution was left to the initiative of the responsible subordinate. Thus, a Führer order in this context was inflexible, whereas the Führer directive was flexible in its application. The directives usually followed a pattern not unlike a prescription, first explaining the condition, then offering remedial instructions, and finally providing some form of answer. Directive No. 46 followed the prescriptive formula and was broad enough to allow dynamic initiative. This was not what made it exceptional.

The thrust of the directive was official confirmation that Nazi Germany outlawed the Soviet partisans as political "bandits." This equated combating partisans with combating gangsters or gangsterism. The rules of engagement covered six points of general principles in forming countermeasures to the "bandit." The first reinforced the strategic status of Bandenbekämpfung. All existing operational headquarters staffs, irrespective of organization or arm, were required to deploy resources to conduct Bandenbekämpfung. The second point ordered the troops to take the initiative against banditry and its supporters, sanctioning all extreme measures. The remaining instructions were concerned with the handling of civilians. The third point recommended that those conducting security operations should regain the confidence of civilians through just treatment. To undermine local support for the "bandits," the fourth point of the directive stipulated that the local populace should receive the minimum level of sustenance. In the fifth point, the troops received a warning to gain the cooperation of the populace. This reflected the stick-and-carrot intent of the directive—rewards for cooperation and collaboration and severe punitive measures for aiding the "bandits." This placed the civilian in an arbitrarily decided position of innocence or labeled him as a "bandit-suspect" (*Bandenverdächtige*). A final contradictory point warned against misplaced confidence in relying on indigenous population, especially among those employed by the Germans.[68]

The strategic orientation of the directive was extermination and mobilization, with an operational emphasis on cooperation between the SS and Wehrmacht. The division of labor was simplified: the army was to clear "bandits" and mobilize civilians in the front area (*Operationsgebiet*), while the SS-Police administered racial cleansing and securing Lebensraum. The directive integrated Zenner's proposal for the transfer of reserves and rear-area depots, thereby turning annexed territory into German lands. A time frame was included in the directive to bring about a repositioning of military assets into the security zone. Four key decisions were placed on the army. The first turned the General Government of Poland into a "Home Forces" area with two reserve army divisions. Second, scheduled for completion by October 15, 1942, Hitler ordered the transfer of five reserve army divisions into the Baltic area and Ukraine. Third, all formations, staff, depots, and military academies stationed in the General Government of Poland redeployed east into rear areas and security zones of occupied Russia by October 1. Finally, a target was set to transfer fifty thousand soldiers from the reserve army into the forward operational areas by the end of October. The directive stipulated that the commander-in-chief of the Luftwaffe should also transfer combat units to areas threatened by "bandits" to reinforce the garrisons already in Russia.

Completing the deployment program and making the directive a national security regulation, the "auxiliary forces," a plethora of Nazi and state organizations, were given license to carry out Bandenbekämpfung. This included the Reich Labor Service (*Reichsarbeitsdienst*), railwaymen security troops (*Eisenbahntruppen*), state foresters (*Reichsforstamt*), and agricultural overseers (*Landwirtschaftsführer*). Hitler ruled that these organizations should be armed to defend themselves.[69]

Early in August 1942, Hitler revealed his impression of combating partisans. He compared it to the struggle waged in North America against "Red Indians." This was a telling remark, possibly originating from his fascination with Karl May novels and offering an insight into his perception of Lebensraum as life on the frontier.[70] The form of Directive 46 was a set of strategic instructions and rules of engagement. Hitler in this directive revealed his Catholic loathing for "banditry," reflecting the received wisdom of the time, and he was at ease with the prospect of burning alive thousands of innocent men, women, and children to exterminate "bandits." He wished to lodge these sentiments in the German mindset by granting the freedom to wage active or passive Bandenbekämpfung. To meet Hitler's sentiments, Himmler had little problem choosing Bach-Zelewski to become his expert.

Following a long meeting between Bach-Zelewski and Himmler, on September 9, the reorganization process took on a new vigor. Bach-Zelewski joined a number of senior SS guests attending a typical Himmler business luncheon and, at 7:00 p.m., discovered the reason for his attendance. Himmler decided to make Bach-Zelewski inspector of Bandenbekämpfung (*Inspekteur für die Bandenbekämpfung im gesamten Ostgebiet*) for the complete eastern area for a trial period.[71] Bach-Zelewski had still to report to both Schenckendorff and Himmler. The OKW officer responsible for monitoring the progress of Bandenbekämpfung was Maj. Gen. Walter Warlimont, deputy chief of the OKW operations department (*Wehrmachtführungsstab*–WFSt) responsible for planning. He was also a logical choice because, since March 1941, he had been involved in drafting the "Barbarossa" regulations, and once the campaign was under way, he had advised Hitler every two weeks on the partisan situation.[72]

The new Bandenbekämpfung regulations did not stop bickering between the Nazis. The SS was directly responsible for policing and guarding the territories designated as Reichskommissariate. The German civilian occupation of Soviet Russia was administered from Berlin by the Reich Ministry of the Eastern Occupied Territories (known as the Ostministerium), which in theory controlled two zones—Ostland (an area comparable with the former Ober Ost) and the Ukraine. Since these lands were to be integrated into the empire, the Reichskommissars were also Gauleiters from Germany and took up permanent residence in their respective territories. The Reichskommissar for the Ukraine, Erich Koch, was Gauleiter of East Prussia, and he extended his power base into the Ukraine through a political land bridge through Bialystok. In other words, Koch's territorial power bisected Bach-Zelewski's security environment. After the Schacht incident of 1935 when Bach-Zelewski protested against Schacht's compliments of Koch, whom he considered inferior and corrupt, relations were permanently marred between Bach-Zelewski and Koch. Since 1941, Koch had depended on two senior SS officers. His HSSPF for both East Prussia and the Ukraine was Hans-Adolf Prützmann. Koch was assigned Jakob Sporrenberg as his security police advisor in 1936. Sporrenberg had calmed the situation after Koch's contretemps with Bach-Zelewski, and in 1941, he became Koch's SSPF-without portfolio until March 1943. Koch had built a reputation as a repulsive and brutal character who exploited his membership of Göring's social clique. The introduction of Bandenbekämpfung and its control by Bach-Zelewski set in train another bout of trouble between the SS and Koch.

On September 27, 1942, Koch summoned Prützmann, and a serious argument ensued. Prützmann reported to Himmler that Koch had contrived the argument. Koch's petulance was defensive, a reaction to keep Himmler from treating him as he treated Hans Frank or Epp. The influence of Bandenbekämpfung, lightly dismissed by Koch as irrelevant, was the crux of the problem. Although the argument centered on who controlled the HSSPF in the field, the Reichsführer-SS or the Gauleiter, Koch demanded "yesmen" as subordinates and expected an elaborate system of reporting to monitor any Bandenbekämpfung operation in his areas so he could retain control over decisions and personnel.[73] Since 1935, Koch had manipulated and milked the loss of face over Bach-Zelewski, but this time, Himmler commented that it was not his style to surround himself with obedient subordinates; still, if that was Koch's way, so be it. Placing the issue of subordinates on hold until after the new year, Himmler mildly rebuked Koch by stating they were too busy for such altercations. Then he made it clear that if Koch wanted to make an issue of this present situation he was quite prepared to accept a fight.[74] On October 2, Prützmann wrote to Koch in his official capacity confirming the implementation of Bandenbekämpfung. He quoted regulation and code to the effect that Führer Directive 46 was in force. Prützmann explained that engaging in bureaucratic procedures prior to a cleansing action was impractical. He added that to be effective, measures must be performed immediately, although local officials would be advised when possible. Prützmann agreed with Koch that holding villages to ransom for money or plunder was a political act with political consequences. He confirmed that the safeguard against errors in collective punishments (*Kollektivstrafen*) was that they could only be made by the commanding officer of the operation. He added, however, that the army commander of the Ukraine had confirmed his orders.[75] The SS, with silent assistance from the army, had neutralized Koch.

## Wehrmacht-SS Initiatives

A significant difference between Directive 46 and other policies was the breadth of its authority, the scale of its tasks, and the manner in which a doctrine was built on it. A mistaken impression has grown since the war that Bandenbekämpfung was specific to the east, was solely under Himmler's authority, and formed a "parallel jurisdiction" with the army.[76] This ignores the cross-fertilization of Nazi policies and the transferability of methods from one front to another. Since 1940, British covert warfare had irritated Hitler. The evening of the directive's release, the British, by a remarkable coincidence, carried out the Dieppe raid. During September and October, the British conducted "pin-prick" raids along the French coast and in the Channel Islands.[77] While the SS-SD countered the SOE, quite effectively in some cases, OKW believed that there was a need to regulate against the commando problem. This was not the same as countering the clandestine SOE and saboteurs dressed in civilian clothes. British and U.S. special forces, commandos, and rangers wore full uniform and carried out military operations. The existing laws of war were quite specific regarding the treatment of soldiers, captured while fighting in uniform or in conventional warfare; they were entitled to the full protection of the Geneva Convention of 1925.

The situation regarding the conventionality of the British commandos was not clear-cut. A former commando confirmed that they were highly trained professional soldiers versed in the ways of the "hardiest and most austere guerrilla."[78] Roger Beaumont was quite scathing about these troops, calling them "mob for jobs."[79] Months before the German army had drawn a category for the "commandos" in their secret handbook of the British army (*Das Britische Kriegsheer*), they identified the commandos as volunteers; its officers were known to be an exclusive group subject to special selection. They trained in handling weapons, using explosives, and surviving inside enemy country. The Germans assumed the British had adopted Russian partisan skills in their training programs. Their weaponry included machine guns and pistols, knives and hand grenades, mortars and flamethrowers. Commando operations included the fleet and the air force in combined operations, with the troops trained to alight from special motor landing crafts or by parachutes. The Germans identified commando tasks as normally seaborne operations in hostile territory, setting up obstacles, destroying war industries, and preparing the way for larger operations. They correctly identified the Special Service Brigades of the Royal Marines and the Special Air Services (SAS) Brigade deployed in North Africa. Thus, in April 1942, the Germans were still not discriminating against the commandos as "bandits."[80] However, by August 1942, OKW and Hitler wanted to discriminate against the commandos in the same manner as they had with the Commissar Order of 1941.

Between August and October 1942, Hitler received a continuous flow of reports about the activities of the allied Special Forces. On August 4, he ordered OKH to issue instructions on the treatment of captured individual allied parachutists.[81] Himmler presented a report to Hitler on September 22, which included details of the sabotage and "bandit war" (*Sabotage und Bandenkrieg*) waged by the British. On October 7, Hitler instructed Jodl to issue an order for the ill-treatment of enemy soldiers captured while "fighting like bandits." In a radio speech the same day, Hitler made this statement: "All terror and sabotage troops of the British and their accomplices, who do not act like soldiers but like 'bandits,' have in future to be treated as such by the German troops, and they must be slaughtered ruthlessly in combat wherever they turn up."[82] The soldier most responsible for preparing the regulations that led to the "Commando Order" was Warlimont. His commanding officer, Alfred Jodl, later explained the reasoning behind the introduction of the Commando Order after the war. "The order arose from Hitler's excitement about two kinds of intensified warfare which made their appearance about the same time in the autumn of 1942. One was the fatal efficacy of excellently equipped sabotage detachments, which landed by sea or were dropped from the air. The other was a special running wild in the fighting methods of enemies who acted singly or in small groups [*sic*]."[83] On October 8, Warlimont received instructions from Jodl to polish Hitler's political announcement into a military format. That same day, Himmler advised Hitler on the continuing incursions by the British. This process led to the introduction of the commando order that superseded the Commissar Order of 1941. The outcome was a less restrictive regulation, applicable to any theater.

On October 18, Hitler explained this new policy to army officers. He opened by stating that "for some time our enemies have been using in their warfare methods which are outside the international Geneva Convention. Especially brutal and treacherous is the behaviour of the so-called commandos, who, it is established, are partially recruited from freed criminals of enemy countries," adding, "orders have been found in which the killing of [German] prisoners has been demanded in principle."[84] Hitler felt that once the soldiers understood the scale of the problem, they would treat the commandos like Soviet partisans. He employed a theoretical example of the destruction of a power plant with the consequential loss of energy that could deprive the Luftwaffe of thousands of tons of aluminium. "The homeland as well as the fighting soldier at the front," he concluded, "has the right to expect that behind their back the essentials of nourishment as well as the supply of war-important weapons and ammunition remains secure."[85]

Hitler, the OKW, and the SS had orchestrated a consistency across the whole of German security policy. The Bandenbekämpfung directive, suitably amended, was applicable anywhere. "Only where the fight against this partisan disgrace was begun and executed with ruthless brutality," Hitler confirmed, "were results achieved which eased the position of the fighting front." The allied commandos, he explained, had been issued with uniforms, but they usually wore civilian clothes to commit acts of sabotage and ran no risk from slaughtering German soldiers except becoming prisoners of war. Many were former prison inmates and had been absolved from their past crimes for volunteering with the commandos. "From now on," Hitler ordered, "all enemies on so-called commando missions in Europe or Africa challenged by German troops, even if they are to all appearances soldiers in uniform or demolition troops, whether armed or unarmed, in battle or in flight, are to be slaughtered to the last man." Hitler expected all executions to be recorded. "The report on this subject appearing in the Armed Forces communiqué will briefly and laconically state that a sabotage, terror, or destruction unit has been encountered and exterminated to the last man."[86] To sustain the secrecy of his instructions, he issued on October 19 the following statement: "This order is intended for commanders only and must not under any circumstances fall into enemy hands." The orders became addendums "a" and "b" of Directive 46.[87] OKH distributed the addendums within seven days of enactment to all German armies, including those in the east. The Kriegsmarine received its copies on October 27, 1942. The chief of staff of the rear area, Army Group South, received a copy of the order, and the war diary of the 3rd Panzer Army recorded the receipt of its copy. The 3rd Panzer Army confirmed the general application of the order to the Eastern Front and sanctioned the killing of soldiers in uniform.

Not surprisingly, with so many Nazi secrets falling into allied hands, it was only a matter of time before the Allies received evidence of the addendums. The British assumed that Hitler was about to revoke the Geneva Convention on prisoners of war. On October 20, Sir Stafford Cripps prepared documentation to charge Germany with breaches in the laws of war. He also began to draw up an operational response if the Germans renounced the Geneva Prisoners of War Convention.[88] Ironically, the concentration of Anglo-American attention on the Commando Order served to artificially divide the Bandenbekämpfung directive in two.[89]

While OKW planned and prepared the Commando Order, in September Himmler prepared the Bandenbekämpfung pamphlet that served as the doctrinal guidelines for all security operations. This insignificant-looking document presents two impressions. Its contemporary style was laced with raw emotion and personified the moral outrage for the ways of the "bandit." As a working document, it motivated the troops into aggressive and wanton acts of revenge and reprisal, but it was ostensibly defensive. The pamphlet was a hodgepodge of ideas strung together without a comprehensible structure yet represented the cutting-edge of security warfare. Bandenbekämpfung served as a rudimentary collection of instructions, brief practical guidelines, for troops assigned to security duties.[90] Several sections exposed its true purpose, which was to enforce Nazi rule beyond the metropolitan centers of occupied Russia. It reflected Zenner's report and the experience of combating Soviet incursion up to that time. Himmler's conclusion was that banditry was set on the dual task of disrupting Nazi control in rural Russia and the destruction of interior lines of communication. The mission was to defy their plans by waging terror across the land, causing "banditry" to wither through attrition.

The pamphlet set out to dehumanize Soviet partisans as criminal "political bandits" and flag bearers of Jewish-Bolshevism. Extracts from SD reports and captured Soviet documents were added to deliberately present a distorted picture. For example, an extract from Stalin's speech of July 3, 1941, calling for a general uprising highlighted these lines: "They shall inflame partisan warfare all over the place. . . . It is necessary to create unbearable conditions for the enemy in the occupied areas. His collaborators must be pursued and eliminated." There was even a comparison of Nazi and Soviet blood oaths. The SS recruits swore an oath to Hitler but the "bandit" oath (*Bandenschwur*) declared "Blood for blood! Death for death!" A supplementary selection of documents was attached to the pamphlet called, "The companion of the 'partisan.'"[91] These documents included excerpts on how the "soviet bandits" measured their success. This served to further dehumanize the "bandits" by implying they were crafty and underhanded with impudence rather than courage being their typical trait. The "bandit" was stereotyped as a practitioner of espionage who ambushed in small groups, used silent weapons to "stab with the bayonet, beat with the shovel and stab with the dagger." The pamphlet concluded by focusing on the Soviet instructions: "Don't leave the initiative to the enemies" and maintain control over the local populations. The Germans were reminded to, "keep one thing in mind: The ground rule of the 'bandit' is: attacking, attacking and again attacking."[92]

The heart of the pamphlet was titled "Reflection on the Fundamental Methods for Combating Bandits" (*Grundsätzliche Betrachtungen zu den Methoden der Bekämpfung der Banden*), and it was about tactics.[93] It had eight subsections. A psychological warfare section began with a warning to the troops to distinguish between the military or conventional formations, stressing the difference between the "bandit" band and the single or opportunist "bandit." The importance of gathering intelligence about the "bandits" was regarded as essential for carrying out a tactical encirclement. The pamphlet warned against "bandit" mobility undermining attempts at the collection of intelligence.[94] To enhance the intelligence capability, the pamphlet recommended placing trusties (*Vertrauensmänner*) within the bands. The preferences included former Soviet POWs, captured "bandits," local dignitaries, young girls, women, grandparents, and children. "Captured bandits" were regarded as a primary source of intelligence, but after intensive interrogation, they were to be executed. Only a month before, Himmler warned, "All women and girls had the potential to be bandits and assassins."[95] An interrogator was permitted to employ mild treatment (*milde Behandlung*) to trick a captured "bandit," in fear for his life, into giving away useful information. This treatment might include the offer of cigarettes and schnapps. The skilled interrogator was expected to exploit the "bandit's" fear of Soviet reprisals against his or her family, which was made worse because the Germans deliberately mislead the community by saying that the "bandits" were paid informers.

Self-protection proposals were collected in a section on preventative measures (*Präventivmassnahmen*). The first stage involved the registration of strangers in a community. The onus of registration was placed with local community leaders; "headman, the village seniors, the inhabitants . . . report every stranger to the police immediately [and threaten them to be] whipped or shot, if they do not." A list of residents, confirmed by the headman, was pinned to the inside front door of houses. The reasoning: "Everything needs to be done to stop migration without purpose and timetable." The pamphlet recommended the introduction of an alarm system, a network of villages connected by messengers, hand signals, and radio-wirelesses. A network of strongpoints placed at critical transport junctions, supported by the communication network, was supposed to protect the interior lines of communication. The ultimate level of prevention was the declaration of security zones. This involved the complete evacuation of all civilians and led to channels of depopulated land running across occupied Russia. The pamphlet recommended further reinforcement of these zones, including the placement of strongpoints, the flattening of terrain features that might provide cover for an ambush and regular patrols.[96]

The prescribed method of "combating the bandits" (*die Bekämpfung*) concentrated on the role of the Waffen-SS, Order Police, and Wehrmacht in the conduct of field operations. The SD and SIPO were assigned supporting roles of field intelligence, conducting interrogations, and punishments. Their job was to keep a constant flow of intelligence to the troops during operations to ensure the complete extermination of the "bandits." To prevent endangering an operation and the "cost of spilling German blood" unnecessarily, it was impressed on the SD to remain diligent in their work. The only tactical goal of an operation was "the extermination of the bandits not its expulsion." The operation had to be quick, with surprise, and projecting dynamism. The main objective was the decapitation of the band leaders: "After losing its leadership, the band is broken." Depending on the circumstances, troops were to establish seclusion zones to conduct plunder and the deportation of the community. The community elders were pressed into enrolling in the Schuma and assisting the patrols. While these actions were under way, an area was supposed to be flooded with propaganda. A Kampfgruppe was to form a security cordon ready to counter any attempt by the bands to break out or break in.[97]

The pamphlet recommended ongoing aggressive counteraction against the "bandits." This included raising hunting teams, formed from local troops, led by SD or SIPO officers, with radio equipment operating in "bandit-infected" (*bandenverseucht*) areas. During the registration (Erfassung) of community populations, "bandit-suspects" *(Bandenverdächtigte)* were executed individually and discretely, to prevent the outbreak of violence. Local collaborators working as *agents provocateurs* were supposed to sow doubt and suspicion throughout the bands. The pacification process, with or without armed action, was always enforced against local dignitaries and village elders, who were to be held hostage. The sanction of revenge actions (*Vergeltungsmassnahmen*) was automatic if an elder failed to adequately explain incursions into his community or if residents had aided the "bandits." Himmler's concern remained the misdirected revenge action but not for humanitarian reasons. He worried that survivors might escape and join the bands. To reduce the possibility of this happening, the commanding officers had to take responsibility for the punishment and ensure the whereabouts of everyone in the community. Few orders were quite so specific in assigning responsibility for the execution of entire communities. Even so, the Germans also tried to develop an "air of willingness to being ruled" in communities as a counter to intimidation of the "bandits." This included a proactive propaganda program and a counter-campaign against "bandit" propaganda. The officer responsible for writing Bandenbekämpfung, Gottlob Berger, sent a copy of the final draft to Bach-Zelewski in November 1942.[98]

## Results

Results can explain a great deal about a policy, even a policy with silences. The success of Bandenbekämpfung as an experiment was accepted by all parties, and Himmler promoted Bach-Zelewski to "Plenipotentiary for Bandenbekämpfung in the East" (*Bevollmächtigter für die Bandenbekämpfung im Osten*) on October 23. The decision was finalized six days after Hitler concluded the amendments "a" and "b" of Directive 46. Bach-Zelewski also received a large number of Jeckeln's security assets and forces.[99] Himmler authorized Bach-Zelewski to represent the Reichsführer-SS in all matters concerning Bandenbekämpfung. To bolster the inspectorate further it was assigned troops: 13th and 14th SS-Police Regiments, all the Schuma formations from HSSPF Russia-Centre, the 1st SS-Infantry Brigade, and the Danish and Scandinavian collaborators (Freikorps Danmark).[100] Bach-Zelewski suggested in his diary that his new status was a demotion to the level of a brigade commander. This was patently untrue. The new position placed him in the key liaison role between the SS and Wehrmacht. His responsibilities also called for the centralization of intelligence and coordination of all security assets applied to security warfare. In terms of actual capability, Bach-Zelewski was on par with an infantry division commander. His functions, however, went far beyond tactical operations with a roving strategic role ranging across the rear areas of the Eastern Front, crossing over both SS and Wehrmacht spheres of authority. His release from administrative and bureaucratic duties was regarded as temporary, and the HSSPF Russia-Centre received another substitute.[101] These were subtle moves because Bach-Zelewski, as Himmler's Trojan horse, was working the scheme toward taking control of security as a whole.

The relationship between the army commanders and the SS in the field remained positive. On October 25, Schenckendorff wrote to Bach-Zelewski regarding the 1st SS Infantry Brigade and the 286th Infantry Division, congratulating them on their efforts during Operation "Karlsbad." One of Bach-Zelewski's first political tasks was to meet with Schenckendorff on October 27 and draw up a broad agreement over joint SS and army operations. The next day, Bach-Zelewski visited the chief of staff, Army Group Centre, Generalmajor Wöhler. They arranged a security agreement over respective spheres of operations. Bach-Zelewski generously agreed to assign the 13th SS-Police Regiment to security protection for the construction of the army group's secondary defense line, an indication of Bach-Zelewski's power of decision.[102] By this time, he was receiving a constant flow of intelligence reports from SD-Oberführer Naumann, in Smolensk, and operational reports from SS-Brigadeführer Kutschera. In the last quarter of 1942, Bandenbekämpfung operations turned toward the Pripyat marshes with the objective of eradicating "bandits," "bandit suspects," and Jews.

On October 28, Himmler sent a message to Wolff, the SS liaison officer in Hitler's headquarters, requesting him to plead with the Führer and Keitel not to transfer his police battalions to the front. He asked Wolff to explain to Hitler that achieving success in Bandenbekämpfung was impossible without the main body of his troops. It was a deliberate "flyer." He knew well enough that the deteriorating situation around Stalingrad forced their transfer. Himmler could hardly lose face with this sentiment but would gain considerable leverage in the acquisition of resources and authority for the coming year, avoiding the problems that occurred in spring 1942.[103] On November 16, Himmler released a communiqué. "In this critical period," he decreed, "all men must be armed to combat the 'bandit.' The harder the fighting now, the sooner the civilian government can begin to work effectively."[104] A month later, he warned Bach-Zelewski that the 1st SS Infantry Brigade was being transferred to the front.[105] In the short time available for their use, Bach-Zelewski led the brigade and Schuma formations in short but harrowing actions to prevent the "bandits" from consolidating their camps before winter. Although Bach-Zelewski had lost his strongest body of troops, he maintained aggressive operations against the partisans with a mix of ad hoc units. He soon came to depend on the SS-Kommando Dirlewanger, assisted by two police armored companies and a collection of Schuma battalions.

The effectiveness of the winter operations has received some analysis, but the various sources present mixed opinions. One report intercepted by the British was poignant. The conclusion of Operation "Hamburg" led SS-Brigadeführer Bassewitz-Behr to release a signal to the RSHA on December

20. The signal was addressed to the chief of Order Police and stated that SS-Brigadeführer von Gottberg had led an exemplary operation. The communiqué announced that "in spite of swamplands like primeval forests, the territory was reopened for the German administration after it had been ruled by 'bandits' for months." The results of the operation itemized the total enemy dead of 6,172: 1,674 were "bandits" killed in action, 1,510 were executed suspects, and 2,988 were "bandit sympathizers," also executed. Ten well-constructed camps were also destroyed, one with the capacity of one thousand men, with modern installations. Large amounts of booty were collected, including four tanks, artillery pieces, and guns. "A great quantity of automatic and no-automatic weapons," Bassewitz-Behr added, "as well as large quantities of artillery and infantry ammunition, which were destroyed there and then, as it is not possible at the moment to get them out of the swamps." He concluded the communiqué with the news that seven German sergeants had been killed and seventeen were wounded (seven police officers) and that Gottberg and Bach-Zelewski received the clasp of the Iron Cross (Second Class). [106]

Meanwhile the Wehrmacht was not complacent during this period. On August 26, OKW ordered all military formations involved in combating the bands to return reports biased toward reconnaissance, intelligence, tactics, and propaganda. The reports also included the treatment of captives, the control of large areas, and the use of local defense and collaboration units for Bandenbekämpfung. The sum of these reports indicated to OKW the soundness of Directive 46 and the comprehensive treatment of civilians. The outcome led to the "directive for combating banditry in the east" (*Kampfanweisung für die Bandenbekämpfung im Osten*), issued in November.[107] These instructions continued to preach the execution of partisans as "bandits" and "bandit suspects," during fighting or in-flight. "Bandit deserters" were treated honorably as prisoners of war, while captured bandits who could prove they were press-ganged into joining the band were sent to hard labor camps. Villages found guilty of aiding the bands were subject to collective reprisals, ranging from increased quotas to total destruction through burning.[108]

On December 1, a conference between Hitler, Keitel, and Jodl confirmed the general approval for Bandenbekämpfung. Keitel initiated discussion on the security issue because OKW was on the point of issuing yet more instructions. Hitler immediately rose to the theme claiming to encourage those who succeeded through brutal means in eradicating the "bandits." He recalled the Zabern Incident (1913) to explain the ineffectual methods adopted in the past to deal with insurrection and insurgency. Hitler explained that in the interwar years, he had observed how the "red bastards" had placed children at the head of their march through Chemnitz in order to dissuade their opponents from attacking. Faced with similar circumstances, an officer, he explained, must be prepared to kill women and children to eradicate the greater menace. Hitler accepted that burning down a house with innocents inside was a military necessity, while Jodl appeared to consider hanging, drawing, and quartering as permissible punishments. Indeed, his only limitation, largely in agreement with Himmler, was to prevent unnecessary after-action measures frightening the populace into supporting the "bandits" en masse. Referring to SS methods, Hitler believed they had more experience in Bandenbekämpfung and were wrongly accused of being brutal. Jodl replied that they only applied the stick-and-carrot, like all forces. Keitel interjected to add that there had been good cooperation between the SS and troops under Bach-Zelewski.[109]

On December 16, Keitel issued the last security order for the year to all commands on behalf of Hitler. It warned that "bandits" fought as "communist-trained fanatics who do not hesitate to commit any atrocity." He added that Hitler had received reports that following Bandenbekämpfung operations some officers had been charged with misconduct for extreme measures. It was time "to be or not to be" (*sein oder nicht sein*) and for measures beyond gentlemanly conduct or the Geneva Convention. Consequently, Keitel believed the conflict in the east and the Balkans was a disease (*Pest*) that demanded brutal measures because of the shortage of forces. The troops were granted the right to use all measures, even against women and children, if it led to success. Any attempt to apply consideration for people in these operations was regarded as a crime against the German people and soldiery. The applications of the Kampfanweisung für die Bandenbekämpfung im Osten was to be carried out without retribution or restitution against the troops. In section 2 of the order, Keitel stated that "no German[s] employed in Bandenbekämpfung can be made responsible for their actions before the courts." All officers and commanders of troops had to be made aware of the order and military judge advocates informed that no sentences against soldiers would be confirmed.[110] This was another blow against Schenckendorff's shrinking authority after he had ordered the arrest of soldiers following an incident in March 1942: "A crowd of soldiers burst into the guards' quarters and lynched four Russian civilians. . . . After prolonged beating with whips the Russians were soaked in petrol and set alight. An officer, a captain, who was present at the lynching calmly looked on at the activities of the soldiers."[111]

In December 1941, Himmler's diary confirmed the combination of a policy for the extermination of Jews and partisans. This was not fully realized until the Wannsee protocol was enacted in January 1942 and the subsequent change in wartime conditions following the rise of Tito and the death of Heydrich. The results from the first phase of Bandenbekämpfung highlighted the continuing mass extermination of Jews alongside the rapidly increasing killing of "bandits" and their supporters. In Himmler's report 51a, passed to Hitler on December 29, the figures present the stark reality behind Prützmann's activities (Table 3.1).[112] It is immediately apparent from the figures that the number of Jews executed outweighed the number of all other groups executed. The number of "bandits" executed after action was far greater than the number of those killed in action. The German and collaborator casualty figures prove the stark imbalance. In January 1943, Daluege itemized the total police casualties for the Order Police in 1942 from all causes as 5,012 dead, a further 9,389 wounded, and 251 believed to be held as prisoners of war.[113]

**Table 3.1: Report 51a, December 1942**

|  | AUGUST | SEPTEMBER | OCTOBER | NOVEMBER | TOTAL |
|---|---|---|---|---|---|
| **Bandits** |  |  |  |  |  |
| Killed in combat | 227 | 381 | 427 | 302 | 1,337 |
| Executed prisoners | 125 | 282 | 87 | 243 | 737 |
| Executed later | 2,100 | 1,400 | 1,596 | 2,731 | 7,827 |
| **Bandit helpers** |  |  |  |  |  |
| Arrested | 1,343 | 3,078 | 8,337 | 3,795 | 16,553 |
| Executed | 1,198 | 3,020 | 6,333 | 3,706 | 14,257 |
| Jews executed | 31,246 | 165,282 | 93,735 | 70,948 | 363,211 |
| Deserters | 21 | 14 | 42 | 63 | 140 |
| **German Casualties:** |  |  |  |  |  |
| Dead | 43 | 16 | 24 | 91 | 174 |
| Wounded | 16 | 5 | 16 | 95 | 132 |
| Missing | 2 | 3 | 3 | 5 | 13 |
| **Schutzmannschaft** |  |  |  |  |  |
| Dead | 67 | 67 | 58 | 93 | 285 |
| Wounded | 34 | 33 | 17 | 43 | 127 |
| Missing | 16 | 10 | 39 | 68 | 133 |

Bach-Zelewski's personal record, as Bevollmächtigter für Banden-bekämpfung, calculated from his diary, confirmed the stark imbalance of casualty figures between Germans and "bandits" (Table 3.2). The accuracy of Bach-Zelewski's figures are also questionable. We know from other sources that Gottberg recorded 1,826 Jews killed during "Nuernberg" but did not include the number burnt alive in buildings. For "Hornung," Gottberg recorded 3,300 Jews killed, and while Bach-Zelewski was again serving at the front, he accounted for 2,958 Jews killed during "Hamburg" (December 1942).[114] As Hitler's war and Bandenbekämpfung entered the final stages, the results from operations aided continuous criminal warfare begun in 1939 by becoming a measure of loyalty to Hitler and proof of conformity to Nazi policy.

## Table 3.2: Bach-Zelewski's record as Bevollmächtigter für Bandenbekämpfung[*]

| FORMATION OR OPERATION | | GERMANS | | | BANDITS | | | |
|---|---|---|---|---|---|---|---|---|
| | Diary Date | Dead | Missing | Wounded | Dead | Shot | POWs | Labor |
| KARLSBAD | 26. 10.1942 | 27 | - | 64 | 546 | - | 33 | - |
| 201st Schuma Battalion | 30.10.1942 | 26 | - | - | 89 | - | 20 | - |
| 54th Schuma Battalion | 30.10.1942 | 3 | - | - | - | - | 5 | - |
| 14th Police Regiment | 30.10.1942 | - | - | 3 | 5 | - | - | - |
| 1st SS Infantry Brigade | 2.11.1942 | 4 | 1 | 3 | 11 | - | ? | - |
| FK - Minsk | 3.11.1942 | 156 | 1 | 62 | 1,003 | 480 | - | - |
| Small unnamed | 3. 11. 1942 | 3 | - | 1 | 22 | - | - | - |
| 'schnell''- Rowanitschi | 10. 11.1942 | 19 | - | 7 | 136 | - | - | - |
| Dirlewanger – "Albert II" | 12. 11.1942 | 3 | 7 | 5 | 176 | - | - | - |
| 14th Police – "Albert II" | 12.11.1942 | - | - | - | 30 | - | - | - |
| "ALBERT II" | 13.11.1942 | - | - | - | 127 | - | 10 | - |
| 20th Panzer Division | 13.11.1942 | - | - | - | 57 | - | - | - |
| MÜNCHEN | 18-20 11.1942 | 1 | | 3 | 105 | - | 3 | - |
| NÜRNBERG | 24-27. 11.1942 | 1 | - | 1 | 524 | ? | 30 | - |
| Minsk area | 28.11. 1942 | 6 | ? | ? | | 353 | - | - |
| 3rd Schuma Battalion | 15. 1.1943 | - | - | 21 | 147 | - | - | - |
| FRANZ | 16. 1. 1943 | ? | 1 | 14 | | 1,143 | - | - |
| 13th Police Regiment | 29.1. 1943 | 6 | - | 17 | 3+ | - | - | 1,308 |
| HORNUNG | 16.2.1943 | ? | - | 7 | ? | - | 104 | - |
| 14th Police Regiment | 23. 2. 1943 | - | - | 2 | 463 | - | - | 1,834 |
| Polish Schuma | 23.2.1943 | 3 | - | - | 20 | - | - | - |
| HORNUNG | 3. 3. 1943 | ? | - | 10 | | 2,074 | 56 | - |
| FOHN | 23.3. 1943 | - | - | - | 543 | - | - | - |
| | Totals | 413 | 10 | 156 | 4,007 | 4,050 | 261 | 3,142 |

*TVDB, 55–95.

# PART TWO
## BANDENBEKÄMPFUNG

# 4

# BANDENBEKÄMPFUNG OPERATIONAL CONCEPT

On September 3, 1947, a two-page document titled "Bandit Fight and the Security Situation" (*Bandenkampf- und Sicherheitslage*) was retrieved by U.S. war crimes investigators from among the captured collection of Himmler's personal papers. A retrieval page, taking the document's place, recorded "Bandenbekampfung N331." The two pages were returned on November 13, 1947, the marker remained in place, and there were no further proceedings.[1] The document was a two-page office memorandum drafted and filed by Himmler at the KSRFSS on June 28, 1943.[2] It recorded the outcome of a meeting held on June 19, 1943, between Heinrich Himmler and Adolf Hitler. The venue was Hitler's idyllic retreat of the Obersalzberg, deep in the Bavarian mountains. The document was cited by Professors Kershaw and Fleming, although they overlooked the wider implications of the memo and as a consequence it has retained its secrets for more than sixty years.[3] This document represented the formulation of a Nazi security policy, prosecuted through the Banden-bekämpfung operational concept, which integrated exterminating Jews with eradicating insurgency.

The memo was broken into two sections. In the first, Himmler set the scene confirming he had presented Hitler with a batch of radio signals received from General Governor Hans Frank (General Government of Poland) on June 18, Reichskommissar Arthur Seyss-Inquart (Holland) on June 18, and Dr. Friedrich Rainer, Gauleiter Carinthia (*Kärnten*), on June 17. All referred to the "bandit situation" (*Bandenverhältnisse*) in Poland, Russia, and an area covering Slovenia, Slovakia, Croatia, and Yugoslavia (known as the *Oberkrain*). Himmler also showed Hitler a copy of his June 11 order that was issued for liquidating Jewish ghettos in the east. Finally, he handed Hitler a "bandit map" (*Bandenkarte*) illustrating the "bandit" situation in the General

Government as of May 31, 1943. Himmler offered Hitler full and personal responsibility for failing to eradicate the "bandits" over the previous winter,
adding that it was a difficult situation worsened by the withdrawal of his
forces to plug the gaps at the front. He made a promise to Hitler: if he was
allowed to keep the forces presently under his command (including the
SS-Cavalry Division, the 1st SS Infantry Brigade, and numerous police formations), as well as return police formations serving in the army's security divisions, he would resolve the "bandit" situation within the year and completely
pacify the areas presently experiencing "banditry."

The second section of the memorandum listed seven decisions made by
Hitler that Himmler recorded as personal commands:

1. The bandit-fight [*Bandenkämpf*] remained the business of the
   Reichsführer-SS, the SS and police.
2. He [Hitler] clearly confirmed that no reproach is held against the SS
   and police because of the growing bandit danger after the transfer of
   forces to the front.
3. He [Hitler] promised to check if the two police regiments, *Griese*
   [based in Marseilles] and *Franz* [based in Finland], could be returned to us.
4. My order of June 11, 1943, was completely correct and gave the order
   to inform the General-Governor it will remain in force.
5. The Führer declared, after my report, that the evacuation of the Jews,
   despite the unrest that would thereby still arise in the next 3 to 4
   months, was to be radically carried out and had to be seen through.
6. The Führer stated clearly that Bandenbekämpfung and questions of
   security were solely the matter and authority of the Reichsführer-SS,
   even in the General-Government.
7. The Führer declined all suggestions to raise Polish formations, following the Katyn propaganda, as some on the German side have
   suggested. The formation of Galician units from the area of Galician
   White Ruthenia is acceptable as this had been part of Austria over
   the last 150 years.[4]

There were many interests at play in this memorandum, while its style
reflected the path taken by the Nazi regime since January 1943. The individual
points isolate how important Bandenbekämpfung had become to Himmler.
They connect Bandenbekämpfung with the Holocaust. These simple notes
also show how a vague agreement could be binding and exploited by one
clique of Hitler's lieutenants against another. However, of particular interest is
the background information. This provides further clues of how Bandenbekämpfung policy was formulated, connecting the "bandit situation" in the
east to the rest of Europe. Whether the dates of the radio signals were deliberately timed to arrive with Himmler, they reveal how he exploited their contents

with Hitler. They also indicate the initial moves in a power play as opportunities were presented. Hans Frank (although ensconced in the General Government—an area subject to intense Nazi administration) was locked in a losing battle with Himmler. Analysis of Bandenbekämpfung conducted in Poland is examined in chapter 8. Regarding Dr. Rainer, who was already in place in southern Europe, and Arthur Seyss-Inquart, who probably wished to return to the region, the situation was less clear. That region was in a state of flux made more uncertain following the collapse of Axis forces in North Africa. The impact of Bandenbekämpfung on western and southern Europe is the subject of chapter 9. Himmler's scene setting also alluded to a "bandit map," which was a lot more important than might appear and is a central theme of chapter 5. That leaves the question of responsibility and development of Ban-denbekämpfung as an operational concept, which is examined in this chapter.

## Total War and Fortress Europe

The events leading to Himmler's memorandum began in January 1943 at a time when the malaise of defeat descended over Germany as pressure mounted from all fronts. Stalingrad caught everyone's attention, and the atmosphere elicited confusion and petulance from Nazi leaders. Hermann Göring's panegyric for the enfeebled soldiers of the shattered 6th Army was the army's "last rites," given during its final death throes. Defeat at Stalingrad coincided with the tenth anniversary of the Nazis' coming to power. Hitler took the opportunity to make a proclamation that reinforced his mission for Germany. He reminded the public of what victory would bring. He reassured the people that their eternal struggle, at least since 1933, had been to build a strong nation, which Germany was. Hitler reiterated that the Jews, the supreme enemy of the state, had been the reason for Germany's downfall in 1918. He comforted the rest of the German people with a promise that this war "would see the final end of Jewry . . . no longer would nations be infected by its curse." Hitler dismissed his earlier military victories as insignificant in this struggle against Bolshevism. The war against Russia had been Germany's, he confessed, but circumstances had transformed it into a European struggle against Bolshevism. Germany, he declared, was the bulwark against the Mongol horde and all that stood between European culture and barbarism. Victory, he explained, would not hail the victor, but the victorious survivors would dictate the future.[5] Hitler's grand scheme for Lebensraum, as envisaged in *Mein Kampf,* was derailed by Stalingrad, and many scholars have argued Hitler's Weltanschauung from this point turned self-destructive.

The opportunity for turning existing gains into a reduced Lebensraum and making occupied Europe slave for the German war effort remained a viable option. At the beginning of 1943, the German position in Russia was still strong even after two seasons of strategic setbacks. Throughout 1942, cliques within the regime attempted to implement various interpretations of Lebensraum;

but they all proved unworkable while the Soviet Union survived. In May 1942, Himmler received the final draft of *Generalplan Ost* from Professor Konrad Meyer, the blueprint for SS colonization of the east.[6] Elsewhere, by the end of the year, there were grumblings within the regime of failures. In October, Otto Bräutigam of the Ostministerium wrote damning reports on the shortfalls of eastern policy. He argued that a struggle against Bolshevism or even a campaign against the moribund Russian Empire might have succeeded, but a struggle for Lebensraum had not fooled the Russian people. He condemned German policies for forcing "both Bolshevists and Russian nationals into a common front against us." Bräutigam pointed out that the war had not brought about a collapse of the Red Army, while the armed forces were not large enough to police the occupation. This had matured into a dire situation, he explained, because the economy of the occupied territories was integral to the success of the war effort.[7] Yet in October, Hitler admitted that if the war were only about colonies he would end it immediately, an indication perhaps of his waning confidence.[8] In December 1942, Bräutigam's Nazi boss, Alfred Rosenberg, hosted a conference for the Wehrmacht, including Schenckendorff, and members of the Ostministerium, to discuss serious issues of the German occupation of Russia. The army blamed the roundup of Russians for labor as encouraging the will to resist. There was growing conviction from some quarters that only Russians (anti-Bolsheviks) could defeat the Russians (Bolsheviks).[9] Schenckendorff hoped to manipulate the conference proceedings to restore his standing in the realm of security. It was flawed judgment to assume that Rosenberg, already declining in the regime's hierarchy of favoritism, could persuade Hitler to change his policy. The ploy failed spectacularly and Hitler admonished them both.[10]

The period from the surrender of Stalingrad (February 1943) to the defeat of Kursk (July 1943) was the watershed of Hitler's war. In the wake of Stalingrad, eyewitnesses described the moment when time stood still, as the shock and calamity of defeat was recognized by everyone. Among Germans, there was a growing realization of the hypocrisy and absurdity of the war, but also a petulant self-denial of the destruction done in their name. The regime required someone to quickly paper over the cracks, pull back the nation from the trance-like spell cast by Stalingrad and move on with the war. Josef Goebbels stepped forward with his "total war" speech in February 1943.[11] Ulrich Herbert called this the "Goebbels initiative," one of many polycratic initiatives from within the regime.[12] The Propaganda Ministry, using advanced techniques to enhance and spotlight subliminal messages, manipulated the presentation. Goebbels called on the German people to rise up and release their storm of victory, while the banners draped around his podium, intended to catch the eye of cinema audiences, declared "total war–rapid war" (*Totaler Krieg–Kürzerer Krieg*). A short total war was an appealing prospect for the German public. However, without a strategic commitment to sustain it,

Goebbels's initiative soon withered, as his diary testified, but his intervention had broken the pallor of defeat.

Hitler, the Wehrmacht, and the SS could stimulate strategic initiatives, but their attention lay elsewhere. The shock of the Red Army's double envelopment at Stalingrad sobered the army to the realities of the war. Superior strategy and tactics on the part of the Soviets had defeated the German army; stealing their precious Cannae, through the exploitation of huge manpower reserves. The German generals wanted to reposition strategy by rebuilding reserves and vigorously defending their existing gains. Hitler proposed the "Fortress Europe" (*Festung Europa*) plan, an economic-warfare driven derivation of Frederick the Great's grand strategy. The Prussian king had effectively held together his military gains through a system of fortresses. Hitler thought solid lines of in-depth fortifications interconnected with fortified cities could blunt Red Army envelopments and offset the Soviet advantage in manpower. Labor and raw materials became the real currency of Fortress Europe as building projects surpassed Roman construction schemes.[13] Defensive walls, such as the "Atlantic Wall" or the "Panther Line" became the construction centerpieces of this strategy. Elsewhere, Albert Speer artificially stimulated the economic life cycle of Germany's war economy through slavery and autarky. The emphasis on cheap mass production released intense competition between agencies and industries for a constant flow of slave labor and exploited materials. The deportation of labor under the Speer-Sauckel directive of March 1942 was intensified in the "Sauckel drive" of 1943. German soldiers and civilians became scavengers scouring Europe for equipment. Economic agencies and industrialists ignored the strategic realities and drove hard to meet performance targets through plunder and labor. By January 1943, Sauckel could publicly boast that 710,000 Ukrainians labored for the German war effort.[14]

One of Hitler's paradigms for victory over the Soviet Union came from Professor Michael Prawdin's study of Genghis Khan, which Hitler recommended to all the members of his inner circle to read.[15] Expediency led Wehrmacht propaganda to make a call to arms for a united (occupied) Europe in the struggle against "Jewish Bolshevism." The German army declared the reintegration of eastern and western European people. Military dogma flooded Russian communities with messages that the defeat of Bolshevism was in everyone's interest and the means to preserving Russian culture. The army attempted to project Stalin—along with Bolshevism—as the common enemy of both Russians and Germans. In an act of "good faith," the Germans stopped all new settlements in Russia. The real purpose behind these messages was to improve Russian willingness to work and to raise volunteers for the armed forces. The question of labor also became a problem for the army, which was forced to be self-sufficient, exploiting local resources. The army ordered insults toward "easterners" stopped and instead praised them for their contribution to the German war effort. References to colonial exploitation or slanderous remarks about Russians as Europe's "Negro" or as "beasts" and "barbarians" were directed to stop. The troops received orders warning them against harsh or unnecessarily violent treatment of Russian civilians.[16] Any positive effect this policy had was undermined by the Wehrmacht's own counter-policy of conscripting labor to maintain its survival in the field.[17]

In July 1942, the German army captured Red Army general Vlasov and since then had allowed him to become the leading personality in the Russian collaboration movement.[18] The growing sense of failure and isolation since 1942 led Max von Schenckendorff toward a curious fate. He was a product of the Schlieffen system and steeped in the noble family military tradition of Frederick the Great and General Blücher. Born in February 1875, by 1914 he was a battalion commander, and by 1918 he was the commander of the 29th Infantry Regiment, one of Bach-Zelewski's former regiments. Since December 1942, he had constantly misread Hitler. When he drifted into the Russian nationalist circle, perhaps convinced that only a Russian could defeat a Russian, he placed himself outside the circle. He encouraged his Feldkommandanturen to support local initiatives that resembled micro-experimentation with Russian self-rule. Soon this turned into a strong relationship with Russian collaborators, which was remembered long after the war. He sponsored a plethora of formations, including the "Order Department" (Ordnungsdienst), Cossack detachments, and communities or settlements with a counter-partisan bias. He gave them weapons and trained their personnel. In April 1943, Schenckendorff jointly hosted a visit to his region by the former Red Army general Vlasov.

In January, Himmler had warned Bach-Zelewski against any ideas of building a new Russian nation. Bach-Zelewski gave his interpretation of Vlasov's visit in a report to Himmler. He encapsulated the proposals of cooperation or colonization. They reflected Himmler's January sentiments.[19] He opened by dismissing out of hand the politically immature German commanders (presumably referring to Schenckendorff) who were embarrassing the situation. In his opinion, if Vlasov had not been captured, he would have become the Red Army commander-in-chief. In his present situation, he was a Russian nationalist pursuing a Russia-only agenda. Vlasov had not endorsed Germanization. Cooperation with the Russians, Bach-Zelewski alleged, could not be honest when German propaganda described the Slavs as a "minor race" (Minderrasse) or declared supreme German mastery. Vlasov was not the answer for many Russians who were increasingly aware of Stalin's order that captured, unwounded soldiers were traitors. The Russian audiences sat in stony silence during Vlasov's speeches. Stalin had already reacted to counternationalistic sentiments by freeing religion and granting other minor political concessions. Bach-Zelewski advised that Vlasov was only honest in small groups, for example when he had told Schenckendorff that Germany would lose the war. Bach-Zelewski believed that the Russians only collaborated while there was no German colonization. He also mentioned that Vlasov thought the mobilization of labor program was disgraceful and that in Russian minds German corruption was worse than Soviet corruption. He concluded that Vlasov "would not take Russian lives until he received confirmation from Hitler of a national Russian state."

On May 14, Schenckendorff, Gehlen (Foreign Armies East), and several Army Group Centre officers held a meeting to discuss the future of eastern policy. They agreed that further discussions should take place before representations were passed to Hitler. Eight days later, a former member of Goebbels's propaganda staff attempted to bring Vlasov into contact with the Nazi governor of Galicia, Dr. Otto Gustav Wächter. On May 25, a conference was hosted by Rosenberg, attended by Bräutigam, Gehlen, Wagner, and other officers from Army Group Centre; the military also brought a letter of endorsement from Kluge in the hope of generating a substantial change in policy. On June 8, Hitler declared he would never build a Russian army and called their ideas fantasy.[20]

Meanwhile, Stalin treated Hitler like King Canute, releasing a tidal wave of partisans through Fortress Europe. The partisans targeted the German communications network in what became known as the "War of the Rails."[21] The German army's main supply collection and distribution centers were joined by an east-west double-track trunk railway line. The supply collection centers were located in Königsberg, Bialystok, Brest-Litovsk, Kovel, and Lvov.[22] From March 1943, the partisans undertook 404 attacks on the railways, blowing up bridges and attempting to cut the German army off from its logistical support. The number of attacks increased monthly and peaked in July with 1,114 incidents. Following the Battle of Kursk, the Soviet plan for late summer of 1943 was to destroy key points along the German rail system. The plan came in two operational phases: Phase 1 (August 1943) caused 21,300 rail attacks, mostly in Byelorussia, carried out by 167 partisan brigades totaling 95,615 partisans.[23] Phase 2 (September 1 to November 1, 1943) deployed 193 partisan brigades totaling 120,000 partisans. The target was the destruction of 272,000 miles of railway. There were mixed opinions at the time about whether the plan succeeded or failed, although the rear area of Army Group Centre recorded 20,505 rails destroyed.[24]

The weakest links in Fortress Europe were Germany's allies, only tolerated by Hitler to sustain the illusion that Germany was not alone in the war. Goebbels was uneasy about the allied strategic threat of invading southeast Europe and gathering support from the Balkan.[25] In 1941, the Axis alliance had divided the spoils of Albania, Yugoslavia, and Greece but security had been an afterthought. Hitler introduced Directive 31 to establish a "clear and unified system of command." It was supposed to engineer cooperation with Italian and Bulgarian forces.[26] The collapse of the *Afrika-Korps* in the latter half of 1942 forced Hitler to reconsider the security for the region. In December, Hitler issued Directive 47 for the "command and defense measures in the South-East." This time he tried to bind the Axis forces operating in the Balkans (Italy, Bulgaria, and Croatia) under a unified but German command. In the summer of 1942, Himmler set Bandenbekämpfung on the Balkans. To raise the political profile of this policy, Foreign Minister Ribbentrop and Keitel met Italian Marshal Cavallero in December 1942. Ribbentrop explained to Cavallero that Croatia required cleansing of a strong British presence. He admitted that "the Führer had declared that the Serbian conspirators were to be burnt out and that no gentle methods might be used in doing this." Keitel immediately interjected that "every village in which partisans were found had to be burnt down."[27] Orders passed to the judge advocate of the German armed forces in southern Europe from OKW demanded the prosecution of aggressive Bandenbekämpfung.[28] On February 21, 1943, Ribbentrop met with the Italian ambassador in Berlin, and they mutually agreed that "the [bands] had to be exterminated, and that included men, women and children, as their continued existence imperiled the lives of German and Italian men, women, and children."[29]

The Nazi political relationship with Vichy France began to deteriorate following the string of defeats in the Mediterranean region. On June 18, 1942, General De Gaulle proclaimed a Free French victory at Bir Hacheim, a small but significant battle in North Africa. Six months earlier, De Gaulle had sent Jean Moulin to occupied France as his representative to stir the resistance into action against the Germans.[30] With events turning against him in the Mediterranean theater, Hitler began to string together a southern theater security strategy. In November 1942, formations of the Waffen-SS led the occupation of Vichy France. The Italians joined the operation and both armies converged on the harbor of Toulon. Territorially, this theater stretched from southern France at its western flank across to Greece in the southeast; Hungary and Italy at the center formed a north and south junction, while Bulgaria and Romania faced east. The bridge to this theater was the "Alpenland," the southern most mountainous range that linked Germany with the south. The southern Mandarins, whether from the Wehrmacht or SS, proved as adept at pulling on the purse strings of the German war effort as their comrades in the east. Two prima donnas formed a dual command in the area: Field Marshal Erwin Rommel (headquartered in Munich, commanding the southern regions) and Luftwaffe Field Marshal Alfred Kesselring. German setbacks in Stalingrad and El Alamein stirred a will to resist especially in northern Italy, Greece, southern France, and Yugoslavia. The Germans thinned out their security forces in the east, to be able to send troops to bolster the Axis in the south. The invasion of Sicily and the dismissal of Mussolini led Hitler to make contingency plans. In July 1943, a British strategic assessment of Hitler's southern flank judged,

German defense of the Balkans and Italy largely hinges on the
security of the German positions in the Istria-Slovenia area which
has been brought under Rommel's command. . . . Further reinforcements have recently arrived in Yugoslavia from France and
Greece, and there is ample evidence that the battle against the
partisans has become Rommel's most pressing commitment.[31]

Frederick the Great is reputed to have said, "To defend everything is to defend nothing," an aphorism that accurately described Hitler's Fortress Europe. In desperation to erect fortifications and feed the arms industries, the
Germans mobilized labor in France, Italy, and the Balkans.[32] Militarily, Fortress
Europe further burdened Germany's reserves, which were distributed across
three theaters of operations, while the Alps served to divide Hitler's empire
north and south.

## Der Chef der Bandenkampfverbände

The new year opened with another bleak military task for Bach-Zelewski:
to hold the line following Soviet breakthroughs around Velikie Luki. He took
charge of the 1st SS-Infantry Brigade within Gen. Kurt von Chevallerie's LIX
Corps. Gottberg, assisted by Bassewitz-Behr, continued to prosecute security operations in his absence. Bach-Zelewski's first impression of Chevallerie
was that he was a ruined man, depressed and suffering involuntary shaking of
the head. Then he discovered that Chevallerie was the former Reichswehr
colonel of the 4th Infantry Regiment in which Bach-Zelewski served as a
lieutenant. His opinion mellowed when the general proved to be brave and so
Bach-Zelewski wrote in his diary that Chevallerie played the part of the "shining god of war" (den strahlenden Kriegsgott markierte). However, this did
not detract from two major problems. The first involved the condition of the
SS brigade, which had little frontline experience and few heavy weapons, was
staffed with ethnic Germans from Hungary, and was led by a small cadre of
Germans. Attached to the brigade was the highly regarded manpower
(Menschmaterial) of the SS-Freikorps Danmark. Irrespective of the redeem-
ing features of this formation, its general command demeanor was low. Bach-
Zelewski believed there were no merits to be gained with these troops: "I
could lose reputation and command qualifications against tanks without antitank guns." He was assigned no further troops and had 14th and 15th SS-
Police Regiments removed from his Bandenbekämpfung command. They were
sent to join another disastrous situation (Schweinerei) in Army Group South.
Bach-Zelewski was informed that the commander of the 14th Regiment, Oberst
der Polizei Buchmann, the man he regarded as his only capable field officer
(refer to chapter 5), had been killed in action. He concluded that the front was
only held because the Red Army did not press its attacks vigorously.

On February 19, Bach-Zelewski attended a meeting, arranged by Himmler, with the general quartermaster of OKH, Wagner.[33] The witnesses to this meeting were Ernst Rode, Wagner's aide Colonel Altenstadt, and SS-Brigadeführer Zimmermann. A record of the meeting from Bach-Zelewski's diary suggests the main topic was the concern that a general uprising could affect the whole rear area of Army Group Centre and HSSPF Russia-Centre. Bach-Zelewski ventured the opinion that in the face of blatant corruption and mounting anarchy within the German civil administration, the only solution was to impose German army authority (*Wehrmachtshoheit*). To bring about a bureaucratic normalization and to secure the army's rear-area supply lines, he recommended declaring a state of emergency (*Ausnahmezustand*). Wagner was of the same opinion.[34] Wagner exposed the underlying political theme of the meeting, when he indicated that the Wehrmacht would endorse a field commander of security. Wagner proposed a new office, based on Bach-Zelewski's existing authority as Bevollmächtigter für die Bandenbekämpfung im Osten, but placed under the command of Army Group Centre.

From the Wehrmacht's perspective, this offer removed two nagging problems. First, they had located an acceptable and energetic replacement for Schenckendorff. Second, this solution returned the control of security warfare to the army. Wagner offered Bach-Zelewski the thinly veiled bribe of a general's rank and a military career, but in political terms, the offer only confirmed the naiveté of the army. Wagner's proposal played into Himmler's hands through the ploy of persuading the army to trust Bach-Zelewski. The ability to gain the trust of opponents and then misuse it was Bach-Zelewski's greatest asset and one he used repeatedly during his lifetime. The army had underrated Himmler and plainly failed to comprehend that control of all security policy was an SS agenda. After the war, he claimed Himmler forced him to refuse the offer, which was patently absurd. This would have been paramount to passing over the top executive job for a line function.[35] Himmler and Bach-Zelewski had conspired and outmaneuvered the army into accepting SS control of security warfare. Taken from another standpoint, in the shadow of Stalingrad, Hitler was unlikely to hand back this authority. On February 24, Bach-Zelewski attended a medal awarding ceremony for senior officers hosted by Schenckendorff. The special guest was Lilian Dagover, a famous German actress, and Bach-Zelewski joined the celebrations.

Once the emergency subsided, Bach-Zelewski began the process of sidelining Schenckendorff. He spent the next five months meeting leaders of the regime. A formal meeting between the SS and the Kriegsmarine was held on April 10 when Bach-Zelewski and Himmler met Grand Admiral Dönitz and senior members of the German navy. The purpose was to bring the navy into coastal and river-based security operations.[36] Throughout April, Bach-Zelewski conversed with Gottlob Berger, whom Robert Koehl referred to as the "Almighty Gottlob."[37] Bach-Zelewski also met with SS-Gruppenführer Winkelmann, the second-most senior police officer in the Hauptamt

Ordnungspolizei, because of Daluege's recurring bouts of illness; they discussed police matters. Daluege, Himmler, and Bach-Zelewski met on May 11, at the KSRFSS; this was probably the last time the three men worked together. On June 1, Bach-Zelewski traveled to the General Government to meet Krüger and Globocnik and to discuss the security situation.

The meeting between Hitler and Himmler, held on June 19, 1943, and discussed earlier, occurred during the final preparations for Operation "Citadel" (Battle of Kursk). On June 21, Himmler issued new orders for fresh initiatives in Bandenbekämpfung.[38] The order opened with a strategic assessment of the general situation. Himmler declared the Eastern Front rear areas and southeastern Europe rife with robbery and banditry undermining German rule and security. He explained that banditry was an historical problem in these areas, which had been intensified through Bolshevism. He blamed the Red Army for having nurtured robbers and "bandits," employing them as partisans. It was his responsibility to restore law and order, military authority, and the security of German interests in these territories. To these ends, he explained that the office of Bevollmächtigter des Reichsführers SS für Bandenbekämpfung, instigated by his order of October 23, 1942, had proved instructive. Experience had shown that permanent successes against the "bandits" were the product of central planning and leadership with the HSSPF directly under his orders. In consequence of this success, Himmler ordered the Bevollmächtigter des Reichsführers SS für Bandenbekämpfung office to be transformed into a high command under Der Reichsführer-SS, und Chef der Deutschen Polizei–Der Chef der Bandenkampfverbände. Himmler remained Chef der Bandenbekämpfung until the end of the war.

Himmler announced Bach-Zelewski's promotion to Chef der Bandenkampfverbände (Ch.BKV) in the presence of Krüger, Kaltenbrunner, and Prützmann.[39] Yet this theme has received little academic scrutiny. Erich Kordt was one of the first and only scholars to mention the Ch.BKV as a stand-alone function.[40] In 1945, the U.S. Army identified SS police, army, Luftwaffe, and naval forces assigned to "antipartisan warfare" as temporarily serving under the Ch.BKV command.[41] F. H. Hinsley, with access to all the decoded signals traffic, referred to the Order Police as "military in character," as an "army of occupation" working closely with the SS, and as reinforcements for the Wehrmacht. He elected to ignore the Ch.BKV even with the amount of signals intercepts.[42] In 1956, Wolf Keilig incorrectly placed the Ch.BKV within the Waffen-SS command structure.[43] Rudolf Absolon, the esteemed German military archivist, referred to Bandenbekämpfung regulations but not its organization.[44] The doyen of military lists, Georg Tessin, completely ignored the subject.[45]

The authority of the Ch.BKV came from Hitler but was defined and engineered by Himmler. The first part of his order was concerned with command tasks. The most important was the absolute control over planning and the decision to commit to operations. These decision-making powers also extended to stopping an operation in mid-flow and redeploying the troops to other pressing assignments. Another task involved exploiting the authority to "calm down" regional commanders from sectors under threat of incursion and incapable of appreciating the "bigger picture." In this context, his authority extended to convincing SS leaders to contain a difficult situation, even suffering a temporary reverse, in order to achieve greater success later. The Ch.BKV was also authorized to command forces in the field during large-scale operations or to intervene in operations if the situation demanded it. The second part of the order addressed command bureaucracy. The Ch.BKV was empowered to raise the headquarters of a high command in parallel with the offices of the Reichsführer-SS. In 7(e) of the order, the Ch.BKV was required to produce the instructions for Bandenbekämpfung and was responsible for training.[46]

This June 1943 order introduced the concept of the "combating-bandits formations" (*Bandenkampfverbände*), discussed in chapter 5, and the "combating-bandits area" (*Bandenkampfgebiet*) discussed in chapter 6. The territorial scope of the Ch.BKV followed the SS regional command structure of HSSPF Russia-North, Russia-South, Russia-Centre, Northeast, Weichsel (Vistula), Croatia, Southeast, Warthegau, Serbia, East (General Government), Northwest (Nederland), and the Alpenland. Later, the HSSPFs in France, Czechoslovakia (Böhmen-Mähren), Norway, and Northern Italy joined the list along with the SD office in Belgium. The territorial scope of the Ch.BKV was defined by Bach-Zelewski. "I was responsible for all partisan reports from the whole of Europe," he later stated.[47] The SS-Hauptämter received instructions to the effect that "all Hauptamt chiefs are instructed to assist and support the Chef der Bandenkampfverbände, who carries out, under my authority, one of the most important tasks of the SS and Police for Germany, in its fight for survival."[48]

On the day the June order was released, Bach-Zelewski was designated with the codename "Arminus." It is uncertain whether this name was bestowed with due reverence or irony or by someone poking fun at Himmler's Romanesque cult.[49] The formal announcement was also unusual by Nazi standards. Aside from Hitler, the entire Nazi Party leadership received a copy of the announcement including Göring, Bormann, Speer, Rosenberg, Frank, Sauckel, and party treasurer Schwarz. The senior officers of the OKW, including Keitel, Jodl, and Warlimont, and the army chief of staff Kurt Zeitzler, Gen. Fritz Fromm, the commander of the reserve army, Adm. Wilhelm Canaris of the Abwehr, and Hitler's army liaison officer, each received a personalized copy. The senior SS officers included Berger, Prützmann, Jeckeln, Korsemann, and Rode, but there appears to have been correspondence to Daluege and Jüttner (chief of staff of the Waffen-SS). The government officials included Hans Lammers (Reich chancellery), Albert Ganzenmüller, and Julius Dorpmüller

(Railways) and Wilhelm Ohnesorge (Post and Telegraph). Bach-Zelewski received the unlimited use of a Junkers fifty-two-passenger transport airplane, with the formal letters of transfer from Hermann Göring.[50] This "gift" of a highly prized aircraft was more than a status symbol and placed the Ch.BKV in the realm of a strategic command.

On September 7, 1943, Himmler, already ensconced as the minister of the interior, issued fresh guidelines for the new Bandenbekämpfung command structure.[51] The system adopted was partly an extension of the KSRFSS and partly a compromise with pseudo-military-security practices. The command structure was multifaceted containing a command (political-military strategic leadership) function, a quartermaster (police-military management) capability, a planning (political) section, and intelligence and communication (political) tasks. The emphasis was information-led security warfare with centralized intelligence and higher mobility and flexibility in the response of the field commander. This set of guidelines followed on from the June order in outlining the operational doctrine of Bandenbekämpfung, listing eight points of strategic and tactical rules. There is an explanation of these tactical rules in chapter 6. Himmler stated that the basis of this doctrine was strict and mobile leadership, which was necessary in large territories with an increasing "bandit" problem. "The ways of the bandit," his second point stated, "can only be mastered by a leadership that is active all of the time." It was deemed crucial that the bands were denied the initiative.

Himmler went on to rouse the SS officer corps into intensifying their efforts through strong leadership. This became a rant over the installation of a staff system. He expected each HSSPF to form a leadership staff for Bandenbekämpfung analysis and planning, irrespective of the level of security risk. In regions declared a Bandenkampfgebiet, they were to form an "antibandit staff" (*Bandenstab*) and combat group (Kampfgruppe).[52] Diagram II (p. 308) provides an indication of how this was organized. Bandenstab manpower was supposed to be located among the existing staff of the HSSPF. He expected the HSSPF to use initiative in staff selection; in certain unspecified circumstances, they might request his assistance.[53] Himmler explained that the Bandenstab was to arrange all Bandenbekämpfung functions including reconnaissance missions, collection of reports, and analysis of the insurgents. During large-scale operations, experts were expected to be attached on an ad hoc basis to supplement local headquarters staffs. Within the command of each Bandenstab, the intelligence (Ic) function was given to SD officers. They were responsible for compiling intelligence reports at the local level and subsequent dispatch to the Ch.BKV for central analysis. The only record of a Bandenstab in operation is examined in chapter 9. The role of the Kampfgruppe is dicussed in chapter 7.

In addition to the main proposals, Himmler included point 7, covering several operational provisions. Each operational commander was warned to establish an efficient signals network. The chief of signals had the authority through Himmler to supervise the signals network. He made the provision for medical services and the safe transportation of German wounded. The senior SS medical officer in the field was to ensure the presence of fully mobile medical teams. The Luftwaffe liaison officer attached to the local HSSPF command had sole control over close-air support and liaison with the air force. This Luftwaffe liaison officer had to be integrated into the planning process to ensure full communications between the SS and Luftwaffe. To assist in signals functions, the Luftwaffe would provide an air location device and detection troops.

## Reshuffles and Scandal

To further explain the authority vested in Bach-Zelewski's command, one needs to examine the changes imposed on the SS organization in 1943. Heinrich Himmler's climb to the most powerful position in Hitler's Germany was beset by petty squabbles and court intrigue. In 1943, he loosened his grip on the workings of the SS organization to become the minister of the interior: this was not a simple task after a routine of control of everyday affairs. In metaphorical terms, Himmler allowed his lieutenants enough rope to succeed or fail, but he also kept a tight hold on the rope. Until 1943, Himmler maintained a strict schedule that relaxed as the confidence in his power grew. He was also forced to loosen his grip if he was to become Hitler's "regent," leading what Robert Koehl called the "inner-German theatre of operations" (*Kriegss-chauplatz Inneres-Deutschland*).[54] This was not a Faustian bargain, the "faithful Heinrich" was being groomed for national leadership.

According to Leonnie Wheeler, 1943 opened for the SS command with internal squabbling. Lines were drawn between the SS main offices (*SS-Hauptämter*) in Berlin and the HSSPFs in the occupied territories. In 1941–42, there had been troubles with Bach-Zelewski, and in 1943, the police became the cause of further difficulties between Daluege and his former protégé. This time Daluege somehow acquired a copy of correspondence (since lost) from Bach-Zelewski to Kurt Knoblauch, chief of staff KSRFSS, regarding criticism of the police troops. Daluege took umbrage and wrote, "I am most grateful for your candid letter to Gruppenführer Knoblauch about the work of my police, General Winkelmann and myself. I am now right in the picture as to the true meaning for the police, of your ceremonial calls. That the police tell lies without stopping is a fact only now revealed to me, their chief. The question of a third battalion will be dealt with by my office."[55] The situation between the two men remained difficult. The continuing Frank–Krüger clash in the General Government of Poland was typical of the troubled relations between some SS and Nazi Party officials. Faced with considerable unrest in the General Government, Krüger made a serious proposal of removing Frank and his inner circle and reorganizing the economy and raising manpower for the war.

On January 2, Himmler informed Bach-Zelewski that he was placing Gottlob Berger in the Ostministerium as state secretary with two tasks: to bring Rosenberg's policies into line over ideology and to tighten the control over the eastern HSSPFs. Interestingly, Bach-Zelewski was asked by Himmler to appraise Bassewitz-Behr as a potential HSSPF.[56] In March 1943, Rosenberg attempted to persuade Hitler to support the idea of focusing on the "bandits" rather than continuing with indiscriminate punishment.[57] On May 25, Himmler explained to Frank that troubles with Jews like the Warsaw ghetto uprising would continue until the last 250,000 Jews were executed. In Russia, the military and the police had largely side-stepped Wilhelm Kube, the civilian commissar for White Russia (*Generalkommissar Weissruthenien*). The relationship between Kube and Bach-Zelewski, former colleagues in the prewar Prussian farming association, began to breakdown. This situation deteriorated further with the onset of a Bandenbekämpfung operation codenamed "Cottbus" and is discussed in detail in chapter 7.

Following the crisis caused by the collapse of Italy, Hitler promoted Karl Wolff as the supreme SS leader in Italy. This marked a new development in SS-Police security policy. Hitler charged Wolff with three tasks: special consultant for all police matters for the puppet Italian Fascist national government; chief of police under the commander of Army Group B and the chief of Army Group South; and commander of the SS regional establishments. After the war, during interrogations by the British, Wolff denied he had been handed these orders.[58] Himmler promoted Wolff "higher-HSSPF" (*Höchste SS und Polizeiführer*) Italy, designated HstSSPF-Italien. It was his first operational task in the war, and with its proximity to Rome, it was largely a political mission.[59] Among Wolff's command was Odilo Globocnik, transferred from Poland as HSSPF Adriatic Coastland (*Adriatisches-Küstenland*).[60] The SS-Police structure in the southern theater initially followed on the coattails of the Wehrmacht, as it had done in Poland and France. In 1942, SS-Obergruppenführer Artur Phleps transferred to the Balkans to raise SS volunteers. Phleps had organized a recruitment agency for the Banat region and, by June 1942, had processed twenty thousand volunteers. According to Berger, Phleps raised a homeland defense regiment (*Heimatschutzregiment*). Phleps was close to the recruitment officer responsible for Serbia, Obersturmbannführer Kecks, an ethnic German from Serbia; they collaborated in raising an SS division. Berger confirmed that Himmler agreed to Phleps' recruitment of men to form an SS mountain division.[61] Himmler transferred his senior SS lieutenants with experience or expertise in the region into positions in the Balkans. The SS establishment in the south expanded to encompass new borders after absorbing Austria and Czechoslovakia. Austria came under two SS authorities— HSSPF Danube in Vienna, and HSSPF Alpenland in Salzburg. Czechoslovakia had been partially annexed with the rump turned into HSSPF Bohemia and Moravia in Prague. Himmler exploited the former Habsburg system as a platform for SS authority and assigned Austrian SS officers to key posts in former empire cities. From January 1944, the southern theater became the largest area of SS political security interests.

After Heydrich's death in June 1942, Himmler had taken personal control of the RSHA. Himmler had resisted passing the job to Bach-Zelewski as Hitler had proposed. Hitler wanted Himmler to find a replacement quickly, probably because the waning powers and authority of the RSHA distracted Himmler from more important duties. Eventually, after six months, Himmler finally passed the position over to Dr. Ernst Kaltenbrunner. The RSHA had lost much of its prestige in the intervening period, and the SD found it was increasingly committed to Bandenbekämpfung-related functions and tasks. Kaltenbrunner imposed strict control over Heydrich's former Young Turks, and became problematic for Himmler. In January 1943, Bach-Zelewski commented in his diary that he thought Kaltenbrunner was accepting a thankless task replacing the doyen of all Germans, Heydrich, with whom he had had fundamental disagreements.[62] Almost immediately after becoming chief of the RSHA, Kaltenbrunner began raising yet another private army. His style of leadership gathering and channeling groups of his Austrian SS into strategic cliques within the regime. Kaltenbrunner's influence spread through Wilhelm Hoettl, Adolf Eichmann, Skorzeny, and Odilo Globocnik, and the commanders of *Aktion Reinhard*.[63] This clique dominated security operations in the south and the Balkans. Kaltenbrunner lacked Heydrich's charisma but tried to emulate his clandestine successes to cut a niche in the Nazi hierarchy. In his first few months as chief of RSHA, Kaltenbrunner turned to his long time friend, Otto Skorzeny, to raise a commando unit dedicated to covert political actions. Only a few weeks earlier, Skorzeny's career appeared finished. He received eight days' house arrest for drinking on the national day of mourning for Stalingrad. Assigned to a reserve transport detachment of the SS-Totenkopfverbände, based in Buchenwald concentration camp, he was about as far away from the war as a member of the SS could possibly be. On April 15, 1943, Skorzeny received a transfer to the RSHA. His arrival immediately sparked differences of opinion with his nominal superior officer SS-Brigadeführer Walter Schellenberg.

The great scandal that shamed the SS-Police came from a totally unexpected source. For several years, Kurt Daluege had been afflicted by a rash of absences caused by bouts of mysterious illness. Then, on July 5, 1943, Daluege officially stepped down. This finally ended the "Himmler-Daluege-Heydrich" triumvirate; Himmler was alone in command of the SS for the first time since 1929. The death of Heydrich in 1942 had rocked the regime; Daluege's demise because of the regressive effects of "congenital" syphilis was a body blow to the SS-Police establishment.[64] Hitler had spent seven pages of *Mein Kampf* arguing for the combating of syphilis and had attributed it to the moral collapse of Germany. He blamed his predecessors: "Particularly with regard to syphilis, the attitude of the leadership of the nation and the state can only be designated as total capitulation. . . . The fight against syphilis demands a fight against prostitution, against prejudices, old habit, against previous conceptions, general views among them not least the false prudery of certain circles."[65] Thus, at the point when Hitler was about to lose the initiative in the war, the man he had written of as "my honour is loyalty" (*Meine Ehre heist Treue*) was cast out in shame. Daluege became a non-person within the regime. Hitler, as good as his word, shunned Daluege for the rest of the war.

Bach-Zelewski immediately broke off his relationship, while Himmler was later forced to warn Daluege not to cause intrigues. The only confirmation of Daluege's circumstances comes from Albert Speer who briefly convalesced with him.[66] Himmler remained embarrassed about Daluege, informing the gathering of senior SS officers at Posen,

> Our old friend Daluege has such severe heart trouble that he has to undergo courses of treatment and now has to retire from active service for one-and-a-half to two years . . . we may hope that Daluege will have recovered in about two years and can then return to the front and get into harness.[67]

Daluege was replaced by Alfred Wünnenberg, a career police officer. Wünnenberg was an accomplished soldier-policeman but not a political soldier of Daluege's calibre. The difference between the two concepts was profound and further indicates why Himmler did not give the job to Bach-Zelewski. The choice of Wünnenberg points the way toward Himmler's thinking: the Order Police was reduced in political stature although its role remained crucial to Bandenbekämpfung. There was another significant change in the Order Police organization: the Kolonialpolizeiamt (discussed in chapter 2) was closed in 1943. Its commander, Pfeffer-Wildenbruch, became a Waffen-SS corps commander.

On August 20, Hitler sacked Wilhelm Frick and replaced him with Himmler as minister of the interior. This centralized the vast German legal and state bureaucracy and the SS completing the Nazi national security state.[68] At the same time, Bach-Zelewski was gradually introduced into the grand circles of the regime as part of his grooming for high office. On August 7, Himmler, no doubt aware of the events to follow, held a meeting with Wolff and Bach-Zelewski, who had taken time out during Operation "Hermann." Seven days after Himmler's promotion, he met with Bach-Zelewski and Prützmann. Bach-Zelewski also held meetings to engage liaison officers from many institutions to his new office, a standard routine within the regime. One venue for these meetings was Göring's Air Ministry building in Berlin. On August 31, Bach-Zelewski met Wünnenberg and Maximillian von Herff to discuss his influence over Order Police personnel policy. Herff was chief of SS personnel and had a major influence over the whole SS-Police organization. Meetings held on September 4 were especially significant because of their strategic prominence. The first discussions involved the role of the Luftwaffe in Bandenbekämpfung operations. Luftwaffe chief of staff General Korten opened discussion on the role of the Luftwaffe in "bandit war" (Bandenkrieg*)*. That evening Bach-Zelewski met with General Wagner. On September 21, Bach-Zelewski met with Artur Nebe, the former Einsatzgruppen commander and associate during the "Barbarossa" pogroms, and Major General Dahlem, another of Göring's senior staff officers. The next day, Himmler and Bach-Zelewski consulted with Grand Admiral Dönitz and three admirals, a continuation from earlier in the year. In October, Luftwaffe colonel Dr. Bormann, a Knight's Cross recipient, became Bach-Zelewski's senior Luftwaffe liaison staff officer. On December 12, 1943, Bach-Zelewski was introduced into Himmler's "circle of friends" (SS-*Freundeskreis*, RFSS), a gathering of industrialists and business leaders, almost certainly to discuss labor matters.[69] However, this ended as the situation on the Eastern Front deteriorated and Bach-Zelewski was ordered to defend Kovel (discussed in detail in chapter 8). In October 1943, Himmler, after a turbulent year, was able to present further expansion from the new office in his presentation of the infamous Posen speech:

> I considered it necessary for the Reichsführer-SS to be in authoritative command in all these battles, for I am convinced that we are in the best position to take action against this enemy struggle, which is a decidedly political one. [He added that this new office had contributed to an increase in the SS organization.] . . . It is notable that, by setting up this department we have gained for the SS in turn a division, a corps, an army and the next step, which is the High Command of an army or even a group . . . [70]

## Bandenbekämpfung and Enemy Classification

A common defense for German security methods by German defendants during the Nuremberg war crimes trials was attributing their brutality to the illegality of the resistance. This argument pinpointed single aspects of the partisan and resistance operations to explain the German campaign. They ignored the racial aspect underpinning German measures, the roundup of labor, and the widespread exploitation. The defendants were well aware that, as the war came to end, German measures had turned more severe. They hoped to steer the prosecution away from focusing on the integrated character of Bandenbekämpfung and its classification of the enemy. Since the trials, academic have consistently compared Soviet and German methods, partisan and antipartisan respectively, finding a common conclusion of mutual brutality. Their picture is one of a vicious cycle of blind terror, cold-bloodedness, and wanton destruction and ignores the rational processes underpinning German behavior in forging policy, irrespective of the opponents. More important, comparative analyses have failed to explain why, as the Germans lost the war, their brutality found greater release for deeper depravity.

Modern Prussia and Imperial Germany were erected on a comprehensive body of state and national laws. In parallel to the national laws, Germany was a proactive participant in the international conventions governing the conduct of warfare. Before 1914, Prussia and later Imperial Germany attended The Hague and Geneva conferences and conventions. Germany was a full signatory of the 1907 Hague Convention IV, "Respecting the Laws and Customs of War on Land." After the First World War, Weimar Germany endorsed the Geneva Protocols on Gas Warfare and Prisoners of War. Hitler conducted law making like a barrack-room lawyer; to whit, laws were only acceptable as long as they worked for his benefit and to the detriment of his enemies. In 1939, he typically promised to abide by the existing precedents of war, while threatening the Jewish race with extinction and practicing ethnic-cleansing against the Polish people. In 1941, Hitler's rules of engagement invading Soviet Russia were encompassed in the infamous Barbarossa directives. By 1943, the Nazi regime was calling forth a different kind of language for the conduct of the war.[71] The shift in the regime's tone was matched by renewed attempts to further circumvent the laws of war.

The circumvention of The Hague conventions had been simplified by the German occupation of Holland, rendering its existence obsolete by right of conquest. The Dutch hoped the Germans would recognize The Hague conventions as binding.[72] When Arthur Seyss-Inquart became the Reichskommissioner for the Occupied Netherlands in 1940, he reported to Hitler that the favorable way to incorporate the Dutch into Hitler's Reich was through economic collaboration. However, Seyss-Inquart declared The Hague Conventions redundant as his administration aggressively ignored their rulings. By 1943, Dutch labor, like labor across occupied Europe, was combed by conscription waves from Sauckel's offices. Eventually, more than a half million Dutch people were conscripted for labor. Seyss-Inquart was also responsible for imposing a catalog of Nazi measures in the persecution of the Jews. In his contribution to the Holocaust he ensured the mass deportation of more than one hundred thousand Jews to extermination camps and ghettos in the east.

The racial impetus of Fortress Europe went in two directions, decided either by "expediency" or extermination. Goebbels's diary in the first six months of 1943 is evidence of how fixated the Nazis were on the "Jewish question" and of their commitment to extermination. In May 1943, Goebbels published an article titled "Der Krieg und die Juden" (The War and the Jews) and pleaded his cause to ensure the "evacuation" of the Berlin Jews.[73] In 1942, the British diplomatic services monitoring German attitudes thought the extermination of Jews was gradually working against the Nazis. One ambassador noted,

> Germans are now beginning to discuss whether perhaps in their treatment of the Jews they have gone too far and to be anxious lest one day they may have to pay dearly for their inhumanity. The conviction is spreading that in any case the future of generations of Germans will have to pay.[74]

The pacification of the Warsaw ghetto uprising in April–May 1943, discussed in chapter 8, from a diplomatic standpoint backfired on the Nazis. In April 1943, the German propaganda service announced the discovery of a site of massacred Polish army officers at Katyn. In 1940, the Soviet secret police had executed more than ten thousand Polish POWs in several killing sites. Goebbels hoped to exploit the incident, but his scheme was undermined. The Germans placed posters in Polish streets denouncing the massacre and listing the names of the Polish officers discovered at Katyn. Many of the victims on the lists were Jewish, and according to Joseph Mackiewicz, the Germans blamed their murdering on "Jewish Bolshevism." The Germans named three members of the Minsk NKVD, all with Jewish names, as responsible for the killings.[75] The Nazis had projected the destruction of Lidice and Warsaw to the world, and the world responded by believing the Nazis had committed Katyn.

After the wave of defeats in February and March 1943, the Waffen-SS delivered a tactical victory at Kharkov. One reward for the battle-scarred veterans was a speech from Himmler, the first in what became a series of important speeches presented through the year. Himmler's speech corresponded to Hitler's mission. "I would like to give it a name: it is the great fortress Europe," Himmler said. "The fortress of Europe with its frontiers must be held and will be held too, as long as is necessary." German success, according to Himmler, was her destiny, but this could only be assured through a political-military victory underscored by security and mass killings. He reiterated the master plan: "The decision . . . lies here in the East; here must the Russian enemy, this people numbering two hundred million Russians, be destroyed on the battlefield and person by person, and made to bleed to death." This tidal wave of human destruction also included the last phase in the extermination of the Jews as he declared,

> Anti-Semitism is exactly the same as delousing. Getting rid of lice is not a question of ideology. It is a matter of cleanliness. . . . We shall soon be deloused. We have only 20,000 lice left, and then the matter is finished within the whole of Germany. . . . We have only one task, to stand firm and carry on the racial struggle without mercy.[76]

In 1943, Dr. Rudolf Thierfelder published a report on the German occupation of France.[77] The thrust of Thierfelder's argument was that German methods adhered to The Hague conventions (1899 and 1907) and the Lieber code. His argument exploited the cyclical interpretation that underpinned any analysis of the laws of war. The Lieber code was spun and weaved to prove Germany was conducting its war within legal limits. The thread of Lieber's code stated, "A territory under military occupation automatically falls under martial law. . . . Martial law in a hostile country suspends criminal and civil law as well as civil administration."[78] Lieber reasoned that "The more vigorously wars are pursued the better it is for humanity. Sharp wars are brief."[79] Lieber's principle underpinned Goebbels's call for rapid and total war. Thierfelder exploited Lieber's interpretation of partisans or "bandits," in the general classification of combatants and non-combatants. Lieber's definition of the partisan was recognized by all belligerents:

> Partisans are soldiers armed and wearing the uniform of their army, but belonging to a corps, which acts detached from the main body for the purpose of making inroads into the territory occupied by the enemy. If captured they are entitled to all the privileges of the prisoner of war.[80]

Lieber was intolerant of guerrillas, whom he deemed robbers and scoundrels, and equated guerrilla war to the horrors of the Thirty Years' War. Guerrilla warfare was defined as criminal banditry: "so much is certain, that no army, no society, engaged in war, any more than a society at peace, can allow unpunished assassination, robbery, and devastation, without the deepest injury to itself and disastrous consequences, which might change the very issue of the war."[81] Thierfelder judged German intolerance of resistance as further proof of Germany's observance of the Lieber code.

In 1942, Directive 46 was introduced to eradicate "banditry" in order to exploit Soviet lands uninterrupted. Addendums "a" and "b" were attached to extend the application of punitive measures to include allied Special Forces (discussed in chapter 3). In May 1944 the OKW issued the formal regulations for Bandenbekämpfung, replacing all prior standing orders or guidelines (discussed in chapter 5).[82] Long before then, the language and principles of Bandenbekämpfung had become routine for the Wehrmacht and SS. A Luftwaffe Eastern Front "bandit-situation" report (*Bandenlage*) from January 1944 provides an example. The report, written by Colonel Kollee, advised that "amongst the bandits the Jews have a certain role, they work according to their nature, and they act as spies. There is an independent Jewish bandit group operating near Leszniow." Kollee went on to discuss the different forms of resistance: "There has been an increase in the number of opportunists' bandits with the minimum of training. Their numbers have increased with the German retreat."[83] The "bandit bands" were identified as composed of Red Army stragglers, enemy troops that infiltrated the front lines, parachutists (*Fallschirmspringer*), POW escapees, German deserters, former collaborators, civilian volunteers, and coerced locals. The larger bands included specialists in their order of battle including bridging units, demolition parties, cavalry detachments, and antitank squads. The bands' signals detachments were known for their superior training, and their capture was highly prized. The Germans particularly singled out armed women (*Flintenweiber*) or females assisting in supply, medical signals functions, and serving as enemy agents. Many reports identified the leaders of the "Bolshevist bands" as "bandits" but then went on to describe them as Red Army officers, political commissars, or public servants. Russian village leaders or Ukrainian chieftains who raised private bands were categorized as "bandit leaders" (*Bandenhäuptling*).[84]

Bandenbekämpfung regulations recognized that some bands were organized as military formations with internal military structures. The Germans often reported in a patronizing way how a band adopted military terms. For example, the Soviets often used "brigade" to identify bands more than a hundred strong, and the Germans believed this was a deliberate misuse of correct terminology. Their language focused on the question of uniforms and discipline. The Germans often referred to the ability of the bands to maintain discipline. The question of uniforms was ambiguous; some bands wore civilian clothing while the Red Army's partisans wore full uniforms. This failure to treat captives in a recognizable uniform as combatants was a clear breach of the laws of war.[85] The Germans described the fighting style of "bandits" as aggressive and destructive. The bands were linked to six tasks. Three were military tasks: attacking strongpoints, depots, transports, marching troops, supply columns, and individual vehicles; attacking German offensives (destroying bridges, mining roads, blocking tracks, and disrupting rail traffic); and disrupting German communications. A fourth task was economic warfare: the bands were ordered to destroy everything of economic value to the Germans, particularly the harvest. The two political tasks of the bands included terrorizing the populace to undermine German authority and administration and undermining the morale of all collaborators. Himmler summarized the picture of the opponent:

> We are dealing with an enemy who simply disregards many of our tactical and strategic experiences. For instance, he just does not care whether he is encircled; it is no importance to him. He attacks at places where our tactical sense, or perhaps we had better say our tactical doctrine tells us that there is no sense in doing so. Still, attack he does, and often enough he is successful.[86]

German regulations officially maligned the "bandit" as a bully, deceitful and cowardly, only attacking troops that were weak. The German soldier was warned that capture would lead to a horrible death. The partisans were accused of mutilating German wounded as a means to stirrup mercilessness in the troops. The "bandit" was described as a saboteur who avoided open combat. A typical tactic of the "bandits" was stopping transport columns by triggering multiple mines and explosives without exposing themselves to German retaliation. They might also conduct a surprise attack with concentrated fire and then quickly disappear. A band suspicious of being surrounded would attack desperately to escape. Decoys might be used to distract the Germans from the main escape route. The "bandits" used camouflage; one particular example seemed to fascinate the Germans because it turned up so many times in reports: "We found bandits, who stood up to their mouths in water, who camouflaged their head with bits of grass or who buried themselves almost completely into the ground." In 1941 and 1942, the governing motivation of German policy was that "all Jews are partisans and all partisans are Jews." From 1943, all armed resistance was "banditry" and all Jews, irrespective of circumstances, were treated as "bandits." By October 1943, Himmler could confidently present a speech to army officers at Bad Schachen exploiting this process of vilification:

> For us the end of this war will mean an open road to the East, the creation of the German Reich we shall be a people of 120 million Germanic souls. . . . We are up against an enemy who uses the laws of war with a sort of Slav cruelty in his own ranks against us. . . . He is capable of cannibalism, of butchering his neighbor, cutting out his liver and keeping it in his haversack.[87]

In 1942, Hitler had warned the troops of placing misguided trust for the civilians of occupied countries (refer to chapter 3). The Lieber Code addressed the position of civilians in war:

> Private citizens are no longer murdered, enslaved, or carried off to distant parts, and the inoffensive individual is as little disturbed in his private relations as the commander of the hostile troops can afford to grant in the overruling demands of a vigorous war.[88]

Given the nature of Nazi rule, it might seem ludicrous to imagine that loyalty was demanded from Russian civilians, but the Germans expected both loyalty and collaboration. Collaboration was measured by membership of the collaboration police (Schuma) or other organizations, while economic productivity proved loyalty. A section of the 1944 regulations, "Treatment of the Population, Bandit Helpers and Bandits" (*Behandlung der Bevölkerung, der*

*Bandenhelfer und der Banditen*), attempted to resolve the ambiguity.[89] The regulations stressed reliance on local German administrators to distinguish between reliable and unreliable civilians. The agricultural economy officer (*Landwirtschaftsführer*) monitored the attitude and mood of civilians. They measured civilian loyalty through the achievement of "production targets" (*Ablieferungszoll erfüllen*). When the Germans announced production targets, they issued "individual produce obligations" (*Ablieferungsleistungen*) and announced penalties for not achieving targets (*Nichterfüllen der Forderung*). The most severe punishment for failure included the confiscation of cattle, or in the case of rotten foodstuff, the substitution by other produce while the farmer received a receipt of his debt to the state to be accounted for in due course. The presence of bands allowed the Germans to designate such areas as diseased or infected and awaiting treatment (discussed in chapter 6). This led to the further classification of civilian disloyalty as the "bandit helper" (*Bandenhelfer*) and the "bandit-suspicious" (*Bandenverdächtigte*). This brought about the enforcement of security through a regime of guilt by association or suspicion. The only mitigating circumstance for civilians under suspicion was if they proved they were pressganged. Initially the Bandenhelfer were executed, but Himmler rescinded this order in January 1943 and incarcerated them in concentration camps instead. Bandenverdächtigte, in another case of confusion, were either executed or enslaved.

The circumvention and manipulation of the Geneva Conventions was, therefore, not surprisingly a major aspect of Hitler's war. The 1941 Barbarossa directives and the 1942 Commando Order challenged the protection offered to soldiers in uniform. Gradually, the number of allied servicemen exposed to ill-treatment or execution included all Special Forces personnel, the random killing of downed bomber aircrew vilified as "terror-fliers" (*Terrorflieger*), and personnel from Poland, France, and Czechoslovakia serving with the allied armies; in particular Poles, French, and Czechs, imprisoned and escaped from German prison camps became subject to the "bullet decree" (*Plan Kugel*) upon recapture.[90]

The confusion caused by these regulations even led some British paratroopers captured at Arnhem to be treated as "bandits" and sent to Auschwitz as labor. In Normandy, Canadian soldiers were executed by Waffen-SS troopers. The allied personnel who escaped from German prisoner of war camps were executed if found. The mass breakout from the Sagen prisoner of war camp led to the execution of fifty recaptured allied officers. In simple terms, a uniform no longer guaranteed protection for captured allied soldiers. The differences between the Lieber Code and Nazi regulation lay in the quest for ethical warfare, a concept that even a gifted Nazi political-warrior like Himmler could barely comprehend:

Military necessity does not admit of cruelty—that is, the inflic-
tion of suffering for the sake of suffering or for revenge, nor of
maiming or wounding except in fight, nor torture to extort confes-
sions. It does not admit of the use of poison in any way, nor of the
wanton devastation of a district. It admits of deception, but dis-
claims acts of perfidy; and in general, military necessity does not
include any act of hostility, which makes the return to peace unnecessarily difficult.[91]

In 1944, following the spate of escape, the Germans issued new regulations for the treatment of POWs, which were posted to all camps. The regulations opened, "escaping from prison camps has ceased to be a sport." It
confirmed that Germany maintained the Geneva Convention but stated that
because "England has besides fighting in an honest manner instituted an
illegal warfare in non combat zones in the form of gangster commandos, terror
bandits, and sabotage troops, even up to the frontiers of Germany." The
statement alluded to the existence of the German handbook for modern irregular warfare, which had two purposes: first, to combat gangsterism and, second, to create strictly forbidden zones, called death zones in which all unau-
thorized trespassers will be immediately shot on the spot."[92] This is positive
evidence that Bandenbekämpfung regulations had been adapted to determine
Hitler's war and the criminal interpretation of the Geneva Convention.

# 5
# DIE
# BANDENKAMPFVERBÄNDE

In his June 1943 Bandenbekämpfung order, Himmler announced the existence of the "combating-bandits formations" (*Bandenkampfverbände*) and the office of the chief of combating-bandits formations (*Chef der Bandenkampfverbände*). This was the final stage in turning Banden-bekämpfung into an operational concept. Christopher Bellamy identified three elements within the operational concept: the moral element that motivates the troops to fight; the physical element, concerned with armies and their logistics; and the conceptual element, the force driving the other two.[1] The physical element of Bandenbekämpfung was the Bandenkampfverbände, with troops from the army, navy, air force, SS-Police, and Waffen-SS, and auxiliaries assigned to security operations for unspecified periods of duty. The moral element of Bandenbekämpfung was personified in Bach-Zelewski, whom Hitler and Himmler believed was their perfect appointment. The third element, the motivation of the troops, came not only from Hitler and Himmler as ideologues or Bach-Zelewski as their commander, but also from the socializing effect of being part of a highly organized and dynamic system. In this sense, the Bandenkampfverbände was a unique idea.

The four components within the Bandenkampfverbände were a commitment to information warfare, central control and coordination of security, the proactive management of troops through the orders of battle, and the command task of molding the troops to reach a common performance standard. As Chef der Bandenkampfverbände, Bach-Zelewski was tasked with regime-wide promotion of Bandenbekämpfung through the projection of positive results, the command of the Bandenkampfverbände across a variety of conflict situations, and the ensurance of consistent performances from the troops.[2]

His fitness for command was decided by Himmler; however, a general observation of his character fails to isolate any superior qualities. Bach-Zelewski was an intelligent man, a Junker, a political opportunist, and a self-confessed serial killer. Bach-Zelewski's military skills were biased toward the infantry, and as a Great War soldier, he was awarded medals associated with heroism and courageous deeds. He was an exponent of modern warfare, security actions, resettlement programs, and mass killing. In addition, he held a close personal relationship with many senior officers of the German army high command; they trusted him. Bach-Zelewski was riddled with self-doubt, including a range of phobias that manifested themselves in his bowel condition. Bach-Zelewski's tasks were onerous. They involved harnessing Bandenbekämpfung doctrine to the existing limits of war leadership (*Kriegsführung*), the conduct of operations (*Kampfführung*), and the formulation of fighting style (*Kampfweise*). He was also responsible for discipline, with powers greater than a typical divisional or corps commander, and the publication of the official Bandenbekämpfung regulations issued by the OKW (1944).[3] Understanding Bach-Zelewski and the Bandenkampfverbände, therefore, are the keys to realizing how important Bandenbekämpfung became as the final manifestation of Germany's concept of security warfare.

## Information Warfare in the Predigital Age

In November 1945, Bach-Zelewski revealed under interrogation that his authority shaped his job as Chef der Sonderverbände. This was, he suggested, a central reporting agency designated to as "Extraordinary Battle Area" *(Sonderkampfgebiet)*. He explained that his powers only extended into being an inspector and that he was without executive powers to counsel the commanders. The one exception, which he did not clarify, was the large-scale Operation "Heinrich" for which he was the commander. In an earlier interrogation, on October 24, he boasted that his staff received upward of fifteen thousand reports daily from across Europe and added, "I think we had three to four hundred thousand soldiers for the fighting of partisans." He explained that agents acquired information from among civilian communities and passed it to the security police. The information service existed in all regions and departments. His intelligence officers were responsible for the collection of this information assisted by the HSSPFs who maintained a system of situation maps. The General Quartermaster was the distribution bureau that transformed the data into operational situation reports.[4] These reports were then passed on a daily basis to Hitler.[5] In 1945, the allied interrogators more than likely misunderstood this testimony. First, the interrogators had little understanding of the internal workings of the German staff system. Second, the Allies had little appreciation of the direction, administration, and practice of Bandenbekämpfung. Third, they could not grasp the strategic importance of Bandenbekämpfung to the German war effort. Martin van Creveld has explained that command has two primary purposes: to arrange and coordinate the needs of the army and to carry out the mission of causing the maximum amount of death and destruction on the enemy. However, in terms of non-conventional warfare, he was obliged to accept some "modification" where the "purely military factors are less important than psychological and political ones."[6] Thus, the Bandenkampfverbände was an exceptional form of information warfare and the driving force of an asset-stripping strategy that encompassed extermination and enslavement.

The German staff system was in a state of constant change and reorganization in the period 1939–45. Geyer's warning of specialization had turned the staff into a regime within the regime. The intelligence services were bloated with bureaucracy and subject to an institutional tug-of-war between the Wehrmacht and SS. The numerous rationalizations examined by the Allies after the war led to the conclusion that it was a ramshackle organization of many "bolted-on" parts. The German army's operations were dominated by cartography. Military cartographers produced a constant flow of maps for every conceivable situation, on a daily basis, sometimes up to four or five times per day. The maps contained details of enemy movements, their order of battle, their reserves, the rapidly changing probing attacks, the development of an offensive, and so forth. Cartographers wrote this data onto maps by hand and then printed the maps for distribution to commanders, including Hitler. After the war, many senior generals comically portrayed Hitler poring over these maps identifying imaginary armies and breakthroughs. The data for the maps came through the long chain of intelligence officers, from the battalion level up to the OKW. Today a laptop computer could scroll through maps and details in minutes, if not seconds; in the 1940s, the Germans used maps of 1 to 100,000-scale, 1 to 200,000-scale, and 1 to 300,000-scale; many were in large format, several square meters. To maximize the flow of information, the staff updated a card-index system, with the cards marked to correspond to map grid-references. In an effort to understand the German concept of intelligence, the Allies made a critical analysis but came up against stonewall testimony as to the role and influence of the intelligence officer. If they had looked harder, they might have discovered that the intelligence services shaped the German command's perception of the war.[7]

## The Halder Initiatives

In 1942, Franz Halder the chief of the Army General Staff introduced two initiatives that had a great bearing on Bandenbekämpfung. One involved acquiring tactical intelligence (*Aufklärung*). The origin of this idea, as far as one can tell, came from German sport hunting techniques, in which small groups of hunters worked in teams to track down and kill game. This idea effectively combined armed reconnaissance with intelligence-gathering tasks. There were two sections to the Jagdkommando order. The first recommended the composition of the Jagdkommando units. All formations in areas threatened by partisans were to raise a Jagdkommando. The typical group included one officer and four troopers. Each group was expected to include a civilian scout, proven in security work. They were armed to inflict a firefight on the partisans. The second section covered the guidelines for Jagdkommandos (*Richtlinien für Jagdkommandos*). The Jagdkommandos were ordered to move only at night, to avoid detection. Upon reaching the "combat" area, they were to emulate the fighting style (*Kampfweise*) of the partisans, scouting and laying traps. The Jagdkommandos adopted "cunning," were led by capable officers initiating ruses (*Kriegslist anwenden*), and were warned to be patient and to await the enemy. In the event of facing superior force, they were advised to signal their senior command and await the arrival of reinforcements. The Jagdkommando served as both an immediate and aggressive reaction to the bands, as well as gathering intelligence. They were particularly suited for reconnaissance-in-force (*gewaltsame Aufklärung*). The presence of Jagdkom-mandos was meant to prevent the bands from resting and was regarded as crucial for maintaining a "bandit-free area" (*bandenfreies Vorfeld*). Each Jagdkommando patrol could last several weeks and range within a twenty-kilometer radius. Halder reiterated in his order that membership of the Jagdkommando was recognized as a "distinction."[8]

The other Halder initiative involved reorganizing Eastern Front military intelligence and involved the Foreign Armies East Department (*Abteilung Fremde Heere Ost,* FHO). In April 1942, Halder promoted Oberst Reinhard Gehlen to command the FHO, making this an independent department and allowing certain freedom of reporting and information collection. The FHO took on the capability of making long-term strategic predictions.[9] Gehlen instigated a bureaucratic process that amassed volumes of data. He remained at his post until the end of the war because he proved highly suited to the changing politics of the war. His late war reports monitored the movements of "bandits" and Jews and were distributed to Hitler and the SS.[10] Post-interrogation studies accumulated by the allied powers show a high degree of German officers' denial over Bandenbekämpfung balanced against an excruciatingly detailed knowledge of how the system worked. Gehlen's memoirs did not include any reference to the monitoring of Jewish bands in the east.[11]

The German army's Intelligence Referat (Ib) was responsible for tracking "bandits" and was under Gehlen's command. This section began by tracking the movements of Soviet partisans, but later this responsibility was expanded to include monitoring all Eastern European resistance. The Referat issued a daily "bandit" situation report based on information from the GFP, signals, and the host of intelligence officers. Its mission was to identify the direction of "bandit activity" (*Bandenschwerpunkte*). It maintained a manual filing system recording the movements of each band, its command chain, its fighting style, its organization, and the extent of its activity. The Referat then created a map of known "bandit activity" (*Karte des Bandeneinsatzes*).[12] The process of mapping was linked to the individual field intelligence officers who worked on 1 to 300,000-scale maps. This level of mapping recorded two forms of information: The first was "bandit" activity, recording positions, camps, command points, landing fields, airfields, the positions of security troops, and the identification of protected convoys. Second, a monthly "bandit" situation map recorded attacks on railways, troops, and civilians; looting; cases of sabotage; and potential threat level. Maps also included levels of loyalty that could be expected from an area so that the appropriate level of security could be applied. Finally, all the situation maps were consolidated into large strategic maps that included industry, populations, reserves, economies, and social reliability. Once a map was redundant, it was destroyed.[13] In 1944, the army intelligence service organized an intelligence instruction course (*Lehrgang*) in Posen. In eighteen days, the intelligence candidates received instruction on every aspect of the war. On April 14, 1944, their day involved studying the role of the intelligence officer in what the Allies translated as "partisan warfare." The "bandit" session was compartmentalized to the strategic direction of the war.[14] This demonstrates that the Germans could, and did, accumulate a large level of information ranging from community loyalty assessment down to economic or book values of property holders. It points toward the main thrust of Bandenbekämpfung, not as a counter-response to partisan incursions, as so often depicted, but as a planned program of asset-stripping security warfare operations. The information available to the commanders and the troops enabled the Germans to precisely pick their targets and conduct operations with the maximum amount of preparation.

## Headquarters and Senior Staff Functions

The tendency of the existing literature has been either to focus on Hitler's headquarters, in the hope of unlocking secrets, or to isolate a well-known German commander and extract a character study from former staff officers. As a result, a patchwork picture has emerged, which paints the staff as faceless men busying around gossiping, conspiring, or doing everything but being inspirational. The German General Staff was a reflection of German state bureaucracy and absorbed a considerable level of institutional inertia. A report on the German General Staff by Karl Allmendinger ignored many truths about German General Staff Corps.[15] One impression that becomes apparent from the records is that the staff work was a very personal affair. Another senior German staff officer, under interrogation, identified the personal qualities of the staff, including "devotion to the commander," even if the commander is "corrupt or unsoldierly" while aspiring to a job well done; "knowledge of the procedures and terminology of command," the issue of clear and understandable orders; and "assistance in command." Staff officers usually were better trained than their commanders; they had the "ability to advise," which some believed, after the war, ran at odds with the Nazi philosophy of Führerprinzip by removing joint responsibility of staff and command; "character"; confidence in the face of defeat; and "knowledge and flexibility."[16] Several staff officers were given "dynamic" missions that side-stepped the bureaucracy. In 1942, Hitler had ordered Generalleutnant Walter von Unruh to undertake a special OKW commission (*Sonderbeauftragter Hitlers und Kommandeur des OKW-Stabes z.b.V*) to investigate the potential for rationalization within the German war effort. Unruh and Warlimont fit that picture perfectly.

The headquarters functions and command purpose of the Ch.BKV created a complex and advanced interpretation of command in the predigital age. Since June 1941, all planning and preparation for SS operations in the east had emanated from the KSRFSS. Under the June and September orders, Himmler arranged for the headquarters of the Ch.BKV to be established alongside the KSRFSS. This placed Bach-Zelewski at the heart of strategy and policymaking, as well as at the hub of the communications system that stretched across Europe. Telephone, signals, and coded communications with the HSSPF, Waffen-SS commands, army groups, armies, military governors, civilian governors, the military districts (*Wehrkreis*), the headquarters of the Luftwaffe, and Kriegsmarine could be connected to the Ch.BKV. This command system remained on high alert, reading signals, analyzing data and making reports on a twenty-four-hour basis. This forced the staff to work shifts. German headquarters replicated many military staff organizations with four senior staff officers assisting the commander, including the chief of staff, the first operations staff officer (designated Ia), the intelligence staff officer (Ic), and the quartermaster. The headquarters complement had four detachments: Operations (Ia), with one general staff officer and five assistants; Intelligence (Ic), with three general staff officers and three assistants; and the Quartermaster detachment, with seven senior staff officers and seven assistants. The Signals function (In) included a senior officer, a radio specialist, and the liaison officer to the army. Bach-Zelewski later testified that his "experts," the Ia and Ic, were in daily communication with OKW/OKH and the HSSPFs.[17]

## The Chief of Staff: Ernst Rode

The role of the chief of staff in the army involved being the commander in chief's aide and confidant. The chief of staff was the senior staff officer, responsible for ensuring the smooth running of the headquarters and setting the pace of work. In the absence of the commander, he usually took over the command. On the occasions when Bach-Zelewski was assigned to other duties, Himmler took overall command until he returned. The chief of staff to Ch.BKV regulated the political-military-security temperature of the commander's activities. The chief of staff issued direct orders, on behalf of Bach-Zelewski, to the HSSPF personally. He controlled the staffs of HSSPFs, police regiments and other fighting formations, ensuring consistent and routine staff performance. Bach-Zelewski's chiefs of staff included SS-Standartenführer und Oberst der Polizei Gölz and SS-Brigadeführer Eberhard Herf (see chapter 7). Perhaps Ernst Rode proved the most effective. Rode was born in 1894 in Silesia, a Protestant. Briefly a member of the Freikorps, he joined the Schutzpolizei in 1920. He was quick to support the Nazi Party from May 1, 1930. In August 1942, Ernst Rode circulated instructions warning of the lack of preparation and slow movement by field commands that had alerted the helpers and supporters of the criminals ("bandits") and enabled them to escape.[18]

## Intelligence Officer (IC): Eduard Strauch

Bach-Zelewski had several officers to undertake intelligence functions on his behalf, but Eduard Strauch was the one for whom he indicated the most concern in Nuremberg. When asked if he knew Strauch, Bach-Zelewski answered, "Yes and keen to meet him," but then qualified this by implying Strauch really worked for Kube and was a mass-murderer by conviction.[19] He had participated in the rounding up and execution of Jews since 1941. In 1942, Kube wrote, "In exhaustive discussions with SS-Brigadeführer Zenner and the exceedingly capable leader of the SD, SS-Obersturmbannführer Dr. (Law) Strauch, we have liquidated in the last ten weeks about 55,000 Jews in White Ruthenia."[20] In his diary, on January 30, 1943, Bach-Zelewski mentioned that SD leader Strauch had informed him that his housekeeper, Helena Bashina, was spying for the "bandits."[21] In 1947, the prison medical services diagnosed Strauch as insane. A lawyer by profession, Strauch joined the SS in 1931. The ability to exterminate was the main quality that the chief of intelligence of the Bandenkampfverbände applied to his work.

Strauch was expected to accumulate information indicating the level of forces required to pacify an area and, more important, the level of disenchantment and resistance in a region. All formations and troops were expected to help collect information, although this was primarily the responsibility of the SD and GFP. Officers from these services collected all possible information on a community. Locating the source of supply to the bandits was imperative. A band with large stores of supplies, using landing strips, and isolated from villages probably worked in isolation from local communities. Bands short on supply and based close to villages raised the level of suspicion. Native inhabitants were questioned carefully, and their statements were measured against the level of band activity. Reconnaissance examined the band camps, road conditions, and the respective strength of the "bandits" as a reflection of civilian loyalty. The three approved methods for reconnaissance included installing agents, and Jagdkommandos and employing slow- flying reconnaissance airplanes. Useful information came from observing the population. The rural leaders, economic experts, and officials of the forestry service monitored workers, collaborators with the German armed forces (known as *Hilfswillige*, or Hiwis for short), and any suspicious people. The flow of Red Air Force traffic to the band indicated its situation and importance.

The SD handled punishments, which usually led to imprisonment or execution. On December 30, 1942, Himmler ordered all captive bandits, sympathizers, and those under the threat of execution to be sent to concentration camps in Germany. On January 6, 1943, correspondence passed from Himmler to SS-Obergruppenführer Oswald Pohl, chief of the SS Economic and Administration Main Office (*Wirtschafts- und Verwaltungshauptamt, WVHA*) regarding the application of the concentration camps to Bandenbekämpfung. "In operations against [bandits] men, women and children suspected of [bandit] activities will be rounded up and shipped to the camps in Lublin and Auschwitz," Pohl confirmed.[22] On January 21, Himmler, in his capacity as chief of the RSHA, requested that all cases of Bandenverdächtigte be placed into slave labor. Four days later, with his request acknowledged, a confirmation was dispatched to OKH enforcing the order throughout the army. The order warned not to communicate the punishment openly as it might reduce those willing to volunteer for labor. Suspects sent to concentration camps or detention centers received an examination as to their suitability for deportation. Jodl believed that like Himmler, who sent detainees to camps in Germany, the army should work to a similar routine. The wheel had turned; the police had given orders to the army.[23] The failure of Russians to "voluntary mobilize" as labor in the German economy led to extensive punitive reprisals against villages. One British interrogation report noted the deliberate destruction of villages in the area of Minsk, including Dubichi, Teplyn, and Zezulevka; the populations of the villages were all burned alive. The village of Staroye Selo was destroyed because it failed to pay its taxes.[24]

Paragraph 162 (1944 regulations) instituted the formal use of execution: "repression and coercion and if necessary, extermination of the political enemy is conducted in the uncompromising and brutal manner typical of any war." The execution of people occurred in the same area but under different circumstances. Public executions usually involved death by hanging with the bodies left dangling from trees, lampposts, makeshift gallows, and even balconies. The bandits killed in action were not guaranteed a quick death. "Finishing off" (*erledigt*) was a common remark in many field reports. Search-and-destroy missions usually involved people collected in a community hall or church, the building was then set on fire and the victims burned to death, while the SS-Police gathered around to ensure no one escaped. Jews were killed as a matter of course when discovered during Bandenbekämpfung conducted by the Wehrmacht or the SS. Taking control (*überholen*) of a "bandit-suspicious" village required experience, and the SD and GFP were the acknowledged experts in this task. The "bandit helpers" were identified, usually by informants, and arrested. The complete deportation of a village became the most appropriate action if "bandit helpers" were repeatedly found in a village. The "special treatment" of a community involved certain rules. The SS-Police leader gave the orders for *Kollektivmassnahmen* against a village, including burning it down. Bach-Zelewski confirmed the form of destruction:

> The village was suddenly surrounded and without warning the police gathered the inhabitants into the village square. In the presence of the local mayor, persons not essential for the local farms and industry were immediately taken off to collection points for transfer to Germany.[25]

## Operations and Survey Officer (Ia): Ernst Korn

In the SS alphabet, "a" did not come before "c." The Ic was the most important staff officer after the COS and next came the operations mandarin. "I had to work on the great, large 'bandit-maps' which I myself had to draw up," Bach-Zelewski mentioned to his interrogators, "and which during the daily situation discussions with the Führer had to be presented to him by Himmler."[26] A few pages that have survived from the operational officer (Ia) war diary (*Kriegstagebuch*) briefly cover the period June 1943 to March 1944. The primary concerns of the section during this time were locating suitable quarters and staffing needs. Initially, part of the section was placed with the KSRFSS in Grossgarten, on August 15, 1943. New staffs were placed in small offices in Kruglanken, but not until October 7, 1943, did the department finally move into a single barracks.[27] By mid July, another four map draftsmen and a statistician joined the department. On June 21, 1943, Oberstleutnant Korn became the director of statistics and maps (*Amt für Statistik und Kartographie*) in the staff of the Ch.BKV under Himmler's direct orders. Korn, his assistant Leutnant Steudle, and a map draftsman were to conduct graphical and statistical assessments of the campaign's successes. In addition to adding details to the maps of Bandentätigkeit and the Bandenlage, they were to create a data bank of maps and statistics of criminals (*Kartothek*), statistics of agricultural produce, and a registration of labor (*Erfassungen von Arbeitskräften*). On October 11, 1943, the department of statistics was renamed Operations Assessments, Ia/Mess (*Messungen*).

The Ia/Mess officer worked primarily on cartographic-based analyses. Alongside the final reports of the operations, a large maps atlas that identified every movement was drawn. This was intensive work. By the end of August, a new work roster was introduced as the first department was divided into Operations and Intelligence. The new sections were allocated new draftsmen, and from October 1943, the operational draftsmen were separated from the mapmakers. The SS-Police leaders were provided with twenty-five thousand examples from 1 to 200,000-scale and 1 to 300,000-scale maps. On September 3, 1943, they began to enter geo-references into the analysis maps. Operation

"Heinrich" had developed such proportions that on October 25, a further three draftsmen were allocated from the command staff to support drawing tasks. By the end of October, German mapmakers had produced 1 to 200,000-scale ordinance maps for use in the Carpathians, Styria (HSSPF Alpenland), Croatia, and Serbia. From November 11, 1943, the teams began work on creating the blueprint for a 1 to 300,000-scale map to allow Himmler and Bach-Zelewski to conduct strategic analysis. That same month, the department received statistical material from the Office of the Four-Year Plan to conduct further research. In March 1944, all the HSSPFs of occupied Eastern Europe and Russia received "bandit" grid maps. These maps were used to plot partisans' movements with grid references that corresponded with Banden-kampfverbände headquarters. In March 1944, the BdOs were instructed to report according to grid reference agreed with the Luftwaffe-net on 1 to 200,000-scale maps. To create uniform reports, a report grid (*Meldegitter*) was established that covered HSSPF Russia-North, Russia-Centre, Russia-South, Ostland, Königsberg, Danzig, and Breslau. The maps were issued in the field, and a report grid was overlaid on the maps to allow units to make their reports in the field from agreed reference points to speed up the process of recognition. On March 12, 1944, the office presented Himmler with the finished atlas: a compilation of Bandenbekämpfung operation maps for 1943.

## The Order of Battle

The concentration of security forces had been a problem for the Germans since 1941. The desired level of total occupation security was impossible to achieve with only a partial occupation of Soviet Russia. The rear-area armies had failed to impose order, while the security divisions had lacked the flexibility in fighting power and the SS-Police battalions and regiments were too small and thinly spread. The introduction of Directive 46 stipulated the allocation and, to a certain extent, the concentration of security forces. This involved the deployment of the SS, the army, the Luftwaffe, the Reserve Army (*Ersatzheer*), and civilian organizations to a common purpose unusual for German regulations. The most significant structural changes caused by the directive were borne by the Reserve Army. This homeland command was responsible for mobilization, replacements, and training. The establishment was known as the military districts system (Wehrkreis), based in the German *Länder*. The rear-area armies were reorganized and renamed. The rear-area army of Army Group Centre became Wehrmachtbefehl-shaber Weissruthenien and received a total manpower displacement of 37,640 men, which was reduced to 30,609 in April 1944.[28] According to one report from February 1944, the Oberfeldkommandantur 400 deployed three security regiments indicating the dispersal of security forces into the communities.[29] The directive also ordered the Reserve Army to detail soldiers and units under training to the east and to release reserve divisions for security zone duties. This dramatically reduced the age of the troops committed to security.[30] After the war, a senior officer commented, "The reserve division was however made up of younger, more dynamic men. Their enthusiasm made up for their lack of experience. Their time on duty (reservists) was between two and three months."[31] OKH and the Reserve Army had also extended the Wehrkreis system into the occupied or annexed territories, including Wehrkreis-XX (Danzig) and XXI (Posen), Wehrkreis-General Government, Wehrkreis XVIII (Salzburg), and Wehrkreis-Bohemia and Moravia (Prague), in effect extending German borders through the presence of military organizations.

## Himmler's HSSPF Empire

By 1943, Himmler's interpretation of the Staatsschutzkorps seemed to have encompassed classical paradigms. He adapted the ancient Roman system of securing empire through rigid centralization and a network of regional power centers. The three key features of the Roman system were the emperor, his regional representative, and the legion. Himmler imitated this system through his HSSPF system, strengthened by SS-Police troops. The June order designated each HSSPF, within an occupied zone, to receive an Order Police regiment. These regiments were similar to those of the Roman legion; both were lightly armed but more powerful than the bands they were expected to combat. The legions were highly maneuverable, the professional backbone of a military organization that also relied on foreign auxiliaries and the centralization of support weapons. In ancient times, the legion served as a political tool of conquest, pacification, Romanization, and the maintenance of law. The SS system performed in the same way for Lebensraum, with pacification, Germanization, and imposition of German rule. The legions policed the empire through a two-tier frontier system that distinguished between the unsettled eastern provinces along the Rhine and the colonized southern territories. The SS lacked the time of the Romans but the impression they have left represents a caricature of antiquity. Lawrence Keppie has suggested the Roman system worked well for two centuries; Himmler expected his system to last a thousand years.[32]

Individually, the three HSSPF in Russia led large formations, but their respective organizational structures were very different. The HSSPF Russia-North, under SS-Obergruppenführer Friedrich Jeckeln, organized a highly regimented structure. The total forces under Jeckeln's command, in October 1942, were 4,428 Germans and 55,562 Schutzmannschaft, of whom 23,758 were serving with Schuma battalions.[33] HSSPF Russia-South came under the command of SS-Obergruppenführer Hans-Adolf Prützmann and was a particularly large region. The establishment was organized bureaucratically but suffered under continual border changes. Prützmann's forces in November 1942, mustered 4,228 German police troops and 15,665 Ukrainian Schuma forces in battalions and regiments; there were a further 5,966 German gendarmerie and 55,094

Ukrainian Hilfspolizei and part-time guards.[34] Eventually, this region raised more than sixty Schuma battalions of at least thirty thousand men, and by July 1943, it commanded thirty-five thousand German police troops. The HSSPF Russia-Centre, the most unstable organization, one that lagged behind other SS security structures, turned out to be the most effective model of Bandenbekämpfung. This region had suffered the most war damage, killing, and exploitation, as Christian Gerlach revealed.[35]

### Table 5.1: Prützmann's Formations*

| SS-Police Regiments | Central Formations | Gendarmerie |
|---|---|---|
| Police Regiment "Gieseke" | 268th Landesschützen Police Battalion | 16 gendarmerie troops (motorized) |
| 37th Police Defense Regiment | Police Landesschützen Battalion *Jehne* | 15 gendarmerie troops (motorized) |
| 35th Police Defense Regiment | | 55 gendarmerie troops (motorized) |
| 33rd Police Defense Regiment | | 3 gendarmerie troops (motorized) |
| 10th Police Regiment | 81st Police Signals Company | 41 gendarmerie troops (motorized) |
| 4th SS-Police Regiment | 83rd Police Signals Company | 51 gendarmerie troops (motorized) |
| 11th SS-Police Regiment | 121st Police Signals Company | 5 gendarmerie troops (motorized) |
| 22nd SS-Police Regiment | | 61 gendarmerie troops (motorized) |
| | Police Cavalry Detachment I | 60 gendarmerie troops (motorized) |
| Tank-hunting company | Police Cavalry Detachment II | 1 gendarmerie troops (motorized) |
| (4th SS-Police Regiment) | | 4 gendarmerie troops (motorized) |
| Heavy company | | 57 gendarmerie troops (motorized) |
| (11th SS-Police Regiment) | | 45 gendarmerie troops (motorized) |

* DDst, record cards of the Kampfgruppe Prützmann 1942–1944.

Himmler's September order stipulated that each HSSPF, in an area designated a Bandenkampfgebiet, was to raise a Kampfgruppe and a Bandenstab. Prützmann issued an example of the internal instructions on the formation of a Bandenstab. His instructions itemized seven points that opened with his justification for doing something this time under Directive 46, the Kampfanweisung of November 11, 1942, and Himmler's orders. In the second and third points, Prützmann's appraisal was for the staff to conduct a thorough analysis of "bandit" combat. The staffs were to introduce protocols for analyses, preparations, plans, and command chains. This "leadership staff" was to enhance the SS-Police command system. In point 4, Prützmann listed ten officers and their jobs. The top three positions followed the known pattern of SS and police staffing: Oberstleutnant der Polizei Engelhaupt was chief of staff, SS-Obersturmführer Schmitz was the Ic, and the Ia was Hauptmann der Polizei Schaufler. There were liaison officers to HSSPF Northeast: Reichskommissar Koch, the Wehrmacht commander in the Ukraine to HSSPF Russia-Centre, and an unnamed officer from the Wehrmacht Ukraine command staff. The next three points explained that assistants would be assigned to field operations located from among available police troops. Prützmann ordered that cooperation with the HSSPF Russia-Centre be conducted without complications. He also explained that Bomhard, the former chief of staff of the Order Police, was assigned to undertake Bandenbekämpfung operations.[36]

## Central and Technical Formations

Signals officers from the army, the SS, the railways, the Luftwaffe, and civilian authorities achieved the highest form of cooperation. After the war, while under interrogation, Karl Wolff was questioned regarding how the SS officers involved in extermination received their orders. His response was, "Whatever these persons had to do with each other was always taken care of by telephone."[37] Through the employment of liaison officers and the telecommunications network, Himmler was able to control his organization very effectively. The British made a study of this system after the war.[38] In 1938, the police constructed an integrated telegraph and radio network. The majority of its operators were women under the command of an inspector-grade police officer.[39] The commander of signals was Generalmajor der Polizei Robert Schlake, who also held the rank of SS-Standartenführer. By June 1941, this network had expanded into a complex structure finally completed in May 1942.[40] The network depended on large transmitters of 20 kilowatts, located in Berlin. Each regional center had a radio station (*Funkstelle*) that used an 800-watt machine and 5-kilowatt machines with ranges of up to 1,000 kilometers. The local stations (*Leitfunkstellen*) used 100-watt transmitters with ranges of up to 100 to 150 kilometers. The Leitfunkstellen and the Funkstellen could cross-communicate within a region. As telephone cables came increasingly under attack through bombing or the partisans, the radio transmitters were sometimes the only form of telecommunications. The radios used both long- and short-wave frequencies, and in the field, officers carried short-wave radio sets, known as tank sets (*Panzergeräte*). The army supplied 10- to 20-watt-powered, voice-operated sets, requiring the minimum of training and pedal-power. The Water Police (*Wasserschutzpolizei*) had special 15-watt sets built into their patrol boats. Mobile communications were organized into companies for battalions and battalions for regiments. The police used radio vans (*Funkwagen*), which were originally designed for emergencies in the cities but which proved valuable in field operations. The motorized gendarmerie used voice-operated sets with a range of up to 150 kilometers. Eventually, the SS-Police regiments, formed from 1942, received a signals company of sixty to seventy men, deployed in close proximity to the commander and staff.[41]

The armored trains (*Panzerzug*) came within the military railway system, under the chief of transportation, and were regarded as critical in Bandenbekämpfung with the emphasis on railway security. The railways formed a unique role within German military traditions: they were the basis of the Etappe system and the single feature of occupation from 1871 to 1945. There were eighty-five armored trains in one configuration or another, with three regimental staffs and a headquarters command.[42] The armored trains were employed in large operations and in independent combat missions within enemy territory, for artillery support and participation in rapid-reaction operations requiring armored cars, an infantry platoon, mortars, and the engineer soldiers.[43] They were deployed to prevent partisans from escaping across railway lines. The radio and signals equipment made armored trains particularly suited for headquarters functions and for serving as the command staff in large operations. They also carried out small and independent security sweeps. The Germans believed they were effective in keeping "bandits" in a permanent state of "nervousness" through their reconnaissance and ambush patrols. Their duties included convoy guard, replacing crews in strongpoints, evacuating wounded, aiding damaged trains, bringing medical assistance, relieving stations under attack, securing construction sites and labor, and distributing propaganda material along the line.

During the July 16, 1941, meeting discussed in chapter 2, Göring suggested the Junkers JU52 transport planes could be configured as bombers to attack the partisans, just as they had been in Spain. The Luftwaffe ground attack airplanes were the Henschel HS126, Junkers JU87, and the Henschel HS129. These airplanes achieved a fearsome reputation for inflicting destruction and panicking civilian refugees. The most important airplane to Bandenbekämpfung was the close liaison Fieseler Fi156, designated Storch (Stork). Designed in 1935, the Storch first saw operational service with the Legion Kondor in Spain. William Green described the special features of this monoplane, which included its high degree of cockpit visibility and the special undercarriage to absorb the shock of short stretch landings from "high vertical descent rates."[44] The few Luftwaffe records to survive the war indicate that the 54th Fighter Group flew round-the-clock missions on the Eastern Front, against partisans. In one report from July 8, 1942, the flyers in fighter-bombers were ordered to angle their bombing precisely. The type of bombs included the single 50- and 10-kilogram fragmentation antipersonnel bombs (*Splitterbomben*).[45]

The Luftwaffe conducted interdiction, strafing, and close air support and also supplied signals and communications monitoring capabilities. Bombing was recommended against fortified strongpoints and camps and to break-up strong concentrations of partisans (*Bandenansammlungen*). In cases in which the "bandits" had only weak anti-aircraft capability, the air force flew strafing attacks against "living targets" (*lebende Ziele*). Dropping propaganda material by air was assumed the best means for turning the population against the bands. All aircrew were instructed to fly with hand weapons to help evade capture and almost certain execution in case of being shot down. Employing parachute troops or air landing forces to encircle the "bandits" or box them in was accepted in special cases.[46]

Cooperation between ground and air forces was also heavily emphasized in the Bandenbekämpfung regulations of 1944. Points 129–139 explained close support from the air force. The physical use of air assets in security operations has received little attention in the copious histories of the Luftwaffe.[47] The guidelines for liaison between ground troops and the air force in Bandenbekämpfung were collected in instructional pamphlets titled "Cooperation Air Force-Army on the Battlefield" (*Zusammenarbeit Luftwaffe-Heer auf dem Gefechtsfeld*). Gerhard Weinberg identified the influence of the Luftwaffe in operations and, in particular, interdiction raids against the bands.[48] For the Luftwaffe, rapidly free-falling into decline, the introduction of Directive 46 was opportune.[49] Tactical air support, in the form of ground-to-air liaison, had been fundamental to mechanized Cannae.[50] German prowess in tactical operations and especially the coordination of combined arms were refined during the Spanish civil war. The German expeditionary force, the Legion Kondor, was an integrated Kampfgruppe of bomber squadrons, armored units, and signals troops.[51] In operational methods, air superiority was regarded as a prerequisite for close liaison operations. The Germans facilitated air-to-ground communications allowing instructions to pass between ground troops and fliers. Luftwaffe liaison officers took to the air to coordinate the signals and strike missions. They mapped and identified the partisans, marked them with colored flares or smoke markers, and directed air strikes.

Airpower granted the SS-Police an advanced capability originally explored in Prussia through the Inspectorate of Flying Troops (*Inspektion der Fliegertruppen*), in August 1919. The Prussian police flying squadron (*Polizeifliegerstaffeln*) began operations with 11 officers, and 106 NCOs and men, and 27 airplanes. They were based in Berlin with outposts in Königsberg, Brieg, Paderborn, and Gotha. The Security Police formed detachments and from their coastline bases operated flying boats. The mission of the Air Police (*Luftpolizei*) was to conduct reconnaissance patrols over the communications network, to participate in combat missions providing morale for the police forces on the ground, to undertake propaganda missions (leafleting, etc.), and to coordinate liaison between different units during an operation. It also worked for the criminal police and the marine police in combating smuggling, solving serious cases of criminal banditry, and hunting escaped prisoners and murderers. In 1920, this service briefly expanded, as was recorded in the diary of Polizei-Hauptmann Erhard Milch, later secretary of state and Luftwaffe field marshal.[52] However, the Allies imposed the Versailles restrictions on the police squadron and forced its disbandment. The police attempted to camouflage the aircraft across Germany. The force survived in a piecemeal format through civilian airplanes until Daluege resurrected the squadron. In 1941, the senior SS-Police commanders used light airplanes to increase their operational capability during Operation "Barbarossa."

In August 1942, discussions were initiated between Himmler and Göring over the centralization of all aircraft under the Luftwaffe, following a rationalization proposal by Unruh. In recompense, Göring offered Himmler support for new aviation missions. This proved to be a weak promise; Himmler was able to acquire a new Fieseler Storch for the new HSSPF Caucasus, but when he requested a Junkers JU52 for flying in poor weather, Göring refused because of the shortages. Only travel space on an airplane could be guaranteed.[53] A decoded message from August 1942 confirmed that the 7th Special Flying Group (Fliegergruppe z.b.V. 7) was transferred to the Luftwaffe. The known structure of the 7th Special Flying Group was its headquarters in East Prussia in Marienwerder (Malbork: Poland) and squadrons (*Staffeln*) dispersed to Cracow, Riga, Minsk, Radzwillow, Agram, Ljubljana, Cottbus, and Oslo. Little is known of its history although considerable reference to its operations can be found in police radio signals intercepted by the British.[54]

The orders for the subordination and operations of the 7th Special Flying Group were issued by Himmler in September 1943. Himmler stated that Bandenbekämpfung and the enlargement of his command into the south and southeast led him to issue these orders. The 7th Special Flying Group came under his direct command; its commander joined his staff. It had certain prescribed objectives to fulfill. The subordination of the flying group to an HSSPF during a reconnaissance or combat operation depended on the Ch.BKV. The concentration of several squadrons within a single operation also depended on the Ch.BKV. Larger transport and reconnaissance planes were set aside for use by main offices and senior commanders. One courier plane was kept at the Lötzen headquarters of the KSRFSS at all times. Himmler's control over the use of the planes was an attempt to restrict them from private use in order to conserve fuel. On the fifth day of each month, the commander of the flying group was to submit a complete log of flights, with details, to the KSRFSS. The flying group was reorganized to maintain its capacity in Bandenbekämpfung, hence the expansion of squadrons in the east and southeast of Europe.[55]

The offices of the RFSS, the CdO, the CdS, and the Ch.BKV each received a Junkers JU52. Each HSSPF was assigned a liaison plane, Storch, while each BdS and BdO within that command shared a Storch. The 7th Special Flying Group eventually moved to Strausberg near Berlin, where the senior's aircraft were maintained and the special duties planes working out of Lötzen (Fi156) were controlled, under the orders of the central offices (four planes, including the FW58) and for training purposes (three Fi156). Some areas like HSSPF Russia-Centre and the other Russian based HSSPFs received an FW58 utility airplane, which could be employed in reconnaissance as well as bombing strikes. The first squadron was based in Kraków, Poland, with eight airplanes; the second squadron was based in Riga, with seven aircraft; the 3rd Staffel was based in Minsk with thirteen aircraft. One airplane (Hs126) was a glider tug for covert operations. Three FW189 were used for reconnaissance and bombing, and five Fi156 were assigned to Bandenbekämpfung. The 4th Staffel was based in Rovno with fifteen airplanes.[56] The expected order of battle for the 7th Special Flying Group was to raise its firepower and standardize the machines. The Staffel were renumbered and were to carry nine airplanes. The 8th Staffel (Minsk) received ten JU87 Stuka airplanes with long towing cables for pulling DFS 230 gliders.[57]

Himmler lost control of the fleet in May 1944 and was obliged to issue further instructions on the use of aircraft. He stated that Göring had ordered a reduction in air operations and that this had been communicated to the HSSPFs. He then pointed out that the *Oberkommando der Luftwaffe* (OKL) had placed checks on fuel usage. He demanded that airplanes be used only in Bandenbekämpfung. Alternatives of motor and railway transportation were to replace the use of airplanes. All flights were to be monitored and examined by Luftwaffe personnel. The control of air missions was confined to the decision of the 7th Special Flying Group's commander.[58]

Covert operations were not new to the SS. In August 1939, they staged a Polish attack against the Gleiwitz radio station before the invasion of Poland.[59] In 1943, SS-Gruppenführer Walter Schellenberg was typical of the youthful, intelligent, and highly motivated SD officers. He came under Heydrich's influence and became the "young Turk" of the SS intelligence faction. He was party to the Heydrich-Wagner agreement that was central to the illegal "Barbarossa" directives. He formed Operation "Zeppelin" (UZ) as a covert RSHA counterintelligence initiative to infiltrate trusties behind Russian lines and within the bands. The British learned all about UZ operations and their commander never realized their secrecy was breached. Alan Bullock once wrote of *The Schellenberg Memoirs* (1956) that, if nothing else, it made a good spy story. Recently, the subject was raised in an article by Perry Biddiscombe focusing on the clandestine activities of spying and sabotage missions.[60] Following the assassination of Heydrich, Schellenberg appears to have stayed in contact with Himmler, awaiting a new boss. Kaltenbrunner proved a disappointment, and Schellenberg had a rocky relationship with him. Kaltenbrunner encouraged Skorzeny to undermine and irritate the upstart intelligence officer at every opportunity. In the last days of the war, Kaltenbrunner succeeded in removing Schellenberg from office, but it was a hollow victory. Schellenberg and other SD evidence presented at Nuremberg contributed to Kaltenbrunner's sentence and execution for war crimes.[61]

Bach-Zelewski and Schellenberg formed a working relationship and met on several occasions. According to Bach-Zelewski's diary, they first met on November 25, 1942, to discuss the subject of trusties.[62] From March 1942, UZ came to play a significant part in the counter-espionage activities of Bandenbekämpfung. The plan behind Zeppelin was to place German agents who were natives in the partisan bands. Each HSSPF in Russia received a detachment of UZ. They worked closely with the Luftwaffe pilots who flew them into drop zones behind the Red Army lines.[63] UZ operations fell between the formation of yet another private army and genuine counterintelligence work. This is confirmed by the rather strange case of the Druzhina I and Druzhina II. The former was a group of former Red Army POWs, trusted to return, and employed in Bandenbekämpfung operations within the German rear area. The latter was a group trusted to conduct subversion operations behind the Russian lines. Colonel Rodionov (known as "Gil") commanded Druzhina I, which gradually grew to battalion size. Deployed under HSSPF Russia-Centre, the formation joined Gottberg's order of battle. In the summer of 1943, they turned on their erstwhile SS comrades, killing more than sixty before deserting back to the Soviets.[64] On June 8, 1943, British codebreakers intercepted an SD signal: "Von dem Bach is informed by RSHA Amt A that the Russian officers company of UZ, Amt VI C Z with 125 Russian officers is ready to set out. Von dem Bach is to inform them of their destination."[65] That same month, Rodionov and Gottberg held further discussion in Berlin, a few days after Bach-Zelewski's promotion. They met on August 21, 1943, to discuss large-scale operations behind Russian front lines.

Bach-Zelewski at various times led troops under his personal command. In 1941, his Police Regiment Centre carried three battalions and numerous support troops. He was granted the support of the SS brigades to conduct the killing actions in Russia. In 1942, his authority progressed into brigade command with several regiments. By 1943, he was leading Korpsgruppe von dem Bach of several brigades and ancillary troops. By 1944, his command authority included corps and divisions. Bach-Zelewski's expertise was not leading troops into combat but coordinating and handling operations, some with complicated configuration.

The SS Special Forces deployed in operations were a direct contradiction to the rules and regulations of Bandenbekämpfung. The Dirlewanger formation, variously called a *Sonderkommando*, *Sondebataillon*, regiment, brigade, and later division, was the most significant unit of the Banden-kampfverbände.[66] In March 1940, Hitler agreed that convicted poachers should be employed in security duties. The Reich minister of justice relocated prison inmates found guilty of poaching to this unit. In 1944, 94 percent of the unit was other prisoners and SS men serving penal sentences.[67] It has often been assumed that Himmler had a widespread policy of using prison manpower; however, in terms of the Waffen-SS, the case of Dirlewanger was an exception, and mostly confined to the central theater of Russia.[68] With some sense of irony, Hans-Peter Klausch found that after the bomb plot in 1944, when Himmler took command of the Replacement Army, soldiers and civilians found guilty of being members of the resistance by the People's Court were sent to the Dirlewanger Brigade. Hitler agreed with Himmler in the development of this formation, as he admitted over dinner in September 1942. By suppressing the poachers and sending them to counter the "bandits," not only did it appear to

Hitler that SS policy was serving a dual purpose, but it also seemed the resulting formation would be a corps of sharpshooters. [69] The record of the formation in hunting "bandits" was exceptional; it was an execution brigade.

Skorzeny's idea for his specialist unit, the SS-Sonderverbände Friedenthal, was to employ criminals serving severe prison sentences. Skorzeny painted a false picture of his unit's organization as the product of the Waffen-SS and the efforts of Hans Jüttner. The reality behind Skorzeny and his "legion" was murky, a lurid tale involving the SS-Totenkopfverbände, the RSHA, and Buchenwald concentration camp. He began raising the unit three months to the day of joining the RSHA. A few documents from the selection process remain in Skorzeny's SS personnel file. One trail indicates the involvement of the SS legal office, under SS-Gruppenführer Bender, and Himmler in the "acquisition" of "volunteers." [70] The men were all long-term prisoners, dishonorably discharged from the SS and serving sentences of hard labor in concentration camps. The first wave of "volunteers" were collected at a training ground in Berlin, part of the depot complex of Adolf Hitler's bodyguard regiment. The men were held under strict control, and the slightest infraction of discipline led to their return to prison. As a temporary expediency, they continued to wear SS insignia, which was removed before combat. The men had already forfeited SS membership, and Himmler would not allow their reinstatement after the war, even if they distinguished themselves. [71] In other words, the men had only a second chance for survival.

Skorzeny was not competing with Dirlewanger although the recruitment of felons and criminals made it appear that way. Himmler held the final decision over postings and did not appear to favor competition to Dirlewanger. Among the cases from Skorzeny's file is Hans Amman, a former SS-Obersturmführer. Thirty-two years old, Amman was first sentenced to death for stealing twenty-eight bottles of champagne that were intended for the wounded of in an SS field hospital. Then his sentence was reduced to fifteen years. Dietrich Nernhardt, a cashiered SS officer, organized the black-market supply of wood in Norway; he was serving a four-year prison sentence since 1942. Andreas Daross, another former SS-Obersturmführer, received a sentence of ten years imprisonment by the SS court of the General Government of Poland. While assigned to an SS courier section, he was discovered "plundering" comrades' personal effects. The other recruits had been involved in cruelty, racketeering petrol, and bringing women into the operational zone. However, two "volunteers" particularly stand out. Hans Steinfurth was a thirty-six-year-old criminal commissioner and SS official. In 1941, while serving in Brünn (Austria), he employed a Jewish baker called Weiss as a Gestapo trusty. Weiss volunteered to conduct investigations into secret finance and the business activities of the Jewish community but also proved duplicitous, taking protection money. Weiss used the money to entertain the SS with drinking binges and orgies. Weiss's punishment remains unknown, but

Steinfurth received a fourteen-year sentence with hard labor. Finally, there was the case of Karl Gebauer, a twenty-year-old SS-Oberjunker from the Waffen-SS. During a Banden-bekämpfung operation in Croatia, in 1943, he and an unnamed SS-Unter-sturmführer, both drunk, attempted to rape a thirty-one-year-old woman. Only briefly foiled, Gebauer moved on to another family and raped their seventeen-year-old daughter in front of her parents. He received a ten-year prison sentence.[72] Himmler assigned Gebauer to Skorzeny; the others were posted to the Dirlewanger Brigade.[73]

## The Combat Formations

There is always a danger when placing elite troops in a position of guardianship over occupied indigenous populations. The Waffen-SS was responsible for many atrocities; they brought their unique combat experience to Bandenbekämpfung. George Stein concluded that the Waffen-SS was a tarnished shield because of its war crimes. He thought the men responsible for the antipartisan campaign did not represent the essence of the Waffen-SS.[74] Bernd Wegner attributed this behavior to the doctrine of destruction the Waffen-SS followed. These political soldiers lived and existed in the belief that they were a "revolutionary fighting order" (*Kampfgemeinschaft*).[75] In the investment of Bandenbekämpfung, Himmler could only call on the limited availability of his elite Waffen-SS divisions. During "Barbarossa," the SS-Police forces were bolstered by Waffen-SS reserves organized into three Waffen-SS brigades. In 1942, a dual process of reorganization began turning the Waffen-SS regiments and brigades into divisions, while the Order Police battalions were turned into regiments and specialists. On July 13, 1942, the Waffen-SS chief of staff, Hans Jüttner, published the Waffen-SS reserve muster order.[76] Himmler had charged Jüttner, with increasing and reinforcing the Waffen-SS order of battle. Jüttner combined the functions of COS, ordnance and equipment, field supplies and raising troops into Waffen-SS orders of battle, and forming of new units. Jüttner had also been quasi-operations officer behind the SS countermeasures in Czechoslovakia during the state of emergency in 1941 and had reported the success of security operations to Himmler.[77]

The role of the cavalry was quite extensive in Bandenbekämpfung. The SS-Cavalry Brigade became the SS-Cavalry Division Florian Geyer and was placed under the command of combat-experienced Waffen-SS officers. Between June 1942 and May 1943, its command passed from Hermann Fegelein to Wilhelm Bittrich.[78] Once the partisans employed heavy weapons, the cavalry division received artillery and an antitank detachment. This turned the division into a nineteenth-century cavalry formation and an advanced mechanized division of modern warfare—mounted troopers riding into combat with self-propelled guns and armored fighting vehicles. The Cossacks raised many formations, and in February 1944, the SS began reforming its brigades. Two regiments remained, but supporting units and the size of independent cavalry

detachments were decreased.[79] This was yet another reversal of a Hitler announcement, "*We must never permit anybody but the Germans to carry arms!*
*. . .* Only the German may carry arms, not the Slav, not the Czech, not the
Cossack nor the Ukrainian!"[80] In February 1943, the infantry elements from
the KSRFSS were formed into an assault brigade (*Sturmbrigade*) Reichsführer-
SS. The SS Operational Headquarters recorded its actual strength at 112 officers, 612 NCOs, and 3,500 men, while the operational or fighting strength was
94 officers, 438 NCOs, 2,168 men, 70 Italian auxiliaries, and 5 ethnic German
NCOs. The brigade eventually became the 16th SS-Division Reichsführer-SS,
and its final complement was 50 percent volunteers, 50 percent conscripts of
German, Austrian, and ethnic descent.[81] In January 1944, the 1st SS-Infantry
Brigade became the 18th SS-Panzer Grenadier Division Horst Wessel. The
infantry brigade still commanded two regiments, the 8th and 10th. The 8th SS-
Infantry regiment was composed of 30 percent volunteers, 50 percent conscripts, and 20 percent Rumanian ethnic German conscripts. The 10th was
comprised of 30 percent conscripts, 40 percent conscripted ethnic Germans,
and 30 percent Germans.[82]

In February 1942, Himmler issued a general order that redesignated the
police regiments into "SS-Police Regiments."[83] These were assembled into
fixed formations using existing police battalions from July 1942 onward.[84]
Twenty-eight regiments were formed, including the 18th SS-Police Mountain
Regiment. The British codebreakers were quick to acknowledge the impact of
this change: "Evidence from Russia and from Holland and Norway suggests
that all Police Battalions will in future be grouped under Regiments, which will
be numbered serially through the Reich and Occupied territories."[85] In January 1943, Daluege presented what proved to be his last annual report on the
Order Police. The fighting contingent of the police represented approximately
15 percent of the overall number. The actual police component was about
180,000 of which 132,000 were reservists, boosted by 301,000 collaboration
auxiliaries. Another 25,000 police were committed to the Wehrmacht, the GFP,
or the Waffen-SS Polizei Division. Daluege announced the total casualties
sustained in 1942 as 5,012 dead, 9,389 wounded, and 251 held as prisoners of
war.[86] According to Georg Tessin, the full complement of the Ordnungspolizei
in 1942 was 276,000 with a Hilfspolizei of 1,991,500.[87] The final accounting for
the 1943 Schutzpolizei complement stood at 117,053 and for 1944 was 126,404.[88]
After a disastrous winter, Himmler was forced to raise more regiments.[89] The
Chef der Ordnungspolizei (CdO) also raised four police rifle regiments. The
commander of 31st Police Rifle Regiment, Oberst der Schutzpolizei Hannibal,
was a senior Hamburg police officer who later formed his own Kampfgruppe.[90]
To compensate for its lack of antitank weapons, the SS-Police raised armored
companies (*Polizei-Panzerkompanien*), which were supplied with captured
tanks and tank-hunting companies (*Polizei-Panzerjäger-Kompanien*) and
trained to use antitank weapons and artillery. A Police Tank Reserve Battalion

was based in Vienna with a strength of eighteen officers and 137 men. Their vehicles included seven French armored cars, eight French tanks, and five Russian tanks including a T-34.[91] In 1944, Bach-Zelewski took control of powerful siege artillery. During the defensive fighting in Kovel (discussed in chapter 8), Bach-Zelewski received armored assault artillery. In the pacification of the Warsaw Uprising in 1944, his special units included flamethrowers, siege mortars for destroying fortifications, armored trains, and tanks.

In September 1942, Daluege issued a standing order for the formation of police guard battalions (*Polizei-Wach-Bataillonen*). This order reflected the new conditions of Bandenbekämpfung and Himmler's regimentation of the Order Police.[92] According to Daluege, the new battalions stood alongside existing police formations as "an alert and elastic in resolving critical war shortages."[93] On September 17, 1942, in line with these reforms, the home police organization was rationalized. The balance between police officials (*Verwaltungspolizei*), security police, and Order Police was reset. As a consequence of the reforms, the manpower surplus from the Verwaltungspolizei was redirected toward policing the occupied zones. The numbers involved fourteen hundred officials and were regarded as significant in 1942.[94]

The Schuma battalions were even more lightweight than the police battalions. In a report from 1943, Daluege justified employment of this force on the grounds of the onerous tasks placed on the Order Police.[95] By this time, the Schuma represented a major factor in Himmler's human resource pool. Over the period of the war, 158 Schuma battalions were raised in the Baltic States, twenty-three in Russia-Centre, sixty-five in the Ukraine, and eleven in the General Government of Poland. Total police troops in 1943 were 181,412, with 117,053 from the Schupo, 49,075 gendarmerie, and the Schuma at 150,000, while volunteers from Italy had raised 100,000, in Croatia 30,000, and Holland 22,000. Tessin estimated that an overall force of 650,000 came under Order Police control, which, if the Hilfspolizei are included, increased the manpower upward to 3,500,000.[96] The Schuma formations came under Daluege's recommendations for the German police battalions in 1942, with a motor-vehicle pool and provision for three armored cars. In terms of firepower, all Schuma battalions were to be fully equipped with infantry field guns, heavy and medium machine guns, and mortars.[97] A report from February 1, 1944, concerned the Ukrainian 204th Schuma Battalion, which was comprised 32 officers (8 Germans), 8 officials (2 German), 232 troopers (58 Germans), 16 translators, and 8 drivers. The German cadre was collected in Wehrkreis XII and organized through BdO Wiesbaden. The men came from the 1896 intake and were not older than forty-eight years old in 1944. Throughout February 1944, the BdO Ostland worked to increase the numbers of German cadres in the Schuma.[98]

Several crossover formations combined elements of the Waffen-SS with the SS-Police. In March 1943, the Waffen-SS raised Ukrainian volunteers for a division. According to Michael Logusz, the initiative for the 14th Waffen-SS

Grenadier Division Galician came from the district governor of Galicia, Dr. Wächter. On March 14, 1943, Wächter discussed the idea with Himmler in Berlin. Following brief correspondence, in which the twin priorities of raising manpower and gathering in the annual harvest were pointed out by Himmler to Wächter, Hitler authorized a Galician (but not a Ukrainian) SS division to be financed through the state of Galicia. The division was to be infantry rather than a police formation. For assistance, Himmler recommended Wächter, Berger, and Krüger in the organizational arrangements. Wächter moved fast and ignored requests by Himmler's adjutant Brandt to remain cautious (Brandt was probably cautious of the racial-political minefield that Wächter was entering).[99] The 14th Division absorbed the 4th and 5th SS-Police Regiments and initially fit the profile of the SS-Polizeiverbände structure rather than the Waffen-SS. On April 12, a conference hosted by Wächter to incorporate the division brought together an interesting group of SS grandees, including SS-Brigadeführer und Generalmajor der Polizei Joseph Stroop Generalleutnant Kurt Pfeffer-Wildenbruch (*Hauptamt Ordnungspolizei*) and the inspector of the colonial police department. Several Nazi Party functionaries and SS administrators assisted them. Recruits mustered through the existing collaboration system were 85 to 90 percent Ukrainian with a sprinkling of former Polish army officers. This entailed the release of men from labor assignment by agreement with local Nazi bosses, the police, and the army's agricultural offices. The expected time frame for the first units to receive volunteers was estimated by Pfeffer-Wildenbruch as May 15, 1943. SSPF Lemberg carried out the division's initial administration during induction.[100] Another crossover force was the Schutzmannschaft-Brigade Siegling, which became 30th Waffen Grenadier Division (*russische Nr.2*). It was formed from Belorussian Schuma battalions in January 1944. This division was commanded by SS-Police officers with Waffen-SS ranks and with a long period of service in Bandenbekämpfung. The division was raised in France, while its family members were housed in German cities.[101]

## The Commander's Influence

Since the war, Bach-Zelewski's command and leadership style has been derided and vilified because of his connection with extermination. However, during the war, he was promoted to high command. In theory, Himmler could have promoted any of his senior Waffen-SS officers to the Ch.BKV. There was confidence in Bach-Zelewski, and it came from other sources besides Hitler and Himmler. Along with a reputation for ruthlessness, he possessed security warfare skills in operations, leadership, and technique.

In 1943, Himmler stated that "the most important precondition[s] to combating the ways of the bandit are strong nerves, a fearless heart, the will and the capability to attack the enemy with very small forces and the necessity to maintain the initiative, rather than to leave it to the enemy, who are poorer quality." To remind the troops of the seriousness of failure he warned, "Cowards amongst the German ranks are to be treated like the bandit, killed."[102] Hitler included instructions to those who failed to carry out the Commando orders: "I will hold responsible under military law, for failing to carry out this order, all commanders and officers who either have neglected their duty of instructing the troops about this order or acted against this order where it was to be executed." The failure of even a non-commissioned officer to carry out these orders was to be reported.[103] In another document Hitler wrote, "I have been compelled to issue strict orders for the destruction of enemy sabotage troops and to declare non-compliance with these orders severely punishable."[104] Personal honor was to be a prerogative of the Bandenkampfverbände; a strong character was equated with being a true National Socialist. Lack of discipline or examples of ill discipline were regarded as personal flaws.

Bach-Zelewski's design for the fighting style of Bandenbekämpfung reflected his political and military experiences. He painted a relentless struggle in the 1944 regulations. The "bandits" had to be located, with hunting dogs, while engineers cleared mines and reconnaissance patrols located "bandit" camps. When engineers were not available, he recommended driving cattle ahead of the troops; there was no advice over what to do if there were no cattle. Deserters, POWs, and locals were to be employed as guides under guard. The troops were expected to undertake total security when entering villages or when hunting "bandits" in swamps, woods, and primeval forests. The troops had to be capable of beating the "bandits" in any environment. The 1944 regulations obliged soldiers to embrace the hardships common to the conflict. Additionally, they should be mobile. All motorized forces and units with pack animals had to employ speed to remain within possible reach of "bandits." The aim of these tactics was to bring combatants to decisive points in an operation, primed for action.

The guidelines for the infantry reflected Bach-Zelewski's military expertise. Because the infantry was the backbone of all military and security operations, Bach-Zelewski demanded superiority over the "bandits" in firefights through strict discipline because the "bandits" in their camouflaged positions presented only the briefest opportunity as a target. Fire discipline had to maintain the element of surprise and required rapidity and accuracy. Officers were warned to prevent random and careless shooting. The infantry was advised to employ support weapons to cover movements, to attack strongpoints, and during counterattacks. These support weapons had to be ready to fire and portable over difficult terrain. Fighting continued into the night. Bach-Zelewski expected the troops to avoid rest at night in villages and other equally "spoiled behavior." The preferred weapons for this "special kind of warfare" included small arms, machine pistols, sniper rifles, machine guns, automatic rifles, light and medium antitank guns, light infantry guns, and flamethrowers. Heavier weapons, such as artillery and anti-aircraft guns, were regarded as essential during blocking encirclement duties.[105] Evacuating wounded from the combat area was regarded as crucial to morale.

As operational commander, Bach-Zelewski was also responsible for the treatment of civilians and was assisted by economic experts. Civilians were taxed and registered, and all goods and produce of economic value in the community collected. Tactical collection teams (*Erfassungskommando*) were formed from among the troops. The registration of plunder was itemized in the 1944 regulations: "Everything, which can be used for our own war economy or is of any use to the bandits, must be removed." The collection operations imposed special security arrangements: "The transports of the registered goods as well as the assembly camps have to be protected . . . [and] the troop has to understand that accounted goods are not booty." The deportation collection camps (*Sammellager*) or depots (*Sammelplätze*) were to be erected prior to an operation and act as holding camps for persons rounded up for deportation to serve as labor in Germany. If the people from villages under suspicion of being partisan supporters survived police action, they were normally deported to Germany as slave labor. The order to remove produce was tempered by the overriding order that "Everything has to be given to the civilians necessary for their livelihood and for the cultivation of the country, if an area is to be permanently pacified." The Erfassungskommando was supposed to be trained in how to conduct this work professionally and was given the assistance of translators. To ensure success in operations, the Erfassungskommando was advised to gather the community leaders, including the mayor, the bookkeeper, or the headman of the village to assist and guide the collection process. The regulations stressed that these actions were a civil-police matter where civilian confidence in the police was determined by respect for the troops and should not cross the threshold of mutual necessity. The troops were warned against being lulled into a false sense of security (*Wachsamkeit einschläfern*). Any suspicious individuals (*verdächtigte Leute*), whether in civilian clothes or German uniform, were handed to the SD and GFP.

## Discipline

Omer Bartov has written of the "perversion of discipline" to explain how German military methods led to brutalizing Germany's own fighting force. Hitler feared a repeat of the breakdown in military discipline as occurred in 1918. Discipline was, according to Bartov, politicized to meet the demands of enhanced military capability and Nazi ideological goals but placed the troops in the difficult position of facing indefatigable commanders and an unbeatable enemy, and so resorted to violence against civilians and POWs.[106] The continuing drift toward brutal regulations was institutionalized through the Operation "Barbarossa" directives and on into the Bandenbekämpfung codes of 1942–43. The SS judicial system handled all disciplinary matters and administered regulations parallel with the German military code. On April 18, 1940, Himmler was granted the legal powers in matters of discipline corresponding to the supreme commander of an army, including signing death warrants, granting pardons, and commuting sentences. The SS code was extended by Führer decree on November 15, 1941, encompassing the SS organization, including the Waffen-SS, SS-Totenkopfverbände, and the SS-Polizeiverbände. The system followed the trickle-down effect with justice divided between field courts (*Feldgerichte*) and tribunals usually held in Germany. There was also the SS-Police special jurisdiction (*Sondergerichtsbarkeit der SS und Polizei*), which held regional court under HSSPF authority. Each SS authority usually included a court or tribunal and catered to secret and honor courts. The SS legal system sentenced men to prisons or concentration camps and arranged executions. Justice was generally swift and meted out with typical severity. Those found guilty were expelled from the SS, sent to serve in penal formations at the front lines, forced into hard labor in a construction battalion, or executed by hanging (dishonorable) or firing squad (honorable), depending on the crime.[107]

Bach-Zelewski's most serious case involved troops under his direct command. The failure of the 14th SS-Police Regiment hit the heart of the command system at the time of Stalingrad. The 14th SS-Police Regiment formed in July 1942 from Police Battalions 51, 63, and 122. Along with the 13th, it was one of two police regiments originally handed to Bach-Zelewski in October 1942. He had already forged a strong relationship to the regiment and its commander when he recorded their activities on August 9. The regiment destroyed a bandit group in a forest near Kutschin; they killed a Jew and a commissar in an exchange of hand grenades. Bach-Zelewski allowed them to use his reconnaissance airplane to ferry four of the wounded to a field hospital. He hosted a coffee meeting, on October 22, 1942, for the first battalion's officers in preparation for the coming campaign. He met with the regimental commander, Oberstleutnant Buchmann, on October 31 regarding an operation in conjunction with Sonderkommando Dirlewanger. On November 7, the 1st Battalion, 14th Police Regiment, stormed and captured a partisan camp northwest of Slutsk following thirty-four hours of continuous fighting. The battalion lost eighteen police officers and a tank. On November 10, the battalion lost seventeen more and suffered an undetermined number of wounded. The regiment remained in action until November 13 before transferring to Minsk to prepare for Operation "München." On November 15, Bach-Zelewski noted the officers of the regiment had a particularly hard day, and so he arranged for the theater in Minsk to be made available for their exclusive use. Two days later, the regiment began deportations of forced labor.

In January 1943, during the Soviet onslaught, the 14th SS-Police Regiment was one of four police regiments destroyed in heavy fighting. The regiment was accused of poor performance by the 8th Italian Army while under attack from an inferior force. It was a political disaster, and the consequences were severe for its commanders. The army COS sent a report to Himmler stating that "the regiment performed badly, allowing itself to be surrounded and only escaped after discarding most of its equipment. It then took up a defensive position where it employed primitive tactics and preparedness; it was surprised and defeated by two Russian companies."[108] As was usual in the German armed forces, commanders dispersed the surviving personnel to other formations or used them as cadres for new regiments and battalions. On February 23, the first battalion of the regiment took part in a reprisal action (*Vergeltungsaktion*) in the area of Bobruisk-Mogilev, shooting 463 partisans and suspects, arresting 1,834 forced laborers, and capturing foodstuffs and 193 horses, while destroying two bandit camps, with a cost of two wounded. At the time, an unnamed Polish Schuma battalion was supporting the regiment. Oberstleutnant Buchmann was killed in action on March 11, 1943.[109]

In April 1943, just prior to his Kharkhov trip, Himmler requested the regiment's papers. Bach-Zelewski wrote to Kurt Daluege, referring to problems of the 14th SS-Police Regiment as his responsibility. He felt their failure was a burden that caused him great personal pain. He confessed to raising the regiment from its baptism of fire and remaining too close with its commander Buchmann.[110] Meanwhile, Himmler issued a further order: "I employ the SS police-court [in] Berlin with the orders for preliminary proceedings of a court martial against the regimental-commander and battalion-commanders because of insubordination and poor service in the field."[111] Himmler was determined to punish even the junior officers. The official listing of those still alive and able to attend the court-martial appeared in the charge sheet of June 17, 1943.[112] The chief of the SS legal department and the SS Police Court in Berlin received full instructions for the case from Himmler. There appears to be no concluding record. On reflection, Bach-Zelewski neither defended nor accused those charged while the new 14th Regiment was handed to Oberst Grieser with no further problems.[113]

However, problems did occur over the handling of collaboration forces. In November 1942, ethnic Germans sent to the Prinz Eugen Division turned problematic, according to a British decode; the Croatian recruits had rebelled and this had raised "political dust." The Croatians were secretly spirited away to Auschwitz, and the ethnic Germans were retained in Germany.[114] On March 4, 1943, a mutiny by the men of a Cossack battalion led them to flee into the Pripyat marshes.[115] In 1943, another Cossack battalion ran amok in Yugoslavia among communities of ethnic Germans, killing, raping, and plundering. Bach-Zelewski referred to it in his diary as the "Terror of the Cossacks." The Cossacks were under the command of Gen. Helmut von Pannwitz, a former leading figure of in the Buchrucker putsch.[116] He and Bach-Zelewski were old acquaintances, and this again illustrates the breadth of Bach-Zelewski's personal network in the higher echelons of the armed forces.[117] Collaboration forces thus proved to be less than reliable. The Galicia Division's reserve battalion was quartered in Tarbes (France); most of its recruits were taken from battalions broken up to raise the division and transferred to France for training. Michael Logusz established that many deserted to the French resistance (*Forces Francaises de Interieur*), known as the *maquis,* or FFI.[118] The most serious case of mutiny also occurred in France within the 13th SS-Division Handschar in September 1943. A group of recruits with contacts to the FFI attempted to kill the SS officers and were set to defect, although this intention was less than clear. Eventually, the SS arrested the ringleaders and shot a dozen.[119]

The case of the 53rd Schuma Battalion is prominent in Bach-Zelewski's diary. It ran into difficulties during a stream of accusations against SS plundering. Criticism leveled by the Germany army's local Feldkommandantur had reached the headquarters of Army Group Centre. Bach-Zelewski's investigation concluded that this was partisan subterfuge. He censored the army major for criticizing the SS and alleged that while everyone was stealing food, only the SS were called plunderers. The same major ignored warnings of a partisan strike in the area. During the attack, the "bandits" killed the major and the 53rd Schuma Battalion rebelled. Bach-Zelewski discussed the situation with Schenckendorff and Himmler and concluded that the continuing German retreat had undermined their morale. "'Bolshevism' appeared to be returning," said Bach-Zelewski. "Soviet propaganda had incited the populous [*sic*], and faith in 'Bolshevism' had become an alibi." Bach-Zelewski claimed these problems had sparked within the Wehrmacht's eastern army (Osttruppen). He argued that Schenckendorff had suppressed the charge against his own troops, ignoring the wider problem among all collaboration forces. He concluded that the soldiers required sifting to remove the rotten elements and the undecided. The Schuma battalions, he continued, could no longer operate under their own authority but must be kept in close proximity to other German troops. The operations officer of the Army Group Centre rear area had also ignored these problems, but Bach-Zelewski accepted the error of judgment on grounds of military necessity. The difficult situation on the front had removed troops from the rear and remaining army units were concentrated railway protection. Bach-Zelewski judged that the partisan leaders in the Mogilev area understood German procedures and had exploited them. The partisans had infiltrated into the 53rd Schuma Battalion, formed a communist cell with two of the battalion's officers, and gradually taken control. They had acquired large numbers of guns and ammunition. This incident had raised problems of covert activities in this area that required further investigation, of which there is no evidence today of the outcome.[120]

## Leadership

Bach-Zelewski's unstructured thoughts on command appear frequently in his diary. In January 1943, he reflected on an argument that had broken out between Gottberg and Bassewitz-Behr. The latter had received the laurels for an operation actually led by Gottberg. This left Gottberg incensed, and while Bach-Zelewski acknowledged this, he commented on how the wrong person could receive merits. He referred to the Battle of Tannenberg, for which Hindenburg received the accolades for Ludendorff's efforts. He felt all his successes had been paid for by bitter disappointments. It was his opinion that selfless action on behalf of the people was rarely rewarded. He hypothesized how the commander of a formation bristling with heavy weapons would receive all the plaudits for a combat success. However, the real heroes were the men of the alarm units—lost, surrounded, and under-equipped—only to be killed in combat or admonished for failure later.[121] Even with his reputation for leading poorly equipped troops, he spent a lot of time bemoaning the situation.

A prime responsibility of the German military leaders was to evacuate "bandit-infected" areas and deport all men aged between sixteen and fifty-five as labor. The term used for this exercise was registration (Erfassung). In January 1943, a conference held in Berlin of senior SS bureaucrats examined the question of labor in occupied territories.[122] Since January, Bach-Zelewski had regular meetings with Gauleiter Sauckel. In February, Fritz Sauckel formerly appealed to Bach-Zelewski for captives from Bandenbekämpfung to be turned over for labor. Himmler agreed in principle but allowed only civilians who had not had contact with the bands to be released. Gradually, Bandenbekämpfung came to depend on labor roundups as valuable commodities. They became less a countermeasure and more a pure realization of financial return. Bandenbekämpfung turned the business of population management into a profitable undertaking. In April 1943, Bach-Zelewski met again with Sauckel. They bartered; Sauckel promised an increased supply of armored cars in return for roundup operations (*Arbeitererfassungsaktion*).[123] Instructions were issued by OKW on July 8 and August 18, treating all captives from security actions as prisoners. The remaining civilians and the unsuitable for deportation were, according to a Himmler order of July 20, to be resettled and put to useful purpose locally.[124] In September 1943, Bach-Zelewski issued instructions to all HSSPFs committed to Bandenbekämpfung regarding the importance of labor to the war effort. He ordered active and vigorous support for operations that conscripted labor. To assist in implementing these instructions, a regional labor controller was assigned to the SS staff. The plenipotentiary general for labor action (*Generalbevollmächtigter für den Arbeitseinsatz*, GBA) was expected to carry out the preparatory work. This included preparing special collection camps for the large numbers of deportees, organizing their transportation, and posting guards. Bach-Zelewski ordered that, henceforth, all Bandenbekämpfung reports were expected to reflect these new requirements. He wanted to know how prisoners were captured and transported, their numbers by sex, and counts of those over and under ten years of age. People unfit for work anywhere were literally "thrown away" (*ausgemustert*), a death sentence, and Bach-Zelewski justified the orders by declaring, "By doing this, without deviation, the nation shall be secured." [125]

Just how far Bandenbekämpfung dogma was assimilated into the German way of war is illustrated in the following army group order:

> The hard fighting at the front demands security of supply and the necessity to secure the transport routes against bandits. All troops in the army and other organisations committed to Bandenbekämpfung are to show aggression in this fight. This battle support's the front. In this context I especially direct Bandenbekämpfung measures for securing trains and roads, bridges and buildings.
>
> The snowfall restricts movement and forces bandits to take shelter in villages and bunkers. Regional operations to seek out the bandit in their camps and in hiding are as important as the immediate action and counter-attack by Jagdkommando following tracks of bandits in the snow; for the destruction of bandits. All units must look for tracks and use the snow to point toward the enemy.
>
> All forces, security services and alarm units must be concentrated to maximum of their ability in the "bandit-fight." The organisation of the Bandit information Service in all places, the special troops and by all soldiers must be monitored and improved. It is important not to waste time. All operations cooperate with Fliegerführer 1. All troop leaders and village commanders are to be made aware of this order.[126]

# 6
# DAS
# BANDENKAMPFGEBIET

The June 1943 order included Himmler's self-appointed authority to declare a "combating-bandits area" (Bandenkampfgebiet). This authority does not seem to have been discussed during his meeting with Hitler on June 19, but the meeting almost certainly engineered it (refer to chapter 4). Himmler decided this would be a fitting senior command function of the Chef der Bandenbekämpfung, a post he retained until the end of the war. This instrument effectively placed Himmler in control over any or all territory experiencing intense partisan incursions or resistance activity. This control was administered either through the offices of the Chef der Bandenkampfverbände or another SS-Police office such as Karl Wolff's in Italy (discussed in chapter 9). These offices would then decide upon the appropriate course of action. The Bandenkampfgebiet had wider operational implications. From the perspective of military history, it was not a major departure from the Etappengebiet introduced after 1872 and regularly utilized until the end of the First World War. During Operation "Barbarossa," Hitler opted for four zones: the combat zone (*Gefechtsgebiet*), the immediate army area behind the front line (*Armeegebiet*), the security zone under the "army rear area" (*Heeresgebiet*), and the political zones under the *Reichskommisariate*.[1] The Bandenkampfgebiet really affected only the political zones in Russia. Ideologically, the Bandenkampfgebiet originated from Himmler's vision for Lebensraum as depicted in the "General Plan for the East." This envisaged a network of colonial estates governing Russia. Thus, common threads linked the Bandenkampfgebiet to both German military traditions and Nazi ideology.

The Bandenkampfgebiet became central to the Nazis' prosecution of Bandenbekämpfung in the last years of the war. It was the Nazi counter to Stalin's partisan challenge over the rightful ownership/control of Russian lands or "space" (*Raum*). In 1942, Himmler proposed eradicating "banditry" through attrition rather than dominating terrain. This represented a compromise to the army's objections over the SS control of security. By the end of 1942, just as in 1918, the devastation of the German occupation had created a wasteland that both Vejas Liulevicius and Christian Gerlach described and that Hannes Heer painted as "death zones" (*tote Zonen*).[2] The situation in the army rear areas continued to deteriorate into an existence dominated by the forces of exploitation and destruction.[3] However, as yet the Bandenkampfgebiet has avoided academic scrutiny.

In 1943, Himmler aligned Bandenbekämpfung policy to the task of dominating terrain for purposes enforcing security by exploitation; the Bandenkampfgebiet, therefore, was a manifestation of Hitler's Fortress Europe strategy. In operational terms, the Bandenkampfgebiet was categorized into three threat levels. The highest threat level, the "bandit-diseased area" (*bandenverseuchtes Gebiet*), was an area wracked with bands or "bandits" openly supported by the indigenous population. If the area contained a military railway line or major road (*Rollbahn*) and the insurgency hindered theater military operations, then it was likely to become subject to a full-scale "cleansing action" (Säuberungsaktion). The mid-threat level, a "bandit-suspicious area" (*bandenverdächtiges Gebiet*), could expect a vigorous investigation of the local community by the SD/GFP. In addition, Jagdkommandos were likely to be dispatched to conduct patrols to gauge the level of "banditry." The lowest threat level, the "bandit-free area" (*bandenfreies Gebiet*), was normally registered only after cleansing operations were completed and was subject to minimum-security scrutiny. In general security terms, the Bandenkampfgebiet signaled the adoption of intense preventative security measures (proposed in the 1942 Bandenbekämpfung manual), the deployment of manpower under training (Zenner's proposal from 1942), and the fusion of both into Bandenbekämpfung operational training. In specific security terms, the difference between 1942 and 1943 was the central role of recruits and training to the prosecution of Bandenbekämpfung and in the domination of terrain.

## Preventative Measures

Simple Bandenbekämpfung practice began with self-security or preventative measures. Himmler first approached this subject in his Bandenbekämpfung pamphlet (1942). The 1944 regulations continued to emphasize defense and protection. In practice, these principles encouraged a strict occupation and heightened an aggressive mood in the occupier. The Bandenkampfgebiet troops within installations, cities, and rural communities were forced into an automatic state of readiness. Regulations stipulated that prior to entering a "bandit-diseased area" the troops should be conditioned as to what awaited them and the bands' location should be plotted on "bandit situation maps" (*Bandenlagekarte*). The advancing troops set patrols, established a skirmish order, and swept their entry points of mines. They entered an area under the cover of machine-guns, ready for combat. When building an encampment in a "bandit-diseased area," they incorporated houses, workshops, and farms within the defensive complex. Strongpoints were stocked with machine guns, flare pistols, and hand grenades with fighting positions (*Kampfstände*) made easily accessible. They cleared strips of forests and scrubland up to 400-meter frontages, setting clear line-of-sight and enfilading killing zones.

The first priority of preventative measures was the protection of lines of communications: railways, roads, and waterways. The civil administration and the SS determined the appropriate level of guardianship to protect the railway lines. Strongpoints were established in stations, at railway block sections or junctions, and at other important installations (bridges, water towers, pump stations, power stations, and railway work facilities). Security landscaping generated a lot of activity among competing Nazi agencies. Deciphered messages reveal that Himmler was active in landscaping: "He wants to know how quickly forestry along supply routes can be cut down as a defense measure," recorded one British signal.[4] In September 1943, Himmler signaled Fegelein, "I order for the building of your defensive task intensive building of positions; you will employ every man available," meaning from the civilian population.[5] After the war, one former German officer indicated that, in principle, they fortified railway installations for rapid defense.[6] The regulations again required a 300-meter-wide exclusion zone, or no-man's-land, on either side of the tracks. The Technische Nothilfe received orders to clear areas up to 500 meters wide on either side of railway lines.[7] The long-distance telephone and signals cables were buried to protect them from attacks.[8] The zone was cleared and posted with warning signs in all relevant languages. The railway command decided which parts of the forests were preserved to protect against snowdrifts. State foresters organized wood removal. Railway gardeners, under guard, attended to the weeds in the zones.

The second priority involved securing the rural communities, economic installations, and important intelligence-connected facilities. Economic facilities, plants, and administration buildings that were important for the German war effort also came within the scope of preventative measures. The civilian authorities decided which buildings were protected. Strongpoint and obstacles were established around key factories. Again the question of loyalty arose in both rural and industrial communities as the Nazis expected civilians to prosecute passive Bandenbekämpfung. The attitude emphasized in the 1944 regulations was that, as a matter of duty (and proof of loyalty), natives granted survival through work should secure their places of work, even after long shifts.

The third priority involved securing agriculture and forestry. The preferred method of securing farming areas was to garrison troops and conduct patrol sweeps. Crops designated for the Germans came under the Nazi civilian administration and its agricultural leaders. They planned and coordinated security levels with the priority of protection and collection of the harvest. Lieutenant General Schwarznecker in a post-war study implied that the SS-Police mission was limited to protecting political issues and the harvests. [9] Another German officer thought that crops, especially Indian corn and rye, were purposefully grown to restrict the movement of "bandits."[10] The "harvest security action" (*Erntesicherungsaktion*) was not only an SS priority. These studies overlook the Wehrmacht and SS prioritization of agriculture as critical in their operational and strategic plans.

The troops and local populace, including those working for the Germans, came face to face in the Bandenkampfgebiet. Civilian status was made more complex than the usual bystander-collaborator-resistor construct. Collaboration was forced on civilians; for example, troops conscripted local watchmen (*Alarmein-heiten*) to raise the alarm. The watchmen's reliability was probably suspect, as they feared the bands more than German terror.[11] Highway security patrols carried out spot checks, entering villages and hamlets to conduct searches. After the war, former German soldiers claimed that many civilians were peaceable, industrious, and uninterested in the conflict. However, the average soldier treated civilians with suspicion and contempt: "Every civilian, every highway and railway worker, especially if those who directed the traffic were natives, was required to have an identification card, the form of which was changed regularly."[12] The villages located in the way of death zones were evacuated and flattened. Native railway laborers (*Eisenbahnhelfer*) and other collaborators were given special consideration in locating a residence. Civilian railway workers received permit papers (*Ausweise*) from the transport duty officers in the town commander (Ortskommandantur) or the territory commander (*Gebietskommandant*) for travel on the railways. Laborers were allowed to enter and to leave the death zones only along designated paths and under guard. Civilians were officially barred from strongpoints and encampments. The emphasis was on rigid social control irrespective of its psychological implications: "The morale of the population has been lowered a good deal by the labor allocation to Germany since the recruiting had to be carried on in most cases by imposing a forced quota on the various communities."[13]

The SS-Police erected complexes across occupied Europe that extended the network of preventative security. Installations were established in Czechoslovakia, Poland, Russia, and Holland—especially field recruit depots (*SS-Feldrekruten-Depot*) and troop training grounds (*Truppenübungsplätze*). In Poland, SS facilities congregated around Warsaw and Debica. By March 1942, the SS-Führungshauptamt operated three Waffen-SS and police supply commands (*Nachschubkommandanturen der Waffen-SS und Polizei*) as the controlling agencies for reserves, supply, and operational training in the east.[14] The Order Police also erected training facilities, including Truppenübungsplatz

Kuznica near Grodno in Belorussia.[15] In March, Himmler decided to extend these facilities as fortified central hubs handling recruits, reserves, and supplies. These were located in Riga, Bobruisk, and Dnepropetrovsk.[16] The construction site of the Bobruisk complex was visited by Bach-Zelewski on his return to duty in May 1942.[17]

In April, Himmler and Wolff discussed the question of Unruh's visit to Warsaw, where SS installations included reserve and supply depots.[18] In May 1942, Unruh conducted an investigation of rear-area functions of the Eastern Front. He visited the SS supply facility in Riga and recommended its closure alongside other SS facilities as wasteful duplication. The SS representative assigned to the party, SS-Sturmbannführer With, attempted to convince Unruh of the necessity for the HSSPF and Waffen-SS to manage their supply facilities independently. Unruh refused to accept any counter-arguments and, on May 11, ordered one company of police and two battalions of Schuma to be placed under Wehrmacht command. With urgently sent a message to Himmler warning him of the implications of the report Unruh intended to put before Hitler.[19] Himmler intervened through Hitler and so prevented any further interference with his forces. Henceforth, Unruh and Himmler treated one another with due circumspection.[20] In a meeting lasting nearly five hours, Hitler, Unruh, Keitel, and Himmler agreed to another rationalization assignment in the General Government of Poland. Himmler cautioned Unruh not to interfere in SS business. Yet some weeks later, Himmler instructed Krüger to provide Unruh with all the assistance necessary to complete his tasks.[21] With's efforts to limit Unruh were appreciated by Himmler, who transferred him to his personal staff to become an internal auditor of SS-Police affairs.[22]

## SS-Waldlager Bobruisk

Himmler's "General Plan for the East" envisaged the creation of colonial estates. This settlement policy (*Siedlungspolitik*) incorporated the vast construction of romanticized Germanic medieval-style burgs across Russia. These burgs were initially integrated into the security system as "armed villages" (*Wehrdörfer*), creating a self-defense network. Even generals of the Wehrmacht applied to Himmler for the right to own a farmstead.[23] There were other SS complexes in the east with the sole purpose of administering security. In March 1943, the intelligence officer (Ic) of Nachschubkommandantur der Waffen-SS Russland-Mitte issued his fourth situation report (the first three are missing). The report concentrated on the "bandit-helpers," the newspaper *Bobruisker Partisanen*, the use of mines as bombs by "bandits," the situation of bandit camps, and heavy mortar attacks.[24] There was little to indicate whether the base was central to SS operations. By the summer of 1943, the Nachschubkommandantur had been redesignated SS-Waldlager Bobruisk. This large, fortified complex straddled several camps in the middle of a forest and alongside the main railway line from Minsk to Bobruisk. Its multiple functions included training, provisioning (protecting the local harvests), and supply.[25] The installation's commander, SS-Standartenführer Rudolf Pannier, was a former businessman and a reserve police officer who had received the Knight's Cross during the winter battles of 1941. By July 1943, the installation was fully operational, and its functions suggested a wider brief than that of an advanced supply and recruit depot. The Waldlager amalgamated headquarters functions and replicated staff positions typically found only within the army Wehrkreis system. The SS-Waldlager Bobruisk was an emerging SS-Wehrkreis (refer to diagram III). The existence of this installation, under Unruh's scrutiny, indicates how Himmler had been able to circumvent OKW policy with minimal resources. Whether this was to become part of an extensive SS-Wehrkreis is open to pure speculation. The advance of the Red Army in the latter half of 1943 eventually led to its abandonment.[26] Yet it demonstrates the extent of SS ambitions.

According to Pannier, a Red Army barracks had formed part of the site, but further work extended and fortified the complex. This involved staggered artillery, infantry, and antitank defenses. The western flank of the complex was protected by flooded and impassable ground, deliberately caused by damming a stream. Recruits assigned to the complex were detailed to building and construction duties. Pannier reported that the men's barracks were homely; the company of artisans had erected latrines and washrooms. Several barracks had been prepared for winter comfort, and cupboards lined the insides. The construction program included a barrack-block for female SS auxiliaries who erected stores for wood and peat, produced locally in Bobruisk. Ninety-two tons were supplied to the complex. A wood and pulp factory was included in the complex and supplied 2,700 cubic meters of construction timber. The recruits sunk a drinking water well of 2 meters, which was later increased to 20 meters with an extraction pump. The complex had sixty-four vehicles, all maintained in the local workshops. The maintenance teams converted some vehicles to use wood-gas, produced on site; this allowed for significant energy savings. The ordnance detachment repaired weapons for use by the installation. Their gunsmiths rebored three captured Pak 45mm antitank guns and replaced their range-finding equipment. In anticipation of winter, there was a program for making skis and snowshoes. The complex installed a central generator to allow the signals equipment to remain functioning even while under attack. In September, the recruits completed the construction a command bunker (*Führer-Bunker*).[27] By October 1943, the Waldlager was a fully functioning and self-sufficient armed complex.

Once the German armies began to retreat, operational and security zones collapsed on top of each other. In October 1943, Pannier observed that Army Group Centre was under pressure to erect defense lines. Clashes broke out between the SS and the army over control of installations and other bases in the Bobruisk area. There was a major disagreement over the SS-Waldlager hospital and medical facilities. Pannier wrote to Field Marshal Model, commander of Army Group Centre, to explain the security situation but did not received a response. He advised Model of significant changes in the tactics of the "bandits" whom he said were no longer roaming independently but operating under military direction. Pannier suggested Model might determine the direction of Soviet attacks by tracking the direction of the "bandits." The bands had exploited the rear-area chaos, and individual "bandits" had mingled with the mass exodus of refugees. The bands also exploited the fears of Hiwis working in headquarters and were able to gather security intelligence.[28] Internal security was a constant problem. The August report mentioned spies within the installation and the arrest of five people for alleged contact with the bands. On August 27, a woman alleged to be a "bandit-helper" was discovered searching desks of an office in the Waldlager. The next day, two more "bandit helpers" were arrested while trying to pass information regarding German troop movements. In each case, they were known to be locals working in the Waldlager. On August 31, six "bandit helpers" were arrested for passing messages about the traffic movements on the Bobruisk-Brosha railway. Similar cases occurred in September as sabotage, espionage, and desertion to the bands increased.[29]

## The Utilization of Manpower

An outline survey of SS-Police manpower indicates a lack of clarity and consistent policy initiatives. This lack stemmed in part from the inability of the SS-Police to take advantage of Germany's conscription program. In 1937, Himmler announced, "I can carry out the all the former tasks of the Landsturm i.e. guarding munitions factories, railroad crossings etc. with civilians over 45, who would be drafted as auxiliary police as planned provided I have as a backbone a troop that is young. For this the Deaths Head Units are provided, ranging in age from 25–35, not older and not younger."[30] From 1939, the SS-Police made concerted efforts to recruit manpower below the German army age limits by offering non-combatant duties as alternatives to combat war service.[31] By 1943–44, the age-range factor became a lottery played out between the Wehrmacht and the SS. In February 1944, all institutions received orders to enlist men in the 1906 age group and younger. The last assessment of police strengths, made under the Wehrmacht replacement plan of 1945, registered 323,300 men and 36,600 women, of which 118,700 were below thirty-eight years of age.[32]

Surviving records from the SS recruiting office in Düsseldorf indicate two trends.[33] First, large numbers of Germans and ethnic Germans continued to volunteer for the SS. Bernd Wegner attributed the end of the all-volunteer force as a contributing factor in the decline in the Waffen-SS as an elite organization.[34] In fact, large numbers of young men continued to volunteer for the SS primarily because of its elite standing. The inducements of lands and farms in the east also helped, while police recruitment in particular seemed to offer a way of avoiding frontline duty. Recruits were indoctrinated into an elaborate vision of the eastern frontier, a wall of armed farmers as a Nazi buffer against the Mongol horde. Bandenbekämpfung was glorified in the recruitment process, portrayed as necessary for eradicating Bolshevism and "bandit" criminality. The pamphlet "With the Sicherheitspolizei in the East" offered the prospect of combating Bolsheviks who habitually murdered and plundered the indigenous people of the east.[35] In "The Spooky Forest" (*Der unheimliche Wald*), the SS candidate was told of the fight against NKVD-led bandit groups in the forests of the east and combat in the camp of the snipers (*Heckenschützenlager*).[36] Thus, the depiction of Bandenbekämpfung at the recruitment point was a youthful exercise in gaining glory cheaply for vast material reward.

Race played an important role in police manpower policy with the 1935 Nuremberg race laws excluding all Jewish constables. The police were administered through the civil code and, as public servants, were obliged to adhere to these race laws. On December 20, 1940, the Hauptamt Ordnungspolizei issued a general notice from Himmler that the anti-Semitic film *Jud Süss* was available for members of the police and their families to enjoy a special viewing.[37] In November 1940, Gustav Lombard, a senior SS-Cavalry officer serving in Poland, ushered his men to attend a private showing.[38] In October 1942, Himmler issued instructions concerning the continuing employment of Jews in the police reserve or the police administration. Those of first-degree mixed German-Jewish blood (*Mischlinge*), that is, with a Jewish mother or father, were expelled from the police. Second-degree Mischlinge (Jewish grandparents) could remain on the police strength only with Himmler's permission. Each police recruit had to sign a document confirming that there were no Mischlinge of first-degree or second-degree status within his or her racial profile. All reports on Mischlinge second degree or police officers married to Jews were collected on December 15, 1942.[39] Women also began to take up important roles within the SS-Police administration. From 1942, women auxiliaries began to replace men in most of the signals functions. Women signals auxiliaries (SS-Helferinnen) had undergone full training in operating skills at a training school (Oberehnheim SS-Reichsschule) in Alsace. The school came under the SS-Police chief of signals. There were three categories of trade for women switchboard operators, teleprinters, and wireless operations. This all-volunteer force was open to women aged between eigthteen and thirty-five. The recruits received a full program of ideological as well as technical training. Trained women were assigned to duties in Germany and the occupied territories. They remained under the direct command and guard of the HSSPF at all times.[40]

From 1940, the Waffen-SS established reserve battalions for recruits; these were usually stationed outside Germany beyond the reach of the army conscription system. The SS-Polizei Division trained in Holland and maintained its reserve depots there. The Waffen-SS installed commands in Poland, Holland, and Czechoslovakia, and the SS-Totenkopfverbände established a central recruitment and reserve depot in Warsaw. The reserve detachments— SS-Reserve Battalion Ost (Zhitomir), SS-Reserve Police Grenadier Battalion I (Hertsogenbosch), SS-Reserve Police Grenadier Battalion II (Amersfoert), Reserve Company Danish Freikorps (Bobruisk), and Reserve Company Norwegian Legion (Mitau)—extended the establishment of occupation by widespread dispersal. The integration of SS and police forces began with induction training. In 1939, three training detachments—SS-Totenkopf Ersatzbataillon I, II, III—were raised for the SS-Totenkopfverbände. These were joined in April 1941 by the SS-Ersatzbataillon Ost, mustered in Breslau. This battalion served as the recruit collection center for all SS-Police formations in the east.[41] The SS-Totenkopf Ersatz battalions eventually served as the recruit collection establishment for all Waffen-SS theaters of operations.[42] The training battalions were joined by specialist military expertise companies to provide support during operations and were supplied with nonstandard equipment.[43]

Basic training for the police was conducted at Koepenick or Fürstenfeldbruck training academies. Four weeks were devoted to fitness, bodybuilding, and self-defense; six weeks were set aside for weapons training (*Waffendienst und Waffenkunde*), which expressed itself in terms of love for the rifle, marching into battle, tactical methods, and marksmanship. Two weeks were devoted to ideological training essentially revolving around a dogma about people and territory titled *Volk ohne Raum—Raum ohne Volk*. The questions of blood and the Nuremberg Laws of September 15, 1935, and an overview of the new Reich and the new leadership were also integral to the tuition. The aim of this part of the course was to build "the police official as a shining example and propagandist" and "the organisation as the highest order of the era." Four weeks were set aside for the study of the police organization and its work. This essentially covered the legal process, policing and taking criminals, as well as the legal system and the prisons; this was followed by five weeks of practical training in the field.[44] By September 1944, the academy was training recruits in the use of rifles and pistols.[45] Four specialist police weapons training schools (*Polizei-Waffenschule*) were established. The first was in Dresden-Hellerau (designated I) and had a capacity to train 300 candidates; Laon (designated II) had a capacity of 200 candidates[46]; Hague (III) had a capacity for 451 recruits; and Maastricht (IV) for 230. On July 30, 1943, the police wanted to erect a weapons school for ethnic Germans from Siebenbürgen, although the records do not indicate if this happened.[47]

The three academies of police officer training were Mariaschein, Fürstenfeldbruck, and Eberswalde.[48] By 1943, the basic training schedule wove politics, security, and Bandenbekämpfung into a single program.[49] The schedule of training began with classes in National Socialism and was followed by tactical and leadership classes. The training instructions stated, "The objective of training must be to achieve ability in fighting capability. . . . The experience of the eastern campaign and the Bandit warfare has to be intensely analysed." Company leadership training, fitness and bodybuilding, air raid protection, laws and legal process, police law, precinct life (*Revierkunde*), and survival techniques were also part of the program. Training continued until December 22, 1944.

To facilitate the rationalization of manpower, the Order Police adopted a city "twinning system" to regulate assignments and deployment. The system linked the precincts of German and Russian cities so that the limited human resources of the police shared administration; this smoothed police duties between German home-front districts with occupied precincts. A report by the BdO Ukraine placed a ratio of Russian homesteads to police officials, and the German twin police department. Kiev, the largest city with 856,000 accounted homesteads, received an Order Police command and a gendarmerie command (denoted as KdO/KdG) of 35 staff officers and 217 Schutzpolizei. Kiev's German twin police home station (*Heimatstandort*) was Hamburg. The next was Dnepropetrovsk, accounting 500,000 homesteads, assigned a KdO/KdG of 35 staff and 123 Schutzpolizei and twinned with Weimar. Krivoi Rog with 197,000 homes was assigned a KdO/KdG of seven staff and 51 Schutzpolizei and twinned with Potsdam. The town of Vinnitsa with 93,000 homes received a KdO/KdG of 7 staff and 26 Schutzpolizei and was twinned with Kaiserslautern.[50] Twinning reduced routine administrative duty within overall operations. The system continued throughout the war and helps explain why the police were able to respond rapidly to strategic emergencies.

Specialist police formations such as the Wasserschutzpolizei (WSP), which took up duties in the east, were also incorporated into the system.[51] WSP-station Bobruisk was formed under HSSPF Russia-Centre with two Wachtmeister and six reservists. Its supply line led to Police Regiment Warsaw. WSP-Kiev had four Wachtmeister and twelve reservists and received its supplies through BdO-Kraków. On February 1, 1944, WSP-Pripyat was dissolved under the instructions of the senior commander of the WSP. These instructions explained how units were broken up and redistributed. Personnel without boats were sent to a troop collection camp in Czechoslovakia. The unit commander and officials reported to WSP-Oder in Breslau. The adjutant and ten reservists returned to their home station in Berlin. The boats were handed over to WSP-Bromberg and then passed on to WSP-Warte/Netze. All motor vehicles and weapons were registered and stockpiled. The men received ten to fourteen days' leave prior to new postings.[52]

Welfare in the SS-Police was the responsibility of officers and senior commanders. Officers, many reservists like their men, ranged across a coterie of demands from finding quarters to arresting a gendarme for the crime of attempted suicide.[53] The troops were issued with cigarettes, vodka (at the cost of RM 5.60 per liter), and wine (free).[54] Official entertainment programs were an important aspect of life for troops in the occupation sectors and rear areas. After-work parties and musical gatherings were a regular feature in Bach-Zelewski's diary. The troops received visits from theater companies or were allowed to attend entertainment programs. The cinema and regular cabaret or variety acts proved popular. In Bobruisk, Pannier recommended historical or training films at the end of a day's work. The HSSPF Russia-Centre brought the SS-Music Corps into Minsk on August 9, 1941, while Police Regiment North encouraged its own war artist, to exhibit his work on July 26, 1941.[55] The troops received the corporate propaganda piece (*SS-Leitheft*) and daily newspapers, and OKW situation reports were displayed on notice boards.

Questions regarding sexual outlets are more difficult to answer or explain. The surviving records do not include sexual details. In the east, the men were forbidden from having free contact with Russian women on racial grounds:

> Ostminister Dr. Wilhelm states that the problem of Ukrainian women who are having children by Germans will be solved by abortion. Men proved to be guilty in this respect will be brought before the party tribunals for forbidden intercourse with Ukrainians. The total number of these children does not amount to 10,000.[56]

Military brothels were organized and administered for all soldiers and troops. Signals intercepts revealed some sexual misdemeanors; for example, an SS man ran off with a prostitute, and they chose to hide in Hamburg's Jewish quarter.[57] Another communiqué referred to sexual orgies committed by SS men of a cavalry squadron in Cholm. Given the social elites who joined the SS-Cavalry, it is not surprising that an official SS lawyer was assigned to defend them.[58] In February 1968, the Wiesbaden county court (*Landesgericht*) heard a case in which the defendant, a former member of Police Battalion 314, was charged with shooting a dancer called "Vera," allegedly the defendant's mistress, during his posting to Kharkov in March 1942.[59]

Reams of signals traffic concerning holidays, sick leave, and bombed-out families in Germany were decoded by the British. The police received leave perhaps more regularly than the army. The operational staff of HSSPF Russia-South found that delays in traveling back to Germany took six days out of ten leave furlough, which they thought left too short a period. The recommendation was fourteen leave days with the added allowance of six traveling days, making twenty days in all. From March 23, 1942, two leave trains twice a week were scheduled to arrive and depart between Germany and the rear area of Army Group South, carrying twelve hundred places.[60] The families of men killed in action were notified through Nazi officials in their hometown. Troopers with relatives killed at home, especially by the bombing, were advised while on duty and were not always granted compassionate leave. In all cases, the bodies of police officers killed in combat were not returned to Germany for burial. By 1943, signals traffic criss-crossed Germany and the occupation sectors advising of death. These messages clearly affected troop morale, and men lived in perpetual fear for their loved ones. The police regiments were mustered from the same neighborhoods and the magnification of their psychological effect perhaps explains, but does not condone, random acts of revenge killings.[61]

Serious losses to disease and sickness had not been planned for by SS-Police operations in Russia during 1941. By 1942, the KSRFSS issued regular monthly casualty returns, including the numbers of those afflicted by common and fatal diseases.[62] An order posted in 1943 by Gottberg's medical officer circulated advice on preventative troop hygiene. Orders about hygiene were read aloud at troop assembly by the duty officer and then were individually issued to each trooper. Troops were ordered to wash regularly and construct steam saunas to combat personal lice. They were advised to repair damaged footwear, warning that small changes in cold and wet weather could lead to frostbite. The men were warned not to wear their boots too tightly and preferably to wear one pair of socks at a time but to change them regularly, especially during very cold weather. In winter, the consumption of alcohol was permitted only inside warm rooms because it caused men to fall asleep and die when outside. The troops were advised to build latrines close to quarters and sheltered from the wind. The battle against vermin (*Ungezieferbekämpfung*) was conducted with traps for rats and disinfectant (*Kresolseifenlösung*) against lice. The troops were warned against entering Russian houses to shelter from the cold because it was believed this was a major cause of contracting disease.[63] Sudden outbreaks of typhoid and spotted fever led the HSSPF Russia-Centre operations officer to make urgent requests for large doses of inoculations in March 1942. Malaria was prevalent in the south, especially in the mining districts.[64] Dysentery plagued police units in Grodno, while typhus blighted the central theater.[65] There were plagues of summer flies and constant calls for delousing equipment and smallpox vaccine.[66] The troops brought their diseases home to Germany, with Frankfurt, Bochum, Lübeck, and Darmstadt particularly badly affected by typhus.[67]

## SS-Waldlager Bobruisk

In July 1943, the first recruits arrived at the SS-Waldlager Bobruisk. They were initially assigned to serve with the Order Police in May, but in July, after some indecision, they were sent to the SS.[68] Pannier's reports pieced together explain why they were unwanted and had drifted. The first impression was pathetic. The recruits were divided evenly between German nationals and ethnic Germans from Rumania. Pannier explained that the recruits were inoculated for smallpox, typhus, dysentery, cholera, and diphtheria, all prevalent in the east.[69] By August, the troops showed some "satisfactory" improvement to the men's fitness. Pannier used hard, energetic training to remove the softness in the men, and this led to a reduction in sick calls. He recorded the overall strength of the complex on July 31 as 11 officers, 102 NCOs, and 2,007 men. This increased in August to 15 officers, 247 NCOs, and 1,972 men. The base had also increased with a company of Latvian Schuma and a number of SS female auxiliaries. There was no indication of any segregation routines.[70] The average age of the recruits stood at twenty-eight, and according to Pannier, they had overcome their personal faults through their strength of character.

The ethnic Germans arrived in the poorest condition. Many had served with the Rumanian army, some with eight years' service and prior combat experience. They were aged between seventeen and forty and carried little or no equipment. They were mostly farm laborers, dull-witted, and inept with formal German (*Hochdeutsch*) because of their local dialects. More than two-thirds of the men were suffering from bad teeth, which caused 166 to suffer stomach and bowel sickness. In Pannier's opinion, approximately 20 to 50 percent of the men were not fit for the demands of soldiering. The most acute problem was untreated illnesses, such as hernias. Many men were previously wounded, or handicapped, and had kept silent about their conditions when signing their recruitment papers. The poorest physical specimens were all collected together into one company. Some recruits required the removal of as many as ten teeth, and in one case sixteen, because of their appalling condition. Pannier proposed dental restoration work because, in his opinion, poor teeth could lead to "upset stomachs and bad testicles."

SS NCOs were brought in from the SS Field Recruit Depot Debica to transform the men into an SS-Jäger Battalion. The perpetual shortage of trained NCOs plagued both the SS and Wehrmacht throughout the war. The NCOs had not served in the field; they were all from administrative branches as a result of Unruh's initiatives.[71] The assessment of the recruits on reception was shaped by the style of military bureaucracy. The reports oozed pathos, masculinity, and indications of military comradeship. Pannier was resigned to the poor quality of NCOs without frontline experience or even the temperament for combat. The arrival of training staff relieved Pannier's NCO shortages.[72] Some NCOs temporarily joined the ranks for retraining. One of the complex's battalion commanders had started the special battle training course for senior NCOs on Mondays, Wednesdays, Fridays (evening), and Sundays (morning). An eight-day special NCO training program on each evening and Sundays was expected to raise their performance in giving orders, leading under fire, and understanding basic principles of military penal codes. Overall training suffered from the shortage of trained platoon leaders, however; the senior NCOs were very young and inexperienced, capable only of garrison duty. Pannier saw little possibility of intensifying training to remove these inconveniences. In September, Pannier reported that he could only rely on nine NCOs for all NCO duties.[73]

The recruits of the SS-Jäger Battalion joined the 1st, 7th, 8th, and 9th companies. The 2nd and 6th companies became the collection points for older recruits, initially identified as difficult cases. Their morale improved once language problems were recognized and resolved. Each company reached their full complement of NCOs of all ranks. At the end of August, the 1st Company, 50 percent of its strength German, had nearly completed its training. They were honed (*vertieft*) for Bandenbekämpfung. Pannier viewed their first experience of that kind of fighting as proving their potential as a professional cadre. The other 50 percent were ethnic Germans (Rumanian), with three weeks' training behind them. The 2nd, 3rd, 4th, and 5th companies had completed three weeks training and were assigned to harvest security duties. The 6th Company had completed five weeks training and eight days of tactical shooting exercises. The troops reached the halfway stage of training and gave every indication of becoming "useful" soldiers. They had absorbed advanced skills training and tougher drilling. In contact with the enemy, they had remained focused and unemotional. Pannier compared their combat temperament with farmers tilling the land—persistent, rugged, and determined.

The 7th, 8th, and 10th companies had received only two weeks training primarily because of the overall lack of weapons. They served on guard duty for the complex, which allegedly sapped their morale and further reduced available training days to only two or three days a week. The 9th Company had become the collection point for all the "useless" men. They included the incapable, wounded, unhealthy, and intellectually deficient. According to Pannier, most of these men failed basic cognitive tests and were plainly clumsy. Many had been deformed through permanent hard labor. The men formed a company for hard labor and camp construction duties, building defenses, command bunkers, and barrack blocks as laborers or as artisans.

Pannier noted that shortages of weapons had only caused a brief interruption in the training, while the older recruits had reached the average standard required after four weeks' training. The equipment manifest listed 326 rifles, 320 bayonets, 9 MG 08s (machine guns), 5 MG 34s (machine guns), 1,058 gas masks, 326 cleaning kits, and 205 shovels. Pannier's August report recorded an improvement in weaponry with 480 rifles, 641 bayonets, 30 MG 42s (machine-guns), 270 shovels, 600 gas masks, 479 cleaning kits, 15 telescopic sights, and 15 sniper rifles. Shooting skills improved dramatically after the second and third exercises. The men had gained trust in their weapons, further raising their level of expertise; Pannier saw the real issue as the poor quality of the Czechoslovak training rifles. From August 20, a new course in the use of antitank weapons was introduced for instructors.[74] The differences in duties and priorities led to confusion and differential levels of training between companies of the battalion. Those troops deployed to sub-camp duties remained on the battalion's strength.[75]

In his September report, Pannier provided more details of the content of training. The recruits were given three to four days practice with machine guns, while the platoon and company training took forty days. There were courses in using antitank (PAK) guns, flak artillery, and heavy machine guns. The 6th Company had undertaken eight days of combat shooting training and had then participated in harvest protection and Bandenbekämpfung. A combat engineer (*Pioniere*) platoon formed for mine-laying, mine-construction, and mine-clearing duties. The base had confiscated more than one hundred horses, enabling the SS-Jäger Battalion to become a horse-drawn unit. There were still problems with equipment such as missing sighting devices and safety catches from weapons. Pannier had discovered that some of the recruits required constant visual training because they did not have the ability to understand lectures and were deemed *Augenmenschen*, literally, "eye people." This forced the SS to conduct constant and repetitive drilling. The situation worsened by the absence of post from home and concern for the families, which had left the recruits in a downcast mood. The food supplied was tasty and the commissariat was efficient in handling rations. The men received sightseeing days when off duty.[76] Pannier referred to two cases of ill discipline, respectively disobedience and drunkenness on duty; these were minor infractions but important enough to be recorded at the time.[77] The question of discipline and mass killing has had some prominence in the debates over Nazi crimes. In one case, a police officer was sent back to Berlin from Russia, after having been found guilty of stealing clothes and food.[78] There were, in fact, considerable numbers of cases of theft and passing fraudulent documents.[79] In the town of Pantschowa, a local police official was charged with embezzlement and fraudulent accounting practices.[80] In 1976, a Hamburg court ruled that Josef Aig. and Wilhelm Eic. from the Nachschubkommandantur Waffen-SS Russland-Mitte were guilty of shooting around fifty Jews and were sentenced to two and twelve years imprisonment, respectively.[81]

## Operational Training

In May 1936, a hypothetical textbook exercise for senior police officials of a police school envisaged an air defense-police battle (*Luftschutz-Polizeikampf*) in the Potsdam-Gröben area.[82] The exercise depicted a situation in which, under the distraction of an air attack, the area of Potsdam came under attack by "bandits." The lecture identified three levels of attack, from the air, plundering, and "banditry." This was the perception of total war in 1936: heavy and low-level air attacks, criminal action of looters and plundering, and terrorist gangs working against the government. The Nazis represented the gangs as left wing and erroneously referred to them as the "misled people of Mr [Karl] Severing." The police were expected, under the circumstances of decision making in a time of total war, to act against enemies from the sky, plunderers, and bandits. A night attack by forty bombers was envisaged. Emergency conditions were to be rehearsed in case of bomb damages and duds, fires, or breakdown of social services. The plundering was expected to be for valuables such as gold and jewelry. Meanwhile the bandits, 150 strong, were to be countered by all means and methods available to the police. The bandits were operating either en masse or in small splinter groups of three. To prevent these small groups from infiltrating the city, the police were expected to employ their motorized assets to the full for rounding them up. Mounted police units were to take up positions across the farmlands and countryside, while the Wasserschutzpolizei were expected to patrol the rivers. The radiotelephone system was expected to be used to coordinate the forces participating in the exercise. The police were divided into groups: those formed to combat bomb damage included members from the technical branches, while a team was formed to handle hospital cases, and several units were deployed as security units. Liaison officers coordinated with air defense personnel.

The 1940 police regulations offered the approved methods for shooting; described as the army way in the correct handling methods for carbines, pistols, and machine pistols. Good performance in shooting was a critical precondition to the police officer's "power to act" (*Schlagkraft*) in both peace and war. These skills were to be maintained through regular exercises in the depots or in ranges while on duty. Weapons competence was expected even from administrative officials and staff.[83] Daluege wrote special missives in the police regulations warning officers to heed their contents, while praising the police for its progress and general improvement. The ideological content of the training programs included race and political awareness classes up to the end of the war. Most of this centered on a National Socialist interpretation of history, philosophy, and culture,[84] and Daluege placed considerable attention on a planned ideological training in which "the fundamentals of National Socialist ideology are taught."[85] Specialist training for serving police personnel was a particular feature with officers and men encouraged to attend training courses to raise their skill levels and potential for command.[86] They were sent to academies that specialized in advanced training like the 3rd Police Weapon School or the Alderhorst Training Battalion based in Holland. In 1942, Police Battalion 256 was typical in enrolling its men in a variety of classes including a sniper course, army engineering, and NCO school. Later, in August, men were sent to a mountaineering course. The police regulations extolled the virtues of maintaining training. In 1940, Himmler indicated his intention to combine formation building with ideological training: "I shall form guard-battalions and put them on duty for 3 months only—to fight the inferior being [*Untermenschen*] . . . it will be the best indoctrination on inferior beings and inferior races."[87]

In September 1941, General of Infantry von Schenckendorff, chief of Army Group Centre's rear area, initiated the first field conference on "combating partisans" (*Bekämpfung von Partisanen*). The participants were battalion commanders or above, from both the SS-Police and Wehrmacht.[88] The proceedings were held in the Mogilev casino over a three-day period. Schenckendorff was the product of the Schlieffen military system, an authority on security, and a virulent anti-Communist. He endorsed the measures of total eradication of the "partisans" as the only solution. The conference organizer was Bach-Zelewski's capable police commander, Oberstleutnant der Polizei Montua, from Police Regiment Centre of HSSPF Russia-Centre. The itinerary covered operational procedures from the commanding general to battalion level. Information presented to the attendees included an evaluation of Soviet "bandit" organization and tactics. Talks and presentations included two from Bach-Zelewski. His first paper was on the "partisan" and the political commissar and why it was necessary to execute them immediately after capture. His second paper explained the importance of gaining collaborators among local Russian communities and agents behind Russian lines as an effective means of gaining intelligence. SS-Gruppenführer Artur Nebe, commander of Einsatzgruppe B, charged with killing operations in Bach-Zelewski's area of central Russia, presented a paper on the role of the SD in the common fight against "partisans" and the "Jewish question." There were two actual exercises on each afternoon of the conference. On the first day, the attendees observed the 9th Company of Police Regiment Centre conduct a security exercise in a village near Mogilev. The company performed cordon and control point exercises and distributed propaganda leaflets to villagers. The troops conducted a search-and-destroy exercise for bunkers in a nearby forest and then practiced the methods for hunting insurgents. On the final afternoon, they traveled by omnibus to the army's 2nd Security Regiment to conduct an antipartisan operation. The plan included the "digging out" (*Aushebung*) of partisans, commissars, and Communists from a preplanned area.[89]

In March 1942, the Order Police issued a combat training ordinance titled, "New Regulations for Training Police Formations in Police Warfare."[90] The primary concern behind the ordinance was to increase the combat readiness of the police. The police battalions endured combat training in case the army employed them in frontline combat. The proscribed methods of combat contrasted with those of the army because the enemy were largely "bandits" and parachutists. The essential training for police action assumed strong fire support from a heavy machine gun. The training had to be conducted in small groups, under live rifle and machine-gun fire. Additionally, the assault forces (*Stosskräfte*) were taught to maintain cohesion and secure flanks and the rear. Reconnaissance was considered crucial because the "partisans" were not identifiable like conventional enemy soldiers. Scouts were trained to operate in groups rather than individually. Experience had taught the police that in this kind of warfare individual scouts never returned from a mission. Experience had also taught that the combination of reconnaissance expertise and veteran troops worked well together. Dividing the search area into small sections was the proven method. Scouts warned troops to thoroughly search trees for snipers and the crowns of larger trees for machine-gun nests. The scouts had to cover every possibility including assessing their own rear when in enemy-occupied territory. In the event of a partisan breakout, scouts were taught to take immediate cover.

In the main exercise, troops were trained to eradicate resistance from houses and woods. The troops were taught how to defend against close-quarter counter-attacks near concealed positions and other "vicious behavior." Instilled into the troops through ceaseless exercises was the principle that even in quiet moments there was the potential of sudden close-quarter action or sniping. The notion of constant watchfulness during operations, the ideas that the "front is everywhere" or the "enemy is all around," were internalized into police standard operating procedure. Security from the opening march route was implanted into the collective mindset of all the troops. Instructions for supply troops, for example, stated that all small war methods could be applied, as there were no rules for combat in darkness, in woods, or in towns. The fundamentals of police combat also absorbed a wide variety of tasks, and training officers needed to accommodate all possibilities. Success was gauged as bringing the partisans into a position from which they could not escape. To achieve this, officers and NCOs were told to apply sensitive orders and patience. In the event of cooperation with the armed forces, they were guided by the Wehrmacht military code. In the event of combating "partisans," they were warned to use strictly controlled fighting squares and chain firing. To understand cooperation and coordination, the officers and NCOs were to learn through table-top war-gaming in what the Germans called sand training boxes (*Sandkästen*). The regulations assured officers that in times of severe combat, the police could expect Luftwaffe dive-bomber "stuka" and army heavy weapons and engineers support, which would open the way for the police to perform as combat infantry.

On August 25, 1942, Otto Winkelmann announced the opening of a new colonial police school in in Vienna-Strebersdorf.[91] In keeping with police practice, the personnel formed a cadre (*Stammpersonal*) with Major der Schutzpolizei Zohm on temporary secondment from Oranienburg until September 5. Apart from his staff, Zohm had a complement of eleven Meister und Wachtmeister. The school was supplied with engineering equipment, eight horses (five for riding, a commander's mount, and two horses for teamwork), and support vehicles. The school was open to registrations from August 20. The colonial officers' role with the Schuma and their tasks requires much more examination than can be included here. The guidelines for military-style action were issued to all colonial police officers. In the opening section, the police officer was offered doctrinal guidance on German colonial policy. The use of armed violence was, in practice common with Imperial Germany, recognized as important in times of emergency. In this context, the war and the nature of conflict was discussed:

> The aims of the fighting in this war: in the west is the destruction of their [Western Allies] abilities to continue fighting; but the war against Bolshevism is to their destruction per se. . . . In colonial war, it will always be a case of having the power to fight [and] the task of battle to solve problems.[92]

The guideline elevated Lettow-Vorbeck as the finest exponent of small war. His use of improvisation was extolled as the best tactic for combating the English. Lettow-Vorbeck's methods were also praised for his use of discipline in combat. The guidelines pressed the colonial cadet to become a leader in the Lettow-Vorbeck mold. To develop this quality, the leader was taught to become skillful in the use of reconnaissance and intelligence. Mindful of security and safety, the colonial leader was advised to use silence, to march with care, and to prepare the attack on the enemy with skill.[93] Although on occasion "milder" forms of retribution might be employed, the colonial guidelines suggested "the occupation of areas, destruction of facilities, placing leaders in exile, sending communities into the deserts, control of water sources, separation of intellectuals, and punishments ranging from taking away the kettle to wholesale destruction of the settlement."[94]

In February 1942, Himmler formed a special task force to attract experts into the police as a special leadership corps. The idea behind this instruction was to bring specialists and skilled professionals into the police reserve. They were to bring instruction and special subjects as degrees.[95] During the war, experience and expertise from colonial service was turned into operational training schedules. After the war, former Oberst der Kolonialpolizei Karl Gaisser provided a report for the U.S. Army Foreign Military Studies Project titled the "Partisan War in Croatia." In the introduction, he recalled his time as a colonial police officer in German Togoland and Cameroon, both noted for outbreaks of guerrilla warfare. In 1933, he emigrated overseas but was repatriated to Germany during the war. In 1942, Gaisser was assigned to the Colonial Police School in Oranienburg, where he had trained police officers and NCOs in guerrilla warfare techniques.[96] Gaisser became the senior police officer in Croatia, where he led Bandenbekämpfung actions. Through the 1950s, Gaisser worked for the U.S. Army and completed a study of the German campaign in the Balkans (refer to chapter 9).[97]

The practice of bringing recruits east began in 1939 when the SS took control of depots in Poland and later in the Low Countries. Following basic training in Germany, recruits transferred to collection centers, located in

Poland, Russia, Holland, Austria, and later Italy. The Deutsche Dienststelle, in Berlin, records the Smolensk bandit school (Bandenschule), established in 1943, as falling within the Ch.BKV's regime. Documents from the final period of German occupation in Russia in 1943–44 also indicate that the school was under their responsibility. Schenckendorff's successor, General of Cavalry von Rothkirch, the commander of the Wehrmachtbefehlshaber Weissruthenien, proved his commitment to its promotion. On January 7, 1944, the rear area of Army Group Centre provided an allowance within its budget for a Bandenschule. The organization of the bandit school is itemized in Table 6.1. The training program relied on small groups of qualified Bandenbekämpfung instructors working closely with an army weapons school (*Armeewaffenschule*).[98] On May 31, Army Group Centre informed Rothkirch that the forthcoming course would include instructors from the 9th Army. The next day, a communication advised that it had not received its quota of instructors. By June 3, panic had set in as Rothkirch's staff were concerned that they had not arrived and the course was to begin on June 11. Later that day, the start date moved forward to June 15. Meanwhile, the Wehrmachtbefehlshaber Weissruthenien ordered five officers to "volunteer" to instruct on fighting tactics by the Russians and bandits. However, misfortune befell the course, as on June 23, Major Shoen, commander of the school, and Major Wawzinek, police specialist for Banden-bekämpfung, were wounded by a Soviet mine. This embarrassment for the school, especially the loss of the course leader, was particularly painful for Rothkirch. On June 28, the school closed and was transferred to Lida as Opera-tion "Bagration," the Soviet offensive, was on the point of liberating Minsk.

In a series of documents from the surviving police files, it seems a serious proposal was being made to build a specialist Bandenbekämpfung school within Germany. Being within Reich borders, this meant the SS-Police were required to seek permission from other state authorities. In 1944, the SS wanted a purpose-built exercise ground for Bandenbekämpfung training. In November, the SS identified the Tucheler Heide as suitable. The Order Police officially contacted the State Forestry Service (*Reichsforstamt*) to landscape a Bandenkampfschule in the forest.[99] The officer charged with responsibility to see the job through was Oberst der Schutzpolizei Eggebrecht, who wrote to Oberforstmeister von Hammerstein on behalf of Himmler to request the build-ing of the Bandenkampfschule. The request required that the school be cam-ouflaged and secluded within the forest and that earth bunkers and support shelters be constructed around the site. The construction involved cutting the trees from the forest, and the police were required to ask for permission to proceed from the Reichsforstamt. The reply was favorable and included the right to cut down trees, but the Reichsforstamt demanded payment of rent for the land and a formal contract of use. The file remained open until February 1, 1945, without any final decision recorded.[100] The teaching programs for Bandenbekämpfung continued until March 1945.

Generalleutnant Lothar von Trotha, 1904, after the "victory"
at the Waterberg. *Author's copy*

Franz Ritter von Epp attending the
conference on colonial affairs at the
Ministry of Italian Africa, Rome,
1938. *Author's copy*

Convergence with Germany's past: the 1939 Nazi Colonial Conference attendees' postcard. Posting the card, to relatives and colleagues, was intended to promote interest in the colonial movement. *Author's copy*

Walter Schellenberg and Otto Skorzeny parade the SS-Sonderverbände Friedenthal following the Mussolini rescue mission, September 1943.
*Courtesy of BA Bild 146-1978-069-07*

From left to right, Hermann Griese, Heinrich Himmler, Rudolf Pannier, and Kurt Daluege, Knights' Cross medal ceremony, Berlin, March 1942. *Courtesy of the NARA Captured German Photographs Collection*

Himmler inspects a detachment of Schutzmannschaft (Schuma) probably in the HSSPF Russia-South, 1942. *Courtesy of BA Bild 146-1982-158-03*

Reinhard Heydrich, 1941. *Courtesy of the NARA Captured Hoffmann Collection*

Bach-Zelewski (center) at the headquarters of the Chef der Bandenkampfverbände in Lötzen, East Prussia, July 1943. *Courtesy of BA Bild 146-2004-0088*

The demonstration of a manhunt. This picture of a small team of one SS officer and two police troopers was almost certainly posed for propaganda or training purposes. It not only depicts a three-man dog team but also SS and police cooperation. *Courtesy of BA Bild 146-2004-0085*

The SS dog handler guides the dog to a cellar as a trooper feigns covering them. The relaxed use of the rifle and the handler's lack of caution amplify the fact that it is a demonstration. *Courtesy of BA Bild 146-2004-0086*

The capture of these two "bandits" barely represents a victory. The laughing troopers, who don't have their fingers on their triggers, reflect the absence of real danger from this exercise. *Courtesy of BA Bild 146-2004-0087*

Two "bandits" or "bandit suspects," tied up, are led away by a happy SS trooper, summer 1943. *Courtesy of BA Bild 146-2004-0082*

Perhaps taking the concept of encirclement a little too far, a squad of SS men surrounds a Russian child during a cleansing action, Russia, 1942–43. *Courtesy of BA Bild 146-2004-0084*

So-called captured Soviet agents photographed for Nazi propaganda purposes and to illustrate the criminality of the partisans, date unknown. *Courtesy of the NARA Captured German Photographs Collection*

"Bandit" or "bandit child" (Bandenkind). A Russian youth, placed under the guard of an SS trooper with damaged trousers, is photographed following a village operation, 1942–43. *Courtesy of BA Bild 146-2004-0081*

An SS field interrogation of captured Soviet partisans, together with bottles of alcohol. *Courtesy of the NARA Captured German Photographs Collection*

The final steps of a Russian accused of being a "bandit" or a "bandit suspect," as members of an SS-Police squad lead him away to his death. *Courtesy of the NARA Captured German Photographs Collection*

The killer is ordered not to waste bullets. *Courtesy of the NARA Captured German Photographs Collection*

A squad of hunters, photographed at the end of a day's operations, taken somewhere in a Russian forest in the summer of 1943. *Courtesy of the NARA Captured German Photographs Collection*

One member of the squad is granted the opportunity by an SS propaganda unit to record his deeds, Russia, 1943. *Courtesy of the NARA Captured German Photographs Collection*

Bach-Zelewski's funeral ovation for General von Schenckendorff, whom he regarded as another father figure, Minsk, July 9, 1943. *Courtesy of BA Bild 146-1983-041-25*

Bach-Zelewski, with Kurt von Gottberg at his right side, marches with the Hitler salute to the parade at Schenckendorff's funeral, Minsk, July 9, 1943. (At Nuremberg, Bach-Zelewski stated under oath that he never adopted the *Hitler Gruss*.) *Courtesy of BA Bild 146-2004-0090*

Bach-Zelewski reconnoiters the Kovel defenses with his staff, January–March 1944. *Courtesy of BA Bild 146-1997-048-04A*

One of Bach-Zelewski's Storch airplanes crashed on landing in deep snow, Kovel, February 1944. *Courtesy of BA Bild 146-2004-0075*

Bach-Zelewski working over maps at his operational headquarters at Kovel, January–March 1944. *Courtesy of BA Bild 146-2004-0077*

Bach-Zelewski receives news from his Luftwaffe pilot, possibly that
he had crashed the Storch, Kovel headquarters, 1944.
*Courtesy of BA Bild 146-1974-076-39*

In adversarial flow, the U.S. Army's prosecutor Col. Telford Taylor, during the
International Military Tribunal, Nuremberg, 1946. *Courtesy of the NARA U.S.
Army Signals Collection*

Posing as a witness, Bach-Zelewski stands by his cell door, Nuremberg, 1946. *Courtesy of the NARA Captured German Photographs Collection*

Walter Warlimont, former general of artillery and Hitler's operations liaison officer. Prisoner mug shot, Nuremberg, 1947. *Courtesy of the NARA U.S. Army Signals Collection*

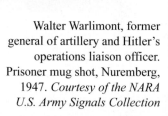

Bach-Zelewski taking the oath of truthfulness at the International Military Tribunal in the main courtroom, January 1946. *Courtesy of the NARA U.S. Army Signals Collection*

Former Bandenkampfverbände intelligence officer (Ic) Eduard Strauch, a defendant in the Einsatzgruppen Trial (USMT-9), gives testimony from the dock, Nuremberg, 1947. A short while later, he was diagnosed as criminally insane and institutionalized. *Courtesy of the NARA U.S. Army Signals Collection*

The only SS officer still in uniform, of sorts, at Nuremberg, Karl Wolff in the dock as a defense witness during Oswald Pohl's trial (USMT-4), 1947. *Courtesy of the NARA U.S. Army Signals Collection*

The memorial to the Warsaw Ghetto uprising, April–May 1943, before which the West German chancellor Willy Brandt knelt on December 7, 1970, Warsaw, Poland. *Author's copy*

The memorial ruins of Oradour-sur-Glane, destroyed by the SS division Das Reich, June 10, 1944, southern France. *Author's copy*

## Table 6.1: The Organization of the Bandenschule (1944)

| SECTIONS | OFFICERS | NCO | MEN | PISTOLS | MPS | RIFLES |
|---|---|---|---|---|---|---|
| Commander | 1 | | | 1 | 1 | |
| Driver | | | 1 | 1 | | |
| Dispatch rider | | | 1 | 1 | | |
| **Training group—Bandit school** | | | | | | |
| Training officers | 2 | | | 2 | 2 | |
| Assistant instructor | | 1 | | 1 | | |
| Assistant instructor | | 2 | | 2 | | |
| Assistant instructor | | | 3 | | | 3 |
| **Training group—Combat Engineer school** | | | | | | |
| Training officers | 1 | | | 1 | | |
| Assistant instructor | | 1 | | 1 | | |
| Assistant instructor | | 2 | | 2 | | |
| Assistant instructor | | | 2 | | | 2 |
| Administration | | | | | | |
| Warrant officer | | 1 | | 1 | | |
| Mail handler | | 1 | | | | 1 |
| Bookkeeper | | 1 | | | | 1 |
| Equipment NCO for bandit school | | 1 | | | | 1 |
| Weapons specialist/instructor | | 1 | | 1 | | |
| Medical orderly | | 1 | | 1 | | |
| Cook number one | | 1 | | | | 1 |
| Cook number two | | | 1 | | | 1 |
| Driver | | | 1 | 1 | | |
| Tailor | | | 1 Hiwi | | | |
| Shoemaker | | | 1 Hiwi | | | |
| Barber | | | 1 | | | 1 |
| Assistant barber | | | 1 | | | 1 |
| NCO Hiwi handler | | 1 | | 1 | | |
| River ferry men | | | 3 Hiwi | | | |
| Building work and moving targets | | | 12 Hiwi | | | |
| **TOTAL** | 4 | 14 | 28 | 17 | 3 | 12 |

## SS-Waldlager Bobruisk

In March 1943, the Soviets launched a campaign since called the "War of the Rails." In March, "bandits" undertook 404 attacks on the railways and blew up the Desna bridges, cutting the line between Gomel and Bryansk.[101] In August, a band attacked the Minsk–Bobruisk railway line. The commander of Einsatzkommando Tatarka, with seven volunteers from an army security detachment (*Wehrmachtsstosstrupp*), undertook an ad hoc preventative action against the band. According to the 608th Security Regiment's after-action report, the SS were praised for their actions in preventing serious destruction for the loss of two wounded. During the early days of August, the Bobruisk–Minsk railway line was the scene of further partisan attacks. Reports from trusties indicated that explosives specialists had been gathering in the area. On August 8–9, 1943, Jagdkommando Wald set ambush positions, fought off a strong band, and killed fifteen to twenty "bandits" at the cost of two SS troopers killed. The SS captured one partisan. Through interrogation, they discovered he had moved into the area only that evening to blow up the railway line. According to Pannier, the railway line was closed for months by "bandits," but through his actions, it was reopened. Operations in the area included the protection of the harvests, maintaining the free access of the railways and the policing of local industries. To these ends, Pannier reported that he had conducted surgical actions against the "bandits" and cleansed the *bandenverseuchtes Gebiet*. Pannier's September 1943 report recorded numerous local Bandenbekämpfung operations arising from securing and protecting the harvest in his area of Bobruisk. All the available troops had been deployed for the protection of the harvest.[102] In his general appraisal of the situation, Pannier indicated that Stalin had ordered an increased level of "bandit" activity in his area. The "bandits" were using communications to coordinate their actions, part of the centralization of the bands, into brigades with liaison staff working directly under orders from Moscow. The range of "bandit" actions included random machine-gun fire, grenades, surprise attacks, laying mines, and the destruction of railways or extensive use of road blocks sometimes more than 1 kilometer long. Pannier mentioned with some concern that the "bandits" no longer fled from a fight but were now looking for a face-to-face battle. His losses were rising but not enough to prevent the completion of his tasks.

The operational priorities of the harvest, local defense against insurgency and running the sub-camps, influenced the training schedule. The 3rd Company was assigned harvest security duties, while another company served in the complex defense lines and another protected the camps. The men on these duties had not received general training, but the companies on guard duty received further individual training in weapons handling, observation, and information gathering, conducted in an ad hoc manner. The conclusion Pannier came to was that even the smallest amount of training had raised the men's "bravery" in combat. The proximity to the bands had raised the level of seriousness of the training exercises. According to Pannier, the troops had responded to the challenge; the 6th Company's performance, in particular, raised the expectations of becoming a solid formation. Pannier's final assessment of the men was 10 percent good, 70 percent mediocre, and 20 percent useless, stated in the most polite terms.[103]

On August 12, 1943, an Einsatzkommando from the central strongpoint of SS-Waldlager Bobruisk conducted a reconnaissance in the vicinity. In the village of Tschikili, they met the command squadron of a band and, after a brief fight, killed five "bandits," one of whom was Senior Lieutenant Pavlo, a scout liaison officer, who had been carrying important papers. The papers included a list of his agents in Bobruisk who were to be arrested. Pavlo had been ordered to employ them in raising a new brigade. The papers also indicated that the bands were being supported by regular groups (*Stammannschaft*) of parachutists under a Major Scharki. On August 14, 1943, Einsatzkommando Bobruisk spent the day removing roadblocks along the route from Makarovichi to Kozlovichi. On the edge of a wood near Makarovichi, the Einsatzkommando stumbled across five mounted "bandits" in full Red Army uniform. This opened an attack on the village that was met with strong opposition. The bands brought up artillery and fired randomly into the Einsatzkommando. Eventually, after suppressing a heavy machine gun, the area was cleansed (*gesäubert*), and the Einsatzkommando moved to Tschikili. The band suffered forty dead and wounded, and the SS had three slightly wounded by a mine explosion that occurred when they were removing a roadblock.[104]

The first section Pannier referenced as falling under the command was the territory called Bandengebiet South Bobruisk. This was a target for concentrated counter-force. On August 18, the 2nd, 3rd, and 5th companies of the SS-Jäger Battalion were deployed to the area Glusk-Kasarichi-Barbarov-Kletno southeast of Bobruisk to secure the harvest. Immediately after their arrival, the "gangs" opened a counter-offensive with all their force. After extensive artillery fire on August 24–25, the "gangs" attacked in several places where the 2nd and 3rd companies were deployed. The "bandits" attacked with two companies, supported by machine guns and tanks. The attack on the 2nd Company was conducted by two tanks and men dressed partially in Red Army uniforms. The 3rd Company managed to force the enemy to stop and retire. They retired from the close-quarter antitank action (*Panzernahbekämpfung*); this led the 3rd Company, joined by the 2nd Company, to counter-attack, sending the gangs in a southwesterly direction. The "bandits" tried to build a fire and retreat, but caught in a pincer (*zangenartige*) movement, they fled. The counter-attack reached a hamlet 500 meters from Kasarichi and stopped at an old factory. The casualties had included three German wounded, one severely, for six "bandits" dead and six wounded. The companies captured various weapons and documents.[105]

The Pannier report also recorded the activities of the SS-Jagdkommando deployed from the Waldlager. They were operating 30 miles east of Bobruisk near the town of Rogachev. An incident, caused by four "bandits" who tripped an alarm at a static security position in the village of Peseva, had flared on August 9, 1943. The "bandits" tried to flee, but one was shot and the Germans captured one of their horses. On the evening August 17–18, the Jagdkommando ambushed what they described as a "bandit" sabotage team leading a Panje wagon. From the ensuing melee, three "bandits" were killed and their equipment was secured, but no explosives were found. Some time later, SS troopers dug out explosives from around the railway line near Kiselevichi. A couple of days later, an SS patrolman (*Aussenstreife*) was shot and killed in Bobruisk.[106] A hunt by the 6th Company of the SS-Jäger Battalion, in the area of Viachovo-Sees located a "bandit" camp. The local collaboration police (Ordnungsdienst Teluscha) had tipped them off. The "bandits" retreated under the pressure of SS firepower, which Pannier attributed to their application of advanced training in combat firing.[107] On August 18, Jagdkommando Wald was assigned to a harvest security action (Erntesicherungsaktion) in the area of Glusha. Their presence was enough to ward off the bands and collection led to the transportation of twenty-five tons of plundered foodstuffs.

To deny the Germans the harvest, the "bandits" had attacked the roads to the collection centers and the men handling the collection. The Soviets had increasingly employed parachutists; they were explosives experts intent on blowing up the railways around the whole area of Bobruisk.[108] The securing of the harvest had taken place inside the band-infected area and thus large quantities of foodstuffs had been denied them. Pannier believed this would force the bands to rely on air supply from Moscow, which could be intercepted. His combating-bands section of the report opened with a summary of the attacks by "bandits" on supply and transportation. They were recorded as using large amounts of explosives to blow up the railway; then they attacked key strongpoints with machine-gun fire and grenades. This slowed down traffic significantly for several days.

Pannier's August report also mentioned Bandenbekämpfung in yet another area, north of Osipovichi, which also concerned the harvest-security action. On August 7, the chief of the Ordnungsdienst in Lapichi requested assistance, and a section from 4th Company, SS-Jäger Battalion, under the command of SS-Hauptsturmführer Reigl, formed up to counter-attack. The detachment chased a band to Pogoreloe, capturing a "bandit" bakery and then proceeded to cleanse the village. The villagers said the "bandits," including the leader, a man called Vorobev, were suffering. Seven days later, on August 14, a scout troop (*Spähtrupp*) advanced toward Greblia, whereupon the "bandits" fled in a northeasterly direction, the Germans following them. Suddenly the band counter-attacked with more than two hundred "bandits," which forced the SS-Jäger Battalion to move back into Greblia, allegedly to cleanse the village. During the firing of the village, explosions were recorded as supposed bandit weapon stores blew up. Twenty bandits were counted dead, but it was known at the time that their losses were greater. The SS suffered one missing, a trooper set upon by eight bandits and presumed dead, and four wounded. On August 31, the Ernteeinsatzkommando of the 4th Company of the SS-Jäger Battalion moved on to the neighboring village of Gomanovka, where they came up against strong "bandit" action. Their own losses included four dead and ten wounded; the losses of the "bandits" were unknown.

According to Pannier's report, operations around Brosha began on August 19–20, 1943, when the strongpoint Bobruisk initiated an action for the rounding up of cattle and agricultural products. This led to a series of firefights near Chikili, which had become the center of band activity, although the "bandits" suffered six wounded. Between August 23 and August 27, the *Ernteerfassungsaktion* continued in the area of Nazdane. This move had allegedly taken the "bandits" by surprise because there had been no interference in the collection process.[109] The gangs attempted to blow up the rails preventing the foodstuff from being transported out, but that failed. They then tried to machine-gun down telephone masts on August 30, hoping to cut German communications. Following an air reconnaissance of the area, the SS instigated a series of bombing decapitation flights. Bandenbekämpfung operations in Brosha caused one band forty dead and wounded, while the SS suffered three slightly injured owing to a mine being removed from a roadblock. On August 24, six airplanes carrying 3,000 kilograms of incendiary bombs and 6,000 kilograms of explosives in an attempt to destroy the headquarters of the brigades bombed the villages of Podgusty-Selenkovichi and Subarevichi. Four days later, Podgusty was attacked with twelve bombs, a combined weight of 1,400 kilograms. On August 31, the village of Berkov was attacked as a probable brigade headquarters with 500 kilograms of explosive bombs.[110]

On August 26, the bands attacked again, this time the Germans held them with well-placed fires. Three days later, elements of the 2nd and 3rd companies, under SS-Untersturmführers Rothmayer and Hassenkamp, approached the village of Zamostosche, which was heavily defended by "bandits." After an hour-long firefight, the village was "captured" at the cost of two dead and three wounded. One of the wounded was Rothmeyer, who subsequently died of his injuries. The "bandits" suffered eleven dead, several weapons and documentation. While this was happening, a brief firefight developed between a scout unit and "bandits" near the hamlet of Podelje. There were no known losses on either side. The papers collected by the SS indicated that the "bandits" were under orders to prevent the Germans from collecting the harvest (*Erfassungsaktion*) at all costs. They were fully aware of the planned SS operation for delivering the harvest (*Ernteeinbring-*

*ungsaktion*). Two "bandit brigades" composed of Polish-Russian border volunteers were joined by the 225th Brigade. This brigade included under its command the "Bogdanovitsce" detachment noted for causing extensive railway damage in the northern area. The bandits had relayed the order to conduct operations against the harvest and carry out large-scale mine-laying activity. They caused the death of SS-Sturmbannführer Beilhack, the SS commander of the Ernteeinbringungsaktion. The brigade had suffered reverses through the deaths of several of its veteran explosives experts. The SS result for the period August 18–31, 1943, was the transportation of a hundred tons of grain and cereals.[111]

Pannier filed his report on September 6, 1943. In all reports, there were evaluations of the German performance. Attached to Pannier's report and his SS personnel file is a letter referring to the death of Rothmeyer. Inaccuracies in reporting were known to happen; whether they were deliberate or not depended on the circumstances. In Pannier's SS personnel file there was a letter dated July 4, 1944, from SS-Untersturmführer Helmich. The letter referred to the Bandenbekämpfung operations the previous year that were covered in page three of the Pannier report. Helmich's letter suggested that the report, which included the death of Rothmeyer, was incorrect. Almost a year later, he felt compelled to draw attention to the inaccuracy of the report. The letter stated that he had been assigned as adjutant to the action on August 26 when Rothmeyer had been killed. With suitable warnings from an Oberleutnant Brockmann about these kinds of actions, they were under the reconnaissance ordered by Pannier. While it attempted to move around the village of Polianki and avoid resistance, a scout troop was surprised and forced to retreat. It was during this clash that Rothmeyer, the troop leader, died of his wounds. With both the officers down, an NCO (SS-Rottenführer) led the scout troop back. In the subsequent report, Pannier suggested that the officers of the 2nd and 3rd companies of the SS-Jäger Battalion had shown cowardice in front of the enemy and during the Erfassung of the village of Kasarichi. Helmich suggested this was not so, that in fact the officers accused fell back under "bandit" pressure. Helmich accused Pannier of using the term pinch (*kneifen*) to imply they had been caught in a pincer movement and run away. The word was erased. Helmich suggested he could still see the imprint of the word on the original report. Helmich posed the question, if both officers were so poor, why were they granted the honor of leading the finest scout troops? To this day, his question remains unanswered.[112]

# 7
# DIE
# BANDENUNTERNEHMUNGEN

In this chapter, the spotlight comes to rest on the Bandenbekämpfung operation. The term *Bandenunternehmungen* could equally mean the "operations of the bandit" and "antibandit operations"; the context determined the interpretation. Bandenunternehmungen involves a hodgepodge of tactics and techniques from sport hunting, conventional warfare, colonial pacification, police actions, and security warfare. Once organized into standard operating procedures and shuffled into a strict code of conduct, Bandenunternehmungen followed the basic principles of warfare.[1] Keith Simpson identified five levels of operations: the defensive measures of strongpoints for local protection (Einzeldienst); the smaller operations (*Klein-unternehmungen*); the large-scale operations (*Grossunternehmungen*); the pacification operations; and the cleansing operations (Säuberungsaktion).[2] His model conforms to the hierarchy of Bandenbekämpfung operations except in three cases. Bandenbekämpfung was fundamentally different because of the inclusion of the "Jewish action" (*Judenaktion*), the "round up of labor action" (*Erfassungsaktion*), and the "harvest-collection action" (Ernteerfassungsaktion). The emphasis of these "actions" distinguished Banden-bekämpfung from Partisanenbekämpfung.

## Tactical Doctrine—Tactical Order

The tactical centerpiece of the Bandenbekämpfung operation was the encirclement (*Einkreisung* or *Einkesselung*). There were other forms of offensive operation, including the flank attack (*Flankangriff*), the envelopment (*Umfassungsangriff*), the frontal attack (*Frontangriff*), the wing attack (*Flügelangriff*), and the penetration (*Einbruch*), but the pièce de résistance remained the encirclement. The encirclement was not only Schlieffen's legacy but also the red thread that ran through all German operational thinking. The opening section of the regulations stated, "We shall always aim for extermination by encirclement." All set-piece security operations were organized to encircle the enemy. There were sound, obvious reasons why the tactic of encirclement suited SS-Police operations. First, encirclement accounted for all the "bandits"; few escaped and then only by chance. Second, this exercise placed the least strain on SS-Police resources, and third, it resulted in fewer German casualties. This standard operating procedure against small and large bands called for the blockading of all escape routes so that the "bandits" were "exterminated systematically." The size of the units deployed were precise, "a thin line of skirmishers is on no account sufficient for encirclement"; hence the size of the combat commands.

The preferred form of extermination of the "bandit" was combat. This involved one of four prescribed methods. The first was "crushing the encirclement" (*Kesseltreiben*), a strangulation maneuver, in which all units converged on the heart of the band, slaughtering all and sundry. The second involved "driving the bandits against pre-prepared firing positions" (*Vorstehtreiben*). This tactic was like a "partridge drive" in which beaters scare birds toward the hunter's gunfire. The third method was to drive an assault wedge into the "heart of the enemy" (*Vortreiben starker Stosskeile*). This wedge, formed out of a combined arms team of infantry and armor or self-propelled artillery, was held in reserve until an opportunity opened to smash into the heart of the band. The final method called for the deployment of an assault group (*Bildung einer Stossgruppe*), released once the encirclement was reinforced. The assault group relied on accurate intelligence and the correct assumption of the band's intended breakout point. These assault groups were more like snatch squads hunting down the "bandits" as they tried to make an escape. Once committed to an operation, the troops were ordered to distract and deceive the "bandits," causing as much confusion as possible to undermine their attempts at interpreting German intentions. The commander was expected to ignore all plausible intelligence from "bandit deserters" regarding the escape or destruction of the band. They were warned to continue the hunt regardless.[3]

The tactical order adopted by all forces in security operations was the battlegroup (Kampfgruppe). The Wehrmacht had been using such formations to integrate armor and mobile infantry to raise their mobility-firepower ratio to counter Soviet breakthroughs and to undertake special operations. The Kampfgruppen were raised from within the available forces assigned to an HSSPF. In July 1945, the British signals and intelligence service wrote a final report on German police signals. The report indicated that "the main unit involved was a Kampfgruppe, a purely ad hoc unit which consisted of anything from a battalion to one or more Police Regiments."[4] The Kampfgruppe performed two functions: they represented the ultimate projection of power and they symbolized the concentration of the many skills and expertise

deployed for Bandenbekämpfung. From the perspective of the Bandenkampfverbände, each Kampfgruppe was named after its commander, indicating a close resemblance to "private" armies. However, it was not just a simple
case of assigning troops to operations. The HSSPF, in forming a Kampfgruppe,
was mindful of retaining a balance between routines and assigning troops to
operations. It was forced to decide whether to maintain a strong grip on local
conditions, thus rationalizing power projection with the wider law and order
requirements of colonial policing.

In June 1943, the HSSPF Russia-Centre deployed its Kampfgruppe for
Operation "Cottbus." The total number of troops committed to "Cottbus"
was 8,709 men, with 3,632 officers and men from the Schuma, and 753 officers
and men from the gendarmerie. The SS-Police headquarters and support functions left to continue regular duties were 4,324 men.[5]

**Table 7.1: HSSPF Russia-Centre during "Cottbus"**

| AUTHORITY | PLACE/COTTBUS | FINAL AUTHORITY | MANPOWER |
|---|---|---|---|
| HSSPF Russland-Mitte | Minsk | HSSPF | |
| Staff company | Minsk | HSSPF | 193 |
| Stabsfahrbereitschaft | Minsk | HSSPF | 79 |
| Signals Company 112 | Minsk | HSSPF | 78 |
| Supply officer | Minsk | HSSPF | 190 |
| NSKK Company Nuremberg | Minsk | HSSPF | |
| Volunteer transport company | Minsk | HSSPF | |
| Volunteer work company | Minsk | HSSPF | |
| Command of SS-Obstbannf. Magill | Minsk | HSSPF | 8 |
| SS-Police Court 17 | Minsk | SS Court Munich | 11 |
| 3rd air liaison officer | Minsk | Luftwaffe | 44 |

The Kampfgruppen were not limited to working under the HSSPF. They
could be raised either locally for an operation or an action or simply through
bringing disparate troops together to form a line. The police continued to
raise combat groups for a variety of missions; Kampfgruppe Hannibal was
raised in April 1944 and continued in frontline action until its surrender in
Königsberg.[6] From July 1944, this particular Kampfgruppe absorbed the police regiments formerly assigned to HSSPF Russia-Centre.

To take the example of the reports from Operation "Hornung," it is noteworthy how forces drawn from the immediate security zone were merged with
units brought in purely for the operation. The plans for "Hornung" were
drawn up by SSPF Weissruthenien in Minsk, with 9,031 troops. The German
element accounted for 6,991 men, including units brought in from the central
reserves, including the 2nd SS-Police Regiment, the 31st SS-Police Rifle Regiment, the SS-Sonderkommando Dirlewanger, an SS-Police armored company,

**Table 7.2: SS-Police Formations Assigned to "Cottbus"**

| SSPF WEISSRUTHENIEN | LOCATION | AUTHORITY | MEN |
|---|---|---|---|
| SSPF | Minsk | HSSPF | 13 |
| 2nd SS Police Regiment | Cottbus | HSSPF | 2,310 |
| 31st Police Defense Regiment | Cottbus | HSSPF | 1,500 |
| 12th Police Armored Company | Cottbus | HSSPF | 131 |
| SS Special Battalion Dirlewanger | Cottbus | HSSPF | 550 |
| Schuma training battalion | Uretsche | HSSPF | 132 |
| Command of the Security Police and SD | Minsk | RSHA | 865 |
| Staff of the farmers associations | Minsk | KdO-Weissruthenien | 2053 |
| Staff of the Gendarmerie Einsatzkommando | Minsk | SSPF -Weissruthenien | 442 |
| Commander of the Orpo Weissruthenien | Minsk | KdO-Weissruthenien | 107 |
| Staff company | Minsk | KdO-Weissruthenien | 150 |
| 11th Signals Company | Minsk | KdO-Weissruthenien | 63 |
| Volunteer music corps Leipzig | Minsk | KdO-Weissruthenien | 45 |
| Commander of the Schuma Minsk | Minsk | KdO-Weissruthenien | 467 |
| Detachment of the department of Schutzpolizei | Baranowitsche | KdO-Weissruthenien | 192 |
| SS Carrier Pigeon Station X | Baranowitsche | KdO-Weissruthenien | 2 |
| Fire Brigade Schuma | Minsk | KdO-Weissruthenien | 152 |
| Fire Brigade Schuma | Baranowitsche | KdO-Weissruthenien | 66 |

**Table 7.3: Gendarmerie Formations Assigned to "Cottbus"**

| COMMANDER OF GENDARMERIE | LOCATION | AUTHORITY | |
|---|---|---|---|
| Headquarters | Minsk | | 42 |
| Gendarmerie Minsk Schuma Patrols | Minsk | KdG | 252 |
| Gendarmerie Baranowitsche Schuma Patrols | Baranowitsche | KdG | 265 |
| Gendarmerie Wilejka Schuma Patrols | Wilejka | KdG | 158 |
| 6th Gendarmerie Troop (motorized) | Cottbus | Gendarmerie Minsk | 36 |
| 7th Gendarmerie Troop (motorized) | Baranowitsche | Gendarmerie Baranowitsche | 36 |
| 11th Gendarmerie Troop (motorized) | Cottbus | . Gendarmerie Minsk | 37 |
| 12th Gendarmerie Troop (motorized) | Cottbus | Gendarmerie Wilejka | 39 |
| 13th Gendarmerie Troop (motorized) | Lida | Gendarmerie Baranowitsche | 41 |
| 19th Gendarmerie Troop (motorized) | Cottbus | Gendarmerie Baranowitsche | 35 |
| 21st Gendarmerie Troop (motorized) | Cottbus | Gendarmerie Minsk | 36 |
| SS-V-Manner Druzhina | Cottbus | SD | 2,500 |
| SS Hospital Minsk | Minsk | SS Leadership Group D | 64 |
| Police supply depot. | Baranowitsche | Gendarmerie Minsk | - |
| Police supply (Russia Centre) | Baranowitsche | Gendarmerie Minsk | - |
| Police riding and driving school | Postavy | Police Commander Ostland | - |
| SS Main Command Zeppelin | Glebokie | RSHA | |

**Table 7.4: Schuma Battalions Assigned to "Cottbus"**

| SCHUMA BATTALIONS | LOCATED | AUTHORITY | MEN |
|---|---|---|---|
| 3rd Lithuanian Battalion | Baranowitsche | KdO-Weissruthenien | 380 |
| 12th Lithuanian Battalion | Hansewitsche | KdO-Weissruthenien | 325 |
| 15th Lithuanian Battalion | **Cottbus** | KdO-Weissruthenien | 603 |
| 254th Reserve Lithuanian Battalion | Sharkovshchina | KdO-Weissruthenien | 158 |
| 271th Lithuanian Battalion | Uretschje | KdO-Weissruthenien | 350 |
| 46th Byelorussia Battalion | Novogrodek | KdO-Weissruthenien | ??? |
| 47th Byelorussia Battalion | Minsk | KdO-Weissruthenien | 630 |
| 51st Byelorussia Battalion | Volozhin | KdO-Weissruthenien | ??? |
| 54th Ukrainian Battalion | **Cottbus** | KdO-Weissruthenien | ??? |
| 102nd Ukrainian Battalion | **Cottbus** | KdO-Weissruthenien | 413 |
| 115th Ukrainian Battalion | Slonim | KdO-Weissruthenien | 537 |
| 118th Ukrainian Battalion | **Cottbus** | KdO-Weissruthenien | 397 |
| 57th Ukrainian Battalion | **Cottbus** | KdO-Weissruthenien | 444 |
| 56th Artillery Battalion | Borissow | KdO-Weissruthenien | 413 |
| 49th Byelorussia Battalion | Minsk | Kdo. Sch. Minsk | 315 |

and the mandatory SD detachment. The balance of forces included 2,040 men drawn from Schuma battalions and the motorized gendarmerie sections. This ratio of Germans to Schuma requires explanation. The balance might suggest German manpower dominated operations, but this is the wrong impression. German forces only dominated the opening moves in a prestige operation, or by ensuring the successful completion of encirclement, or by conducting the vigorous fighting required against well-armed bands. The Schuma and collaborator forces then were filtered into the encirclement or replaced the stronger combat units when the fighting had tailed off. The system worked on shifts, enabling local troops and visiting units to rest and refit regularly. This also allowed the enforcement of the required level of policing in a region. In Operation "Hornung," the troops at the disposal of SSPF Weissruthenien were assigned to compass-point combat commands (Ost, Nord, West, Süd). This was the prerequisite for an encirclement operation.

> *Kampfgruppe Ost*: under the commander of the 2nd SS-Police Regiment, with the Russian collaboration Battalion Rodjanoff, field battery Borissow from the 1st SS-Infantry Brigade, and a tank section from the 18th SS-Mountain Police Jäger Regiment.
> *Kampfgruppe Nord*: under the commander of 1st Battalion 23rd SS-Police Regiment, with SS-Kommando Dirlewanger, Schuma Battalion 57, Police Signals Company 112, and the 12th SS-Police Tank Company.

*Kampfgruppe West*: under the commander of the 13th SS-Police
Regiment (less the 3rd Battalion), Schuma Battalion 18, a field
battery from Schuma Artillery Detachment 56, and the mine-clear-
ing and bridge-building Technische Nothilfe Detachment II.
*Kampfgruppe Süd*: under the commander of the 10th SS-Police
Regiment (less the 1st Battalion), with a detachment 11th SS-
Police Regiment (originally from Schuma battalion 103), Balten
Battalion 1, and heavy company Kohlstadt.
*Kampfgruppe Südost*: two battalions from the army's 101st Infan-
try Regiment.
*Gottberg's command*: detachments from the Bomber Flying School
Bobruisk, SS-Police Signals Company 11. An SD-Sonder-
kommando was attached to each battalion.[7]

Following the organization of the tactical order the commanding officer
issued the tactical instructions necessary to meet the demands of an operation. A set of instructions issued by Otto Hellwig, SSPF Shitomir, illustrates
their format.[8] The instructions opened with a warning that there could be no
departure from their strict application. There was no opportunity for interpretation, deviation, or equivocation. Operations had to conform with official
channels of reporting, with daily situation reports passed to the regional
police commander, either the KdO or BdO. They in turn would issue an overview report for the district commissar (*Gebietskommissar*) belonging to the
Nazi civilian administration. The reports had to contain simple details of which
bandit bands had been located and attacked and the German (plus allied)
formations that had participated. The report should list the villages subjected
to actions and the reasons for their treatment, as well as those villages des-
tined for destruction on the grounds of preventative action (*Präven-
tivgründen*). Hellwig stressed in point two of his instructions that preventative burning of villages containing nests of bandits could only be carried out
with prior approval of the Gebietskommissar. When it was decided to destroy
a village, the entire population was to be subject to registration (Erfassung)
for deportation and forced labor. Villagers found with weapons that had fired
on the police were executed on the spot. The registered civilians were led to
the nearest town where the local police conducted their dispersal to work
details or transportation to Germany. Raising transportation was the responsibility of the general commissioner (*Generalkommissar*), and police officers
not already committed to Bandenbekämpfung operations assisted him. All the
troops were instructed to "leave the people with something," although precisely what was not stipulated. The Germans accounted for items removed
from the villagers through a billing system (*Behandigungsschein*) and handed
out a receipt (*Quittung*) to the "former" owner. Hellwig warned the troops that
wanton acts of destruction imperiled the Reich's war effort. Plundering and

serious breeches of the instructions would lead to the death penalty. Hellwig expected disciplined behavior and threatened regular checks and enforcement by the police. He also warned that the instructions were also binding on the Lithuanian, Latvian, Ukrainian, and other auxiliary troops, stressing this point by underlining the text.[9] Hellwig's instructions conformed to the Bandenbekämpfung directive and the 1942 guidelines. The process of the collection of goods and the roundup of labor (Erfassungsaktion) was articulated as the correct form of punishment for disloyal civilians.

## Operations

Ruth Bettina Birn's study of operation "Winterzauber" concluded with the opinion that the SS-Police concept of professionalism was the strongest motivation in the performance of operations.[10] In arriving at this conclusion, Birn dismissed the notion that ideological pressures, whether political, economic, or social, applied to antipartisan operations warfare, as had been suggested by Hannes Heer.[11] She also disagreed with Christian Gerlach's argument that economic and agricultural exploitation largely determined the application and intensity of Bandenbekämpfung operations.[12] In 1941, the response to the partisan was subject to competing priorities such as the outright defeat of the Soviet Union. In this period, the level of response fluctuated. In the period leading to the introduction of Directive 46, the army employed large-scale operations to eradicate the "bandits" during the campaign season. After Directive 46 was introduced, large-scale operations were continued but the target range was widened to include civilians. In practice, this policy was directed toward wrestling the initiative away from the bands and reducing their effectiveness by causing them attrition losses.

Bach-Zelewski became associated with large-scale operations beginning with "Adler" (July 15–August 7, 1942). This operation offered all the promise of new ideas and based on experience gathered since June 1941. "Adler" was followed by Operation "Greif" (August 14–20) and then by Operation "Sumpffieber" (August 22–September 21), completing a string of operations that heralded the issue of the Bandenbekämpfung directive. The first indication was the success of employing large bodies of formations committed to a single operation. From August 1942, Hitler received Bandenbekämpfung reports compiled by Himmler. In effect, they were a summary of the after-action reports sent to the KSRFSS. One of the first reports to Hitler concerned Operation "Greif," which listed ninety-eight "bandits" killed, twenty prisoners, with six "bandit" deserters. This list included large quantities of material captured from the "bandits," including several field guns. The German losses were one dead and three wounded. A subsequent report for "Greif" accounted seven dead "bandits" and ten prisoners and the death of two Germans.[13] Irrespective of losses, Stalin was prepared to accept such attrition if it denied the Germans freedom to rule. The following case studies of Bandenbekämpfung operations from 1943 provide an indication of the range of actions involved in forming a Bandenunternehmungen.

## Municipal Action

The police specialized in the application of close-order tactics in towns and cities. With their Weimar experiences, they were long-time exponents of armed street fighting. The use of close-order tactics was a police expertise confined to villages, conurbations, and cities. In 1943, the incumbent HSSPF Russia-Centre, SS-Obergruppenführer Gerrett Korsemann, planned Operation "Zauberflöte" for the city of Minsk. The plan entailed rooting out "bandits, Bolshevik terror and saboteur troops, operatives and helpers, signallers and deserters" through the systematic search of 130,000 homes and the war ruins of the city.[14] The operation, timed for April 17–22, 1943, was supposed to permanently cleanse the city through the eradication of resistance, the arrest of German deserters, and the mass deportation of laborers to Germany, by winkling them out of their hiding places (*Schlupfwinkel*). This complex operation envisaged the coordination of simultaneous cordons systematically sweeping all six-city districts, with an outer security encirclement collapsing onto an inner security ring. This operation contained two generic components: the search for or hunting of fugitives and the criminal registration and punishment element.[15]

The police experienced the strains of quelling crowd violence during Hitler's rise to power. They also had a reputation for using weapons to impose law and order. In 1906, riots in Hamburg awakened fears of looming revolution, and the police used arms to restore law and order.[16] The Freikorps became deft at conducting full-scale street battles with heavy weapons. In 1927, the police had treated the question of street and house-to-house fighting (*Strassen- und Häuserkampf*) in its official journals. Richard Bessel suggested that the police rehearsed and practiced closing streets and neighborhoods to prevent demonstrations by proletarian agitators and Communist sympathizers. In 1929, the Berlin police revealed their capability in city action against Communist activists who had occupied a housing district. The action led to the death of thirty-three agitators and 198 agitators were injured, but there were no police casualties.[17] Police close-order tactics involved tight cordons of troops and were manpower-intensive exercises. Operation "Zauberflöte" was the most comprehensive plan for a city action.

The organization of forces for "Zauberflöte" was as usual detailed. The planned operational period was five days and depended on the highest level of cooperation between the Wehrmacht and SS-Police. A series of complex maneuvers led the troops along parallel actions with the commander conducting them toward the complete choking off of all escape routes. The plan required the army to form an outer cordon with troops from the 141st Reserve Division and units of the Minsk garrison commander (Ortskommandantur).

The SS-Police, working the inner cordons, committed elements from two regiments, and the SS-Sonderkommando Dirlewanger was placed on a system of strict rotation. Five hundred and sixty men from the 2nd SS-Police Regiment took up the first watch on April 17. The 13th SS-Police Regiment followed on April 18 with 470 men. The subsequent watches saw fluctuations in manpower commitment: the 2nd with 640 men on April 19, the 13th with 540 men on April 20, the 2nd with 470 men on April 21, and finally, the 13th with 490 men on April 22. Precise instructions were handed to the SS-Sonderkommando Dirlewanger. They were to encircle the Jewish ghetto and provide guards detachments for their columns of laborers leaving and returning to the ghetto. Korsemann chose to openly admonish Dirlewanger by adding to the preparatory orders the warning that any plundering by his men would be punishable through the severest means.[18]

Operation "Zauberflöte" was timed to start at 4:00 a.m. on April 17, with the army exploiting the cover of darkness and maximizing surprise to blockade the first district. The men of the 2nd SS-Police Regiment took up their positions. The cordon of two men at 50 meters required a total of 268 men. During the initial maneuver the cordons required each man to cover an area either side 50 meters from the next man. Fifty meters appears a fair-sized gap until it is realized that this was the guaranteed kill zone for troops shouldering the standard German army rifle. On main roads, this number was increased to two men per 50 meters. On April 18, the army received the order to relieve the police by 7:00 p.m. By the evening of April 18, the central part of the city was encircled by the army, and on April 21, this allowed the police to conduct the final searches. Meanwhile, the search and hunting teams roamed the district. Six hundred men, from the 2nd, 13th, and 1st battalions of the SS-Police Regiment, were assigned to search floors and cellars to find weapons and Soviet propaganda. The teams assigned to searching no-man's-land (*Sperrgebiet*) numbered 120 men. In one sense, they were like beaters in a hunt driving victims toward the walking killing zone.

The second part of the operation involved registration. The police set up regular checkpoints (*Durchgangsstellen*) and assigned twenty men each. Their job was to conduct the first screening. Persons found in possession of official SS or SSPF documents were allowed to continue their lives uninterrupted. Others without such documentation on them were taken to collection points for registration and possible deportation. Korsemann's plan also integrated what became the central checkpoints, each handled by one SD officer, a police official, a translator from the Security Police, and ten ordinary police officers from the Order Police. The job of registration for deportation was handed to a hundred-man detail at the collection points (*Sammelplätze*), with another fifty men policing the transports. For the climax of the operation, Korsemann had anticipated the encirclement being completed by April 22. He also projected that day as the moment when the fugitives in desperation would make their strongest attempt to break out. As a precaution, therefore, he increased the number of guards by two men every 50 meters strengthening the city cordon. The attempted breakout actually came at night on April 19–20, but it was crushed. Resistance, when offered, caused houses to be burnt down, booty destroyed, and underground presses collected.

During the operation, on April 19, Bach-Zelewski met Fritz Sauckel in Minsk to hold discussions on foreign labor, as mentioned in chapter 4.[19] The overall result was 76,000 persons processed, 52,000 persons taken to collection points for further processing, and another 22,400 rail travelers inspected for traveling without a ticket as "black travelers" (*Schwarzfahrer*). Five hundred and fifty people were sent to Germany as laborers, 712 regarded as unsuitable to be sent to Germany were sent as laborers to Minsk, 39 were arrested, and 2 suffered "special treatment" (*Sonderbehandlung*). The police confiscated materials identified as saboteur materials, including acid, batteries, copper and fuse wire, rifles, gas masks, cameras, and medical kits, as well as a miscellaneous selection of clothing. To mark the completion of the operation and acknowledge their resounding success, a closing ceremony was arranged for 11:00 a.m. on April 23, 1943. Bach-Zelewski declared "Zauberflöte" a bandit operation (Bandenunternehmungen), remained in Minsk to preside over a march-past of 136 officers and 3,705 non-commissioned officers, and men of the "SS- und Polizeiverbänden," and then gave a speech.[20]

## Security Cannae

An almost perfect example of Cannae occurred in an operation named "Nasses Dreieck" ("wet triangle"), which took place by the River Desna and close to Kiev. Himmler had ordered Prützmann to take charge of cleaning the area of a significant bandit incursion.[21] A band led by a Russian farmer named Naumenko was reputed to be eight hundred to one thousand strong. At first, the members of the band had been drawn from local villages and were volunteers. Post-operation interrogations discovered that "Band Naumenko" had in fact three hundred men armed with rifles, six machine guns, fifteen light machine guns, four mortars, and thirty automatic weapons. The Germans learned that Naumenko had forced locals into a second detachment of about 250 and were led by his brother or sister, though neither was certain. A Captain Spenatzky, a Red Army officer, organized another detachment of about 250 with heavy and light machine guns, automatic rifles, and Russian rifles. The regional bandit commissar was said to be Lieutenant Kim, a thirty-five-year-old specialist sent by Moscow and openly declared the overlord of the rayon (district). This band was known but its strength was not recorded. An element of confusion was added to the assessment of the "bandit" forces by the disappearance of the collaboration Cossack Battalion 121, which was believed to have joined the bands.[22]

The field commander assigned to eradicate the bandits was Oberst Römer, the local Luftwaffe garrison commander. The terrain bisected the River Desna, included forested swampland, and came under the command of the regional authorities of the Wehrmacht and SS-Police. The intelligence on the bands, prior to Operation "Nasses Dreieck," indicated to the Germans that they required larger forces. Römer planned a coup de main with a three-sided encirclement using the river as a barrier to "bandit" mobility. He also incorporated deception into the plan to conceal his shortfall of troops and heavy weapons. The bluff appeared to work. "Our strength was overestimated," Römer boasted later. "The bandits believed that we had 2,000 Cossacks and several regiments." The troops available allowed the formation of the ad hoc Kampfgruppe Römer. On May 6, Römer organized the Kampfgruppe into five attack detachments (*Stosstrupps*), three deploying antitank and anti-aircraft weapons. Constrained by manpower, he elected to eschew clearing the forest and avoided the swamp to maintain his operational mobility. During the preparation phase, Römer received reports that the "bandits" had occupied four villages, Darniza, Wysschaja Dubetschnja, and Lebedov Chutor and were in control of crossing points over the river. He decided that they would become his first and priority objectives. Römer called on Wasserschutzpolizei Kiev to form a riverine force of three motor patrol boats and retake control of the river crossings.[23]

Römer chose the classical Cannae tactic, incorporating the river to anchor the progress of his mobile units, making them perform a closing door maneuver. The operation began on May 9, 1943, with the units moving into their designated positions. One group occupied positions to the north near to the occupied villages, while a detachment of Cossacks rode hard to close the southern flank. A third detachment formed up a screen at the front of the forest to prevent any of the "bandits" from escaping. The last maneuver involved the Wasserschutzpolizei patrol boats moving into position to close off the river crossing points. This confirmed a loose encirclement. For security purposes Römer designated one detachment to secure the march, by protecting the supply routes and guarding signals land lines. The 120th Luftwaffe Signals Regiment set up the operational communications network and began monitoring bandit communications. The encirclement was then strengthened on May 10, when the Germans brought up heavier weapons to reinforce the northern detachment positioned near the villages. A heavy mortar detachment took up positions on the far side of the river. Realizing their predicament, the bandits tried to force an escape by attacking the bridge, but they were repulsed. This caused damage to the bridge, and operations waited for five hours, while German army engineers carried out repairs.

The "bandit" action triggered a German attack, and the Germans soon captured several villages. Slowly they began crushing the bandits like an anaconda slowly constricts its prey. The lack of air support forced the Germans to press the "bandits" in a direction that brought them within range of the mortars. This singularly successful tactic caused serious losses for the "bandits" and drove them deep into the swamp.[24] After this climactic fighting, the Germans proceeded with a slow and deliberate cleanup action. On May 11, a detachment proceeded in a north-northwesterly direction systematically clearing bandits from houses and cellars of villages. That evening Römer recorded that a flight of Stuka dive-bombers joined in an attack on one of the villages, to "cleanse it of enemies and return to its legal standing."[25] The cleanup of the area continued the next day, with the Technische Nothilfe locating and marking minefields. The encircling troops were briefly stalled in the swamp by resistance and another minefield near the villages of Nowosselki-Oschitki. Elsewhere, the Wasserschutzpolizei cleared the river islands and executed fourteen captured bandits without trial. Reports to Römer indicated that the main body of the band had fled deep into the woods and swamps. Over the next two days, supporting Hungarian troops captured high ground. This gave Römer time to prepare his forces for the final *Schwerpunkt*. On May 15–16, the "bandits" were officially recorded as destroyed:

> With short pauses, the bandits up to their necks in water in the swamp were unmercifully attacked by mortars, heavy artillery and heavy machine-guns. The result was that many bandits tried to escape but were destroyed in the process. A large number were found dead caused by iron and swamp water.[26]

Römer wrote in his operational report that "in the period the May 9–16, approximately twelve hundred bandits and bandit-helpers were shot, more than 50 percent during the attempt to break out of the swamp." He added, "one must add to this the large number shot during the fighting in the swamp morass of at least 800 to 1,000." He noted that 843 "bandits" were killed in the fighting and two hundred apparently unaccounted for in the swamp. Römer surmised that "all the armed bandits had fled into the swamp, the prisoners had confirmed this. There are still individual bandits attempting to evade capture seeking protection as refugees." He ordered the woods combed for escapees and any found were punished.[27] The question of "bandit" weaponry came into the report: "According to the calculation, there was only a small amount of captured weapons, only 10 guns and other equipment. This is explained because the bandits were in the swamps and they either lost their weapons or buried them."[28] Also in passing Römer acknowledged the presence of the GFP and the execution by shooting of 205 Bandenverdächtigte.

Römer reserved his highest praise for the Cossacks in both their reconnaissance and combat roles. They were "the perfect troops for pacification," in his opinion, because "they ride fast and fight hard." He commended the excellent relationship with community leaders and a local schoolmaster. They assisted in the efficient deportation of civilians and two thousand cows.

Römer finally judged the shortfall of German propaganda to be at fault. "The reason for the rise in banditry," he said, "was the failure of our own propaganda that the civilians were to be slaughtered or sent to Germany, which was worse than Siberia," Römer judged. "Our propaganda failed. In Wypolsowo, the propaganda detachment played music and distributed leaflets of pictures of the Führer. The inhabitants said if our propaganda had worked, then Naumenko would never have been able to develop."[29] Römer's observations partly explain the nature of the relationship between political killing and military capability within a Bandenbekämpfung operation. However, they do not explain Bach-Zelewski's apparent rant against the operation. In his diary, after the completion of the operation, he complained that Prützmann was not militarily trained. He ranted that it was alright for the Reichsführer to pass on orders to others while passing the responsibility for the nation on to him but that sometimes leaders had to rise above their careers and do the right thing. He argued that under this dictatorship, the nation accepted authority from above, but had no real idea of the uninterrupted fight for power that was taking place below. He was in a powerful position but struggled to maintain his influence.[30] Bach-Zelewski should not have been so paranoid: a month later, he was promoted to Ch.BKV.

## Pursuit

The least desired eventuality for an SS-Police operation was a pursuit. This was in contrast to the army, which considered pursuit a positive outcome. The pursuit offered the "bands" some chance of escape, a burden for the SS because it extended their operational commitment, placed strains on men and equipment, and heightened the potential for casualties. Operation "Wehrwolf" involved a pursuit that turned out to be one of the most dramatic episodes of all SS-Police Bandenbekämpfung operations in the east. The matching sources of evidence from German reports and the partisan leader's memoirs heighten the drama.[31] Soviet partisan policy for the Ukraine changed in 1942, and one plan was to employ long-range raids deep inside German occupied territory.[32] One such raid was led by Maj. Gen. Sidor Artemevich Kovpak. It resembled a Mongol invasion rather than a modern insurgency force.

The objective of the raid has been the subject of speculation. Armstrong believed they planned to destroy oil fields. Another opinion suggested that it was an attempt to assess the condition of the Ukrainian partisans on their home ground, although Kovpak himself noted strong resistance from the UPA, one of several Ukrainian nationalist resistance groups, to his presence in their region. Captured "bandits," under interrogation, stated their objective was to reach either Hungary or Rumania. The Germans could not determine if the raid was to re-establish Soviet power and authority in the minds of the people of the occupied zones or if it was planned as a military-style operation.

The German files contain handwritten remarks that indicate some among the staffs believed the raid was an attempt to link up with Tito. The Kovpak band adopted a quiet routine until it reached the Galician borders, even passing strategic oil fields without any attempts at sabotage. The band adopted "hit-and-run" tactics while continuing westward and retaining the initiative.

Kovpak was a long-serving member of the Communist Party and a veteran of the Russian civil war. In the interwar years, he had served as mayor of the Poltava municipality. When the German army arrived in 1941, Kovpak formed a partisan band of more than three thousand well-armed men and women. His deputy was the ruthless political commissar Gen. Semyon Rudnev, who ordered execution for any partisan found plundering during the raid. The regimental organization and logistics of the raid were based on mobility and self-sufficiency. The band's order of battle included five battalions of partisan infantry and an artillery company with nine field guns (76mm and 45mm caliber guns). Each battalion received twenty machine guns. The flak detachment was armed with 20mm anti-aircraft guns, and the mortar section carried medium-size mortars. Each battalion was assigned up to fifteen explosives experts for sabotage. The cavalry squadron, with more than one hundred twenty mounts, carried out the regiment's advance reconnaissance and screening patrols. Signals were the responsibility of a Red Army officer and his two daughters, who expertly maintained contact with Moscow and liaised with the Red Air Force. The Germans' signals monitoring service reported that the bands maintained strict radio routines and never deviated from preset security procedures. Female partisans walked along lanes pretending to be simple country folk while identifying landmarks, suitable air-landing fields, and regimental collection points. The headquarters staff, together with a scout company, and the supply function pooled three hundred motor vehicles. The band's march route took it through communities and villages. The inhabitants were required to work for the band in gathering supplies and scouting. Wounded were flown out from air-landing points when air support was available. The supply formed forage teams to locate and acquire provisions. Like a nomadic tribe, the band drove three hundred head of cattle and many more sheep and carried crates of chickens. Once airdrops became unavailable, the regiment resorted to replenishment by attacks on police stations and small military depots.

On March 26, 1942, Kovpak set off from Bryansk, and after a brief fire fight with the Germans, his band found sanctuary in the Smolensk forest and took up residence. Months later in October, at the head of his band, Kovpak set off toward the west. By early 1943, they had passed Rovno and then Dubno and arrived on the Galician border. Along the way, the band liberated Jews from the Skalat labor camp and absorbed a group of young people into the "Jewish company." To disguise the breakthrough, the bandits dressed in

German uniforms and so passed villages without interference. All captured Axis troops were stripped and killed. After the raid, the Germans found a collection of different uniforms and papers. The march was disciplined, with quiet routines and the skirting of German strongpoints. They crossed into Galicia via forests, traveling at night and resting under camouflage. For seven months, the incursion failed to attract any serious attention from the Germans.

Politically, the raid was a serious challenge to Bach-Zelewski's authority. The route of Kovpak's march not only triggered a response from the respective spheres of SS competence but had touched on the highly sensitive issue of the extermination program in Poland. Bach-Zelewski's field commanders were the unlikely pairing of Globocnik and Krüger. The plan the SS concocted called for a rapid series of maneuvers to decapitate the bandit leadership. The SS placed a rich bounty on Kovpak's capture, turning him into a Robin Hood figure. To match the SS projection of initiative with available forces, the SS command initially chose to pump units into the area like a drip feed, collecting them at strategic points, but all they did was commit units piecemeal and sustain losses. They thought this might reduce Kovpak's options while allowing them to concentrate their forces, but Kovpak foiled their plan with his continuous movement.

A distinctive feature of Operation "Wehrwolf" was the SS-Police order of battle, which crossed several nationalities including Russian, Italian, German, Ukrainian, Polish, and Hungarian. The first Kampfgruppe Dorsch, a total of 16 officers and 267 men, included a gendarmerie squadron, the Tarnopol Schutzpolizei, the 3rd Battalion 23rd SS-Police Regiment, and a detachment of Ukrainian police. These units were later joined by the SS-Police Battalion Breslau and the Galician Cavalry Squadron. This Kampfgruppe was broken up on July 11, 1943, and replaced by Kampfgruppe Hauptmann Karl, which contained Landesschützen Battalion 543, an SS-Police signals detachment (Kraków), the surviving members of Kampfgruppe Dorsch, a squadron of reconnaissance airplanes, and troops from the army's Reserve Grenadier Battalion 425. The total complement including staff was eighteen officers and 622 men. On July 12, the 4th SS-Police Regiment as a complete formation joined the fray. The SD-Einsatzgruppe Piper was dispatched from Reichskommisariat Ukraine with seven officers and 450 men.

The Germans first realized the implications of the raid on July 7, 1943, when aircraft from Luftwaffe Regional Command (*Luftgau*) VIII located the band 30 kilometers southeast of Tarnopol. The band ran for cover 15 kilometers southeast into the forest of Ivankovce, but the Germans were already prepared and attempted encirclement. Kovpak later wrote that a German or Axis ally blocking force countered his every move. "Having paved highways and motor transport at their disposal, the Hitlerites quickly sealed all the exits from the mountains and began to close the ring of encirclement."[33] Although the Germans had insufficient numbers they continued to attempt encirclement, and the bandits kept escaping. The breakout of the evening July 12–13 led to the decisive commitment of the Luftwaffe.

From the beginning of the German reaction, the 7th Special Flying Group was committed with 6 Fieseler Storch airplanes. The commander of Luftgau VIII ordered the Luftwaffe School Deblin to assign two flying groups. [34] The first was a ground-attack group (*Schlachtflieger-Gruppe*) with five of the newly arrived Henschel HS129 airplanes. With its heavily armor-protected cockpits, a 20mm cannon, and four machine guns, the HS129 was a deadly opponent for a bandit force. The other group, flying nine of the old heavy-type fighter aircraft, the ME110 destroyer (*Zerstörer*), was recorded as pilots under training for night-fighter duties.[35] Both aircraft types had twin engines, and this led Kovpak to recall being continuously under observation and attack from Messerschmitts. Monitoring the results of these sorties, a Luftwaffe command team made up from senior officers flying an HS129 or a Fieseler Storch observed the attacks. Using their wireless location devices and plotting ranges on their 1 to 100,000-scale maps, the Luftwaffe again found the band under cover in a forest south of Tarnopol. The air attacks inflicted on the band caused high losses, which were confirmed by a local SIPO officer but not detailed. The band moved on, through forests and across the River Dniester, blowing up the bridge in their wake.

The band found deep cover but was located on July 16–17, and again the Germans attempted encirclement. It fought its way to Medynia but air attacks killed more than 150 horses. The "bandits" fled toward the Carpathian Mountains again destroying bridges desperate to hamper the German's progress. They inevitably began to slow because of the combined effects of exhaustion and the sapping of morale by permanent air attack. To increase mobility they stripped down their motor vehicles from four wheelers to two wheelers (it this was never explained how). It was a costly decision. They faced encirclement with the added difficulty of rolling air attacks. In the fierce fighting, the rearguard of the band was destroyed and large amounts of supplies were lost. One air attack caught the forage teams in the open, and they came under repeated bombing and strafing. In desperation they offloaded their artillery pieces to increase their speed, but thereby deprived themselves of all anti-aircraft defense.

Just when it seemed Kovpak was finished, he responded heroically with an act that no doubt saved the remnants of the band. On July 18, 1943, Kovpak correctly identified elements of the 4th SS-Police Regiment in the town of Rosulna. He sent a small force to attack them (both sides confirm this). It was almost certainly a decoy attack. The Germans reported a small but sneak bandit attack at 11:40 p.m. The shock hit the 7th Company of the regiment unprepared. Krüger later reported that the bandits attacked with heavy machine-gun, mortar, and antitank gunfire. This was perhaps an exaggeration, as the earlier pages of his report clearly stated that the bandits had dumped their artillery. Kovpak did not explain the content of the attack but claimed the SS had been "exterminated," which was another exaggeration. The results reported by the Germans grudgingly confirmed a fleeting bandit success. One bandit was killed and another wounded, at the cost of eighteen German dead and seventeen wounded. The arrival of the 6th Company relieved or rescued, depending on one's opinion, the 7th Company and saved the regiment from further shame.[36] The effect of the attack allowed Kovpak to move. The German response was to deploy more troops. On July 24, the 13th SS-Police Regiment arrived, assisted by Jagdkommando Galician. They amassed between them fifteen hundred men, but more important, they were specialist bandit hunters. On August 1, a contingent of the 26th SS-Police Regiment with 40 officers and 1,764 men joined in the operations. Anticipating Kovpak's run toward Red Air Force support, Himmler's 1st RFSS Flak Battalion was deployed to hinder any aerial support for the bandits.

In August, Kovpak simply disappeared. On August 11, Bach-Zelewski made a scathing attack on the lethargy of the SS-Cavalry Division and added insult to injury by overly praising Kovpak's ability.[37] After the war, Kovpak described German tactics: "The enemy remained on the defensive. He reckoned on wearing us down, compelling us to expend all our ammunition, and meanwhile so to strengthen the solidity of the ring [encirclement] that not a single man would be able to break out."[38] Kovpak's constant movement, even running away, saved him from capture, although these were certainly not the politically correct descriptions for his 1947 memoirs. Kovpak left behind his deputy, General Rudnev, killed on August 3–4, 1943, 641 "bandits" killed, and a hundred captured. The German's estimated another 450 wounded remained behind, and it seems a significant number became undercover agents.[39] The German casualties from "Wehrwolf" were 141 dead and 129 wounded (including 4 missing); the Axis allies sustained 7 dead and 4 wounded. The largest loss was suffered on July 8, 1943, with 42 dead and 6 wounded. After the war, Bach-Zelewski embellished Kovpak's reputation:

> [T]here wasn't a Kolpak [Kovpak] man who went into capture. They were the most fanatical and courageous partisans that I have ever seen. They were strictly disciplined that if one of them was wounded, his comrade had to shoot him so that he did not get into German capture and betray any secrets.[40]

## Victims and Violence

In examining Operation "Winterzauber," Birn found a series of actions that revolved around "special treatment." The Schuma committed the destruction of villages when the SD or GFP were unavailable. The executions were ordered carried out in the villagers' houses, with the corpses covered in straw and set alight. Birn stated that evidence from Russian sources indicated that many victims were deliberately burned alive.[41] The question of whether witnesses were allowed to live or die has yet to be established. Birn noted that the Schuma Battalion 279 had been rounding up civilians and had released a mentally disturbed woman into their "care." Eventually a Latvian Schuma trooper had brought the woman to the German security police. The German in command reported that this woman required long-term "special treatment" and said, "I think that it's a great danger if one person knows of our methods and can lead to disaster."[42]

Prior to the Bandenbekämpfung directive, killing Jews in security operations was usually phrased as "Jew-hunts," while in 1943, Kutschera warned the troops to accept the justice of dealing with the Jewish members of bands.[43] Generally, the terminology settled on the presumption that all Jews were bandits and vice versa, and when Jewish bandits (*Juden-Banden*) were encountered, they suffered excruciating death. A Luftwaffe sergeant reported the details of one cleansing action (Säuberungsaktion): "we had orders to kill all persons over 5 years of age." He added, "we found a bunker in the forests. They were destroyed."[44] Later, "on June 28, 1943, three houses with Jews inside were set on fire. We sensed the Jews had munitions in the top floor, because explosions were heard." The following day, a further report stated, "on 29 June we searched a larger area of forest where fifty bandits had escaped. At 7:00 p.m., the wood was encircled and the Luftwaffe companies began a search. By 8:00 p.m., the Luftwaffe and police forces had joined signifying the destruction of all the bandits."[45]

There were many cases of assassination in Russia. In November 1942, Himmler's pilot was killed in what Bach-Zelewski coolly described as a "serious day for the Reichsführer."[46] The capture of assassins and agents led to execution after brutal interrogation. Captives not killed in the field but subject to execution were brought into the towns for public or secret execution. The public execution in Russia was hanging. This entailed makeshift gallows. The use of lampposts, telegraph posts, and even balconies has been recorded. There is little evidence to show how long the bodies were left to hang. The bodies sometimes had placards fixed to them to deter would-be bandits. The British codebreakers found that captured parachutists were killed with drugs or gas. There appear to be only snippets of evidence as to the instructions for executing these prisoners in the field. An interception from May 1942 indicated that the police were warned to have the gas equipment prepared for handling enemy air-landing troops.[47] The SSPF Dnjepropetrowsk made a request to the SS-Sanitätsdienst in Berlin:

> Experiments to date of injecting parachutists with scopolamine were successful. Therefore experiments with mescaline are to be undertaken, since three injections produce an enhanced effect

through intoxication. The principal experiment is to be carried out with from 0/4 up to 0/6 grams in equal measure with an interval of half an hour. The effect lasts up to 5 hours. For the experiment with 50 to 100 persons, 50 grams of Mescaline Hydrochloride in solid form are needed.[48]

French MacLean located an example where Dirlewanger and his men gathered an audience around groups of captive Jewish females. The females were made to remove their clothes and then injected with strychnine while the onlookers watched them die.[49] After the war, Squadron Leader Vera Atkins located missing women SOE operatives and discovered their fate:

> It has now been definitely established that the four women who were killed at Natzweiler . . . were killed on 6 July 1944. They were given a narcotic injection, probably Evipan, and were immediately cremated. They were unconscious but probably still alive when thrown into the oven.[50]

Birn discovered the registration process was not purely a rounding-up of potential laborers or deportees to Germany. There was a screening process that distinguished those able to work (*arbeitsfähig*) and those incapable of work (*arbeitsunfähig*). This classification included their fitness, health, age, and suitability. Birn identified that the handicapped, the infirm, and the aged were subjected to "special treatment," the euphemism for execution. Many people were isolated from the mass of deportees and sent to concentration camps. In June 1942, Himmler instructed Rösener to conduct the first Bandenbekämpfung operation in Slovenia, and children from the cleanup were ordered sent to Austria for their assessment as racially suitable for resettlement. Very soon the child victims of Bandenbekämpfung, separated from families or orphaned, became under SS terminological orthodoxy "bandit children" (*Bandenkinder*). In January 1943, Himmler ordered plans for schooling and training Bandenkinder. They were to be assessed for this schooling on grounds of their racial and political potentials. The children were to be trained in all manner of field and manual work. Their schooling was to be limited to the basic needs: count to a hundred, know the traffic code, and be prepared for field and manual labor. From this initial planning, the intention had been to erect special camps for children under sixteen. The rest of the appraisal report outlined the decision-making process, which indicated that the SD-Einsatzgruppen was rounding up the children to be transported to the camps.[51]

We can now begin to understand the real meaning of Säuberungsaktion. The first concerned the seemingly minor point that burial teams were never part of the organization plans. With such comprehensive and detailed sets of plans and instructions, it seems such a small matter to deal with. The other involved the perception of "bandit-diseased" communities or localities. Once measures were completed, with everything of economic value stripped away, villages were set on fire with the evidence, the dead or dying disappearing in the ashes. Was this what Curt von Gottberg meant by his instructions for "Hornbung," which pointed toward the real purpose behind the action? "With regard to the treatment of persons and villages I refer to the verbal instruction of February 7, 1943. The recording of the agricultural products is carried out simultaneously with the cleansing."[52] Following "Cottbus," the Reichskommissar Ostland wrote to his Nazi boss complaining about SS methods. He noted that during cleanup operations it was difficult to "distinguish friend from foe." "Nevertheless," he continued, "it should be possible to avoid atrocities and to bury those who have been liquidated."[53] Säuberungsaktion was quite literally cleansing through fire.

The roundup and killing of so many adults for labor had a subsequent effect on the children (Bandenkinder). The SS found a solution. Himmler initially told Pohl,

> The Higher SS and Police Chiefs will arrange the shipments with the Chief of Security Police, the Chief of SS Main Economic and Administrative Office and the Inspectorate of the Concentration camps. The chief of the SS main economic and Admin Office in agreement with the Chief of the Security Police and SD, suggest the establishment of collective camps for children and adolescents in Lublin.[54]

Another paper trail, involving Bach-Zelewski, Kaltenbrunner, and Himmler, makes it possible to glimpse the policy management for Bandenkinder. Their primary concern was to relocate the children to a purpose-built camp where they would become labor for agriculture. The trail began when an order was transmitted from Himmler's offices on July 10, 1943, demanding that the senior SS officers manage the problem and make it work.[55] In a memo from July 23, Kaltenbrunner was instructed to ensure that all females and orphans in the detention center (*Auffangslager*) at Konstantynow worked on the state farms, tending and gathering kok-sagys rubber plants. Further instructions came from Himmler on July 28, concerning the minimum treatment of Bandenkinder, again referring to the original letter of July 10 and stating that the matter had to be resolved. Himmler declared that the presence of Russian activists operating in the Warthegau did not affect the intention to erect buildings for the education of Bandenkinder. The erection of buildings to accommodate Bandenkinder in the General Government was linked to the order to use the children on the state farms in the Ukraine. Himmler insisted that Russian Bandenkinder had to be separated from the Latvian children's homes and the

Russian families. These children should also be employed on state farms. The rules applied to children under fifteen years of age. Accommodating the children was not considered an SD responsibility.[56]

Communication was then established between Bach-Zelewski and Kaltenbrunner on the subject of Bandenkinder through a cable of September 22, 1943. The building of refugee camps for "bandit women" (*Bandenfrauen*) and Bandenkinder had been agreed to by Bach-Zelewski. Kaltenbrunner confirmed that Konstantynow camp had been erected as an SD center, so that the process of moving the children could begin. Bach-Zelewski had been asked to establish stores and conduct the collection of Bandenfrauen and Bandenkinder. The processing of the children was meant to be accelerated as collecting them on to state farms had not happened. On February 9, 1944, an SS-Obersturmbannführer on Himmler's personal staff, at the KSRFSS, wrote to SS-Sturmbannführer Werth reminding him "of this issue as it has become topical again. I would like to reopen communications on this subject as it has developed further since 9 September 1943." On that day, Kaltenbrunner informed Himmler that the SD concentration camp of Konstantynow had been erected and transfers were to begin soon.[57] There the correspondence ended with full compliance to the codes and regulations, but little interest in the conditions in which the children lived.

## Body Counts and Baubles

Report writing in Bandenbekämpfung was an administrative art form, blending petty German bureaucracy and SS stereotyping. For all manner of reasons, the accounting process could make or break careers. Reporting procedures married Hitler's political soldiers to the regulatory habits of public servants (*Beamten*). The rigid application of the ubiquitous 5:00 p.m. daily limitation on returns smacked of bureaucratic petty-mindedness (*Beamtenmentalität*). In such circumstances, it was, therefore, predictable that this task became the most controversial aspect of Bandenbekämpfung. The question turned on the accuracy of the figures. Scholars have taken considerable interest in the Nazi's statistical records. "The considerable discrepancy between the number of 'bandits' killed and the German casualties on the one hand," Jürgen Förster has written, "and the minor difference between the number arrested and those later executed, point to the dialectical dimension of the Wehrmacht's reprisal policy."[58] When Himmler took control of Bandenbekämpfung, he introduced a new reporting system. This system represented his plan to force attrition of the bandits, and so casualties were recorded and accounted in a form since known as the body count. Himmler wholeheartedly believed every act of the partisan had to be countered by greater firepower, greater manpower, and harsher measures. Himmler depended on the expertise and abilities of his lieutenants, as well as their truthfulness, to determine levels of success. Himmler also relied on body counts: simple data of enemies killed, rounded-up labor, and plunder. Instead of using this data, he endeavored to guarantee its accuracy.

Since the beginning of the war, German combatants had accounted for their victories with set rules and criteria. Within the administrative routine of the Bandenkampfverbände, the collection of numbers continued beyond purely "bandit" casualties. There was a listing of everything, prescribed through the introduction of a masterpiece in the bureaucracy of security bookkeeping.[59] The numbers of "bandits" killed in combat, "bandits" killed after combat, and suspects dispatched, and even on occasion details of the animals killed deliberately, were all recorded. After the numbers of killed came the number of prisoners and laborers rounded up, divided by men, women, and children. Finally, the numbers of farm animals taken in the "registrationaction" (Erfassungsaktion) were then formally accounted.[60]

One issue that arose was whether the "bandits" were armed. On February 13, 1943, following the completion of "Sternlauf," the operations officer of the SS-Cavalry Division issued a report that contained a huge booty list. Alongside the dead—654 partisans, 119 civilians, and 32 women—there was a list of captured booty, including rifles, cannons, tractors, field kitchens, machine guns, pistols, maps, and papers. There was also a sack of hats, 2 sacks of salt, 100 kilos of flour and 300 kilos of bread, 10 wooden mines, explosives, 4 cows, 45 horses, and so forth. The number of prisoners was 126 partisans, 142 civilians, and 241 women and children.[61] To conform to strict bureaucratic reporting and for the sake of efficiency, the same list was typed again for the divisional tactical report and again for the OKW. On February 8, the Wehrmacht's XXXXI Panzer Corps, under which the SS-Cavalry division was serving, recorded 1,317 "bandits" killed; 566 "bandit suspects," including 96 women, finished off (erledigt); and 150 "bandit" prisoners, 40 deserters, and 917 civilians (623 women) deported. The corps also recorded 220 bunkers destroyed; they captured tons of equipment, including horses, ski shoes, field guns, and mortars.[62]

Following "Draufänger II," SS-Sonderkommando Dirlewanger posted an after-action report. During May 5–6, they had destroyed 33 bunkers, killed 386 "bandits," and "finished off" 294 "bandit-suspects." They "harvested" 3 men, 30 women, 117 horses, 248 children, 140 sheep, 14 pigs, and 120 tons of foodstuffs. They had suffered 4 wounded men and captured 1 machine gun, 110 rifles, and 16 mines among all the equipment listed as booty. Dirlewanger recorded the villages of Starzynki, Brygidowo, Lubon, Baturyn, Krzeminiec, and Januszkowicze as destroyed.[63] Extended reporting allowed Dirlewanger to accumulate his figures from a two-week period. He itemized 14,000 dead and 39 prisoners accounted for by encirclement and extermination. His losses included a German officer and 2 men killed with 12 wounded. For his Hiwi collaborators, the losses were 7 dead and 21 wounded.[64]

In July 1943, Himmler issued a general order for the monthly return of casualty figures. These instructions stipulated the manner in which reports had to be completed following an action. The monthly collection of casualties included the formal manner in which reports were to be produced following an action.[65] The original format for reporting casualties begun by listing German losses, divided into officers and men, dead, wounded, and missing; collaborator and Axis forces followed the same format but included deserters. Then came enemies killed in combat, executed "bandit helpers" and "bandit suspects," prisoners, and wounded; finally all booty was listed to complete the form. In July 1943, there had been a discrepancy over the collection and reporting figures. It had led to a number of allegations of deliberate false accounting. Bach-Zelewski had been forced to conduct an investigation that had led to the introduction of a new format for recording figures. The intention behind the new report form was to prevent "double counting" (*Doppelerfassung*) or fraud. The field commanders were expected to identify the intentions of the bands, details of their leaders, the strength of band forces, equipment, details of how and when they were combated, and how casualties were caused. While there may have been an indication of discrepancy in figures before July 1943, this was hardly the case afterward and confirmed the rising level of terror.[66]

"Hermann"(July 13–August 11, 1943) was an example of a larger-scale operation embracing the complete range of Bandenbekämpfung tasks. Each participating unit compiled a report for the central accounting. The 31st SS-Police Rifle Regiment killed twelve bandits in combat and shot another two for no losses. It managed to capture 44 rifles and registered 101 men, 111 women, 102 children, 4 horses, 3 cows, and a calf, though apparently most of the sheep were lost in the swamp. Agricultural experts later collected 95 cows, 12 horses, 6 calves, and 256 sheep. The Gendarmerie-Einsatzkommando z.b.V posted a report on August 6, 1943. They accounted for 14 large camps destroyed, 66 other camps destroyed, 98 "bandits" killed in action, 23 "bandits" shot, and 11 prisoners. They captured mortars, machine guns, and rifles, but alleged they had destroyed this booty because of the difficult terrain. Their registration included 1,878 people (listed without age or sex), 89 horses, 378 beef cattle, 47 pigs, and 413 sheep. The commander, a Hauptmann, added congratulations for his men for a job well done. Dirlewanger scored the highest number. His command killed 1,067 in fighting, finished off a further 550, and took 33 prisoners. They destroyed 64 camps, 48 fighting positions, 11 bunkers, and 2 medical facilities. The battalion captured 5 artillery pieces, 5 mortars, 17 machine guns, and over 250 rifles and pistols. They destroyed a further 39 machine guns, 3 mortars, 169 rifles, and a variety of other equipment, including a field kitchen and radios. Dirlewanger also registered 929 men, 1,631 women, 395 children, 588 cows, 178 horses, 477 sheep, 8 pigs, and 115 vehicles. The reporting of figures at the operational level was not quite as clear-cut as has been led to believe. In the reports made by the SS formation Dirlewanger following "Hermann," new figures were being reported two weeks after its close.[67]

In March 1943, General Schmundt wrote to Himmler to confirm Hitler's decision that certain medals could be issued in his capacity as Chef der Bandenbekämpfung. This authority was limited to the Iron Cross (Second Class), applicable only to the east and confined to junior officers, army, and SS-Police troopers. For the Iron Cross (First Class), he still had to receive confirmation from OKH. Probably a little unconvinced that Bandenbekämpfung deserved medals, Schmundt stressed that "we indicate the measurement of awards against measurements used for troops on the eastern front." Himmler was required to report all medal confirmations by the twentieth of each month.[68] In his final report of January 1943, Daluege announced that frontline and operational success was demonstrated by the issue of military awards, a plentiful collection of 716 Iron Crosses (First Class), 7,819 Iron Crosses (Second Class), and 2,200 Infantry Assault Badges.[69] On January 30, 1944, Hitler agreed to the issue of the "combating-bandits badge" (*Banden-kampfabzeichen*) as an official military award. It was struck as a merit badge of evidence of "courage and achievement and proof of fighting against bandits" and was given based on the number of days in combat. All members of the Wehrmacht and SS could receive the badge; the issuing authorities were Himmler, the Ch.BKV, the HSSPFs, division commanders, Wehrkreis and Luftgau senior officers, and the Kriegsmarine high command. After May 1, 1944, days counted toward this badge were not allowed to be accounted for other military awards such as the infantry combat badges; but they could be combined with individual bravery badges like the destruction of tanks if they occurred within the same operation.[70]

The Bandenkampfabzeichen came in bronze, silver, or gold and was worn on the left breast. The designer of the award remains unknown, but the symbolic intentions behind the medal are clear. The badge portrayed a many-headed hydra, coiled around the blade of a sword, with a swastika on the hilt, that had been driven into its heart. The hydra represented the bandits. The snakes and the hydra had been commonly used to depict, especially in Freikorps medals, the enemy from hell. The basic depiction of a sword pointing downward with a swastika on the grip came from the Thule Society. The sword used in the badge was styled on those used by the Vikings but was also commonly used in heraldry to denote the instrument of execution. The swastika on the hilt of the sword and the skull lying on the oak leaf were intended to complete the symbolism. There were sun wheels on the hand guard to divine the beginning and end of life. The sword placed in a vertical position pointing downward represented the juxtaposition between heaven and earth, and the elixir of life and death of the hero. The sword is wielded even in the face of dangerous and dark powers. The sword is the one Siegfried used to kill the dragon. The links between earlier memorabilia and the Banden-kampfabzeichen make its political meaning all too clear. Between 1914 and 1916, a monument was erected to Siegfried's sword denoting the new and the reborn. The sword and the circular swastika had been the central symbols of the Thule Society, a forerunner to the Nazi Party. The fight against the snake had been a dominant theme in Nazi myth, projected by Arno Breker, a signifi-cant artist of the Third Reich. Finally, the sword and shield of similar propor-tions had been heraldic symbols of the Silesian Freikorps medal of 1919. This medal used the sword to signify death brought to the troops of hell.[71] At the same time, the newspapers portrayed the recipients of Germany's highest medals as the nation's new heroes.

Bandenbekämpfung accreditation was critical to the participants' war records. Medals were also recommended for the troops involved in Banden-bekämpfung. Pannier highlighted in his reports especially outstanding per-formances during operations. The award of medals sometimes came with a sense of irony. Bach-Zelewski's record as the commander of the Banden-kampfverbände makes interesting reading (Table 7.5). On July 3, 1944, he was awarded the Bandenkampfabzeichen in Bronze based on twenty-eight days of accredited combat. Realizing that Bach-Zelewski would take this as an affront, Himmler wrote of his courage and selfless acts as rewards themselves.[72] On June 28, 1944, Himmler's personal staff received a message from Field Marshal Busch, the commander of Army Group Centre, recommending the Knights Cross for von Gottberg. Busch commended von Gottberg for "his leadership of the Kampfgruppe, formed from police and a multitude of subordinate forces from the army, he was outstanding, in planning, participation and execution of the operations." He also congratulated him for capturing large amounts of enemy equipment and plunder, releasing troops to fight at the front (owing to his success) and his ruthless (*rücksichtslos*) perseverance of victory.[73] Some medals were of greater value than just a campaign badge.

Table 7.5: Bach-Zelewski's Command Record*

| OPERATION | | GERMAN | | | BANDITS | | | |
|---|---|---|---|---|---|---|---|---|
| | Diary Date | Dead | Missing | Wounded | Dead | Shot | POWs | Labor |
| Cottbus | 23.6.1943 | 39 | 4 | 525 | - | - | - | - |
| Seydlitz | 23.7.1943 | 34 | - | 53 | 2,768 | | 603 | 6,817 |
| Hermann | 11. 8. 1943 | - | - | - | 4,199 | - | 2,329 | 5,500 |
| Fritz | 8. 10.1943 | 20 | - | 63 | 668 | 410 | - | 15,730 |
| Heinrich | 20.11.1943 | 389 | 72 | 1,535 | 5,146 | 46 | 136 | - |

* TVDB, 72–117.

## Political Ramifications

On April 25, 1943, Bach-Zelewski joined Schenckendorff and his chief of staff, Colonel Hielscher, to plan the large-scale operation designated "Cottbus."[74] In the final stages of "Cottbus," a set of partial results found their way into the hands of the Generalkommissar Weissruthenien, Gauleiter Wilhelm Kube. They were interim figures and came from Curt von Gottberg's SSPF Weissruthenien headquarters staff. Under Himmler's first rules for post-operational reporting, the protocols for the official release of figures normally followed a series of informal confidence tests and confirmations. These were raw and unconfirmed figures. Without inquiring into their validity, on June 5, 1943, Kube felt compelled to write to Gauleiter Hinrich Lohse, Reichskommissar Ostland and his Nazi superior. Kube titled the letter "Results of police operation 'Cottbus' as reported so far for the period June 22 to July 3, 1943." The figures listed 4,500 "bandits" killed, 5,000 "bandit suspects" executed, 2,412 men and women rounded up for labor, and 250 imprisoned. The casualties were 59 dead and 267 wounded Germans with 22 dead and 120 wounded Schuma. There were lists of booty including 530 horses, 67 wagons, an airplane, 12 gliders, 10 large field guns, antitank guns, and so forth. The town of Begoml, in spite of its reputation for collaboration, suffered the full impact of deportation and was bombed to destruction by the Luftwaffe. Kube singled out Dirlewanger's reputation for "destroying many human lives"; among those executed as suspects were women and children.[75] Lohse passed the report to Reichsminister Alfred Rosenberg, his Nazi boss in Berlin. His covering letter complained that the incident might draw unfavorable parallels with the Katyn atrocity. Rhetorically, he pondered what would happen if the Allied powers found out the true nature of security operations.[76] "The fact that the Jews receive special treatment requires no further discussion," he continued. "However it appears hardly believable that this is done in the way described in the report of the Generalkommissar of 1 June 1943! What is Katyn against that?"[77]

The paper trail came to an end with Himmler through his senior SS liaison officer to Rosenberg, Gottlob Berger. After the war, Berger testified to the effect that he forced Rosenberg to conduct an investigation. Berger's evidence pointed at the brutality of Bandenbekämpfung:

> I know that over there in the East people were fighting severely, and particularly one thing happened several times, that civilian population was chased into barns and were all shot, and it repeatedly happened that the barns were set on fire.[78]

Berger, however, confessed there was a discrepancy in the figures of "Cottbus" with 492 rifles counted among the six thousand "bandit" dead. The Rosenberg investigation focused on the validity of the figures, but according to Berger, the real issue was the tension between the SS and the Nazis within Rosenberg's administration. Berger claimed that "Cottbus" was a politically disastrous operation, although Bach-Zelewski hailed it as a success. Berger insisted the Nazi officials request that Schenckendorff intervene and conduct an investigation in his capacity as the senior army commander. Berger believed Schenckendorff found that the German casualties were deliberately reduced. There were not 28 but 50 Germans killed and 140 wounded. Schenckendorff also discovered irregularities in the transmission of figures, and Berger felt compelled to lay the blame with the SS: "the figures that were all made up by these HSSPFs, you cannot imagine."[79]

The local planning for "Cottbus" was conducted by HSSPF Russia-Centre, SS-Gruppenführer Gerret Korsemann. On March 24, 1943, Korsemann replaced Carl Graf von Pückler-Burghaus, a temporary substitute. Prior to his posting, Korsemann had served as SSPF Stanislav-Rostov, under the command of Prützmann, HSSPF Russia-South. On June 1, Oberstleutnant der Schutzpolizei Ernst Korn requested a transfer from Korsemann's command staff.[80] Korn had established a respectable police career since the First World War. Between December 16, 1941, and January 18, 1942, Korn was a battalion commander of the 1st Police Rifle Regiment of the SS-Polizei Division. He became HSSPF Russia-Centre's operations officer (Ia), and in September 1942, he was regularly issuing operational instructions for Bandenbekämpfung. On January 11, 1943, six months short of his forty-fourth birthday, he was turned down from frontline service with the Waffen-SS. However, some weeks later, he was promoted Oberstleutnant der Schutzpolizei (February 1, 1943) and was Bach-Zelewski's temporary chief of staff until March 27. On May 17, Korn received the conciliation of career confirmation of his police leadership ability.[81] His resignation from Korsemann did not blight his career because he was promoted to operations officer (Ia) for the KSRFSS. On June 21, he returned to Bach-Zelewski's realm, as discussed in chapter 4. The resignation pointed to problems with Korsemann. Under Himmler's direct orders, Korn became director of the staff section responsible for the production of statistics and maps (*Amt für Statistik und Kartographie*). We cannot prove any connection between Korn's posting and Himmler's reaction to the controversy over the falsification of figures, but it does appear more than a coincidence.[82] Korn left neither a "Cottbus" report nor testimonial evidence at Nuremberg.[83]

Following Korn's resignation, Korsemann's problems appeared to spiral out of control. On June 30, 1943, against Bach-Zelewski's advice, Korsemann wrote a letter of complaint to Field Marshal von Kleist about the Wehrmacht rumor mill and protesting accusations that he was a drunk.[84] We know little either of the content or of Kleist's response, but the tone of the letter caused Himmler to take offense with Korsemann. On July 4, Himmler ordered Bach-Zelewski, as the commanding officer, to prepare a report on Korsemann. The next day, Korsemann was suspended from all his positions. Himmler wrote to the chief of SS personnel, Maximillian von Herff, on July 6, requesting details of other incidents said to have arisen during Korsemann's time in the Caucasus. Korsemann's seniority drew to a close in September 1943 when Himmler finally cast his decision:

> Too much alcohol in his life, too much fraternising with regular German army officers, too many parties with alcohol and regular army officers, too lazy in his duties as Chief of Police, too quick to retreat from the Caucasus when trouble arose and all together he is now degraded to the Waffen-SS.[85]

During interrogations in Nuremberg, Ernst Rode referred to Himmler's preference for getting rid of people by playing one off against another. He indicated that this was the case with Korsemann.[86] The threads did not end there. In a signal deciphered by the British in October 1943, there was evidence of ill-feelings about this case lingering within the corps. The intercept showed Rudolf Pannier criticizing Gottberg regarding the Korsemann case, as "he [Gottberg] has already once tried to worm his way into the structure, when I should have been made chief of staff to [Korsemann] the officer body to which I belong, have to keep silent in the face of naked reality."[87]

Evidence of Gottberg's role in the case is limited and largely circumstantial. On June 28, 1943, SS-Gruppenführer Korsemann issued the final details for "Günther," an operation that placed Kampfgruppe Korsemann in overall command. The records show that since the beginning of January 1943, SSPF Weissruthenien, under SS-Brigadeführer Curt von Gottberg, had been leading operations with Kampfgruppe Gottberg. The internal politics involved a clear line of seniority with Gruppenführer Korsemann (HSSPF) senior to Brigadeführer Gottberg (SSPF). Korsemann had not slated Gottberg to participate in "Günther," but following Korsemann's departure, Kampfgruppe Gottberg took over the operation. The HSSPF controlled the central formations such as the SS-Sonderkommando Dirlewanger and the SS-Police Regiments. Therefore, line officers like Dirlewanger had more than a passing interest in their senior officers. Dirlewanger's impression of what was happening to Korsemann raises some interesting evidence.

"Zauberflöte" exposed the ill feelings between Dirlewanger and Korsemann. Korsemann had openly circulated precise instructions to Dirlewanger and his men. The order then warned against plundering, which would be punishable with the severest means (schärfsten Mitteln geahndeten). All participants in the operation read this order, which snubbed Dirlewanger's command as a group of uncontrollable plunderers.[88] Following "Cottbus" but prior to "Günther," Korsemann issued specific orders again to Dirlewanger warning him against any repeat of the destruction of suspected "bandit villages" (*Banditendörfer*) that had occurred before, most probably during "Cottbus." Later, Dirlewanger issued a most illuminating experience report (*Erfahrungsbericht*) on July 14, 1943, that left no doubt about his contempt for Korsemann. Writing under the heading of "Günther," Dirlewanger responded to the criticism raised about his performance during "Cottbus." In preparation for "Günther," Korsemann had ordered that certain "peaceable peasant villages" to be spared. Reconnaissance had proved that the villages were rife with resistance. An alleged SD report had also confirmed this, according to Dirlewanger, stating the villages were "full of bandits and the roads and fields littered with mines." The SD requested that the order to stay action against the villages be rescinded. Korsemann sent an unclear reply to spare the villages, even though the SD had been shot at and the roads were littered with mines. Dirlewanger's 2nd Company had approached one of the villages and was fired on from all the houses, sustaining two dead and two wounded. Dirlewanger stated that such losses could have been prevented if his one year of unquestioned experience of bandit fighting had been trusted. Dirlewanger's swipe at Korsemann concluded, "It seems, therefore, appropriate to employ leaders with Bandenbekämpfung experience to issue decisive orders, to prevent unnecessary losses."[89]

In the heat of security politics, Dirlewanger was not content to comment solely about Korsemann. The deportation measures required the involvement of officials from Sauckel's GBA. These rarely conformed to the will of either civilian administrators or the army high command, and deported labor at will. Once labor officials joined security operations, they attracted criticism. On July 14, 1943, Dirlewanger reported the performance of labor officials attached to his command during the "harvesting" (Erfassung) phase of "Günther" after its "military" phase. He caustically remarked, "we have made a new experience, the uniformed *Beamten*. . . . They like to boast that they receive 15 Reichsmark per day. This harmfully reduces the mood of the troops." The report described how Dirlewanger's troops had rounded up two thousand to three thousand people, hundreds of horses and cattle, but no collection camp or transport had been organized. In the absence of labor officials, the armed forces and the SS-Police were forced to process the deportees and arrange their transportation. The arrangement of these facilities was supposed to be made in advance. Concluding on a venomous note, Dirlewanger pondered whether Erfassung operations in the future might be conducted on Saturday afternoons or Sundays when the labor officials were off duty.

Turning to Bach-Zelewski's diary for this period, we are offered another perspective on the events as they unfolded. Since his promotion to the full command of all Bandenkampfverbände on June 19, Bach-Zelewski had been running a tight schedule. "Cottbus" was implemented prior to his taking command, but its results came under his control. On June 29, 1943, he visited the

1st Police Grenadier Regiment to observe their operational performance. He traveled to Minsk on July 3, to join Korsemann, Gottberg, and SS-Brigadeführer Hermann, commander of 1st SS-Infantry Brigade, while they were preparing "Hermann." The next day, he attended a meeting with the Grand Mufti of Jerusalem, arranged by Himmler, to raise a formation of Muslim recruits from the Balkans. The following day, when Korsemann was relieved, he briefed Field Marshal von Kleist on the overall security situation. It is likely that Kleist passed comment on Korsemann's letter during Bach-Zelewski's visit. The next day, Bach-Zelewski received news of Schenckendorff's death by heart attack. As a mark of respect, he secured Himmler's approval for the Breslau Police band to perform a full military funeral service. This took place on July 9 with due pomp and ceremony and with Bach-Zelewski accepting the march past.[90] A week later, after a brief visit to the Balkans, he met with War-limont on July 16, to plan a large-scale operation in the Polotsk region of Russia. From there, he visited the command of "Hermann" to observe the progress. Apparently satisfied, he flew to Bialystok, to confer with Gauleiter Sauckel, regarding the new quotas for forced labor. On July 19, he flew back to Minsk only to return to Poland (Lublin) the next day to assist SS-Gruppenführer Globocnik in the handling of "Wehrwolf" against the Kovpak band. This travel ranged across Rovno, Lvov, Kraków, Breslau, and Warsaw until he returned to his headquarters at Lötzen on July 26.

In the midst of all this activity, SS-Brigadeführer und Generalmajor der Polizei Eberhard Herf arrived on the scene. Eberhard Herf was a member of Himmler's personal staff and had undertaken what might be loosely termed time and motion studies of SS performance in the east. Herf had already attracted British codebreaking activity in January 1942 when Himmler wrote to him via HSSPF Russia-North. It seems Herf had a quarrel with Zenner, and Jeckeln had been asked by Himmler to investigate the case. Herf had re-quested a transfer, but Himmler quashed that decision until the investigation had been completed. Himmler was particularly angry because he had expected Herf to report to him with any troubles.[91] This was an omen of things to come.

Bach-Zelewski first met Eberhard Herf, on July 1, 1943, in his quarters at Lötzen. They spent the best part of two days together, discussing the com-mand system and meeting with the staff, before Bach-Zelewski departed for Minsk. During Bach-Zelewski's absence, Herf was presumably left to settle into his prestigious assignment as chief of staff but found the operational procedures did not meet with his standards. On July 19, 1943, in a famous letter first discussed by Hans Buchheim in the 1960s, and often referred to since, Herf wrote to his friend and namesake SS-Obergruppenführer Maxi-millian von Herff, the chief of SS-Personnel Main Office (*SS-Personalhauptamt*), relating an accusation that there were serious problems within Banden-bekämpfung reporting. From the outset, Herf confirmed his disapproval of German policy in the east and the security measures in particular. He had "misgivings over the colonization process," which he felt would lead to defeat in the winter of 1943–44 as resentment continued to swell support for the partisans. He was particularly unhappy at the practice of keeping the body count figures "artificially low" to highlight the "successes." Herf believed the figures sent to Himmler were "cooked." To add weight to this comment, he said that rumors circulating during his time in the Ukraine were being broadcast by Kube and Lohse as fact. Herf indicated that Kube and Lohse had in fact got hold of secret reports and were openly denouncing the failings of a system that recorded that 480 rifles were found on 6,000 dead "partisans." In other words, the reports had not been distributed to them through the usual channels. The number of rifles had been fudged, according to Herf, "to swell the figure of enemy losses and highlight our own 'heroic deeds.'" His investigation of the numbers led to the common excuse that the insurgents destroyed their weapons and disguised themselves as innocent civilians to escape from the police. Herf was not convinced, reflecting on the severity of the fighting. "How easy it must be to suppress these guerrillas—when they destroy their weapons!"[92]

The Herf to Herff correspondence continued. On July 21, the police general wrote, "since yesterday I am in a completely different position. The RFSS has asked me to write to him about the situation. . . . I explained starkly with statistics how the situation is deteriorating."[93] Following his return on July 27, Bach-Zelewski discussed matters with all the staff, which was clearly unsatisfactory for Herf. The next day, he wrote again to his friend regarding the meeting. "Bach is back. He said he felt that I wanted to rule here (*Ich würde hier die Zügel der Regierung in die Hand nehmen*)." Herff replied that as chief of staff he had greater authority than what was being granted. In his diary for July 28, 1943, Bach-Zelewski wrote, "report to the RFSS, my chief of staff is not suitable for the position." The following day, Herf wrote again to his SS friend, in what was the final letter:

> Alea sund [*sic*] jacta! [The die is cast!] These are the facts I can disappear here. They will find somebody else for this job as they did before. Their explanation was classical "too much commander and not enough chief of staff" who has to be flexible and considerate. "You want to rule yourself. The RFSS needs to have someone to shout at, but you are too old and too old to report to him everyday." I wrote to you of the real motives. [94]

Herf decided to leave, commenting that even his request for genuine reports when they projected no deterioration were denied by the reluctant staffs. "It was openly told to me how everybody could guess the strategy," he continued. "They offered me a Kampfgruppe." Herf was fed up but filed Bach-Zelewski's final comment. "Reconsider your decision said Bach, you can lose reputation and honor, or as well achieve honour."[95] Bach-Zelewski's final words on Herf are in his diary. "Lectured to by the RFSS. My chief of staff has been recalled, because he has not matched up to the task."[96] Heinz Lammerding (see chapter 9) became Bach-Zelewski's chief of staff on August 13, 1943, a choice with which he was very content.[97] So often depicted as an upstanding German officer in the "Cottbus" case, Generalmajor der Polizei und SS-Brigadeführer Eberhard Herf returned to his position as KdO Minsk. He had been KdO Minsk since 1941 and had received the order from Kube, on January 29, 1942, for the "second wave" of Jewish extermination, of the Minsk ghetto. He was hanged after being found guilty of war crimes during the Minsk trial in 1946.[98]

What can be gleaned from these events? In the summer of 1943, these incidents represented the most extraordinary behavior. The shopping list of ranks highlights two Nazi ministers (Himmler and Rosenberg), a field marshal, four senior officers (a general from the army and three SS-Obergruppenführer), two Reichskommissars, five general rank or equivalent officers, and at least three senior line officers. The butchers' bill included one senior officer disgraced, a state secretary killed, and a general dead of a heart attack. New accounting regulations, discussed in chapter 6, were issued to the Bandenkampfverbände on July 12, 1943, three days after Herf's first letter. [99] As for Rosenberg and his motley crew, their castigation of the SS was hard-faced politics. Their selectivity in highlighting some victims over others is revealed in the telling disclaimer of the letter from June 18, 1943, that "the fact that Jews receive ['special treatment'] *Sonderbehandlung* requires no further discussion." Gerald Reitlinger suggested that not until July 10, 1943, did Himmler receive Kube's report. This might indicate Himmler had been planning new accounting rules before the "Cottbus" incident. Reitlinger also suggested that "Cottbus" was the clearing of the "Partisan Republic of Lake Palik," which might have triggered the extreme measures. Later, Kube told Strauch that this action was unworthy of a nation that had produced Kant and Goethe. In response, Strauch accused Kube of not handling disciplinary charges against Jews properly and of not removing the electrician who had bugged his telephone line. Kube was blown up by his chambermaid on September 23, 1943; Strauch had all seventy Jews under Kube's control killed in reprisal, and another thousand Jews were slaughtered in Minsk. Adding a final twist to the remarkable series of coincidences, Himmler told Bach-Zelewski that Kube's assassination was "a boon to the German people."[100]

The timely death of Schenckendorff on July 6, during the investigation of the falsification allegations, was a perhaps too fortuitous coincidence.[101] Field Marshal von Kluge wrote to Schenckendorff's wife for the first time in years with condolences for his former comrade. The heart of the case was between Korsemann, Gottberg, and the position of HSSPF Russia-Centre. Were the real culprits Gottberg in league with Dirlewanger to prevent the timely release of reports? From the perspective of the Nazi's total war effort, this incident caused the highest loss, decapitating the German security command in the east for the entire war. From the standpoint of professionalism, we discover that the etiquette of careerism, based on the principles of social Darwinism, was not confined to the SS organization. All the ranting and reengineering brought superficial success but failed to unhinge the Allies' grand strategy or to hamper the long-term direction of the war. In many ways, rationalization, professionalization, and standardization were highly successful at perpetuating Hitler's war. Internally, the Nazis were unable to overcome their character traits or behavioral patterns. Personal greed and self-gratification were the reaction to calls for total war and collective effort received a short-sighted response. Nazism was undone by its social Darwinist motivations. In 1943, Hitler's empire was like a giant sand-castle facing the incoming tides. As the tides breached the walls, the Nazis worked like ants to rebuild their barriers. In this process, sand suffers from liquefaction and eventually becomes useless. The real breaches in the Nazi edifice dissolved from within. Thus, as the regime grandstanded total war, a new round of polycratic competition and opportunism opened between the hangers on.

The only person to succeed from the affair was Gottberg. He was awarded the German Cross in Gold, a highly cherished medal that was regarded as political recognition for services to the state. The award of the German Cross in Gold for Gottberg (July 1943– August 25, 1943) led to a service epistle by Bach-Zelewski: "von Gottberg with the SS-Polizeiverbände, army and Luftwaffe has carried out effective operations against the bandits. The show piece was the Grand Operation 'Cottbus' [*Grossunternehmen Cottbus*] where in critical days it was his leadership that saw it through." Thus:

NÜRNBERG: November 19–25, 1942, between Glebokie and Vilno; 1st SS-Infantry Brigade, 14th SS-Police Regiment, 2 Schutzmann-schaft-Battalions, and local gendarmes.
HAMBURG: December 10–12, 1942, in forests north of Slonim; 2nd SS-Police Regiment, 1st Battalion 23rd SS-Police Regiment, and 1st Battalion 24th Regiment, 3 Schuma Battalions; 3,186 combined enemy dead; 3 tanks, 7 artillery pieces, 5 sub-machine guns, 12 light machine-guns, and 367 rifles captured; 19 bandit camps destroyed.
ALTONA: December 22–23, 1942, south of Slonim; 1,059 enemy dead.
FRANZ: January 5–14, 1943, east of Osipovichi; 1,349 enemy dead; 280 rifles, 3 cannons, and large amounts of ammo captured; 9 camps destroyed
ERNTEFEST: January 18 to February 5, 1943, military road Minsk-

Slutsk; 3,721 enemy dead; 433 rifles, 2 artillery pieces, mortars, and 28 machine guns captured.

HORNUNG: February 8–26, 1943, Pripet marshes south of Slutsk; 2 SS-Police Regiments, 2 SS-Police Battalions, and 5 Schuma; 9,662 enemy dead.[102]

The last entry of Gottberg's accreditation list was Operation "Cottbus." Bach-Zelewski listed that it took place from April 28 to June 21, 1943, to the north of Borissow. He called it the largest operation in HSSPF Russia-Centre involving 16,662 men from the Wehrmacht and police. The enemy suffered 6,042 killed in action, 3,709 "bandit suspects" executed, and 599 prisoners. The Germans suffered 127 dead (3 officers) and 535 wounded (10 officers). The captured booty included 29 pieces of artillery, 18 mortars, 61 machine guns, 16 antitank guns, 45 submachine guns, but, most revealing of all, only 905 rifles.

# PART THREE
## CLIMATIC DECLINE

# 8
# POLAND

Wither Bandenbekämpfung? In July 1944, Victor Klemperer observed, "We had now not three, but five fronts: Russia, France, Italy, also the home front of the bombing attacks and the bandit-front."[1] Chapter 4 explains how Nazi national security was reengineered by the SS, through institutional machinations and political opportunism, to turn Bandenbekämp-fung into an operational concept. The subsequent chapters explain how Bandenbekämpfung developed in an effort to eradicate the Soviet partisan. Outside of the war against the Soviet partisan, there was a more complex situation than even Klemperer could encapsulate. Hitler's strategy did indeed incorporate five central fronts, among them Bandenbekämpfung, but each engendered a different set of priorities and agendas. In terms of operational security policy, the last years of the war saw Bandenbekämpfung adapted as a catchall solution for a range of issues, not all related. The exponents of Bandenbekämpfung struggled to maintain consistency against differing territorial conditions and the interests of rival agencies. Their greatest problem was uncertainty caused by Hitler's continual reinterpretation of how victory might be achieved. This uncertainty swept through Nazi organizations. Military setbacks inflicted by the Red Army, the bombing of German cities, and the allied invasions in the west were answered by faith in static fortifications and concrete obstacles, the ongoing extermination of the Jews, and the determined pacification and eradication of resistance. Hitler's war was turning in on itself.

In the summer of 1944, Poland once again attracted the attention of the world. Poland's geo-political position made it the key buffer against Soviet invasion and incursion. Since 1939, Poland had been exposed to a combination of occupation, genocide, and corruption. From April 1943 to January

213

1945, Poland was on the receiving end of intensified Bandenbekämpfung, including blocking or preventing Soviet thrusts into Poland to destroy strategic junctions, securing and participating in the continued extermination of Jewry, and destroying Polish nationalism by eradicating the resistance movement. The underlying operational factor in these tasks was the SS reliance, even piggybacking, on the traditional Wehrmacht occupation structure, which enabled extensive administration of genocide, enslavement, and exploitation. Bandenbekämpfung tasks were completed despite obstacles. There were hurdles from leadership quarrels regarding the regime's policy toward Poland, but the Bandenkampfverbände developed a dynamic capability for multitasked command, coordinating and completing ideological, political, and security tasks within their operations. The SS ingeniously organized operations by interweaving them with older security methods. In addition, the SS internalized "Hitler's will" as the logic of command. The abundance of the "Führer's will," in real terms translated as faith and fanaticism, substituted for the lack of replacement armies and equipment shortages and was supposed to bolster the troop's sagging morale. The presence of this faith and fanaticism coincided with a growing expectancy for high-end results from operations. The demands by Hitler, the SS, the Nazi Party, and German institutions lost all semblance of reality except the administration of destruction and revenge. Germany, so it seemed, was fighting a different kind of war from the other belligerents.

## SS-Police in Poland

Revenge was a common Nazi slogan. The Nazis reaped "revenge" against Poland for the Versailles Treaty, the war-guilt clause, and the creation of the "new" Poland. After dismantling Poland, the Nazis used the rump, the General Government, as their base to prosecute their ongoing race war against the Jewish people and the eradication of Polish national identity. Himmler held Poles in utter contempt and was only concerned for Poland's fate insofar as it undermined internal security in the wake of Germany's waning fortunes. Himmler's idea of security regarding Poland rarely wavered from widespread killing. In 1940, in a speech to Hitler's Waffen-SS bodyguard, he explained how killing actions were fraught with hardship. In freezing weather, he recalled, "we had to haul away thousands, tens thousands, hundred thousands . . . to shoot thousands of leading Poles, where we had to have the toughness, otherwise it would have taken revenge on us later." Additionally, he did not differentiate between SS-Police security actions and military operations:

> [I]t is much easier to go into combat with a company than to suppress an obstructive population of low cultural level in some area with a company or to carry out executions, or to haul away people, to evict crying and hysterical women, or to return our

German racial brethren across the border from Russia and to take care of them.[2]

By the end of 1943, Himmler's opinion had remained fundamentally unchanged, while his suspicion over Polish intentions was reinforced when he recalled the border battles of 1919:

> The fight for Germandom stretched across the Warthegau, Oberschlesien, West Prussia, and small areas of the borders. This was a fight against the bandit and our soldiers and the defense was successful. But where had the Polish expertise come from. . . . The Polish nation used good organization. Their troops were excellent fighters, the men's careers included award of the Iron Cross first class, some were old Prussian senior sergeants, there were veteran sergeants, many had been taught in German schools. . . . They had been willing to learn peoples war [Volkskrieg], they were prepared to give up blood and they knew how to use German order and precision against us. This game plan must never be allowed to be repeated.[3]

He told his audience, "Every little fire will immediately be stamped out and quenched and extinguished otherwise—as in the case of a real fire—a political and psychological surface-fire may spring up among the people."[4] His words proved prophetic.

Himmler had good reason to be concerned. Captured Polish partisans and slave laborers from the east escaped and formed bands. Himmler went to extraordinary lengths to ensure that escapees were apprehended.[5] Internal security was undermined from the combined effects of the transfer of home police troops and the rise of "foreigner bands" inside German cities.[6] In 1942, the Stuttgart police were alerted to the activities of a Polish resistance faction working within Germany. The Germans infiltrated "trusties" among slave laborers and were able to identify and arrest the leader Leonhard Kendzierski (along with his brother and a courier) in Cologne. Under interrogation, Kendzierski confessed that the resistance movement was rooted in the foreign labor force in Germany. He, his brother, and the courier also gave away their comrades' identities, and this led to further arrests. In August 1943, criminal commissar Kurt Bethke was transferred to Cologne to contain this problem. Bethke believed the strategic position of Cologne, the major crossing point over the Rhine, as well as the bombing, influx of slave laborers, and reduction of police resources had all undermined the city's social cohesion.[7] In April 1944, a Polish resistance courier arrived in Cologne with orders that all members of the resistance were to join with approaching allied armies from the west. In the event of an uprising within Germany, they were expected to stand aside and let matters take their course. In the event of a general collapse, they were to disperse into groups of one hundred to two hundred and make their way back to Poland. By August 1944, the situation in Cologne had deteriorated into open acts of violence such as killing police officers, party members, and German army soldiers. In response, the security police planned a Bandenbekämpfung-style operation, which led to sporadic street fighting and raging gun battles across districts of the city.[8]

The Nazi reorganization of Poland was reflected by the HSSPF command system. "Northeast," covered the extended state of eastern Prussia, HSSPF "Weichsel" (Vistula) administered the Reichsgau of Danzig-West Prussia, and HSSPF Warthe covered the Warthegau with all states incorporated into the Reich. The General Government was administered separately by the HSSPF East, under SS-Obergruppenführer Friedrich-Wilhelm Krüger and was divided into five SSPFs—Kraków, Lublin, Radom, Warsaw, and Lemberg. The scale of policing assigned to this territory is listed in Table 8.1 and highlights how many large formations were deployed to this command. In addition, there were at least seventeen Order Police battalions, including an artillery battalion, as well as gendarmerie and technical specialists. The SS-Police signals stations network, as elsewhere, connected Warsaw, Radom, Kielce, Tschenstochau, Lublin, Biala-Podlask, Zamocs, Rzeszow, and Danzig.[9]

Corruption was an ever present problem facing the SS in Poland. In 1941, SSPF Lublin under SS-Gruppenführer Odilo Globocnik was handed responsibility for *Aktion Reinhard*, the plan to exterminate Polish Jewry. To

Table 8.1: Friedrich-Wilhelm Krüger's Formations[*]

| SS-Police Regiments and Training Formations | Named Police Battalions |
|---|---|
| 2nd SS-Police Regiment | Police Battalion *Gaarsche* |
| 4th SS-Police Regiment | Police Battalion *Gaier* |
| | Police Battalion *Krüger* |
| 14th SS-Police Regiment | Police Einsatz Battalion *Kunhardt* |
| 15th SS-Police Regiment | Police Bicyclist Battalion *Nord* |
| 22nd SS-Police Regiment | Police Battalion *Schirmeck* |
| 25th SS-Police-Regiment | Police Battalion *Südost* |
| | Police Battalion *Tietz* |
| Police Training Battalion Warsaw | Police Battalion *West* |
| Police Training Battalion West Prussia | Police Battalion *Wittmann* |

*DDST, record cards of the Kampfgruppe Krüger, Tessin.

facilitate this plan, extermination camps were erected at Belzec, Sobibor, and Treblinka. Globocnik had been removed from his previous post because of corruption, and immediately recognized the potential for personal gain from the new posting. In the fall of 1940, SS-Sonderbataillon Dirlewanger was posted to SSPF Kraków to conduct security duties. The battalion was then posted to SSPF Lublin. In a bizarre twist, Oskar Dirlewanger, Globocnik, Berger, and Krüger became entangled in a serious case of corruption. Officially, Dirlewanger received a promotion on the recommendation of Krüger and Globocnik for services against smugglers, illegal trade, and Polish resistance. However, Krüger also tipped off the SS legal officer, Dr. Konrad Morgen, about Dirlewanger's behavior, including wanton acts of murder, extortion, and the crime of sexual relations with Jews (*Rassenschande*). Krüger probably hoped to divert Morgen from investigating Globocnik and himself. The tip backfired, and Krüger was forced by SS etiquette, if not by self-interest, to protect Globocnik as his lieutenant and SSPF against Morgen. Berger pledged faith in Dirlewanger. Morgen was blamed, consequently reduced in rank, and forced to serve in a Waffen-SS unit.[10] Dirlewanger moved east to join Bach-Zelewski in 1942. Himmler's suspicions of Globocnik lingered into 1943 and his backing of this protégé only lasted while he was politically useful.

Elsewhere, security merged with policing in the first stages of establishing Bandenbekämpfung operations Poland. In one example from November 29, 1942, a *Gendarmerie-Hauptmannschaft* from Radom conducted actions in the forest area of Lubionia, south of Ilza, against "Polish-Jewish bandits."[11] The motorized gendarmerie detachment had three companies, with a platoon of Schutzpolizei and an additional twenty gendarmes from guard duty. Fifteen German foresters from Lubionia and forty Polish foresters from Forsterei Marcule assisted them. They shot three "armed Jews" in the forest and then a firefight ensued. The final casualty list was forty-one "bandits" killed and one arrested. The police collected fifteen Polish rifles, a hunting rifle, and grenades. They took reprisal actions against the villages in the area as a matter of course. The German analysis of the security situation in Poland, recorded a growing tendency of the fight for freedom. In January 1943, Luftwaffe Colonel Kollee's "bandit situation report," previously discussed in chapter 4, described the Polish predicament, "they fight for their independence. . . . The Poles know that they have no possibility for independence from Germany, nor Russia."[12] These two examples contrast the extremes of security in Poland.

## Lemberg and Warsaw

Two aspects underlying Nazi ethnic cleansing in Poland have hitherto received only the briefest of research attention—the link between SS security measures and the Holocaust and the impact of operational training to prepare troops for genocide-based operations.

## Lemberg

In 1939, Fritz Katzmann became the senior SS representative assigned to the 14th Army prior to the invasion of Poland. Katzmann then served as SSPF Radom but, in April 1942, was transferred as SSPF Lemberg based in the Galician city of Lvov.[13] He was tasked with extermination of the Galician Jews. His final report to Krüger was a chilling example of Nazi thoroughness.[14] Katzmann explained that the "evacuation" of Jews from the district was systematic from April 1942. By November 10, exactly "254,989 Jews had been evacuated [*ausgesiedelt*]." On June 23, 1943, the report concluded that 434,329 had been "evacuated" and that the remaining Jews (21,156) were confined in twenty camps. All confiscated valuables and property had been handed over to the Special Staff Reinhard. Katzmann's description of the task was depraved. He explained how the SS-Police forces and Ukrainian police were "exposed to physical and mental strains" of having to overcome the "nausea" of entering "dirty and pestilential Jewish holes." Bizarrely, Katzmann described in diabolical terms how he overturned an absurd biological warfare plot, "during the searches there has been found, moreover, a number of leaflets in the Hebrew language, inciting the Jews to breed lice carrying spotted fever, in order to destroy the Police Force." Katzmann gathered together a suitably large police force inoculated against spotted fever; he went into action "to destroy this plague boil."[15]

Irrespective of his preparations, Katzmann's men suffered 120 cases of spotted fever, and eighteen died. He described searching for Jews in concealed places such as chimneys, sewers, cellars, and inside furniture. They seized weapons from the Jews that had been purchased from Italian soldiers. They also discovered bunkers "masterly" concealed from detection. There was evidence that Italian soldiers stationed in the area had helped Jews to escape for large sums of Polish Zloty and even U.S. dollars. On May 13, 1943, an armed Jewish band hijacked a Luftwaffe vehicle and its driver. The driver offered to help them escape but drove them into a local NSKK barracks, where they were disarmed. Their weapons again proved to be Italian. After an interrogation, another large group of Jews was located in woods near Brody; these Jews were declared members of the Polish resistance movement. A search was initiated by the gendarmerie, Ukrainian police, and two companies from the army. During what appeared to be a firefight, thirty-three Jewish "bandits" were shot dead. A Polish gamekeeper, working for the Germans, was killed, and an SS man wounded. On May 21, another "Jewish band" was overwhelmed; they were also armed with Italian small arms. Ten days later, an additional Jewish band of 139 members existing in six bunkers was hunted down and killed. In June, the SS again combed the area and discovered more traces of Jews trying to escape into Hungary. After further Bandenbekämpfung in the area, the cleansing action counted twenty thousand Jews rounded up and three thousand Jews who had committed suicide. Katzmann reported losses of 11 dead and 137 injured. "Only thanks to the sense of duty of every single leader and man have we succeeded to get rid of this PLAGUE [*sic*] in so short a time," he concluded his report.[16]

## Warsaw

Christopher Browning, in his study of the Order Police, raised the issue of the "initiation to mass murder" as the first step toward mass extermination.[17] Browning had little available evidence to work his ideas beyond general interpretation. Bandenbekämpfung, it was explained in chapter 6, combined training and the "baptism of fire" with operational security. The modus operandi of Bandenbekämpfung rarely included frontline battalions and regiments; the allocation of manpower was generally ad hoc. Bach-Zelewski's expertise was in maximizing the operational capability of diverse and limited resources. The rationalization of training, after 1942, forced the Wehrmacht and the Waffen-SS to establish common goals and outcomes. Bandenbekämpfung ensured rapid completion of recruit training through their "baptism of fire" prior to frontline posting. After 1942, specialist facilities, such as the SS-Waldlager Bobruisk, were constructed to rush recruits through basic and advanced training. Poland was the perfect hunting ground for racial "enemies of the state," granted the potential for "blooding" that was encouraged by both the SS and Wehrmacht. Uprisings or revolts in Poland became an opportunity to place recruits in an earlier baptism of fire.

The proscribed training set by the German armed forces for street fighting involved flanking and encircling maneuvers. The idea was to waste defenders by cutting off access to water, food, and energy supplies. The Germans saturated defenders and defensive positions with continual artillery and aircraft bombardment. Once identified, sections of streets or houses were repeatedly assaulted until isolated as pockets of resistance so they could be destroyed piecemeal. Another German tactic was to drive through a municipality, cut off the escape route, and then traverse over the town, combating the enemy among the population. The Germans also fought on two levels, through cellars and sewers, knocking holes through walls to maintain their momentum. After capturing an area, they sealed it up with mines and barbed wire to prevent the defenders from returning. During the fighting, the Germans forced civilians to clear the streets to allow armored vehicles to be brought forward to support the fighting.[18] These principles were twice applied to Warsaw.

The importance of on-the-job training was apparent in the suppression of the Warsaw ghetto uprising (April 20–May 16, 1943). The heroic stand by the Jewish community against deportation to the death camps was pacified by a young security force. The subsequent Warsaw ghetto report by the SS commander, SS-Brigadeführer Jürgen Stroop, detailed the daily actions and the pacification process.[19] This was a lesson in SS methods of suppression and the prevailing security thinking in 1943, as well as the SS skills of coordinating a mixed force of police and Wehrmacht troops. The Polish historian Andrej Wirth's introduction to the infamous "Stroop report" was overly concerned by what he viewed as the cynical use of youth in killing. Wirth thought involving the youthful SS troops only added to the scale of the tragedy; he did not grasp that it was a conscious act. The pacification of the Jews in the Warsaw ghetto was, for the Nazis, a baptism by fire for German youth. The report was a meticulous description of the daily activities in the process. To the SS, the report was instructional and illustrated the expertise required for the command and coordination of mixed force security actions. The Stroop Report detailed the deliberate employment of recruits in a Judenaktion and was, therefore, a training manual.

The report also offers insight into the character of SS professionalism. It both explained and reported use of flamethrowers and anti-aircraft guns to destroy pockets of resistance. This professionalism, however, was inverted; the fire brigade and the Technische Nothilfe participated in the pacification by conducting controlled fire-raising and closing down water supplies. This corruption of socially beneficial expertise (rescue services) was first adapted during the "Night of Broken Glass" of November 1938, when the German police started fires in synagoges. The same units in Warsaw blocked sewers, denying free movement to the resistors. The fire brigade assisted the troops in placing heavy weapons to minimize the damage to surrounding buildings. One aspect of the report that was unusual, given the concentration on firepower, was the relatively small proportion of heavy weapons utilized during the operation.

The report's coverage of casualties provides a limited survey of manpower. Jewish losses included five thousand to six thousand killed in the fighting, 56,065 captured, and 13,929 killed in Nazi extermination camps.[20] Total German casualties were seventeen dead and eighty-five wounded. The SS-Police troops deployed were collected from five separate force pools. The Order Police assigned units from the 22nd SS-Police Regiment, a detachment of Technische Nothilfe, a troop of gendarmerie, and the fire brigade. The average age of police casualties was thirty-one, the oldest thirty-seven, and the youngest twenty. The SS-Totenkopfverbände committed two battalions, the 3rd SS-Panzer-Grenadier Training Battalion (Warsaw), and the SS-Cavalry Training Battalion (Warsaw). Their casualties averaged twenty-four years of age; the eldest forty-two (a senior NCO) and the youngest, a seventeen-year-old private, among a total sample of sixty-four casualties. A collaboration battalion of Trawniki police from the SSPF Lublin had a casualty ratio averaging twenty-six years of age, although the eldest was fifty-one. The German army sent a flak battery, a company of regular engineers, and a reserve engineer battalion; they worked alongside railway troops. An SD detachment was present, as usual in all such actions. Stroop declared that the young men of the SS deserved special commendation. With only three to four weeks training behind them, they had acted with a devil-may-care (*Draufgängertum*) attitude. Stroop also commended the officers and men of the police who were already experienced in this kind of "front fighting."

The testimony of SS-Grenadier Willi Hansen, a batman for SS-Obersturmbannführer Nowak, has left some idea of the preparations to destroy the Warsaw ghetto. Hansen's job was to serve Nowak while training with the 1st Company of the 3rd SS-Panzer-Grenadier Training Battalion (Warsaw) from November 1942 to August 1943. In conversations with Nowak, Hansen alleged that the SS received orders from Berlin to destroy the ghetto because of attacks by the inmates on the German garrison. From April 11–22, the members of the Totenkopf training unit were mobilized every morning for "partisan warfare." Nowak was not officially part of the suppression forces but unofficially took part in looting the ghetto.[21] SS-Oberscharführer Anton Schaffrath, born in 1918, was a railwayman. He joined the Allgemeine-SS, called up in May 1943, and was then sent to NCO training with the 3rd SS-Panzer-Grenadier Training Battalion (Warsaw). He participated in the pacification from May 14, his 2nd Company assigned to blocking around the ghetto. Schaffrath stated that members of the SD had executed Jewish prisoners, and he witnessed many women and children deported via the railway station. Schaffrath listed the approximate ages of his fellow NCOs as ranging from twenty-four to forty, with an overall average of thirty-two years.[22] SS-Sturmann Erwin Maletz trained as a nineteen-year-old recruit in the 4th Company of the 3rd SS-Panzer-Grenadier Training Battalion (Warsaw). Captured in August 1944, Maletz told his British interrogators that SS-Unterscharführer Warth had forced men to shoot Jews, while SS-Sturmann Erlach delighted in killing Jews and "the more the merrier" was his motto.[23] Franz van Lent, a Dutchman, served as an SS-Sturmann and was captured by the British army in Normandy in 1944. He volunteered a statement to the British. His first posting was the 1st SS-Panzer Grenadier Regiment Totenkopf. On April 18, 1943, the regiment sent its 1st, 2nd, 3rd, and 4th companies into the Jewish ghetto in Warsaw. They remained there until May 18, he explained:

> During this time they shot 45,000 Jewish men, women and children. The Germans murdered their victims either in groups with machine-guns or singly by shooting them with pistols in the back of their heads. . . . Six Poles of the Polish Underground movement who had tried to help the Jews were arrested and shot in Sieges Allee where their bodies were left for several days to frighten the public.[24]

The uprising surprised Hitler if not the SS leadership.[25] It is in this context that the relevance of the Bandenkampf und Sicherheitslage June 1943 memo, discussed in chapter 4, is made apparent.[26] Stroop inadvertently hastened Jewish extermination by highlighting the importance of preemptive strikes to prevent future resistance. Point 5 of the memo reflected Hitler's mood to see the security mission through. Within Nazi circles, thwarting a general Jewish uprising compared closely with preventing a 1918-style internal collapse. The consequential review of security measures served to undermine the ill-fated Bialystok ghetto resistance and highlighted the thinking behind "Zauberflöte," discussed in chapter 7. According to Lucy Dawidowicz, the Germans had changed their tactics: "Everywhere the Germans employed lies, surprise and stealth to liquidate the ghettos. Sudden encirclements at night, or at dawn, prevented organised combat groups from mobilising and coordinating their units."[27] These events signified that the combined efforts to eradicate "banditry" alongside the extermination of the Jews was the crux of the Bandenbekämpfung operational concept.

## Lublin

The incidents in Warsaw and Lemberg, continued criticism of Hans Frank, and increasing resistance of Jews and Poles caused Hitler and Himmler to instigate radical decisions. On June 21, 1943, the General Government of Poland and former Polish territories annexed into the Reich, renamed the Warthegau and Weichsel-Pommern, were declared Bandenkampfgebieten.[28] Since March 1943, Richard Wendler, governor general of Lublin, had urged Himmler to remove Globocnik:

> Above all, I thank you for clearing the air regarding the SS and Police Leader Lublin and trust you will transfer him somewhere else. This is the only noble and possible solution. I must even ask you today, to transfer Gruppenführer Globocnik within the shortest time to his new field of activity and to remove him from here.[29]

The suppression of the Warsaw ghetto uprising was followed by the Bialystok ghetto revolt. On August 15, 1943, Globocnik sent small teams of police into the ghetto to take control of the SS factories. The following day, fighting broke out, and the Germans rapidly succeeded in reducing the resistance into small pockets. It spelled the end of the revolt although troubles continued into September, and the last Jewish captives were deported in November.[30] Globocnik's performance in combating the Kovpak incursion was also less than inspiring.[31] Himmler's concerns grew. The Jewish uprisings and the escalating resistance, reinforced by the Treblinka revolt (August 1943), finally sealed Globocnik's fate.[32] He was replaced by an officer at the pinnacle of SS professionalism.

In January 1943, Himmler had ordered Pohl's concentration camp system to absorb the intake of "bandit suspects," mentioned in chapter 7. The prisoners were sent to camps in Lublin and Auschwitz, placing pressure on the facilities and their working efficiency. By November 1943, given the troubles, these camps were bulging with prisoners. The appointment of SS-Gruppenführer Jakob Sporrenberg, as SSPF Lublin, was opportune. Sporrenberg was captured by the British in Norway, in 1945, and was eventually turned over to war crimes investigators.[33] He spun tales that his trained interrogators found difficult to believe. He had served in the SD and, in 1937, took command of the security police in Königsberg. On April 10, 1941, he lunched with Himmler, Bach-Zelewski, and SS-Gruppenführer Schmauser.[34] During the proceedings, he was confirmed as SSPF Minsk, under Bach-Zelewski.[35] He later served in the Hauptamt Ordnungspolizei to study police procedures in preparation for the invasion of Russia. His period of service at the SSPF Minsk was from July to August 1941. Then, he served as SD special assignments officer attached to Gauleiter Koch until March 1943.

On February 1, 1943, Sporrenberg alleged he was posted again to serve with Bach-Zelewski, in Minsk. During a meeting with Bach-Zelewski, Sporrenberg said he was told not to regard service in Bandenbekämpfung as a punishment. It was explained that he would serve in the ranks of the 2nd SS-Police Regiment. He was to receive the temporary police rank of Oberwachtmeister for the duration of his Bandenbekämpfung service. Sporrenberg recalled that during one operation his battalion was surrounded and the officers killed. The troops pleaded with him to take command. He did so and saved the battalion, and Bach-Zelewski praised him. Sporrenberg told the British that he served six months combating the partisans. Bach-Zelewski's diary is silent on all these matters. Sporrenberg alleged he went home on compassionate leave as his wife was suffering from cancer of the face. Himmler, however, recalled him for improperly taking leave and posted him as SSPF Lublin as a punishment. Bach-Zelewski did record that on September 8, 1943, a meeting was held with Dr. Wendler, Lublin governor general, and Sporrenberg.[36] On October 19, Frank convened a meeting with Krüger, Sporrenberg, SS-Oberführer Bierkamp (BdS Lublin), and Generalmajor der Polizei Hans Grünwald (BdO Lublin). Krüger presented them with the fait accompli, Himmler's orders confirming executions:

> The Jews in the Lublin District have developed into a serious danger. This state of affairs must be cleared up once and for all. I have charged the "unit Globocnik" with the execution of this matter. The Higher SS and Police Leader East, and the SS and Police Leader Lublin, are requested to assist Globocnik with all resources at their disposal.[37]

The resulting operation began on November 3, 1943, and lasted for two more days. Aktion Erntefest represented a startling new level of security capability and a frightening determination to complete the destruction of the

Jews in quick time. The action called for the rapid extermination of Jews in the Lublin district, incarcerated in the Trawniki, Poniatowa, and Majdanek concentration camps. On the evening of November 2, Sporrenberg brought together all his commanders and detailed how the killing operation was to be conducted. The manner of execution was mass shooting. The SS-Police units were to conduct themselves as in a Bandenbekämpfung exercise, first surrounding the camps. The Jews were then led from the camps to pits already dug for the purpose, made to undress, and then shot. Music was played to smother the sounds of shots. The slaughter lasted three days and was regarded as a major achievement by the SS-Police in Poland. Christopher Browning identified the units employed in the operation.[38] They included the 22nd SS-Police Regiment (Kraków) and the 25th SS-Police Regiment (Lublin), Waffen-SS detachments from Warsaw, the Lublin police, and experts from the SS-Totenkopfverbände controlling the camps. Sporrenberg's position in Lublin was as absolute as Globocnik's had been. He personally commanded the 25th SS-Police Regiment and Security Police. Browning found witnesses who stated that during the action, Sporrenberg monitored progress by flying around in a Fieseler Storch. Aktion Erntefest concluded, with the SS-Police having executed 42,000 people in three days.

Gerhard Weinberg observed, "When murdering 42,000 Jews in three massacres in the Lublin area during a few days in November 1943, the Germans made certain to catch their victims completely by surprise and returned to the procedure of mass shootings that had characterized the early stages of the killing program in 1941."[39] In recompense for the deed, Friedrich-Wilhelm Krüger was assigned to the SS Division Prinz Eugen in November 1943 to train for command of an SS division. Jakob Sporrenberg and members of his team were transferred to Norway. One can only surmise why Sporrenberg packed off to Norway, but perhaps more important, one wonders why Himmler did not repeat Aktion Erntefest.

## Kovel

Today, Kovel is a Ukrainian city, part of territory annexed from Poland by Stalin after the Second World War. Between 1919 and 1939, Kovel was a Polish city on the Soviet border, a strategic railway junction. Kovel's terrain is bisected by the River Styr, surrounded by forests, and located on the southwest tip of the Pripyat marshes. In the winter of 1943–44, the mild weather caused the ground between the forests to turn swamp-like. The roads were impassable even for tracked armored vehicles. Kovel was first occupied by the Red Army in 1939 and then by the Wehrmacht in 1941. Alexander Werth referred to the Soviet occupation of Kovel on September 20, 1939, noting that it had caused internal hostilities.[40] The German occupation can be measured by the crimes of two former German police officers, Erich Kassner and Fritz Manthei, both of whom received lifelong prison sentences after the war.

Between 1942 and 1943, they were responsible for the civil administration of the District of Kovel (*Zivilverwaltung Gebietskommissariat Kowel*) and the gendarmerie in Kovel. Their crimes included mass killing, destruction of the Kovel ghetto, and hunting down escapees in hiding. They committed a reprisal action against a local community when a Ukrainian militia unit defected to the partisans.[41] In January 1944, Kovel became the key strategic junction of the Eastern Front. The railway lines linked Germany with Hungary and Rumania; Kovel was a supply hub and part of the central German defense line. The situation in Kovel, threatened by Soviets, was deadly for Hitler, who feared the loss of allies and resources.

On January 14, 1944, Hitler ordered Bach-Zelewski to form a rapid reaction command and assault group, Stossgruppe von dem Bach, to defend Kovel.[42] The command team included SS-Standartenführer Gustav Lombard (chief of staff), Oberstleutnant der Gendarmerie Reimpel (operations officer), and SS-Standartenführer August Zehender (commander of 17th SS-Cavalry Regiment).[43] The Stossgruppe was composed of the 17th SS-Cavalry Regiment, an army pioneer battalion, an army self-propelled assault-gun detachment, and an army artillery detachment. Hitler's orders granted Bach-Zelewski the authority to act "ruthlessly, with brutality, and to act with strength of personality." Bach-Zelewski arrived in Kovel on January 16 from Warsaw and remained in command until March 16. Within the remit of his command, he took control of the city's troops, placing them on a defensive posture after a tactical meeting with the army's Feldkommandantur and local Nazi Party bosses. On January 23, his team completed the building of their tactical headquarters. His Fieseler Storch was used to ferry Lombard and Reimpel to meet with the commanders of the Hungarian army, the German army's XIII Corps, and the HSSPF Russia-South.[44] On January 29, he was briefly caught up in the fighting and came under machine-gun fire.

At first the Russians advanced rapidly, pushing north and south of the city, crossing the railway line toward Sarny. After capturing the rail junction, the Soviets concentrated their forces. German reinforcements made a timely arrival, were hastily detrained, formed into a weak Kampfgruppe, and hurled against the Russians. The shock stalled the Soviets and halted their efforts to concentrate. The Kampfgruppe withdrew and prepared for the defense. To protect the city, the main body of Bach-Zelewski's troops formed a security line across the central railway embankment. While the Germans conducted their defensive preparations, Soviet partisan bands increased their attacks along the railway lines. Bach-Zelewski described the numbers of partisan attacks, "in masses of red lines" covering his maps. The Germans received continual reports from local informers identifying Soviet attempts to concentrate to the north of the city. The Red Army pressed three rifle divisions to force a way through to the northeast riverside. They directed their drive through the swamps to capture the main road severing connections with the west. In coordination with this drive, the partisans attempted a double encirclement of Kovel, masking their intentions by marching more than 30 kilometers north and sweeping around the city.[45] German reconnaissance over-flights disclosed the Soviet intentions. This situation indicated to Bach-Zelewski that he had no choice but to deliver a spoiling attack against the Soviets. His decision plunged the Stossgruppe into bloody fighting but proved the correct decision as the Soviets withdrew. Bach-Zelewski placed troops on either side across the river, forming a bridgehead. The Stossgruppe continued to repulse Soviet attacks but was once again forced to withdraw across the river. The post-action report concentrated on the west bank defensive line at Zareèje because it encompassed old First World War fortifications.[46]

In February, the Germans attempted to counter-attack and push forward to Lutsk. A strike force of SS-Cavalry, combat engineers, and flak batteries attempted to breakthrough Soviet lines. During the attack, Soviet counter-attacks halted the Germans. When the SS-Cavalry stopped to rest, they were surprised by hundreds of partisans. This led to intense house-to-house fighting. The remaining troops of the Stossgruppe, supported with tanks, were forced to rescue the cavalry. The casualties counted on February 23 and on February 26 amounted to forty-five enemy dead.[47] On the Central Front, the Soviets collected strong forces against the river railway bridge, while infantry concentrated in the forests. Heavy defensive fighting held off the Russians supported by a German armored railway train that was brought forward. Bach-Zelewski later alleged the Red Army had a 10 to 1 advantage and was, therefore, able to complete the encirclement of the city. The Germans likened the Soviet attack to a door being levered with the gendarmerie and supply troops desperately protecting the right wing of the Stossgruppe.

Supporting the Stossgruppe was the 7th Special Flying Group, which conducted a variety of sorties throughout January and February. The flying group commander, Oberstleutnant Heinzius, was based in Lublin and reported daily to Himmler. A continuous period of mild weather enabled the Germans to exploit aerial reconnaissance without Red Air Force intervention. There were transport and glider-towing missions bringing in supplies and reinforcements. The ground fighting allowed the airmen to pinpoint enemy movements during bombing missions. Air attacks were directed at breaking up the bands, destroying their camps, or interdicting their supply routes. A message from January 16 referred to "special-operation Bach" (*Sonderunternehmen Bach*), which included at least six squadrons. In February, Bach-Zelewski's diary referred to the opening of an extended period of air force operations. On February 7, signals emanating from a squadron of Stukas were deciphered by the British.[48] Five days later, signals confirmed an attack squadron of Stuka airplanes had joined these air operations.[49]

By March 11, Bach-Zelewski's defensive battle was over; his efforts proved reasonably skillful, employing bluff, diversions, and counterstrokes.

Gustav Lombard passed Bach-Zelewski's Kovel defense report to Fegelein, Hitler's representative. The report fulfilled the Führer's order to stop the Soviet advance and defend Kovel. Bach-Zelewski attributed his success to the assault-gun (*Sturmgeschütz*) detachment, which he used to bluff the Red Army. Captured Soviet POWs divulged that they had estimated the number of German tanks at two hundred. Bach-Zelewski also praised the 662nd Pioneer Battalion, 17th SS-Cavalry Regiment, and the artillery. Lombard added to the report. He recalled a counter-attack by the German army's XIII Corps in an attempt to close the gap between Prützmann and Bach-Zelewski. It was stalled because of a Soviet offensive that began at the same time. The Russians threw back the weak German forces but were in turn assaulted by the full weight of an attack led personally by Bach-Zelewski. The Red Army swarmed against the Stossgruppe.[50] After Bach-Zelewski departed from Kovel, the Soviet operations intensified. Eventually, the Red Army passed north and south, reinforcing the encirclement by March 17. SS-Obergruppenführer Gille was ordered to defend the city, and the encirclement was broken by the 5th SS-Panzer Division Wiking.

During the Kovel operations the Polish resistance movement conducted incursions in the area that attracted SS-Police reactions.[51] Two SS troopers confessed to shooting civilians in Kolki and in another village near Kovel:

> Our squadron took part in the shootings of civilians in the small town of Kolki. I personally participated in shooting three civilians. Then we burnt down part of the town. During the retreat, after crossing the River Styr, we burnt down the first village beyond the river. In that village our second platoon under Untersturmführer Korn shot 25 persons. I myself shot two persons. Women were among those shot. Of the men of our platoon, those particularly active in the shootings were Rottenführer Waneck, Unterscharführer Polin, Unterscharführer Steikdel, troopers Schirmann and Faut. The shootings were done on the orders of Regimental commander Standartenführer Zehender.[52]

Andrew Borowiec has suggested there was communication between an SS general and the Polish resistance in March 1944. This area came under the Polish 27th Resistance Division, highly regarded for its fighting ability. The division suffered grievous losses at the hands of the Wiking. Later, en route to the Warsaw uprising, it was surrounded by Soviet troops and disarmed.[53]

Although it is difficult to identify real or lasting friendships within the SS, it does appear that Himmler and Bach-Zelewski shared a common bond. Another bout of Bach-Zelewski's health problems provides evidence of some bonding. Prior to his Kovel assignment, a medical examination in December passed Bach-Zelewski as fit. The doctor even commented that his energy made it difficult to prevent him from being at the front.[54] On March 12, Himmler wrote to Bach-Zelewski,

> I can only acknowledge that in spite of this heavy health handicap you stood so outstandingly with your Kampfgruppe. Lombard will give you the plan in detail. In general it might be said that SS-[Obergruppenführer] Gille will command the re-building of the SS-Division *Wiking* and he will in the next few days takeover your Kampfgruppe. Lombard will stay on for "special tasks."[55]

Bach-Zelewski was examined again on March 22, and the diagnosis indicated a return of his bowel problems although his hemorrhoids operation remained a success.[56]

Hitler almost certainly held Bach-Zelewski in disdain for leaving Kovel on the spurious grounds of his ill health. The change of command in Kovel caused problems between the remaining Bandenkampfverbände team and the incubant Waffen-SS staff. On April 15, Reimpel wrote to Bach-Zelewski,

> My position has seen a change because of the arrival of the *SS-Wiking*, no longer the deputy, and have to be loud to be heard. The Gruppenführer [Gille] is a man to look up to but he is not quite what it takes. The influence of the young-blood staff officers is a problem. My tasks are finished and I wish to leave as fast as possible. As long as my men are bleeding here, this is my place. The co-operation of the staff in the first days was great. The Führer has interfered and sacrificed that capability.[57]

On April 24, Himmler wrote to Bach-Zelewski, "The general without luck does not hold true for you; that Kovel could be held was partly down to Gille and partly down to you."[58] Former Waffen-SS veterans liked to extract their battle of Kovel, from Bach-Zelewski's battle. The working notes of the operations officer from the office of the Chef der Bandenkampfverbände, for March 20, 1944, prove that Kampfgruppe Gille received drawing materials to produce its Bandenbekämpfung maps for Himmler's collection in keeping with other Bandenkampfverbände.[59] In April 1944, Gille was awarded the Knight's Cross from Hitler, the highest military award Germany could bestow. Bach-Zelewski received the Bandenkampfabzeichen in Bronze, for twenty-eight days in combat, from Himmler on July 3, 1944. It was scant consolation.[60]

## Collapse in the General Government

By January 1944, the Germans were reporting many cases of Polish "bandits" in the Danzig-West-Prussian forests.[61] The assassination of SS-Brigadeführer Franz Kutschera on February 1, 1944, by a twenty-year-old resistance fighter was a shock for Himmler and Bach-Zelewski.[62] On July 19, 1944, an SS liaison officer informed the German Foreign Office that the HSSPF East had issued an order enforcing the collective responsibility of family members of assassins and saboteurs.[63] The deteriorating situation forced the SS to act. The execution of all male relatives of assassins and saboteurs was ordered, and females were sent to concentration camps. This situation rapidly escalated as the Polish will to resist increased and Nazi officials became assassination targets. According to Richard Lukas, these attacks reached more than six hundred assassinations per year by 1944.[64]

Military intelligence monitored the resistance and their links with Polish governments in exile. Gehlen maintained a detailed and meticulous analysis with comprehensive organization charts of the resistance and their controlling authorities. His assessment of the Polish resistance movement in February 1944 identified categories of political allegiance. Gehlen's analysis of the communist resistance focused on the Polish Workers Party, which he estimated had seventy-five hundred volunteers. They were organized through a rigid hierarchical structure and controlled from Moscow. The central cadre was in Warsaw with eleven cells, and there were a further seven cells within its city districts. However, Gehlen's information concerning the Polish People's Army (*Armja Ludowa*) with its regional offices across Poland was sparse. He located their headquarters in Biala Podlaska and guessed that their combat units were each formed into five cells organized into companies 120 fighters strong, but that was all.[65]

The German intelligence services also monitored the possibility for a Polish revolt. A few weeks before the Warsaw uprising, Gehlen warned of an impending revolt. On July 1, 1944, he identified the Polish resistance movement as encouraging the population to employ all means hostile to the Germans. His report stated that the forests were swarming with splinter groups in hiding. As was his habit, Gehlen concentrated on the political motivations within the resistance movement. He advised of tensions between the Polish government-in-exile (in London) and the Soviet-sponsored Lublin government that splintered the rank-and-file membership into factions. The peasantry was judged to have sided with the English-backed anti-Communist movement. The Germans confirmed the growing enmity between Polish and Ukrainian populations within Galicia and their political diversities. Gehlen summarized the situation: "In our judgement the plans for revolt, given the Polish character, inclines toward a strong but not over-estimated possibility, given the general political and military situation."[66]

Lower in the intelligence hierarchy, resistance monitoring became the responsibility of German army district commanders. Major General Haseloff, chief of staff of the General Government's military district, regularly circulated security reports that itemized incursions, summarized casualties, listed wireless interceptions, identified propaganda issues, and recorded security operations. Haseloff's reports from December 1943 to July 1944 began as monthly releases but increased to weekly with the upsurge of "banditry."[67] In December, there were 6,392 incidents conducted by 6,050 resistance units organized into groups of 100 insurgents. The balance of casualties was 39 Germans killed against 1,016 Poles killed. At least thirteen main railway lines were attacked, especially from Warsaw to Minsk, Radom, and Demblin.[68] By April 1944, insurgents had attacked thirty-four main railway routes. There had been 6,322 reported attacks, carried out by 5,897 operatives. Haseloff's report confirmed 4,961 "bandits" captured and 1,000 shot, while the Germans suffered 267 killed and more than 560 wounded.[69] The resistance groups, it was confirmed, were standing and fighting.

This rising level of resistance was recorded elsewhere in a miscellaneous collection of reports that covered various levels of army command. A report on behalf of the OKW Operations Staff assessed the overall situation from the perspective of the central sector.[70] On July 10, 1944, considerable numbers of attacks occurred along the railway lines between Kraków and Warsaw. Further deterioration in the General Government was indicated by sporadic shootings against German vehicles in the area of Lublin on July 17, 1944. Around Sparozew, the Germans identified an eight-hundred-man "bandit" group but could do little about them. Northeast of Lublin, a band of more than one thousand operated with impunity, as did the "bandit" group "Stalin," three hundred strong, operating around Bilgoraj. Reports from "trusties" flooded in from the Lemberg area. One reported the presence of a "bandit" group of Polish Jews, two thousand strong and reputedly air-landed into the area. Another group, eight hundred strong, was operating in the south, while the police were combating yet another group of four hundred "bandits," the so-called Tschepigia-Bande.[71] The evidence of the scale of the Polish threat also emerged from a report by the rear-area commander of Army Group Centre that stated,

> Since the opening of Operation "Frühlingsfest" from the Naliboki forest along the route Minsk–Baranovichi, and also the Slutsk district was an area dominated by concentrations of bands. Unlike the Soviet bands, the entire Polish strength has tripled in a few weeks to about 4,500 men. The procurement of arms for the greater Polish bandit movement is their major problem. Further growth in the Polish resistance movement can be depended upon.[72]

## Warsaw Uprising

On July 31, 1944, Gen.Tadeusz "Bor" Komorowski, commander of the Polish Home Army (*Armja Krajowa*), known as the AK, agreed to start the uprising to liberate Poland. On August 1, 1944, at 5:00 p.m. fighting broke out in the streets of Warsaw. The uprising was set just as the Soviet offensive ran out of steam. The German "victory" over Warsaw has become another lost battle having virtually disappeared from the annals of German military history.[73] After the war, the prolific writings of German generals collectively disowned or at least marginalized the battle. A collective malady of amnesia afflicted former SS and Wehrmacht veterans of the battle. Yet the suppression (*Niederkämpfung*) of the uprising by Bach-Zelewski, and his lieutenants was the zenith of Bandenbekämpfung. The German order of battle through the disposition of units to destroy the uprising indicated a more complex theater-wide operational plan. It came at a time of intensive German intelligence warnings. Strategically, the Germans were not surprised. Rather, Germans were prepared and wanted to exploit the uprising. It remains unclear whether Hitler or his generals manipulated German forces for a drive against the Soviets, but the possibility changes the given interpretation of events surrounding the uprising.

The crushing Soviet offensive, Operation "Bagration," opened on June 22, 1944, and caused wholesale collapse of Army Group Centre followed by pursuit of its remnants through Poland. Losses included twenty-eight divisions, three hundred fifty thousand men, and mortal wounding of the Wehrmacht in the east. German centers during the occupation of Soviet Russia such as Vitebsk, Orsha, Mogilev, Bobruysk, and Minsk were overwhelmed and liberated. Hitler's faith in static fortifications proved illusionary as the "Panther line" crumbled. After strenuous efforts, Field Marshal Model wrestled to stabilize the Central Front before Warsaw.[74] He ordered the 3rd SS-Panzer Division Totenkopf to hold a line 50 miles east of Warsaw. This division held long enough to allow the 2nd Army to escape Soviet encirclement. On July 28, the division gradually withdrew while conducting a series of punishing counter-attacks. On August 11, the division crossed the River Vistula northeast of Warsaw and took up positions on the western bank. During the next seven days, the Totenkopf along with the Wiking held off repeated Soviet assaults,[75] actions that paralleled the Waffen-SS-inspired victory at Kharkov in April 1943 because of the number of panzer divisions. On June 22, 1944, there were few armored reserves available to Army Group Centre to counter "Bagration." However, by August 1, eight panzer divisions had gathered around Warsaw.[76]

The Soviets encountered a dilemma. To seal off Warsaw, assaults across the River Vistula would involve facing German siege artillery and intensive defensive firepower, thus sustaining serious losses. The Soviet predicament, therefore, was either securing the front line and allowing the Polish resistance to collapse or capturing Warsaw and placing the Soviet central front inside the jaws of Germany's armored forces. Hitler had metaphorically placed Stalin under the "Sword of Damocles" since the Red Army's finest assault troops, committed to capturing the city, would be left exposed to the German armored forces concentrated against their flanks. The conditions offered the Germans a classic Cannae with the Red Army pressed against a river. The Soviet dilemma had diplomatic implications; Stalin faced growing allied suspicions over Soviet territorial ambitions. Strategically the overall military situation, since the opening of "Bagration," had lost momentum as the Germans forced a stalemate through vicious counter-attacks and probes. Stalin also faced another problem—the Germans held the advantage of shortened internal lines and could use the telephone system instead of military signals. "Ultra" and the German police signals went silent causing the Allies intelligence gaps.

The German response in 1944 compared to the 1943 uprising appeared slow more so because Himmler had received warnings within a half hour of the opening shots. Richard Lukas rhetorically asked why the Germans were so unprepared.[77] His explanation of the slow response came from German testimony after the war. These testimonies generally confirmed that the uprising triggered a crisis among the Nazis. Norman Davies relied on evidence from former SS-Untersturmführer Gustav Schielke given in 1949.[78] Schielke told his Polish interrogators that the Germans expected the uprising but were physically unprepared. In 1972, Günther Deschner suggested that the Germans had left Warsaw largely unprotected, having withdrawn or evacuated bases and depots.[79] The situation was frantic; German troops were hastened to the front, while rear-area formations were withdrawn. According to most sources, the Germans had approximately two thousand troops of differing caliber garrisoned in Warsaw at the time of the outbreak. The experience of the Warsaw ghetto uprising taught Himmler that the way to defeat armed resistance was to support a garrison in place, using it to divide the attention of the resistance. Thus, instead of a necessarily rapid response, Himmler's response was measured and predictable. He had complete confidence in the capability of the SS-Police. The SS evidently believed that they had contained the uprising within ten days of its start. The SS reaction, therefore, was party to the Wehrmacht's operational intentions of an armored Cannae.

From the beginning, the Germans adopted widespread "kill and destruction" tactics. Hans Frank notified Berlin that "Burning down the houses is the most reliable means of liquidating the insurgents' hideouts."[80] Himmler told a gathering,

> I simultaneously gave orders for Warsaw to be totally destroyed. You may think I am a fearful barbarian. If you like I am one, if I have to be. My orders were to burn down and blow up every block of houses. As a result, one of the biggest abscesses on the eastern front has been removed.[81]

The Allies, after the war, believed August 5 was the day the brutalities officially ended. Joanna Hanson found the killing continued until at least August 12 before the Germans attempted more subtle methods to defeat the Poles.[82]

In this context a couple of questions need to be asked: what were Bach-

Zelewski's movements prior to the uprising, and when did he receive the command? Virtually all accounts accept that he took command on August 5, 1944, which correlates his version of the events. His diary, however, makes interesting reading. The week prior to the uprising he spent visiting East Prussia defenses and formations. On July 30, 1944, he lunched with Himmler and von Gottberg. On July 31, he joined Himmler (recently promoted to commander of the reserve army) to meet with Col. Gen. Heinz Guderian. The latter was promoted to chief of the General Staff of the Army on July 20, 1944, following the bomb plot against Hitler. Bronislav Kaminski, leader of the Russian National Liberation Army, was also present. On August 1, Bach-Zelewski's diary referred to a meeting with Katzmann in Danzig, which was plausible because the latter had become HSSPF Weichsel. His diary referred to the events in Warsaw on August 2, a day he spent relaxing, swimming, and reflecting by the sea at Zoppot. He recalled with sentimentality that thirty years earlier he had been in the same place with two friends, both killed in the First World War. In 1934, while visiting Zoppot, he received orders to travel to Berlin to participate against the "Röhm putsch." Thus it was that, while in Zoppot, he heard of the "great mess" (*grosse Schweinerei*) in the General Government.[83] On August 3, he took his airplane through stormy weather to reach the KSRFSS in Lötzen. This appears a strange move, not because the offices of the Chef der Bandenkampfverbände and the KSRFSS had been relocating to southern Germany since March 1944 but because, by staying where he was within Reich borders (East Prussia), there was complete access to Hitler, Himmler, and any SS facilities via telephone.[84] Then, according to his diary, on August 4, he traveled to Kraków to meet Himmler and, while en route, received word that he had been ordered to take command. Bach-Zelewski added that he later received official notification from Himmler by telephone. Bach-Zelewski wrote down that it was a suicide mission (*Himmelfahrtskommando*), as in Kovel earlier that year.[85] After the war, Bach-Zelewski told interrogators that he had made representations to the KSRFSS but was told Himmler had gone to Posen to conduct operations personally. Not wishing to be ignored, Bach-Zelewski said he spoke directly with Hitler's headquarters. Fegelein told him the situation was being contained by Himmler and Luftwaffe Lt. Gen. Rainer Stahel. They expected an early collapse, but some days later, Fegelein telephoned Bach-Zelewski.

> I was told furthermore that the full power which I had requested of the Führer was granted, and that I should put down the uprising quickly and forcefully. Replacements could not be counted upon, because the Russian breakthrough at Minsk tied up all forces as far as the Vistula River.[86]

Not surprisingly, therefore, Bach-Zelewski's diary and his post-war testimony record his command beginning on August 5. The general lack of urgency also did not change with Bach-Zelewski's command. He established his command post outside the city in Sochaczew to the west. On August 6, he observed the street fighting in Warsaw and wrote that he saved many Polish civilians through deportation. He observed that one of his Kampfgruppe commanders, SS-Gruppenführer Heinz Reinefarth, was fighting with "stronger nerves" than himself. The next day, following Luftwaffe air raids, Bach-Zelewski witnessed scenes of vicious street fighting, masses of corpses, and burning buildings. He ordered assault guns to reduce Polish barricades. One intercepted signal requested flamethrowers and incendiary bombing of the city by Luftwaffe.[87] On August 8, Bach-Zelewski met Gen. Nikolas von Vormann, commander of the 9th Army and the Wehrmacht commander for the city. He then drove to Warsaw, took a nap before lunch, met with Dirlewanger, and received report updates. The Germans regarded the situation contained by August 9, and that same day, Bach-Zelewski again met with Vormann. In his notes, however, he seemed more concerned over the loss of his chief of staff Gölz in a traffic accident. The measured pace of life continued. On August 21, Bach-Zelewski received a message from Himmler to meet with Guderian. He arrived in Lötzen early so he went swimming in the nearby lake. At 5:30 p.m., as he awaited Himmler, he decided to go to the cinema. The next day, while still waiting for Himmler's arrival, he went off to the hairdresser. Senior command of this political-military battle meant regular politicking with Nazi bosses. Bach-Zelewski complained in his diary that, until 4:00 p.m. each day, he was under hostile enemy fire and was then forced to brave a dangerous flight, in foul weather, to meet with party bosses. On August 23, he noticed blood in his stools for first time since his operation. He was concerned was about inflamed hemorrhoids or possibly cholera, then spreading among his troops.

Bach-Zelewski's command gradually increased the size of its order of battle during the pacification. Initially two Kampfgruppen were formed, the smaller under Major General Rohr and the larger under SS-Gruppenführer Reinefarth. Kampfgruppe Reinefarth was further broken down into three attack groups (*Angriffsgruppe*) under SS-Oberführer Dirlewanger, Major Reck (from the Infantry School in Posen), and Colonel Schmidt (commander of 608th Security Regiment). Each attack group was assigned eight flamethrowers.[88] Bach-Zelewski's reputation for achieving solid performances from mixed-quality troops enabled the Germans to economize their efforts. It allowed the gradual release of frontline formations from the wasting effects of street fighting. The Germans employed a massive array of specialist units whose purpose was wholesale destruction. An interrogation report of Lt. Eduard Kunze, an engineer, on May 1, 1945, revealed that the Germans had released a gas into airtight buildings or tunnels and ignited it. This gas he claimed was called "A-Stoff" and was odorless and colorless.[89] On October 5, 1944, the final order of battle of Korpgruppe von dem Bach was,

*Corps level formations*: 34th SS-Police Rifle Regiment and the I SS Flak Detachment (KSRFSS).

*Kampfgruppe Rohr*: 10th Mixed Wehrmacht Police Battalion; 906th Artillery Battalion; 944th Security Battalion; 1st Battalion, 17th SS-Police Regiment; and 246th Landesschützen Battalion.

*Kampfgruppe Reinefarth*: SS-Brigade Dirlewanger (with 2 battalions of easterner Muslims), 501st SS-Jäger Regiment, Police Regiment Schmidt, Police Battalion Burghardt, Police Regiment *Reck*; Sturm-Pionier Regiment Herzog, Police Battalion Sarnow; 3rd Cossack Regiment; 2nd Azerbaijan Battalion; Police Flamethrower Battalion; 302nd Panzer Detachment (and 218th Assault Panzer Company); 2nd Sturmgeschütz Detachment; 1000th Assault Mortar Company; 2nd Battery Heavy Artillery; 201st Heavy Fortifications Mortar Battery; 695th Railway Battery; and the 5th Armored Train.

*Supporting organizations*: 25th Panzer Division; Kampfgruppe Bernhard (Korück 532); and 1st Luftwaffe Division. [90]

During the uprising, Bach-Zelewski as a senior force commander was responsible for enforcing discipline and maintaining troop morale. On August 28, he was instrumental in ordering the drumhead court-martial (*Standgerichtssitzung*) and the execution of Bronislav Kaminski. This self-styled tribal leader of anti-Bolshevik Russians had successfully collaborated with the Germans since 1942. His success in eradicating Soviet partisans in the forests of Bryansk even garnered praise from Hitler. When the German army retreated, Kaminski's horde and their dependents went with them. In the early days of the uprising, Kaminski and Dirlewanger appeared to compete for the crown of the most abominable behavior, including drunkenness, killings, rapes, and pillage.[91] Bach-Zelewski wrote of Kaminski's trial in his diary mentioning that it was conducted in Litzmannstadt (Lodz, Poland). After the war, Guderian claimed Bach-Zelewski eliminated Kaminski because he was a dangerous witness.[92] Under allied interrogation, Bach-Zelewski admitted to spiriting Kaminski away with three of his staff officers in a ruse. An SS court-martial declared Kaminski (an SS-Brigadeführer) guilty of the misdemeanor of failing to obey orders. Bach-Zelewski also admitted that once new and better units became available he could afford to dispense with the Kaminski Brigade.[93] Sven Steenberg, formerly a German army interrogator with the Russian émigrés, later claimed the execution was hushed up and a rumor spread that Polish partisans had killed Kaminski. Kaminski's men demanded a visit to the scene of the supposed incident. Kaminski's command car was allegedly driven into a ditch, riddled with machine-gun bullets, and liberally daubed with goose blood.[94] Evidence also suggests that Kaminski had lost control of his men, and the SS feared a repeat of Gil-Rodionov's Druzhina mutiny of 1943.

Perhaps it was for this reason that they executed him. There again Bach-Zelewski also breached German law four days before on August 24 to overhear his name being announced on the BBC. On September 9, the BBC broadcast that he had joined the list of allied war criminals. "What honour!" he exclaimed in his diary. "Just for Warsaw, where I have shown the extreme humanity before God!"[95]

Examining Bach-Zelewski's actual combat and leadership performance in Warsaw reveals predictable behavior. Since August 29, the SS-Police had been awaiting an assault by the Red Army; that same day, Luftwaffe Col. Gen. Ritter von Greim visited Bach-Zelewski. The Germans were still waiting on August 30 when Bach-Zelewski observed Dirlewanger's performance clearing houses on the northern bank of the city. He made another inspection of the defenses and discussed the placement of antitank units with his troop commanders. Eventually the Soviet attack came on September 2; Bach-Zelewski was barely left with time to record the events. He later recorded that the German repulse was his greatest success to date, while his command watch period stretched from early morning to late night. He informed Himmler that the northern encirclement of the city was complete and that Kampfgruppe Rohr had captured Czerniakov and advanced to the south of Siedlce. In the message, he boasted having "driven through prisoners of war while standing-up in the car to end the fighting. I guaranteed their lives. This was the only way to control prisoners with so few guards." Was he implying that at other times the captives were simply executed? He concluded his message by confirming the capture of 60 percent of Warsaw although "he was still in competition with the Bolsheviks." His written commentary on the fighting over three days from September 5 in the southern part of city was erratic. He confirmed, "The Poles are fighting like heroes." Then he wrote a cryptic line: "We have to hurry because of the Bolsheviks. Better here than in the west" (no doubt meaning the campaign in France where the Germans were losing). On September 6, he took time out to visit Pruszkow transit camp, which was being used as a collection point for Polish partisans.

There was a break in Bach-Zelewski's diary entries until September 13, 1944. Filling that gap is Reinefarth, who took the opportunity to conduct some hearty politicking. Reinefarth wrote to Himmler on September 9, expressing his gratitude for the kind words the Reichsführer had bestowed on his troops through Bach-Zelewski. He explained the reason for the operation's success:

> Our duty would not have been possible without the reckless and never ending support of SS-Obergruppenführer von dem Bach. We thought highly of him, in spite of his own suffering, he stayed amongst the Kampfgruppe even though gastric flu spread like a plague amongst the troops. He looked after himself only when physically forced to do so.[96]

Prior to the uprising there had been little contact between the two men, but Reinefarth wanted to redress this with his version of events:

> After 12 years as an old colleague, Bach remained in the front line providing motivation to the troops. The SS-Obergruppenführer is not able to tell you about his reconnaissance flights over Warsaw, because you will prohibit his flying. I am sorry for writing this way, but I thought it was my duty because von dem Bach is owed recognition for his efforts in the harsh fight for Warsaw.[97]

However, Bach-Zelewski was wise to Reinefarth's shenanigans. On September 21, he held a meeting with Guderian. It seems Reinefarth had also kept Guderian suitably informed about activities in Warsaw. This meeting closed the contact between Reinefarth and Guderian. Bach-Zelewski was also angry that Reinefarth's Kampfgruppe had "taken ill-deserved laurels."[98]

During heavy fighting on September 13, the Red Army took the district of Praga. Bach-Zelewski recorded that the fighting was like Kovel, from all directions. He signed off his diary, "I have had enough of Warsaw." The next day, he reported to Himmler on the occupation of the Siedlce district and the capture of Fort Legionowo.[99] On September 16, he transferred quarters closer to the city. The Red Army, having taken control of the riverbank and Praga, exposed his former headquarters to direct attack. He was confirmed a full corps commander (Korpsgruppe von dem Bach), and the 19th Panzer Division passed to his command. He recorded that his new command post was a villa with a vegetable garden. At 5:30 a.m. on September 17, he was awakened by a "Bolshevik" attempt to cross the river with the "Polish-Soviet Berling Army." That evening the Red Army made another attempt to breach his riverbank defences. The Germans had observed Red Army preparations to arrange pontoons, indicating a large attack.

All evening Bach-Zelewski led the defense against Soviet assaults and recorded it in his diary on September 18. It was a "night full of excitement," he declared. The Soviet attempts to breach the riverbank were twice repulsed. One assault of nine hundred Soviet troops in the north, at Zoliborcz, was defeated. A factory site in the south was captured under Bach-Zelewski's leadership during a lunchtime action. The Germans were frightened when American four-engine bombers approached the city. The bombers, however, dropped supply canisters, and most fell to the Germans, owing to the direction of the wind. Later, Bach-Zelewski met with army commanders to discuss the next Soviet attack. Early on September 20, he attended a conference with Guderian and met with Himmler. Later, serious news arrived from Warsaw, however, interrupting his lunchtime nap. The Soviets released a smokescreen along the riverfront to disguise a large-scale attack. German artillery destroyed twenty-seven assault boats, but still the Red Army managed to reach the opposite bank of the city center. German reserves were sent in and destroyed the Soviet bridgehead. The counter-attack forced the Soviets back from the west bank. The SS-Police captured 180 Russians and sustained three hundred dead and wounded. The last day, September 21, the heaviest Soviet assaults against the Totenkopf occurred, and this corresponded with events inside Warsaw.

On September 22, Bach-Zelewski flew around Warsaw signifying total German control of the city. The next day, the southern perimeter and encircle- ment were finally cleansed. The fighting over the last houses of resistance remained a difficult task because Soviet artillery continued to support the resistance. Among the captive Soviet troops were forty armed women (*Flinten- weiber*). Later, Bach-Zelewski held a meeting with foreign office officials, Luftwaffe division commanders, and Reinefarth. He sent representatives to parley with the last Polish defenders of the Mokotow district and received a positive response. A partial armistice was negotiated, and civilians were evacu- ated from the combat area. He wrote:

> I save lots of people. Now I know why God saved me! In this time
> of blood and tears I shall hold high the banner of humanity. It
> fulfils me with deep happiness to be able to do so much good.

On September 26, the attacks on the Mokotow district were renewed. The brief armistice had allowed the evacuation of 4,500 civilians. The next day, Bach-Zelewski sat and awaited the final victory. At 1:30 p.m., the capitulation confirmation was sent to Himmler. At 7:30 p.m, Himmler called to confirm Hitler's award of the Knight's Cross to Bach-Zelewski and Dirlewanger; Reinefarth, already a recipient of this most coveted medal, received the Oak Leaves cluster. They held a medal party in lieu of the overall capitulation on September 28, but the Poles spoiled the celebrations with sporadic fighting. On September 29, Bach-Zelewski's comments were deep:

> In these days I become part of history and I am so proud for my
> sons. I negotiated with the Poles who received instructions from
> London. This is really big politics!

On September 30, he reported to Himmler that the 19th Panzer Division had captured Zoliborcz after two days' fighting. Resistance officially ended at 7:00 p.m. when eight hundred Poles laid down their arms and fifteen thousand civilians came out of hiding.

The final instrument of Polish surrender was drafted in phrases corre- sponding to the Geneva Convention of 1929. Bach-Zelewski later alleged that he manipulated events to ensure Himmler did not break this agreement. He also said Hitler confirmed the surrender document. The Poles have a different record of the surrender; their delegation of four officers was driven to Bach-

Zelewski's headquarters in Ozarow, a country house full of portraits of the Polish aristocracy. They discussed surrender with Bach-Zelewski and his chief of staff, Oberst der Polizei Göltz. When the document was signed, Bach-Zelewski gave a short speech about how the act would save more lives and then telephoned Himmler with the news. The surrender and subsequent treatment of the Poles had wider implications. Bach-Zelewski's orders, from Hitler and Himmler, required the killing of all captured insurgents whether or not they were fighting within the terms of the laws of war, the non-combatants (women and children) were to be executed, and the whole city was to be razed to the ground.[100] Why had he been allowed to receive a formal surrender? If the Geneva Convention was appropriate for Polish resistors, then it was also applicable to partisans across Europe and allied Special Forces personnel. Bach-Zelewski alleged that he intervened to protect civilians by organizing a Polish commission to run the prison camp, hospitals, and kitchens. The Pruszkow transit camp officially came under the authority of the governor of Warsaw, Dr. Fischer, but Bach-Zelewski said he acted outside Fischer and claimed that he procured provisions. Camp hygiene, he suggested, was handled by the Polish Red Cross, the Swiss Red Cross managed supplies, and the Polish administration, from Kraków, monitored treatment. The insurgents, he said, had been allowed to visit the camp before the surrender negotiations.[101] Many Polish POWs were to perish in the coming months. The surrender terms were cosmetic, a means to ending it quickly, so that Bach-Zelewski could be rested for his next political assignment.

The final results illustrate the true scale of horror behind Bach-Zelewski's work. Andrew Borowiec estimated the population of Warsaw before 1939 at approximately 1.2 million, with 352,000 Jews and 819,000 of Christian faith; 48 percent were laborers and artisans.[102] The industrial workforce was 100,000, with 90,000 listed as professionals and 20,000 unemployed. The population following the 1943 ghetto uprising stood at 974,745, including a total German civilian population of 24,222.[103] A final tally for the fighting is taken from Bach-Zelewski's diary:

> German losses: killed—73 officers, NCOs and men 1,453. Wounded —242 officers, 8,196 NCOs and men.
> Polish losses: killed—1,559 (identified), 100,000 (estimated killed). Wounded—15,000 Prisoners—5 generals, 2,028 officers, and 17,443 others.
> Evacuated (*Evakuierte*) Poles 309,716: 70,023 (to Germany), 61,856 (unfit for work), 135,830 (unfit for work and kept in the General-Government), 3,503, (others) and 29,504 sick.[104]

Why, if the Germans were being humane, did Bach-Zelewski continue to distinguish between those fit for work and those who were not? The final twist,

Bach-Zelewski's recommendation for the Knight's Cross, included August 1, 1944, as the date he took command.[105] This makes Bach-Zelewski officially responsible for the first twelve days of killing, the worst period, which he never attempted to amend on the citation. After the uprising, a sleeve-shield was manufactured but it proved less popular with the troops than the Bandenkampfabzeichen.

Himmler believed that Warsaw was the final historic battle between Poland and Germany:

> Warsaw, the capital city, the brain, the intelligence of this 16–17 million strong Polish nation will have been obliterated, this nation which has blocked our path to the east for seven hundred years and since the first battle of Tannenberg, has always been in the way.[106]

"It is the hardest battle we have fought since the beginning of the war," he added. "It is comparable with the house to house fighting in Stalingrad." According to Heinz Reinefarth, who had spent most of 1942 and 1943 behind a desk in Poland, the Battle of Warsaw was "revenge for Stalingrad."[107] On October 25, 1944, SSPF Warsaw arranged for a party of seventy police officer cadets to ride over the Warsaw battleground.[108] The country, however, was in ruins. In October, the SS-Police reported a rash of corruption and black marketing schnapps, bread, and butter as the trade of "banditry."[109] As the Red Army wrestled for control over the last German strongholds, the SS conducted a final act of barbarism with the extermination of the Hungarian Jews, transported to Auschwitz in November. By December, the SS-Police in Poland had dwindled to a single detachment assigned to dubious special cleanup duties.[110] Eventually the last pockets of German resistance in Poland were eradicated in February 1945. After the war, the former SS leadership from Poland experienced mixed fortunes. Jakob Sporrenberg and Jürgen Stroop were tried in Warsaw in 1950 and 1952 respectively. Friedrich-Wilhelm Krüger committed suicide in May 1945. Julian Scherner was dismissed and posted to the Dirlewanger for corruption and died in combat in 1945. Otto Hellwig died in retirement in Hannover in 1962, as did Fritz Katzmann who died at home in 1957. Heinz Reinefarth died in retirement in 1979 after a political career as a mayor in Schleswig-Holstein.[111]

# 9
# WESTERN EUROPE

The last years of the war in western and southern Europe have generally not attracted the attention they deserve from scholars of the Third Reich. The law of large numbers has concentrated minds on the Eastern Front. This has distorted our understanding of how Hitler strategized his war. The war in the west and south caused the Germans to implement a complex occupation administration and sweeping security measures. Hitler's 1943 appeal to defeat Bolshevism and survive the war inevitably meant the rest of Europe had to be not only pacified but also exploited. Hitler also reassured German public opinion that the Axis alliance was strong and that they were not fighting alone. His strategy also involved erecting a north-south axis of buffer states, including Norway and Italy, connected by strategic corridors. Denmark in the north and the "Alpenland" in the south became lynchpins. These strategic corridors allowed the free movement of troops and materials for "fire-brigade"-like operations. The corridors were also crucial to an east-west Axis, anchored in the west (behind the Atlantic wall and the English Channel) and allowing the movement of troops east to quell troubles. Ultimately these corridors served as escape routes for Hitler's armies. In conceptual terms, Hitler's late war strategic gamble was to stoke eastern fires with western fuels. It was highly effective until the allied invasions in Italy (1943) and then France (1944). The threat of collapse in the west forced Hitler to divert key personnel and resources to conduct Bandenbekämpfung in the west and south of Europe. The outcome, although predictable, proves just how far Bandenbekämpfung was open to interpretation at the local level.

The vast scale of German security operations, conducted in western Europe, means this chapter can concentrate only on key Bandenbekämpfung issues. The central issues, aside from the protection of strategic corridors, were the consistency in the implementation of measures set against a back-drop of command quarrels and institutional rivalry. The character of security operations produced a cocktail of tactical ingenuity and the continued faith in traditional methods. Underscoring all operations were the highest expectations, almost unrealistic, in the results. Hitler's southern flank was politically troubled with the strategic situation always in constant flux. Whether alliance or occupation, by 1943, it seemed like Germanization in the mindset of the indigenous populations. SS race experts had worked swiftly and systematically to deport or exterminate the Jews of southern Europe.[1] Across the region including France, Italy, and Greece, wholesale exploitation of manpower and resources had been imposed by Nazi and collaboration agencies.[2] The surge of the SS-Police presence in the west and Italy, in particular, increased Himmler's influence further. Collectively the SS command in western Europe quickly erected a balanced cross-section of expertise that included policing, covert actions, and Bandenbekämpfung operations. Long after the war, SS apologists alleged atrocities in this region were aberrations and one-off incidents, forced on them by the extremis of provocation. A variety of sources now show, however, that Bandenbekämpfung was widespread in support of Hitler's western Europe strategy, thus proving the SS apologists incorrect.

## Praetorians in the South

Bandenbekämpfung in western Europe shaped the rules of the engagement under which it was conducted. In effect, Hitler was unable to stop adjusting these rules, which he introduced, then amended.[3] Part of the reason for Hitler's continual interference lay with allied covert methods, which were waged across all Europe and in league with the resistance. Fitzroy MacLean later confessed that covert methods contravened the laws of war, but the German response was disproportionate.[4] Bandenbekämpfung was further shaped by the prominence of command quarrels and rivalries that exposed the rules of engagement to undue influence at the local level. Commanders continually overstretched themselves in security operations in what Kershaw has described as "working towards the Führer." By the spring of 1944, therefore, these two issues ensured that the violence of German security operations spiraled.

### The Politics of Engagement

Since October 1942, Hitler had instructed the Wehrmacht and SS on how to treat captured soldiers from the allied Special Forces.[5] One such example driving Hitler to distraction occurred on March 21, 1944. The chief of the Gestapo reported the capture of French SAS soldiers. They had parachuted into France to conduct sabotage against railway targets in the Rennes area but were captured one by one. Following intensive interrogations, the

Gestapo learned of extreme covert training facilities in England and recommended that these captured commandos be killed after interrogation.[6] The timing of the April 1944 Bandenbekämpfung regulations was opportune in this respect but Hitler continued to tinker.[7] In June 1944, Warlimont confirmed on Hitler's behalf that the original Commando Order of October 1942 was still enforceable, although the Allies were sending individuals (indicating they were to be treated as spies or saboteurs). On June 23, a conference was called to consider the "treatment of commando men"; it set guidelines for operations in the west. The allied invasion in Normandy forced reconsideration. Troops captured in "open" battle remained POWs, but in doubtful cases, the captives were to be handed over to the SD for decision. An example of the new guidelines was the case of allied parachutists in Brittany. The Germans declared them saboteurs because they operated beyond the boundaries of conventional fighting in Normady and thus could be "massacred in combat."[8] Similar confusion over the treatment of paratroops occurred during the Battle of Arnhem when the SS sent British POWs to Auschwitz. Another OKW circular of June 26 instructed that allied commandos captured beyond the beachhead must be killed "in combat" or in special cases turned over to the SD. The German high command in the west was ordered to make a daily return of the figures for prisoners and their executions.

Hitler was also distracted by the question of allied military missions attached to resistance movements. On July 22, 1944, new guidelines addressed the treatment of British, American, and Soviet soldiers, in or out of uniform, working alongside the partisans. The military section of the RSHA requested handing them over for interrogation. Warlimont confirmed this, adding a postscript that the Commando Order had not been instrumental against the missions thus far, but

> the principle must be adopted from the start that all members of partisan groups, even in the south-east are fundamentally insurgents. Indeed they are treated as prisoners of war for reasons of expediency, in order to obtain the largest possible number of deserters and workers.

On July 30, OKW issued instructions that allied military missions were henceforth treated as commandos.[9] That same day, Hitler and the judge advocate of the Wehrmacht released instructions for occupation security stating, "Those who attack us from the rear at the decisive stage of our fight for existence deserve no consideration." Any acts of violence by non-German civilians were to be immediately dealt with by troops from the SS and Wehrmacht. Captives were to be handed over to the SS. Women were to be enslaved, although the children were "spared."[10]

To ensure the various parties adhered to Bandenbekämpfung

regulations, Bach-Zelewski monitored overall performance. "He spent two days receiving voluminous reports," wrote Karl Gaisser after the war, "and then gave it as his opinion that, compared with the eastern front, fighting the partisans in Croatia was child's play, pointing out that the partisans never made a stand but ran away whenever they were energetically attacked."[11] Gaisser accused of Bach-Zelewski of only once visiting the region, but British decodes and Bach-Zelewski's diary indicate otherwise. From early July 1943, when Bach-Zelewski took his first appraisal tour of security in southeastern Europe, he became a regular visitor. There were at least fourteen visits. He traveled to Belgrade on November 29, 1943, to assess the general security situation and the imminent threat of allied invasion.[12] During one trip, Bach-Zelewski experienced a partisan attack against his train in Croatia. He later wrote in his diary, "Swines! The train in front has driven over a torpedo [German term for a mine], and the train behind mined and has been bombarded. We drove clear of the skirmishes."[13] This suggests Bach-Zelewski did not delay to witness the partisans leaving.

The visits were interrupted when Hitler summoned Bach-Zelewski to Kovel (chapter 8) in January 1944. He did not return until May 1944. During this absence, the SS field command in the east was relocated to the region. Between March and June 1944, the KSRFSS moved to Glasenbach near Salzburg, while the headquarters of the Chef der Bandenkampfverbände moved to Königssee, a small lakeside town near Berchtesgaden.[14] According to Ernst Rode, these moves were intended to improve the liaison between HSSPF Alpenland, HSSPF Adriatic Coastland, HSSPF Croatia, and their centralization under HstSSPF Italy.[15] Bach-Zelewski took two trips back to back on May 20–26, 1944, and on June 1–17; he was forced to tour by road transport owing to allied air superiority. Later, expectations for his arrival in Laibach on July 9 were the prelude to a special drive against the partisans.[16] After the war, Bach-Zelewski summarized his work: "I found out on the spot in the southeast about the band fighting and I myself took part actively with the Wehrmacht in a partisan operation in Croatia."[17]

## Command and Control Tantrums

By July 1943, Hitler had judged Italian reliability suspect and, in the expectation of their defection, initiated extensive planning for intervention. Operation "Axis" (*Achse*) was undertaken to seize Italian military assets, capture the navy, and form defensive positions against allied invasion.[18] On September 3, 1943, British troops landed on the Italian mainland across the straits of Messina. The German army responded quickly, deploying armored and infantry divisions, while the SS-Police sent in twenty thousand troops to secure northern Italy. On September 8, 1943, as allied forces were set to invade mainland Italy at Salerno, General Eisenhower informed his soldiers that Italy had surrendered. Three days later, Luftwaffe Field Marshal Albert Kesselring declared martial law in Italy. Elsewhere, both the Germans and the partisans raced to disarm Italian troops. Each side declared success and shared the booty. This boosted Tito's influence and inspired Communist partisans in Italy to revolt. A domino effect was set in motion; Communist-led resistance movements in southern France took up arms and renewed outbreaks of violence in Greece, Albania, Slovakia, and Croatia. This was the consequence of German failure to defeat Tito militarily and as a popular figure. German sentiment railed against Italy as emotions ranged from calculation to vengence to cold-bloodedness. Bach-Zelewski noted in his diary the impending problems with Italy on July 26; however, by September 9, he had begun describing the Italians as "traitors."[19] Skorzeny stole media attention by rescuing Mussolini from captivity in an airborne commando raid.[20] This enabled Hitler to construct an Italian puppet government around Mussolini. Then the reshuffles followed. In October 1943, Field Marshal Erwin Rommel was transferred to France and the overall supreme command in the southeast passed to Kesselring.

The relationship between the SS, Wehrmacht, and Nazi agencies remained relatively stable in the region until April 1944. One postwar study outlined the different authorities in Italy. There were three principal offices, the Foreign Office under ambassador Dr. Rahn in Rome, the Wehrmacht under Albert Kesselring, and the SS-Police under SS-Oberstgruppenführer Karl Wolff. In addition to representatives and staffs from the food requisition agency (army authority), chief of ordinance (army authority), propaganda units (embassy staff), "Reich Foreign Labour Service," and the Organization Todt, there were also layers of rear-area and headquarters formations.[21] In France, Holland, and elsewhere, the various agencies found a working compromise that suited all. This was the case in Italy at the end of 1943. Wolff and Kesselring appeared to have established a professional working relationship. However, circumstances contrived to undermine their relationship.

Hitler caused complications when he confused the strategies for southern Europe. During the winter of 1943–44, he granted Kesselring unlimited command over forces in the south, including the SS. Then he issued three directives. In January 1944, he issued Directive 52 for the defense of Rome. Fear of the outflanking of German fortifications caused Hitler to make provisions for defending the Alpine areas. Another string of instructions from Hitler led to Directive 60. This ordered the construction of fortifications, effectively weaving Istria, Trieste, and the Gulf of Venice into a defensive network stretching across northern Italy. Hitler's orders were addressed to civilian and military authorities alike, mobilizing labor and construction gangs. Then in August 1944, Hitler stipulated that HstSSPF in Italy was to continue aggressive operations against "banditry" in cooperation with the Wehrmacht. In September, Hitler issued Directive 65 for the construction of defenses in Austria and Slovakia. This time, Wehrkreis XVIII and Gauleiters Dr. Rainer in Carinthia and Uiberreither in Styria were to cooperate in constructing defenses.[22]

Himmler added to the complications by declaring upper and middle Italy Bandenkampfgebieten on April 3, 1944,[23] and by handing out political mandates to his cronies who used their positions to pursue conflicting decisions. For example, Kesselring opposed the Bandenkampfgebieten, but his alternate strategy was risky in Nazi terms. He wished to use tactical withdrawals entwined with rigid defensive strongpoints. His plan was to frustrate the Allies by slowing or stalling the pace of the advance. The problem came during withdrawal; large military formations entered the security zones and declared Bandenkampfgebiet, thereby reducing SS control and authority. Thus, Himmler placed the SS and Wehrmacht at odds by exposing contradictory priorities. Kesselring's semi-flexible strategy and the rigid SS security policy caused friction within high command circles. Bach-Zelewski observed on April 20, "The Army-Bandenkampfverbände relationship in the Adriatic coast and Italy area had been declared a *Bandenkampfgebiet* by 'Wölffchen.'" He added, "Discussions had followed with the OKW and the final chance of clarification was lost. Only areas where the RFSS [Himmler] himself declared a *Bandenkampfgebiet,* it actually happened. There were strained relations when the HSSPF were subordinated to the army."[24] Bach-Zelewski wrongly attributed the decision, but the actual situation was far less clear-cut. "Wölffchen," as his comrades called Wolff, was yet another senior SS leader blighted by ill health. In March 1944, Wolff was absent on sick leave. Hans-Adolf Prützmann, redundant as HSSPF Russia-South since the Soviet advance during the winter of 1943–44, deputized for Wolff until late July 1944. With Wolff absent (and possibly reluctant to face up to Kesselring), Himmler took the opportunity to declare Italy a Bandenkampfgebiet.[25]

On May 1, 1944, Field Marshal Keitel initially confirmed Kesselring's stance and authority over the SS. Then on May 4, he equivocated and decided the commander of the larger forces held automatic seniority over field operations. Opportunism led Kesselring to wait until June 17 to issue new guidelines, "New Measures for Bandenbekämpfung." They aligned Kesselring to Hitler and the war of extermination on all fronts. The guidelines followed the familiar mixture of observations, advice, and orders but were also loaded with cringing political overtones. Kesselring blamed the "bandits" for the deteriorating situation in Italy, endangerment of the troops and supply lines, and Germany's exploitative economy. His only answer was to impose measures "of the utmost severity." He referred to Hitler's directive that enacted Achse to justify his decision. The troops were pressed to carry on regardless of "mistaken" actions rather than not to act at all. Responding to the growing awareness that the Allies intended to prosecute war crimes, Kesselring advised, "I will protect any commander who exceeds our usual restraint in the choice of severity of the methods he adopts against the partisans." These security arrangements acknowledged a balance between "passive and active" measures, but emphasized the need for aggressive responses. Command proportioning was also sanctioned; the commander of the larger field force was granted overall command but insisted that SS-Police troops were restricted to the security zones.[26] Kesselring ordered his chief of staff to erect transit camps to hold suspects and civilians. He recommended an extensive propaganda program to support exterminating the "bandits." Kesselring had woven Hitler's tinkering and Keitel's indecision into his machinations.

Kesselring was not content to grant carte blanche to the armed forces to conduct brutal actions. Three days later on June 20, he issued more orders. They reflected Hitler's September 16, 1941, order (chapter 3). The troops were to conduct reprisals against all males in villages and to publicly execute captured band leaders. Kesselring warned against allowing Mussolini's fascists to participate in reprisals, while confirming that plunderers (meaning partisans) would be punished. He judged that the dignity of the German soldier demanded such orders.[27] A public announcement was made to the Italian people to deter them from joining the "bandits." Complying with these orders on July 11, the German commander of Covola posted an announcement to the community: "For every soldier or civilian killed, One Hundred men also taken from the locality of the crime, will be shot."[28]

After the war, the British investigations of Wolff's command concluded that there was wholesale destruction of villages on the flimsiest grounds of "bandits." Wolff attempted to defend his actions in Italy:

> I represented the type of "political general," and despite all my prowess in the leadership of troops in anti-guerrilla actions and the independent defence of the Franco-Italian alpine passes at the Mont Cenis and west of Turin in Autumn 1944, my main activity lay solely in the political and administrative sphere.[29]

Wolff tried to contend that as an administrator, he had no real authority over people's lives. On the contrary, Wolff had the power of life and death over the whole area of SS operations. In July 1945, Wolff was overheard saying, "During the one and a half years I was here in Italy, I never sent a single report to my superiors, neither as HstSSPF to Himmler, nor as Military Plenipotentiary to Keitel. . . . I never played a heavy hand here."[30] After interrogations, the British concluded, "Wolff cannot be regarded as a completely reliable witness."[31] Reprisals remained common practice with the ratio pitched at 10 to 1 until August 1944 when Mussolini intervened to end them.

On November 30, after a recommendation from Kesselring, Wolff was awarded the German Cross in Gold, the Nazi political medal. Closer archival inspection indicates that Wolff received the Iron Cross in May 1944. The following month, he received a "letter of appointment" (*Ernennungsurkunde*) to the Bandenkampfverbände, a statement of proficiency from Bach-Zelewski personally. The details are sparse but indicate consistent patterns of behavior. A large-scale operation in the western Alps in August 1944 in the areas of Domodossola and Monte Grappa northwest of Udine proved Wolff's ability as a practitioner of Bandenbekämpfung. The operations were a response to the allied landings on the south coast of France (Operation "Dragoon") that triggered widespread guerrilla action. The operation spread across the Franco-Italian border as Wolff tried to dislodge the guerrillas from the mountain passes. Wolff's butchers' bill itemized 1,634 enemy dead, including two "bandit" leaders, one political commissar, and one Italian colonel. There were 1,461 prisoners taken during the fighting, including one "bandit" leader, two English officers, and six German deserters. Added to these were another 1,902 arrested under the suspicion of banditry, 2,454 taken for labor in Germany, and 810 taken because they were between fourteen and twenty-seven years old and thus of military age. The German losses included 51 dead (2 officers). There were 218 wounded, including a major of the NSKK, and 6 missing. The Italians, fighting with the Germans, suffered 34 dead, 107 wounded, and 29 missing.[32] This was, apparently, a command feat worthy of addition to the Bandenkampfverbände roll of honor.

Awards were also granted to Wolff's lieutenants; one in particular to Willi Tensfeld provides yet more evidence of what Bandenbekämpfung meant in Italy. On September 10, 1941, Tensfeld joined a fourteen-day course on how to become an SSPF, working with the Order Police and security police. His peer group included Curt von Gottberg and Walter Schimana. Prior to becoming SSPF-Upper Italy West, he served as SSPF-Kharkov (August 1941–May 1943) and as SSPF-Stalino (May 1943–September 1943), and in 1943, he briefly served in Lublin. In February 1945, he received the German Cross in Gold for the following operations:

NACHTIGALL: July 29, 1944, twenty-three days of "hard" mountain fighting.

STRASSBURG: September 5–October 5, 1944 (460 enemy dead and 295 prisoners).

BERNI: October 5–November 4, 1944, in the mountains, where he was personally involved in leading the fighting (51 enemy dead and wounded 511 prisoners).

AVANTI: October 9–November 4, 1944, handled the skills of the enemy in a severe bloody fight in the area of Cannobino, Viggerro, Ossolatal-Lago-Magiore development battle (565 enemy dead and 387 prisoners).

KOBLENZ: November 15–December 22, 1944 (162 enemy dead and 1,628 prisoners).

HOCHLAND: January 12, 1945, an ongoing operation (124 dead and 816 prisoners reported so far).

The totals for all Tensfeld's efforts were 1,254 enemy dead and 6,083 prisoners and the usual amount of booty.[33]

## Rösener's Bandenstab

Bandenstab Rösenor, based in Laibach, controlled the lynchpin province of the Alpenland in Hitler's southern flank. Today Laibach is the Slovenian capital of Ljubljana, an important geo-political city at the confluence of Austria, Croatia, and Slovenia. In 1900, the major cities of this area were Salzburg, Agram (Zagreb), Laibach, and Trieste, and all were part of the Austro-Hungarian Empire. The Versailles settlement redrew the map of the region and ceded these cities to Italy, Yugoslavia, and Czechoslovakia, ignoring identities and the indigenous populations. Following the Austrian Anschluss, Germany absorbed this region. In June 1939, SS-Oberabschnitt Alpenland administered the southern alpine districts of Carinthia, Styria, and the Tyrol, headquartered in Salzburg.[34] Himmler authorized the formation of the HSSPF Alpenland covering Salzburg and Laibach and the HSSPF Croatia based in Agram, in January 1942. This was part of the steadily growing SS operational jigsaw that encompassed Serbia, Greece, Vienna, and Budapest. By 1943, the strategic junctions and key cities were interwoven into a security network that covered Graz, Klagenfurt, Marburg, Laibach, Agram, and the peninsula of the Karst in Istria.[35] Analysis of Bandenstab Laibach provides the only near complete record of a working Bandenstab operation.

SS-Obergruppenführer Erwin Rösener joined the SS in 1929. In March 1933, he became police president of Aachen and reached a unique level of bureaucratic pedantry, even by Nazi standards, by issuing official orders to himself.[36] Rösener was appointed HSSPF Alpenland on December 16, 1941. In keeping with many of his colleagues, Rösener suffered a catalog of health problems. Physically tall and lean and with great physical strength, his problems were all related to "nerves." In 1938, Rösener was diagnosed with an ulcer. He was thirty-six years old and had worked himself into a state of psychological collapse. A workaholic, his condition was aggravated through a total lack of rest and recuperation. Marital problems also blotted Rösener's copybook; he had three marriages in five years. Himmler ordered Rösener to make regular visits to his third wife, who lived in Berlin, a long journey from Alpenland. To make sure he followed these instructions, Wolff kept a log of each visit. Rösener included SS-Obergruppenführer Maximillian von Herff in his inner circle. Increasingly his duties as HSSPF Alpenland concentrated on Banden-bekämpfung, which proved stressful. In an attempt to escape these duties, Rösener tried, through Herff, to position himself for the HSSPF Vienna job after Kaltenbrunner moved to the RSHA. Rösener's intrigues failed, and he was denied transfer because of his success in prosecuting Bandenbekämpfung. Rösener's story was about success in Bandenbekämpfung in spite of health problems.

The link between HSSPF Alpenland and Bandenbekämpfung had been formalized in June 1942 (refer to chapter 3). Insurgency had plagued the SS since 1941, and on October 5, 1942, what was to become the Banden- stab Laibach began the routines of coordinated reporting and responses.[37] Rösener's right-hand stooge in formulating procedures was SS-Standarten- führer Otto Lurker, a long-serving SD officer. Lurker joined the SS in 1929 and moved in prestigious circles; his first superior was Prützmann. Lurker had perfect First World War credentials, was awarded the severe combat wound badge, and had joined the Freikorps. Among the details of his SS officer ap- praisal there is the comment, "probably the best leader of an SD section." He was Hitler's former prison warder and prison assistant, later writing the book *Hitler Behind Prison Walls*.[38] The former jailer was a proponent of raising local armed militias for self-defense.[39] As the wave of panic about the partisan threat swept over the region, one director of local mining operations wrote with concern to Rösener. He was fearful of "communist activity" against his mines not only because of the potential loss of production but also because it might undermine the morale of the workers (*Arbeitsmoral*).[40] It was the kind of letter on which the SS thrived, and Lurker was quick to take advantage.

From October 24, 1942, Lurker adopted common forms of Banden- bekämpfung reporting. In November, he organized a meeting of all the section chiefs in Marburg, but the proceedings were marred by a case of indiscipline. There had also been a "wild slaughter party" of farm animals by members of the Order Police, and meat had gone wasted. Himmler heard about it and responded immediately, warning that breaches in ration regulations would result in punishments without mercy. Months earlier, in February 1942, there was a serious breach of discipline in Veldes, Yugoslavia. Suspicion fell on the 4th Company of Police Battalion 181 of aiding local "bandits" and defacing a picture of Hitler in their mess canteen.[41] The military governor initiated court- martial proceedings; the troopers were disarmed and imprisoned in Graz. This time, the BdO Alpenland was forced by Himmler to issue a standing order on December 17 on the punishments for abuses of local population rations.[42] This problem only distracted Lurker and Rösener for a short time, because by the end of the month, British intercepts recorded the senior conference had taken place at the BdO headquarters.[43] This was the beginning of the Banden- stab Laibach.

Following the new year lull, serious partisan incursions began in Febru- ary 1943. Many SS signals deciphered by the British indicated that three battalions of the 19th SS-Police Regiment were fully engaged in northern Yugoslavia. By March, the fighting had spilled over into the HSSPF Alpenland, as a tactical situation report from Lurker indicated. He warned of the presence of a band, fifty strong, fully armed with rifles and machine guns, and recom- mended full-scale operations to the north, south, east, and west: encirclement in all but name. He added that since March 2, bands up to thirty strong were streaming into the territory under Tito's orders. The security commando "Karl" had arrested seven "bandits" and their leader, and through interrogations, it was discovered that another twenty "bandits" were raiding for food.[44] "The outstanding feature of these operations," the British observed, "has been the ability of partisans to keep the Germans continually on the move; no sooner has an area been cleared or an attack on a strong point beaten off than the partisans appear again in or near the same area. The Germans reckon that the partisans are short of arms but at the same time are always calling for help themselves."[45]

In his May report, Lurker concentrated on the increasing infiltrations into the Veldes area. "Bandit" activity had increased markedly. Large-scale Bandenbekämpfung operations had fractured the bands, but the "bandits" kept their numbers intact by press-ganging (*Zwangsrekrutierungen*) terrorized members of the local population. The bands had replenished their weapons and had donned a pseudo-German uniform. The May Day celebrations were interrupted by cases of arson in towns, ambushes, and bonfires on hilltops (beacons for the partisans). Lurker included a casualty record: "bandit" losses were twenty-three shot dead, eleven prisoners, and twenty-seven deserters. German casualties were twenty-nine dead, ten wounded, and one missing.[46] That month, Rösener deployed two companies of Order Police to combat the *Moraeutscher Bande*. There followed 48 hours of intensive fighting in coordinated operations with the army, gendarmerie, and border troops (*Zollgrenzschutz*). General Brenner, the military district commander, and Rösener joined forces to increase the effectiveness of the operations. Rösener later complained that their actions were compromised by a lack of an early warning system, allowing only short lead times to counter the bands. This indicated that civilians were becoming reluctant to raise the alarm over the presence of bands. He complained about the poor quality of his troops, who were ill prepared for such operations, causing mixed results. On May 19, Rösener, in an act of bureaucratic self-protection, reported to Himmler that the troops were still conducting Bandenbekämpfung against the Moraeutscher Bande.[47]

The intensity of partisan incursions continued through June 1943. A series of "bandit" attacks formed the centerpiece of an Order Police situation report. On June 2, eight battalions of "bandits" were identified preparing for an attack on the gendarmerie in St. Martin (Styria); allegedly their plan also involved plundering the Reich-Slovenia border. The gendarmerie was warned that support was unavailable, and on June 13, a superior "bandit" force surrounded them. The next day, "bandit" attacks were delivered against the strategic railway line near Lichtenwald station. The bands had removed track pins along a large section of line, disguising their actions by resting the rails in position, but causing a 15mm misalignment. This was enough to derail a passenger train. The locomotive and two carriages tumbled down an incline, injuring twelve soldiers. Police troops had patrolled that area two days before and found nothing out of the ordinary. The line was back in service the next day, and two battalions of the 19th SS-Police Regiment were ordered to patrol the line.[48] The British identified further activity in Virovitica area on June 17. This time the sheer weight of German counter-attacks forced the partisans to withdraw.[49]

By coincidence, the growing intensity of Tito's incursions peaked just as Hitler and Himmler met to discuss the Bandenkampf- und Sicherheitslage (discussed in chapter 4). On June 21, 1943, Himmler declared the Alpenland a Bandenkampfgebiet, writing letters to all interested parties. He made Rösener deliver the confirmation documents to the Gauleiters personally.[50] During the meeting with Hitler, Himmler was offered the vague promise that the SS-Police Mountain Regiment "Franz" might be returned to his command. On the strength of this, Himmler informed the Gauleiter Rainer of Carinthia that this regiment would be assigned to his district.[51] In his general instructions on Banden-bekämpfung of June 1943, Himmler advised forming a Leadership Headquarters *(Führungsstab)* for all districts involved in Bandenbekämpfung. Thus the Bandenstab Laibach reported to Bach-Zelewski command staff and so Rösener became part of the Bandenkampfverbände by default. The Bandenstab Laibach became responsible for coordinating all Bandenbekämpfung in the Alpenland, Croatia, and the Karst (Istria) region. Tracking the constant organizational changes from September 1943 to May 1945 shows that Rösener came under the command of Bach-Zelewski, Wolff, and Prützmann at different times.

In July, Rösener received a frosty letter from Himmler. He was accused of not informing the wife of a senior SS comrade, in person, of her husband's death and was rebuked for his military shortfalls. Himmler wrote, "I am not at all happy with your Bandenbekämpfung. Please don't try to calm me with your excuses of not enough troops." He added, "Stay in your main district more and don't drive so much to Berlin. Take care personally and things will improve. Please be reminded to keep up your marriage and be cautioned—I am not waiting for a third disaster." Rösener was contrite, apologizing for everything, although his excuses were plausible. He replied that a senior SS officer had gone in his place, a man who had lost two sons to the war and who understood her grief. He explained away his absences as having to attend on Bach-Zelewski in Agram and being engaged in combat against the "bandits." He also reminded Himmler that his trips to Berlin were part of his marital relations duties, ordered by the Reichsführer, and that they were still monitored by Wolff.[52]

In comparison with the HSSPFs in the east, the HSSPF Alpenland operated under tight economies of troops, materials, and cooperation from the Wehrmacht. The Order Police use was prioritized, and Rösener's command was rationed. He received packets of formations and equipment. For example, on August 6, 1943, the Hauptamt Ordnungspolizei organized an artillery company "Alpenland" to provide heavy weapon support for police opera-tions.[53] The unit was made up of career police officers and conscripts. The company commander, a career Oberleutnant, came from the Hamburg police department. The battery officer was a lieutenant from the Halle police depart-ment who was to command recruits from the 1st Police Weapons Training school (Polizei-Waffenschule I). In keeping with usual practice, this police company was assigned to Klagenfurt for its home depot.[54] The company re-ceived eight pieces of field artillery: the 75mm Light Infantry Gun 18, produced by the Rheinmetall Company in Düsseldorf and configured for employment in mountain operations. Highly maneuverable, these guns could provide accu-rate fire support from restricted ground positions and were also simple to train gunners with. Again following usual procedures, the company joined the com-munications network organized by the 181st SS-Police Signals Company. This integrated its battery fire liaison communications to other police units.[55]

The intensification of incursions, in May 1943, led Rösener's staff to pressure General von Unruh into releasing two or three captured French ar-mored vehicles. This caused the routine paper war involving the army's in-spector of armored troops (Heinz Guderian), Unruh's personal staff, the KSRFSS, and Winkelmann at the Hauptamt Ordnungspolizei. Eventually, the vehicles, Hotchkiss armored cars and Renault tanks, were released but had to be engineered to conform with German munitions standards. The SS was also expected to collect the vehicles from Gien-on-the-Loire and transport them.[56] The combination of manpower issues and Bandenbekämpfung guidelines gave rise to some strange decisions. In July 1943, following the guidelines to the letter, the district commissioner (*Landrat*) of Cilli telexed Rösener's staff, to confirm three Jagdkommando teams had been raised and were operating in his area. They included an SD-Jagdkommando, an army Jagdkommando, and a civil-service (Beamten) Jagdkommando. Each Jagdkommando had been mus-tered through by rugged selection and were patrolling in six-week stints, avoid-ing contact with safe villages. No doubt Rösener was reassured that German civil servants (Beamten) were aggressively hunting down Tito's partisans.[57]

The Bandenstab Laibach's overall situation changed after Italy's sur-render. The Italian army representative in the area of Laibach, General Ceruli, handed over his weapons to Tito's partisans. This allowed Tito to renew his operations and incursions. A gendarmerie situation report from Styria in Sep-tember recorded mayhem in the Warasdin-Toplitz area. On September 5, two Croatian women laden with peaches were accosted by partisans. The "ban-dits" ordered them to hand over the fruit to the poor; the women refused. The partisans shaved their heads and then released them; the next day, fighting broke out between German soldiers and "bandits." Six hundred troops came under repeated attacks lasting for three hours with barrages from "bandit" artillery. The Germans were forced to retreat, suffering eight dead and six wounded; afterward, the "bandits" stripped the dead. At midnight on September

7, an air raid alarm served as a decoy for a mass breakout and desertion of officer cadets from a local cavalry depot. The cadets joined the partisans.[58] A week later, the 19th SS-Police Regiment warned BdO Marburg that reconnaissance had identified the presence of the Kalniki-Bandit Brigade, reinforced by the 12th Slovenian Brigade. They estimated five thousand "bandits" approaching the Alpenland area. They carried heavy weapons, including four artillery pieces, and were "advancing toward the Reich border." The "bandits" had not cut the telephone cables but had caused numerous train derailments. They stopped one locomotive, removed the crew, locked the passengers in the carriages, and sent the train hurtling down the line toward Laibach.[59]

The impact and influence of Bach-Zelewski and Wolff on operations in the region can be contrasted with heightened operations from September 1943. One report discovered from a large-scale operation, conducted on the Italian border (September 21–23), is incomplete but provides a small but significant indication of the changes. The central fighting component, the 19th SS-Police Regiment, was joined by several smaller auxiliary and collaboration troops. There were indicators of the coordination of ad hoc forces, including antitank detachments and squadrons of tanks—all working toward a common mission. Although casualties are not known, the report recorded that the bands used mortar barrages, while the "bandits" were emboldened to stand against the Germans.[60] From September 30, 1943, thirteen thousand Slovenian partisans from the 2nd Partisan Corps, arranged into five brigades, attempted to surround Warasdin, and lay siege. The fighting forced them out of Styria only after pulverizing attacks by Stuka dive-bombers.[61] Information passed by a "trusty" to the gendarmerie on October 1, 1943, indicated a large body of bandits, up to four thousand strong, entering the area.[62]

On October 8, 1943, Bach-Zelewski attended a meeting with Rösener, SS-Oberstgruppenführer Paul Hausser, and Odilo Globocnik, in Trieste.[63] The presence of the elite Waffen-SS commander indicated how determined the SS were to finally crush Tito. On October 15, Rösener assembled the troops for a cleansing action of a large "bandit" force concentrated by the Agram–Laibach railway. They crossed the Reich border by traveling along the River Save and came close to threatening the coal-mining districts. The "bandits" were reputed to have five thousand in number and be heavily armed with artillery. Rösener's plan involved blockading the river, fighting free-form (freikämpfen) to liberate St. Georg, and finally destroying the "bandits," or at least preventing them from entering Austria. Rösener's main force was the 19th SS-Police Regiment; its 2nd Battalion was ordered to enforce a blockade and to place an armed reconnaissance on the heights overlooking St. Georg. The fighting escalated into running battles as the Germans struggled to comprehend that they were outnumbered and outgunned. The Luftwaffe was urgently requested to provide Stuka support to break up the "bandit" attacks.[64] Efforts to pacify the vicinity of Laibach intensified, with the Wehrmacht and SS-Police employing armored forces. The partisan response was to hit back even harder. For seven days until November 14, a police battalion was surrounded in Rudolfswerth, a town lying between Laibach and Agram. The battalion was kept alive and fighting by regular resupply from the air. The presence of elite units made the difference. Troops from the 9th SS-Panzer Division and the 16th SS-Panzer Grenadier Division supported by Luftwaffe dive-bombers destroyed the partisans on November 15. Five days later, two battalions from the reconstituted 14th SS-Police Regiment destroyed five hundred partisans.[65]

Political squabbles added to Rösener's stress. On October 28, 1943, Himmler received a serious complaint about him from Gauleiter Uiberreither. A bandit incursion had breached the Reich's borders by up to five kilometers and threatened the strategic Agram–Laibach railway. Uiberreither, following Himmler's general instructions for Bandenbekämpfung to the letter and raised ad hoc police, army, and militia units under the command of an SS-Sturmbannführer. The troops were passed on to an Order Police major in Agram. Uiberreither was then informed that the force was not large enough, so he contacted the army, receiving a mountain Jäger company and several field howitzers to his growing order of battle. He roused the local Luftwaffe representative into dispatching a flight of Stuka dive-bombers and flak units. Taking the imitative further, Uiberreither raised nine companies of militia and formed a special train to transport them. Uiberreither explained to Himmler that without his political influence the troops could not have been moved with such speed. Rösener, according to Uiberreither, interfered in the process, upsetting many people and undermining the cooperation between the parties. Rösener and Uiberreither's differences, couched in typical Nazi polycratic terms, lay in their perspectives; Rösener held a lofty "birds-eye view," while Uiberreither believed he projected a "front-line perspective." Rösener made a counter-complaint that Uiberreither was insulting and demanded his replacement. Himmler soothed troubled waters by ordering Rösener to apologize.[66]

Partisan activity grew in intensity throughout 1944. In response, German operations increased in scale. By August 1944, Rösener was promoted to SS-Obergruppenführer and was working on joint operations with Globocnik. The British identified the growing close relationship between Rösener and Globocnik as distinct: "Evidently there is close liaison among the Germans on this frontier to meet such Partisan cooperation."[67] The Bandenstab Laibach received a squadron from the 7th Special Flying Group based in Laibach. During another bout of illness in August, Rösener fretted over the level of air support the Bandenstab was receiving.[68] On September 13, Bach-Zelewski instructed Rösener to safeguard all rail traffic in his area. A conference was held on railway security and a liaison officer from the Railway Police (Eisenbahn-Polizei) was seconded to Rösener's staff. The railway police were to monitor luggage and take protective measures inside guard vans against bombs.[69] The railway line between Laibach and Postumia was brought under the protection of the SS-Police, as ten thousand rolls of barbed wire and boxes of nails were ordered to seal the exclusion zone. In November, Rösener was advised that, because of the changing military situation, his region was the safeguard for all connections between the southern and eastern fronts. With growing surety, Rösener pressed for urgency from his lieutenants and ordered SS-Oberführer Harm to inflict greater damage on the partisans during cleansing actions north of Laibach. Later in November, he ordered the Gestapo and the 13th SS-Regiment to annihilate "bandits" and enemy parachutists near Klagenfurt. The seriousness of the situation led all leave to be cancelled until the "bandit menace" had been eradicated.[70]

On August 18, 1944, Rösener was proposed for the German Cross in Gold medal, through an accreditation report, prepared by Bach-Zelewski.[71] The report delighted in praising Rösener's success as a Bandenbekämpfung leader, commanding troops against overwhelming enemies in unfamiliar terrain. Covering January 30 to June 1944, this report confirmed Rösener's total "score"of 6,297 "bandits" killed in combat, 2,779 captured "bandits," 1,344 "bandit" deserters, and 5,930 arrested "bandit" suspects. Bach-Zelewski cited six actions to confirm Rösener's leadership qualities. In February, Rösener's daredevil (*Draufgängertum*) actions under severe conditions broke up the advance of the XIV Partisan Division, with 1,200 "bandits" into Styria. In the hard fighting that followed, 600 "bandits" were killed, 163 were taken prisoner, and large amounts of booty were captured. In March, Rösener was judged responsible for destroying the IV Battalion of the Canker Bandit Brigade in Jurowitz, where his "excellent" leadership resulted in 132 "bandits" killed. From that same month, Bach-Zelewski drew attention to operations in Rakitowitz. Under difficult conditions, Rösener had personally led his troops to victory, with the destruction of a band four thousand strong. The assault involved hand-to-hand combat or close-fighting (*Nahkämpfe*), and many "bandits" were killed in burning buildings. In April, Rösener led reconnaissance assaults to breaking up concentrations of bands and destroying hundreds of "bandits." The report concluded with Rösener's actions of June 23, 1944, when he had commanded SS and Wehrmacht troops with great success and personal courage (*persönliche Tapferkeit*). Bach-Zelewski concluded, "I think HSSPF Rösener is worthy of the German Cross in Gold because of his merit in leading troops and his particularly repeated dignified courage." Rösener's accreditation was refused on October 15, 1944, confirmed in writing by the liaison officer (IIb) of the Chef der Bandenkampfverbände, Bach-Zelewski's office. Rösener's achievements were recognized along with confirmation that he had reached the required statistics. In recompense, he received the Bandenkampfabzeichen in Silver for time served on August 12, 1944. On January 27, 1945, Rösener finally received the German Cross in Gold.[72]

In September 1944, Rösener was diagnosed as suffering from paratyphus and forced to take an extended leave of absence. The doctor thought the illness was psychosomatic. There was considerable evidence for him to make this judgment. From an earlier medical examination, in May 1944, it was noted that Rösener's parents came from Westphalian peasant stock and were not regarded as fit and healthy by SS standards. His father died from the lingering effects of gas poisoning suffered during the Great War, and his mother, a diabetic, died at the age of sixty-one. His present health problems were blamed on "Bandenkampf causing great nervous and psychological stress." The physician remarked, "He has heartbeats without realizing he has a heart." His symptoms included acute nervous stress and serious palpitations, which caused lethargy, coughing bouts in the morning, periods of moodiness, and, low work achievement despite working throughout the night. Today, we might call his condition "burnout" (*Ermüdungserscheinungen*).[73] He was forced to take a period of extended leave. However, the proposed candidate substitute for Rösener, SS-Obergruppenführer Wappenhans, had been placed in SS reserve following the end of his duty in HSSPF Russia-South. Wappenhans received a routine SS medical at Dachau, was diagnosed as being in a severe state of nervous collapse, and was declared unfit to replace Rösener.

## Tactical Ingenuity and Old Methods

The techniques and tactics employed by the Germans against the resistance in the western theater demonstrated tactical ingenuity but regularly resorted to traditional measures. The usual pattern of SS command preceded operations. The SS had installed an extensive police communications network. The British observed, "It was not until the middle of September 1942 that the Police W/T [wireless transmission] network was extended to Yugoslavia."[74] In January 1943, there were three regional police stations in southern Europe: the Laibach headquarters of BdO Alpenland, the Belgrade headquarters of BdO Serbia, and the central police signals station in Graz. The British reported that "on 17 September 1943 the German Police were first noted in Northern Italy. Control was located at Verona which became the headquarters of HstSSPF-Italy." On October 8, 1943, HSSPF Alpenland was connected to Wolff's HstSSPF network.[75] By November 1943, the SS network in the southern theater was complete. This communications net allowed the SS-Police to prosecute rapid deployment of units and coordinate complex missions in the latter-day form of realtime. On the strength of this system the SS-Police were able to adopt surprisingly ingenious measures to defeat the resistance.

### The Balkans

In 1943, Bandenbekämpfung operations conducted in the southern theater followed all the usual patterns. Winston Churchill and the British War Cabinet received reports on the conditions in southern Europe. One report gave an impression of the scale of the atrocities that blighted the region. It recorded that by May, eight thousand civilians (including women and children) had been executed; others were forced to pay ransoms or were taken to concentration camps. There was widespread plundering and exploitation; people were forced to flee or were exposed to the mountainous wastes. The form of the atrocities makes a revolting comparison with the enormity of the killings in the east. Men were locked into burning churches; a captured Croatian carried a sack full of human eyes; children were dashed to death against walls; bodies were mutilated; pregnant women had their fetuses ripped out; children were tied to burning haystacks; women were made to dig graves, raped, and then killed; villages were burned down; crops were wasted; and clergy were executed. Himmler's visit to Zagreb coincided with sporadic acts of violence. Serbian civilians suspected of acts of sabotage were rounded up. Two trainloads were deported to a concentration camp. The Gestapo chief of Kraljevo executed 140 women and children, and other executions took place in Kozevi and Belgrade. In the district of Jablanica, fourteen villages were destroyed, and two thousand captives were deported to Germany. The British reports noticed that the Axis press continued to report these incidents as reprisals. In June, the partisans killed eight German police officers and wounded seven others, and this initiated a reprisal that included 575 people. The reports were equally scathing of the Germans, Italians, Croats, and Hungarians, accusing them all of involvement in the atrocities.[76]

The SS fighting formations in Yugoslavia suffered from leadership difficulties. Artur Phleps had become commander of the V SS-Mountain Corps. His corps included the 7th SS-Mountain Division Prinz Eugen and the Bosnian-Moslem 13th SS-Mountain Division Handschar. Phleps had built a shameless reputation for groveling correspondence with Himmler. A situation report for May 7, 1944, was typical of his leadership character. He began with a business-like approach, opening with a list of problems that required addressing, including leadership, manpower, and performance within the corps. The shortage of manpower affected both divisions. This problem worsened because the SS planned to raise an Albanian division of volunteers, drawing officers and NCO cadres from both divisions. Phleps was irate at the general quality of the recruits in training because they were unable to speak German and were unschooled. The second part of the report referred to Phleps's relationship with his chief of staff, Dr. Gustav Krukenberg. This quickly turned into a personal rant. Krukenberg was a Himmler favorite and direct appointee; Phleps could not have him removed easily. Phleps declared Krukenberg a bureaucrat, a depressive and untrustworthy, a jurist, a "nose in everyone's business" pedant who lacked warmth and issued embarrassing orders. He blamed Krukenberg's elderliness, his commercial business-mindedness, and his inability to recognize personal failings. Phleps indicated that SS-Sturmbannführer Eberhardt, the operations officer of the Prinz Eugen Division, had formed a clique with Sauberzweig, commander of the 13th SS-Division, against Krukenberg. Phleps, however, was careful to praise SS-Oberführer Otto Kumm, the newly promoted (February 1944) commander of the Prinz Eugen, who had brought a lust for battle and "a new happy spirit."[77] Phleps's record appeared effective but closer scrutiny indicates otherwise.

The operational record of the Prinz Eugen Division from Operation "Weiss" (January 1943) through to Operation "Waldrausch" (January 1944) identified the continued confidence in encirclement as the sole means to destroy the partisans. In April 1944, the spring campaign opened with Operation "Maibaum" to eradicate partisans in Bosnia. The Bosnian SS-Division Handschar, under the V SS-Mountain Corps, conducted a blocking operation to prevent a large partisan force from crossing the River Drina and joining forces with Tito in Serbia. The Prinz Eugen Division and Croatian forces worked with the Handschar Division. In typical fashion, the Germans deployed in river valleys and on roads trying to press the partisans against the blockade and force them into encirclement. Many partisans escaped across the mountains, and the division sent out Jagdkommandos to hunt them down. The Bosnians remained in position, holding the blockade and ensuring there was no encroachment by the partisans.[78] Since arriving in northeastern Bosnia in February 1944, the division had been carrying out "cleansing" actions and turning the area into a secured zone. The division's commander had organized the area into an SS-sponsored client Muslim state. Operation "Maibaum" opened in April to clear the area of all partisans but ran into Operation "Maiglöckchen" in May, where the division supported by Èetnik collaborators, encircled partisans, although they escaped.[79]

In May 1944, the Germans located Tito in Drvar. The German commanding general for the Balkans, Field Marshal von Weichs, agreed to initiate "Rösselsprung" ("Knight's Move") on May 6. In previous operations during 1943, the Germans had attempted to exterminate the partisans en masse. Operation "Schwarz" (May–June 1943) involved massive Axis forces in a large-scale encirclement of the partisans, but Tito and the bulk of the partisans escaped. However, their escape was possible only because they left behind their wounded to be butchered by the Germans.[80] In 1944, during the wave of intense security activity, the Germans planned a hammer-and-anvil operation against Tito. "Rösselsprung" involved an airborne covert action coordinated with a conventional encirclement by ground forces. The Germans also committed their dwindling combat aircraft to support the forces on the ground with bombing and close liaison sorties. The scale of air cover provided by the Luftwaffe involved more than four hundred combat missions. The airborne hammer—decapitating Tito, his command staff, and the allied military missions—was expected to be delivered by the SS in one fell swoop. The operational commander was General von Leyser of XV Mountain Corps, who was responsible for the coordination of the SS, the army, the Luftwaffe, and the collaborator troops.[81] The timing of the operation was set for May 25, 1944, Tito's birthday.

The formations, an airborne assault battalion with snatch teams, had been concentrated around Agram and in Serbia since February 1944. Included among the units were elements of the Abwehr's 1st Brandenburger Regiment, a Special Forces formation, which had conducted covert operations since 1939. The Prinz Eugen Division, according to Otto Kumm, received its orders for "Rösselsprung" on May 21. The orders stated that the operation was regarded as critical to bringing about a decision in the region. The division was to form into Kampfgruppen and attack on a broad front, forming blocking actions, capturing supply points, and preventing the partisans from escaping through the area of Banja Luka. Their principle objective was to reach the airborne assault troops, rapidly rendering them support. The ground troops were to link up, using control techniques, to bring about and finally seal the encirclement.[82]

The German version of what happened starts with the early hours of May 25 when a heavy air strike was delivered against Tito's headquarters. At 7:00 a.m., the first assault wave landed, in two parts—a parachute drop of 314 troops and a glider force of 340 troops (including a detachment of Abwehr from Agram). The glider assault had two elements: the first of five platoons, riding in DFS230 gliders pulled by HS126 biplanes and the second element of three platoons also riding in DFS230 gliders but towed by Stukas. These men were organized into teams: Panther (110 men) tasked with snatching Tito; Draufgänger (70 men) tasked to capture the partisans' signals station; and three teams, Greifer, Stürmer, and Brecher, tasked with capturing the allied military mission.[83] Air support was supplied by the Croatian air force flying German airplanes, including fighter-bombers and dive-bombers. The Panther group gliders landed within their target area, but Tito and the allied missions escaped. The partisans, initially surprised, fled for cover. A lieutenant from the Abwehr captured Tito's propaganda equipment. The second assault wave landed at noon, and the Germans took up defensive positions awaiting the arrival of the ground troops.

At 6:00 p.m., the airborne commander was wounded when the partisans began a series of vigorous escape assaults against the SS defensive positions. The attacks continued throughout the night with a concentrated attack at 3:30 a.m. on May 26. At 5:00 a.m., the Luftwaffe conducted air strikes against the partisans. About two hours later, the lead elements from the Prinz Eugen Division made contact with the airborne troops. The Prinz Eugen Division experienced mixed results in arriving at the site of Tito's abandoned headquarters. They had managed to push the partisans back and repulsed several counter-attacks but allied air superiority had displaced Luftwaffe support. This airpower had attacked all movement on the roads and hindered all motorized forces' mobility. Regardless of the lack of air cover and the growing intensity of the partisan attacks, the Prinz Eugen Division had little choice but to press on if the partisans were to be destroyed. The SS commander liberally used words such as "tenacious" and "fierce" to describe the partisan's actions while referring to the allied air cover as "lively." Using the terrain to their advantage, the partisans set clever traps; this ensnared the Germans in delays as they grew more cautious and partisans escaped. On May 31, members of an SS regiment discovered Randolph Churchill's rucksack among twenty dead soldiers reputed to be from the allied military mission. That evening, Phleps and his V SS-Mountain Corps headquarters held a party for SS-Obersturmbannführer Eberhardt, who had received a transfer. The next day, Phleps ordered "free hunting" for the Prinz Eugen Division following the partisan escape. The German casualties were recorded by the XV Army Corps as 213 killed, 881 wounded, and 57 missing. The body count of partisans was 1,916 killed, 161 prisoners, 35 deserters, and the usual amounts of booty.[84] Operations ended on June 6 when the Prinz Eugen Division moved into reserve.

The British impression of what happened followed the German reports, although they were clearly affected by the shock of the raid. Fitzroy MacLean later claimed that he learned of the attack while in London and described the signals at the time as the kind that "took one's breath away." The Germans had spent three days prior to the attack conducting overflights of the partisan positions from two thousand feet up. Following on the last wave of bombers, the German airdrop followed with parachutists and gliders.[85] Michael McConville, among others, mentioned that on May 23, a German aircraft made several passing runs over the headquarters taking photographs. The British mission believed a bombing raid was expected and deployed to positions in the foothills. The air raid preceded the airborne assault, which had taken the partisans by surprise. As sporadic fighting broke out, Tito made his way to a cave and many of his staff fought to join him there. A party of twenty collected around Tito and retreated through a prearranged escape route. They then broke up into smaller groups to complete their escape. Eventually, more partisans and allied mission members, one of whom had salvaged a radio, collected together. The British were contacted and diversions arranged while Tito was on the run. He was eventually spirited away to Italy (June 3) and did not return to Yugoslavia until September 21. Tito lost contact with his partisans for the duration of "Rösselsprung," but this did not prevent them from defense or from remaining intact as a significant force.[86]

The Prinz Eugen Division commander later wrote of the lessons learned from "Rösselsprung." Otto Kumm identified problems of transportation discipline and poor maneuvering through the mountains. The division had found it difficult to prepare at night and had lost communications with its strike battalion. Communications routines were poor from the beginning of the operation with signals routed through the V SS-Mountain Corps to reach XV Army Corps.

Kumm concluded that his combat leaders required a wider perspective of the fighting and should not focus only on their parts in the operation. The

Germans had not pushed scouts forward and had failed to reconnoiter the withdrawal of the partisans. Kumm also noticed that combat commanders failed to concentrate their forces for counter-attacks or to make rapid decisions when they realized partisan intentions. He was particularly critical of the high levels of ammunition expended by German troops. Infantry firing was too early and at too great a distance to have any effect. He indicated a lack of training by suggesting that the troops needed more practice before such methods became a routine. He noted that the heavy weapons barrages rarely achieved concentration on a major target. The overexpenditure and poor supply of ammunition led to extended periods without heavy weapons support. The greatest problem was the division's near total lack of spatial awareness in relation to neighboring formations. Critical in the encirclement maneuver, there were several cases of SS troops firing on German forces. An attack by one battalion was stalled by fire from a Jagdkommando, both from Prinz Eugen Division. The command and coordination of the division was also sidetracked from the mission by minor matters such as railway and road security. The problem of communications became acute with the lack of useable radios and the absence of signals capability at nighttime. Kumm's list also included problems in personal equipment supplies, lack of Luftwaffe support, poor medical facilities for the wounded, lack of central supply, poor weapons and rations, and lack of draft-animal equipment. Praise was limited to the worth of the combat engineers, capability of the animal handlers, and importance of the mountain field guns.[87] Given the scale of the problems, one can only wonder what the division had been doing during the years when it was under Phleps's direct command. Actually, Phleps's bureaucratic opportunism had disguised his incompetence in turning the Prinz Eugen Division into a professional fighting force.

## Italy

In Italy the SS-Police and Wehrmacht had divided their activities appropriately. The SS had a free hand over security operations, mobilizing labor and deporting Jews and Gypsies. The Wehrmacht led a spirited defense against the Allies. Then, in the space of two days, everything changed. On March 23, 1944, a bomb triggered in Rome's Via Rasella and killed twenty-eight German policemen, wounded four (who subsequently died of their wounds), and later one more who had died was added to the count, making a total of thirty-three killed for German reprisal calculations. Hitler demanded reprisals within 24 hours, but they did not take place until August 24, when 335 men were executed in what has become known as the Ardeatine Caves atrocity. On the morning of March 24, 1944, after a brief firefight, German soldiers captured an American OSS team. The team's mission was to blow up a tunnel along the Genoa–La Spezia railway line on Italy's northwest coast. The team was captured by soldiers of the 135th Fortress Brigade (*Festungsbrigade*). The brigade came under Gen. Anton Dostler's LXXV Army Corps, which in turn came under the command of Army Group von Zangen, which covered northern Italy. The OSS team wore U.S. Army uniforms and included fifteen men of Italian extraction. Dostler, following a brief discussion with his chief of staff, ordered the fifteen men executed on March 25 under the terms of the "commando order." The execution order was passed to a senior lieutenant from the fortress battalion to make the preparations and included charging an NCO to dig the men's graves. In the early hours of March 26, a twenty-five-man firing squad with two officers arrived from the fortress battalion. At 7:30 a.m., each "commando" received a pistol shot to the back of the neck. They were buried in their uniforms in a communal grave.[88]

On June 29, 1944, the men of Civitella Della Chiana, a small town in Italy, were executed by German troops. The incident was sparked by the killing, possibly murder, of two German soldiers and the wounding of a third. Historian Erich Hosbawm commented on this atrocity and argued that historians should adopt caution when examining of such incidents. He found that many villagers thought local boys were responsible for the deed and not the resistance movement, and their foolish act had brought reprisals to the village.[89] Michael Geyer also examined the killings; within a broad study of Hitler's war of extermination, Geyer concluded that the German army conducted cold, calculated executions interspersed with cases of wild slaughter. Based on the limited documentary evidence of some military maps highlighted to show "bandit" activity, Geyer's conclusion attributed the outburst of reprisals and massacres to the collective effects of war-weariness showing incipient disintegration of the German army as they built an "emotional horizon" of massacres between killers and killed as the war ended. The facts do not confirm Geyer's conclusion, but correspond to Hosbawm's warning.

A report written by British Intelligence after the war listed nineteen reprisal atrocities between March 24 and November 27, 1944. They included a "conservative" estimate of seventy-five hundred men, women, and children executed. Included in the numbers were the Ardeatine Caves atrocity in Rome, during which 335 men were shot, and Civitella, where 212 men, women, and children were executed. The Ardeatine Caves massacre was begun by an attack on troops of the Police Regiment Bozen.[90] In Civitella, the victims' ages ranged from one to eighty-four, and all the executed women were found naked. There was the usual evidence of burning of buildings, as the British report confirmed: "approximately 100 houses were destroyed by fire; some of the victims were burned alive in their homes." The fighting formations potentially responsible included the Luftwaffe's Herman Göring Panzer Division and 1st Parachute Division, the 114th Light Division, and the 16th SS-Panzer Grenadier Division Reichsführer-SS. Each formation had conducted reprisals and atrocities. Only two weeks earlier in Pisa, troops of the Hermann Göring Division collected eighty hostages and "indiscriminately seized and hanged them on nearby trees."[91] The Hermann Göring Division had regularly conducted atrocities since its deployment in North Africa. Geyer elected to judge the Reichsführer-SS, "an autonomous formation if ever there was one," as the chief culprit. This indicated a fixation over its honorary title rather than its actual operational status.[92] Indeed, the troops of the Reichsführer-SS had conducted the "Marzabotto Massacre" as reprisal for the feverish activity of the "Garibaldi Partisan Brigade." Between August and September 1944, the Reichsführer-SS's reconnaissance detachment was responsible for killing upward of two thousand civilians.[93] Circumstantial evidence does not make the Reichsführer-SS responsible for the Civitella Della Chiana massacre.

Elsewhere, in northeast Italy, Globocnik had adopted a strategy to regulate and maintain north-south communications. This enabled the conduct of east-west Bandenbekämpfung actions preventing a linkup by Italian and Yugoslav partisans. A Bandenstab was established to carry out operational planning led by SS-Sturmbannführer Ernst Lerch. Globocnik's forces were a mix of SS-Police and Italian collaborators. The police units included the 2nd Italian Militia Regiment, a detachment of German gendarmerie, and some Carabinieri; in all, a Kampfgruppe of 1,630 men. Attached to Globocnik's forces was the SS-Karstjäger Battalion (*SS-Karstwehrbattallion*). The Karst is a distinct geological feature of Istria, in northern Italy or the northwest corner of Yugoslavia. The idea of raising this battalion came from SS-Standartenführer Professor Brandt, a noted geographer and caving specialist. Brandt wished to place the men from this region, noted for their Fascist support, into a security battalion, and so they became known as the *Karstjäger*. The initial mustering raised 964 men; the officer cadre came from SS geological detachments. The battalion began Bandenbekämpfung actions in the Trieste area on December 1, 1943, under the command of Odilo Globocnik. It quickly established a reputation for shooting partisan suspects. The battalion was later turned into the 24th Waffen-Gebirgs Division der SS Karstjäger merging with the SS-Italian Brigade of nine thousand Italian collaborators.[94]

Under Globocnik, two operations of note were initiated at this time, "Osterglocke" (April 1944) and "Braunschweig" (May 1944). Heinrich Blaser, a senior police lieutenant, transferred to Globocnik's command staff on January 19, 1944. He testified after the war that "Braunschweig" lasted seven days in mid-May and had the objective of encircling an Italian partisan band and liquidating their leaders.[95] The British decodes proved accurate about the purpose of these operations; they were part of an intensive exercise to round up labor of military age on the grounds of preventing revolts. Those arrested from Communist areas were deported to Mauthausen and Buchenwald concentration camps.[96] Skorzeny assisted Globocnik in both operations, and this partly explains why he was not involved in "Rösselsprung." The post-war interrogation of Friedrich Dupont, a former SS-Obersturmführer of the SS-Totenkopfverbände, testified to Skorzeny's work with Globocnik. Dupont joined the Skorzeny-Jagdverbände, and he explained their job as conducting intelligence gathering and carrying out counterintelligence.[97]

Why had it suddenly "blown up" in Italy? There is no clear-cut answer. The breadth of security operations conducted across the whole southern flank was extensive. After the war, Kesselring was questioned over the reasons for this period of extreme brutality. He excused the behavior of German troops on the grounds of the ill feeling generated by Italy's treachery. He argued that the partisans were really criminal bandits, the worst elements of Italian society, and blamed the Allies for encouraging them.[98] Geyer attributed the cruelties to vague notions of war-weariness but was hindered by being unable to decipher symbols on a Bandenbekämpfung map. Blaming the atrocities on Hitler's tinkering, Himmler's Bandenkampfgebiet decision, the rivalry between military strategy and security policy, and German resentment over Italian treachery seems shallow and inadequate. Finding an adequate explanation for the abrupt end to the atrocities after September 1944 is also virtually impossible.

## France

The events in the Balkans and Italy spilled over into southern France. Bandenbekämpfung methods were widespread in France, imposed alongside labor and extermination policies. German army prisoners of war confirmed the scale of security activities in southern France. A consolidated report from former NCOs from 978th Grenadier Regiment mentioned that an "anti-terrorist training course" (*Terroristenbekämpfungslehrgang*), almost certainly a Bandenkampfschule, was organized near Avignon in May 1944. The course lasted for fourteen days and took two participants from each unit of the regiment. The attendees "made one excursion against the partisans, but without success." The 978th Grenadier Regiment also experienced severe partisan attacks near Dijon while en route to Normandy.[99] The SS deployed detachments to combat growing resistance activities. The 18th SS-Panzer Grenadier Training Battalion transferred to southern France. This battalion had been involved in Bandenbekämpfung operations in the Ukraine since December 1942. In January 1944, it undertook security assignments in White Russia and then in April was redeployed to Prague. On June 23, 1944, it began a period of service in southern France where it remained until September.[100]

Georg Gerhager, an SS-Rottenführer serving with the 2nd SS-Flak Detachment, remembered his participation in actions against the resistance during an interview with British intelligence officers. A Kampfgruppe of infantry and flak artillery was formed by the 2nd SS-Panzer Division Das Reich to combat resistance in the area of Montauban. SS-Brigadeführer Heinz Lammerding, Bach-Zelewski's former chief of staff, was the commander of Das Reich, regarded as an elite armored division. Gerhager confirmed that the infantry surrounded a forest where the resistance was concentrated and was then shelled by the artillery.[101] SS-Grenadier Marcel Meith, an Alsatian serving in the 11th Company of 4th SS-Panzer Grenadier Regiment 4, Der Führer, part of Das Reich, revealed that he had participated in extensive security duty since mid-April 1944. He was involved in rounding up Frenchmen suspected of working with the resistance and transporting them to a camp near Montauban. Their activities ranged as far as 120 kilometers from Montauban. Meith recalled being an interpreter in the interrogation of a Frenchman, who had tried to escape, was shot three times in the chest, but remarkably remained alive. The SS examined the man's papers and beat him when he refused to talk. Eventually the wounded man died.[102]

The most infamous of incidents was the destruction of Oradour-sur-Glane on June 10, which involved killing 642 men, women, and children.[103] Elements of the Der Führer Regiment destroyed the town and the inhabitants on a Saturday afternoon. They conducted a textbook Cannae encirclement, rounded up the defenseless civilians, and paraded them in the square. The SS forced apart the men from their families and led them away to barns and large buildings. They machine-gunned them and then set alight the buildings using straw strewn over the bodies to accelerate the burning. The women and children were herded into the town church. The combination of benzene and a carton of explosives transformed the stone building into a crematorium—a raging inferno that burnt so hot the church bell melted into the stone floor. Those attempting escape through the windows were shot; few escaped.

In July 1944, in Vercors, a mountainous plateau region near the Italian and Swiss borders, an allied military mission and French resistance gathered together, secure in the belief that their position precluded them from suffering a sudden and direct attack. General Wiese, commander of 19th Army, who was responsible for operations in the area of southern France, thought otherwise. The Germans decided to encircle the resistence by combining an air-landing segment of parachutists and glider troops with ground forces.[104] Wiese handed over tactical command to Gen. Karl Pflaum, the commander of the 157th Reserve Division, which was reinforced by the 9th Panzer Regiment and miscellaneous units, including mountain troops. The 157th had been in France since the Italian collapse. Pflaum passed the planning of the operation to Colonel Schwehr, the mountain infantry regiment commander, to lead Banden-bekämpfung operations against the Vercors mountain plateau. His orders were to "find the gangs of terrorists and exterminate them completely."[105] The Germans deployed between five thousand and fifteen thousand soldiers as well as a contingent of four hundred troops from General Student's parachute corps. The Luftwaffe supplied various combat and reconnaissance aircraft. The SS brought "Mongol" troops from Vlasov's army and French collaborators to conduct security.[106]

On July 14, German gliders landed among the allied encampments while mountain and panzer troops encircled the mountain base.[107] The predictable softening-up began with strike missions of single-engine fighter-bombers (witnesses thought Focke-Wulf 190) and reconnaissance overflights. Roads were blockaded, tunnels were blown, and bridges demolished to seal up the plateau's occupants. The air landing took the resistance by surprise, partly because it was expecting an allied supply drop. The results were predictable. Panic led to chaos, and the resistance was unable to form an effective counter-attack. The Allies could not provide air support as in the Balkans, nor could they disrupt the Luftwaffe's air umbrella. Sporadic fighting broke out, but the Germans overwhelmed the resistance and beat captives to death on the spot. The after-operation punishment included locking up surviving resistance captives in burning buildings; a fourteeen-year-old girl was raped eleven times; a young girl was disembowelled and her intestines wrapped around her throat; and one woman was raped by seventeen soldiers while a German doctor ensured she remained conscious. A church was used as a collection center for captives and labor. One observation of the roundup of livestock was likened to a Texan cattle drive: three thousand cattle, three hundred pigs, and three hundred horses, as well as hay, apples, and wheat. The Germans continued patrols to round up escapees, hunting them down with dogs.[108] On July 15, Eisenhower questioned the Germans as to the combat status of the resistance. Field Marshal Rundstedt responded on July 24, denying the resistance combatant status on the grounds of the Franco–German armistice conditions of 1940. He maintained the official line that the resistance was made up of francs-tireurs and should be treated brutally. On August 15, 1944, the American forces conducted Operation "Dragoon" and were able to bring direct support to the resistance.

There is a chilling, absolute silence among the former German armed forces regarding Vercors. Oradour has been subject to criminal investigation and scholarly debate since June 1944. Charles Sydnor elected to blame Heinz Lammerding, with his extensive experience of Bandenbekämpfung operations in Russia, and his responsibility for killing fifteen thousand Soviet partisans and more civilians.[109] After the war SS apologists described their Bandenbekämpfung actions against the French resistance in the modern parlance of antiterrorism. Former SS veterans of the regiment believed they had a plausible excuse. They insisted that the regiment had been severely mauled in Russia and took its replacements from Alsace-Lorraine. These men were not volunteers but conscripts, and many deserted. The German contingent, with families in Germany, were badly shaken by the continual reports of bombing made worse by the lack of leave, heightening their general state of frustration. The large number of "bandit" incidents and the general state of resistance made their "normal" life intolerable. The brutal murder of their SS comrades was an act illegal under the laws of war. There had been "bandit" attacks in the neighboring town of Tulle. They even blamed the deaths of the women and children on the accidental discharge of explosives ("bandit" weapons) blowing up in the town and burning down the church from within (which cannot explain why they sealed the church, preventing escapes). Another story claimed that the officer responsible for Oradour had somehow atoned by risking his life for his comrades and was killed in combat in Normandy.[110]

Today, evidence held by the Public Records Office in London is available for scholars to examine. From June 1944, large numbers of German prisoners of war were brought to Britain for interrogation. On July 2, 1944, twenty-two men of SS-Panzer Grenadier Regiment 4, Der Führer, were interrogated at Kempton Park Camp by Capt. "Bunny" Pantcheff of the Prisoner of War Intelligence Section (PWIS). All reputed to be Alsatians, they confirmed that when their division moved north there were serious incidents with partisans. They maintained that a village by River Garonne had been searched (a map was drawn) and the men dragged into the square. There were no interrogations of the citizens. They alleged that on June 11, the commander of the 3rd Battalion had been captured by partisans. They maintained that all houses were searched; explosives were found in one, and that house was destroyed.[111] Later in August 1944, POW Jean Ertle, formerly of the 10th Company, Der Führer, stated that SS-Sturmbannführer Kämpfer had been kidnapped by Frenchmen.[112] On July 7, Pantcheff had the fortune to interview four SS panzer grenadiers from the 3rd Platoon of the 3rd Company, Der Führer. They indicated that the 3rd Platoon had formed a cordon around Oradour on June 10. The 1st and 2nd platoons had shot the men with machine guns. The women and children collected in the church received machine-gun fire and grenades. The church was deliberately set on fire, "the screams of the victims [who survived the machine-gun and grenade assault] could be heard quite clearly outside the church." During the interview, one incident was remembered in which a twelve-year-old girl jumped from a window, broke her ankle, and was shot. Pantcheff recorded, "The village doctor with his wife and three children returned later from Limoges and were shot immediately. . . . The village was then burned to the ground. The entire population of almost 500 was completely wiped out."[113]

In follow-up interrogations, other men from the Der Führer regiment revealed further information about the performance of the regiment. SS-Mann Rene Banzet, captured on June 17 in Normandy, was an eighteen-year-old Alsatian who had deserted with Martin Müller; both were from the 1st Company. Banzet had witnessed men of the 1st, 2nd, and 3rd companies hanging women from telegraph poles. Men were machine-gunned to death in village squares allegedly for membership in the Maquis.[114] Georg Wolber, an SS-Sturmann from the 2nd Company, was interviewed in a POW hospital and admitted to overhearing gossip regarding the atrocity. He believed SS-Sturmbannführer Kämper's staff car was "found shot up in the village."[115] On October 11, SS-Sturmann Fritz Ehlev (12th Company), a nineteen-year-old from Insterburg in East Prussia, confessed to Captain Kettler that he had heard of the Oradour massacre. He said gossip from his comrades, SS-Rottenführer

Budre and SS-Sturmann Hinz, attributed the crime to the 4th Company. He also confessed to having "observed" SS-Unterscharführer Wust (12th Company), a Dresdener, raping two French girls in the village of Yuret.[116] Adalbert Lutkemeier, an SS panzer grenadier from the 10th Company, related various incidents in southern France. He admitted to watching two Frenchmen being hanged by their wrists, while SS-Unterscharführer Rätsch and SS-Rottenführer Wolters (1st Company) beat them with sticks to exact information.[117] Finally, in June 1945, SS-Oberscharführer Karl Lenz (3rd Company) stated under interrogation that the headquarters platoon of the 1st Battalion was in the village. This unit was composed of thirty-five SS troopers but was strengthened with men from other companies. He believed that the 1st Company was not implicated but that the 2nd, 3rd, and 4th companies had cordoned off the village. The 2nd Platoon of the 3rd Company was "located at the time on high ground and was able to see what was going on in the village, i.e. women being locked up in the Church, the burning of the Church etc." Lenz mentioned SS-Sturmbannführer Dickmann (commanding officer of the 1st Battalion) but judged SS-Hauptsturmführer Kahn (Dickmann's second in command and officer commanding the 3rd Company) as "the leader implicated in the atrocity."[118] In an East Berlin courtroom in 1982, former SS officer Heinz Barth was found guilty of leading a detachment of troops from the Der Führer during the Oradour atrocity as well as of participating in the five killing actions in Czechoslovakia following Heydrich's assassination. It is perhaps not surprising, therefore, to find that his first muster formation was Reserve Police Battalion Kolin.[119]

## Collapse

In August 1944, an uprising broke out in Slovakia. This uprising, one of the least known events of the war, has been overshadowed by the Warsaw uprising in the historiography. It lasted between two and four months, although scholars remain undecided over its precise duration.[120] "On 23 August," Reitlinger wrote, "a black day that saw the loss of Paris and the surrender of Rumania, rebellion broke out in the small republic of Slovakia. This was a still more dangerous situation than that of Warsaw, because the rebellion cut off the retreat of the routed German 8th Army in Galicia."[121] The Slovakian version of the uprising identifies three phases: initial uprising, guerrilla warfare, and the final phase when the Red Army entered Slovakia.[122] Walter Laqueur, however, argues that the uprising was bungled and badly timed.[123] Hitler placed SS-Obergruppenführer Gottlob Berger in command to suppress the revolt. In similar circumstances to Bach-Zelewski's notification of command over Warsaw, Berger testified in 1947 that he received word of his new command by telephone from Fegelein.[124] The situation was unclear to the Germans, concerned for the wider impact on military and economic matters in the region. Berger set off for Vienna, arriving the evening of September 1, and was immediately advised of the considerable forces under his command, according to French MacLean.[125] Berger recalled that his orders were "the immediate disarmament of the Slovak Army . . . the setting up of labor battalions; the arrest of General Caclo; the safeguarding of President Tiso."[126] The uprising dragged on into 1945. The Germans sent in the Dirlewanger formation, under the command of Walter Schimana. During the fighting, an allied military mission was captured. According to the German press, the men received a court-martial, were found guilty, and were executed. The reverberations reached London and Washington, D.C. Henry Stimson, U.S. secretary of war, in correspondence with the secretary of state, explained the meaning of Hitler's Commando Order and its implications and expressed outrage that their men were in uniform but treated as spies.[127]

Since December 1943, the situation in Hungary had concerned Hitler. The Red Army had revealed just how sensitive the Germans were about the area with the efforts to block Kovpak. The Red Army's autumn 1943 onslaught had brought them to within striking distance of the region. This caused Hitler another dilemma; not only was Hungary part of the Axis, the oil fields of Rumania represented his last strategic oil reserve. Gehlen had been gathering information about the movement of partisans from Russia toward Hungary, and in March 1944, he advised Hitler that a band of six thousand Jews was threatening the oil fields.[128] It is hard to know if this triggered the last extensive atrocity of the Jews, but its proximity to events seems more than coincidental. In March, Hitler ordered Operation "Margarethe," four German army corps, to Hungary. Himmler sent Winkelmann to become HSSPF Hungary.[129] In April, Himmler reproached Winkelmann, saying, "He is not to ask continually for orders but to act. His activity is too little in evidence; he is to show ruthless energy in this grave hour by grasping and organising affairs; he must be guided by sound sense and honour."[130] Again this corresponds with Himmler's interference elsewhere.

By September 1944, with two uprisings on either side of Hungary, Hitler was again concerned about potential defection. The British noted,

Jews are still rounded up and deported to Poland. BdS Hungary informs RSHA Berlin that a special train is leaving Sarvar on 4 August for Auschwitz with 1,296 Jews, no doubt for the concentration camp there. Of their treatment nothing is said in these sources, but it may be noted that a message about chemicals for use in malarial districts and therefore to destroy mosquitoes is addressed to Auschwitz for the attention of Himmler's special commissioner for the combating of animal pests.[131]

To secure Hungarian loyalty, Hitler dispatched his notorious double-act of Bach-Zelewski and Skorzeny.[132] The consequences have become legend. The story told by Skorzeny was that Bach-Zelewski intended to destroy Budapest with the siege artillery used in the destruction of Warsaw. According to Skorzeny, Bach-Zelewski wanted to exact revenge on the Hungarians for their official complaint to Hitler over his use of Ukrainians in Warsaw. Skorzeny conducted a daring raid, kidnapping Horthy's son and blackmailing the father into remaining loyal. Bach-Zelewski, made redundant by Skorzeny's actions, was sent packing to Germany to prepare for command in the Ardennes offensive.[133] It was in Skorzeny's interest to accuse Bach-Zelewski, but his bravura performance came at a time when he himself was facing criminal charges.[134] It is more likely that Skorzeny planned the subterfuge while Bach-Zelewski threatened city-wide destruction and that both were enough for Horthy to remain loyal. Bach-Zelewski was reticent about the subject and mentioned in passing that Hitler had given him the assignment personally; his diary indicates only his arrival and departure from Budapest.[135] Later, in evidence in the Eichmann trial (1961), he confessed that Hitler ordered him to Budapest to form a military government. He alleged that it was through his urging that Horthy capitulated at 6:00 a.m. on October 16, 1944.[136]

Just as the accordion-like German occupation system extended with victory, so too it contracted with collapse. The British began to scent a general collapse as early as November 1944 when they noted that German refugees were, in fact, ethnic Germans trying to escape partisan vengeance.[137] In Hungary the situation around Budapest deteriorated rapidly. The Waffen-SS took command of the city under Pfeffer-Wildenbruch, commander of IX SS Corps, no longer responsible for SS-Police colonial affairs. The IX SS Corps included the 8th SS-Cavalry Division Florian Geyer, the last incarnation of the SS-Cavalry Brigade. On December 21, two hundred German parachutists landed in the Hunyadi district, behind Russian lines, in an attempt to conduct sabotage and political warfare and stall the advance of the Red Army. Winkelmann requested Jüttner to hand their control over to the RSHA and to form an SS-Jagdverband.[138] The city was surrounded by the Red Army and a state of siege announced by the Schutzpolizei on December 27. The SS garrison surrendered on February 11, 1945. Felix Steiner, a former senior Waffen-SS officer, praised Pfeffer-Wildenbruch's performance for his tenacious "6th Army-like," Stalingrad-style defense of the city.[139]

Collapse left a surfeit of redundant headquarters units. From August 1944 onward, all across Europe, staff formations mass migrated to the safety of the Reich.[140] The final weeks saw Himmler's police command system fracture into a north-south divide with Wünnenberg in overall command in Berlin.[141] They became the Chef der Ordnungspolizei Nord (Flensburg) and the Chef der Ordnungspolizei Süd (Tyrol) and continued to operate for weeks after the war.[142] As late as February 1945, Carinthia was declared a Bandenkampfgebiet. Along with other band-infested areas of the region, the SS began to wage Bandenbekämpfung inside Austrian borders.[143] In March, Gehlen issued his last official "bandit situation reports." This covered the period

November 1944 to February 1945; it presented a broad picture of partisan incursions joining the advancing allied armies. Gehlen identified Polish, Czech, Croat, Slovak, and Russian "bandits" flocking to the fronts. He continued to categorize nationalist and Communist bands and made the usual derogatory remarks about Jewish bands and their tendency for intensified criminality.[144] The British monitored 10th SS-Police Regiment, SS-Police Regiment Bozen, an Italian volunteer police battalion, and 12th SS-Police Regiment, all in action against Italian partisans. Rösener and Globocnik had formed a Bandenstab, in Prevalko, to stabilize operations in Istria. Rösener received a message from the 4th Section Signals Interception Detachment, warning that Tito had declared a general mobilization of the Save district.[145] On April 6, Rösener reported that German armed forces were mutinying and requested assistance in preventing arms from reaching the partisans. Later, Rösener reported that he had introduced the training of five Wehrwolf detachments.[146]

In the last days of the Nazi regime, there were outbreaks of open opposition to Hitler stirred by the absence of armed authority.[147] In March 1945, Ritter von Epp attempted to make contact with OSS agents offering to negotiate with the German army in the south to end all fighting.[148] In April, the Bavarian liberation movement (*Freiheitsaktion Bayern*) surfaced. The rebels declared a "pheasant hunt" (*Fasanenjagd*) of Nazi officials.[149] They approached Epp to endorse their uprising; he equivocated. German security forces swiftly crushed the insurrection. Through denunciation, arrest, and the threat of execution, they defeated the rebels. A drumhead court-martial, convened by the commandant of Munich, imposed death sentences against Count Rittberg, a staff officer from Army Group South, and Major Caracciola, the Wehrmacht liaison officer assigned to Epp, who coincidently was the rebel leader. In the end, Epp proved his true character by surrendering quietly to the Americans. The SS continued to execute civilians, including a vicar and a teacher, for hoisting the blue and white flag of Bavaria above the church tower of Götting.[150] They imposed their authority over Münstertal (Baden), on April 15–20, when the SS-Jagdverbände-Süd executed two deserters and a priest for making insulting and inflammatory remarks about the deteriorating military situation.[151] On April 10, Skorzeny took himself off to Vienna, to rescue his family. His memoirs referred to crossing the Floridsdorf Bridge in Vienna and forcing a sergeant in the army to surrender a truck full of furniture to nobly carry German wounded.[152] British intercepts indicate that he sent a signal ordering the execution of three officers he personally judged traitors. The men were hanged from the same Floridsdorf Bridge, but this episode was not mentioned in his memoirs, nor was the fact that the bridge served to affect his escape.[153]

Skorzeny also failed to comment that he remained with Kaltenbrunner to the end. He planned, if Hoettl is to be believed, to become the general of Nazi resistance; Kaltenbrunner called him "the partisan Napoleon."[154] On April 22, Ernst Rode was requested to attend a meeting with Kaltenbrunner in Aigen, near Salzburg. During the meeting, it came to light that Karl Wolff was about to surrender in Italy. Peter Black noted that Kaltenbrunner had stumbled over Wolff's secret because he himself had tried to make contact with the OSS.[155] The discussion, however, turned on Austria. Berger, in communication to the meeting from Munich, claimed parallel authority with Kaltenbrunner and control of southern Germany. Rode reputedly told both Berger and Kaltenbrunner that their authorities were worthless and sent a message of that effect to Himmler. He then took it on himself to deliver Himmler's train to the OKW south for use as a mobile headquarters.[156] With the SS operational headquarters safely ensconced in Augsburg, the SS-Police commands divided, and all out of reach of the Red Army, the SS began their final acts of betrayal and self-protection. In Berlin, Fegelein absented himself from Hitler's bunker on April 27, 1945. He was found in civilian clothing; Hitler ordered his execution for cowardice.[157] Two days later, the BBC announced that Himmler had attempted to negotiate a separate peace.[158] Himmler later excused his betrayal on the grounds that "Hitler was insane. It should have been stopped long ago."[159]

To many across Europe, the war ended on May 8; this was not the case in southern Europe. Wolff surrendered the SS-Police forces to the Allies on May 2, 1945. Ordered not to pass weapons to Italian partisans by Field Marshal Alexander, he proved the exception.[160] Delaying actions offered precious hours for German soldiers, civilians, and collaborators to escape partisan gun law. The SS-Division Galician marched into British captivity on May 10, 1945, in Austria.[161] The Bosnian Handschar Division disintegrated; some went home, others stayed with their German officers and tried to effect capture by the Anglo-Americans. Some were set upon by Austrian freedom fighters or Tito's partisans. The rump surrendered to the British on May 15.[162] The Prinz Eugen Division, fighting the partisans on May 6, desperately tried to escape toward Austria. Caught up among the masses of frightened refugees and fleeing remnants of German forces, it continued rearguard actions until May 15. In a surreal world of chaos and collapse, collective memories of this time include final farewell parades by unit commanders and vicious firefights with partisans. The remnants eventually surrendered along with one hundred fifty thousand German troops taken into captivity by Tito's partisans.[163] On May 12, Kaltenbrunner was located in hiding and arrested by the U.S. Army. Fear had kept the fighting in effect until May 15, 1945, when Rösener and the Bandenstab Laibach finally surrendered. For all of Rösener's failings, his forces were the last of the Bandenkampfverbände to lay down their arms. On May 18, Skorzeny surrendered to the U.S. Army in Styria. On May 23, Himmler committed suicide in Schleswig-Holstein; Prützmann had a few days earlier; both did so while in British captivity. Globocnik fled to Carinthia and, on May 31, was cornered by British troops; he also chose suicide.[164] To the great relief of the rest of the world, it was over.

# 10
# DENIABILITY

The history of Bandenbekämpfung did not end with Erwin Rösener's surrender on May 15, 1945. The Allies were determined to judge Nazi war crimes, avoiding the sham of the 1921 Leipzig trials.[1] Nuremberg became a world stage, the test whether international law could be made to work. The Allies arrived in Nuremberg with different agendas. The Soviet Union, obviously used to political show trials, plodded through Nuremberg as the Grand Alliance disintegrated into Cold War rivalries. Inside their occupation zone, the Soviets imposed massive reparations and a vigorous denazification program.[2] The British, contrary to received opinion, prosecuted an active program of investigation and justice. They were hindered at first by having to dismantle the temporary pseudo-Nazi local governments introduced by American civil affairs teams in areas designated for British administration.[3] They also administered the region with the greatest industrial capacity and the largest numbers of former foreign laborers, suitably relabeled displaced persons (DPs), and were in a race against the onset of winter to build adequate food stores. The British arrived in Nuremberg as the standard-bearers of the fight against Nazism but were suffering under the pressures of a national decline. American occupation authorities descended on Germany, marketing democracy as a viable political alternative. They had administered a contradictory policy of destroying the Nazi system and replacing it with institutions managed and administered by former Nazis. Parallel to official policy, the U.S. Army, the State Department, and a host of other organizations dispatched teams of competing scavenger investigators with contradictory agendas. Some targeted advanced technology reparations, while others gathered together former German generals into the Foreign Military Studies Program.[4] The American prosecutors came to Nuremberg imbued with grandiose ambitions to dispense liberal justice. Newly liberated countries like Poland and France were only allocated minor bit parts in the main event. German defendants arrived bewildered but determined to formulate an effective defense strategy. The senior officers of Bandenbekämpfung treated Nuremberg as the final bitter battle.

In 1998, a German police official published an article that accused the allied administration of a lack of due diligence in the pursuit of justice against Bandenbekämpfung. He blamed the Allies for not bringing Bach-Zelewski et al. to book. Wolfgang Kahl criticized the Allies for allowing Bandenbekämpfung to be treated as antipartisan warfare and consequently as a reasonable legal defense. The Nuremberg court, he noted, had agreed to the literal transcription-translation of Bandenbekämpfung as Partisanenbekämpfung. Kahl recognized that the German defendants had a common interest in propagating the milder interpretation. This manipulation of terminology was, in Kahl's opinion, the willful avoidance of justice.[5] His criticism of Nuremberg ignored some of the facts. In 1946, Nuremberg passed judgment on the SS, declaring it an illegal organization and

> Under the guise of combating partisan units, units of the SS exterminated Jews and people deemed politically undesirable by the SS, and their reports record the execution of enormous numbers of persons. Waffen SS divisions were responsible for many massacres and atrocities in occupied territories such as the massacres at Oradour and Lidice.[6]

The origins of Kahl's views lie in what Norbert Frei has called the "policy for the past" postured under the first West German government of Konrad Adenauer. This was the symbolic break from the Nazi past and the period of post-war allied occupation. Germany's new beginning came at the cost of disengagement with the past.[7] West Germany adopted the legal principles that safeguarded everyone's civic rights, circumvented the Nuremberg judgements as victor's justice, and allowed mass murderers to conduct their lives unmolested by law. This made trials of Nazis and SS war criminals a curious hit-and-miss affair.[8] A judicial review of the term Partisanenbekämpfung, carried out by the federal legal service in 1967, made any corrective judgement of Bandenbekämpfung virtually impossible.[9] In this chapter, we examine how the fallacy of antipartisan warfare expunged the record of Bandenbekämpfung. The post-war period was inundated with evidence purposefully constructed to ensure the plausible deniability of crimes. This was not a story of the big lie, but the massaging of half-truths and half-lies into plausible explanations. The written history remains littered with their examples. Questions will remain as to why Bandenbekämpfung was not tried at Nuremberg and why it was allowed to become a platform for the process of denial. Perhaps a simple answer to the hurdle of serving justice against men like Bach-Zelewski was the fear they stirred long after the war.

## Breaking with the Regime

The story of the last six months of the war has been the product of incomplete records, unreliable testimony, and dubious literature. These *final days*, as a media theme, have plummeted the depths of wild speculation, most dreamt up by the SS to further stir rumor and exaggeration. The end of Bach-Zelewski's war began with the conclusion of his mission in Budapest, which was followed by a brief period of leave. He was recalled to duty in November 1944. Himmler had become commander of Army Group Upper Rhine, and he placed Bach-Zelewski in command of XIV SS Corps. The staff of the Ch.BKV remained with him. The corps of twelve thousand men, supplied with captured Russian guns and the same siege artillery used to destroy Warsaw, was emplaced in defensive positions around Baden Baden in southwestern Germany. There were several familiar formations including the 2nd SS-Police Regiment with a heavy artillery company, one battalion of border guards and cadets from the Police School Ettlingen. On January 4, 1945, the corps joined Operation "Nordwind," the final southern flank attack of Hitler's Ardennes offensive. After momentary surprise successes, the corps retreated under heavy U.S. counter-attacks.[10]

In the impending doom, Himmler transferred east to take command of Army Group Vistula, with Heinz Lammerding as his COS. This army group was positioned around Falkenburg in Pomerania. The army group deployed two corps, XVI SS Corps commanded by Heinz Reinefarth based in Küstrin and Bach-Zelewski's X SS Corps assembled around Deutsch Krone. The staffs for the headquarters of X SS Corps came from the Ch.BKV and were under Oberst der Schutzpolizei Gölz.[11] The corps was forced out of Schneidemühl by superior Red Army forces and then formed a series of oblique defensive positions with northern and western wings. On February 8–9, the corps suffered severely under attacks from the 1st Polish Army, which breached the defenses of the northern wing. The Germans were routed, and the front was only restored by the intervention of small combat teams from the army. Bach-Zelewski faced charges for breaching Hitler's "no retreat" order, and Himmler forced him to explain in an official report. Bach-Zelewski blamed his troops for withdrawing without orders. His only solution was that the army should assume field command. He also stated that in the ensuing chaos, the soldiers in Deutsch Krone had been unexpectedly relieved. In a thinly veiled reference to Himmler's poor leadership, he added that the army had pressed him to return the corps to its original positions, but the retreat of the army group (Himmler) made that impossible. These lame excuses marked the passing of their partnership.[12]

In March 1944, after commanding operations in the Kovel area, Bach-Zelewski was again afflicted with bowel problems. Medical examination failed to confirm a return of his complaint, but by then, Bach-Zelewski had been spirited away from the threat of Soviet encirclement. Correspondence between Bach-Zelewski and Himmler at that time indicated a close bond. Himmler's first message was handed to Bach-Zelewski en route to the hospital: "My dear Bach, I am glad you are in Lublin. After your heavy fighting in Kovel, I await your trip to Karlsbad."[13] Twelve days later, Bach-Zelewski received a letter from Rode. "More than anything," he wrote, "it was a joy that you are on the way to reconstitution. RFSS was also happy about it, he is still concerned about your well-being. He wants to hear the news about you all the time. For the duration of your absence, RFSS has taken command again as Ch.BKV, is there a better solution?" Two days later Rode wrote again: "he [Himmler] is very concerned for you. . . . The RFSS only did this [temporarily assume command] one time before, after Heydrich's death, while he organized the SD. This is a friendly hint of its importance."[14] In April, Himmler wrote to Bach-Zelewski in the hospital: "I want to heartily thank you for your letter. . . . I am happy you are returned to health. . . . I no longer want you terrorising the doctors but that you will be fully cured." He advised Bach-Zelewski that "to terminate the cure fourteen days early makes no sense at all. I call upon your intelligence and obedience, and expect you around 15 May and not before." Himmler signed, *Your loyal Heinrich*, very different from his usual style.[15]

Breaking with Himmler in the final weeks proved easier than escaping from Hitler's grasp. After the war, one observer noted that Hitler thought well of him. "That Bach-Zelewski is a clever chap," Hitler said. "When we had a job breaking down Communist resistance somewhere I would bring him alone and he would put it across them!"[16] Bach-Zelewski remained true to Hitler, although in January 1942, in his unhinged drug-induced condition, he recorded certain gossip that at the height of the crisis "he [Hitler] spent his New Year's Eve alone in his winter garden until four in the morning."[17] Later in a diary entry, there is a copy of a letter he had couriered to his wife. It was entitled "The unknown God" (*Dem unbekannten Gott!*). "What is true and untrue— loyalty to Adolf Hitler and as an officer I accept my fate, having taken god's way. . . . I beg for the life of Adolf Hitler and victory for the nation," Bach-Zelewski wrote. Of Himmler, he wrote, "grant me merciful salvation, strength and power never to be afraid of the intrigues of the RFSS; and that I am not afraid."[18] These were strange sentiments for his political benefactor and the godfather of his children and his commanding officer. Allegedly, Hitler told Keitel in the last days that "if Bach-Zelewski was here, I would be entirely at ease. He would scrape up prisoners of war, convicts, everything."[19]

On February 17, Hitler transferred Bach-Zelewski to command of the Oder Corps, in positions south of Stettin, around Schwedt-on-the-Oder. The corps was made up of stragglers, dregs, and the 1st Naval Division of the Kriegsmarine. Bach-Zelewski was reunited with Skorzeny and the remnants of the SS-Jagdverbände. Remarkably, the corps, strengthened by the presence of the 3rd Panzer Army, briefly stalled vigorous Red Army attacks across the River Oder. On April 16, Hitler addressed his final Directive 74 to the soldiers on the Eastern Front. He warned that the deadly Jewish-Bolshevik enemy was determined to destroy Germany and exterminate the German people. In this final fight to the death, he extolled the troops to stand firm as a sworn brotherhood and force the enemy to bleed to death at the gates of Berlin.[20] Nine days later, the Oder front collapsed, and Bach-Zelewski and Skorzeny went their separate ways. Bach-Zelewski was finally apprehended by the U.S. Army, in Sonthofen, on the Austrian–Italian border, on August 1, 1945.

## Expert Witness

Following incarceration, Bach-Zelewski was interrogated, and a preliminary report recorded,

> He is an ardent disciple of Hitler and the Nazi doctrine. He is quite anxious to relate his role on the Eastern Front, taking great pains to point out his alleged fair treatment of Poles, Russians and Jews.[21]

After an initial period of investigation and negotiation, the decision was taken to use Bach-Zelewski as a witness for the allied prosecution. The U.S. prosecutor, Brig. Telford Taylor, and the British investigator, Squadron Leader Peter Calvocoressi, concluded that Bach-Zelewski could testify against the leading Nazis. In the face of opposition from colleagues, Taylor was forced to seek approval from Robert Jackson, the U.S. chief prosecutor, and it was granted.[22] For several months, Bach-Zelewski underwent intensive interrogation to strengthen his evidence prior to entering the courtroom. The shock for the defendants when he entered the courtroom, in January 1946, was one of the defining moments of the trial. The feeling of the defendants was summed up by Göring, who called Bach-Zelewski a swine. The impact not only affected the defendants. One judge thought the neatly dressed man was little more threatening than "a mild and rather serious accountant."[23] Most observers were unable to associate this pathetic character with heinous crimes.

The adoption of Bach-Zelewski as an expert witness begs several questions. The first concerned whether he was a genuine turncoat, a coerced stool pigeon, or if instead he gave testimony for the prosecution in a ploy to avoid the law and extradition to the Soviets. The other question was of the value and reliability of his evidence, which is discussed later. The allied prosecutors, and in particular Taylor, had been on the distribution list of British decodes of German police signals. Taylor was fully cogent with Bach-Zelewski's pivotal role in security warfare and the Holocaust.[24] Bach-Zelewski was generally known as the commander of Bandenbekämpfung and had been publicly denounced as a war criminal by the BBC. Bach-Zelewski faced many serious charges, including responsibility for the destruction of Borki, a village on the Bobruisk–Mogilev highway.[25] He also testified that, at the end of 1942, Dirlewanger executed the population of a village along the Mogilev–Labrunisk road.[26] Skorzeny suggested that Bach-Zelewski flattered Colonel Andrus, the U.S. Army commander of the prison guard responsible for the witnesses and defendants.[27] During one case, Berger stated,

> I experienced it. Bach-Zelewski was on the first floor on Criminal 1. Our cells were directly opposite each other. I saw Bach-Zelewski come from the interrogations. I saw this collapse, his attacks of weeping. In addition then the Protestant chaplain came to me and questioned me about Bach-Zelewski. And then I saw that quite suddenly all this stopped and that he was quite calm.[28]

The soundness of Bach-Zelewski as a witness seems ill-judged.

By October 1946, Taylor was confident enough in Bach-Zelewski's reliability to request from him, through the interrogation officer Walter Rapp, a report on the prisoner's response to the judgments handed down by the court. The report began with the army: "Most prisoners, with the exception of those who are members of the SS, consider the verdict against [Alfred] Jodl a judicial crime. . . . There is no sympathy for Keitel and everybody considers the sentence against him as just." The acquittal of the German General Staff led to great jubilation among the inmates, as did the decisions against Göring, Ribbentrop, Rosenberg, Frank, Sauckel, and Funk. The judgment against Kaltenbrunner was regarded as just, and Bach-Zelewski coolly remarked that he had still been unable to accept the responsibility of his crimes. The defendants were apparently surprised that the SA was acquitted as a criminal organization and felt the Allgemeine-SS deserved similar treatment. When asked if there had been an upsurge of religiosity among the prisoners, Bach-Zelewski denied it. Rapp added to the findings that "[Bach-Zelewski] feels a great guilt and he only hopes that he could pay with his life for what he considers his past errors—but at the same time he says 'as long as you [Walter Rapp] are here I don't think that I will be tried because I seem to be more valuable as a witness than as a defendant.'" The report's findings were distributed among members of the U.S. government.[29]

## The Expert Antipartisan Warfare Officer

In 1951, a British army legal expert tried to explain the German justification for Germany's behavior during the war: "the defense commonly rested on the argument that, under the conditions prevailing, i.e. guerrilla warfare—in the occupied countries, reprisals were justified as the only means of enforcing law and order, and of protecting the lives of the troops in rear of the fighting zone."[30] There was no limit to the number of professional legal opinions that challenged, in spirit, Bach-Zelewski's membership of the prosecution. However, the real test must be the reliability of his testimony, the value it added to the known facts, and the degree of previously unknown information revealed by his designated expertise. There were four cases pertinent to Bach-Zelewski's expertise: labor policies, the treatment of Jews, the treatment of partisans (bandits), and the Warsaw uprising.

Both Sir Stafford Cripps in Britain and Henry Stimson in the United States had reviewed the implications of the Commando Order. In January 1946, Bach-Zelewski received general questions regarding Bandenbekämpfung and was asked to comment on the *Kampfweisung für die Bandenbekämpfung im Osten*.[31] Behind this question lay particular circumstances pertinent to his answer. Only months before, the U.S. Army found Gen. Anton Dostler guilty for causing the execution of American servicemen in Italy. He was executed by a U.S. Army firing squad on December 1, 1945.[32] The British were preparing a trial against Col. Gen. Nikolaus von Falkenhorst to begin in July 1946. The proceedings were to examine the criminal intent of the Commando Order. The evidence included Falkenhorst's order that "if a man is saved for interrogation he must not survive for more than twenty-four hours."[33] The British interrogator wrote, "I reminded him of the ghastly deeds which had followed his zealous interpretation of Hitler's orders."[34] The answer to this question was regarded as particularly important. Without hesitation, Bach-Zelewski explained that the Kampfweisung was a general order to shoot partisans in line with the Commando Order. Taylor later explained that there were no illusions as to its purpose other than as a "blanket order of extermination," "a flagrant violation of the laws of war and a capital war crime."[35] This might indicate that Bach-Zelewski was being truthful, but his absence from the western theater made it relatively easy for him to be honest in this case.[36]

In the case of reprisals and revenge killing, however, Bach-Zelewski's replies were less consistent. He thought reprisals were not efficient. They only worked if the local populace was forced into submission. Troops actually required the population to be well meaning for their own protection. In October 1945, in regards to revenge actions, he stated that there was no central order, that they were purely a reaction to German losses, and although Schenckendorff had declared no revenge actions, he had not formally issued an order. In Bach-Zelewski's opinion, revenge actions were on the conscience of field commanders. He alleged that he had tried to prevent them through conferences with commanders but he was not very successful. Then he said, "there were thousands of cases like that." The interrogator immediately responded, "what you mean is there were thousands of cases where people suspected of partisan activity were executed?" "Yes," said Bach-Zelewski, "there have been numerous cases. Looking at all Europe . . . I am quite convinced of that." Then he added that the guilt remained, not with the soldiers, but with the men hanging around Hitler who did not tell him what was going on.[37]

During one trial, Bach-Zelewski introduced the categories of the "house partisan" and the "wild partisan." They had no military training. This "partisan movement," he said, "was a people's insurrection. . . . Such people's insurrections, of course, being unrest not only the noble motives of a nation." They asked him if all partisans were combated in the same manner. Bach-Zelewski's answer in full was,

> No. The partisans, to the extent to which they were organized, were combated according to military and tactical concepts. This combating according to military regulations was a matter of the operations. Apart from those there were, however, the "house" partisans and the so-called "wild partisans," who made use of the whole of the whole of the partisan fighting. These were small groups or individual personalities which were active on the fringes of the area of the original partisan movement. These so-called "house" partisans were not combated according to military tactical aspects, but instead this combating was a matter carried out according to police and security principles.[38]

Did this mean the strategic profiles were wider than first realized or was this just a ploy to quash the question with a plausible answer?

The issue of foreign labor placed Bach-Zelewski in the position of having to contend with the question of the treatment of Slavs. He employed his Polish ancestry to dodge the question with political and racial rhetoric:

> My family comes from Western Prussia. They have been living there for centuries. It is of course natural that, based on the Versailles treaty, many of the members of my own family who remained in Western Prussia at the time became Poles. That is to say, they became Polish citizens. Therefore, I realize that I felt that in the individual national groups, even my own family, some of the families were found to be racially superior or of value and they were permitted to keep their property and were declared Germans upon my instigation with the Reichsführer-SS.[39]

He stated that beginning in 1943, captured partisans were to be sent to the Reich as labor. He said he was ordered by Sauckel to go to Minsk to receive the directives on labor. He did not mention the agreement he made with Sauckel during their meeting (see chapter 6). Bach-Zelewski explained that the idea was to resolve the partisan problem by removing civilians from a trouble zone. This also led to so-called antipartisan operations being used as a disguise for collecting labor. Many thought this policy would reduce the bloodthirsty state of affairs. SS and army alike were used to round up labor. This led to a rise in the numbers of partisans. The problem of shortages of guards at rail centers led many to escape to become partisans.[40] Bach-Zelewski was able to remove the issue of labor from his responsibility, but in regards to the Jews, he faced a greater challenge.

## The Roots of Holocaust Denial

During one interrogation, Bach-Zelewski made a curious remark regarding the Holocaust: "The thing that most touched me in all this terror was the fact that they just let themselves be led to the slaughter like cattle, entirely without opposition."[41] Bach-Zelewski dismissed the victims as livestock. This raises the question of Bach-Zelewski's denial as a mass murderer. His statements were loaded with pathos, sentimentality, and nostalgia. He was a self-confessed serial killer and faced his interrogators with his need for a father figure and his craving for attention. During the courtroom proceedings, Bach-Zelewski turned himself and his family into victims. A clash manifested itself between his quest for reputation, which had dominated his life, and the development of his newfound victimhood. From January 1946, he changed his name again to Erich von dem Bach-Zelewski. This allowed him to reflect with detachment on *Erich von dem Bach* as a different person with a different past.[42] Three impressions of his family emerged from these performances. His family roots were Hohenzollern, neither Prussian nor German-Polish, which made him a neutral.

His father was responsible for a large family, and they lived on an East Elbian estate built by his grandfather. Poverty was a perennial problem for the family, and his father became an insurance salesman to bring in cash; he died in Dortmund in 1911 while working as an insurance clerk. As nobles, Bach's family lived a hand-to-mouth existence until army success allowed Bach-Zelewski to be at one with his peers.[43] He also acknowledged his colonial connections, claiming that "the brother of my father was the first commander of the German Protection Troops under Dr. Karl Peters."[44] He did not mention Emil Zelewski's defeat and disgrace. He further told his interrogators that he left the army because of a boycott set against him when his sisters wedded Jews.[45] He repeated over and over again, "I had to give up active service in 1924 when two of my sisters married Jews." He alleged that one sister, a saleswoman in Wertheim near Berlin, had "married a poor Jew." The other sister married a successful Jewish businessman who had the appearance of a "Nordic" man.[46] They allegedly lived in Bialystok.[47] This reconstruction of his life even wrapped up the events of 1935, albeit amended to fit the new purpose. The disagreement with Gauleiter Koch was turned into a matter of combating corruption and maladministration, and Schacht's presence became incidental. It is noticeable that at no time did Schacht refer to the incident during the trial process. Turning to 1939, when he was the central figure in the SS race and resettlement process in Poland, he told the interrogators of his fundamental opposition to Himmler and Heydrich. Working with the Gauleiter of Silesia,

Josef Wagner, he said he composed a paper on the inadvisability of erecting Jewish ghettos. Himmler, however, dashed their hopes because of military security concerns, Jewish opposition to National Socialism, and the Jewish predilection for resistance.

The worthlessness of Bach-Zelewski's evidence and his cynical manipulation of his interrogators were already present in November 1945. He declared,

> I was opposed to Himmler's exaggerated racial and Germanic ideas as early as 1934 when his pronouncements were becoming clearer and clearer. At the beginning of the Polish campaign and after Himmler's speech at the Wewelsburg I was filled with the profoundest misgivings because I saw that my national status would be questioned by reason of my half-Slav descent and my Jewish relations.[48]

Focusing purely on this interrogation transcript, we can see how he embellished his story. He qualified Himmler's extermination policy of the Jews of Europe by saying "not the Jews but the Slavs." Every crime became an alibi for everything else. "Moreover," he said, "the fight against partisans was gradually used as an excuse to carry out other measures, such as the extermination of Jews and Gypsies . . . the systematic reduction of the Slavic peoples by some 30,000,000 souls [in order to ensure the supremacy of the German people], and the terrorization of civilians by shooting and looting." The decision to exterminate the Jews, he alleged, came after the failure at Moscow and the Katyn discoveries. "It certainly came late and all SS and Army generals confirm this," he alleged. "Today, I am of the opinion that the order must have originated from Hitler himself." He first heard rumors in 1943, and then he alleged that a commission came to build a gas plant to make gas in his area. They wished to use a factory complex repairing captured weapons in Mogilev. The "rumors of gas vans in Posen were quite strong," he said.[49]

Bach-Zelewski was shown a copy of Meldung 51a (see chapter 3). He denied responsibility for the numbers of Jews shot, admitting that he tried to discriminate between the "Jewish question" and the "bandit problem."[50] According to Bach-Zelewski, the Pripyat marshes killing actions of 1941 went against his original plans. He explained to the interrogators that his Jewish brother-in-law and family happened to live in Bialystok. He tried in vain to get them to leave, which they did, but then they returned a month later believing the killing was over. This, he explained, was the common belief among the Jews, that the Nazi actions were like Russian pogroms—short and deadly. The Jews, he decided, were reluctant to leave, especially those with money or wealth; only the working-class Jews left with the Red Army. He said he went to the chief rabbi of Bialystok to explain that the reprisals were Himmler's response for Soviet scorched-earth policies. His recommendation was for the

Jews of Bialystok to escape. Bach-Zelewski embellished the tale by asking the interrogator, "why have no Rabbis been giving testimony?"[51] He had offered to the rabbi keeping the front lines open on either side of the Pripyat marshes. The Jews could then flee through the marshes without worry of encountering German soldiers and could reach the safety of the Red Army lines. This would have involved a months-long trek in the middle of the security campaign. The proposed escape failed on account of a surprise Red Army cavalry counter-attack that attempted to destroy the German rear areas. Bach-Zelewski was forced to close the gap, and the killings began under Einsatzgruppen commander Artur Nebe. Bach-Zelewski then explained that by revealing the Pripyat marshes incident, he had turned traitor to the German people, but he also recognized that some day the story would surface. Not content to leave the story alone, he explained that Rabbi Barnovdez's house became his headquarters. He even added that "a Jew" worked for him in the Minsk hotel, another headquarters. This person made the fires and did other menial tasks and was denounced by a Russian chambermaid (presumably Helena Bashina) because he received "special benefits."[52]

The truth was less palatable and involved familiar characters. In 1939, Bialystok came under the Soviet occupation following the Nazi-Soviet dismemberment of Poland. The Jewish population swelled with refugees from Warsaw. On June 27, 1941, Field Marshal von Bock and Heinz Guderian led the German invasion through Bialystok. On the first day, the Great Synagogue was set on fire with eight hundred Jews locked inside. On July 11, the Germans rounded up four thousand males, led them into the forest, and shot them. The ghetto was established on August 1, housing upward of fifty thousand persons.[53] From 1941, Bialystok was a central supply center for HSSPF Russia-Centre. On July 1, 1941, Bach-Zelewski received the first reports of the encirclement battle of Bialystok. A week later, he joined Bock and Schenckendorff for coffee. That evening, for their parting dinner, Bach-Zelewski supplied prawns.[54] On July 14, he began the preparations for the cleanup of the forest area of Biaełowieźa, near Bialystok. Preparations involved questioning Schenckendorff and Oberst der Polizei Montua as to how this might be best achieved.[55] In 1943, resistance in Bialystok led to six days' fighting and marked the end of Globocnik in Poland. Bialystok served as a jumping-off point for killing actions in the surrounding communities. The total number of Jews killed from this region reached 240,000.[56]

In terms of the treatment of Jews as partisans and vice versa, Bach-Zelewski was quite equivocal; some Jews were partisans but they were not in significant proportion to the whole number. He referred to the resistance by the Jews in the Warsaw ghetto but dismissed it, stating that fifty German casualties did not make a strong case. He said he was sacked by Hitler and Himmler for not deporting the Hungarian Jews when he was in Budapest, in 1944. He then launched into a tirade in which he said he was a victim of the

"Dagger" proposition. The interrogator corrected him, "the stab in the back?" Bach-Zelewski replied, "yes, the stab in the back." He then explained that everyone was blaming Himmler because he was dead and they could exonerate themselves. The "Jewish problem," he said, was not handled by a single policy but by many, some of which were in conflict. Bach-Zelewski then explained how in 1944–45 Schellenberg had tried to save the last remaining Jews under Himmler's sanction. They had all worked together with a "General Franz Schenckendorff." The only other general in the German army with a similar name was Heinrich von Schenckendorff. [57]

Bach-Zelewski's argument over the wider treatment of the Jews delved into Nazi economics and the exclusion of the Jewish communities from their livelihoods. This meant they were deprived of food. By forcing the Jews to build camps, Bach-Zelewski astounded the interrogator by suggesting, Himmler was in fact offering them a livelihood, the opportunity to work for Germany and food. He assumed the "free" (presumably he meant Aryan) population would never buy anything Jewish, and for this reason, the Jews had to be made to work for Germany. He had established watchmakers', tailors', and shoemakers' workshops and granted Jewish unions under Oberpräsident Schmeldt. The Jews repaired all the broken watches from the Reich; German watchmakers were particularly happy because they no longer had access to skilled manpower because of conscription. Bach-Zelewski rounded off his story by adding that the "Eastern Jews were a passive people."[58] Bach-Zelewski was an unrepentant Nazi. After 129 Nuremberg interrogations, countless more by West German Federal prosecutors, and numerous courtroom and written statements, he never once accepted his guilt for the thousands of murders he was responsible for.

### The Warsaw Debacle

One of the most detailed collections of interrogations and documents of pre-trial preparations were those concerning the Warsaw uprising of 1944. The significance of the uprising lay with the possible defendants and witnesses. With the exception of Hitler, Himmler, and Dirlewanger, all the leading German participants were in allied custody; some in Poland, but the majority at Nuremberg. The single most important military personality was Col. Gen. Heinz Guderian. The SS was of course represented by Bach-Zelewski, and the Nazi civilian administration by General Governor Hans Frank. On the next level, there was General Vormann, the army commander in Warsaw; Ernst Rode, the chief of staff of the KSRFSS; and Heinz Reinefarth, the Kampfgruppe commander at the center of the street fighting. Waiting in the wings with due trepidation were Warlimont, Hitler's dynamic advisor; Wolff, Himmler's former adjutant; and Dr. Ludwig Fischer, the Nazi governor of Warsaw. There were a host of field officers and operatives of varying ranks, including the SS commander of the Warsaw security police. Telford Taylor chose to focus the case on German army responsibility for the destruction of Warsaw rather than to place the key defendants on trial for war crimes. This led to perhaps the most bizarre example of what happened when expert witnesses were granted too much leeway.

On July 20, 1944, hours after the bomb plot against Hitler, Guderian became chief of the General Staff of the Army. The former armored warfare specialist "Fast Heinz" Guderian cut a shabby picture in Nuremberg. Confinement did not call forth his finest hour. He spent much of the first part of his incarceration with other senior army defendants attempting to form a united and Nazi defense. When his coup failed, he broke ranks and elected a legal defense of denial. Guderian denied everything, concocting implausible stories especially about his part in Warsaw.[59] His vehement denials caused his complexion to become puce or to redden with severe palpitations, indicating that perhaps Hitler had taught him something after all. His subsequent 1952 memoirs failed to mention his dramatic performances.[60] Guderian's bizarre behavior continued when on January 29, 1946, he was interrogated by a Polish army officer. It seems Guderian attempted to locate a "mutual understanding" by suggesting his old family home had been within 1919 Polish borders. He said he rarely passed by Poland, meaning the General Government, preferring to visit his family in the Warthegau, a territory of western Poland annexed to the Reich in 1939. Unable to grasp the insensitivity of his remarks, he then changed tack and stated that he came from a long family line of German Junkers with a homeland that had been Prussian for hundreds of years. The Polish officer's reply was calm but firm, reminding Guderian that the area had been Polish long before it had been German.[61] On this footing the less than cordial interrogations concerning the Warsaw uprising proceeded.

Guderian denied any planning responsibilities and claimed that he had only met Hitler on a few occasions, "none of which had any political significance." This was interesting for the interrogators because his promotion to chief of the general staff was made by Hitler personally, after the July 20, 1944, bomb plot. Guderian stated that Bach-Zelewski received orders from Hitler to destroy Warsaw. Bach-Zelewski's units were of doubtful quality, "highly evil," and conducted "ruthless actions." Guderian claimed that the implementation of the Geneva Convention in the surrender negotiations was his idea. Regarding the razing of the city and the shooting of civilians, he said, "this order concerning human beings is not known to me. The order concerning the razing of the town I heard from Hitler myself."[62] Guderian was then presented with a section of Hans Frank's diary. On August 3, 1944, at 9:10 p.m., Guderian had called Frank on the telephone and said, "in the city of Warsaw a verdict is to be accomplished with all ruthlessness." He denied that any such discussion had taken place and suggested that the phone call in the diary entry concerned the Luftwaffe's bombing of Warsaw. Again, Guderian blamed Bach-Zelewski for the destruction of Warsaw. The interrogator then referred to a telegram Bach-Zelewski received from Guderian on October 11, 1944, ordering him to "raze Warsaw to the ground. . . . I notify you of this since this new Führer order about the destruction of Warsaw is of the greatest importance for any further policy in Poland."[63] Contrast this with his 1952 memoirs: "I requested that Warsaw be included forthwith in the military zone of operations; but the ambitions of Governor-General Frank and the SS national leader Himmler prevailed with Hitler."[64]

A confrontation broke out in the cells between Guderian, Ernst Rode, and Bach-Zelewski. The interrogators asked Rode for his version of the events. According to Rode, the order was distributed through OKH to 9th Army and through Himmler on behalf of the SS-Police. The actual route was from Guderian to General Vormann to Bach-Zelewski. Rode stated that a conference had taken place between Hitler and Guderian, which preceded the destruction order. Guderian offered Bach-Zelewski siege artillery both to defeat the Polish resistance and to destroy the city. Bach-Zelewski had asked Guderian if the order could be rescinded but was told it was a direct Hitler order. Thus Bach-Zelewski had tried to persuade General Bor, commander of the Polish resistance, to prevent this from happening by surrendering under the Geneva Convention. Rode contended that this operation had also fallen under the authority of the army because Bach-Zelewski's commendation for the Knight's Cross came from General Vormann. Guderian would meet Bach-Zelewski only with Major-General Wenck as a witness while Bach-Zelewski in turn took Rode. The interrogators asked why Bandenbekämpfung had been practiced in the operational sector, and Rode explained that the fighting had broken out behind the German lines and only later became part of the "operational area" (*Operationsgebiet*).[65] This appeared to be regarded as convincing testimony from an objective and professional senior police officer.

On August 9, 1946, Ernst Rode was interrogated regarding the operational circumstances for the Warsaw uprising. Rode gave an explanation that wrapped the SS command system under the Wehrmacht and the army. He told his interrogators that Guderian and Bach-Zelewski took witnesses to their meetings, which is why he was able to testify authoritatively. The combating of the partisans was supposed to be Himmler's responsibility. Rode placed Guderian in overall command, with Himmler commanding Dirlewanger and Bach-Zelewski under the dual commands of the SS and the army. Rode said Bach-Zelewski had tried to prevent the destruction of Warsaw but implied that Guderian refused to intervene to prevent it. He said the army was always in command and this was proved in the issue of the highest medals. Rode said Bach-Zelewski reported directly to Hitler for resources and decisions. The atrocities committed by Dirlewanger's and Kaminski's troops were not sanctioned by Bach-Zelewski. Later, Bach-Zelewski summarily executed Kaminski and had Dirlewanger and his troops removed.[66]

On August 14, 1946, Bach-Zelewski stated that the Polish uprising initially attacked the local German garrison. Then Himmler intervened and sent

Reinefarth to quell the uprising although the German 9th Army under Vormann was in control of Warsaw. Bach-Zelewski insisted that his only conferences with Guderian were when Rode was present. Guderian had offered him heavy artillery to destroy the city. Bach-Zelewski contended that he had tried to change Guderian's mind in regard to the reduction of Warsaw, but the latter reacted very coolly and said it was a Hitler order. Bach-Zelewski insisted that Guderian fully appreciated Hitler's destruction order in detail. He continued by stating that the destruction order was already in progress on his arrival in the city. Guderian, Bach-Zelewski alleged, had informed Vormann and Stahl of the destruction order and therefore the army was responsible. On September 22, Bach-Zelewski maintained that he knew everything in great detail but was responsible for nothing. During this interrogation, he explained how a large-caliber railway mortar and one hundred flamethrowers were used to suppress the uprising. Then, two days later, he alleged that Himmler was very taken with Guderian and they formed a strong working relationship; not unlike Bach-Zelewski and Himmler, it might be noted. On October 5, 1946, Bach-Zelewski was again questioned over the army's responsibility for the destruction of Warsaw. Bach-Zelewski alleged that Vormann had not been forceful enough to clarify the chains of command or to control the flow of orders. He continued that this weakness made him directly responsible for the deaths. For this reason, the first fourteen days of German counteractions were the responsibility of Vormann and Stahl. Bach-Zelewski then added that the Warsaw Shield had been granted to the men by Hitler but he did not believe they were worthy of it.[67]

When Nikolaus von Vormann gave evidence on September 21, 1946, he began by stating his command period for the 9th Army: June 25 to September 30, 1944. This confirmed that he was the senior army commander. He then stated that political control originated with the General Government. Vormann stated that the army came under SS control and that the roles were only reversed in terms of military operations. He stated that Kaminski was a disaster for the operations and wanted him removed. Guderian, he alleged, promised good troops but sent a rabble. Vormann added that Bach-Zelewski had received elements of an armored division under his central command. Troops inside the city were under Stahel's command while troops outside were under Bach-Zelewski, over whom he had no control.[68] On October 2, 1946, Vormann alleged that he complained of the atrocities to Army Group Centre and that it was he who had Kaminski removed from Warsaw. He stated that Bach-Zelewski was directly subordinate to Himmler, which was why the men received the Bandenkampfabzeichen, distributed by Bach-Zelewski, instead of the Iron Cross. He was asked the direct question, "In your position as Operational Commander in Chief were you authorized to give orders to [Bach-Zelewski]?" Vormann replied that if Reinefarth and Bach-Zelewski had not complied with his requests, he could overrule them, although he confirmed they were not under his command.

Heinz Reinefarth was questioned on September 19 and 20, 1946. He had arrived in Warsaw on August 5 or 6, 1944, reporting to Vormann on his arrival. He was given command of one army battalion and one police battalion. Reinefarth confirmed that Bach-Zelewski told him of Hitler's order to destroy the city. Stahel had set up a combat headquarters in Warsaw that was already functioning. He then met Kaminski who was in the uniform of an SS-Brigade-führer; his men were in German army uniforms. According to Reinefarth, Vormann told him that he had given Kaminski the authority to loot Warsaw, which Reinefarth opposed. But Vormann said this was an inducement to fight, as he was well aware of Kaminski's behavior. Reinefarth firmly stated that Kaminski came under Vormann's command. Bach-Zelewski had informed Reinefarth of the women and civilians shot and burned. Kaminski was under the command of Rohr, who wanted rid of him because of the behavior of his troops, including rape and murder. Rohr had lost control of Kaminski and his men, who were regularly found inebriated and refused orders. For this reason, Bach-Zelewski decided to remove Kaminski through subterfuge, having him arrested and then executed. Reinefarth finally stated that Bach-Zelewski all along wanted to settle with the Poles through political rather than armed means. But Bach-Zelewski was under Vormann's command and this constrained his movements.

The end of the Warsaw interrogations and the International Military Tribunal did not end the Warsaw debacle. A most unusual situation arose when Bach-Zelewski was sent, under American immunity but with Polish army guards, to give evidence in a trial of war criminals in Warsaw. Having been responsible for the destruction of Warsaw and the deaths of many Poles, this was indeed ironic. He traveled on February 14, 1947, and remained in Warsaw for four weeks. He provided a report on his return. On arrival in Warsaw, he was taken to the large collection prison of Mokotow, whose inmates included both Poles and Germans. The defendants included Dr. Fischer, Warsaw governor; Otto Meisinger, commander of the Warsaw security police; and Philip Bouhler, who had been involved in the euthanasia program. He gave little evidence in regard to the destruction of Warsaw. A command chart was written down by Bach-Zelewski (refer to Diagram V) and offered into the proceedings. It was intended to portray a confusion of authorities in order to disguise his authority. It appeared to work. True to their word, the Poles returned Bach-Zelewski to the Americans. Thus the destroyer of Warsaw had been protected from a Polish request for extradition. One can only admire the good grace of the Polish people to have suffered such an inequitable situation; it was just another of the many injustices never healed at Nuremberg. Following his evidence, the U.S. ambassador Murphy was passed the testimony on March 3, 1947. A clue to the treatment of the Poles can be found in this testimony:

Since there was no supply department attached to my staff and I had no supply organizations at my disposal, I had to hand over control to the civil administration but the question of efficiency was not affected. . . . Finally I state that hundreds of thousands of civilians and tens of thousands of soldiers of Polish nationality owe their lives due to my sense of responsibility alone. For this, my humane victory over crime, Himmler gave me the reward in the form of a communication by a notary, that my brother Victor had died insane in the Boldeschwing Institution, near Bielefeld.[69]

The subject of Warsaw was again aired, albeit briefly, in the "Hostages" trial, case seven in the military tribunals at Nuremberg. This was prosecuted by the U.S. Army against German officers involved in antipartisan warfare principally in Yugoslavia. It was a strange case because the Yugoslavs had their own war crimes process, while the Americans imprisoned all the leading commanders of the Wehrmacht but had not elected to extradite them. The trial did not attempt to distinguish between antipartisan warfare, Banden-bekämpfung, or crimes committed by the Nazis in the name of security. It was another attempt by Taylor to bury the German army in further shame. Bach-Zelewski again appeared as Taylor's expert witness. To parry his testimony, the defendants attempted to raise the questions of Warsaw in the court proceedings. By this time, Bach-Zelewski was well versed in manipulating the courtroom into believing his version of events. Immediately after being questioned about Warsaw, he said, "I crushed the insurrection in two months fighting and my troops had ten thousand casualties. . . . I bear responsibility for my corps in Warsaw then and today and when I was in command of troops I bear all responsibility."[70] Bach-Zelewski was asked if he was in Hitler's confidence at this time; he replied in the affirmative but stated he was not in Himmler's. He was asked if he had tried to "exert pressure against the supreme leadership," to which he replied, "certainly not, sir." The losses for Warsaw had also changed. In January 1946, Bach-Zelewski claimed he had saved "hundreds of thousands of civilians and tens of thousands of soldiers of Polish nationality."[71] In October 1945, he estimated total losses in six weeks of combat, "20,000 German and Poles 10,000 military and 40,000 civilians."[72] This contrasts with the figures from his dairy listed in appendix 5.

During the proceedings, Bach-Zelewski was reunited with Ernst Korn. Under interrogation, Korn had provided some evidence to Taylor but had not criticised Bach-Zelewski. Upon leaving Bach-Zelewski, Korn explained that he became chief of staff to the HSSPF in Croatia. He remained in that position until April 1944, when he was relieved of command. He told the story that the HSSPF had few resources when he arrived in Agram; there were no troops or equipment to wage a campaign against the partisans. He confessed to organizing an operation in Croatia; he described it as a security operation to protect the local ethnic German population. He said he was supported in guns and equipment by the German commander, Colonel General Rendulic. He denied that he was responsible for rounding up hostages and that the Order Police had formed independent execution squads under his command. He swore an oath to the truthfulness of his comments.[73] In the courtroom he admitted to handling Operation "Ferdinand," in October 1943, with police and infantry. "A German Regular Police on its own initiative could not undertake any operation independently, as regards the planning orders and execution," he stated in his concluding remarks.[74]

After years of diligent disruption and misinformation, Bach-Zelewski finally had his day in court regarding Bandenbekämpfung. Bach-Zelewski opened his testimony by stating that "after various front assignments, at the turn of the year 1942–1943—that is, at the beginning of January 1943—I became Chief of the Band Combating Units. That was a Central Office with the Reichsführer-SS for the combating of bands. This position of Commander of Anti-Partisan Units never ended and the staff carried on to the end. Primarily it was a central report office which worked in close cooperation with the OKW and the OKH." He said he was "responsible for all partisan reports from the whole of Europe, which arrived at this office, and I had to work on the great, large, band-position maps which I myself had to draw up and which during the daily situation discussions with the Führer had to be presented to him by Himmler." He accepted some responsibility for his command. "As the fighting itself went," he claimed, "I was in charge of operations only in the east, but since I was responsible for the drawing up of a new band fighting regulation of course I found out on the spot in the southeast about the band fighting and I myself took part actively with the Wehrmacht in a partisan operation in Croatia."[75]

In perhaps one of the most remarkable put-downs in legal history, the judge's summation of Bach-Zelewski was "the witness is not a military expert in this connection." The defense counsel, Dr. Sauter, grasped the moment and argued that "the witness Bach-Zelewski is of course the typical SS representative," continuing, "we had no idea, during the presentation of our case, that exactly an SS leader would be sent here to talk about the regulations for band warfare and particularly that the SS leader who is regarded as mainly responsible for the millions of murders in Russia," concluding, "the witness Bach-Zelewski must of course give from his point of view in order to save whatever there remains to be saved from the SS."[76] After years of waiting, Bach-Zelewski's defining lifetime moment was dashed by a lawyer—another historical irony.

## Foreign Military Whitewash

After Bach-Zelewski, the foremost economist of the truth was Franz Halder, the former chief of the General Staff of the Army. As a model of Schlieffen professionalism, Halder has left a considerable mark on the post-war history of Germany's security warfare. After the war, he became the chief consultant for the Foreign Military Study (FMS) Program under the U.S. Army's Historical Branch. Hitler "sacked" Halder in the summer of 1942 at the time of the introduction of the Bandenbekämpfung directive. Halder had issued the Jagdkommando order in one of his final acts as army chief of staff. He ensured that Bach-Zelewski, Himmler, and even Bandenbekämpfung were written out of the "official" history. Under Halder's guidance terms like Partisanen replaced Banden while Partisanenbekämpfung was artificially reinstated over Bandenbekämpfung, to serve up a sanitized version of German military history. In effect, Halder wanted to pretend that German military traditions remained unaffected under Nazism. Halder also had the ambition to complete a Wehrmacht history like the Reichswehr's official history of the Imperial Army during the First World War. Fortunately for him, U.S. military tradition dictated that some form of foreign military study should follow this war, as it had all previous American wars. Unchecked and unverified, Halder was able to produce his semi-official history financed and resourced by the Americans.

While the technical reports within the FMS collection have a value, the studies connected with partisan warfare or Bandenbekämpfung were a political whitewash. Bach-Zelewski's only contribution, a brief report of his command of the 14th SS Corps on the Western Front, suggests his complicity. The report confirmed that his Ch.BKV from Warsaw became the corps staff. Ernst Rode contributed a report on the KSRFSS, confirming its policing role and thereby removing the record of its links with Bandenbekämpfung. Field Marshal Kesselring provided a study of the campaign against the Italian guerrillas arguing, "its origin and its method was contrary to international law and turned the previous comradeship (between Italians and Germans) in arms into brutal murder."[77] The argument formed the basis of his war crimes defense:

> Guerrilla bands were a motley crew, made up of soldiers of the Allies, Italians, Balkan nations, also German deserters, male and female elements of the population of diverse occupations and ages, with greatly varying moral conceptions lacking any unity based on mutual ethical standards.

The direction of his attack made no reference of remorse for the killings and only contempt for the court. "A soldier," he argued, "upon whose life an attempt may be made in the most dastardly manner, sees 'red' and reacts differently from a pettifogging prosecutor or judge behind the protective cover of his writing desk."[78]

Former field commanders also participated in the FMS Program. In 1947, former Lt. Gen. Arthur Schwarznecker, who had worked closely with Bach-Zelewski from 1943 to the winter of 1944, wrote a study of security within "enemy territories" in the area of Army Group Centre. Schwarznecker, the commander of Oberfeldkommandantur 392 and Korück 582, was at the forefront of Bandenbekämpfung in the east. His study was critical of SS responsibility for antipartisan warfare beyond the combat zone, arguing that "if their activity had been confined to purely political tasks, to which their training and capacity had prepared them, they would have been able, in cooperation with the available police force, to carry out their missions, without the weakening influence of unreliable elements."[79] Gustav Hoehne observed that "in the Polish area . . . partisans were present, for which the mal-administration of these territories must be partly blamed. The civil administration had expropriated personal property on a large scale in several areas, causing the Polish population thus rendered homeless to band together in small groups, which caused a great deal of damage." He concluded that "the rules for hunting game with beaters make the best directive," for combating partisans. Halder's opinion of Hoehne's study stated that it was "a worthwhile contribution to the study of the partisan movement in Russia. . . . It is also interesting because it is based on the personal experiences of the author. I approve of the essay in general."[80] Even the man most responsible for the Vercors atrocities, Karl Pflaum, was granted the opportunity to write reports of his operations in the south of France in 1944. Pflaum wrote two reports on the 157th Reserve Division, the first from a general perspective and the other on operations in August–September.[81] Some years later, Lt. Gen. Paul Schirker published another study in 1951 covering the division's operations in September 1944.[82]

The pièce de résistance was a study from former Generalmajor der Polizei Alexander Ratcliffe. "In several valuable contributions," Halder wrote glowingly, "General Ratcliffe has proved his good ability of observation and clear judgement of the Russian as an enemy." Ratcliffe recommended sound socialization so that a future army, presumably American, fighting in the east was well prepared in advance:

> To European minds Russia is a sinister land . . . with respect to the peculiarities of nature, climate and the inhabitants. The hopelessness of the vast Russian expanses, the severity of the Asiatic winter and the endlessness of the Eastern forests call for strong hearts. The additional strain of a merciless partisan war will be more easily borne if the fear of the unknown has been overcome.

Halder wrote that the study did not bring anything new but "because of its limitation to principles and clear distinction of the essentials I consider it valuable and believe that I can recommend the purchase of this study to the Historical Division."[83] Scrutinizing Ratcliffe's career details a little more closely, it seems he was a colonial soldier with Lettow-Vorbeck in East Africa and joined the police after the war. He was involved in the organization of police units and served under Daluege until 1937, when he joined the army, retaining his general's rank. In 1942, he served with the 207th Security Division and, in 1944, was the Kommandantur of Orscha. Captured by the Russians in 1944, he did not return to Germany until 1949. Ratcliffe was not the only *Kolonialmensch* involved in the FMS Program. In one study of antiguerrilla operations in the Balkans, the U.S. Army accepted and promoted the writings of Karl Gaisser discussed in chapters 5 and 9.[84]

By the mid-1950s, Halder's fictions and the needs of U.S. Army operational research had found harmony. The U.S. Army's Center of Military History published government publications on such themes as antiguerrilla operations, Soviet partisans, and German rear-area security.[85] A former U.S. Army intelligence officer, James Critchfield, has written about the formation of Germany's post-war defense and intelligence establishment.[86] Critchfield, like many U.S. military operatives, must have known how far Gehlen and other German generals were steeped in criminal behavior. The captured files were loaded with evidence of hunting Jews, mass killings, and the wholesale terror of civilians. While expediency in the light of the Cold War represents a reasonable argument for former times, it is more difficult for objective observers to be anything other than bemused by the decision to let so many war criminals go free.

## Alles Vorbei

If the newly founded state of West Germany had internalized the principles established by Nuremberg, then ongoing war crimes justice might have been routine. However, the timing of the last American tribunal, the execution of the last war criminals in U.S. custody, and the Federal Republic's assertion of its own legal destiny coincided at a critical point in time. Norbert Frei has explained how Adenauer and West Germany circumvented the judgments of Nuremberg and ensured that the legal system avoided its precedents.[87] The first officials of the Federal German legal system were uncomfortable with Nuremberg; it smacked of victor's justice, but then many within the judiciary were the products of the Third Reich. Politicians and jurists alike successfully circumvented the Nuremberg judgments on the spurious grounds of avoiding the Nazi policy of punitive judgments. It is in this context that one has to weigh Wolfgang Kahl's criticism of Nuremberg.

In 1950, the former U.S. military governor of Germany, Lucius Clay, wrote that "the police were screened thoroughly to exclude Nazis."[88] The reconstruction of the German police led down some bizarre turns. Ulrich Herbert's study of Dr. Werner Best explains why there was such resistance toward trials. Herbert discovered that the former SS established self-protection cliques and that Best, a lawyer by profession, vigorously defended the commanders of Einsatzgruppen.[89] He was not alone. In 1946, Bomhard was released from American custody, as he was not regarded as a real war criminal. He went home with his personal archive of SS-Police documentation. This archive formed the basis for his post-war career as defense advisor to police officers on "trial" before state ministries of the interior attempting to denazify the Federal police. Bomhard became an acceptable headache for the state authorities.[90] In the 1950s, he defended police officers against the loss of pension rights and status. Armed with his collection of records and files, he successfully prevented attempts to denazify the police. He still retained powerful friends. After the war, Winkelmann became the deputy to the chief of police for southern Germany; he retired in 1965 on a full state pension and became president of the retired police officers' association.[91] In the German Democratic Republic, the notorious *Braunbuch* was published in 1965, listing former Nazis and their prominence as elites within the Federal system (refer to appendix 4).[92] In 1978, Leonard Mahlein attempted to raise opposition to the influence of the SS in Federal Germany by publishing a pamphlet explaining the scale of the movement.[93]

Matters did not just rest with the law. The SS old boy network proliferated and released a market for literature of denial. Just as after the First World War, there was much industry devoted to the publication of memoirs and SS unit histories. The apologists for the Waffen-SS, led by Paul Hausser, tied themselves in knots shunning the criminal activities of the Bandenkampfverbände while claiming several of its "lost victories" for their own record. In 1953, Guderian, no longer blaming everyone, showed his true colors by openly endorsing the Waffen-SS and writing the foreword to Hausser's book. He opened his endorsement with the SS motto, which had been granted by Hitler in 1931 to Daluege and Bach-Zelewski for suppressing the Stennes revolt. Guderian praised the stoicism of Waffen-SS veterans in the face of post-war castigations and blame. He credited the Waffen-SS with originating the idea of a united Europe and with staunching the Bolshevization of Europe.[94] In 1957, a publication challenged this increase of denial among the SS. It gave the names and addresses of the SS veterans' associations. Nearly all the SS formations were listed, including the Dirlewanger old boys association in Duisburg.[95] Bomhard played his part in this historical process. He advised historians of the Bundesarchiv in the publication of a study of the police in wartime and wrote the foreword for a turgid history of the 18th SS-Police Mountain Regiment. In the foreword, he briefly recalled the heady days of the *Alpenkorps* in Serbia conducting its fighting withdrawal in October 1918 under Ritter von Epp. Calling the regimental history an "opus of memory," he deigned to refer to both the partisans and the bandits and declared that the regiment was the pride of the German people.

A life of obscurity after Nuremberg was an unbearable sentence for Bach-Zelewski in the 1950s. He was shunned by the likes of the Waffen-SS veterans' association, in which men like Berger, Bomhard, and Winkelmann were granted the status of minor celebrities. He claimed to have lied at Nuremberg. He alleged smuggling poison to Göring, but in reality his life had become the loneliness of a nightwatchman for an industrial concern.

Unable to keep quiet about events, he was tried for the 1934 murder of Anton von Hohburg und Buchwald. He thought his subordinate accomplices, SS driver Paul Zummach and SS-Hauptsturmführer Reinhardt, were dead so he denied the charge. Zummach turned up and so Bach-Zelewski confessed. He then retracted his confession when Zummach committed suicide in his cells.[96] Bach-Zelewski received ten years of house arrest. In 1961, he gave evidence for the Eichmann trial in Israel. The case jolted the Federal Republic's legal authorities into action, leading in the first instance to the 1965 Auschwitz trial in Frankfurt. The trial received considerable attention both at the time and later, but it confined the question of war crimes to one camp and one group of guards. In 1962, Bach-Zelewski was finally charged with killing three Communists in 1930; he was found guilty, received life imprisonment, and died in prison in 1972. Wolff received a fifteen-year jail sentence for his part in the extermination of the Jews but was released on grounds of ill health. Once released from prison, Wolff continued to meet and travel with former SS colleagues like Klaus Barbie, the "Butcher of Lyons," and pontificated as a celebrity in television documentaries like the "World at War" in the 1970s.[97]

A case against the SS-Cavalry was conducted in Brunswick. In 1963, a legal review into the crimes of the 2nd SS-Cavalry Regiment carried out in Russia in 1941 had taken place. The case was held against Franz Magill and the men of the 2nd SS-Cavalry Regiment. The review made many interesting points, a summary of which can be mentioned here. The court was not convinced that Magill and his cohorts were killers, declaring them tools and assistants of someone else unknown. The manner of their contribution was based on their level of involvement in actions that led to fifty-two hundred Jews to be killed. The accused were known to have acted in the murder of the Jews, but it was unclear how independent their actions were. Under the Roman code of law, the court could not determine a clear answer to their criminality. The court turned to the military legal code (*Militärstraf-gesetzbuch*) in force from the outbreak of war in 1939. Under the prevailing military code, a subordinate knowingly carrying out an illegal order was guilty of criminal behavior. The accused had confessed that their orders had little to do with war. This had disturbed the troops, and the troops had also confessed to shooting Jews on the grounds only that they were Jews. This was recognized as racial policy and therefore illegal; thus, the men should have refused to carry out the order. The review stated that there were no exceptions and that the adjutant of the regiment, Walter Bornschauer, had no defense for "only" signing the orders. The review recommended proceedings against the cavalrymen.[98]

In March 1964, Gustav Lombard, the former commander of the 1st SS-Cavalry Regiment, found his way into the courts through a parallel review process. Martin Cüppers tracked down Lombard's case and found that the courts became entangled in whether the orders and the reports had been faked by Hermann Fegelein against Lombard's wishes. After nine years of proceedings, fifty files, and 230 witnesses, the case against Lombard ended. The state lawyers could not establish a strong enough case; there was just not enough proof of Lombard's personal desire to kill.[99]

Heinz Reinefarth was declared immune from prosecution because the British and Americans were not prepared to extradite him to Poland. The Poles requested his extradition in 1947 along with four other generals, including Heinz Guderian and Ernst Rode. The Americans placed a protective veil over these men, declaring them material witnesses to their trials. "These five generals are outstanding German military personalities and have been utilized during the past two years by the Historical and Intelligence agencies in Europe to prepare detailed studies on German operations during the past war," the U.S. Army declared in 1948. "In this capacity they have made positive valuable contribution to our intelligence effort on the USSR and satellites."[100] Many of the papers from the uprising have disappeared but just enough have survived to gain a picture of Kampfgruppe Reinefarth. By chance in 1958, Reinefarth became embroiled in a legal battle with Professor Thieme from Freiburg. On September 19, 1946, Reinefarth lied under oath to U.S. Army interrogators about his role in Warsaw, even denying that Dirlewanger was under his command.[101] Thieme challenged Reinefarth's evidence from Nuremberg. An article in *Der Spiegel* had mentioned Reinefarth and the Warsaw uprising. A reader had sent a letter, which had been published, and Reinefarth had sought legal redress. The evidence began to form that Reinefarth had ordered attacks on the Polish population. The records collected for the proceedings indicated that Reinefarth's denazification process had probably been incorrect; a polite way of suggesting that it was undermined by lies.

The *Spiegel* article posed three questions: had Reinefarth any connection with Dirlewanger; had he been involved in any war crimes; and could a case be made? Regarding the command relationships, the situation should have been clear-cut: Dirlewanger was under the command of Reinefarth.[102] French MacLean suggested the two hated each other so much that they nearly came to a duel.[103] Dirlewanger's personnel file includes his recommendation for the Knight's Cross from Reinefarth and endorsed by Bach-Zelewski. The recommendation included actions from April 24 and July 7, placing Reinefarth on the spot.[104] Reinefarth praised Dirlewanger's Warsaw performance as "daredevilry and pluck" (*Draufgängertum und Schneid*). This was confirmed by Bach-Zelewski, who mentioned that Dirlewanger had been wounded eleven times, confirming Reinefarth's opinion that he was only 50 percent fit. The record of incidents in Warsaw included the first day's fighting on August 5, in particular the storm of Litzmannstadtstrasse following Stuka and tank attacks; the capture of Adolf Hitler Platz and the relief of the army's Feldkommandantur on August 8; and the continuous fighting of September 3–5, 1944. All the while Reinefarth praised Dirlewanger's courage, leadership capability, and example to the troops. The 1958 article confirmed Reinefarth had been Dirlewanger's commander; but it then delved into more serious matters. Reinefarth pleaded innocence of any involvement in burnings and shootings. He claimed he had left Warsaw on September 3, 1944. Yet in his Knight's Cross award recommendation, it had been noted that he had personally directed the Stuka attacks, by the Luftwaffe on September 4–7, 1944. As to shootings, the article recommended that the judges reassess the records and examine an order signed by Reinefarth for the shooting of 196 civilians and the burning of another 155. The article thought that Reinefarth's offer on September 12, 1944, to Himmler of two captured sacks of tea required evaluation. The article blamed the leading German political parties, the CDU and SPD, for condoning Reinefarth. Calling Reinefarth the executioner of Warsaw (*Henker von Warschau*), it was suggested that with a thousand deaths to his name, he might have to reconsider his legal position. In the end the scandal led to nothing, and Reinefarth died in 1979, in retirement.

In 1974, two years after the death of Bach-Zelewski in the Landsberg prison, Judge Rudolf Ilgen recalled a long forgotten incident from a Sunday evening in the spring of 1933. Ilgen was sent to investigate the murder of a minor SPD functionary. Several men, believed to be SS, had called at the man's house and ordered him to attend an interrogation. The SS interrogated the victim near his house about the whereabouts of the "Iron Book" (*eiserne Buch*), allegedly containing a list of opponents to Nazism. Shots were overheard and the man was killed. The killers attempted to dump the body in a lake but were disturbed. The victim's body was recovered, and three SS men were arrested. The commanding officer of Frankfurt on the Oder SS-Standarte was SS-Oberführer Bach-Zelewski, and he arrived on the scene armed with a pistol. He requested details from Ilgen, who, although not obliged to, informed him of what had happened. Bach-Zelewski's immediate response was to dismiss as allegations any SS involvement, but he appeared to accept Ilgen's handling of the case and duly left the building. A short while later, Bach-Zelewski returned and advised Ilgen that he had investigated the scene and found evidence of the mark of three arrows, the symbol of the Iron Front, which he said proved they had carried out the killing. But there was no further proof of this, and by evening, the evidence confirmed that at least one of the SS men was guilty.

Bach-Zelewski left again only to return shouting that he would not allow the arrest of one of his men. This time, he refused to leave and began threatening Ilgen. All the while, an SS truck cruised around the justice building with the occupants ominously screaming, "Sieg Heil." Bach-Zelewski changed tack, requesting the accused men be placed under his custody and offering his word of honor that they would not escape. The senior court officials agreed, probably in fear of their own lives; they stated they did so under duress. Meanwhile, the main culprit was spirited away by Ilgen into full police custody. Realizing he had been duped, Bach-Zelewski lost all control and his face began to make nervous twitches (*zuckte*) from behind his spectacles. He abruptly composed himself and said, "I cannot go back, I fought the Poles to save Germany. In Upper Silesia, an old woman threw hot water out of the window at me. I ordered my comrades to 'beat her to death.'" Ilgen could only reply that that was war and this was murder and such behavior had to stop. Bach-Zelewski countered by suggesting that in two years this incident would be forgotten.[105] This book opened with Heinrich Heine's warning against the police, Thule, and the historical school and ends with William Shakespeare's observation, "The evil that men do lives after them."[106]

# CONCLUSION

In 1972, Erich von dem Bach-Zelewski, a lonely and decrepit old man, died in a German prison hospital. Eighty-one years earlier, his uncle was killed in a colonial skirmish that rendered shame on the German army and disgraced his family. In 1911, his father, an East Elbian Prussian Junker, died penniless in Dortmund. Four years later, his "stepfather" chaperoned him into war as a child soldier in the German army. Between 1915 and 1945, the boy was nurtured into a serial murderer and mass executioner. This dysfunctional family bred a man who was encouraged by Hitler to disfigure German history. Bach-Zelewski exploited his past to build a career. He exploited a flair for violence to produce favorable outcomes for his political leaders. In war, he was responsible for mass extermination across continental Europe. In his wake, West Germany suffered serious bouts of political violence. The challenge of the student revolution of 1968 inspired the Baader–Meinhof gang to acts of terrorism and crime. In 1972, during the Munich Olympic Games, a Palestinian terrorist hit squad killed Jewish athletes from the Israeli team. Detachments of German police and soldiers once again conducted procedures for Bandenbekämpfung to suppress the violence. These conditions seemed a fitting memorial to the godfather of Nazi Bandenbekämpfung, as well as a historical test of German democracy. Eventually, order was restored, Germany found confidence in democracy, and another old Nazi disappeared from memory.

Current thinking on the SS has rightly focused on its brutal methods during the occupation of Europe in the Second World War. Whether this was caused by Partisanenbekämpfung or Bandenbekämpfung is immaterial to the victims. Words, however, do matter, and the differences between the two concepts were significant. The key to understanding their differences lies in understanding security warfare. Nineteenth-century Western nationalism

301

encouraged the convergence of industrial society with the drive of imperialism and advances in warfare. One outcome saw the rise of the professional soldier; the other saw the formulation of security warfare. The great powers exploited security warfare for different ends: America to build the nation, Britain to expand the empire, and France to recapture Napoleonic grandeur. The German variety had origins drawn from the Thirty Years' War, but the Franco–Prussian War refined it. Germany institutionalized security to reinforce unification and install a guardianship of national interests. The German army later used the African colonies to hone its security warfare methods; it learned to practice brutality as a routine and extermination as a punishment. In 1914, this system was instrumental in sustaining Germany in total war against five other great powers and their empires. Thus, security warfare was a proven and reliable system in the mindset of professional German soldiers. It was, therefore, logical that Adolf Hitler trusted German security warfare in 1939.

Taken from another viewpoint, in the years just before the First World War, Germany looked set to craft the twentieth century. German science and industry had overtaken Britain and France. The education system supported Germany's drive to compete with the British Empire in international management ventures. German philosophy, music, and other cultural exploits were the envy of Europe. The economy had achieved an unusual mix of heavy industry, agriculture, and a fine sprinkling of modern financial and capital markets. Only America represented the greater power, but Germany had become the engine of Europe. Some scholars have argued that Germany took a wrong turn, while others have argued that Germany followed a "special road" that led to calamity. In 1989, after five regimes and two world wars, the much reduced borders of Germany were reunified. This seemed to confirm the "wrong turn" or the "wrong path"; however, which would have been the correct way? In one hundred years, from 1814, Germany followed a road from Napoleonic occupation through the defeat and occupation of France and a renewed invasion of France, along the way threatening the world with its military prowess. Defeat proved its weaknesses, revolution exposed its political frailties, and democratic politics served to shield Hitler until he came to power.

Bandenbekämpfung played its part in these events, through security warfare, and suited a growing preoccupation with guardianship. In 1870, Bismarck succinctly stated that two hundred years of French aggression had ended, but he failed to mention that it heralded forty-four years of obsessive security paranoia. Germany had been periodically ravaged by wars and, during the Thirty Years' War, had become a slaughterhouse, which left deep scars. After 1871, Germany joined a select band of great powers but trembled under growing self-doubt. This self-doubt, fixated on Germany's great power status, was rife in society by 1900. It was exaggerated. However, faced with competing notions of the national ideal, such as America's "manifest destiny," Germany responded with control of the population, society, and politics and economics. German Lebensraum in comparison to manifest destiny was reactionary and based on fears of failure or backwardness. Both concepts had tragic consequences for those swept away in their wake, but the American was generated from hope, whereas the German came from the harvest of despair.

What were the implications for Bandenbekämpfung? The two prominent features—an absence of technical "modernity" and the preponderance of "old school"–trained operatives—made Bandenbekämpfung that soul mate of Lebensraum. By 1872, Bandenbekämpfung was synonymous with countering guerrillas, or the franc-tireur. This idea was still being flaunted by Field Marshal von Rundstedt in 1944 to disqualify the French resistance from humane treatment. Small war principles were also drafted onto Bandenbekämpfung techniques to formulate the pursuit as a routine of security warfare. German operational rehearsals in the colonies had long-term consequences. The first was the adoption of search-and-destroy measures into Bandenbekämpfung techniques. The second found the protagonists of guerrilla warfare and their families as the first victims of genocide. There was no external intervention or army of liberation in Namibia (1904–12) to prevent the extermination of the Herero. By 1914, Bandenbekämpfung had established itself.

The First World War ensured the cruelties of colonial warfare were visited on continental Europe. In 1914, the German army conducted widespread executions of civilians excused on the grounds that the victims were franc-tireur. In East Africa, Germany's "Lion of Africa," Lettow-Vorbeck, conducted a sideshow guerrilla campaign. Upon arrival at home, his role in the Freikorps was to conduct an antiguerrilla campaign just as he had in Namibia in 1904–5. Lettow-Vorbeck was proved to be a military anachronism by the exploits of Franz Ritter von Epp. Epp helped develop security warfare beyond the experiences of China (1900) and Namibia (1904–7) and operations from the Great War to Munich (1919). Epp turned Bandenbekämpfung into a political weapon. The First World War ensured that security warfare was the preferred means of occupation, pacification, and intervention. The long-term impact of the security Cannae at Munich led to the continuation of Schlieffen dogma and the eventual adoption of Bandenbekämpfung as mainstream Nazi security policy.

Research for this book revealed some interesting parallels, the most pertinent being the impact of historical writing on the development of operational doctrines. Two dominating military thinkers of their time—American naval strategist Alfred T. Mahan and German chief of the general staff Alfred von Schlieffen—were reading Theodor Mommsen's *History of Rome* around the same time. Both took ideas from Hannibal's campaigns but arrived at very different conclusions.[1] Their interpretations not only shaped their respective national armies but came to influence the direction of the twentieth century. Roman antiquity was a popular means of erecting lessons for the future that were expounded by historians and teachers and left an indelible mark on the men who became the Nazi leadership. They were the product of an education system that stirred them to equal or surpass the past. Who can deny the power of historical writing on the future? The irony of Mommsen's classical interpretation serving as the engine for German and Nazi ambitions of empire is only surpassed by his continuing influence over the U.S. armed forces. In 1991, General Schwarzkopf, U.S. Army commander in Kuwait, attributed his victory over Iraq to the inspiring example of Hannibal and the Battle of Cannae. One day, soldiers and historians alike will realize the battle was only a Pyrrhic victory and the onset of defeat.

Where does this leave research into Bandenbekämpfung? As far as evidence, documentary and oral evidence have been interwoven. The documentary evidence was compiled from surviving captured records, including manuals, pamphlets, speeches, and various kinds of reports. The oral evidence was collected from a variety of sources. The SS-Police signals traffic generated decryption, translation, and interpretation. The content of the signals themselves ranged from orders to commit or report mass killings and simple personal family messages. There were also interrogation reports from the British and U.S. armies. Some military personnel had written memoirs of varying quality. Oral testimony included interrogations, expert witness statements, and courtroom testimony from war crimes trials. Because of concerns over the reliability of oral history, signals and interrogation testimony provided the vehicle for "overhearing" the perpetrators.

In 1979, a former member of the Prinz Eugen Division—witholding his given name—told some stories from his past. Using his nickname, "Bozo" explained that he had been an expert in the use of the flamethrower. He volunteered for the SS when he was eighteen years of age and transferred to the Prinz Eugen Division in 1943. Bozo's expertise included climbing mountains to reach the caves where members of Tito's partisan bands might be hiding. In the time of a quick "zap-zap," he sent two squirts of flame into the cave to "cook" everything. He had to ration the squirts, otherwise he would have had to spend the day climbing up and down the mountain to refuel rather than hunting across the peaks for the partisans. There was no talk of prisoners of war or white flags; just location, arrival, squirt, and on again. The procedure was explained in a snappy way, giving the impression of military precision. The story, although unpleasant, parallels to similar behavior by combatants from other countries during the war. There was one exception. Bozo became an "expert" in turning anyone who ran into a hurtling ball of flame. The effects of his work thirty-six years later caused him nightmares and flashbacks.[2] On June 5, 1994, a former member of the 2nd SS Panzer Division entered the German military cemetery of Le Cambe on the Normandy battlefield, walked directly to a particular grave, fell to his knees, and burst into uncontrolled tears. This story raises questions, such as should we be concerned with whether perpetrators suffer from post-traumatic stress disorder? Do we care?

Where did Bandenbekämpfung go? It is commonly understood that human experiences can pass through generations. It is perhaps conceivable that children who have absorbed the stories from their father's wartime experiences translate them into games. Two games played by German children have remarkable correlation with Bandenbekämpfung. The first was called *A-zerlatschen*, the aim of which was to destroy the "A." The "A" represented a prison camp (Arbeitslager), and when it was destroyed, all the inmates were freed. The other game was *Bandenkriegen*. The aim was to catch as many of the "Banden" as possible to win the game. In contrast, as a child growing up in Britain, I recall playing Robin Hood with my school friends. Could such games be, among other things, a means of historic transfer from one generation to the next?

Since my first gripping encounter with Christopher Browning's book *Ordinary Men: Reserve Police Battalion 101 and the Final Solution in Poland*, I have remained deferential to Browning's expertise. Although a constant companion to my research, Browning's book began to reveal its limitations. Its greatest drawback is its reliance on testimonies made over twenty-five years after the events. The "ordinary men" thesis cannot explain how Bozo did his job. It cannot rationalize his methods or his motivations. We still know little of where Nazi policy began, how it was implemented, or how it answered questions about resource marshaling, management decisions, and training methods. We need to know much more about the functions within organizations and work routines of German people of that time. This does not make the "ordinary men" thesis redundant. Rather, it forms part of the foundation for a deeper explanation of Nazism.

What are the implications for the study of post-1945 Bandenbekämpfung themes? It was a deliberate decision on my part to avoid comparisons with other countries and other wars. Counterinsurgency or asymmetric warfare represents a modern adaptation of British, French, and American security warfare traditions. For example, the circumstances of the U.S. Army's actions in Vietnam around 1968 might contain fleeting moments of patterns of behavior similar to the Germans' in occupied Russia in 1943, but they were not the same. The German troops differed in so many ways from the American soldiers that a separate book would be required to explain them all. While some American soldiers committed crimes in Vietnam, the majority of German troops committed to Bandenbekämpfung were guilty of heinous crimes. Indeed, they were officially encouraged to commit crimes. Where the study of security warfare beyond 1945 remains important is in how it was scattered into the many strands of modern security and warfare.

Munich was gripped by revolution in 1919 and by terrorism in 1972. The response of the new Weimar democracy in 1919 was to unleash Bandenbekämpfung. The Federal government's response in 1972 was to once again turn to Bandenbekämpfung. A nation gripped by terror will overreact. When the September 11 terrorist attacks turned security and insecurity into the key issues of the twenty-first century, we all became a little more imprisoned. The interventions in Iraq and Afghanistan in the name of security have contributed to further global disorder. The impulses to turn to Bandenbekämpfung still resonate. To extend security, raise response levels, stamp an official footprint on civil rights, and exploit the public's susceptibility to psychological pressure by governments: these are the phenomena that originally gave Bandenbekämpfung release. Scholars of the post-September 11 world, examining our perceptions of security, might examine the military abuse and political manipulation of Bandenbekämpfung.

# DIAGRAMS

## I. Organization of the Kommandostab Reichsführer SS (1941)

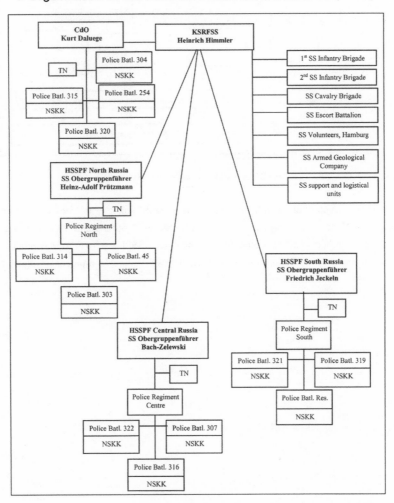

**Source:** Based upon documents from archives, the Rode testimony, and the KSRFSS diary of 1941.

## II. Chef der Bandenkampfverbände (Ch.BKV) June 1943

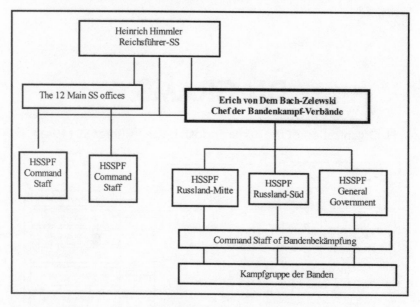

**Source:** Himmler's June 1943 order mentioned in chapter 4.

This diagram shows the establishment of the three HSSPF in the east (the exclusion of Russland-Nord was not explained), with the Bandenbekämpfung command staff and the formation of the Kampfgruppe. Each of the other HSSPF's were to form command staffs, but not a Kampfgruppe unless their territory was declared a Bandenkampfgebiet (a territory under antibandit warfare).

**III. Nachschubkommandantur der Waffen-SS und Polizei**

**SS-Obersturmbannführer Rudolf Pannier**
**Commander**
**Nachschubkommandantur der Waffen-SS und Polizei**

Latvia Scuma Company - 1 Officer, 7 NCOs, 134 Men

Labour Operations and Detachment - 1 Officer, 4 NCOs, 52 Men

Prison Camp and Base officer - 2 Officers, 1 NCO, 1 Man

**V** SS-O'stuf. Koing & SS-U'stuf Söllner — 16 NCOs, 81 Man
- Transport
- Motor vehicles

**IN** SS-H'stuf. Thon — 13 NCOs, 65 Man
- Signals
- Communication

**IVb** SS-O'stuf's. Dr.Schwaner & Dr. Reha — 1 NCO, 4 Men
- Medical Services
- Dental
- Surgeon

**VI** SS-O'stuf. Koch — 1 NCOs, 3 Man
- Propoganda

**IVa** SS-O'stuf's Wogler & Kanzy — 8 NCOs, 2 Men
- Commissary
- Pay
- Supplies
- Finance
- Buildings
- HIWIs

**IIa/b** SS-O'stuf Neupert — 5 NCOs, 7 Men
- Staff Company
- Adjutantur
- Officers
- Personnel
- Orders of the day
- Orders of the base

**Ic/III** SS-O'stuf Von Baer — 1 Man
- Ic: Intelligence, Recce, Defence, Bandit situation, Administration of regulations
- III: Justice and discipline, Arrests

**W.u.G** SS-O'stuf Schäfer — 6 NCOs, 22 Men
- Ordnance and Maintenance
- Workshops
- Advanced and basic weapon training
- Inspections
- Liaison with the army
- Vtl Dachau

**Ib** SS-O'stuf Walwarta — 1 NCO, 2 Men
- 8th Company CO
- Construction: Exercise grounds
- Training ground preparation
- Specialist live firing positions

**Ia** SS-Stumbaf. Beihack — 2 NCOs, 1 Man
- 2nd Company CO
- Cadre group supervisor
- Operations
- Security
- Transportation

**Source:** Found in chapter 7: NARA, RG242, BDC, A3343-SSO-364A, Rudolf Pannier, Tätigkeitsbericht für den Monat August, 6 September 1943. Military History Archive Prague (MHAP)/USHMM RS-48.004/roll 6, Ic Mitteilungen Nr.4, 5 March 1943. MHAP/USHMM RS-48.004/roll 6, Tätigkeitsbericht, 8 August 1943.

## IV. From Thule Society to Bandenkampfabzeichen

### Symbol of the Thule Society

The Thule-Gesellschaft (Thule Society) was founded in 1918 by Rudolf von Sebottendorff. He was an occultist, but his membership included Epp and other Nazis. Thule became the symbol for a German empire beyond Germany's existing borders.

### Bandenkampfabzeichen

The lineage of the Bandenkampfabzeichen is reveald. This illustrates how Himmler and Bach-Zelewski had sealed Epp's past and Germanic mythology into a medal for Lebensraum.

## V. Bach-Zelewski's Chain of Command, Warsaw (1944)

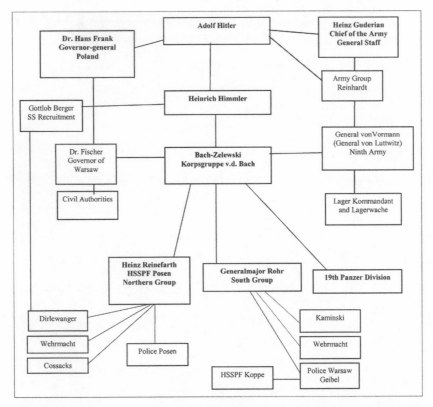

**Source:** Bach-Zelewski's evidence presented at the Polish war crimes trial in 1947, in Warsaw. This model was intended to explain why he had virtually no responsibility for the destruction and killing. His personal war diary tells a different story.

# APPENDIX 1:

## GLOSSARY OF BANDENBEKÄMPFUNG AND RELATED TERMINOLOGY

**Allgemeine-SS:** the General SS and central part of the SS, composed mainly of part-time volunteers.

**Arbeitererfassungsaktion:** Bandenbekämpfung action to round up labor under the pretext of security.

**Bagration:** Soviet name for the 1944 summer offensive.

**Banden:** bands.

**Bandenaufklärung:** bandit reconnaissance.

**Bandenbekämpfung:** bandit fighting or combating bands.

**Bandenfrauen:** women working with the band.

**Bandenhäuptling:** chieftain or leader of a locally raised and inspired band.

**Bandenkampfverbände (BKV):** combating band formations.

**Bandenkampfvorschrift:** instructions to combat the bands.

**Bandenkinder:** children from destroyed villages.

**Bandenlage:** bandit situation report.

**Bandentätigkeit:** band activity.

**Bandenunwesen:** band (criminal) activities.

**Bandenverdächtige:** bandit suspects.

**Bandenverseucht:** bandit diseased area.

**Banditen:** bandits.

**Barbarossa:** codename for the German invasion of Russia, June 22, 1941.

**Befehlshaber der Ordnungspolizei (BdO):** field or regional commander of the uniformed police.

**Befehlshaber der Sicherheitspolizei (BdS):** field or regional commander of the security police.

**Chef der Bandenkampfverbände (Ch.BKV):** commander of the formations for the combating of bands.

**Chef der Ordnungspolizei (CdO):** chief of the Order Police.

**Cottbus:** Bandenbekämpfung operation in Byelorussia in May–June 1943.

**Einsatzgruppen:** Task force, action group, SS/SD killing teams.

**Erfassungs:** registration of people, farm animals, and produce during Bandenbekämpfung.

**Ergänzungstelle:** recruiting center.

**Erledigt:** finished off; used to denote the killing or finishing off of persons.

**Ernteerfassungsaktion:** registration of harvests for plunder.

**Feldkommandantur:** Regional military government office.

**FHO:** Fremde Heere Ost; Foreign Armies East. The organisation for intelligence gathering in the east.

**FHQ:** Führerhauptquartier; Hitler's headquarters.

**Franc-tireur or frank-tireur:** French guerrillas during the Franco–Prussian War of 1870.

**Freikorps:** Free Corps or state-sponsored irregulars.

**Freischärler:** the freedom fighters (guerrillas).

**Frülingsfest:** Spring Festival; Bandenbekämpfung operation Byelorussia (April 1944).

**Führer:** Adolf Hitler or a leader in the SS; sometimes the commanding officer of an action or operation.

**Führerbefehl:** Hitler order.

**Führererlass:** Hitler decree or edict.

**Führer-Weisung:** Hitler directive.

**Gauleiter:** district leader of the Nazi Party responsible for administering a region or district (Gau).

**Gebirgsjäger:** mountain soldier.

**Geheime Staatspolizei (Gestapo):** Secret State Police.

**Geheimen Feldgendarmerie (GFP):** Secret Military Police.

**Generalgouvernment:** General Government of Poland, which was occupied rather than annexed by Germany.

**Generalstab:** chief of staff.

**Guerillakrieg:** guerrilla warfare.

**Hilfswillige (Hiwi):** Russian auxiliaries serving with German units on the Eastern Front.

**Höchste SS- und Polizeiführer (HstSSPF):** Supreme SS- and Police Leader Italy.

**Höhere SS- und Polizeiführer (HSSPF):** Higher SS and Police Leader.

**Ia:** first general staff officer operations officer.

**Ib:** second general staff officer (Supply).

**Ic:** third general staff officer (Intelligence).

**IN:** general staff officer (Signals).

**IO:** general staff (Ordnance).

**Kampfgruppe:** battle group.

**Kommandantur:** garrison headquarters.

**Kommandostab RFSS (KSRFSS):** Command Staff RFSS Headquarters staff of the Reichsführer-SS.

**Konzentrationslager (KZ):** concentration camp.

**Kriminalpolizei (Kripo):** criminal police division.

**Kugelblitz:** Bandenbekämpfung operation in Surazh Rayon, Belorussia (February 1943).

**Landespolizei:** state police.

**Landesschützen (Ldsch):** local defence force or a unit of Landwehr.

**Landsturm:** German reservists aged over thirty-nine.

**Landwehr:** German reservists up to age thirty-nine.

**Lebensraum (living space):** the concept of migrationist colonialism.

**Luftwaffe:** German air force.

**National Sozialistisches Kraftfahr-Korps (NSKK):** Nazi motor corps.

**Oberfeldkommandantur (OFK):** administrative headquarters in occupied territory.

**Oberkommando der Wehrmacht (OKW):** German High Command of the Armed Forces.

**Ordnungspolizei (Orpo):** Order Police, the Nazi regular uniformed beat police.

**Organisation Todt (OT):** a construction agency founded under Reich Minister for Armaments.

**OSS:** Office of Strategic Services, U.S. covert operations organization.

**Partisanen:** partisan

**Partisanenkrieg:** partisan warfare.

**Partisanentätigkeit:** partisan activity.

**Partisanenüberfall:** partisan operations.

**Polizei:** Police.

**Polizeigebietsführer (PGF):** police area commander, a title employed in Croatia by the SS-Police.

**Polizeiverwaltung (PV):** police administration, usually applied to precinct, district, or region.

**Quartiermeister (Qu):** quartermaster.

**Rasse- und Siedlungs-Hauptamt (RuSHA):** SS Main Office for Race and Settlements.

**Reichsarbeitsdienst (RAD):** Reich Labor Service.

**Reichskommissar:** the chief administrative officers of German occupied territories.

**Reichskommissariat Ostland:** administering Estonia, Lithuania, Latvia, and Byelorussia.

**Reichskommissariat Ukraine:** administering the Ukraine and occupied southern Russia.

**Reichssicherheitshauptamt (RSHA):** Main Office of State Security.

**Rückwärtigen Heeresgebiet (RHG):** Rear Area Command.

**Schutzmannschaften (Schuma):** collaboration units raised in Eastern Europe, Russia and the Ukraine.

**Schutzstaffel (SS):** guard squad of the Nazi Party.

**Schutztruppen:** German colonial troops raised in the colonies from the indigenous population.

**Sicherheitsdienst (SD):** SS intelligence service.

**Sicherheitspolizei (Sipo):** security police part of the SS.

**Sicherungs:** Security.

**Sicherungsdivision (SichD):** Security Division.

**Sicherungsregiment (SichR):** Security Regiment.

**Sonderkommando:** special command.

**SS-Totenkopfverbände**: Death's Formations.

**Volksdeutsche:** ethnic or racial Germans.

**Wach-Bataillon (WB):** watch battalion or guard battalion.

**Wasserschutzpolizei (WSP):** the Prussian river and coastal police force.

**Wehrmacht:** armed forces.

**Wehrmachtführungsstab:** Armed Forces Operations Staff.

**Weissruthenien:** White Ruthenia, Byelorussia, and Belorussia; western Russia.

**z.b.V.:** "zur besonderen Verwendung," usually attached to unit names to designate assignment to "special purposes."

# APPENDIX 2:

## GERMAN RANK STRUCTURES

| RANKS | ARMY | SS[1] | POLICE[2] |
|---|---|---|---|
| **Generals** | | | |
| Field Marshal | Generalfeldmarschall | Reichsführer-SS | |
| | | | Chef der Ordnungspolizei |
| Colonel General | Generaloberst | SS-Oberstgruppenführer | Generaloberst der Polizei |
| Brigadier General | General der Infanterie | SS-Obergruppenführer | General der Polizei |
| Lieutenant General | Generalleutnant | SS-Gruppenführer | Generalleutnant der Polizei |
| | Generalmajor | SS-Brigadeführer | Generalmajor der Polizei |
| | | | Polizeipräsident |
| **Field Officers** | | | |
| Colonel | Oberst | SS-Oberführer | Oberst |
| Lieutenant Colonel | Oberstleutnant | SS-Standartenführer | Oberstleutnant |
| Major | Major | SS-Obersturmbannführer | Major |
| | | SS-Sturmbannführer | |
| | | | |
| **Captain** | Hauptmann | SS-Hauptsturmführer | Hauptleute |
| | Rittmeister | | Hauptmann |
| | | | Bezirkshauptmann |
| | | | |
| **Lieutenants** | Oberleutnant | SS-Obersturmführer | Oberleutnant |
| | Leutnant | SS-Untersturmführer | Leutnant |
| | | | |
| **Senior NCOs** | Stabsfeldwebel | SS-Sturmscharführer | Meister |
| | Oberfeldwebel | SS-Hauptscharführer | Hauptwachtmeister |
| | Feldwebel | SS-Oberscharführer | Revieroberwachtmeister (Schupo) |
| | | . | Bezirksoberwachtmeister (FSP) |
| | | | |
| **Junior NCOs** | Unterfeldwebel | SS-Scharführer | Oberwachtmeister |
| | Unteroffizier | SS-Unterscharführer | Wachtmeister |
| | | | |
| **Troopers** | Stabsgefreiter | SS-Stabsrottenführer | |
| | Obergefreiter | SS-Rottenführer | Rottwachtmeister |
| | Gefreiter | SS-Sturmmann | Unterwachtmeister |
| | Oberschütze | SS-Oberschütze | |
| | Schütze | SS-Schütze | |
| | | SS-Mann | Anwärter |
| | | | Hilfspolizisten |

These are only the main ranks. There were many others that would make this table impractical.

1. All SS ranks began with the initials SS (SS-Obergruppenfuhrer).
2. All police general ranks concluded with "der Polizei" (Generalleutnant der Polizei).

# APPENDIX 3:

## THE PERPETRATORS

This is not an exhaustive list of all the men studied during this research, but a representative hall of shame.

**Bach-Zelewski, Erich von dem** (SS-Obergruppenführer): Born March 1, 1899, in Lauenberg (Lebork). HSSPF Russia-Centre (1941–44), Ch.BKV (1943–45). Died in prison in 1972, while serving a life sentence.

**Bader, Kurt** (Generalmajor der Ordnungspolizei und SS-Brigadeführer): Born February 26, 1899, studied law at Freiburg University. Served in the Great War as a Leutnant, took his doctorate in 1929. Expert in police law and regulation, joined the police in 1929, the Nazi Party in May 1932, and the SS in April 1933. Member of the Hauptamt Orpo administering codes of conduct of the police.[1]

**Becker, Herbert:** born May 13, 1887, in Torgau; served in the Great War as a Leutnant; and in 1919 he became a police captain in Marienwerder. He remained a senior police officer until captured by the U.S. Army in 1945.

**Berger, Gottlob** (SS-Obergruppenführer): born 1876. One of Himmler's favorites. Member of the main office of the SS; responsible for manpower and recruitment. Received a twenty-five-year sentence following the Ministries Trial No. 12.

**Bomhard, Adolf von** (Generalleutnant der Ordnungspolizei und SS-Brigadeführer): Epp's former regimental adjutant and Daluege's deputy. Be-

---

1. NARA, T1270/23/1602, interrogation of Kurt Bader, Generalmajor der Orpo, March 25, 1947.

came inspector of training schools and downplayed his participation in Nazi crimes and was released as unimportant to the war crimes process. In the 1950s, he defied all attempts by the Federal Republic of Germany to denazify the Federal police.[2]

**Daluege, Kurt Max Moritz** (SS-Oberstgruppenführer): born in Kreuzburg in Upper Silesia, September 15, 1897. Chef der Ordnungspolizei (1936–43). His nickname was "Dummi-Dummi." Executed in Prague in 1946.

**Dirlewanger, Oskar Dr.** (SS-Oberführer): born 1895. Commanding officer of Special Battalion Dirlewanger (1942–44). Killed while in captivity 1945.

**Epp, Franz Ritter von:** born in Munich, October 16, 1868. Former soldier and later the Nazi state leader of the Colonial Political office; represented the party in the Reichstag and governor of Bavaria. Died in U.S. captivity December 31, 1945.

**Fegelein, Hermann** (SS-Gruppenführer): born 1906. Commander of SS cavalry division Florian Geyr and from 1943 Himmler's adjutant to Hitler. Hitler ordered his summary execution for cowardice in April 1945.

**Frank, Karl Hermann** (SS-Gruppenführer): born 1898. Protector of Bohemia-Moravia from 1943. Executed in Prague in May 1946.

**Gempp, Friedrich** (Generalmajor): born in Freiburg/Br in July 1873. He joined the army in 1893 and became a Leutnant in 1895. He served throughout the period 1893 to 1943. For the majority of that time, he was with the German army intelligence service under Oberst Nicolai and later Admiral Canaris. Missing since 1946.

**Globocnik, Odilo** (SS-Gruppenführer): born in Trieste in 1900. Responsible for *Aktion Reinhard* the systematic murder of the Jews in Poland. Committed suicide in May 1945. His nickname was "Globus."

**Gottberg, Curt von** (SS-Obergruppenführer): Gottberg became Bach-Zelewski's substitute as HSSPF Russia-Centre in the latter half of 1942 and also replaced Wilhelm Kube as Reichskommissariat in 1943. Committed suicide in May 1945.

**Hannibal, Heinrich Friedrich Wilhelm** (Oberst der Schutzpolizei and SS-Standartenführer): born November 19, 1889, Protestant, served through-

---

2. NARA, T1270/23/0519, interrogation of Adolf von Bomhard, June 27, 1945.

out the Great War. Joined the Hamburg Schutzpolizei on July 16, 1920, and the Nazi Party on February 1, 1932. Initially in the SA, on May 1, 1939, he became an SS-Sturmbannführer. Formed Kampfgruppe Hannibal, subject to one of Hitler's last recorded military conferences. Surrendered in Königsberg in February 1945.

**Jeckeln, Friedrich** (SS-Obergruppenführer): born in 1895; became a professional soldier. Early member of the SS and Nazi Party, the HSSPF Russia-North. He was hanged in Riga in 1946.

**Jedicke, Georg Bruno** (Generalleutnant der Ordnungspolizei and SS-Gruppenführer): born March 26, 1887, in Dresden. Regarded as seventh in line from Daluege. In 1940, he became Befehlshaber der Ordnungspolizei (BdO) Saarland, Elsaß, and Lothringen and BdO Ostland, 1941–44.

**Jüttner, Hans** (SS-Obergruppenführer): born 2 March 1894 in East Prussia, the son of a schoolteacher. Chief of staff of the Waffen-SS (1940–45). Himmler's deputy in the Reserve Army after July 20, 1944. Died in the 1970s.

**Kaltenbrunner, Dr. Ernst** (SS-Obergruppenführer): born in 1903, in Austria. Joined the Austrian SS in 1931. In 1943, he was promoted to take Heydrich's position at the RSHA. He brought Skorzeny to the SD in June 1943. He was regarded as the significant SS representative at Nuremberg, found guilty of war crimes in 1946, and executed.

**Korn, Ernst** (Oberstleutnant der Schutzpolizei): born June 11, 1899. Served in the army in the 8th Jäger Battalion (1917–18) as a lieutenant. Served with 213th Security Division and then as battalion commander of the 1st Police Rifle Regiment. During the Nuremberg Tribunals, he was the only witness to testify against Bach-Zelewski in the courtroom.

**Krüger, Friedrich-Wilhelm** (SS-Obergruppenführer): born May 8, 1894, in Alsace. A professional soldier (1913); served in the Freikorps and joined the Nazi Party in 1925. Became HSSPF Ost and controlled the police and security in the General Government. Committed suicide in May 1945.

**Lammerding, Heinz** (SS-Brigadeführer): born in Dortmund August 27, 1905, and qualified as building engineer from the Munich Technical University. He was a highly regarded protégé of Theodor Eicke and rose through the rank of the SS officer corps. Died in Germany in 1970.

**Lettow-Vorbeck, Paul von** (General of Infantry): The "Lion of East Africa" was born in 1870. He served under von Trotha in China and Namibia. Took command of the German East African Schutztruppen in 1914. Participated in the Freikorps attempted coup, Kapp putsch; critical of the Nazis but not a major opponent. Died in Hamburg in 1962.

**Lombard, Gustav** (SS-Brigadeführer): born April 10, 1895, and joined the SS May 1, 1933, and the Nazi Party April 1, 1933. March 1941 to December 28, 1943, was with the 1st SS-Cavalry Regiment. On January 15, 1944, became commander of Stossgruppe v.d.Bach.

**Lurker, Otto** (SS-Standartenführer): born July 28, 1896, in Griesheim. A businessman with two semesters at commercial school. He joined the SS on April 1, 1929. Rösener's chief of intelligence 1941–44?. He had the notoriety of being Hitler's prison warder at Landsberg.

**Pannier, Rudolf** (SS-Standartenführer): born July 10, 1897, in Gera, protestant, businessman by profession. Served 1917–18, served in a Reserve Battalion on the Eastern Front. Was in the Freikorps 1919–20. Between May 1943 and April 1944 he was the supply officer for the HSSPF Russia-Centre.

**Pannwitz, Helmut von** (general of cavalry): commander of all Cossack forces under German command; an acquaintance of Bach-Zelewski and a senior participant in the Buchrucker putsch of 1923. Hanged in Moscow in January 1947.

**Pfeffer-Wildenbruch, Karl von** (SS-Obergruppenführer und Generalleutnant der Polizei): "top soldier" of the Order Police. Joined the army in 1907 as an artillery officer, served on the Eastern Front, in the military mission to Baghdad in 1917, and on the Western Front. In 1919, joined the Prussian Schutzpolizei, served in staff positions, became member of the Nazi Party in 1932, assigned to Chile during the Chaco War and became inspector of police training schools. In 1938, he joined the SS and took command of the SS Polizei Division in 1939. Became inspector of the colonial police and served as an SS corps commander. Died in retirement in 1965.

**Phleps, Artur** (SS-Obergruppenführer): born in Siebenbürgen, Rumania, in 1881. A career soldier from 1896, first with the Austrian army, then as a general of the Rumanian army, and finally with the Waffen, from 1941. Killed while serving as SS V Mountain Corps commander in 1944.

**Prützmann, Hans-Adolf** (SS-Obergruppenführer): Joined the SS and Nazi Party in 1930. Became HSSPF Russia-South, later the leader of the Wehrwolves. Committed suicide in British captivity in May 1945.

**Reinefarth, Heinz** (SS-Gruppenführer): born 1903 in Cottbus, a Protestant later turned believer (*gottgläubig*). Studied law in Jena and, in 1932, joined the SS and the Nazi Party. He was a member of the German Police Comrades Association (*Kameradschaftsbundes Deutscher Polizeibeamten*) where he came into contact with Kurt Daluege, for whom he conducted legal work. Served with the army in Poland and France; he received the Knight's Cross. In January 1942, he joined Himmler's staff, rising to the rank of SS-Brigadeführer and Generalmajor der Polizei. In February 1944, he became the HSSPF Warthegau, an area of Poland. After the war, he was elected town mayor in Schleswig-Holstein and died in 1979.[3]

**Rode, Ernst** (Generalmajor der Ordnungspolizei und SS-Brigadeführer): born in 1894, in Silesia. A Protestant, Freikorps (1919), Schutzpolizei (1920), Nazi Party (May 1930), and the SS. Chief of staff to both the KSRFSS and Ch. BKV.

**Rösener, Erwin** (SS-Gruppenführer): born 1902, joined the Nazi Party in 1926 and the SS in 1929. Served in the Aachen SA until 1929, became the president of Aachen police and HSSPF Alpenland (1941). Executed in Yugoslavia in 1946.

**Schenckendorff, Heinrich Moritz Albert von** (general of infantry): born in 1875. By 1914, a battalion commander; commander of the 29th Infantry Regiment (1918), 13th Border Defence Guard (1939), and general of infantry (1940). Became commander of the rear-area command of Army Group Centre on the May 15, 1941. Died in service of a heart attack in July 1943.[4]

**Skorzeny, Otto** (SS-Obersturmbannführer): born in 1908, Catholic, in Austria. He joined the Nazi Party in 1932 and the SS in 1934. He escaped from Nuremberg, and justice, in 1946, and remained in exile for the rest of his life and died in 1975.

**Sporrenberg, Jakob** (SS-Gruppenführer): SS officer. Born in Düsseldorf, in 1902. In 1923, under the French occupation authorities, he was given two years' imprisonment for illegal activities associated with the Nazi Party in the Ruhr. He served in Russia from August 1941 as SSPF Minsk under Bach-Zelewski. Joined the 2nd SS-Police Police Regiment in 1943 to gain Bandenbekämpfung experience. In August 1943, Sporrenberg became SS and Police Leader in the Lublin district. Responsible for the implementation of Aktion Erntefest, the killing of 42,000 Jews. Captured by the British and subsequently executed by the Polish government in 1952.

---

3. NARA, RG242, BDC, A3345-OSS-231, Heinz Reinefarth.
4. BA-MA, MSg 109 / 10852.

**Strauch, Eduard** (SS-Obersturmbannführer): born in Essen in August 1906, he joined the SS in 1931. Was a lawyer by profession and became one of Heydrich's senior SD officers. In February 1942, he was the commander of the SIPO and SD in Russia-Centre. In July 1943, he was assigned to Ch.BKV as intelligence officer (Ic). Diagnosed insane in 1947.

**Streckenbach, Bruno:** born 1902 and served in the Freikorps. He joined the Nazi Party and the SS. He rose to seniority in the RSHA (Office I personnel). He led Einsatzgruppe I in Poland. Joined the Florian Geyer, SS Cavalry Division. Captured by the Russians, he remained a prisoner until 1955. Avoided criminal proceedings in 1973 owing to ill health and died in 1977.

**Stroop, Jürgen** (SS-Gruppenführer): born September 26, 1895, in Detmold. Served in the infantry in the Great War and joined the Nazis in 1932. Rose steadily through the SS ranks and served in several SSPF functions in Poland prior to the uprising in 1943. Captured in 1945, he was executed in Warsaw in 1952.

**Tensfeld, Willy** (SS-Obergruppenführer): born November 27, 1893, in Schleswig-Holstein. He served in the navy from 1909 to 1923 as a sailor, in the U-Boat service, and in the Freikorps. He joined the SS on September 1, 1931, and the party in November 1931. SSPF Upper Italy until 1945.

**Trotha, Lothar von** (general of infantry): born July 3, 1848, in Magdeburg, studied at Gymnasium and the University of Berlin. Between 1865 and 1871 von Trotha's career developed from officer cadet to battalion adjutant with the 47th Infantry Regiment. He joined the military expedition to China. He came home to become commander of the 16th Infantry Division in Trier. He took command of the expedition to German South-West Africa on May 16, 1904. On May 21, 1906, he was placed in reserve. He died in retirement, in Bonn, in 1920.[5]

**Warlimont, Walter** (general of artillery): born in 1894, in Westphalia. Operations officer (Ia) of the operational orders department (*Wehrmachtführungsstab* or WFSt.) of the OKW, carrying out planning behind strategies and operations.

**Winkelmann, Otto** (Generalleutnant der Polizei und SS-Obergruppenführer): born in 1894, studied law, and became a professional soldier. He became a police officer with the Schutzpolizei. He joined the Nazi Party in 1932 and the SS in 1938. He joined Daluege's Hauptamt Ordnungspolizei, respon-

5. BA-MA, MSg 109 10872

sible for the command group. He became HSSPF Hungary until transferred to police operations in southern Europe; he died in 1977.[6]

**Wolff, Karl** (SS-Oberstgruppenführer): born in Darmstadt in May 1900. In April 1917, he became a Leutnant from September 1918 (having been a cadet for a year), in the 116th Hessian Life Guards. At the end of the war, he served in the Hessian Freikorps in 1919. He joined the SS and Nazi Party in 1931, becoming Himmler's personal adjutant.

**Wünnenberg, Alfred** (SS-Gruppenführer and Generalleutnant der Ordnungspolizei): born in 1891 in Saarburg, in the Lorraine region. Alfred Wünnenberg took over the Ordnungspolizei in 1943 when Daluege was forced to retire.

**Zelewski, Emil von:** uncle of Bach-Zelewski. The Schutztruppe commander in Tanzania, he was killed in 1891 at the Battle of Rugaro, by members of the HeHe tribe. A memorial for him was erected by Carl Peters, but he was always remembered for his disastrous performance in the battle that led to his death.[7]

**Zenner, Carl** (SS-Brigadeführer und Generalmajor der Polizei): born in 1899. A veteran of the First World War and the Freikorps. Former Aachen president of police became SSPF Weissruthenien until May 1942. Ended the war in SS requisitioning. Received a five-year sentence in 1945 and a fifteen-year sentence in 1961.[8]

---

6. Mark C. Yerger, *Allgemeine-SS: The Commands, Units and Leaders of the General SS* (Winnepeg, Canada: J. J. Fedorowicz, 1997), 58.
7. A story of Emil von Zelewski, written by Carl Peters, can be located in the personnel file of Bach-Zelewski.
8. Yerger, *Allgemeine-SS*, 112.

# APPENDIX 4:

## THE MIXED FORTUNES OF FORMER BANDENKAMPFVERBÄNDE IN 1965[1]

**Erich von dem Bach-Zelewski:** serving a life sentence in Landsberg prison.

**Friedrich Beck:** SS-Sturmbannführer, commander Bandenkampfschule; in 1965 Polizeirat in Darmstadt.

**Erich Haasche:** former Gendarmerie Hauptmann, in Lutsk and Warsaw uprising; in 1965, police director in Lower Saxony.

**August Hanner**: commander of the III Battalion, Police Regiment "Todt" and commander of 105th Schutzmannschaft Battalion; in 1965, Polizeirat Hamburg.

**Ludwig Hödel:** SS-Untersturmführer in Bandeneinsatz, Hauptmann in 3rd SS-Police Regiment; director of the Bavarian Border Police.

**Kurt Huhn:** Hauptmann, company commander in 14th SS-Police Regiment; in 1965, police official, group commander of U.S. sector in West Berlin.

**Helmut Kiehne:** Oberleutnant der Schupo, mounted police section BdO Ukraine, conducting Bandeneinsatz; in 1965, chief police commissioner, Hamburg.

**Hermann Kraiker:** Major der Schupo, Kampfgruppe Prützmann; in 1965, police official in Bochum, Ruhr.

**Hubert Marbach:** company commander of an SD-Einsatzgruppen and member of the 2nd SS-Police Regiment; in 1965, director of the Landespolizei school in Bonn.

**Paulus Meier:** mass-murder operations while battalion commander, 9th Police Battalion and II Battalion, 14th SS-Police Regiment; in 1965, Polizeirat Bonn.

1. DDR (ed.), *Braunbuch: Kriegs- und Naziverbrecher in der Bundesrepublik*, (Berlin: Staatsverlag Der Deutschen Demokratischen Republik, 1965), 86–103.

**Konstantin Neher:** Gendarmerie Hauptmann in the 30th Waffen-SS Grenadier Division; in 1965, director of Landespolizei District Commissar, Württemberg.

**Herbert Poethke:** SS-Hauptsturmführer and Oberleutnant der Schupo, Einsatzkommando in the east; in 1965, Polizeioberkommissar in Mönchengladbach.

**Karl Pötke:** Hauptmann der Schupo, Einsatzkommando, commander II Battalion, 16th SS-Police Regiment; in 1965, director of Schupo (Ia) in Hamburg.

**Heinz Reinefarth:** HSSPF Warthe, Warsaw uprising; in 1965, mayor of Westerland/Sylt.

**Friedrich Röhl:** BdO Riga, Hauptmann der Gendarmerie; in 1965, director of the Landespolizeischule Rheinland-Pfalz.

**Christian Steeger:** 27th SS-Police Regiment and III Battalion, 15th SS-Police Regiment; in 1965, senior police official in Linz.

**Werner Terrèe:** Leutnant der Schupo, II Battalion 2nd SS-Police Regiment in Bialystok; in 1965, director of a police section in the district of Osnabrück.

**Otto Winkelmann:** director of the Hauptamt Ordnungspolizei, HSSPF Hungary; in 1965, retired police official on a full pension.

# NOTES

## Preface

1. Woodruff D. Smith, *The Ideological Origins of Nazi Imperialism* (Oxford: Oxford University Press, 1986).
2. Fritz Fischer, *Germany's Aims in the First World War* (New York: Norton, 1967). See also Oleh S. Fedyshyn, *Germany's Drive to the East and the Ukrainian Revolution 1917–1918* (New Brunswick, N.J.: Rutgers University Press, 1971).
3. Frank Ebeling, *Geopolitik: Karl Haushofer und seine Raumwissenschaft 1919–1945* (Berlin: Akad-Verlag, 1994); and David T. Murphy, *The Heroic Earth: Geopolitical Thought in Weimar Germany 1918–1933* (Kent, Ohio: Kent State University, 1997).
4. Ian Kershaw, *Hitler 1889–1936: Hubris* (London: Allen Lane, 1998), 249.
5. Adolf Hitler, trans. Ralph Manheim, *Mein Kampf*, Intro. D. C. Watt (London: Pimlico, 1992), 598.
6. *Brockhaus' Konverations–Lexicon* (Leipzig: Brockhaus Verlag, 1908), 338–9.
7. Uwe Danker, "Bandits and the State: Robbers and the Authorities in the Holy Roman Empire in the Late Seventeenth and Early Eighteenth Centuries," in Richard J. Evans, *The German Underworld: Deviants and Outcasts in German History* (London: Routledge, 1988), 75–107.
8. Victor Klemperer, *LTI [Lingua, Tertii, Imperii]: Notizbuch eines Philologen* (Leipzig: Reclam, 1985), 168–70; Martin Brady (trans.), *The Language of the Third Reich* (London: Continuum, 2002), 172–3; and Josephus, trans. G. A. Williamson, *The Jewish War* (London: Penguin, 1978). According to the librarians of the Augustus Bibliothek, in Wolfenbüttel, the book first entered the German university system in Lübeck (1475) and was later translated into German.
9. Alfred Andersch, *Der Vater eines Mörders* (Zurich: Diogenes, 1980), 38.
10. Heinrich Clementz, *Geschichte des Judischen Krieges*, (1900), republished (Fourier Verlag, Wiesbaden, 1997).
11. *Table Talk*, 253.
12. Martin Van Creveld, *On Future War* (London: Brassey's, 1991), 129.
13. Richard Overy, *Interrogations: Inside the Minds of the Nazi Elite* (London: Allen Lane, 2002), 482 and 486.
14. *Der Grosse Brockhaus, Handbuch des Wissens* (Leipzig, Brockhaus, 1929), 273.
15. Philip W. Blood, "Bandenbekämpfung, Nazi Occupation Security in Eastern Europe and Soviet Russia, 1942–45," (PhD diss., Cranfield University, 2001).

16. Philip W. Blood, "Kurt Daluege and the Militarisation of the Ordnungspolizei," in Gerrard Oram (ed.), *Conflict and Legality: Policing Mid-Twentieth Century Europe* (London, Francis Boutle, 2003).

## Chapter 1: Security Warfare

1. Harold D. Lasswell, "The Garrison States," *American Journal of Sociology* 46, (1941), 455–68; and "The Garrison-State Hypothesis Today," in Samuel P. Huntington (ed.), *Changing Patterns of Military Politics* (New York: Free Press, 1962), 51–70.
2. Gordon A. Craig, *The Politics of the Prussian Army 1640–1945* (New York: Oxford University Press, 1955), 52–3.
3. Hans-Ulrich Wehler, *The German Empire 1871–1918* (Warwickshire: Berg, 1985), 57–8.
4. Alfred Vagts, *A History of Militarism: Civilian and Military* (Toronto: Meridian, 1959), 382.
5. Craig, *The Politics of the Prussian Army*, 252–3.
6. Jeffrey Verhey, *The Spirit of 1914: Militarism, Myth and Mobilisation in Germany* (Cambridge: Cambridge University Press, 2000).
7. John Shy, "Jomini," in Peter Paret (ed.), *Makers of Modern Strategy: From Machiavelli to the Nuclear Age* (Princeton: Princeton University Press, 1986), 143–85.
8. Michael Howard, *War in European History* (Oxford: Oxford University Press, 1976), 96.
9. Crane Brinton, Gordon A. Craig, and Felix Gilbert, "Jomini," in Edward Mead Earle (ed.), *Makers of Modern Strategy: Military Thought from Machiavelli to Hitler* (Princeton: Princeton University Press, 1971), 77–92.
10. Edwin A. Pratt, *The Rise of Rail Power, In War and Conquest* (London: P. S. King, 1915); and Martin van Creveld, *Supplying War: Logistics from Wallenstein to Patton* (Cambridge: Cambridge University Press, 1977).
11. Albert von Boguslawski, *Der kleine Krieg und seine Bedeutung für die Gegenwart* (Berlin: Luckardt, 1881). The lectures presented to the German Military Society in Posen in 1880.
12. Lonsdale Hale, "Partisan warfare," *Journal of the Royal United Services Institute* 30 (1885), 135–64.
13. Ibid., 137.
14. Francis Lieber, "Guerrilla Parties Considered with Reference to the Laws and Usages of War," was written at the request of Maj. Gen. Henry W. Halleck (August 1862). For a broader study of Lieber and his work, see Richard Shelly Hartigan, *Lieber's Code and the Law of War* (Chicago: Precedent, 1983).
15. Ian F. W. Beckett, *Encyclopaedia of Guerrilla Warfare* (Santa Barbara, Calif.: ABC-CLIO, 1999), ix.
16. J. H. Morgan, *The War Book of the German General Staff: Being "The Usages of War on Land,"* Issued by the Great General Staff of the German Army (New York: McBride, Nast, 1915).
17. Ernst Fraenkel, *Military Occupation and the Rule of Law* (Oxford: Oxford University Press, 1944).
18. Morgan, *The German War Book*, 64.
19. Manfred Botzenhart, "French Prisoners of War in Germany, 1870–71," in Stig Förster and Jörg Nagler (eds.), *On the Road to Total War* (New York: Cambridge University Press, 1997), 588.
20. Geoffrey Best, *Humanity in Warfare,* (London: Routledge, 1980), 194.
21. Alon Confino, *The Nation as a Local Metaphor: Württemberg, Imperial Germany and National Memory, 1871–1918* (Chapel Hill: University of North Carolina, 1997).
22. Theodor Lindner, *Der Krieg gegen Frankreich* (Berlin: Asher, 1895), 42.
23. Ibid., 77.

24. Ibid., 43.
25. Mark Stoneman, "The Bavarian Army and French Civilians in the War of 1870–1871: A Cultural Interpretation," *War in History* 8 (2001), 271–93.
26. Lindner, *Der Krieg gegen Frankreich,* 102–15.
27. Ibid., 113–15.
28. Ibid., 30–1.
29. Robert T. Foley, *Alfred von Schlieffen's Military Writings* (London: Frank Cass, 2003), 219–26.
30. Gunther E. Rothenberg, "Moltke, Schlieffen and the Doctrine of Strategic Envelopment," in Paret (ed.), *Makers of Modern Strategy,* 313–15.
31. Telford Taylor, *Sword and Swastika: Generals and Nazis in the Third Reich* (New York: Barnes and Noble Books, 1995), 12.
32. Foley, *Alfred von Schlieffen's Military Writings,* xv.
33. Wehler, *The German Empire,* 148–52, reference to the "modern Cannae."
34. Volker Berghahn, *Imperial Germany 1871–1914: Economy, Society, Culture and Politics* (Oxford: Berghahn, 1994), 88–9.
35. "Peter Purzelbaum" and H. C. von Zobeltitz (eds.), *Das Alte Heer: Erinnerungen an die Dienstzeit bei allen Waffen* (Berlin: Heinrich Beenken, 1931).
36. Foley, *Alfred von Schlieffen's Military Writings,* 208–218.
37. Christopher Dandeker, "The Bureaucratisation of Force," in Lawrence Freedman (ed.), *War* (Oxford: Oxford University Press, 1992), 118–23.
38. Justus Hashagen, *Das Rheinland und die Französische Herrschaft* (Bonn: Hanstein, 1908).
39. Michael Howard, *The Franco–Prussian War* (London: Rupert Hart-Davis, 1961), 377–8.
40. Creveld, *Supplying War,* 75–108.
41. "Instruktion, betreffend das etappen- und eisenbahnwesen und die obere leitung des feld-intendantur – feld sanitäts-, militär-telegraphen- und feld-post wesens im kriege [*sic*]" (Berlin, 1872), trans. Wilbraham Lennox, trans. Donatus O'Brien, *Prussian Etappen Regulations* (London: W. Lennox, 1875).
42. Rudolf Thierfelder, *Die Verwaltung der besetzten französischen Gebiete 1870/73,* (Darmstadt: Wittich, 1943), 9–13.
43. Michael Rowe, "German Civil Administrators and the Politics of the Napoleonic State in the Department of the Roer, 1798–1815," Sidney Sussex College, Cambridge, Ph.D. diss., 1996, 344–57.
44. Refer to Thierfelder, *Die Verwaltung.*
45. Dieter Fricke, *Bismarcks Prätorianer: Die Berliner politische Polizei im Kampf gegen die Deutsche Arbeiterbewegung (1871–1898)* (Berlin: DDR, 1962), 23.
46. NARA, RG319, IRR, Wilhelm Krichbaum (Chef der GFP) and Franz Groshek (GFP director) Geheime Feldpolizei (1947).
47. Fricke, *Bismarcks Prätorianer,* 24–5.
48. BA MA, RW 5/v, series of Kriegsministerium Papers from the office of Generalmajor z. V. Gempp; Geheimer Nachrichtendienst und Spionageabwehr des Heeres, book 654 (hereafter referred to as the Gempp papers).
49. Ibid, 118–31.
50. Arne Perras, *Carl Peters and German Imperialism 1856–1918* (Oxford: Oxford University Press, 2004), 129. Zelewski allegedly desecrated a mosque when he marched inside with his boots on wearing his hunting dogs.
51. Jan-Bart Gewalt, "Learning to Wage and Win Wars in Africa: A Provisional History of German Military Activity in Congo, Tanzania, China and Namibia," African Studies Centre, Leiden, The Netherlands, ASC Working Paper No. 60, 2005.
52. Perras, *Carl Peters,* 201; Kirsten Zirkel, "Military Power in German Colonial Policy: The Schutztruppen and Their Leaders in East and South-West Africa, 1888–1918," in David Killingray and David Omissi (eds.), *Guardians of Empire: The Armed Forces of the Colonial Powers c.1700–1964* (Manchester: Palgrave, 2000), 91–113; and Mann, *Mikono ya damu: "Hands of Blood."*
53. Walter Goerlitz, trans. Brian Battershaw, *History of the German General Staff, 1657–1945* (New York: Praeger, 1957), 125.

54. Gerd Fesser, "Pardon wird nicht gegeben!" *Die Zeit* Nr. 31, July 27, 2000, 17.
55. Josef Krumbach, *Franz Ritter von Epp: Ein Leben für Deutschland* (Munich: Brunnen, 1938), 175.
56. Ibid., 169.
57. Max Menzels, *Dienstunterricht des deutschen Infanteristen* (Berlin: R.Eisenschmidt, 1913), xxvi.
58. Gerhardus Pool, *Samuel Maherero* (Windhoek: Gamsberg Macmillan, 1991), 269, 272–4.
59. Kurd Schwabe, *Der Krieg in Deutsch-Südwestafrika 1904–1906* (Berlin: Weller, 1907), 372.
60. Ibid., 306.
61. Helmut Bley, *Namibia under German Rule* (Hamburg: LIT, 1996).
62. Horst Drechsler, *"Let us die fighting": The Struggle of the Herero and Nama against German Imperialism* (London: Zed Press, 1980); and "The Hereros of South-West Africa (Namibia)," in Frank Chalk and Kurt Jonassohn, *The History and Sociology of Genocide: Analyses and Case Studies* (New Haven, Conn.: Yale University Press, 1990), 242.
63. Tilman Dedering, "A Certain Rigorous Treatment of All Parts of the Nation, The Annihilation of the Herero in German South-West Africa, 1904," in Mark Levene and Penny Robert, *The Massacre in History* (New York: Berghahn, 1999), 223–46.
64. Ibid., 215–18.
65. Schwabe, *Der Krieg in Deutsch-Südwestafrika,* 374.
66. Ibid., 375.
67. Menzels, *Dienstunterricht des deutschen Infanteristen,* xxvi.
68. Schwabe, *Der Krieg in Deutsch-Südwestafrika,* 376.
69. Menzels, *Dienstunterricht des deutschen Infanteristen,* xxvii–xvi.
70. Patricia Hayes, Jeremy Silvester, Marion Wallace, and Wolfram Hartmann (eds.), *Namibia under South African Rule: Mobility and Containment, 1915–46* (Abington, Oxon: James Currey, 1998), 17.
71. Hayes et al. (eds.), *Namibia under South African Rule,* 60–7.
72. Jürgen Zimmerer, *Deutsche Herrschaft Über Afrikaner: Staatlicher Machanspruch und Wirklichkeit im kolonialen Namibia* (Münster: LIT, 2001).
73. Bley, *Namibia under German Rule,* 163.
74. Schwabe, *Der Krieg in Deutsch-Südwestafrika,* 36.
75. Gesine Krüger, *Kriegsbewältigung und Geschichtsbewußtsein: Realität, Deutung und Verarbeitung des deutschen Kolonialkriegs in Namibia 1904 bis 1907* (Göttingen: Vandenhoeck & Ruprecht, 1999), 62–3.
76. Bley, *Namibia under German Rule,* 167.
77. Krumbach, *Franz Ritter von Epp,* 179.
78. John Horne and Alan Kramer, *German Atrocities 1914: A History of Denial* (New Haven, Conn.: Yale University Press, 2001); and John Horne and Alan Kramer, "War Between Soldiers and Enemy Civilians," in Roger Chickering and Stig Förster, *Great War, Total War: Combat and Mobilization on the Western Front, 1914–1918* (Cambridge: Cambridge University Press, 2000), 16.
79. Vejas Gabriel Liulevicius, *War Land on the Eastern Front* (Cambridge: Cambridge University Press, 2000), 7; and Norman Stone, *The Eastern Front 1914–1917* (London: Penguin, 1975).
80. Carl von Clausewitz, ed. and trans. Michael Howard and Peter Paret, *On War* (London: Penguin, 1993), 233.
81. Horne and Kramer, *German Atrocities,* 74.
82. Reichsarchiv, *Schlachten des Weltkrieges: Die Eroberung von Nowo Georiewsk* (Berlin: Lodz, 1925).
83. Paul Hechler and Walter Kunrath, *Ehrentafel der im Weltkrieg 1914–1918 gefallenen Angehörigen des Preussischen Landwehr–Infanterie Regiments Nr. 6* (Berlin, 1931).
84. NARA, RG242, OKH, T78/6/677220-677309, Heeresarchiv, Kommandierenden General der Sicherungstruppen, der Deutschen Okkupation, 1917–18.
85. IWM, GAFWW, box 13, file number 34848. The Mobile–Etappenkommandantur 140, in Buseigny (France).

86.  IWM, GAFWW, box 13, file number 34903.
87.  Charles Townsend, *The Oxford History of Modern War* (Oxford: Oxford University Press, 1997), 225.
88.  Ernst Jünger, trans. by Michael Hoffmann, *Storm of Steel* (London: Penguin, 2003), 55.
89.  Gempp papers, book 40, 21.
90.  Gottfried Benn, "Wie Miss Cavell erschossen wurde. Bericht eines Augenzeugen über die Hinrichtung der englischen Krankenschwester," in Friedrich Felger (ed.), *Was wir vom Weltkrieg nicht wissen* (Berlin: Andermann, 1930), 113–7; and Reinhold Grimm and Jost Hermand, *1914/1939: German Reflections of the Two World Wars* (Madison: University of Wisconsin Press, 1992), 22–36.
91.  Holger H. Herwig, "The Immorality of Expediency: The German Military from Ludendorff to Hitler," in Mark Grimsley and Clifford J. Rogers, *Civilians in the Path of War* (Lincoln: University of Nebraska Press, 2002), 167–7.
92.  Helen McPhail, *The Long Silence: Civilian Life under the German Occupation of Northern France, 1914–1918* (London: IB Taurus, 1999), 37–54.
93.  BA MA, PH30 I/ Deutsche Ortskommandantur und Passabteilung im Kortyryk and Wytschaede in Flanders, Belgium.
94.  McPhail, *The Long Silence,* 38–54.
95.  Liulevicius, *War Land,* 7.
96.  Paul Roth (ed.) *Die politische Entwicklung in Kongress-Polen während der deutschen Okkupation* (Leipzig: K.F.Koehler, 1919), 140–181.
97.  BA MA, PH30II/61/62/63, Kaiserliches Generalgouvernement Warschau.
98.  Gempp papers, book 42.
99.  Ibid., book 45, 175–363.
100.  Ibid., 157.
101.  Ibid., 155.
102.  Liulevicius, *War Land,* 8–9.
103.  IHR, lecture, February 25, 1999; and Margit Szöllösi-Janze, *Poison Gas, Lice and Mites: Fritz Haber (1868–1934) and the Uses and Abuses of Science* (Munich and St. Antony's: Oxford University Press).
104.  Gempp papers, 387.
105.  Ibid., 308.
106.  BA MA, PH3/410, GFP in Russia, "Die Arbeitsweise des russischen Nachrichtendienstes nach den Erfahrungen der geheimen Feldpolizei Ob. Ost, August bis Oktober 1916.
107.  Gempp papers, book 1.
108.  Alex Vanneste, *Kroniek van Een Dorp in oorlog Neerpelt 1914–1918* (Antwerp, The Netherlands: Universitas, 1998).
109.  Martin Herzog and Marko Rösseler, "Der große Zaun," *Die Zeit,* Nr. 17, April 16, 1998.
110.  IWM, GAFWW, box 13, file 34900, Etappen-Inspektionen 1, April 5, 1917, Zusatzbestimmung der Etappen-Inspektion zu AOK 1, file 37648 vom, March 28, 1917, Betr: Organisation der Arbeitskräfte der Zivileinwohner.
111.  IWM, GAFWW, box 3, file 43799, order Ic. Nr. 170, Hauptmann Freiherr von Ende, February 4, 1918.
112.  Verhey, *The Spirit of 1914,* 219–33.
113.  Ibid., 63–81.
114.  Ibid, 12.
115.  J. R. Sibley, *Tanganyikan Guerrilla: East African Campaign 1914–18* (New York: Ballentine, 1971).
116.  Paul von Lettow-Vorbeck, *Meine Erinnerungen aus Afrika* (Berlin: K.F. Koehler, 1926).
117.  Adolf von Bomhard, *Das K. B. Infanterie-Leib-Regiment: Nach d. amtl. Kriegstagebüchern bearb. im Auftr. d. ehem. Infanterie-Leib-Regiments* (Munich: Selbstverl., 1921).
118.  Münchener Stadtmuseum, *München-"Hauptstadt der Bewegung"* (Munich: Klinkhardt & Biermann, 1993), 54–5.

119. Nigel H. Jones, *Hitler's Heralds: The Story of the Freikorps 1918–1923* (London: Murray, 1987), 138–41. Details of the operation can be found in Friedrich von Oertzen, *Die Deutsche Freikorps 1918–1923* (Berlin: Spaeth & Linde, 1937), 337.
120. Oertzen, *Die Deutsche* Freikorps, 246. See also Felix L. Carsten, *The Reichswehr and Politics, 1918 to 1933* (Oxford: Oxford University Press, 1966).
121. Krumbach, *Franz Ritter von Epp,* 60.

## Chapter 2: The New Order

1. Hans Grimm, *Volk ohne Raum* (Munich: Albert Langen, 1926).
2. Karl Haushofer, *Geopolitik Des Pazifischen Ozeans: Studien Über Die Wechselbeziehungen Zwischen Geographie und Geschichte* (Berlin: Kurt Vowinckel, 1927), 96.
3. Martin Schmitz, "Schülerzahlen der gewerblichen kaufmännischen Schulen von 1923 bis 1933," Diplom. essay, RWTH-Aachen, 2001.
4. H. W. Bauer, *Kolonien im Dritten Reich* (Köln: Gauverlag, 1936).
5. Hayes et al. (eds.), *Namibia under South African Rule,* 97.
6. Fraenkel, *Military Occupation and the Rule of Law.*
7. Henry T. Allen, *My Rhineland Journal* (Boston: Houghton Mifflin, 1923), 405.
8. Walter Warlimont, *Inside Hitler's Headquarters 1939–45* (Navato: Presidio Press, 1964); and Craig, *The Politics of the Prussian Army.*
9. Detlev Peukert, trans. Richard Deveson, *The Weimar Republic: The Crisis of Classical Modernity* (London: Penguin, 1991).
10. Thomas G. Mahnken, *Uncovering Ways of War: U.S. Intelligence and Foreign Military Innovation* (Ithaca, N.Y.: Cornell University Press, 2002), 89.
11. NARA, IRR319, German Army, vol. 1, 01-FIR/25, The German General Staff 1804 to 1934, Walter Warlimont, December 28, 1945.
12. Ibid.
13. Hermann Geyer, "Kriegserfahrungen und Cannae im Weltkriege," *Militärwissenschaftliche Mitteilungen,* Heft, August 5, 1924, 24.
14. NARA, T78/368/6330495-706, Oberleutnant von Ziehlberg, Berlin, May 1, 1930.
15. Bruno Ernst Buchrucker, *Im Schatten Seeckt's; die Geschichte der "Schwarzen Reichswehr"* (Berlin: Kampf, 1928); Craig, *The Politics of the Prussian Army,* 402–4; Jones, *Hitler's Heralds,* 227–30; and BZ-IMT, December 17, 1945.
16. The following were instructive: Alf Lüdtke, *Police and State in Prussia, 1815–1850* (Cambridge: Cambridge University Press, 1982); Frank Thomason, "Uniformed Police in the City of Berlin under the Empire," in Emilio C. Viano and Jeffrey H. Reiman (eds.), *The Police in Society* (Lexington, Mass: D.C. Heath, 1975); Jürgen Thomaneck, "Police and Public Order in the Federal Republic of Germany," in John Roach and Jürgen Thomaneck (eds.), *Police and Public Order in Europe* (London: Croom Helm, 1985); Herbert Reinke, "'Armed as if for a War': The State, the Military and Professionalization of the Prussian Police in Imperial Germany," in Clive Emsley and Barbara Weinberger (eds.), *Policing Western Europe: Politics, Professionalism and Public Order, 1850–1940* (Westport, Conn: Greenwood Press, 1991).
17. NCA document 2050-PS, Reichsgesetzblatt, August 1919.
18. NARA, RG319, IRR, box 6, CINFO reports 2, Political analysis of the Weimar Republic, December 10, 1945.
19. Stadtarchiv Aachen (StaA), Regierung Aachen, Akte 4/7/I, *Arbeiter und Soldatenrat 1918–1923, Das besetzte Rheinland*; and Ulrich Kluge, *Soldatenräte und Revolution: Studien zur Militärpolitik in Deutschland 1918–1919* (Göttingen: Vandenhoeck & Ruprecht, 1975).
20. Otto Loening, *Deutsche Rechtsgeschichte* (Leipzig: Hirschfeld, 1929), 30.
21. Fricke, *Bismarcks Prätorianer,* 23–30.
22. Richard Evans, *Rereading German History 1800–1996: From Unification to Reunification* (London: Routledge, 1997), 65–86.

23. Richard Bessel, "Policing, Professionalization and Politics," in Emsley and Weinberger (eds.), *Policing Western Europe*, 187–217.

24. Ibid., 202.

25. Ibid., 187–8.

26. Loening, *Deutsche Rechtsgeschichte*, 40.

27. James M. Diehl, "No More Peace: The Militarization of Politics," in Roger Chickering and Stig Förster (eds.), *The Shadows of Total War: Europe, East Asia and the United States 1919–1939* (Washington, D.C.: German Historical Institute, and Cambridge: Cambridge University Press, 2003), 97–113.

28. Münchener Stadtmuseum, *München-"Hauptstadt der Bewegung"* (Munich: Klinkhardt & Biermann, 1993), 52.

29. HStaD Regierung Aachen, file 22757, documents 34, 86, and 87.

30. HStaD Regierung Aachen, file 22757, document 71.

31. HStaD Regierung Aachen, file 22757, document 97, Bericht March 1933, Hilfspolizei Ausbildung. This training was divided between the practical (*Praktische Ausbildung*), rudimentary weapon skills and the conduct of police patrols, and the theoretical (*Theoretische Ausbildung*), providing a basic knowledge of German law and penal code.

32. Franz Seldte, *Der Stahlhelm: Erinnerungen und Bilder aus den Jahren 1918–1933* (Berlin: Stahlhelm, 1932).

33. Gerald Reitlinger, *The SS: Alibi of a Nation 1922–1945* (London: Faber & Faber, 1956); and Robert Koehl, *The Black Corps: The Structure and Power Struggles of the Nazi SS* (Madison: University of Wisconsin, 1983).

34. The relationship between the SS and Hitler has been extensively covered by Martin Broszat, *The Hitler State* (London: Longman, 1983); Alan Bullock, *Hitler: A Study in Tyranny* (London: Penguin, 1990); Joachim C. Fest, *Hitler* (New York: Knopf, 1977).

35. Heinz Höhne, *The Order of the Death's Head: The Story of Hitler's SS* (London: Penguin, 1969), 135.

36. Jeremy Noakes and Geoffrey Pridham, *Nazism 1919–1945: A Documentary Reader*, III (Exeter: University of Exeter Press, 1998), 185, hereafter referred to as Noakes & Pridham and volume.

37. Blood, "Kurt Daluege and the Militarisation of the Ordnungspolizei," 95–120.

38. Hans Speier, "Ludendorff: The German Concept of Total War," in Earle (ed.), *Makers of Modern Strategy*, 306–21.

39. Erich Ludendorff, *Der totale Krieg* (Munich: Ludendorff, 1935).

40. Hew Strachan, "Total War in the Twentieth Century," in Arthur Marwick, Clive Emsley, and Wendy Simpson, *Total War and Historical Change: Europe 1914–1955* (Buckingham: Open University Press, 2001), 255–83.

41. Wilhelm Deist, "The Road to Ideological War: Germany 1918–1945," in Williamson Murray, Macgregor Knox, and Alvin Bernstein, *The Making of Strategy: Rulers, States and War* (New York: Cambridge University Press, 1994), 359–60.

42. NCA document 2284-PS, SS-Standartenführer Gunter d'Alquen, History, Mission and Organization of the SS, 1939.

43. Ernest K. Bramstedt, *Dictatorship and Political Police* (London: Routledge, 1945); Helmut Krausnick, *Hitler's Einsatzgruppen: Die Truppe des Weltanschauungskrieges 1938–1942* (Frankfurt: Fischer, 1985); Robert Gellately, *The Gestapo and German Society* (Oxford: Clarendon, 1991); and George Browder, *Hitler's Enforcers: The Gestapo and SS Security Service in the Nazi Revolution* (Don Mills, Ontario: Oxford University Press, 1996).

44. Koehl, *The Black Corps*, 46.

45. Andersch, *Der Vater eines Mörders*; and Peter Padfield, *Himmler: Reichsführer-SS* (London: Heinemann, 1990), 3–19.

46. Robert Koehl, *RKFDV: German Resettlement and Population Policy 1939–1945,* (Cambridge, Mass.: Harvard University Press, 1957).

47. Koehl, *The Black Corps*, 48.

48. NARA, RG242, A3343-SS0-023, Bach-Zelewski.

49. Kurt Ernst Gottfried von Bülow, *Preussischer Militarismus zur Zeit Wilhelm II* (Schweidnitz: Scweidnitz, 1930).

50. Bülow, *Preussischer Militarismus*, 229–30.
51. IWM, IMT, interrogation, No. 2599, June 27, 1947.
52. BZ-USMT, January 17, 1946.
53. BA, SS personnel file, Bach-Zelewski. On the side of the SS family tree (*Ahnentafel*), the SS Race and Resettlement Office (RuSHA) representative inscribed the date in pencil and spelled his name in the Polish form, "Zelewsky."
54. NARA, RG242, A3343-SS0-023, Bach-Zelewski, letter to Himmler, October 23, 1940.
55. BZ-IMT, October 25, 1945.
56. NARA, RG242, A3343-SS0-023, Bach-Zelewski, report from Daluege, March 16, 1933. The word *hemmungslos* could also mean wild and unscrupulous.
57. BA, SS personnel file, Bach-Zelewski.
58. NARA, RG242, A3343-SS0-023, Bach-Zelewski, document Nr. 26335, Himmler's list of birthday presents included toys, ice cream, and a dog, from 1935 to 1944.
59. Tuviah Friedman, *Bach-Zelewski: Dokumentensammlung* (Haifa: Institute of Documentation, 1996), 2–6.
60. John Weitz, *Hitler's Bankier: Hjalmar Schacht* (New York: St. Martin's Griffin, 1998), 257. Recalling the incident years later, Schacht said that when Bach-Zelewski got up to protest, he wanted to say, "The men's toilets are along the corridor, second door on the right."
61. NARA, RG242, OKW T-77, roll 795, report from Roschmann of Kriegs-marinedienstelle, Königsberg, Prussia, to Oberbefehelshaber der Kriegsmarine, August 20, 1935; report from the Chief of Staff of Wehrkreiskommando I, Königsberg, Prussia, to Oberbefehelshaber des Heeres, August 20, 1935; and Hjalmar Schacht, Reichsbankpräsidenten und beauftragten Reichswirtschaftministerium, zur Eröffnung der Deutschen Ostmesse, August 18, 1935.
62. BA-ZNS, L 85247, pension file, Georg Liedl.
63. Terry Charman, *The German Home Front 1939–45* (New York: Philosophical Library, 1989), 114.
64. Kershaw, *Hubris*, 249. See Derwent Whittlesey, "Haushofer: The Geopoliticians," in Earle (ed.), *Makers of Modern Strategy,* 388–411. See also Murphy, *The Heroic Earth*.
65. NCA document 1708-PS, National Socialist Yearbook 1941, edited by Robert Ley.
66. In 1934, Epp attended Josef and Magda Goebbels' wedding as an official witness, alongside Hitler.
67. Hermann Weiss, *Biographisches Lexikon zum Dritten Reich* (Frankfurt am Main: Fischer Taschenbuch, 2002), 112.
68. Alan Wykes, *Himmler* (New York: Ballentine, 1972), 51–4.
69. Peter H. Merkel, *Political Violence under the Swastika: 581 Early Nazis* (Princeton: Princeton University Press, 1975), 108–9.
70. Krumbach, *Franz Ritter von Epp,* 245–64.
71. Bauer, *Kolonien im Dritten Reich*, 56.
72. Noakes & Pridham, III, 667–75.
73. Michael Mann, *The Dark Side of Democracy: Explaining ethnic cleansing* (Cambridge: Cambridge University Press, 2004), 308–11.
74. PRO, WO208-4300, Report on the interrogations of PW LD 1136 SS Gruppenführer Jakob Sporrenberg.
75. NARA, RG 319 IRR Case Files: U.S. Army Intelligence papers, list number 544, Kurt Daluege, source document, "Nazis in the News" May 25, 1942.
76. BA R19/414, *Rheinische Landeszeitung* cuttings from the May 14–15, 1937, Kolonialtagung in Düsseldorf.
77. HStA Düsseldorf. Denazification prozess. Virtually 100 percent of Rhineland industrialists joined the RKB.
78. Richard J. Overy, *War and Economy in the Third Reich* (Oxford: Clarendon, 1994), 188–204.
79. Ibid., 191.
80. BA R19/414, Letter from Major (Schupo) Kummetz nach Düsseldorf (Kolonial-politische Schulung der Polizei), May 19, 1937.

81. Gellately, *The Gestapo and German Society*, found the Gestapo complements for Düsseldorf—126; Essen—43; Duisberg, 28.
82. Krumbach, *Franz Ritter von Epp*, 270–1.
83. Ibid, 300. The commemoration of the fiftieth anniversary of the colonial association (*Kolonial Gesellschaft*) fueled the atmosphere of rejuvenating political interest in the colonies.
84. Woodruff D. Smith, *The German Colonial Empire* (Chapel Hill: University of North Carolina, 1978), 233.
85. NCA, document 3058-PS, letter from Heydrich to Göring: Subject: Action against the Jews, November 11, 1938. Heydrich reported 191 synagogues on fire, 76 destroyed, and many subsidiary buildings damaged. The Nazis had 20,000 Jews arrested and 36 killed. Looting had broken out and the police had arrested 174 persons.
86. Noakes & Pridham, II, 553–65.
87. BA R19/414, letter Himmler to Bormann, Betr. Berufschule January 17, 1939.
88. Creveld, *Supplying War*, 142–7.
89. NCA, document PS-2322, Hitler's speech to the Reichstag, September 1, 1939.
90. Noakes, IV, 137–8.
91. Michael Burleigh and Wolfgang Wippermann, *The Racial State: Germany 1933–1945* (Cambridge: Cambridge University Press, 1991), 63–4.
92. NARA, RG242, BDC A3345-OS-5045, Vortrag über Die Deutsche Ordnungspolizei, Generalmajor der Polizei Querner, BdO Hamburg, September 2, 1940 (referred to as the Querner report).
93. NARA, RG242, BDC, A3345-B-171, Karl Lautenschläger, Handbuch für den Hilfs-Polizeibeamten (Berlin, 1939). Interestingly, Krichbaum adapted the same source to itemize the duties of the GFP in Russia and France, mentioned in NARA, RG338, FMS, C-029, The German Secret Field Police, Oberst Wilhelm Krichbaum, May 18, 1947.
94. NCA, document 647-PS, Führer directive, August 17, 1938.
95. Ruth Bettina Birn, *Die Höheren SS-und Polizeiführer: Himmlers Vertreter im Reich und in den besetzten Gebieten* (Dusseldorf: Droste, 1986).
96. NARA T1270/23/0519, interrogation of Adolf von Bomhard, June 27, 1945.
97. Noakes & Pridham, III, 928.
98. Alexander B. Rossino, "Destructive Impulses: German Soldiers and the Conquest of Poland," *Holocaust and Genocide Studies* 2 (Winter 1997), 351–65. See also Alexander B. Rossino, *Hitler Strikes Poland: Blitzkrieg, Ideology and Atrocity* (Lawrence: University of Kansas, 2003).
99. NARA, RG242, T580, numerous incidents of banditry in the Polish forests in 1940, handled by the Gendarmerie.
100. TVDB, 132–3; Wolfgang Jacobmeyer, *Das Diensttagebuch des deutschen Generalgouverneurs in Polen 1939–1945* (Stuttgart: Deutsche Verlags-Anstalt, 1975); and Jan Tomasz Gross, *Polish Society under German Occupation: The Generalgouvernment 1939–1944* (New Haven, Conn.: Princeton University Press, 1979), 162.
101. Leonie Wheeler, "The SS and the Administration of Nazi Occupied Eastern Europe, 1939–1945," (Phil. diss., University of Oxford, 1981), 63–76.
102. Czeskaw Madajczyk, *Die Okkupationspolitik Nazideutschlands in Polen 1939–1945*, (Stottgary: Akademie, 1987).
103. Noakes & Pridham, III, 924.
104. PRO, HW16/6, MSGP 18, October 3, 1940.
105. Mark C. Yerger, *Allgemeine-SS: The Commands, Units and Leaders of the General SS* (Winnepeg, Canada: J. J. Fedorowicz, 1997), 37.
106. NARA, RG242, A3343-SS0-023, Bach-Zelewski, letter April 26, 1939.
107. Friedman, *Bach-Zelewski*, 8.
108. Wanda Machlejd (ed.), *War Crimes in Poland: Erich von dem Bach* (Warsaw: Zachodnia Agencja Prasowa, 1961), 27–31. Wanda was seventeen when she served in the resistance during the Warsaw uprising (refer to chapter 8) and, after her capture, managed to survive Belsen concentration camp. She was released in 1945.
109. NARA, RG242, A3343-SS0-023, Bach-Zelewski, letter to Himmler, December 4, 1940.

110. Ibid, Bach-Zelewski. Himmler replied wishing him success, December 23, 1940.

111. BA R19/414, Daluege to Adolf von Bomhard, Betr. Kolonialpolizeigesetz, July 3, 1940.

112. The Querner Report; NCA, document 2168-PS; and Ernst Bayer, *Die SA* (Berlin: Luennhaupt, 1938). See also John R. Angolia and David Littlejohn, *NSKK and NSFK: Uniforms, Organisation and History* (San Jose, Calif.: Bender, 1994).

113. BA R19/15, Adolf von Bomhard, July 2, 1940. Betr. Meister (SB) und Wachtmeister (SB) der Schutzpolizei des Reiches, der Gendarmerie und der Schutzpolizei der Gemeinden, die sich fuer den Kolonialdienst gemeldet haben.

114. BA R19/15, Daluege, RFSS O.Kdo PII (2e) 1 Nr. 1/40, Betr. Kolonialpolizei, October 31, 1940.

115. PRO, HW16/6, MSGP 23, November 17, 1940.

116. PRO, HW16, GPD104-105-106-107, December 3, 1940.

117. NCA document D-665; also in Martin Broszat and Hemut Krausnick, *Anatomy of the SS State* (London: Collins, 1968), 264–5.

118. Bramstedt, *Political Police*, 87–90; Bracher, *The German Dictatorship*, 442.

119. George H. Stein, *Waffen-SS: Hitler's Elite Guard at War, 1939–1945* (Ithaca and London: Cornell University Press, 1966).

120. NARA, RG242, T580, roll 216, Ansprache des Oberbefehlshabers der Ordnungspolizei anläßlich der Tagung der Inspekteure der Ordnungspolizei, January 21, 1941.

121. Mark C. Yerger, *Waffen SS Commanders: The Army, Corps and Division Leaders of a Legend-Augsberger to Kreutz* (Atglen, Pa.: Schiffer, 1997), 146–8.

122. NARA RG242, T175/13/2515813-90. Eventually, there were two colonial police academies, in Berlin-Oranienburg and Vienna.

123. NARA, RG242, T580, roll 216, Ansprache des Chefs der Ordnungspolizei anlässlich der Tagung der Inspekteure der Ordnungspolizei am January 21, 1941, 24.

124. BA R19/36, Errichtung eines Kolonialpolizeiamtes beim Hauptamt Ordnungspolizei, 0-HB 53 Nr2/41, Chef der Ordnungspolizei, March 6, 1941. See also BA R470.

125. Wheeler, "The SS and the Administration of Nazi Occupied Eastern Europe," 76.

126. The essential companion on this subject is Rolf-Dieter Müller and Gerd R. Ueberschar, *Hitler's War in the East 1941–1945: A Critical Assessment* (Oxford: Berghahn, 1997); and Horst Boog et al., trans. Dean S. McMurray, Ewald Osers, and Louise Willmot, *Germany and the Second World War: The Attack on the Soviet Union,* vol. 4 (Oxford: Oxford University Press, 1998), hereafter referred to as DZWK.

127. Christian Streit, *Keine Kameraden: Die Wehrmacht und die sowjetischen Kriegsgefangenen 1941–1945* (Stuttgart: Deutsche Verlags-Anstalt, 1978), 83–125; Christian Streit, "The German Army and the Policies of Genocide," in Gerhard Hirschfeld, *The Policies of Genocide: Jews and Soviet Prisoners of War in Nazi Germany* (London, 1986), 1–14.

128. The Barbarossa directives are collected in the following NCA documents: 446-PS, Directive 21, Operation Barbarossa, December 1940; 872-PS, Conference of "Fall Barbarossa" and "sonnenblume," February 3, 1941; 874-PS, diversionary preparations with Fritz Todt, March 9, 1941; 873-PS, Conference with "Chief L" April 30, 1941; 876-PS, Deception of the enemy, May 12, 1941, and IMT C-50; and 886-PS Decree for the conduct of courts martial in the district "Barbarossa" and for special measures of the troop, May 13, 1941.

129. Hamburger Institut für Sozialforschung (ed.), *Verbrechen der Wehrmacht: Dimensionen des Vernichtungskrieges 1941–1944* (Hamburg: Hamburger Edition, 2002); and Christian Gerlach, *Kalkulierte Morde: Die deutsche Wirtschafts- und Vernichtungspolitik in Weissrussland 1941 bis 1944* (Hamburg: Hamburg Edition HIS, 1999).

130. Michael Reynolds, *Steel Inferno: 1st SS Panzer Corps in Normandy* (Staplehurst: Perseus, 1997).

131. PRO, HW16/6, MSGP 28, September 12, 1941.

132. PRO, HW16/6, MSGP 29, October 22, 1941.

133. IWM, IMT, interrogation, Nr.2599, June 27, 1947. Bach-Zelewski alleged he was the ordnance officer of the 29th Infantry Regiment commanded by Schenckendorff after the First World War, under Wehrkreis III.

134. NARA, FMS, B-629, "The Sphere of Duties of the Command Staff of the RFSS and the Chief of German Police and their collaboration with the OKW," Ernst Rode (July 18, 1947).

135. Yehoshua Büchler, "Kommandostab Reichsführer-SS: Himmler's Personal Murder Brigades in 1941," *Holocaust and Genocide Studies* 1 (1986), 11–25.

136. Unsere Ehre Heist Treue, *Kriegstagebuch des Kommandostabes Reichsführer-SS Tätigkeitsberichte der 1. Und 2. SS-Inf.-Brigade, der 1. SS-Kav-Brigade und von Sonderkommando der SS* (Vienna: Europa Verlag, 1965).

137. Charles Sydnor, *Soldiers of Destruction: The SS Death's Head Division, 1933–1945* (Princeton: Princeton University Press, 1977), 122.

138. Stein, *Waffen-SS: Hitler's Elite Guard at War,* 120; Michael Burleigh, *The Third Reich: A New History* (London: Macmillan, 2000), 613. For the police units, see Edward B. Westermann, "'Friend and Helper': German Uniformed Police Operations in Poland and the General Government, 1939–1941," *Journal of Military History* 58 (October 1994), 643–61; "Himmler's Uniformed Police on the Eastern Front: The Reich's Secret Soldiers, 1941–1942." *War in History* 3 (1996), 309–29; and "'Ordinary Men' or 'Ideological Soldiers'? Police Battalion 310 in Russia, 1942," *German Studies Review* 21 (February 1998), 41–68.

139. NCA, document L-221, Martin Bormann memorandum, July 16, 1941; and Peter Longerich, *The Unwritten Order: Hitler's Role in the Final Solution* (Stroud: Tempus Publishing, 2001), 69–74.

140. NARA, RG242, T175/3/2503430/639, Orpo HQ, subject: Richtlinien für Partisanenbekämpfung, orders signed by Winkelmann, Daluege's chief of staff, November 17, 1941. Although BA R19/305 Schnellbrief, Winkelmann, Betr. Richtlinien für Partisanenbekämpfung, October 17, 1941.

141. NCA, IMT, L-221, op cit.

142. BA MA, RH13/ v. 37, Berlin April 1938 (Wehrmachtsakademie Nr. 871/38 g.k).

143. BA-MA, RW41/4, Abschrift, RFSS, July 25, 1941: "schutzformationen" in den neubesetzten Ostgebieten, July 31, 1941.

144. BA R19/281, CdO, Betr. Schutzmannschaften in des Ostgebietes, November 6, 1941. Under the police code the Schuma were formed thus: Schutzmannschaft (*Einzeldienst*) dem Städten (known as the *Stadtschutzmannschaft*); the Schutzmannschaft (*Einzeldienst*) auf dem Lande (known as the *Landesschutzmannschaft*); Schutzmannschaft in geschlossenen Einheiten; the Feuerschutzmannschaft; and the Hilfsschutzmannschaft. The Schuma were granted three number categories 1 to 50 for those raised in HSSPF Russia-North; 51 to 100 for battalions raised in HSSPF Russia-Centre; and 101 to 200 for those created in HSSPF Russia-South. They were also granted the capability of raising specialist and technical branches using the appropriate technical term.

145. Martin Dean, *Collaboration in the Holocaust: Crimes of the Local Police in Byelorussia and Ukraine, 1941–1944* (New York: St. Martin's, 2000), 27.

146. PRO, HW16/6, MSGP 28, September 12, 1941.

147. BA R19/281, BdO Ostland - HA-Orpo, Betr. Gliederung der Schutzmannschafts-Btl. December 4, 1941.

148. PRO, HW16/45, GPD492, December 9, 1941.

149 Klemperer, LTI [Lingua, Tertii, Imperii]: Notizbuch eines Philologen, 254

150. PRO, HW16/45, GPD 292, July 18, 1941.

151. PRO, HW16/6, MSGP 29, September 13, 1941.

152. Ibid.

153. NCA, document 3257-PS, report to Chief of the Industrial Armament Department from the Armament Inspector Ukraine, December 2, 1941.

154. Nicholas Terry, "Conflicting Signals: British Intelligence on the 'Final Solution' Through Radio Intercepts and Other Sources, 1941–1942," *Yad Vashem Studies* (2004).

155. PRO, HW16, MSGP 27, August 21, 1941.

156. PRO, HW16, MSGP 29, October 22, 1941.

157. PRO, HW16, MSGP 30, November 14, 1941.

158. PRO, HW16/6, MSGP 27, August 21, 1941. A light-hearted moment in the British decipher, "Fashion note. 56th Police Battalion, fitting its men out, sends for 396 steel helmets, 376 pairs of hand-cuffs, and 415 bathing-drawers."

159. PRO, HW16/6, MSGP 27 August 21, 1941.
160. Ibid.
161. TVDB, 4–6.
162. PRO, HW16/6, MSGP 29, October 1941.
163. PRO, HW16/6, MSGP 27, August 22, 1941.
164. PRO HW 16/32, August 18, 1941, GPD 326 No.2 Traffic, to HSSPF Posen. SS-Hauptsturmführer Herbert Lange was been in charge of the euthanasia gas vans. Refer to Noakes & Pridham, III, 1138–9; and Michael Burleigh and Wolfgang Wippermann, *The Racial State: Germany 1933–45* (Cambridge: Cambridge University Press, 1991), 102.
165. Staatsanwaltschaft des Landgericht Braunschweig, "Schwurgerichtsanklage gegen Angehörige des SS-Kav.Regt.2 (Erschiessung von Juden im Gebiet der Pinsker-Sümpfe August 1941" (Braunschweig, 1963). The case has also been referred to in Ruth Bettina Birn, "Two Kinds of Reality," in Bernd Wegner (ed.), *From Peace to War: Germany, Soviet Russia and the World, 1939–1941* (London: Berghahn Books, 1997), 277–92. See also Karla Müller-Tupath, *Reichsführers gehorsamster Becher: Eine deutsche Karriere* (Berlin: Aufbau, 1999), 27–56. The swamp was not deep enough to cause drowning so the SS troopers returned to shootings.
166. TVDB, 4; and *Unsere Ehre Heist Treue*, 30-2.
167. Soviet Embassy (London), *Soviet Government Statements on Nazi Atrocities,* (London: Hutchinson, 1946), 46. The account also mentioned the 6,504 persons shot by the brigade under the regimental order of July 27, 1941. A further order 37 by Himmler demanded daily reports of the numbers shot. Copies of the reports discovered in the Toropets area, in January 1942, left behind by the SS Cavalry Brigade when it fled from the Soviet advance.
168. Ibid.
169. NARA, T501, roll 1, Der Befehlshaber des rückw. Heeres-Gebietes Mitte, Korpstagesbefehl Nr. 28, September 16, 1941.
170. PRO, HW16, MSGP 29, October 22, 1941.
171. BA-MA, RW41 and NARA, RG242, roll T501, Korpesbefehl Nr. 53, Erfahrungsaustausch (Kampf gegen Partisanen), September 16, 1941.
172. TVDB, 4–6.
173. PRO, HW16/6, MSGP 27, August 21, 1941.
174. Ibid.
175. TVDB, 6.
176. PRO, HW16/6, MSGP 28, September 12, 1941.
177. NARA, RG242, A3343-SS0-023, Bach-Zelewski, letter from commander 252nd Infantry Division, August 19, 1941.
178. TVDB, 24.
179. TVDB, 30 and PRO, HW16/6, MSGP 32, February 14, 1942.
180. TVDB, 31 and PRO, HW16/6, MSGP 32, February 14, 1942. The virtual replication of Bach-Zelewski's diary with the British cipher confirms the strength of evidence.
181. Ibid, 26.
182. Ibid, 27, commenting, "He [Hitler] spent his New Year's Eve in his winter garden until 4 a.m."
183. Ibid, 28.
184. Ibid, 30.
185. Hermann Geyer, *Ostfeldzug. XI Armeekorps* (Neckargemünd: Kurt Vowinckel, 1967).

## Chapter 3: Hitler's Bandenbekämpfung Directive

1. NCA, document C-148, Communist Insurrection in occupied territories, September 16, 1941. NARA, T1270, GB War office negatives, "Hitler's Speeches," MI14/52, Kommunistische Aufstandsbewegung in den besetzten Gebieten.
2. PRO, *SOE: Operations in Eastern Europe, Guide Booklet* (n.d.).

3.   M. Conway, "The Rexist movement in Belgium 1940–1944," (Phil. Diss, University of Oxford, 1989).

4.   Derek Wood and Derek Dempster, *The Narrow Margin: The Battle of Britain and the Rise of Air Power, 1930–1940* (London: Hutchinson, 1961), 226–315.

5.   Hugh R. Trevor-Roper, *Hitler's War Directives 1939–1945* (New York: Doubleday, 1966), 101–4.

6.   Ibid, 122–5; and Rudolf Absolon, *Die Wehrmacht im Dritten Reich, Band V* (Boppard am Rhein: Harald Boldt, 1969–95), 410.

7.   Williamson Murray, "The Collapse of Empire: British Strategy, 1919–1945," in Williamson Murray, MacGregor Knox, and Alvin Bernstein, *The Making of Strategy: Rulers, States and War* (Cambridge: Cambridge University Press, 1994), 399–425.

8.   Patrick Howarth, *Intelligence Chief Extraordinary: The Life of the Ninth Duke of Portland* (London: Bodley Head, 1986), 108–10. The intelligence reports were sent to Lieutenant Colonel Holland of the guerrilla warfare section in the War Office. Eventually the British conducted covert operations, smuggling arms and finance into Abyssinia.

9.   F. H. Hinsley, *British Intelligence in the Second World War: Its Influence on Strategy and Operations*, vol. I (London: Europa, 1980).

10.  M. R. D. Foot, *Resistance: European Resistance to Nazism, 1940–45* (London: Methuen, 1976); John Shy and Thomas W. Collier, "Revolutionary War," in Paret (ed.), *Makers of Modern Strategy*, 832. Shy and Collier referred to the presence of George C. Lloyd (British colonial secretary) and J. C. F. Holland at the founding of the SOE. They were friends of T. E. Lawrence. Holland served with Lawrence in Arabia and took part in covert operations during the Abyssinia crisis. Also refer to W. E. D. Allen, *Guerrilla War in Abyssinia* (Harmondsworth Middlesex: Penguin, 1943).

11.  Stephen Badsey, "Commandos," in Richard Holmes (ed.), *The Oxford Companion to Military History* (Oxford: Oxford University Press, 2001), 213–4.

12.  PRO, HS 4/36, Reports on the internal situation and Nazi atrocities, 1939–43.

13.  PRO, FO371/30897, Conditions in Germany 1942, case 70, Dr. Benes and the collapse of the German army in December 1941.

14.  David Mountfield, *The Partisans* (London: Hamlyn, 1979), 29.

15.  PRO, HS 4/50, Operation Bivouac, 1942.

16.  DKHH, 415.

17.  Ibid, 429 and 433.

18.  PRO, SOE files are HS 4/18, 19, 22, 24, and 39, Operation Anthropoid.

19.  DKHH, 437–84.

20.  "Ein Vergeltungsschlag von besonderer Wildheit," *Berliner Morgenpost*, June 2, 1942.

21.  Peter Hoffmann, *Hitler's Personal Security: Protecting the Führer, 1921–1945* (New York: De Capo, 2000).

22.  *Table Talk*, 512; and Hoffmann, *Hitler's Personal Security*, 64.

23.  NARA, RG242, T580/222/09995, Reinhard Heydrich's funeral oration by Kurt Daluege, June 7, 1942.

24.  John Bradley, *Lidice: Sacrificial Village* (New York: Ballentine, 1972); Richard Livingstone, "A Final Lesson: The Destruction of Lidice," *Purnell's History of the Second World War*, 3, 1024–9; and Günter Deschner, *Reinhard Heydrich. Statthalter der totalen Macht* (Munich: Heyne, 1980).

25.  JNSV, case 644, case against members of Polizei Kampfgruppe Dietrich des HSSPF Russland Mitte.

26.  Rab Bennett, *Under the Shadow of the Swastika: The Moral Dilemmas of Resistance and Collaboration in Hitler's Europe* (Basingstoke: Macmillan, 1999), 238–68.

27.  TVDB, 29.

28.  PRO HW 16/46, signal from Bach-Zelewski to the chief SS medical officer, January 29, 1942.

29.  Machlejd, *War Crimes in Poland*, 22.

30.  TVDB, 34.

31. NARA, RG242, T175/125/2649909-18, letter from Dr. Grawitz to Himmler, March 4, 1942.

32. Richard Breitman, *The Architect of Genocide: Himmler and the Final Solution* (Hanover, N.H.: University of New England Press, 1991). Höhne, *The Order of the Death's Head*, 334.

33. NARA, RG242, A3343-SS0-023, Bach-Zelewski, letter from chief SS medical officer to Himmler, March 9, 1942. The symptoms associated with nervous condition included inferiority complex (*Minderwertigkeit-svorstellungen*), a high level of sensitivity to pain (*Schmerzempfindlichkeit*), an inability to look after oneself (*Sichgehenlassen*), and the inability to concentrate (*mangelnde Willenskonzentration*).

34. NARA, RG242, T175/125/2649909-18, Himmler to Grawitz, referred in the Nuremberg process, NCA document P-632.

35. NARA, RG242, T175/125/2649909-18, Himmler to Grawitz, referred in the Nuremberg process.

36. NARA, RG242, A3343-SS0-023, Bach-Zelewski, letter, March 31, 1942, from Bach-Zelewski to Heinrich Himmler.

37. NARA, RG242, A3343-SS0-023, Bach-Zelewski letter, April 6, 1942.

38. TVDB, 35.

39. Ibid, 38.

40. NARA, RG242, T501/15/302-313, Befehlshaber des rückwärtigen Heeresgebietes Mitte Ia, Vorschläge zur Vernichtung der Partisanen im rückw. Heeresgebiet und in dem rückw. Armeegebieten, 1.3.42, Schenckendorff.

41. Theo Schulte, "The German Army and National Socialist Occupation Policies in the Occupied Areas of the Soviet Union 1941–43" (Ph.D. diss, University of Warwick, 1987), 74, BA-MA, RH 22/230, DRZW-4, 1224–5.

42. Hannes Heer, "The Logic of the War of Extermination," in Hannes Heer and Klaus Naumann, *War of Extermination: The German Military in World War II 1941–1945* (New York: Berghahn, 2000), 106–9.

43. Ibid., 112–3.

44. Ibid., 110–4.

45. NARA, RG242, T175/81/2601626-30, Partisanenbekämpfung report from SSPF Weissruthenien SS-Brigadeführer Carl Zenner to HSSPF Ostland Friedrich Jeckeln, June 13, 1942 (hereafter referred to as the Zenner report).

46. NARA, RG242, T175/81/2601626-30, the report also listed the killing of two members of the collaboration police (*Ordnungsdienst*) and five wounded.

47. Ibid. The total number of battalions was based on the existing and expected new battalions and support units.

48. PRO, HW16/6, MSGP 37, August 11, 1942. Zenner was quite astute and aware of his declining popularity; in April, he sent Hitler a birthday greeting and received a kindly response. He was still working with Jeckeln and Jedicke in June and July 1942; and Roger James Bender and Hugh Page Taylor, *Uniforms, Organization and History of the Waffen-SS* (San Jose, Calif.: Bender, 1971), 10. Zenner was eventually transferred to BII in the SS-Main Office (requisitioning supplies).

49. PRO, HW16/6, MSGP 27, August 21, 1941.

50. Milovan Djilas, trans. Michael B. Petrovich, *Wartime* (London: Harcourt Brace Jovanovich, 1977).

51. BA R19/320, RFSS, Tgb. Nr. 1a 323/42 (Geheim) KSRFSS, Befehl–für die Unterdrückung der Bandentätigkeit in den Gebieten Oberkrain und Untersteiermark, June 25, 1942.

52. Ibid, Tgb. Nr. 1a 323/42 (Geheim) KSRFSS, Befehl Richtlinien für die Durchführung der Aktion gegen Partisanen und sonstigen Banditen in Gebieten Oberkrain und Untersteiermark, June 25, 1942.

53. TVDB, 39–40.

54. NARA, RG242, BDC, A3345-OSS-096B, Dr. Erhard Schöngarth; and, Helmut Krausnick, *Hitler's Einsatzgruppen: Die Truppe des Weltanschauungskrieges 1938–1942* (Frankfurt am Main: Fischer, 1985), 157 and 204.

55. Heer, "The Logic of the War," 111, n84.

56. DKHH, 437–84.

57. NARA-RG242, T175/81/2601616, letter Himmler to Daluege, July 28, 1942.
58. NARA, RG242, BDC A3345-DS-J007, frames 0689-1843, collected sources on Bandenbekämpfung.
59. NARA, RG242, T175/74/2591672. This order was first issued during a visit to Helsinki, February 17, 1942.
60. NARA, RG242, T175/74/2591686-706, Gedanken über das Wort "Partisanen."
61. NARA, RG242, T175/135/22287909-12, Der Reichsführer-SS, Order No. 65, August 12, 1942.
62. NARA, RG242, BDC A3345-DS-J007, frames 0689-1843.
63. NARA, RG242, T175/74/2591688, letter from the personal staff of the RFSS to SS-Standarte "Kurt Eggers."
64. William L. Combs, *The Voice of the SS: A History of the SS Journal "Das Schwarze Korps"* (New York: Peter Lang), 376–7.
65. NARA, RG242, T175/3/2503430-39, Betr. Richtlinien für Partisanenbekämpfung, circulated by Chef der Ordnungspolizei, November 17, 1941.BA-BL, R19-318, Bandenbekämpfung, Winkelmann's confirmation approval for Richtlinien für Partisanenbekämpfung, November 17, 1941, see also DRZW, 1201–3.
66. NARA, RG242, T175/140/2668141-355, Weisung Nr. 46: Richtlinien für die verstärkte Bekämpfung des Bandenunwesens im Osten, Der Führer, OKW/WFSt/ Op. Nr. 002821/42g.K., Führerhauptquartier, August 18, 1942. Refer to Walter Hubatsch, *Hitlers Weisungen für die Kriegführung 1939-1945: Dokumente des Oberkommandos der Wehrmacht* (reprinted by Osnabruck, 1999), 201–9; and Trevor-Roper, *Hitler's War Directive*, 197–202.
67. Kershaw, *Hubris*, 27–91; and Geoffrey Megargee, *Inside Hitler's High Command* (Lawrence: University of Kansas, 2000), 63–4.
68. BZ-IMT, October 25, 1945.
69. Trevor-Roper, *Hitler's War Directives*, 197–202.
70. *Table Talk*, 621.
71. DKHH, 542–4.
72. Warlimont, *Inside Hitler's Headquarters*, 254–5.
73. NARA, T175/56/2571332, Aktenvermerk über Besprechung mit Gauleiter Koch, Prützmann, September 27, 1942.
74. NARA, T175/56/2571327, letter Himmler to Koch, October 9, 1942.
75. NARA, T175/562571324-5, letter Prützmann to Koch, Betrifft: Banden- bekämpfung, October 2, 1942.
76. Truman O. Anderson III, "Germans, Ukrainians and Jews: Ethnic Politics in Heeresgebiet Süd, June–December 1941," *War in History* 7, no. 3 (July 2000), 325–52.
77. Peter Young, *Commando* (New York: Ballentine, 1969), 114–27.
78. C. E. Lucas Phillips, *The Greatest Raid of All* (London: Heinemann, 1958), 157.
79. Roger A. Beaumont, *Military Elites* (New York: Walker, 1976), 44–5.
80. Oberkommando Des Heeres, *Das Britische Kriegshee*. Gen St d H/Abt. Fremde Heere West, Secret Nr. 3000/42, April 10, 1942, 425–6.
81. NCA, document 8553-PS, Combating of single parachutists, August 4, 1942.
82. USMT-12, 36.
83. NCA, document, Jodl, affidavit, October 1946.
84. NCA, document, 498-PS and document C-179, Führer order, October 18, 1942.
85. Ibid.
86. Ibid.
87. Hubatsch, *Hitlers Weisungen für die Kriegführung 1939–1945*, 206–9.
88. PRO, FO371-/30924, case 12246 papers, war crimes litigation.
89. PRO, WO208/4294, Scotland Papers.
90. Der Reichsführer-SS und Chef der Deutschen Polizei, Bandenbekämpfung, I Ausgabe (RSHA, September 1942); also located on NARA, RG242, BDC, A3345-DS-J007, frames 0689-1843.
91. Ibid., 1.
92. Ibid, 21–4.
93. Ibid., 8–21.
94. Ibid., 10–13.

95. NARA, RG242, T175/112/2710259, August 17, 1942.
96. Ibid, 13–15.
97. Ibid., 14–16.
98. NARA, RG242, T175/81/2601880, Brandt to Holfeld, November 22, 1942.
99. NARA, 175/140/8160, RFSS Befehl, October 23, 1942; and TVDB, 65. Bach-Zelewski received the confirmation on October 24, als Bevollmächtigter des Reichsführers SS für Bandenbekämpfung.
100. TVDB, 51–2.
101. Substitution enabled a career SS officer to experience senior responsibility, while the officer officially responsible for the position was released for other duties.
102. Ibid, 65.
103. NARA, RG242, T175/81/2601501-2034, message from RFSS to Karl Wolf, at Hitler field headquarters, October 28, 1942.
104. Ibid, wireless message, Himmler to Bach-Zelewski, November 16, 1942.
105. TVDB, 52–84.
106. PRO, WO235-389, United Nations Charges against German War Criminals, The Fühlsbüttel Prison Case, July 1947, evidence against HSSPF Hamburg Georg Henning Graf von Bassewitz-Behr.
107. NCA, document NOKW 1067 *Kampfanweisung für die Bandenbekämpfung im Osten,* and Oberkommando d. Wehrmacht, Kampfanweisung für die Bandenbekämpfung im Osten, Merkblatt 69/1 (Berlin, November 11, 1942).
108. CMH Pub 104-19, *The Soviet Partisan Movement, 1941–44* (Washington, D.C., Center of Military History, 1956), 119–21.
109. Warlimont, *Inside Hitler's Headquarters,* 289–92.
110. NCA, document UK-66, Document marked "A" dated January 1, 1943, originating from NCA document NOKW 068, Combating of Partisans, December 16, 1942; and Gert Meyer (eds.), *Wehrmacht Verbrechen: Dokumente aus Sowjetischen Archiven* (Köln: PapyRossa, 1997).
111. Soviet Embassy, *New Soviet Documents on Nazi Atrocities,* (London: Hutchinson, 1943) 49. Schenckendorff had the soldiers arrested and the officer reduced to the ranks.
112. NARA, RG242, T175/ 81/2601524, Meldung, 51a, December 1942.
113. NARA, RG242, T175, roll 3. Dienstbesprechung der Befehlshaber und Inspekteure der Ordnungspolizei January 1943, Berlin.
114. Raul Hilberg, *The Destruction of the European Jews* (New York: Holmes & Meier, 1985), 148.

## Chapter 4: Bandenbekämpfung Operational Concept

1. NARA, T175 Roll 70/2586870, USMT, N331, Bandenbekampfung, September 3, 1947.
2. NS19/1433, "Bandenkampf- und Sicherheitslage." Vortrag des Reichsführers-SS bei Hitler auf dem Obersalzberg am 19 June 1943 see also NARA, RG242, T175/ 70/2586239-60 and T175/81/2601501-2034, Reichsführer-SS, 28 June 1943.
3. Ian Kershaw, *Hitler 1936–45: Nemesis* (London: Penguin, 2000); and Gerald Fleming, *Hitler and the Final Solution* (Berkeley and Los Angeles: University of California, Oxford, 1986).
4. Kershaw, *Nemesis,* 589.
5. NARA, RG242, T312/18/4758799-4758803, Proklamation des Führers, January 30, 1943.
6. Werner Brill, *"Mitleid ist fehl am Platz" Über Vernichtungskrieg und Gewalt* (Saarbrücken: Blattlaus-Verl, 1999), 40–1.
7. NCA, document 294-PS, document 1381-PS, and Noakes & Pridham, III, 912.
8. *Table Talk,* October 18, 1942, 74.
9. BA-MA, RW41/4, Geheime Reichssache, SS-Brigadeführer Zimmermann, Berlin 4 January 1943.

10. Timothy Patrick Mulligan, *The Politics of Illusion: German Occupation Policy in the Soviet Union* (New York: Praeger, 1988), 50–1.

11. Noakes, IV, 490–4; and Richard Bessel, *Nazism and War* (London: Weidenfeld & Nicholson, 2004), 115.

12. Ulrich Herbert, *Hitler's Foreign Workers: Enforced Foreign Labor in Germany under the Third Reich* (Cambridge, Berg, 1997), 257–61.

13. Michael Thad Allen, *Hitler's Slave Lords: The Business of Forced Labour in Occupied Europe* (Chapel Hill: University of North Carolina, 2002).

14. Soviet Embassy, *Soviet Government Statements on Nazi Atrocities,* 66–7. The *Münster Zeitung* announced that since 1942 2,000,000 million Russians had been deported to Germany.

15. Breitman, *The Architect of Genocide,* 39–43.

16. NARA, RG242, T354, roll 650, Behandlung der europäischen Völker, 23 April 1943.

17. Refer to Nicholas M. Terry, "The German Army Group Centre and the Soviet Civilian Population, 1942-1944," (PhD diss., University of London, 2005).

18. TVDB, 75.

19. NARA, RG242, T175/128/2654189-92 Himmler to Bach-Zelewski, memo on Vlasov, January 1943.

20. Alexander Dallin, *German Rule in Russia 1941–1945: A Study of Occupation Policies* (London, Macmillan, 1957), 582–8; and Höhne, *The Order of the Death's Head,* 467.

21. J. J. Baritz, "War of the Rails," *Purnell's History of the Second World War,* 7, 1973, 2857–67.

22. Klaus Hildebrand, "Die Deutsche Reichsbahn in der nationalsozialistischen Diktatur 1933-1945," in Lothar Gall und Manfred Pohl (eds.), *Die Eisenbahn in Deutschland von den Anfängen bis zur Gegenwart* (Munich: C.H. Beck, 1999), 165–249. See also Hans Pottgiesser, *Die Deutsche Reichsbahn im Ostfeldzug 1939–1944* (Neckargemünd: Kurt Vowinckel, 1975); Andreas Knipping and Reinhard Schulz, *Reichsbahn hinter der Ostfront 1941–1944* (Stuttgart: Transpress, 1999); Alfred B. Gottwaldt, *Heeresfeldbahnen: Bau und Einsatz der militärischen Schmalspurbahnen in zwei Weltkriegen* (Stuttgart: Motorbuch, 1998).

23. NARA, RG338, FMS, D369, Railroad Transportation, Operation Zitadelle 1943, Herman Teske (1948).

24. NARA, T78/556/789205 to end OKW records, map of railway attacks, September 1943.

25. Goebbels, *Diary,* 272.

26. Trevor-Roper, *Hitler's War Directives,* 125–29; Absolon, *Die Wehrmacht,* V, 411.

27. NCA document D-735, Foreign office file note, 23 December 1942, 194.

28. NCA, document UK-66, attachment from 1 January 1943.

29. NCA, document D-741, Memorandum regarding the discussion between Reich Foreign Minister and Ambassador Alfieri in Berlin on 21 February 1943, 196–7.

30. Richard Holmes, *Bir Hacheim: Desert Citadel* (London: Pan Ballantine, 1971), 6 and 142–58.

31. PRO, CAB 176-2, Joint Intelligence Committee papers, Telegraphic report, November 18, 1943, Annex—Situation in the Balkans Mid-September to End of 1943 Note on Strategic Importance of Istria-Slovenia area.

32. Herbert, *Foreign Workers,* 273–82.

33. IWM, USMT-7, Bach-Zelewski suggested the first conference between General Schenckendorff and Wagner had taken place in 1942, when the Wehrmacht recommended he become the commander of antipartisan forces.

34. TVDB, 69–70.

35. BZ-IMT, 25 October 1945 and USMT-7, 8930.

36. TVDB, 73.

37. Koehl, *The Black Korps,* 236.

38. NARA, RG242, T175/128/2654007, SS-Befehl, 21 June 1943. BA BL, NS19/1706, SS-Befehl vom 21 June 1943 zur Bandenbekämpfung, insbes. Zuständigkeit des Reichsführers-SS und Umwandlung der Dienststelle des "Bevollmächtigten für die Bandenbekämpfung" in "Der Reichsführer-SS und Chef der Deutschen Polizei,

Der Chef der Bandenkampfverbände" sowie Ernennung von SS-Obergruppenführer von dem Bach zum Chef der Bandenkampfverbände. Hereafter referred to as the June 1943 order.

39. TVDB, 77. The meeting was held at the KSRFSS on June 19, 1943.

40. Erich Kordt, *Wahn und Wirklichkeit* (Stuttgart: Union Deutsche Verlagsges, 1948), 307.

41. War Department Technical Manual TM-E 30-451, *Handbook on German Military Forces* (Washington, 1945), section VIII-6.

42. F. H. Hinsley (ed.), *British Intelligence in the Second World War: Its Influence on Strategy and Operations* (London: Her Majesty's Stationary Office, 1981), vol. 2, app 5, "The German Police Ciphers," 670.

43. Wolf Keilig, *Das Deutsche Heer 1939–1945: Gliederung, Einsatz, Stellenbesetzung,* (Bad Nauheim, Hans-Henning Podzun, 1956), sections 140–9.

44. Absolon, *Die Wehrmacht,* VI.

45. Georg Tessin and Norbert Kannapin, *Waffen-SS und Ordnungspolizei im Kriegseinsatz 1939–1945,* (Osnabrück: Biblio Verlag, 2000), 527–666.

46. The June 1943 Order.

47. IWM, IMT-7, 8917.

48. NARA, RG242, T175/128/2654007, SS-Befehl, 21 June 1943.

49. "Arminius" was the young Germanic tribesman who led an army to victory over the Roman army commanded by Varus at the Battle of the Teutoburger Wald in the 9 AD.

50. NARA, RG242, A3343-SS0-023, Bach-Zelewski.

51. NARA, RG242, T175/128/2654007, SS-Befehl, 7 September 1943, hereafter referred to as the September order.

52. Ibid.

53. Ibid.

54. Koehl, *Black Corps*, 157.

55. PRO, HW16/1, MSGP 42, February 7, 1943.

56. TVDB, 65.

57. Wheeler, "The SS and the Administration of Nazi Occupied Eastern Europe."

58. PRO, WO311–359, Statements of German Generals in Italy. Wolff stated, "Hitler nor Himmler ever gave me an order, or intimated to me that the struggle against the partisans was to be used as reason or pretext for the extermination or decimation of the Italian population. They only requested in general and as a deterrent the taking of energetic measures in cases of sabotage and acts of terrorism."

59. NARA, BDC, A3343-SS0-010c, Karl Wolff. His full title was Höchste SS- und Polizeiführer Italien, orders dated 23 September 1943.

60. Gitta Sereny, *Into That Darkness: From Mercy Killing to Mass Murder* (London: Pimlico, 1995). Thus the leading mass killers of the SS found themselves working one last time together in the Balkans and Italy.

61. USMT-11, 6713.

62. TVDB, 65.

63. Ruth Bettina Birn, "Austrian Higher SS and Police Leaders and Their Participation in the Holocaust in the Balkans," *Holocaust and Genocide Studies* 6, 351–72, 1991; Peter R. Black, *Ernst Kaltenbrunner: Ideological Soldier of the Third Reich* (Princeton: Princeton University Press, 1984), 178.

64. NARA, RG242, T175/78/2596827-892, correspondence from Himmler regarding Daluege and his wife's illness. NARA, RG 319 IRR case file K. Daluege.

65. Hitler, *Mein Kampf*, 224.

66. Albert Speer, *The Slave State* (London: Weidenfeld & Nicolson, 1981), 9.

67. NCA, document 1919-PS.

68. Jürgen Huck, "Ausweichstellen und Aktenschicksal des Hauptamtes Ordnungspolizei im 2. Weltkrieg," in Hans-Joachim Neufeldt, Jürgen Huck, Georg Tessin, *Zur Geschichte der Ordnungspolizei 1936–1945,* (Koblenz, 1957), 119–27.

69. TVDB, 62–90.

70. NCA, document 1919-PS; Himmler's Posen Speech, October 1943.

71. Klemperer, *The Language of the Third Reich*.

72.  Gerhard Hirschfeld, *Nazi Rule and Dutch Collaboration: The Netherlands under German Occupation, 1940–1945* (Oxford: Berg, 1988), 17, 211, 221–22.
73.  Goebbels, *Diary*, 194–318.
74.  PRO, FO 371/30899, case 4948, Embassy Berne to Foreign Office, May 13, 1942.
75.  Joseph Mackiewicz, Murder of Katyn, (London, Hollis& Carter, 1951), 158–9.
76.  NCA, document 1918-PS, Kharkov, April 1943.
77.  Thierfelder, *Die Verwaltung der besetzten französischen Gebiete.*
78.  Lieber General Order, section I, points 1.
79.  Ibid, section I, points 12.
80.  Ibid, section IV, partisans, armed enemies" point 81.
81.  Lieber, *Guerrilla Parties*, 22.
82.  Oberkommando d. Wehrmacht, Bandenbekämpfung: Merkblatt 69/2, Berlin, 6. May 1944, hereafter referred to as the 1944 regulations.
83.  BA MA, RL 21/243, office of Oberst Kollee, from the 1 January 1944, folder 20, Ic-situation report (FeldLuftGauKommando XXV Gruppe Ic), January 9–15, 1944.
84.  The 1944 regulations.
85.  BA MA, RW41, Generalkommando Rothkirch, Wehrmachtsbefehlshaber Weissruthenien, various reports, December 1943 to June 1944.
86.  NCA, document L-70, Himmler at Bad Schachen, October 14, 1943, also referred to in Bramstedt, *Dictatorship and Political Police,* 243.
87.  NCA, document L-70, Himmler at Bad Schachen, October 14, 1943.
88.  Lieber, General Order No. 100, section I, points 23.
89.  The 1944 Regulations, part four, section E, paragraphs 157–62.
90.  PRO, WO208-4294, Lt. Col. Scotland's papers, Plan Kugel.
91.  Lieber, section I, points 15, 16.
92.  IWM, prisoners of war exhibition, 2004. Document referred to as the "German announcement against escapes."

## Chapter 5: Die Bandenkampfverbände

1.   Christopher Bellamy, *The Evolution of Land Warfare* (London: Routledge, 1989).
2.   NARA, BDC, A3343-SS0-023, Bach-Zelewski, letter from Himmler, July 30, 1943.
3.   The 1944 regulations.
4.   NARA, IMT, October 25, 1945 and BZ-IMT-7, 8917.
5.   BZ-IMT, October and November 1945 interrogations.
6.   Martin Van Creveld, *Command in War* (Cambridge, Mass.: Harvard University Press, 1985), 262.
7.   U.S. War Department, Military Intelligence Division, *German Military Intelligence 1939–1945* (Washington, D.C.: University Publications of America, 1984).
8.   BA-MA, RH27-1 /98, 1st Panzer Division, general orders August 18–September 10, OKH Nr. 11058/42 Zusammenstellung von Jagdkommandos zur Bandenbekämpfung (August 13, 1942).
9.   Geoffrey P. Megargee, *Inside Hitler's High Command* (Lawrence: University of Kansas, 2000), 175.
10.  Reinhard Gehlen, *Der Dienst, Erinnerungen, 1942–1971* (Munich: Droemer, 1971).
11.  NARA, RG242, OKW papers, T78, roll 556, Vortragsnotiz: Abrücken jüdischkommunistischer Bandengruppen von Galizien nach Ungarn, March 16, 1944.
12.  U.S. War Department, *German Military Intelligence*, 13–25.
13.  Ibid, 86–8.
14.  Ibid, appendix 7.
15.  NARA, T1270, roll 23, "The Character of the German General Staff 1925 to 1945," December 28, 1945.
16.  Ibid, report on the German General Staff by Bogislaw von Bonin, December 28, 1945.
17.  IWM, USMT-7.

18. NARA, RG242, T175/135/2662194-390, Rundschreiben, Spionage, Sabotage und Politische Zersetzung, August 8, 1942.

19. BZ-IMT, March 25, 1946.

20. NCA document 3428-PS, letter from Kube to Lohse, Combating of Partisans and action against Jews in the District General of White Ruthenia, July 31, 1942.

21. TVDB, 67.

22. USMT–4, 39–40.

23. NCA, documents, PS-1786, War diary of the deputy chief of armed forces operations staff, March 14, 1943.

24. PRO, WO208-4295, Report on German atrocities in Eastern Europe, M.I.9, July 6, 1944.

25. BZ-USMT, October 26, 1945.

26. NARA, IMT, October 25, 1945.

27. NARA, RG242, T175/222/2759241-272, Kriegstagebuch der Abteilung Ia/Mess.

28. BA MA RW 41/59a/75/58/60 Wehrmachtsbefehlshaber Ukraine, document 191.

29. BA MA, RW 41//59a/75/58/60 Wehrmachtsbefehlshaber Ukraine, documents 41 and 42.

30. IWM, German Army Box 3, file number 35849.

31. Heinz Krampf, FMS, D-257, Protection of the Railroad Lines Brest Litovsk–Gomel and Brest Litovsk–Kovel (1943), (n.d.).

32. Lawrence Keppie, *The Making of the Roman Army: From Republic to Empire* (London: BT Batsford, 1984), 190. See also Graham Webster, *The Roman Imperial Army of the First and Second Centuries AD* (London: Grosvenor, 1969); Roy W. Davies, *Service in the Roman Army* (Edinburgh: Edinburgh University Press, 1989); and J. B. Campbell, *The Emperor and the Roman Army, 31 BC–AD 235* (Oxford: Oxford University Press, 1984).

33. Tessin et al., *Waffen-SS und Ordnungspolizei*, 581.

34. Ibid., 592–3.

35. Refer to Gerlach, *Kalkulierte Morde*, for more detailed examination.

36. BA R19/281, Hans-Adolf Prützmann HSSPF-Russland-Süd. Betr. Führung in de Bandenbekämpfung – Tgb. 8/43(g) Geheimen, January 25, 1943.

37. IWM, Karl Wolff, interrogation Nr. 4573, January 28, 1948.

38. PRO, HW 16/98, History of the German Police W/T Network, July 1945, 1–2. HW16/93, Police Radio Network, July 18, 1942; HW 16/95, Notes on German Police W/T organization.

39. NARA, RG238, T1270, roll 31, consolidated interrogations of police operations by U.S. 12th Army, June 4, 1945.

40. NARA, BDC, A3345-B-170, Die Nachrichtenmittel der Ordnungspolizei, 1940; and, NARA, RG242, T175, roll 16, KSRFSS, Standorte und Nachrichtenverbindung, May 22, 1942.

41. Ibid.

42. Wolfgang Sawodny, *Die Panzerzüge des Deutschen Reiches 1904–1945* (Freiburg: EK-Verlag, 1996).

43. The 1944 regulations.

44. William Green, *The Warplanes of the Third Reich* (London: Macdonald and Co., 1970), 165–8.

45. BA-MA, RL10-290, Luftwaffe Flying Operations, JG 54 Kriegstagebuch, November 1942, anti-partisan operations between July 11 and August 11, 1942. The III/KG 55, September 28, 1942 to February 27, 1943, flew Heinkel HE 111 bombers and ME 108 (training aircraft), attacked partisans around Leningrad supporting ground troops.

46. The 1944 regulations.

47. Hans-Ulrich Rudel, *Trotzdem* (Oldendorf, 1981); Raymond F. Tolver and Trevor J. Constable, *The Blond Knight of Germany* (Blue Ridge Summit, Pa.: Aero Pub., 1985); and Adolf Galland, *Die Ersten und die Letzten: Jagdflieger im Zweiten Weltkrieg* (Munich: F. Schneekluth, 1953).

48. Gerhard L. Weinberg, "Airpower in Partisan Warfare," in John A. Armstrong (ed.), *Soviet Partisans in World War II* (Madison: University of Wisconsin Press, 1964), 361–88.

49. Trevor-Roper, *Hitler's War Directives*, 197–202.
50. G. A. Shepperd, "Ground to Air Liaison: Strategy and Tactics," *Purnell's History of Second World War* 8 (1975), 3217–20.
51. BA-MA RL 35/1, Kriegstagebuch, Hauptmann Christ (Ia), Generalstab der Legion Condor, January 6–June 30, 1938; RL 35/ 12, German staff officers in Spain; RL35/13, Officers serving with S/88 including advisors and civilians; RL35/ 38, Kriegstagebuch General Richtofen.
52. Johannes Buder, *Die Reorganisation der preussischen Polizei 1918–1923* (Frankfurt am Main: Lang, 1986), 99–103.
53. NARA, RG242, T175/65/2581292, Besprechung Reichsmarschall Göring, Oberst Meister, August 13, 1942.
54. PRO, HW16/6, MSGP 37, August 11, 1942.
55. BA NS19/3717, KSRFSS, Betr. Unterstellung und Einsatz der Fliegergruppe z. b.V. 7, September 25, 1943.
56. BA NS19/1165, KSRFSS, Betr. Einsatz der Flugzeuge des Fliegergeschwaders z.b.V.7, May 27, 1944, Analge 2, Betr. Einsatz der Gruppe mit den zur Zeit zur Verfügung stehenden Flugzeugen.
57. Ibid, KSRFSS, Betr. Einsatz der Flugzeuge des Fliegergeschwaders z.b.V.7, May 27, 1944, Analge 3, Betr. Standorte und Stärke der einzelnen Staffeln im Endzustand.
58. BA NS19/1165, KSRFSS, Betr. Einsatz der Flugzeuge des Fliegergeschwaders z.b.V.7, May 27, 1944.
59. Reitlinger, *The SS*, 21; Walter Schellenberg, *The Schellenberg Memoirs* (London: Andre Deutsch, 1956), 68–72; and Padfield, *Himmler*, 267.
60. Perry Biddiscombe, *"Unternehmen Zeppelin*: The Deployment of SS Saboteurs and Spies in the Soviet Union, 1942–1945," *Europe-Asia Studies* 52, no. 6 (2000), 1115–42.
61. NCA document 2939-PS, affidavit Walter Schellenberg, November 17, 1945. NCA document 3838-PS, affidavit Martin Sandberger, November 19, 1945.
62. TVDB, 62.
63. Schellenberg, *Memoirs,* 309–20.
64. Alexander Dallin and Ralph S. Mavrogordato, "Rodionov: A Case-Study in Wartime Redefection," *The American Slavic and East European Review* 1 (1959), 25–33.
65. PRO, HW16/13, file covering the reaction to the bomb plot, July 20, 1944.
66. Hans-Peter Klausch, *Antifaschisten in SS-Uniform: Schicksal und Widerstand der deutschen politischen KZ-Häftlinge, Zuchthaus- und Wehrmachtstrafgefangenen in der SS-Sonderformation Dirlewanger* (Bremen: Edition Temmen, 1993); French MacLean, *The Cruel Hunters: SS-Sonderkommando Dirlewanger, Hitler's Most Notorious Anti-partisan* (Atglen, Pa.: Schiffer Military History, 1998).
67. MacLean, *The Cruel Hunters*, 42.
68. Ibid.
69. *Table Talk*, 682.
70. NARA, RG242, BDC A3343-OSS-139B, Otto Skorzeny, correspondence Himmler and Bender April–June 1944.
71. Ibid, letter, Bender to Himmler, May 13, 1944.
72. Ibid, letter, Bender to Himmler, April 22, 1944.
73. Ibid, letter, Bender to Himmler, May 13, 1944.
74. Stein, Waffen-SS: Hitler's Elite Guard at War, 291.
75. Wegner, *The Waffen SS*, 3.
76. NARA, RG242, T175/135/149539, SS-Führungshauptamt, Verzeichnis der zuständigen Ersatztruppenteile der Waffen-SS.
77. NCA, document 1972-PS, Intermediate report on the civilian state of emergency.
78. NARA, RG319, IRR, investigation of Wilhelm Bittrich, 1945–54.
79. NARA, RG242, T175/9/2511009-53, various battalions' correspondence, January–July 1944.
80. NCA, document L-221, July 1941. Translator's italics.
81. PRO, HW16-100, Waffen SS decode reports, Q.18, November 13, 1943; and PRO, WO208-4359, History of the Waffen-SS division: MI.14 notes on the composition and history of the SS divisions.

82. PRO, WO208-4359, History of the Waffen-SS division: MI.14 notes on the composition and history of the SS divisions. The reports were based upon the interrogations of captured Waffen-SS men.

83. Tessin et al., *Waffen-SS und Ordnungspolizei,* 557.

84. BA R19/103, Schnellbrief, Daluege, Betr. Zusammenfassung der Polizei bzw Res Polizei Bataillon zu Polizei Regimentern und Bestimmung neuer Heimatstandorte, July 9, 1942.

85. PRO, HW16/6, MSGP 37, August 11, 1942.

86. NARA, RG242, T175/3/2503430-2, Dienstbesprechung der Befehlshaber und Inspekteure der Ordnungspolizei im Januar 1943 in Berlin.

87. Tessin et al., *Waffen-SS und Ordnungspolizei,* 652.

88. BA R19/94 Rechnung Schutzpolizei, 1944.

89. BA R19/103, Schnellbrief, Winkelmann, Betr. Neuaufstellung der SS Polizei-Regimenter 14, 15, 26 and Todt, April 6, 1943.

90. BA R19/111, 23 November 1943, CdO, Schnellbrief, Betr. Aufstellung des Polizei-Schütz Regiments 37.

91. BA, R19/331, Polizei Panzer Ersatz Abteilung Wien, August 23, 1944. See also Ruggenberg.

92. NARA, RG242, T175/199/2740020-60, formation of the Police Battalion 311.

93. Ibid, Schnellbrief: Aufstellung von Polizei-Wach-Bataillon, CdO, September 9, 1942.

94. BA R19/91, report on manpower wastages in the Verwaltungspolizei, Sicherheitspolizei and Schutzpolizei, September 17, 1942.

95. NARA, RG242, T175/3/2503379-416, Dienstbesprechung der Befehlshaber und Inspekteure der Ordnungspolizei im Januar 1943, in Berlin. Bericht des Chefs der Ordnungspolizei, über den Kräfte- und Kriegseinsatz der Ordnungspolizei im Kriegsjahre 1942.

96. Tessin et al., *Waffen-SS und Ordnungspolizei,* 652–3.

97. Ibid., 652–3.

98. NARA, RG242, T175/9/2511009-53, various battalions" correspondence, January –July 1944.

99. Michael O. Logusz, *Galicia Division: The Waffen-SS 14th Grenadier Division 1943–1945* (Atglen, Pa.: Schiffer Military History, 1997), 52–6.

100. Ibid., 56–9

101. PRO, WO208-4359, History of the Waffen-SS division: MI.14 notes on the composition and history of the SS divisions.

102. NARA, RG242, T175/222/2759241-9715, SS order, June 21, 1943.

103. NCA, document 498-PS, Hitler's Commando order, October 18, 1942.

104. NCA, documents 503-PS Hitler's statement on the changing nature of the war.

105. The 1944 regulations.

106. Bartov, *Hitler's Army,* 59–105.

107. CMH, SHAEF G2 Reports, "The Allgemeine-SS," Annexe L Hauptamt SS Gericht, 1945.

108. NARA, RG242, BDC, A3343-SS0-023, Bach-Zelewski, letter to Kurt Daluege, January 8, 1943; and IWM, RFSS papers, Chef des Generalstabes des Heeres, Auszug: aus einem Bericht des Ia der 365 JD über die Kämpfe bei der 8. italienischen Armee, March 23, 1943.

109. TVDB, 73, although Daluege maintained a missing person file on him until June 1943.

110. NARA, RG242, BDC, A3343-SS0-023, Bach-Zelewski, letter to Kurt Daluege, January 8, 1943.

111. IWM, Persönlicher Stab Reichsführer, "Himmler papers", letter of May 6, 1943.

112. IWM, Himmler papers, list of surviving and dead officers of the 14th SS-Police Regiment issued through the Hauptamt Ordnungspolizei (June 17, 1943).

113. PRO, HW16/6, MSGP 52, a new 14th SS-Polizei Regiment was recreated out of Police Regiment Griese, December 12, 1943. Oberst der Ordnungspolizei Griese should not be confused with Oberst der Kolonialpolizei Karl Gaisser.

114. PRO, HW16/6, MSGP 40, November 9, 1942.

115. PRO, HW16/6, MSGP 44, April 8, 1943.

116. Buchrucker, *Schwarze Reichswehr,* 32.
117. TVDB, 80.
118. Logusz, *Galicia Division,* 403–11.
119. George Lepre, *Himmler's Bosnian Division: The Waffen-SS Handschar Division, 1943–1945* (Atglen, Pa.: Schiffer Military History, 1997), 81–108.
120. TVDB, 71–2.
121. TVDB, 65.
122. NCA, document 705-PS, Minutes of the conference (January 12, 1943).
123. NCA, document PS-204, this document became a subject of a major disagreement between Bach-Zelewski and Fritz Sauckel, the latter attempting to disguise his control of labor round-up operations.
124. BA, NS/19/3717, Keitel, Betr. Unterbringung von Zivilbevölkerung, July 24, 1943.
125. NARA, RG242, T354, roll 650, Gewinnung von Arbeitskräften fur die deutsche Rüstungs- und Ernährungswirtschaft bei der Bandenbekämpfung, RFSS und Chef der Deutschen Polizei – Der Chef der Bandenkampf-Verbände, September 1, 1943.
126. BA MA, RW41/60, Field Marshal Busch, Obkdo.H.Gr.Mitte, Ia Nr.15 598/43 g.Kdos, December 1943.

## Chapter 6: Das Bandenkampfgebiet

1. DZWK, 1192.
2. Liulevicius, *War Land on the Eastern Front,* described how in the First World War the Germans had caused hardship for the indigenous population, 207–9; Hannes Heer, *Tote Zonen: Die Deutsche Wehrmacht an der Ostfront* (Hamburg: Hamburger Edition, 1999), refers to the killing fields in the east, 11–40; whereas Gerlach, *Kalkulierte Morde,* explained how the Eastern Front was transformed into a desert of people and economy, while in "German Economic Interests, Occupation Policy, and the Murder of the Jews in Belorussia," in Ulrich Herbert (ed.), *National Socialist Extermination Policies: Contemporary German Perspectives and Controversies* (Oxford: Berghahn, 2000), he reinforced his argument by summarizing that "Economic interests and crises were far more important influences on the tempo of the liquidation of the Jews," 227.
3. Terry, "The German Army Group Centre and the Soviet Civilian Population, 1942–1944," entwines Soviet and German history in his study of the Army Group Centre occupation zone to explain his view of the economic geography of a region under occupation. He suitably described this as "The Quartermasters' State," implying that the quartermaster of the army group was all powerful, 36–57.
4. PRO, HW16/6, 43, February 6–March 6, 1943.
5. PRO, HW16/100, Waffen SS, report CX/MSS/Q1, October 9, 1943.
6. NARA, RG338, FMS, D-157, "Protecting supply lines in the Southern Ukraine," Generalleutnant Ludwig Keiper (Luftwaffe), hereafter referred to as the Keiper study.
7. BA R19/304, CdO, Schnellbrief, Betr. Besondere Massnahmen zur Partisanen-bekämpfung, July 14, 1942.
8. NARA, RG338, FMS, D-224, 'securing lines of communication in enemy country," Generalleutnant Arthur Schwarznecker, hereafter Schwarznecker report.
9. Ibid.
10. Keiper study.
11. Ibid.
12. Schwarznecker report.
13. USMT-12, 10148, reference to the methods of the 285th Security Division, June 8, 1943.
14. NARA, RG242, T175/135149539, SS-Führungshauptamt Organisation, June 1, 1942.
15. BA R19/325, CdO, Schnellbrief, Betr. Aufstellung eines Wachzuges für den Polizei-Truppenübungsplatz, June 2, 1943.
16. DKHH, 377.

17. TVDB, 35.
18. DKHH, 402.
19. NARA, RG242, T175/66/2562721; SS-Sturmbannführer With, Bericht für die Zeit, May 16–21, 1942.
20. DKHH, 423.
21. DKHH, 485, 493.
22. Wegner, *The Waffen-SS*, 302–3.
23. NARA, RG242, T175/42/1, the application from Lieutenant-General Ramcke for a farmstead in the east. Refer to Rolf-Dieter Müller, *Hitlers Ostkrieg und die deutsche Siedlungspolitik. Die Zusammenarbeit von Wehrmacht, Wirtschaft und SS,* (Frankfurt a. M, 1991) for a more detailed examination.
24. Military History Archive Prague (MHAP)/USHMM RS-48.004/roll 6, Ic Mitteilungen Nr. 4, March 5, 1943. The copy of this report kindly provided by Nicholas Terry.
25. NARA, RG242, BDC, A3343-SSO-364A, Rudolf Pannier, Tätigkeitsbericht für den Monat August, September 6, 1943, hereafter referred to as Pannier's August report.
26. MHAP/USHMM RS-48.004/roll 6, Tätigkeitsbericht, August 8, 1943. The copy of this report kindly provided by Nick Terry and is hereafter referred to as Pannier's July report.
27. NARA, RG242, BDC, A3343-SSO-364A, Rudolf Pannier, Tätigkeitsbericht für den Monat August, September 6, 1943.
28. MHAP/USHMM RS-48.004/roll 6, Tätigkeitsbericht für den Monat September, October 8, 1943. The copy of this report kindly presented by Nick Terry and is hereafter referred to as Pannier's September report.
29. Pannier's August report.
30. NCA document 1992-A-PS, National Political Course for the Armed Forces, January 15–23, 1937.
31. Guido Knopp, "Die SS—Eine Warnung der Geschichte" (ZDF television, 2003).
32. NARA, RG242, T77/780/5506284-568, Wehrmacht Ersatzplan 1945.
33. BA ZNS, trooper's personnel records.
34. Wegner, *The Waffen-SS*, 303–9.
35. RFSS, *Dich ruft die SS*, 81.
36. Ibid., 83.
37. NARA, RG242, T175/5/2505208-6228, organizational of the Technische Nothilfe, December 20, 1940.
38. Martin Cüppers, "Gustav Lombard – ein eingagierter Judenmörder aus der Waffen-SS," in Klaus-Michael Mallman and Gerhard Paul (eds.), *Karrieren der Gewalt: Nationalsozialistische Täterbiographien* (Darmstadt: Wissenschaftliche Buchgesellschaft, 2004), 147.
39. BA R19/467, RFSS Ch.d.Dts Pol, Betr. Jüdisch Versippte im der Polizeireserve, Polizei-Reservisten and Polizeibeamte, October 27, 1942.
40. CMH, SHAEF G2 Reports, Reichsschule SS, Oberehnheim in Elsass, 1945.
41. NARA, RG242, T175/135/2662194, SS-Führungshauptamt Organisation, March 1942. See also Wolfgang Vopersal, "Die SS-Ersatzbataillone in Breslau und dass SS-Ersatzbataillon, Ost," in *Der Freiwillige* 4 (March 1973), 22–23; and *Der Freiwillige* 5 (April 1973), 18–19.
42. NARA, RG242, T175/135/2662194-389, SS-Führungshauptamt Organisation, March 1942.
43. NARA, RG242, T580, roll 222, an order from November 1939, armored cars for occupation forces, CdO.
44. BA R19/266, Richtlinien für die Ausbildung der in die Schutzpolizei des Reiches und der Gemeinden eingestellten Polizeireservisten, March 6, 1940.
45. BA R19/327, CdO, Schnellbrief, Ausbildung WSPK, September 9, 1944.
46. BA R19/325, CdO, Schnellbrief, Betr. 2 Lehrgang für Kampfausbildung der Bez. Offz. Anw. an der Pol. Waffenschule II in Laon, May 8, 1944.
47. BA R19/325, CdO, Schnellbrief, Betr. Auffüllung der Polizei-Waffenschulen durch Volksdeutsche aus Siebenbuergen, July 30, 1943.
48. BA R19/26, Offiziere Ausbildung, Hauptamt-Ordnungspolizei, Amtsgruppe II.
49. BA R19/10, RFSS, Betr. Offiziernachwuchs, Anlage 2, Richtlinien für den Offizieranwärterlehrgang für Revier—und Bezirksoffiziere, March 28, 1943.

50. BA R19/121, Polizeiverwaltungsbeamte im Bereich des BdO Ukraine (Rowno) 1941–2, Heft 1. Following Chernigov 67,000, 35 officials and 58 officers, home station Karlsruhe, Zhitomir 95,000, 35 officials, and 26 officers, home station Plauen; Nikolaiev 167,000 homes, 35 officials, and 42 officers, home station Aussig; Poltava 130,000, 7 officials, and 46 officers, home station Mönchen-Gladbach-Rheydt; Kremenchug 89,000, 7 officials, and 25 officers, home station Wittenberg; Berdichev 66,000, 7 officials, and 23 officers, home station Hamm; Kirovograd 100,000, 7 officials, and 27 officers, home station Würzburg; Korsun 97,000, 7 officials, and 27 officers, home station Koblenz; Dnjeprodserchinsk 148,000, 7 officials, and 39 officers, home station Oppeln; Nikopol 57,000, 7 officials, and 23 officers, home station Lübeck.

51. BA R19/327, Schnellbrief, Betr. Wasserschutzpolizei-Kommando "Dnjepr," October 23, 1941.

52. BA R19/327, CdO, Schnellbrief, Betr. Auflösung Wasserschutzpolzei Kommando "Pripjat, February 1, 1944

53. PRO, HW16/6, MSGP 40, November 9, 1942.

54. NARA, RG242, T354, roll 648, Dirlewanger Brigade order for the issue of alcohol and cigarettes.

55. PRO, HW16/6, MSGP 30, November 14, 1941.

56. PRO, HW16/6, MSGP 47, July 9, 1943.

57. PRO, HW16/6 MSGP 26, July 24, 1941.

58. PRO, HW16/6, MSGP 30, November 14, 1941.

59. JNSV, case 663, *Landesgericht* Wiesbaden, February 23, 1968.

60. PRO, HW16/6, MSGP 31, January 22, 1942; and, MSGP 34, April 11, 1942.

61. PRO, HW16/6, MSGP 34, April 11, 1942; HW16/38, July 11–November 3, 1943; HW16/39, 1943–44; HW16/42, August 6, 1944–February 13, 1945.

62. NARA, RG242, T175/16/2519790, reports from KSRFSS titled "Verluste, Infektionen, Seuchen," contains many examples from January–March 1942.

63. NARA, RG242, T354, roll 648, Kampfgruppe von Gottberg orders of the day, February 1943.

64. PRO, HW16/6, MSGP 35, May 24, 1942.

65. PRO, HW16/6, MSGP 36, July 17, 1942.

66. PRO, HW16/6, MSGP 37, August 11, 1942.

67. PRO, HW16/6, MSGP 53, January 12, 1944.

68. PRO, HW16/6, MSGP 44, April 8, 1943.

69. Pannier's August report.

70. Pannier's September report.

71. Pannier's July report.

72. Pannier's August report.

73. Ibid.

74. Pannier's September report.

75. NARA, RG242, BDC, A3343-SSO-364A, Rudolf Pannier.

76. Ibid.

77. Pannier's August report.

78. PRO, HW16/6, MSGP 34, April 11, 1942.

79. PRO, HW16/6, MSGP 38, cases of forged ration cards and security passes, September 7, 1942.

80. PRO, HW16/6, MSGP 40, November 9, 1942.

81. JNSV, case no. 830.

82. NARA, RG242, T175/9/2511009-52, Besprechung der Prüfungsarbeit für Major-Anwärter (Mai 1936) in Polizeiverwendung (von Polizeioffizierschule aufgestellt).

83. NARA, RG242, BDC, A3345-B-171. Vorschrift für die Verwendung der Schutzpolizei und der Gendarmerie (Einzeldienst) im täglichen Dienst, Teil 1, Berlin 1940 with the attached Vorschrift für die Waffen- und Schiessausbildung der Ordnungspolizei, Teil 3, Berlin 1940.

84. Richard Schulze-Kossens, *Militärischer Führernachswuchs der Waffen-SS: Die Junkerschulen* (Osnabrück: Munin, 1982); and Jay Hathaway, *In Perfect Formation: SS Ideology and the SS-Junkerschule-Tölz* (Atglen, Pa.: Schiffer, 1999).

85. NARA, RG319 IRR, case file Kurt Daluege.
86. PRO, HW16/6, Chief of Staff Rode request to encourage further training and identify future leaders.
87. NCA, document 1918-PS, Himmler's Metz speech, 1940.
88. BA-MA, RW41 and NARA, RG242, T501/1/1-464, Korpsbefehl Nr. 53, Erfahrungsaustausch (Kampf gegen Partisanen), September 16, 1941.
89. This course contributed to the regulations introduced on October 25, 1941, referred to in chapter two.
90. NARA, RG242, T175/9/2511053-63, CdO, Merkblatt für die Ausbildung der geschlossen Polizeinheiten im Polizeikampf, March 1941.
91. BA R19/10, RFSS, O-Kdo I O (3) 1 Nr. 210/42, Winkelmann, Betr. Auflösung der Kolonialpolizeischule in Wien, August 7, 1942.
92. NARA, RG242, T175/13/2515813-90, Richtlinien für die kolonialtaktische Ausbildung an den Kolonialpolizei-Schulen (1942).
93. NARA, RG242, T175/13/2515813-90, Die Völker der Erde.
94. NARA, RG242, T175/13/2515813-90, general lecture notes.
95. BA R19/467, RFSS, Besondere Aufgaben der Ordnungspolizei erfordert Aufstellung eines Sonderfährenkorps aus Polizeireserve bzw., February 17, 1942.
96. NARA, RG338, FMS, P005b, Partisan Warfare in Croatia, Karl Gaisser (April 1951), later became the basis of the Gaisser study.
97. Gaisser study.
98. BA MA, RW41/76, January 7, 1944, diary entry, 20.
99. BA R3701/2038, Reichsforstamt, Geplante Bandenkampfschule in Tucheler Heide, November 2, 1944.
100. BA R19/321, on November 23, 1943, Richard Hildebrandt wrote to Himmler explaining that Forstamtmann Erich Bachus responsible for the Tuchler Heide was an exceptional officer. Explaining that his father had been assassinated by "bandits" on November 10, 1943.
101. Baritz, "War of the rails," 2857–67.
102. NARA, RG242, BDC, A3343-SSO-364A, Rudolf Pannier.
103. Ibid.
104. Ibid.
105. Pannier's August report.
106. Ibid, the shooting took place on the evening of August 20–21.
107. Ibid.
108. Ibid.
109. Ibid, the collection included twenty-six tons of cereals, four tons of hay, twenty-three horses, fifty-five cows, twenty-four calves, twelve sheep, and one pig.
110. Ibid.
111. Ibid.
112. NARA, RG242, BDC, A3343-SSO-364A, letter SS-Untersturmführer Helmich, July 4, 1944.

## Chapter 7: Die Bandenunternehmungen

1. Bellamy, The Evolution of Land Warfare, 18–20.
2. Simpson, "The German Experience of Rear Area Security on the Eastern Front," 43.
3. The 1944 regulations, sections 72–79.
4. PRO, HW 16/98, History of the German Police W/T Network, July 1945, 2.
5. NARA, T353, roll 650, Kräftebereicht Stand vom June 1, 1943, HSSPF, June 3, 1943.
6. BA-MA, RS4/1066, Auszug aus einem Bericht Ia der Kampfgruppe "Hannibal": Major Friedrich Neumann, Ludwigshafen, April 1956.
7. NARA, RG242, T-354, roll 650, Bataillons-Befehl für das Unternehmen "Hornung," February 7, 1943.

8. NARA, RG242, T175/81/2601501, Abschrift von SSPF Shitomir, Banden-bekämpfung, January 27, 1943.

9. Ibid.

10. Ruth Bettina Birn, "'Zaunkoenig' an 'Uhrmacher.' Grosse Partisanenaktionen 1942/43 am Beispiel des 'Unternehmens Winterzauber,'" in *Militaergeschichtliche Zeitschrift* 60 (2001), Heft 1, 99–118.

11. Heer und Naumann et al, *Vernichtungskrieg, Verbrechen der Wehrmacht 1941 bis 1944,* 104–38.

12. Gerlach, *Kalkulierte Morde,* 859–1055.

13. NARA, RG242, T175/81/2601529, Meldung 2, August 24, 1942.

14. USHMM, RS22.007M (State Archive of the Russian Federation Trophy Documents), Gefechtsbericht für des Unternehmen Zauberflöte, April 24, 1943. I would like to thank Nick Terry for providing a copy of this final report.

15. NARA, RG242, T354, roll 649, Unternehmen Zauberflöte, April 17–22, 1943.

16. Richard Evans, *Rethinking German History: Nineteenth Century Germany and the Origins of the Third Reich* (London: Allen & Unwin, 1987), 248–90.

17. Bessel, "Policing, Professionalization and Politics," 201.

18. Ibid.

19. TVDB, 74.

20. TVDB, 75. USHMM, RS22.007M, Gefechtsbericht für des Unternehmen Zauberflöte, April 24, 1943.

21. TVDB, 76.

22. BA-MA, RL20/302, Unternehmen Nasses Dreieck, May 5–16, 1943.

23. Ibid.

24. Ibid.

25. Ibid.

26. Ibid

27. Ibid.

28. Ibid.

29. Ibid.

30. TVDB, 76–7.

31. Sidor A. Kovpak, *Our Partisan Course* (London: Hutchinson, 1947). The German after action files have survived and can be found in NARA, RG242, T175/222/2759715-865, Abschlussbericht über die Bekämpfung der Kolpak-Bände, September 2, 1943. Krüger to the army commander in the General-Government Hereinafter referred to as Krüger's report to the army. Also BA-MA RL20/284, SS report to Luftwaffe commander in Lemberg.

32. Armstrong (ed.), *Soviet Partisans,* 11; and O. A. Zarubinsky, "The 'Red' Partisan Movement in Ukraine During World War II: A Contemporary Assessment," *The Journal of Slavic Military Studies* 9 (June 1996), 399–416.

33. Kovpak, *Our Partisan Course,* 115.

34. BA-MA RL20/284, the SS report as administered by the Luftwaffe commander in Lemberg.

35. Cajus Bekker, trans. Frank Ziegler, *The Luftwaffe War Diaries* (London: Stackpole Military History, 1972), 379–81.

36. The Germans recorded Kovpak's name as Kolpak. There was an Oberst Kolpak who commanded a German Freikorps Battalion in the Baltic, in 1919, Oertzen, *Freikorps,* 28.

37. PRO, HW16/6, MSGP 49, September 9, 1942.

38. Kovpak, *Our Partisan Course,* 115.

39. Peter J. Potichnyj, "Pacification of Ukraine: Soviet Counterinsurgency, 1944–1956," Conference paper, Russian Experience with counterinsurgency, University of New Brunswick, Center for Conflict Studies, October 1987.

40. BZ-IMT, testimony, October 24, 1945.

41. Birn, "Zaunkoenig", 111.

42. Ibid.

43. NARA, RG242, T354, roll 648, Kampfgruppe Kutschera, operational order for Unternehmen Franz, January 4, 1943.

44. BA-MA, RL 20 302—Kriegstagebuch 3 Kdr. Fl. Bau 4/XIII—Commander Oberst Altermann 1943, documents, 63–4.

45. Ibid.

46. TVDB, 53. Walter Schellenberg confirmed this incident, explaining that Himmler's long-serving Bavarian pilot had been warned not to go into a Russian village. He ignored the warnings and was, according to Schellenberg, killed by partisans in what was obviously a cruel manner.

47. PRO, HW16/6, MSGP 36, July 17, 1942.

48. PRO, HW35/42, German Police, July 24, 1942.

49. MacLean, *The Cruel Hunters*, 61–2. Their corpses were cut up, mixed with horse meat, and boiled into soap.

50. PRO, HS8-882, Vera Atkins. The women had been captured in Paris between June and November 1943 and sent to Natzweiler in May 1944.

51. NARA, RG242, T175, roll 81, Übersicht über bisherige Anordnungen und Anregungen betr. Banenkinderunterbringung, July 13, 1943.

52. NARA, RG242, T-354, roll 650, Bataillons-Befehl für das Unternehmen "Hornung," February 7, 1943.

53. IMT, R-135, letter from Reich Commissar for the Eastland to Reich Minister for the Occupied Eastern Territory, June 18, 1943.

54. Ibid.

55. NARA, RG242, BDC, A3345-DS-J007, Himmler to Chef der Bandenkampfverbände, HSSPF Ukraine and HSSPF Russland-Mitte, July 10, 1943.

56. NARA, RG242, T175, roll 21, Himmler to Kaltenbrunner, Chief of RSHA July 28, 1943.

57. Ibid.

58. Jürgen Förster, "The Relation between Barbarossa as an Ideological War of Extermination and the Final Solution," in David Cesarani, *The Final Solution, Origins and Implementation* (London: Routledge, 1994), 97–8.

59. NARA, RG242, T354, roll 648, central document for the listing of casualties and results, 1943.

60. Ibid., Tactics against Bandits, unnamed company commander, Dirlewanger Brigade, September 5, 1943.

61. NARA, RG242, T175/70/2547404-750, Gefangenen- und Beutezahlen im *Unternehmen Sternlauf,* February 13, 1943.

62. NARA, RG242, T175/70/2547404-750, Korpstagesbefehl, January 3–February 12, 1943.

63. NARA, RG242, T354, roll 649, Unternehmen Draufänger II, reports, May 1943.

64. NARA, RG242, T354, roll 649, Gefechtsbericht der Einsatzgruppe Dirlewanger fuer die zeit vom May 20– June 2, 1943 (June 25, 1943).

65. NARA, RG242, T354, roll 648, Monatliche Zusammenstellung der Verluste (feindliche und eigene) und Beute, July 12, 1943, HSSPF Russland-Mitte, Operations Officer.

66. NARA, RG242, T354, roll 648, HSSPF Russland-Mitte, Monatliche Zusammenstellung der Verluste (feindliche und eigene) und Beute, July 12, 1943.

67. NARA, RG242, T354, roll 649, Unternehmen Hermann reports.

68. NARA, RG242, T175/81/2601501-2034, Letter from General Schmundt OKW to Himmler, March 15, 1943.

69. NARA, RG242, T175/3/2503430-2, Dienstbesprechung der Befehlshaber und Inspekteure der Ordnungspolizei im Januar 1943 in Berlin.

70. Absolon, *Die Wehrmacht,* VI, 489, and 789.

71. Eric Lefebre and Jean de Lagarde, "Das Bandenkampfabzeichen 1944–1945," *Internationales Militaria,* January 1999, 36–41.

72. TVDB, 104.

73. NARA, RG242, BDC A3343-SSO-24A, Curt von Gottberg.

74. TVDB, 75.

75. NCA, document, R-135, Results of police operation Cottbus, June 22–July 3, and June 5, 1943, 206–7.

76. Ibid, letter from Hinrich Lohse to Alfred Rosenberg, June 18, 1943, 205.

77. Ibid, Diary no. 3628/43, letter from Reichs Commissar for the Eastland, to Personal-Staff RFSS, June 18, 1943.

78. IWM, USMT-11, Berger's testimony, 6121.

79. Ibid, Berger's defence evidence, 6133–412.

80. NARA, RG242, BDC, A3345-OSS-202A, Ernst Korn. NARA, RG242/18/2521387, Korn's request was acknowledged by Himmler, June 1, 1943.

81. NARA, RG242, BDC, A3345-OSS-202A, Generalmajor Klinger, Kommandeur der Schutzpolizei, Hauptamt Ordnungspolizei, May 17, 1943.

82. NARA, RG238, M1019, roll 37. Korn remained in this position until September 14, 1943, when replaced by his assistant Leutnant Steudle.

83. PRO, HW16/6, MSGP 55, April 13, 1944. Korn sent a signal that was intercepted by the British on March 10, 1944, when he was chief of staff of the *Bandenstab Croatia*.

84. TVDB, 80.

85. NARA, RG242, BDC, A3345-OSS-202A Gerrett Korsemann. PRO, HW16/6, MSGP 40, October 1–31, 1942, one of the many personal messages from Korsemann to Himmler, this time wishing him a happy birthday, November 9, 1942.

86. NARA, RG238, M1270/26/798, Ernst Rode interrogation report, October 22, 1945, Annex II Rode's relationship with Himmler.

87. PRO, HW16/100, Waffen SS decode reports, November 1, 1943. Also refer to TVDB, 91.

88. NARA, RG242, T354, roll 649, Unternehmen Zauberflote, April 17–22, 1943.

89. NARA, RG242, T354, roll 649, Erfahrungsbericht "Unternehmen Günther," July 14, 1943.

90. TVDB, 79–80; and BA-KA, the photographic collection, Koblenz.

91. PRO, HW16/6, MSGP 33, March 17, 1942.

92. Broszat and Krausnick, *Anatomy of the SS State*, 346–7: A copy of the original can be found on NARA, RG242, T175, roll 38, with the subsequent correspondence.

93. NARA, RG242, T175/38/2548284, Letter Herf to Herff, July 21, 1943. Herff continued, "The success now is that I can request everyone to report, no matter if Bach-Zelewski is about or not. This changes the position 380 degrees. I am free again from this business of fraud."

94. NARA, RG242, T175/38/2548288, letter, Herf to Herff, July 29, 1943.

95. Herff left office, believing his honor remained intact.

96. TVDB, 81.

97. Ibid, 82.

98. Manfred Messerschmidt, "Der Minsker Process 1946," in Heer and Naumann (eds.), *Vernichtungskrieg*, 551–68; Alexander Victor Prusin, "'Fascist Criminals to the Gallows!': The Holocaust and Soviet War Crimes Trials, December 1945–February 1946," *Holocaust and Genocide Studies* 17 (2003), 1–30; and Eric Haberer, "The German Police and Genocide in Belorussia, 1941–1944," *Journal of Genocide Research* 3 (2001), 23–24.

99. NARA, RG242, T354, roll 648, HSSPF Russland-Mitte, Monatliche Zusammenstellung der Verluste (feindliche und eigene) und Beute, July 12, 1943.

100. Gerald Reitlinger, *The Final Solution: The Attempt to Exterminate the Jews of Europe* (New York: Perpetua Edition, 1961), 287–90. See also PRO, WO208-4295, Report on German atrocities in Eastern Europe, M.I.9, July 6, 1944.

101. BA-MA RW41/4 letter from Kluge to Schenckendorff's wife.

102. NARA, BDC, A3343-SS0-24A, Curt von Gottberg.

## Chapter 8: Poland

1. Victor Klemperer, *To the Bitter End: The Diaries of Victor Klemperer 1942–45*, II, (London: Penguin, 1998), 405.

2. NCA document 1919-PS, Metz speech, May 1940.

3. NCA document 1919-PS, Bad Schachen, October 14, 1943.

4. NCA document 1919-PS, Sonthofen speech 1943.

5. NARA, RG242, T175/13/2515629-782, Gendarmerie arrest instructions for slave labourers in the area of Strasbourg border guard posts in 1943.

6. Herbert, *Foreign Workers*, 364–70; Eric A. Johnson, *Nazi Terror: The Gestapo, Jews and Ordinary Germans* (London: John Murray, 2002), 310.

7. NARA, RG242, T1270, roll 23, the interrogation of criminal commissar Bethke.

8. Interview with Frank Gierllen, May 10, 2000. Gierllen, a veteran Belgium resistance fighter, confirmed Soviet resistance factions operated across the German border near Aachen.

9. PRO, HW 16/98, History of the German Police W/T Network, July 1945, 20.

10. MacLean, *The Cruel Hunters*, 57–66. During his time in Kraków, Dirlewanger was known to have conducted security actions against insurgents rooted in the Polish forests.

11. BA R19/462, Gendarmerie-Hauptmannschaft Radom, Einsatzbericht über den Einsatz am 29 November 1942 im Walde ostwaerts Lubionia 12 km südlich von Ilza, 30 November 1942.

12. BA-MA, RL 21/243, office of Oberst Kollee, from January 1, 1944, Ic-situation report (Feldluftgaukommando XXV Gruppe Ic), January 9–15, 1944.

13. Yerger, *Allgemeine-SS*, 39.

14. NCA, document L-18, Final Report on the Solution of the Jewish Question in the District of Galicia, 756–70.

15. Ibid.

16. Ibid.

17. Christopher Browning, *Ordinary Men: Reserve Police Battalion 101 and the Final Solution in Poland* (New York: First Harper Perennial, 1998), 104.

18. U.S. Army, Handbook, section, IV-VIII.

19. Jürgen Stroop, "Es gibt keinen jüdischen Wohnbezirk in Warschau mehr!" published as *The Stroop Report*, trans. Sybil Milton and introduction by Andrej Wirth, (London, 1980).

20. NCA, document 1061-PS, concluding repor May 24, 1943.

21. PRO, WO208-4295, Scotland Papers, Report on interrogation of PW KP 2084.34 SS-Gren. Willi Hansen, March 10, 1945.

22. PRO, WO208-4295, Report on interrogation of PW CS/689 SS-Oschaf. Anton Schaffrath, November 25, 1944.

23. PRO, WO208-3625, PWIS(H)/KP/525, PWIS Interrogations, Kempton Park, December 1944. Report written on December 4, and signed Major MacCloud.

24. PRO, WO208-3625, PWIS(H)/KP/239, PWIS Interrogations, Kempton Park, August 1944. Report written on August 11, and signed Major MacCloud.

25. Mark Mazower, *Inside Hitler's Greece: The Experience of Occupation 1941–1944.* (New Haven, Conn.: Yale University Press, 1995), 222–4.

26. NARA, RG242, T175/70/2586239-60 and T175/81/2601501-2034, Reichsführer-SS, 28 June 1943 and NS19/1433, "Bandenkampf- und Sicherheitslage." Vortrag des Reichsführers-SS bei Hitler auf dem Obersalzberg am 19 June 1943.

27. Lucy Dawidowicz, *The War against the Jews, 1939–45* (London: Penguin, 1975), 394–8.

28. NARA, RG242, T175/81260280, Order RFSS to Hans Frank and Bach-Zelewski, June 21, 1943.

29. Robin O'Neil, *Belzec: Prototype for the Final Solution; Hitler's Answer to the Jewish Question*, at http://www.jewishgen.org/yizkor/belzec1/bel000.html

30. Reuben Ainsztein, *Jewish Resistance in Nazi-Occupied Eastern Europe* (London: Elek, 1974), 518–47.

31. TVDB, 81.

32. NCA, document 1517-PS of November 1941, and IMT-BZ, March 25, 1946, where Bach-Zelewski admitted to engineering Globocnik's removed.

33. PRO, WO208-4300, Scotland Papers, Report on interrogation of PW LD 1136 SS-Gruppenführer Jakob Sporrenberg, February 25, 1946.

34. Schmauser was Bach-Zelewski's replacement at HSSPF-Southeast.

35. DKHH, April 10, 1941, 148.
36. TVDB, 84.
37. PRO, WO208-4300, Scotland Papers, Sporrenberg.
38. Browning, *Ordinary Men*, 137-42.
39. Gerhard L. Weinberg, *Germany, Hitler and World War II: Essays in Modern German and World History* (Cambridge: Cambridge University Press, 1995), 228-9.
40. Alexander Werth, *Russia at War, 1941–1945* (London: Pan, 1965), 77 and 149.
41. JNSV, case 638. They both received life sentences from the court in Oldenburg in 1966.
42. TVDB, 92-3, the Kovel Order for rapid deployment, January 14, 1944.
43. Cüppers, "Lombard," 149.
44. NARA, RG242, BDC, A3343-SSO-275A, Gustav Lombard.
45. Bellamy, *Evolution of Land Warfare*, 20.
46. TVDB, 99-103.
47. NARA, RG242, T175/81/2601886, Miscellaneous Bandenbekämpfung papers. The body count amounted to one dead, seven wounded, and one missing, from the Waffen-SS; the army, seven dead (one officer), forty-one wounded, and four missing; and the police, two officers killed, twenty-six wounded, eighty five missing (including an official and a doctor).
48. PRO, HW16/39, GPD2383, February 2, 1944, No 1 traffic.
49. PRO, HW16/6, MSGP54, March 14, 1944 and HW16/39, GPD2378, GG3, No 1 traffic.
50. TVDB, 98.
51. PRO, WO 311/10, Black List of German Police, SS and Miscellaneous Party and Paramilitary Personalities, Report, September 1945.
52. Soviet Embassy, *Soviet Government Statements on Nazi Atrocities,* 171. The town of Kolki today still stands on the River Styr, 50 kilometres east of Kovel.
53. Andrew Borowiec, *Destroy Warsaw! Hitler's Punishment, Stalin's Revenge* (Westport, Conn.: Praeger, 2001), 73–76.
54. NARA, RG242, A3343-SS0-023, Bach-Zelewski, letter from Dr. Rapport, 11 January 1944.
55. TVDB, 96, the letter was copied into Bach-Zelewski's diary.
56. NARA, RG242, A3343-SS0-023, Bach-Zelewski, letter from Dr. Rapport, 22 March 1944. The letter stated, "The problem of SS-Obergruppenführer von dem Bach is the lack of concentration when on the toilet. He must concentrate or the sphincter cannot work."
57. TVDB, 98-9.
58. TVDB, 99.
59. NARA, RG242, T175/222/279241, Kriegstagebuch der Abteilung Ia/Mess., 21 June-21 November 1943.
60. TVDB, 100.
61. BA R19/321 Schnellbrief on the activities of bandits, January 21, 1944.
62. TVDB, 74.
63. NCA, document L-37, Collective responsibility of members of families of assassins and saboteurs, July 19, 1944.
64. Richard C. Lukas, *Forgotten Holocaust: The Poles under German Occupation 1939–1944* (New York: Hippocrene, 1997).
65. NARA, RG242, T78, roll 560, OKH, Generalstab des Heeres, Fremde Heere Ost, Die Widerstandsbewegung im Gebiet Des Ehem. Polen, 9 February 1944.
66. NARA, RG242, T78, roll 562, OKH, Generalstab des Heeres, Fremde Heere Ost 1 July 1944.
67. NARA, RG242, T77, roll 1421, Wehrkreiskommando Generalgouvernement, Generalmajor Haseloff, Lage im Generalgouvernement im Monat Dezember 1943, 6 January 1944.
68. NARA, RG242, T77, roll 1421, Wehrkreiskommando Generalgouvernement, Generalmajor Haseloff.
69. NARA, RG242, T77, roll 1421, April 1944.
70. NARA, RG242, T77, roll 1421, Reisebericht, Oberstleutnant Ziervogel und Hauptmann Cartellieri, 25–26 July 1944.

71. NARA, RG242, T78 roll 562, OKH, Generalstab des Heeres, Fremde Heere Ost, 1 July 1944.
72. BA-MA, RW 41/60, Wehrmachtbefehlshaber Weissruthenien, Anlagen 1-99 zum kriegstagebuch Nr. 6 (1 January 1944 to 30 June 1944). Grundlegender Befehl Nr.22 of 1 January 1944: Bandenlage.
73. Matthew Cooper, The German Army, 1933-1945, (Lanham: First Scarborough House, 1990), 476. Evan Cooper barely mentioned the battle.
74. Carlo D'Este, "Model" in Correlli Barnett (ed.), Hitler's Generals (London: Weidenfeld & Nicolson, 1989), 319–34.
75. Sydnor, Soldiers of Destruction, 306.
76. W. Victor Madeja, Russo-German War: Summer 1944, vol. 33 (Allentown: Valor, 1987), 50.
77. Lukas, The Forgotten Holocaust, 195.
78. Norman Davies, Rising" 44: The Battle for Warsaw (London: Macmillan, 2003), 251-2 and 728.
79. Günther Deschner, Warsaw Rising (London: Pan, 1972), 21-2.
80. Ibid, 251.
81. Noakes & Pridham, III, 952.
82. Joanna K. Hanson, The Civilian Population and the Warsaw Rising of 1944 (Cambridge: Cambridge University Press, 1982).
83. TVDB, 106-7.
84. TVDB and NARA, RG242, T175/222/2759241-50, papers referring to the transfer from the east to Salzburg.
85. TVDB, 106 and BZ-USMT 14 August 1946.
86. BZ-IMT, 29 January 1946.
87. PRO, HW16/6, MSGP 60, May 1945.
88. Janus Piekalkiewicz, Kampf um Warschau: Stalins Verrat an der polnischen Heimatarmee 1944 (Munich: F.A. Herbig, 1994) and Hans von Krannhals, Der Warschauer Aufstand 1944 (Frankfurt: Bernard & Graefe Verl.f. Wehrwesen, 1964), 300-1.
89. PRO, WO208-3629, PWIS(H)/KP/685, PWIS Interrogations, Kempton Park, May 1, 1945.
90. TVDB, 114-5.
91. Sydnor, Soldiers of Destruction, 305, NARA, RG242, T312/343/7916427-6431, Ninth Army special report "Zum Warschauer Aufstand"
92. Guderian, Panzer Leader, 356.
93. BZ-IMT, 29 January 1946.
94. Sven Steenberg, Vlasov (New York: Alfred A. Knopf, 1970), 171-2, also Reitlinger, The SS, 377, Padfield, Himmler, 527.
95. TVDB, 108.
96. NARA, RG242, BDC, A3345-OSS-231, Heinz Reinefarth, letter to RFSS, 9 September 1944.
97. Ibid.
98. NARA, RG242, BDC, A3345-OSS-231, Heinz Reinefarth, and TVDB, 110.
99. PRO, HW16/6, MSGP 61, September 1–October 31, 1944. The message was confirmed. A reply was not decrypted, sent on September 17. Himmler signalled his acknowledgment of the capture of the fortress and ordered the troops to continue attacks. He was ordered to destroy the uprising soon as everyday counted. TVDB, 110. Bach-Zelewski added in his diary, "I am curious how long we can hold Warsaw and hopefully we can have soldiers luck. Everyday is a success."
100. Hanson, The Civilian Population and the Warsaw Uprising of 1944, 85–6.
101. BZ-IMT, January 29, 1946; and Bruce, Warsaw Uprising, 201.
102. Borowiec, Destroy Warsaw! 94.
103. Ibid, 95.
104. TVDB, 115. The discrepancy in the figures, Borowiec indicated 974,745 in 1943; indicating a total of 528,994 missing people.
105. TVDB, 107.
106. Noakes & Pridham, III, 952.
107. NARA, RG242, BDC, A3345-OSS-231, Heinz Reinefarth., October 1944.

108.  PRO, HW16/6, MSGP61, October 25, 1944.

109.  BA R19/321 Schnellbrief on the activities of bandits, October 14, 1944.

110.  BA R19/328, CdO, Schnellbrief, Aufstellung der SS-Pol Abt. Z.b.V. (mot) beim BdO Krakau, 12 December 1944.

111.  Refer to Mark C. Yerger, *Allgemeine-SS*, for a more detailed study of the SS commanders in retirement. Sereny, *Into That Darkness*, commented that Globocnik took Franz Stangl and his team of killers to Trieste. This compares with Sporrenberg and his team of killers who were sent to Norway. The reasoning behind these postings remains unexplained.

## Chapter 9: Western Europe

1.  Walter Manoschek, "The Extermination of the Jews in Serbia," in Herbert, *National Socialist Extermination Policies*.

2.  Cf. Mazower, *Inside Hitler's Greece*.

3.  IWM, IMT-7, 24-65.

4.  Fitzroy MacLean, *Eastern Approaches* (S.I., Cape, 1949), 275, PRO, HW16/6-MSGP 56, May 8, 1944, and PRO, HW16/6-MSGP 54, March 14, 1944.

5.  NCA, document PS-508, various correspondence concerning allied incursions in Norway including: the landing of British Freight Gliders in Norway (November 21, 1942), confirmation of the October 18, 1942 order (December 4, 1942), sparing captured commandos for interrogation (December 13, 1942), reference to a formal complaint by the Red Cross over German policy (December 14, 1942). Warlimont signed off all of these orders into OKW regulation as well as confirming the execution (special treatment) of three captured commandos (November 7, 1943) none of which was mentioned in his memoirs.

6.  NCA, document PS-7276, Commando operations, March 21, 1944.

7.  NCA document RF411, Bandenbekämpfung: Instructional pamphlet 69/2 comes into force for the Wehrmacht on 1 April 1944. Instructional pamphlet, for service use only 69/1 "Combat instructions for the Combating of Bands in the East."

8.  NCA, document PS-532, Treatment of commandos, June 23, 1944.

9.  NCA, document PS-537, Treatment of members of foreign "military missions," captured together with partisans, July 30, 1944. The order included the soldiers from British, American, and Soviet missions.

10.  NCA, document D-762, Combating of terrorists and saboteurs in the occupied territories, July 30, 1944.

11.  CMH, *German antiguerrilla operations in the Balkans (1941–1944)* (Washington D.C.: Center of Military History, 1954), referred to here as the Gaisser study.

12.  PRO, HW16/6, MSGP 49, September 9, 1943.

13.  TVDB, 89.

14.  TVDB and NARA, RG242, T175/222/2759241-50, papers referring to the transfer from the east to Salzburg.

15.  NARA, RG238, M1270/26/798, Ernst Rode interrogation report, October 22, 1945.

16.  PRO, HW16/6, MSGP 59, August 8, 1944.

17.  IWM, USMT-7, 8917.

18.  Trevor-Roper, *Hitler's War Directives*, 214–6.

19.  TVDB, 106.

20.  Wilhelm Hoettl, *The Secret Front: The Inside Story of Nazi Political Espionage* (London: Weidenfeld & Nicolson, 1953), 318. Hoettl was scathing about Skorzeny's taking the laurels for the raid. The planning according to Hoettl was conducted by his adjutants Radl and Folckersam, while there is evidence the original plan was drawn up by Luftwaffe parachute Gen. Kurt Student.

21.  NARA, RG338, FMS, B289, Alfred Zerbel, November 18, 1950. Zerbel almost certainly confused the title of the GBA with its function of rounding up labor.

22.  Trevor-Roper, *Hitler's War Directives*, 255–62.

23. NARA, RG242, T175/81/2601886, declaration of Upper and Middle Italy, April 3, 1944.

24. TVDB, 97.

25. NARA BDC, A3343-SS0-010c Karl Wolff. He suffered Nephrotomie, Pyetomie, and heart disease and, like Bach-Zelewski, underwent convalescence in Hohenlychen and Karlsbad. Right up to the very last days, Wolff ensured he was fully paid-up for all his benefits and entitlements.

26. NCA, document UK-66, "New Measures in connection with operations against Partisans" June 17, 1944, 576–80; and Gerhard Schreiber, "Partisanenkrieg und Kriegsverbrechen der Wehrmacht in Italien 1943 bis 1945," in *Beiträge zur Nationalsozialistichen Gesundheits- und Sozialpolitik, Band 14, Repression und Kriegsverbrechen: Die Bekämpfung von Widerstand und Partisanenbewegungen gegen die deutsche Besatzung in West- und Südeuropa* (Berlin: Schwarze Risse, 1997), 93–129. Schreiber referred to the original title "Neuregelung in der Bandenbekämpfung," 107.

27. NCA, document UK-66, combating partisans, June 20, 1944, 581.

28. NCA, document UK-66, Commander Covolo area headquarters, July 11, 1944, 582.

29. PRO, WO311–359, Statements of German Generals in Italy, September 17, 1946.

30. NARA, RG319, IRR, overheard prison cell conversation Karl Wolff, July 7, 1945.

31. PRO, WO 311/28, Allied Force Headquarters (British Section). Report on German Reprisals for Partisan Activity in Italy, July 9, 1945. The report considered 20 cases, "The Special Position of the SS," 21.

32. NARA, RG242, BDC, A3343-SSO-010C, Karl Wolff. Führungsstab BB-Ia-Nr.3096/ 44 g: Betr.: Abschlussmeldung in der "Bandenbekämpfungswoche."

33. NARA, BDC, A3343-SS0-090C, Willi Tensfeld, February 24, 1945.

34. Hoettl, *The Secret Front*, 157.

35. Brunner und Voigt, *Deutscher Handelsschulatlas*, (Berlin: B. G. Teubner, 1925), 14–15.

36. HSta Düsseldorf Regierung Aachen, file 22757, document 57, letter March 7, 1933. Rösener wrote to himself confirming his promotion to SS-Sturmbannführer. He also instructed himself to remain in the same office, no.257, from where he sent the letter.

37. NARA, RG242, T175/10/2511956, Zusatzbefehl 1, October 5, 1942.

38. NARA, RG242, BDC, A3343-SSO-285A, SS-Standartenführer Otto Lurker (*Hitler hinter Festungsmauern*, Berlin, 1933).

39. NARA, RG242, T175/10/2511958, regular five-day reports for all Alpenland activities.

40. NARA, RG242, T175/10/2511824-5, Energieversorgung Südsteiermark, October 17, 1942.

41. PRO, HW16/6, MSGP 33, March 17, 1942.

42. NARA, RG242, T175/10/2512274, BdO Alpenland in Marburg, Stabsbefehl 20, December 17, 1942.

43. PRO, HW16/6, MSGP53, January 12, 1943.

44. NARA, RG242, T175/10/2512023, Bandentätigkeit, SD report, Lurker, March 22, 1943.

45. PRO, HW16/6, MSGP54, March 14, 1944.

46. NARA, RG242, T175/81/2601501-2034, Bandenlage im Bereich des HSSPF im Wehrkreis XVIII Veldes, May 1943.

47. NARA, RG242, T175/81/2601501-2034, Message from Rösener to Himmler, May 19, 1943. The stenographer made several errors in the message not least the salutation "heil titler."

48. NARA, RG242, T175/10/2512025, BdO Marburg, June 19, 1943.

49. PRO, HW16/6, MSGP 47, July 9, 1943.

50. NARA, RG242, T175/81//2601501-2034, Oberkrain and Untersteiermark declared Bandenkampfgebiet.

51. NARA, RG242, T175/81//2601501-2034, collection of papers concerning the raising of forces for HSSPF Alpenland.

52. NARA, RG242, BDC, A3343-SSO-042B, Erwin Rösener, correspondence July 1– 23, 1943.

53. BA R19/305, CdO, Schnellbrief Betr. Aufstellung der Polizei Infanterie Geschützkompanie "Alpenland," August 6, 1943.

54. BA, R19/305, Schenllbrief, Betr. Heimatstandort der Pol. Inf. Gesch Komp "Alpenland," September 25, 1943.

55. Terry Gander and Peter Chamberlain, *Small Arms, Artillery and Special Weapons of the Third Reich* (London: Macdonald and Janes', 1978), 286.

56. NARA, RG242, T175/81//2601501-2034, letter to Winkelmann, May 29, 1943.

57. NARA, RG242, T175/10/2512021-2. Landrat Kreis Cilli to SD Untersteiermark, July 7, 1943.

58. NARA, RG242, T175/10/2512154, Vorfälle durch Banden in der Umgebung Warasdin-Toplitz, September 12, 1943.

59. NARA, RG242, T175/10/2512171, Fernschreiben from 19th SS-Police Regiment, September 14, 1943.

60. NARA, RG242, T175/10/2512641-3, Gefechtsstand 19th SS-Polizei Regiment, September 30, 1943.

61. PRO, HW16/6, part two, MSGP50, October 7, 1943.

62. NARA, RG242, T175/10/2512183, Gendarmerieposten Friedau, Untersteiermark, October 1, 1943.

63. TVDB, 86.

64. NARA, RG242, T175/10/2512100-3, Befehl zur Säuberung des Grenzraumes südlich der Save im Abschnitt Ratschach-Steinbrück-Trifail-Sava, Führungstab für Bandenbekämpfung, October 15, 1943.

65. PRO, HW16/6, MSGP52, December 15, 1943.

66. NARA, RG242, BDC, A3343-SSO-042B, Erwin Rösener. Gauleiter Uiberreither to Himmler October 28, 1943.

67. PRO, HW16/6, MSGP60, September 7, 1944.

68. PRO, HW16/6, MSGP58, July 3, 1944.PRO, PRO, HW16/6, MSGP59, August 8, 1944, PRO, HW16/6, MSGP61, November 5, 1944, and HW16/6, MSGP62, December 31, 1944.

69. PRO, HW16/6, MSGP61, November 5, 1944.

70. PRO, HW16/6, MSGP62, December 31, 1944.

71. NARA, RG242, BDC, A3343-SSO-042B, Erwin Rösener. The document was signed but not dated by Bach-Zelewski, allowing Himmler to use the report as and when required.

72. NARA, RG242, BDC, A3343-SSO-042B, Erwin Rösener.

73. Ibid, Erwin Rösener. Report by Dr. Braitmair, May 29, 1944 and Dr. Fahrenkamp, November 1944.

74. PRO, HW16/98, "History of the German Police W/T Network," July 1945, 21.

75. NS19/1165, KSRFSS to Der Höhere SS- und Polizeiführer Alpenland, October 8, 1943.

76. PRO, CAB 120-732, Recent Activities and Present Strengths (July 1943) of Opposing Forces in Yugoslavia, Albania and Greece, Joint Intelligence Sub-Committee for the War Cabinet.

77. NARA, RG242, BDC, A3343-SSO-378A, Artur Phleps, letter to Himmler, May 7, 1944.

78. Lepre, *Himmler's Bosnian Division*, 187–94.

79. Ibid, 198.

80. BBC series, SOE: the interview with Bill Deakin former mission commander with Tito. Michael McConville, "Knight's Move in Bosnia and the British rescue of Tito: 1944," *RUSI Journal*, December 1997, 61–9.

81. Otto Kumm, *Prinz Eugen: The History of the 7. SS-Mountain Division "Prinz Eugen"* (Winnipeg: J. J. Fedorowicz, 1995), 117–48.

82. Ibid, 117–21.

83. S. Kunzmann-Milius, *Fallschirmjäger der Waffen-SS* (Osnabrück: Munin Verlag, 1986), 77.

84. Kumm, *Prinz Eugen*, 123–7.

85. Maclean, *Eastern Approaches*, 450–1.

86. McConville, "Knight's Move in Bosnia," 61–9.

87. Kumm, *Prinz Eugen*, 129–38.

88. NCA, document 2610-PS, sworn testimony of US army Major Frederick W. Roche judge advocate in the case against General Dostler. Karel Margry, "The Dostler Case," *After the Battle Magazine*, no. 94 (1996), 1–19; see also NARA, RG-319, German General Staff vol. IV, boxes 13 and 14.

89. Eric Hosbawm, *On History* (London: Weidenfeld & Nicolson, 1997), 267.

90. PRO, WO32-12206, Crimes by German Forces Against Italian Partisans. NCA, document UK-66, Report of British War Crimes Section of Allied Force Headquarters on German Reprisals for Partisan Activities in Italy, undated (probably 1945).

91. PRO, WO208-4295, Interrogation of Luftwaffe Gefreiter Mattias Kerschgens, from Aachen, October 25, 1944.

92. Michael Geyer, "Civitella Della Chiana on June 29, 1944," in Heer and Naumann, *War of Extermination*, 175–216.

93. Roger James Bender and Hugh Page Taylor, *Uniforms, Organization and History of the Waffen-SS*, vol. 3 (San Jose, Calif.: Bender Publishing, 1975), 105–26.

94. Stein, *Waffen-SS*, 298 and PRO, WO208-4359, History of the Waffen-SS division: MI.14 notes on the composition and history of the SS divisions.

95. NARA, RG238, IMT, T1270/23/0367-0386, Heinrich Blaser, interrogation (27 February 1946), case S0799.

96. PRO, HW16/6, MSGP57, June 5, 1944.

97. NARA, IMT, T1270, roll 23, interrogation Friedrich Dupont, August 24, 1945.

98. PRO, WO311/359. Voluntary statement by PWD LD 1573 Generalfeldmarschall Albert Kesselring, The Partisan War in Italy from 1943 to 1945.

99. PRO WO 208-3648, PWIS(H)/LF/429, PWIS Interrogations, Lingfield Park, August 1944. Report written on August 4, and signed by Major MacCloud.

100. Wolfgang Vopersal, "Die SS-Ersatzbataillone in Breslau und das SS-Ersatzbataillon "Ost"," in *Der Freiwillige*, April 1973, issue 5, vol. 19, 18–19. This is the in-house journal of the association of former SS (HIAG).

101. PRO WO 208-3634, PWIS(H)/LF/440, PWIS Interrogations, Lingfield Park, August 1944. Report written on August 5, and signed by Major MacCloud.

102. PRO WO 208-3647, PWIS(H)/LDC/429, PWIS Interrogations, London District Cage, August 1944. Report written on August 5, and signed by Captain G.C. Sinclair.

103. Sarah Farmer, *Martyred Village: Commemorating the 1944 Massacre of Oradour-sur-Glane* (Berkeley: University of California Press, 1999); Robert Hébras, *Understand Oradour-sur-Glane drama* (Editions C.M.D. site pamphlet).

104. Richard Marillier, *Vercors 1943–1944: Le malentendu permanent* (Clamecy: Armançon, 2003), 114–5.

105. Michael Pearson, *Tears of Glory* (London: Macmillan, 1978), 89.

106. E. H. Cookridge, *They Came from the Sky* (London: Corgi, 1976), 156–62.

107. Pearson, *Tears of Glory*, 90.

108. Ibid, 91.

109. Sydnor, *Soldiers of Destruction*, 320.

110. Otto Weidinger, *Comrades to the End: The 4th SS Panzer-Grenadier Regiment "Der Führer" 1938–1945* (Atglen, Pa.: Schiffer Pub., 1998).

111. PRO WO 208-3624, PWIS(H)/KP/95, PWIS Interrogations, Kempton Park, July 1944. Report written on July 3, and signed Captain T.X.H. Pantcheff.

112. PRO WO 208-3647, PWIS(H)/LDC/294, PWIS Interrogations, London District Cage, August 1944. Report written on August 28, and signed by Captain H.K. Kettler.

113. PRO WO208-3624, PWIS(H)/KP/113, PWIS Interrogations, Kempton Park, July 1944. Report written on July 3, and signed Captain T.X.H. Pantcheff.

114. PRO WO 208-3648, PWIS(H)/LDC/327, PWIS Interrogations, London District Cage, September 1944. Report written on September 9, and signed by Captain H.K. Kettler.

115. PRO WO 208-3648, PWIS(H)/LF/334, PWIS Interrogations, Lingfield Park, July 1944. Report written on July 21, and signed by Major MacCloud.

116. PRO WO 208-3649, PWIS(H)/LDC/406, PWIS Interrogations, London District Cage, October 1944. Report written on October 11, and signed by Captain H.K. Kettler.

117. PRO WO 208-3649, PWIS(H)/LDC/439, PWIS Interrogations, London District Cage, October 1944.
118. PRO WO 208-3657, PWIS(H)/LDC/741, PWIS Interrogations, London District Cage, June 14, 1945.
119. JNSV, DDR, case no. 1009.
120. Foot, Resistance, 208–9. Reitlinger, The SS, 377–80; and Karel Krátký and Antonin \nejdárek, "The Slovak Rising," Purnell's History of the Second World War 7, 1968, 2157–66.
121. Reitlinger, The SS, 377–8.
122. Krátký et al., "The Slovak Rising," 2157–67.
123. Walter Laqueur, Guerrilla: A Historical and Critical Study (London: Weidenfeld & Nicolson, 1977), 220–221.
124. IWM, USMT-11, Berger's testimony, 6094.
125. Maclean, The Cruel Hunters, 199.
126. IWM, USMT, case 11, Berger's testimony, 6095–9. He went to some pains to deny that the operations included anti-Jewish operations: "There were no anti-Jewish operations—not at the time and Himmler's declaration that it was a Jewish rising is not true." German Wochenshau newsreels from the period went to great efforts to depict captured Slovakian Jewish partisans with Bolshevik intentions.
127. PRO, WO204-10184, Slovakia, letter from Henry Stimson, March 6, 1945.
128. NARA, RG242, OKH records, T77, roll 556. Vortragsnotiz. Abrücken jüdischen-kommunistischer Bandengruppen von Galizien nach Ungarn, March 16, 1944.
129. Birn, Die Höheren SS-und Polizeiführer, 297–304; Black, Kaltenbrunner, 150–1; Yerger, Allgemeine-SS, 48; Reitlinger, The SS, 350–51. Reitlinger incorrectly attributed Winkelmann as Daluege's replacement in 1942; Winkelmann represented Daluege at conferences when the bouts of sickness forced his absence.
130. PRO, HW16/6, MSGP 66, June 30, 1945.
131. PRO, HW16/6, MSGP 60, September 7, 1944.
132. NARA, RG238, T1270/1. The relationship between these two men became hostile once they were in America in captivity after the war. Skorzeny remained one of Bach-Zelewski's loyal subordinates; in the last days of the war, they fought together in Schwedt on the Oder.
133. Otto Skorzeny, trans. David Johnson, My Commando Operations (Atgeln, Pa.: Schiffer Press, 1995), also Perry Pierik, Hungary 1944–1945: The Forgotten Tragedy, (Nieuwegein: Aspekt, 1996).
134. In preparation for the Ardennes offensive, Hitler requested that Skorzeny conduct covert operations behind the American lines in U.S. Army uniform. Another circumvention of the laws of war that suited Hitler.
135. BZ-USMT, April 14, 1947; and TVDB, 116.
136. "Details of The Testimony of Erich von dem Bach-Zelewski," Nizkor Project Website, http://www.nizkor.org/hweb/people/e/eichmann-adolf.
137. PRO, HW16/6, MSGP 61, November 5, 1944.
138. PRO, HW16/6, MSGP63, February 13, 1945.
139. Felix Steiner, Der Freiwillige: der Waffen-SS Idee und Opfergang (Rosenheim: Deutsche Verlagsgesellschaft, 1958). Overall, a tedious tome by a former senior SS officer.
140. Ibid, 339–58. Steiner along with his former comrades depicts a heroic retreat into eventul captivity. The evidence is savory, as German forces fled in a rout to escape from capture, particularly by Tito's partisans or the Red Army, firing wildly on civilians and randomly destroying amenities, not so much to implement "scorched earth" as to cause misery.
141. NARA, RG319, IRR, Gottlob Berger, appendix I-A, SS-Hauptämter. There are grounds to suggest Kaltenbrunner had become responsible for all policing.
142. PRO, HW16/98, History of the German Police W/T Network July 1945, 40. The police signals traffic only began to decline in April; the last messages were sent out on May 8.
143. PRO, HW16/6, MSGP64, April 2, 1945.
144. NARA, T78/562/000402-54, Übersicht über die Bandenlage in der Zeit (November 1944–February 1945), March 6, 1945.

145. PRO, HW16/6, MSGP63, February 13, 1945.
146. PRO, HW16/6, MSGP66, June 30, 1945. Perry Biddiscombe, *Wehrwolf! The History of the National Socialist Insurgent Movement, 1944–1946* (Cardiff: University of Wales, 1998), 29.
147. PRO, HW16/6, MSGP 66, June 30, 1945.
148. Bradley F. Smith and Elena Agarossi, *Operation Sunrise: The Secret Surrender* (London: Andre Deutsch, 1979), 62.
149. David Clay Large, *Where Ghosts Walked: Munich's Road to the Third Reich* (New York: W.W. Norton, 1997), 344–5.
150. JNSV, Final Phase Crimes, cases 005,037, 073, 103 and 599.
151. JNSV, Final Phase Crimes, case 062.
152. Skorzeny, *My Commando Operations*, 429.
153. PRO, HW16/6, MSGP 65, May 29, 1945.
154. Hoettl, *The Second Front*, 317.
155. Black, *Kaltenbrunner*, 242–3.
156. NARA, RG238, T1270, roll 26, Ernst Rode interrogation report, October 22, 1945.
157. NCA, document PS-3734, Hanna Reitsch summary of interrogation, October 8, 1945.
158. Charles McMoran Wilson, *Winston Churchill: The Struggle for Survival, 1940–1965: Taken from the Diaries of Lord Moran* (London: Constable, 1966), 250.
159. Hugh R. Trevor-Roper, *The Last Days of Hitler* (London: Pan, 1973), 277–8: Trevor-Roper committed an appendix (1) of his well known book to the execution of Fegelein. He questioned whether the execution was due to Fegelein's cowardice or "guilt by association" with the treasonous rumblings among the SS. NARA, BDC, A3343, SSO, 198, Hermann Fegelein. Fegelein's personal failure in the last hours of the war does not quite reconcile with his "bravery" earlier in the war that led to the awards of the Knights' Cross and close-combat assault badges.
160. PRO, HW16/6, MSGP66, June 30, 1945.
161. Logusz, *Galicia Division*, 360.
162. Lepre, *Himmler's Bosnian Division*, 302–14.
163. Kumm, *Prinz Eugen*, 266.
164. Gitta Sereny, *The German Trauma: Experiences and Reflections 1938–2000* (London: Penguin, 2000), 195–215.

## Chapter 10: Deniability

1. Claud Mullins, *The Leipzig Trials* (S.I, H.F. & G. Witherby, 1921).
2. Timothy R. Vogt, *Denazification in Soviet-Occupied Germany: Brandenburg 1945–1948* (Cambridge, Mass.: Harvard University Press, 2000).
3. Constantine Fitzgibbon, *Denazification* (London: Norton, 1969); H.st.D. Entnazifizierung files; and RO FO record groups 935, 942, and 1013.
4. Richard Breitman, Norman J. W. Goda, Timothy Naftali, and Robert Wolfe, *U.S. Intelligence and the Nazis* (Cambridge: Cambridge University Press, 2005).
5. Wolfgang Kahl, "Vom mythos der 'Bandenbekämpfung': polizeiverbände im zweiten weltkreig," *Die polizei. zentralorgan für das sicherheits- und ordnungswesen aus*, 1998, J. 89, Nr.2, 47–56.
6. MSO, Judgement of the International Military Tribunal for the Trial of the German Major War Ciminals Nuremberg September 30 and October 1, 1946, Miscellaneous no. 12 (1946).
7. Norbert Frei, *Adenauer's Germany and the Nazi Past: The Politics of Amnesty and Integration* (New York: Columbia University Press, 2002).
8. Helge Grabitz, "Problems of Nazi Trials in the Federal Republic of Germany," *Holocaust and Genocide Studies* 3 (1988), 209–22.
9. "Geisel und Partisanentötungen im zweiten Weltkrieg: Hinweise zur rechtlichen Beurteilung" (Ludwigsburg: Zentrale Stelle der Landesjustizverwaltungen, Februar 1968), hereafter referred to as ZStL Legal Report 1968.

10. NARA, RG242, FMS, B-252, "The XIV SS Corps: November–December 1944," December 7, 1946, Lieutenant General von dem Bach-Zelewski.

11. Bender and Taylor, *Uniforms, Organization, and History of the Waffen-SS*, vol. 2, 27–49.

12. NARA, RG242, A3343-SS0-023, Bach-Zelewski report, February 9, 1945. Himmler ensured that a copy of the report was attached to Bach-Zelewski's personnel file.

13. TVDB, 96.

14. TVDB, 97.

15. TVDB, 99.

16. Warlimont, *Inside Hitler's Headquarters*, 292.

17. TVDB, 30.

18. TVDB, 63.

19. Reitlinger, *The SS*, 398.

20. Trevor-Roper, *Hitler's War Directives*, 300–1; and Rudolf Absolon, *Die Wehrmacht im Dritten Reich*, 403.

21. NARA, RG238, T1019-4 Record of the United States War Crimes Trials Interrogations 1946–1949. Evidence Division of the Office, Chief Counsel for War Crimes (OCCWC) Headed up by Walter H. Rapp, Chief Prosecutor was Telford Taylor. HQ Third United States Army Intelligence Center, office of the assistant chief of Staff, G-2, APO 403, Preliminary report, August 22, 1945, referred to as IMT-BZ, August 22, 1945.

22. Taylor, *The Anatomy of the Nuremberg Trials* (London: Bloomsbury, 1993), 259.

23. Ibid.

24. PRO, HW16/6, parts one and two, circulated to Telford Taylor.

25. BZ-IMT, January 20, 1946.

26. BZ-IMT, November 27, 1945.

27. Skorzeny, *My Commando Operations*, 443.

28. IWM, USMT-11, 6,004.

29. NARA, RG238, T1019, roll 4, report from Walter Rapp to Telford Taylor, October 2, 1946.

30. D. A. L. Wade, "A Survey of the Trials of War Criminals," *The Royal Institute of International Affairs* 96 (1951), 66–70.

31. BZ-IMT, January 17, 1946, NCA document NOKW-067.

32. Karel Margry, "The Dostler Case," *After the Battle* 94 (1996), 1–19.

33. E. H. Stevens, *Trial of Nikolaus von Falkenhorst: Formerly Generaloberst in the German Army* (London: William Hodge, 1949), xiv.

34. A. P. Scotland, *The London Cage* (London: Evans Brothers, 1957), 165–166 and 170–71.

35. Taylor, *The Anatomy of the Nuremberg Trials*, 253–5.

36. Of all the allied powers, only the French war crimes investigators attempted to place the Bandenbekämpfung directive on trial through the ill-fated Oradour-sur-Glane proceedings.

37. BZ-IMT, October 25, 1945.

38. BZ-USMT-7, 8930.

39. USMT-8, 396.

40. BZ-IMT, January 17, 1946.

41. BZ-IMT, March 23, 1946.

42. BZ-IMT, January 17, 1946.

43. BZ-USMT, April 14, 1947.

44. IWM, USMT-7, 8994–5.

45. BZ-IMT, November 27, 1945.

46. IWM, IMT, Bach-Zelewski, interrogation, no. 1975, April 14, 1947.

47. BZ-IMT, March 23, 1946.

48. BZ-IMT, November 27, 1945.

49. Ibid.

50. BZ-IMT, January 15, 1946.

51. BZ-IMT, March 25, 1946.

52. BZ-IMT, interrogations March 23–25, 1946.

53. Tomasz Wisniewski, *Jewish Bialystok and Surroundings in Eastern Poland* (Ipswich, Mass.: Ipswich Press, 1998), 37–8.
54. TVDB, 3.
55. TVDB, 4. Konrad Kwiet, "From the Diary of a Killing Unit," in John Milful (ed.), *Why Germany? National Socialist Anti-Semitism and the European Context* (Oxford: Berg, 1993), 75–91.
56. Wisniewski, *Jewish Bialystok*, 48.
57. BZ-IMT, March 24, 1946.
58. BZ-IMT, March 23, 1946.
59. Heinz Guderian, *Panzer Leader* (London: De Capo, 1952), 355–6. Guderian wrote that on July 20, 1944, he flew to Lötzen, which of course was code for visiting Himmler prior to a meeting with Hitler.
60. NARA, RG319, IRR, Heinz Guderian.
61. NARA, RG242, T1270, Nuremberg testimonies, Guderian interrogations.
62. Ibid.
63. Ibid.
64. Guderian, *Panzer Leader,* 355–6.
65. NARA RG238, M1019/58/7847-68, Rode interrogation no. 19.
66. NARA RG238, M1019/58/7847-68, Rode, August 9, 1946.
67. BZ-IMT, October 5, 1946.
68. BZ-IMT, September 21, 1946.
69. BZ-IMT, January 29, 1946.
70. IWM, USMT-7, 8977.
71. BZ-USMT, January 29, 1946.
72. Refer to chapter 8 for the losses Bach-Zelewski inflicted on Warsaw.
73. NARA, RG238, M1019, roll 37, Ernst Korn testimony, August 1, 1947.
74. IWM, USMT-7, 9349.
75. BZ-IMT-7, 8917.
76. IWM, IMT-7, 8922–23.
77. NARA, FMS, C-032, "The War behind the front: guerrilla warfare," Albert Kesselring, July 28, 1947.
78. Kesselring, 1947, 7.
79. Schwarznecker report.
80. NARA, FMS, C-037, "Haunted Forests: enemy partisans behind the front," Gustav Höehne, 17–19.
81. NARA, FMS, A-946, Activities of the 157th Reserve Division (1946); and FMS, B-237, Southern France (1946).
82. NARA, FMS, B-331, 157th Reserve Division: September 1944 (1951).
83. NARA, RG338, FMS P-055c, Lessons Learned From the Partisan War in Russia, Alexander Ratcliffe 1952.
84. CMH Pub 104–18, *German Anti-guerrilla Operations in the Balkans (1941–1944)* (Washington, D.C., Center for Military History, 1954).
85. CMH Pub 104-19, *The Soviet Partisan Movement 1941–1944* (Washington, D.C.: Center for Military History, 1956); and CMH Pub 20-240, *Rear Area Security in Russia: The Soviet Second Front behind the German Lines* (Washington, D.C.: Center for Military History, 1951).
86. James H. Critchfield, *Partners at the Creation: The Men behind Postwar Germany's Defense and Intelligence Establishments* (Annapolis: Naval Institute, 2003).
87. ZStL Legal Report 1968.
88. Large, *Where Ghosts Walked,* 255.
89. Ulrich Herbert, *Best, Biographische Studien über Radikalismus, Weltanschauung und Vernunft 1903–1989* (Bonn: Dietz, 1996); and Friedrich Wilhelm, *Die Polizei im NS-Staat* (Paderborn: F. Schoeningh, 1997).
90. Florian Dierl, "Adolf von Bomhard—'Generalstabschef der Ordnungspolizei,' in Klaus-Michael Mallman and Gerhard Paul (eds.), *Karrieren der Gewalt: National-sozialistische Täterbiographien* (Darmstadt: Wissenschaftliche Buchgesellschaft, 2004), 62–3.
91. Neufeld et al., *Zur Geschichte der Ordnungspolizei,* 115; and Yerger, *Allgemeine-SS,* 58.

92. DDR (ed.), *Braunbuch: Kriegs-und Naziverbrecher in der Bundesrepublik* (Berlin: Staatsverlag Der Deutschen Deomokratischen Republik, 1965), 91–104.

93. Leonard Mahlein, *Waffen-SS in der Bundesrepublik: Eine Dokumentation Der VVN-Bund Der Antifaschisten* (Frankfurt am Main: Roderberg, 1978).

94. Paul Hausser, *Waffen-SS im Einsatz* (Oldendorf: Pless, 1953).

95. DDR, *SS im Einsatz: Eine Dokumentation Über Die Verbrechen Der SS* (Berlin: Staatsverlag Der Deutschen Deomokratischen Republik, 1957), 591.

96. Friedman, *Bach-Zelewski: Dokumentensammlung*, 12.

97. ZDF, 2003, Television series, "Die SS-Eine Warnung der Geschichte," programme 6: Mythos Odessa, produced by Guido Knopp.

98. Staatsanwaltschaft an dem Landgericht Braunschweig, Schwurgerichtsanklage gegen Angehörige des SS-Kav. Regt.2 (Erschiessung von Juden im Gebiet der Pinsker-Sümpfe August 1941), June 15, 1963. 58–64.

99. Cüppers, "Lombard," 151–2.

100. NARA, RG319, file marked "Extradition of Former German Officers to Poland."

101. NARA, RG319, Extradition of former German officers to Poland. Unfortunately the Americans had refused to extradite Reinefarth (along with Guderian, Rode, and Vormann) to Poland in 1947 and 1948.

102. NARA, RG242, BDC, A3345-OSS-154, Dr. Oskar Dirlewanger.

103. Maclean, *The Cruel Hunters*, 188.

104. NARA, RG242, BDC, A3345-OSS-154, Dr. Oskar Dirlewanger, Vorschlag für die Verleihung des Ritterkreuzes des Eisernen Kreuzes, Kampfgruppe Reinefarth, September 10, 1944.

105. Rudolf Ilgen, *Mein Zusammenstoss mit SS-Oberführer von dem Bach-Zelewski als Richter im Fruhjar 1933 in der Neumarkt* (Koblenz: Wolfgang Lomüller, 1980). Formal testimony set down in Koblenz in August 1974.

106. William Shakespeare, *The Collected Works* (London: Cook & Wedderburn, 1982), 765.

## Conclusions

1. Russell Weigley, *The American Way of War: A History of United States Military Strategy and Policy* (Bloomington: Indiana University Press, 1973), 176.

2. Interview, April 17, 1979.

# SELECTED BIBLIOGRAPHY

Tim Mason once wrote that "All good written history begins at the end" (*Social Policy in the Third Reich* ). So finally, we come to a review of the sources. There is not a single collection of all Bandenbekämpfung documents and records. Many records were deliberately destroyed at the war's end or deliberately misfiled long after the war; one might wonder which was worse. There is no way of "guesstimating" what the contents of these records were, however suspicious one has become of the ways of the Bandenkampfverbände. This, however, is the smallest problem for anyone studying this subject. The remaining evidence is finely distributed in the United States, Russia, Germany, and Britain, and to a lesser extent in France, Belgium, Holland, Poland, and Hungary. The vast majority of the evidence came from documentary sources. The documents are not weighted equally. Signals or deciphered messages do not surpass a complete policy document. However, a series of interrogations can reveal a lot more about how things were done than a bland policy statement. Synthesizing them, as in the section on the Bandenstab Rösener in chapter 9, brings great rewards. There is also the problem of accuracy and deceit: Bach-Zelewski's diary, for example, inaccurately describes his war crimes, as we might expect. Fortunately, his intercepted messages reveal his actual killing "scores." Yet, Bach-Zelewski's diary also provided evidence that more than padded the gaps in areas not directly associated with war crimes and that assists in explaining certain behavior patterns. "Lumping" together evidence on key issues extended the number of perspectives and minimized our reliance on "flaky" single documents. What do not fit in the blow-by-blow account are the visits to memorial sites and meetings with perpetrators or victims. The sheer size of the Auschwitz complex or the acreage of Oradour-sur-Glane gives an impression of the Nazi ambition. Unfortunately, this picture cannot be added to the list of footnotes.

## Unpublished Sources

The National Archives and Records Administration (NARA), Washington D.C., College Park Annex microfilm and documents collections includes the captured German records group. This includes the near complete record of Himmler's papers. How complete the collection is will never really be known, and we must assume that a certain amount of weeding out took place before Karl Wolff handed the documents over to the Americans. The total number of record groups consulted includes:

RG242 Captured German documents
Berlin Document Centre (BDC) microfilm of SS personnel files
RG 238 World War II war crimes record group
RG319 U.S. Army Intelligence record group
RG338 U.S. Army Historical Branch Foreign Military Studies

There is a cautionary tale. Not all the papers discovered on the microfilms were labeled in the finding guides. On my third visit to the archives, the vast majority of my time was spent examining the 642 SS microfilms for misplaced and unmarked documents. America has other fine collections including the U.S. Holocaust Memorial and Museum, with its library and document collections, and the Center for Military History, U.S. Army (Pennsylvania), with its collection of G5 McSherry papers and documents from the U.S. Army occupation of Germany (1944–47).

The German Federal archives are located in Berlin-Lichterfelde, Koblenz, Freiburg im Breisgau, and Kornelimünster near Aachen. The files of the Nazi Party and SS are located in Berlin. The military papers of the Wehrmacht and Waffen-SS records are kept in the Bundesarchiv-Militärarchiv (BA-MA) in Freiburg im Breisgau, in southwest Germany. They hold the Abwehr papers of Major General Gempp. Often overlooked is the Deutsche Dienststelle in Berlin, which was originally the Wehrmacht's personnel record with muster rolls for all the Wehrmacht, Waffen-SS, and SS-Police. The Hauptstadtarchiv-Düsseldorf proved exceptionally helpful in assisting the search for key denazification papers that provided background on the level of Reichskolonialbund membership among industrialists.

Britain has a fine collection of documents. The Public Record Office in London changed its name to the National Archives. To avoid confusion, I have elected to continue to use PRO. The archives holds a unique series of documents that includes:

German Police Decodes (HW16 series)
Foreign Office papers (FO series)
CSDIC collection including the PWIS and WCIU papers (WO series)
The papers of Lieutenant Colonel A. P. Scotland (WO series)
British war crimes papers (WO series)

The Imperial War Museum has the only complete set of Nuremberg documentation in Britain. The Wiener Library contains a small but valuable collection of documents.

## Published Sources

There is an abundance of mainstream literature dedicated to the study of the Third Reich. By contrast, there is next to nothing regarding Bandenbekämpfung, although there is a large body of scholarship on Partisanenbekämpfung. The body of literature interwoven into this book is not replicated here. This is only a brief overview of the main literature that has influenced this research.

Since the late 1950s, scholarship has diligently tried to piece together an explanation of the totality of Nazi crimes in Eastern Europe and the former Soviet Russia. Christian Streit (*Keine Kameraden*) and Omer Bartov (*The Eastern Front, 1941–1945*, and *Hitler's Army*) in their different approaches identified the German army's complicity to Nazi ideological doctrine and war crimes. The façade of the German army's professional morality was later exposed by the exhibition, "The War of Destruction and the Crimes of the Wehrmacht" (*Vernichtungskrieg. Verbrechen der Wehrmacht 1941 bis 1944*) of 1995 (Hamburg Institut für Sozialforschung, *Verbrechen Der Wehrmacht*). Refer to Bill Niven, *Facing the Nazi Past*, for the story of the exhibition). Hannes Heer, the former director of the exhibition, advanced the literature with essays and books on Nazi security policy. Christian Gerlach's research focused on the occupation of Belorussia. His doctoral thesis has transformed our collective impression of the scale of German behavior in the occupied Soviet Union. He examined such practices as collective reprisals and hostage taking, the German army's consistent security responses to resistance since 1871. Gerlach highlighted the large Bandenbekämpfung operations of 1942–43, explained the connections between security and economic pressures on German policy and the exploitation of industrial and agricultural zones (*Kalkulierte Morde,* and see also *Krieg, Ernährung, Völkermord*). Another important country-specific study of Nazi occupation is Mark Mazower's examination of Greece (*Inside Hitler's Greece*). He isolated the transfer of SS specialists from the east to parts of southern Europe; this extended the realm of extermination and exploitation among Hitler's Axis allies.

Although Bandenbekämpfung was about empire building, many post-war interpretations tended to equate German antipartisan warfare with military security. This requires some explanation. In addition to the influence of the Nuremberg war crimes trials, the U.S. Army, in keeping with its traditions, established a pseudo-academic study of the war in Europe. It employed many of its former enemies, senior German officers living in the spotlight of war crimes justice, to write reports on aspects of Hitler's war. Understandably those selected to write about the security campaign described their deeds as antipartisan warfare. Ironically, many were unable to break with the past or certain words and phrases; the foreign military reports are littered with references to "Banden," "Banditen," and "Bandenbekämpfung." Their influence shaped the Cold War years, as Western scholars in the field of security studies concentrated on the power of the Soviet and Yugoslav partisans. Few acknowledged Himmler's central role, preferring to embellish the story of the highly professional German army and the failure of its "antiguerrilla" measures. In 1960, John Armstrong and his colleagues published a timely definitive study of the Soviet partisan movement. They viewed Hitler's security policy as subject to the "overriding objective of destroying Soviet military power within a very short time," and said that the "German command regarded the partisans as crucially important only insofar as they impeded the German war effort." In Armstrong's opinion, German and Soviet methods were barely separable: "The combination of Soviet and German objectives produced a situation in which measures of almost unparalleled ruthlessness became the norm of guerrilla and antiguerrilla warfare alike" (*Soviet Partisans in World War II*, 6–7). The force of this opinion still emerges in the literature. Given the tensions of the Cold War world, it is perhaps not surprising that scholarship used the past to judge contemporary conflicts, in particular Vietnam.

In 1976, Keith Simpson stepped away from this trend with his article about German military security policy ("The German Experience of Rear Area Security on the Eastern Front 1941–45"). Simpson isolated the German tradition of security from the Franco–Prussian tradition through the First World War and into Weimar. He disagreed with the thesis of failure and thought German methods were brutal but "very effective," and were for that reason maintained. Simpson explained Weimar's pivotal role in his analysis, "because of the polarization in politics between nationalists and communists, the weaknesses of the central government, and the need to establish an effective police force which was capable of maintaining internal security." During Weimar, he argued, "paramilitary *Schutzpolizei* gained experience from internal security operations during the communist uprisings of 1918 and 1923."

The publications in press and discussed in 1997 were particularly germane to this book. Christopher Browning's extremely harrowing account of the activities of a police battalion in Eastern Europe has had the most profound impact upon the research for this book (*Ordinary Men: Reserve Battalion 101 and the Final Solution in Poland*). Browning assessed the Nazi Order Police (Ordnungspolizei) as the product of repeated German attempts to introduce a militarized police, rather than of nazification. He also noticed the tendency of the police troops to improve with their killing experience. Ulrich Herbert's magnum opus of Dr. Werner Best was a primer for examing Himmler, Daluege, and Bach-Zelewski (*Best, Biographische Studien über Radikalismus, Weltanschauung und Vernunft 1903–1989*). Having discovered that Edward Crankshaw was party to what is now referred to as the PRO HW16 series German Police Decodes, his study of the Gestapo took on a new pallor. Daniel Jonah Goldhagen's *Hitler's Willing Executioners* briefly turned the historical establishment on its head. Goldhagen expounded a suspicion, long dismissed by leading historians, that the Nazis had awakened a character trait of the German people, "eliminationist anti-semitism." The response to Goldhagen was quite remarkable with equal amounts of deprecation and support. In retrospect, ten years later, *Hitler's Willing Executioners* was about exploiting the German media, forcing the German people to face their past, the Holocaust in particular, the combination of which many more eminent scholars found distasteful. (See Ulrich Herbert, *Nationalsozialistische Vernichtungspolitik, Neue Forshungen und Kontroversen.* These published lectures highlight how far research has come in explaining Nazism and show that simple answers are not satisfactory in this complex subject. See also Norman Finkelstein, *The Holocaust Industry.*) Fewer books published today refer to Goldhagen, while his books, in German shops, gather dust.

Since I completed the PhD in 2001, several scholars have emerged with some bearing here. Ben Shepherd and I met in 1997. I have read his work from the PhD thesis ("German Army Security Units in Russia, 1941–1943: A Case Study") through to his book *War in the Wild East.* He conducted an in-depth study of a security formation, the 221st Security Division, which served in the rear area of Army Group Centre on the Eastern Front. The book purports to be a study of the perpetrators following on from the work Christopher Browning. In some respects, this places our work in the same genre. His archive base and analysis ends in 1943, just at the time when Bandenbekämpfung was about to peak. In practical terms, this forces a separation between our researches. In general terms, his findings that the Germans were fixated with the Soviet "guerrilla" is only half the story. In the quest for colonization and victory, the partisans were an obstacle to the Germans; the absence of partisans and even collaboration did not end the German terror. I am not convinced that in his research Shepherd was able to break through the fundamental walls of his subject. Is his book about a division or about perpetrators? In his thesis, Shepherd alleged the partisans "regularly flouted three of the four criteria of lawful combatant status laid down in the 1907 Hague Convention" and that "partisan outrages were calculated to provoke vicious German reprisals." He rounded off the section, "How far this behaviour was compelled by German terror in the first place is of course another question." In the first instance, Shepherd implies Soviet complicity in the horror, which ignores the fact that Hitler's armies invaded Russia brandishing the Barbarossa directives and wildly circumventing the laws of war (refer to chapters 2, 3, and 4 in this book).

Secondly, in legal terms, if the rules of land warfare were breached, then the onus was on the Germans to establish a thorough investigation and set legal proceedings against the Soviets before committing reprisals. It is unclear what he meant by "another question"; isn't the purpose of a German perpetrator study to focus on Nazi terror, almost to the exclusion of all others? Ultimately, how are extenuating circumstances applied in regard to the laws of warfare, when the laws are deliberately circumvented by either party?

Edward Westermann's *Hitler's Police Battalions* has examined the Order Police. In many respects, there is overlap between our findings, but Westermann and I will probably have to agree to disagree. The difference between our two books lies in emphasis. Westermann has carried through a perpetrator study from an organizational perspective. He argues, with considerable merit, that the police established an organizational culture that enabled it to perform many of its tasks without remorse. He has concentrated on the influence and impact of the Nazis' ideology as the root cause of their killing; this is ground upon which we differ. He experimented with organizational theory and adapted it quite well. Westermann did not take this very far, and some of his analysis comes to an abrupt halt. In terms of the overall study of the police, his book still represents an important work and is essential reading on the subject.

The latest developments have come in the field of German colonialism. Colonial warfare is often treated as a cul-de-sac of military history, explained away as those "savage little wars of modern peace." The works of Jürgen Zimmerer (*Deutsche Herrschaft Über Afrikaner*) and Jan-Bart Gewalt (*Herero Heroes* and "Learning to Wage and Win Wars in Africa") deserve special mention for their efforts in revealing the full extent of German savagery in Namibia. The German pacification of the Herero ensured that Bandenbekämpfung thereafter traveled the road of extermination and enslavement. Isabel Hull's study of the German army in Namibia (formerly German Southwest Africa) was awaited with anticipation and published as *Absolute Destruction: Military Culture and the Practices of War in Imperial Germany*. This book has disappointed those who cling to the tired notion that the German army was an honorable estate bewitched and corrupted by Nazism. Hull's analysis of the Imperial German Army, its military culture, and its professionalism explodes the myth of a clean professional army ill-prepared for war in August 1914. It also examines the resort to genocide, by the army in Namibia, against the Herero.

## Published Primary Sources

Absolon, Rudolf, *Die Wehrmacht im Dritten Reich, Schriften des Bundesarchivs* (Boppard am Rhein: Harald Boldt, 1969–95), vols. 1-6.

Boberach, Heinz, Rolf Thommes, and Hermann Weiss, *Ämter, Abkürzungen, Aktionen des NS Staates* (Munich, 1997).

*Brockhaus' Konversations–Lexicon* (Leipzig: Brockhaus Verlag, 1908).

Brunner und Voigt, *Deutscher Handelsschulatlas* (Berlin: B.G. Teubner, 1925).

CMH Pub 104-18, *German Anti-guerrilla Operations in the Balkans (1941–1944)* (Washington, D.C.: Center for Military History, 1954).

CMH Pub 104-19, *The Soviet Partisan Movement 1941–1944* (Washington, D.C.: Center for Military History, 1956).

CMH Pub 20-240, *Rear Area Security in Russia: The Soviet Second Front Behind the German Lines* (Washington, D.C.: Center for Military History, 1951).

DDR (ed.), *Braunbuch: Kriegs-und Naziverbrecher in der Bundesrepublik* (Berlin: Staatsverlag Der Deutschen Demokratischen Republik, 1965).

————, *SS im Einsatz: Eine Dokumentation Über Die Verbrechen Der SS* (Berlin: Staatsverlag Der Deutschen Demokratischen Republik, 1957).

"Erich von dem Bach-Zelewski," Nizkor Project Website, http://www.nizkor.org/ hweb/people/e/eichmann-adolf.

Friedman, Tuviah, *Back-Zelewski: Dokumentensammlung* (Haifa: Institute of Documentation, 1996), 2–6.

"Geisel und Partisanentötungen im zweiten Weltkrieg: Hinweise zur rechtlichen Beurteilung" (Ludwigsburg: Zentrale Stelle der Landesjustizverwaltungen, Februar 1968).

Hinsley, F. H., and C. A. G Simkins. *British Intelligence in the Second World War: Security and Counter-Intelligence* (London: HMSO, 1990), vol. 4.

Hinsley, F. H., et al., *British Intelligence in the Second World War: Its Influence on Strategy and Operations* (London: HMSO, 1979–84), vols. 1–3.

HMSO, Judgement of the International Military Tribunal for the Trial of German Major War Criminals, Nuremberg, 30 September and 1 October 1946, Micellaneous no. 12 (1946).

Holmes, Richard (ed.), *The Oxford Companion to Military History* (Oxford: Oxford University Press, 2001).

Hubatsch, Walter. *Hitler's Weisungen für die Kriegführung 1939–1945: Dokumente des Oberkommandos der Wehrmacht* (reprinted by Osnabruck, 1999).

"Instruktion, betreffend das etappen- und eisenbahnwesen und die obere leitung des feld-intendantur—feld sanitäts-, military-, telegraphen- und feld-post wesens im kriege" (Berlin, 1872), in Wilbraham Lennox and Donatus O'Brien (trans.), *Prussian Etappen Regulations* (London: W. Lennox, 1875).

International Military Tribunal, *Trial of the Major War Criminals*, 42 vols. (London, 1949–51).

Justiz und NS-Verbrechen, Nazi Crimes on Trial, German Trial Judgements Concerning National Socialist Homicidal Crimes 1945–1999, compiled by Prof. Dr. C.F. Rüter and Dr. D.W. de Mildt of the Institute of Criminal Law, University of Amsterdam.

Nazi Conspiracy and Aggression, vols. 1–8, Supps. A and B. Office of the U.S. Chief of Counsel for Prosecution of Axis Criminality (Washington, D.C.: Government Printing Office, 1946–48).

Noakes, Jeremy, and Geoffrey Pridham, *Nazism 1919–1945: A Documentary Reader*, III (Exeter: University of Exeter Press, 1983), vols. 1–3 and Noakes, vol. 4.

Oberkommando d. Wehrmacht, *Bandenbekämpfung: Merkblatt 69/2* (Berlin, May 6, 1944).

Oberkommando Des Heeres, *Das Britische Kriegsheer*, Gen St d H/Abt. Fremde Heere West, Secret Nr.3000/42, April 10, 1942.

O'Neil, Robin, *Belzec: Prototype for the Final Solution; Hitler's Answer to the Jewish Question*, at http://www.jewishgen.org/yizkor/belzec1/bel000.html.

PRO, *SOE: Operations in Eastern Europe, Guide Booklet*, (n.d.).

Reichsführer-SS, *Bandenbekämpfung* (Berlin: Reichssicherheitshauptamt, 1942).

————, *Deine Zukunft* (Berlin: Reichssicherheitshauptamt, 1944).

————, *Der Untermensch* (Berlin: Reichssicherheitshauptamt, 1942).

————, *Dich ruft die SS* (Berlin: Reichssicherheitshauptamt, 1943).

————, *Die Schutzstaffel als antibolschewistische Kampforganization* (Munich, 1936).

Reichssicherheitshauptamt, *Meine Ehre heist Treue, Reinhard Heydrich, 7 März 1904– 4 Juni 1942* (Berlin, 1942).

Schmitz, Martin, "Schülerzahlen der gewerblichen kaufmannischen Schulen von 1923 bis 1933," Diplom. Essay, RWTH-Aachen, 2001.

Schwabe, Kurd, *Der Krieg in Deutsch-Südwestafrika 1904–1906* (Berlin: Weller, 1907).

Soviet Embassy (London), *New Soviet Documents on Nazi Atrocities* (London: Hutchinson, 1943).

Staatsanwaltschaft dem Landgericht Braunschweig, Schwurgerichtsanklage gegen Angehörige des SS-Kav.Regt.2 (Erschiessung von Juden im Gebiet dem Pinsker-Sümpfe August 1941), June 15, 1963.

Tessin, Georg. *Verbände und Truppen der deutschen Wehrmacht und Waffen-SS im Zweiten Weltkrieg, Erster Band: Die Waffengattungen-Gesamtübersicht* (Osnabrück: Biblio Verlag, 1977).

Trevor-Roper, Hugh R. (intro.), *Hitler's Table Talk 1941–1944* (London: Phoenix, 2000).

———. *Hitler's War Directives 1939–1945* (New York: Doubleday, 1966).

*Unsere Ehre Heisst Treue, Kriegstagebuch des Kommandostabes Reichsführer-SS Tätigkeitsberichte der 1. Und 2. SS-Inf.-Brigade, der 1. SS-Kav.-Brigade und von Sonderkommando der SS* (Vienna: Europa Verlag, 1965).

U.S. War Department, Military Intelligence Division, *German Military Intelligence 1939–1945* (Washington, D.C.: University Publications of America, 1984).

———, Technical Manual TM-E 30-451, *Handbook on German Military Forces* (Washington, D.C.: Government Printing Office, 15 March 1945).

U.S. Government Printing Office, *Nazi Conspiracy and Aggression* (Washington, D.C., 1946–48), vols. 1–8.

———. *Trials of the War Criminals before the Nuremberg Tribunal* (Washington, D.C., 1949), vols. 1–12.

Zentrale Stelle der Landesjustizverwaltungen in Ludwigsburg. *Geisel- und Partisanentötungen im zweiten Weltkrieg: Hinweise zur rechtlichen Beurteilung* (1968).

## Oral Sources

BBC series, SOE: (1983), interview with Bill Deakin, former commander with Tito.

"Bozo," interview, April 17, 1979.

Frank Gierllen, interview, May 10, 2000.

ZDF, 2003, Television series, "Die SS-Eine Warnung der Geschichte," programme 6: Mythos Odessa, produced by Guido Knopp.

## Unpublished Sources and Academic Theses

Conway, M., "The Rexist Movement in Belgium 1940–1944," Phil. diss., University of Oxford, 1989.

Rowe, Michael, "German Civil Administrators and the Politics of the Napoleonic State in the Department of the Roer, 1798–1815," PhD diss., Sidney Sussex College, Cambridge, 1996.

Schulte, Theo, "The German Army and National Socialist Occupation Policies in the Occupied Areas of the Soviet Union 1941–43," PhD diss., University of Warwick, 1987.

Shepherd, Ben, "German Army Security Units in Russia, 1941–1943: A Case Study," PhD diss., University of Birmingham, 2000.

Terry, Nicholas M. "The German Army Group Centre and the Soviet Civilian Population, 1942–1944," PhD diss., University of London, 2005.

Wheeler, Leonie, "The SS and the Administration of Nazi Occupied Eastern Europe, 1939–1945," Phil. diss., University of Oxford, 1981.

## Secondary Sources

**Before 1945**

Allen, W. E. D., *Guerrilla War in Abyssinia* (Harmondsworth Middlesex: Penguin, 1943).

Bauer, H. W., *Kolonien im Dritten Reich* (Köln: Gauverlag, 1936).

Bayer, Ernst, *Die SA* (Berlin: Luennhaupt, 1938).

Benn, Gottfried, "Wie Miss Cavell erschossen wurde. Bericht eines Augenzeugen über die Hinrichtung der englischen Krankenschwester," in Friedrich Felger (ed.), *Was wir vom Weltkrieg nicht wissen* (Berlin: Andermann, 1930).

Boguslawski, Albert von, *Der kleine Krieg und seine Bedeutung für die Gegenwart* (Berlin: Luckardt, 1881).

Bomhard, Adolf von, *Das K. B. Infanterie-Leib-Regiment: Nach d. amtl. Kriegstagebüchern bearb. im Auftr. d. ehem. Infanterie-Leib-Regiments* (Munich: Selbstverl., 1921).

Buchrucker, Bruno Ernst, *Im Schatten Seeckt's; die Geschichte der "Schwarzen Reichswehr"* (Berlin: Kampf, 1928).

Bülow, Kurt Ernst Gottfried von, *Preussischer Militarismus zur Zeit Wilhelm II* (Schweidnitz: Scweidnitz, 1930).

Fraenkel, Ernst, *Military Occupation and the Rule of Law* (Oxford: Oxford University Press, 1944).

Goebbels, Josef, *Diary*.

Grimm, Hans, *Volk ohne Raum* (Munich: Albert Langen, 1926).

Hale, Lonsdale, "Partisan Warfare," *Journal of the Royal United Services Institute* 30 (1885), 135–64.

Hashagen, Justus, *Das Rheinland und die Französische Herrschaft* (Bonn: Hanstein, 1908).

Haushofer, Karl, *Geopolitik Des Pazifischen Ozeans: Studien Über Die Wechselbeziehungen Zwischen Geographie und Geschichte* (Berlin: Kurt Vowinckel, 1927).

Hechler, Paul, and Walter Kunrath, *Ehrentafel der im Weltkrieg 1914–1918 gefallenen Angehörigen des Preussischen Landwehr–Infanterie Regiments Nr. 6* (Berlin, 1931).

Hitler, Adolf, trans. Ralph Manheim, *Mein Kampf*, intro. D. C. Watt (London: Pimlico, 1992).

Krumbach, Josef, *Franz Ritter von Epp: Ein Leben für Deutschland* (Munich: Brunnen, 1938).

Lasswell, Harold D., "The Garrison States," *American Journal of Sociology* 46 (1941).

Lettow-Vorbeck, Paul von, *Meine Erinnerungen aus Afrika* (Berlin: K. F. Koehler, 1926).

Lieber, Francis, "Guerrilla Parties Considered with Reference to the Laws and Usages of War," written at the request of Maj. Gen. Henry W. Halleck (August 1862).

Lindner, Theodor, *Der Krieg gegen Frankreich* (Berlin: Asher, 1895).

Loening, Otto, *Deutsche Rechtsgeschichte* (Leipzig: Hirschfeld, 1929), 30.

Ludendorff, Erich, *Der totale Krieg* (Munich: Ludendorff, 1935).

Menzels, Max, *Dienstunterricht des deutschen Infanteristen* (Berlin: R.Eisenschmidt, 1913).

Morgan, J. H., *The War Book of the German General Staff: Being "The Usages of War on Land," Issued by the Great General Staff of the German Army* (New York: McBride, Nast, 1915).

Mullins, Claud, *The Leipzig Trials* (S.I, H.F. & G. Witherby, 1921).

Oertzen, Friedrich von, *Die Deutsche* Freikorps *1918–1923* (Berlin: Spaeth & Linde, 1937).

Pratt, Edwin A., *The Rise of Rail Power, In War and Conquest* (London: P.S. King, 1915).

Reichsarchiv, *Schlachten des Weltkrieges: Die Eroberung von Nowo Georiewsk* (Berlin: Lodz, 1925).

Roth Paul, *Die politische Entwicklung in Kongress-Polen während der deutschen Okkupation* (Leipzig: K.F.Koehler, 1919).

Schwabe, Kurd, *Der Krieg in Deutsch-Südwestafrika 1904–1906* (Berlin: Weller, 1907).

Seldte, Franz, *Der Stahlhelm: Erinnerungen und Bilder aus den Jahren 1918–1933* (Berlin: Stahlhelm, 1932).

Soviet Embassy, *New Soviet Documents on Nazi Atrocities,* (London: Hutchinson, 1943).

Thierfelder, Rudolf, *Die Verwaltung der besetzten französischen Gebiete 1870/73,* (Darmstadt: Wittich, 1943).

Zobeltitz, H. C. von, and "Peter Purzelbaum," *Das Alte Heer: Erinnerungen an die Dienstzeit bei allen Waffen* (Berlin: Heinrich Beenken, 1931).

**After 1945**

Ainsztein, Reuben, *Jewish Resistance in Nazi-Occupied Eastern Europe* (London: Elek, 1974).

Allen, Henry T., *My Rhineland Journal* (Boston: Houghton Mifflin, 1923).

Allen, Michael Thad, *Hitler's Slave Lords: The Business of Forced Labour in Occupied Europe* (Chapel Hill: University of North Carolina, 2002).

Andersch, Alfred, *Der Vater eines Mörders* (Zurich: Diogenes, 1980).

Anderson, III, Truman O. "Germans, Ukrainians and Jews: Ethnic Politics in Heeresgebiet Süd, June–December 1941," *War in History* 7, no. 3, July 2000, 325–52.

Angolia, John R., and David Littlejohn, *NSKK and NSFK: Uniforms, Organisation and History* (San Jose, Calif.: Bender, 1994).

Armstrong, John, *Soviet Partisans in World War II* (Madison: University of Wisconsin Press, 1964).

Badsey, Stephen, "Commandos," in Richard Holmes (ed.), *The Oxford Companion to Military History* (Oxford: Oxford University Press, 2001), 213–4.

Baritz, J. J., "The Phantom War: Occupied Russia 1941/1943," *Purnell's History of the Second World War* 4, 1365–72; and, "War of the Rails," *Purnell's History of the Second World War* 7, 2857–67.

———, "War of the Rails," *Purnell's History of the Second World War* 7, 2857–67.

Barnett, Correlli (ed.), *Hitler's Generals* (London: Weidenfeld & Nicholson, 1989).

Bartov, Omer, *Hitler's Army: Soldiers, Nazis and War in the Third Reich* (New York: Oxford University Press, 1992).

Bartov, Omer, *The Eastern Front, 1941–1945: German Troops and the Barbarisation of Warfare* (London: Palgrave Macmillan, 1986)

Beaumont, Roger A., *Military Elites* (New York: Walker, 1976).

Beckett, Ian F. W., *Encyclopaedia of Guerrilla Warfare* (Santa Barbara, Calif.: ABC-CLIO, 1999).

Bekker, Cajus, trans. Frank Ziegler, *The Luftwaffe War Diaries* (London: Stackpole Military History, 1972).

Bellamy, Christopher, *The Evolution of Land Warfare* (London: Routledge, 1989).

Bender, Roger James and Hugh Page Taylor, *Uniforms, Organization and History of the Waffen-SS,* vols. 1–5 (San Jose, Calif.: Bender Publishing, 1975).

Bennett, Rab, *Under the Shadow of the Swastika: The Moral Dilemmas of Resistance and Collaboration in Hitler's Europe* (Basingstoke: Macmillan, 1999).

Berghahn, Volker, *Imperial Germany 1871–1914: Economy, Society, Culture and Politics* (Oxford: Berghahn, 1994), 88–9.

Bessel, Richard, *Nazism and War* (London: Weidenfeld & Nicholson, 2004).

———, "Policing, Professionalization and Politics," in Emsley and Weinberger (eds.), *Policing Western Europe.*

Best, Geoffrey, *Humanity in Warfare* (London: Routledge, 1980), 194.

Biddiscombe, Perry, "*Unternehmen Zeppelin*: The Deployment of SS Saboteurs and Spies in the Soviet Union, 1942–1945," *Europe-Asia Studies* 52, no. 6, 2000, 1115–42.

———, *Werwolf! The History of the National Socialist Insurgent Movement, 1944–1946* (Cardiff: University of Wales, 1998).

Birn, Ruth Bettina, "Austrian Higher SS and Police Leaders and Their Participation in the Holocaust in the Balkans," *Holocaust and Genocide Studies,* 6 (1991), 351–72.

———, *Die Höheren SS-und Polizeiführer: Himmlers Vertreter im Reich und in den besetzten Gebieten* (Dusseldorf: Droste, 1986).

———, "Two Kinds of Reality," in Bernd Wegner (ed.), *From Peace to War: Germany, Soviet Russia and the World, 1939–1941* (London: Berghahn Books, 1997), 277–92.

———, "'Zaunkoenig' an 'Uhrmacher.' Grosse Partisanenaktionen 1942/43 am Beispiel des 'Unternehmens Winterzauber,'" in *Militaergeschichtliche Zeitschrift* 60 (2001), Heft 1, 99–118.

Black, Peter R., *Ernst Kaltenbrunner: Ideological Soldier of the Third Reich* (Princeton: Princeton University Press, 1984).

Bley, Helmut, *Namibia under German Rule* (Hamburg: LIT, 1996).

———, *South West Africa under German rule, 1898–1914* (London: Heinemann, 1996).

Blood, Philip W., "Kurt Daluege and the Militarisation of the Ordnungspolizei," in Gerrard Oram (ed.), *Conflict and Legality: Policing Mid-Twentieth Century Europe* (London: Francis Boutle, 2003).

Boog, Horst, et al., trans. Dean S. McMurray, Ewald Osers, and Louise Willmot, *Germany and the Second World War: The Attack on the Soviet Union,* vol. 4 (Oxford: Oxford University Press, 1998).

Borowiec, Andrew, *Destroy Warsaw! Hitler's Punishment, Stalin's Revenge* (Westport, Conn.: Praeger, 2001).

Botzenhart, Manfred, "French Prisoners of War in Germany, 1870–71," in Stig Förster and Jörg Nagler (eds.), *On the Road to Total War* (New York: Cambridge University Press, 1997).

Bradley, John, *Lidice: Sacrificial Village* (New York: Ballentine, 1972).

Bramstedt, Ernest K., *Dictatorship and Political Police* (London: Routledge, 1945).

Breitman, Richard, *The Architect of Genocide: Himmler and the Final Solution* (Hanover, N.H.: University of New England Press, 1991).

———, *Official Secrets: What the Nazis Planned, What the British and Americans Knew* (New York: Hill and Wang, 1999).

Breitman, Richard, Norman J. W. Goda, Timothy Naftali, and Robert Wolfe, *U.S. Intelligence and the Nazis* (Cambridge: Cambridge University Press, 2005).

Brill, Werner, *"Mitleid ist fehl am Platz" Über Vernichtungskrieg und Gewalt,* (Saarbrücken: Blattlaus-Verl, 1999), 40–1.

Brinton, Crane, Gordon A. Craig, and Felix Gilbert, "Jomini," in Edward Mead Earle (ed.), *Makers of Modern Strategy: Military Thought from Machiavelli to Hitler* (Princeton: Princeton University Press, 1971), 77–92.

Broszat, Martin, *The Hitler State* (London: Longman, 1983).

Broszat, Martin, and Hemut Krausnick, *Anatomy of the SS State* (London: Collins, 1968).

Browder, George, *Hitler's Enforcers: The Gestapo and SS Security Service in the Nazi Revolution* (Don Mills, Ontario: Oxford University Press, 1996).

Browning, Christopher, *Ordinary Men: Reserve Police Battalion 101 and the Final Solution in Poland* (New York: First Harper Perennial, 1998).

Büchler, Yehoshua, "Kommandostab Reichsführer-SS: Himmler's Personal Murder Brigades in 1941," in *Holocaust and Genocide Studies* 1 (1986), 11–25.

Buder, Johannes, *Die Reorganisation der preussischen Polizei 1918–1923* (Frankfurt am Main: Lang, 1986).

Bullock, Alan, *Hitler: A Study in Tyranny* (London: Penguin, 1990).

Burleigh, Michael, *The Third Reich: A New History* (London: Macmillan, 2000).

Burleigh, Michael, and Wolfgang Wippermann, *The Racial State: Germany 1933–1945* (Cambridge: Cambridge University Press, 1991).

Campbell, J. B., *The Emperor and the Roman Army, 31 BC–AD 235* (Oxford: Oxford University Press, 1984).

Carsten, Felix L., *The Reichswehr and Politics, 1918 to 1933* (Oxford: Oxford University Press, 1966).

Cesarani, David, *The Final Solution, Origins and Implementation* (London: Routledge, 1994).

Charman, Terry, *The German Home Front 1939–45* (New York: Philosophical Library, 1989).

Chickering, Roger, and Stig Förster, *Great War, Total War: Combat and Mobilization on the Western Front, 1914–1918* (Cambridge: Cambridge University Press, 2000).

Chickering, Roger, and Stig Förster (eds.), *The Shadows of Total War: Europe, East Asia and the United States 1919–1939* (Washington, D.C.: German Historical Institute, and Cambridge: Cambridge University Press, 2003).

Clausewitz, Carl von, ed. and trans. Michael Howard and Peter Paret, *On War* (London: Penguin, 1993).

Clementz, Heinrich, *Geschichte des Judischen Krieges* (Fourier Verlag, Wiesbaden, 1997).

Combs, William L., *The Voice of the SS: A History of the SS Journal "Das Schwarze Korps"* (New York: Peter Lang, 1986).

Confino, Alon, *The Nation as a Local Metaphor: Württemberg, Imperial Germany and National Memory, 1871–1918* (Chapel Hill: University of North Carolina, 1997).

Cookridge, E. H., *They Came from the Sky* (London: Corgi, 1976).

Cooper, Matthew, *The German Army, 1933–1945* (Lanham: First Scarborough House, 1990).

———, *The Phantom War: The German Struggle against Soviet Partisans* (New York: Viking, 1977).

Craig, Gordon A., *The Politics of the Prussian Army 1640–1945* (New York: Oxford University Press, 1955).

Crankshaw, Edward, *Gestapo: Instrument of Tyranny* (London: Putnam, 1956).

Creveld, Martin Van, *Command in War* (Cambridge, Mass.: Harvard University Press, 1985).

————, *On Future War* (London: Brassey's, 1991).

————, *Supplying War: Logistics from Wallenstein to Patton* (Cambridge: Cambridge University Press, 1977).

Critchfield, James H., *Partners at the Creation: The Men behind Postwar Germany's Defense and Intelligence Establishments* (Annapolis: Naval Institute, 2003).

Cüppers, Martin, "Gustav Lombard—ein eingagierter Judenmörder aus der Waffen-SS," in Klaus-Michael Mallman and Paul Gerhard (ed.), *Karrieren der Gewalt: Nationalsozialistische Täterbiographien* (Darmstadt: Wissenschaftliche Buchgesellschaft, 2004).

Dallin, Alexander, *German Rule in Russia, 1941–1945: A Study of Occupation Policies* (New York: Macmillan, 1957).

Dallin, Alexander, and Ralph S. Mavrogordato, "Rodionov: A Case-Study in Wartime Redefection," *The American Slavic and East European Review* 1 (1959), 25–33.

Dandeker, Christopher, "The Bureaucratisation of Force," in Lawrence Freedman (ed.), *War* (Oxford: Oxford University Press, 1992), 118–23.

Danker, Uwe, "Bandits and the State: Robbers and the Authorities in the Holy Roman Empire in the Late Seventeenth and Early Eighteenth Centuries," in Richard J. Evans, *The German Underworld: Deviants and Outcasts in German History* (London: Routledge, 1988).

Davies, Norman, *Rising 44: The Battle for Warsaw* (London: Macmillan, 2003).

Davies, Roy W., *Service in the Roman Army* (Edinburgh: Edinburgh University Press, 1989)

Dean, Martin, *Collaboration in the Holocaust: Crimes of the Local Police in Byelorussia and Ukraine, 1941–1944* (New York: St. Martin's, 2000).

Dedering, Tilman, "A Certain Rigorous Treatment of All Parts of the Nation, The Annihilation of the Herero in German South-West Africa, 1904," in Mark Levene and Penny Robert, *The Massacre in History* (New York: Berghahn, 1999).

Deist, Wilhelm, "The Road to Ideological War: Germany 1918–1945," in Williamson Murray, Macgregor Knox, and Alvin Bernstein, *The Making of Strategy: Rulers, States and War* (New York: Cambridge University Press, 1994), 359–60.

Deschner, Günter, *Reinhard Heydrich. Statthalter der totalen Macht* (Munich: Heyne, 1980).

————, *Warsaw Rising* (London: Pan, 1972).

D'Este, Carlo, "Model," in Correlli Barnett (ed.), *Hitler's Generals* (London: Weidenfeld & Nicolson, 1989).

Diehl, James M., "No More Peace: The Militarization of Politics," in Roger Chickering and Stig Förster (eds.), *The Shadows of Total War: Europe, East Asia and the United States 1919–1939* (Washington, D.C.: German Historical Institute, and Cambridge: Cambridge University Press, 2003).

Dierl, Florian, "Adolf von Bomhard—Generalstabschef der Ordnungspolizei," in Klaus-Michael Mallman and Paul Gerhard (ed.), *Karrieren der Gewalt: Nationalsozialistische Täterbiographien* (Darmstadt: Wissenschaftliche Buchgesellschaft, 2004).

Djilas, Milovan, trans. by Michael B. Petrovich, *Wartime* (London: Harcourt Brace Jovanovich, 1977).

Drechsler, Horst, "The Hereros of South-West Africa (Namibia)," in Frank Chalk and Kurt Jonassohn, *The History and Sociology of Genocide: Analyses and Case Studies* (New Haven, Conn.: Yale University Press, 1990).

Drechsler, Horst, trans. Bernd Zollner *"Let us die fighting": The Struggle of the Herero and Nama against German Imperialism*, (London: Zed, 1980).

Ebeling, Frank, *Geopolitik: Karl Haushofer und seine Raumwissenschaft 1919–1945* (Berlin: Akad-Verlag, 1994).

Emsley, Clive, and Barbara Weinberger (eds.), *Policing Western Europe: Politics, Professionalism and Public Order, 1850–1940* (Westport, Conn: Greenwood Press, 1991).

Evans, Richard, *Rereading German History 1800–1996: From Unification to Reunification* (London: Routledge, 1997).

Evans, Richard, *Rethinking German History: Nineteenth Century Germany and the Origins of the Third Reich* (London: Allen & Unwin, 1987).

Farmer, Sarah, *Martyred Village: Commemorating the 1944 Massacre of Oradour-sur-Glane*, (Berkeley: University of California Press, 1999).

Fedyshyn, Oleh S., *Germany's Drive to the East and the Ukrainian Revolution 1917–1918* (New Brunswick, N.J.: Rutgers University Press, 1971).

Fesser, Gerd, "Pardon wird nicht gegeben!" *Die Zeit*, Nr. 31 (July 27, 2000), 17.

Fest, Joachim C., *Hitler* (New York: Knopf, 1977).

Fischer, Fritz, *Germany's Aims in the First World War* (New York: Norton, 1967).

Fitzgibbon, Constantine, *Denazification* (London: Norton, 1969).

Fleming, Gerald, *Hitler and the Final Solution* (Berkeley and Los Angeles: University of California, Oxford, 1986).

Foley, Robert T., *Alfred von Schlieffen's Military Writings* (London: Frank Cass, 2003).

Foot, M. R. D., *Resistance: European Resistance to Nazism, 1940–45* (London: Methuen, 1976).

Förster, Jürgen, "The Relation between Barbarossa as an Ideological War of Extermination and the Final Solution," in David Cesarani, *The Final Solution, Origins and Implementation* (London: Routledge, 1994).

Frei, Norbert, *Adenauer's Germany and the Nazi Past: The Politics of Amnesty and Integration* (New York: Columbia University Press, 2002).

Fricke, Dieter, *Bismarcks Prätorianer: Die Berliner politische Polizei im Kampf gegen die Deutsche Arbeiterbewegung (1871–1898)* (Berlin: DDR, 1962), 23.

Friedrich, Wilhelm, *Die Polizei im NS-Staat* (Paderborn: F. Schoeningh, 1997).

Gall, Lothar, and Manfred Pohl (eds.), *Die Eisenbahn in Deutschland von den Anfängen bis zur Gegenwart* (Munich: C.H. Beck, 1999).

Galland, Adolf, *Die Ersten und die Letzten: Jagdflieger im Zweiten Weltkrieg* (Munich: F. Schneekluth, 1953).

Gander, Terry, and Peter Chamberlain, *Small Arms, Artillery and Special Weapons of the Third Reich* (London: Macdonald and Janes', 1978), 286.

Gehlen, Reinhard, *Der Dienst, Erinnerungen, 1942–1971* (Munich: Droemer, 1971).

Gellately, Robert, *The Gestapo and German Society* (Oxford: Clarendon, 1991).

Gerlach, Christian, *"Kalkulierte Morde*: German Economic Interests, Occupation Policy, and the Murder of the Jews in Belorussia," in Ulrich Herbert (ed.), *National Socialist Extermination Policies: Contemporary German Perspectives and Controversies* (Oxford: Berghahn, 2000).

———, *Kalkulierte Morde: Die deutsche Wirtschafts- und Vernichtungspolitik in Weissrussland 1941 bis 1944* (Hamburg: Hamburg Edition HIS, 1999).

———, *Krieg, Ernährung, Völkermord: Forschungen zur deutschen Vernichtungspolitik im Zweiten Weltkrieg* (Hamburg: Pendo Publishing, 1998).

Gewald, Jan-Bart, *Herero Heroes: A Socio-political History of the Herero of Namibia 1890–1923*, (London: James Currey, 1999).

———, "Learning to Wage and Win Wars in Africa: A Provisional History of German Military Activity in Congo, Tanzania, China and Namibia," African Studies Centre, Leiden, The Netherlands, ASC Working Paper No. 60, 2005.

Geyer, Hermann, "Kriegserfahrungen und Cannae im Weltkriege," *Militärwissenschaftliche Mitteilungen*, Heft, August 5, 1924, 24.

———, *Ostfeldzug. XI Armeekorps* (Neckargemünd: Kurt Vowinckel, 1967).

Geyer, Michael, "Civitella Della Chiana on June 29, 1944," in Hannes Heer and Klaus Naumann, *War of Extermination: The German Military in World War II 1941–1945* (New York: Berghahn, 2000), 175–216.

Goerlitz, Walter, trans. Brian Battershaw, *History of the German General Staff, 1657–1945* (New York: Praeger, 1957).

Goldhagen, Daniel Jonah, *Hitler's Willing Executioners: Ordinary Germans and the Holocaust* (London: Little, Brown, 1996).

Gottwaldt, Alfred B., *Heeresfeldbahnen: Bau und Einsatz der militärischen Schmalspurbahnen in zwei Weltkriegen* (Stuttgart: Motorbuch, 1998).

Grabitz, Helge, "Problems of Nazi Trials in the Federal Republic of Germany," *Holocaust and Genocide Studies* 3 (1988), 209–222.

Green, William, *The Warplanes of the Third Reich* (London: Macdonald and Co., 1970).

Grenkevich, Leonid D., *The Soviet Partisan Movement, 1941–1944: A Critical Historiographical Analysis* (London: Frank Cass, 1999).

Grimm, Reinhold, and Jost Hermand, *1914/1939: German Reflections of the Two World Wars* (Madison: University of Wisconsin Press, 1992).

Grimsley, Mark, and Clifford J. Rogers, *Civilians in the Path of War* (Lincoln: University of Nebraska Press, 2002).

Gross, Jan Tomasz, *Polish Society under German Occupation: The Generalgouvernment 1939–1944* (New Haven, Conn.: Princeton University Press, 1979).

Guderian, Heinz, *Panzer Leader* (London: De Capo, 1952).

Haberer, Eric, "The German Police and Genocide in Belorussia, 1941–1944," *Journal of Genocide Research* 3 (2001), 23–24.

Hamburger Institut für Sozialforschung (ed.), V*erbrechen der Wehrmacht: Dimensionen des Vernichtungskrieges 1941–1944* (Hamburg: Hamburger Edition, 2002).

Hanson, Joanna K., *The Civilian Population and the Warsaw Rising of 1944* (Cambridge: Cambridge University Press, 1982).

Hartigan, Richard Shelly, *Lieber's Code and the Law of War* (Chicago: Precedent, 1983).

Hathaway, Jay, *In Perfect Formation: SS Ideology and the SS-Junkerschule-Tölz* (Atglen, Pa.: Schiffer, 1999).

Hausser, Paul, *Waffen-SS im Einsatz* (Oldendorf: Pless, 1953).

Hayes, Patricia, Jeremy Silvester, Marion Wallace, and Wolfram Hartmann (eds.), *Namibia under South African Rule: Mobility and Containment, 1915–46* (Abington, Oxon: James Currey, 1998).

Hébras, Robert, *Understand Oradour-sur-Glane drama*, (Editions C.M.D. site pamphlet).

Heer, Hannes, "The Logic of the War of Extermination," in Hannes Heer and Klaus Naumann, *War of Extermination: The German Military in World War II 1941–1945* (New York: Berghahn, 2000), 106–9.

———, *Tote Zonen: Die Deutsche Wehrmacht an der Ostfront* (Hamburg: Hamburger Edition, 1999).

Heer, Hannes and Klaus Naumann (eds.), *Vernichtungskrieg: Verbrechen der Wehrmacht 1941 bis 1944* (Hamburg: Hamburg Edition HIS, 1995).

———, *War of Extermination: The German Military in World War II 1941–1945* (New York: Berghahn, 2000).

Herbert, Ulrich, *Best, Biographische Studien über Radikalismus, Weltanschauung und Vernunft 1903–1989* (Bonn: Dietz, 1996).

————, *Hitler's Foreign Workers: Enforced Foreign Labor in Germany under the Third Reich* (Cambridge: Berg, 1997).

———— (ed.), *National Socialist Extermination Policies: Contemporary German Perspectives and Controversies* (Oxford: Berghahn, 2000).

Herwig, Holger H., "The Immorality of Expediency: The German Military from Ludendorff to Hitler," in Mark Grimsley and Clifford J. Rogers (eds.), *Civilians in the Path of War* (Lincoln: University of Nebraska Press, 2002).

Herzog, Martin, and Marko Rösseler, "Der große Zaun," *Die Zeit*, Nr. 17 (April 16, 1998).

Hilberg, Raul, *The Destruction of the European Jews* (New York: Holmes & Meier, 1985).

Hildebrand, Klaus, "Die Deutsche Reichsbahn in der nationalsozialistischen Diktatur 1933-1945," in Lothar Gall and Manfred Pohl (eds.), *Die Eisenbahn in Deutschland von den Anfängen bis zur Gegenwart* (Munich: C.H. Beck, 1999).

Hirschfeld, Gerhard, *Nazi Rule and Dutch Collaboration: The Netherlands under German Occupation, 1940–1945* (Oxford: Berg, 1988).

————, *The Policies of Genocide: Jews and Soviet Prisoners of War in Nazi Germany* (London, 1986)

Hoettl, Wilhelm, *The Secret Front: The Inside Story of Nazi Political Espionage* (Weidenfeld & Nicolson: London, 1953).

Hoffmann, Peter, *Hitler's Personal Security: Protecting the Führer, 1921–1945* (New York: De Capo, 2000).

Höhne, Heinz, *The Order of the Death's Head: The Story of Hitler's SS* (London: Penguin, 1969).

Holmes, Richard, *Bir Hacheim: Desert Citadel* (London: Pan Ballantine, 1971).

Horne, John, and Alan Kramer, *German Atrocities 1914: A History of Denial* (New Haven, Conn.: Yale University Press, 2001).

————, "War Between Soldiers and Enemy Civilians," in Roger Chickering and Stig Förster, *Great War, Total War: Combat and Mobilization on the Western Front, 1914–1918* (Cambridge: Cambridge University Press, 2000).

Hosbawm, Eric, *On History* (London: Weidenfeld & Nicolson, 1997).

Howard, Michael, *The Franco–Prussian War* (London: Rupert Hart-Davis, 1961).

————, *War in European History* (Oxford: Oxford University Press, 1976).

Howarth, Patrick, *Intelligence Chief Extraordinary: The Life of the Ninth Duke of Portland* (London: Bodley Head, 1986).

Hull, Isabel von, *Absolute Destruction: Military Culture and the Practices of War in Imperial Germany* (Ithaca: Cornell University Press, 2005).

Ilgen, Rudolf, *Mein Zusammenstoss mit SS-Oberführer von dem Bach-Zelewski als Richter im Fruhjar 1933 in der Neumarkt* (Koblenz: Wolfgang Lomüller, 1980).

Jacobmeyer, Wolfgang, *Das Diensttagebuch des deutschen Generalgouverneurs in Polen 1939–1945* (Stuttgart: Deutsche Verlags-Anstalt, 1975).

Johnson, Eric A., *Nazi Terror: The Gestapo, Jews and Ordinary Germans* (London: John Murray, 2002).

Jones, Nigel H., *Hitler's Heralds: The Story of the Freikorps 1918–1923* (London: Murray, 1987).

Josephus, Flavius, trans. G. A. Williamson, *The Jewish War* (London: Penguin, 1978).

Jünger, Ernst, trans. Michael Hoffmann, *Storm of Steel* (London: Penguin, 2003).

Kahl, Wolfgang, "Vom mythos der 'Bandenbekämpfung': polizeiverbände im zweiten weltkreig," *Die polizei. zentralorgan für das sicherheits- und ordnungswesen aus*, 1998, J. 89, Nr. 2, 47–56.

Keilig, Wolf, *Das Deutsche Heer 1939–1945: Gliederung, Einsatz, Stellenbesetzung*, (Bad Nauheim: Hans-Henning Podzun, 1956).

Kenkmann, Alfons (eds.), *Villa ten Hompel: Sitz der Ordnungspolizei im Dritten Reich – Vom "Tatort Schreibtisch" zur Erinnerungstatte?* (Duisberg: Agenda Verlag, 1996).

Keppie, Lawrence, *The Making of the Roman Army: From Republic to Empire* (London: BT Batsford, 1984)

Kershaw, Ian, *Hitler 1889–1936: Hubris* (London: Allen Lane, 1998).

———, *Hitler 1936–45: Nemesis* (London: Penguin, 2000).

Killingray, David, and David Omissi (ed.), *Guardians of Empire: The Armed Forces of the Colonial Powers c.1700–1964* (Manchester: Manchester University Press, 2000).

Klausch, Hans-Peter, *Antifaschisten in SS-Uniform: Schicksal und Widerstand der deutschen politischen KZ-Häftlinge, Zuchthaus- und Wehrmachtstrafgefangenen in der SS-Sonderformation Dirlewanger* (Bremen: Edition Temmen, 1993).

Klemp, Stefan, *"Freispruch für das Mord-Bataillon." Die NS-Ordnungspolizei und die Nachkriegsjustiz* (Münster: LIT, 1998).

Klemperer, Victor, *LTI [Lingua, Tertii, Imperii]: Notizbuch eines Philologen* (Leipzig: Reclam, 1985).

———, trans. Martin Brady, *The Language of the Third Reich* (London: Continuum, 2002).

———, *To the Bitter End: The Diaries of Victor Klemperer 1942–45*, II (London: Penguin, 1998).

Kluge, Ulrich, *Soldatenräte und Revolution: Studien zur Militärpolitik in Deutschland 1918–1919* (Göttingen: Vandenhoeck & Ruprecht, 1975).

Knipping, Andreas, and Reinhard Schulz, *Reichsbahn hinter der Ostfront 1941–1944*, (Stuttgart: Transpress, 1999).

Koehl, Robert, *The Black Corps: The Structure and Power Struggles of the Nazi SS* (Madison: University of Wisconsin, 1983).

———, *RKFDV: German Resettlement and Population Policy 1939–1945* (Cambridge, Mass.: Harvard University Press, 1957).

Kordt, Erich, *Wahn und Wirklichkeit* (Stuttgart: Union Deutsche Verlagsges, 1948).

Kovpak, Sidor A., *Our Partisan Course* (London: Hutchinson, 1947).

Krannhals, Hans von, *Der Warschauer Aufstand 1944* (Frankfurt: Bernard & Graefe Verl.f. Wehrwesen, 1964).

Krátký, Karel, and Antonin \nejdárek, "The Slovak Rising," *Purnell's History of the Second World War*, vol. 7 (1968), 2157–66.

Krausnick, Helmut, *Hitler's Einsatzgruppen: Die Truppe des Weltanschauungskrieges 1938–1942* (Frankfurt: Fischer, 1985).

Krüger, Gesine, *Kriegsbewältigung und Geschichtsbewusstsein: Realität, Deutung und Verarbeitung des deutschen Kolonialkriegs in Namibia 1904 bis 1907*, (Berlin: Vandenhoeck & Ruprecht, 1999).

Kumm, Otto, *Prinz Eugen: The History of the 7. SS-Mountain Division "Prinz Eugen,"* (Winnipeg: J. J. Fedorowicz, 1995).

Kunzmann-Milius, S., *Fallschirmjäger der Waffen-SS* (Osnabrück: Munin Verlag, 1986).

Kwiet, Konrad, "From the Diary of a Killing Unit," in John Milful (ed.), *Why Germany? National Socialist Anti-Semitism and the European Context* (Oxford: Berg, 1993), 75–91.

Laqueur, Walter, *Guerrilla: A Historical and Critical Study* (London: Weidenfeld & Nicolson, 1977).

Large, David Clay, *Where Ghosts Walked: Munich's Road to the Third Reich* (New York: W.W. Norton, 1997).

Lasswell, Harold D., "The Garrison-State Hypothesis Today," in Samuel P. Huntington (ed.), *Changing Patterns of Military Politics* (New York: Free Press, 1962).

Lefebre, Eric, and Jean de Lagarde, "Das Bandenkampfabzeichen 1944–1945," *Internationales Militaria*, January 1999, 36–41.

Lepre, George, *Himmler's Bosnian Division: The Waffen-SS Handschar Division, 1943–1945* (Atglen, Pa.: Schiffer Military History, 1997).

Levene, Mark, and Penny Robert, *The Massacre in History* (New York: Berghahn, 1999)

Liulevicius, Vejas Gabriel, *War Land on the Eastern Front* (Cambridge: Cambridge University Press, 2000).

Livingstone, Richard, "A Final Lesson: The Destruction of Lidice," *Purnell's History of the Second World War* 3, 1024–9.

Logusz, Michael O., *Galicia Division: The Waffen-SS 14th Grenadier Division 1943–1945* (Atglen, Pa.: Schiffer Military History, 1997).

Lüdtke, Alf, *Police and State in Prussia, 1815–1850* (Cambridge: Cambridge University Press, 1982).

Lukas, Richard C., *Forgotten Holocaust: The Poles under German Occupation 1939–1944* (New York: Hippocrene, 1997).

Machlejd, Wanda, *War Crimes in Poland: Erich von dem Bach* (Warsaw: Zachodnia Agencja Prasowa, 1961).

Mackiewicz, Joseph, *Murder of Katyn* (London: Hollis & Carter, 1951).

MacLean, French, *The Cruel Hunters: SS-Sonderkommando Dirlewanger, Hitler's Most Notorious Anti-partisan* (Atglen, Pa.: Schiffer Military History, 1998).

Madajczyk, Czeskaw, *Die Okkupationspolitik Nazideutschlands in Polen 1939–1945*, (Stottgary: Akademie, 1987).

Madeja, W. Victor, *Russo-German War: Summer 1944*, vol. 33 (Allentown: Valor, 1987).

Mahlein, Leonard, *Waffen-SS in der Bundesrepublik: Eine Dokumentation Der VVN-Bund Der Antifaschisten* (Frankfurt am Main: Roderberg, 1978).

Mahnken, Thomas G., *Uncovering Ways of War: U.S. Intelligence and Foreign Military Innovation* (Ithaca, N.Y.: Cornell University Press, 2002).

Mann, Michael, *The Dark Side of Democracy: Explaining Ethnic Cleansing* (Cambridge: Cambridge University Press, 2004).

Manoschek, Walter, "The Extermination of the Jews in Serbia," in Ulrich Herbert, *National Socialist Extermination Policies: Contemporary German Perspectives and Controversies* (Oxford: Berghahn, 2000).

Margry, Karel, "The Dostler Case," *After the Battle Magazine*, no. 94 (1996), 1–19.

Marillier, Richard, *Vercors 1943–1944: Le malentendu permanent* (Clamecy: Armançon, 2003).

Marwick, Arthur, Clive Emsley, and Wendy Simpson, *Total War and Historical Change: Europe 1914–1955* (Buckingham: Open University Press, 2001).

Mason, Tim, *Social Policy in the Third Reich: The Working Class and the National Community* (Oxford: Berg, 1997), 1.

Mazower, Mark, *Inside Hitler's Greece: The Experience of Occupation 1941–1944* (New Haven, Conn.: Yale University Press, 1995).

McConville, Michael, "Knight's Move in Bosnia and the British Rescue of Tito: 1944," *RUSI Journal*, December 1997, 61–9.

McPhail, Helen, *The Long Silence: Civilian Life under the German Occupation of Northern France, 1914–1918* (London: IB Taurus, 1999).

Megargee, Geoffrey P., *Inside Hitler's High Command* (Lawrence: University of Kansas, 2000).

Merkel, Peter H., *Political Violence under the Swastika: 581 Early Nazis* (Princeton: Princeton University Press, 1975).

Messerschmidt, Manfred, "Der Minsker Process 1946," in Hannes Heer and Klaus Naumann (eds.), *Vernichtungskrieg: Verbrechen der Wehrmacht 1941 bis 1944* (Hamburg: Hamburg Edition HIS, 1995), 551–68.

Mountfield, David, *The Partisans* (London: Hamlyn, 1979).

Müller, Rolf-Dieter, *Hitlers Ostkrieg und die deutsche Siedlungspolitik. Die Zusammenarbeit von Wehrmacht, Wirtschaft und SS* (Frankfurt a. M, 1991).

Müller, Rolf-Dieter, and Gerd R. Ueberschar, *Hitler's War in the East 1941–1945: A Critical Assessment* (Oxford: Berghahn, 1997).

Müller-Tupath, Karla, *Reichsführers gehorsamster Becher: Eine deutsche Karriere* (Berlin: Aufbau, 1999).

Mulligan, Timothy Patrick, *The Politics of Illusion: German Occupation Policy in the Soviet Union* (New York: Praeger, 1988).

Münchener Stadtmuseum, *München-"Hauptstadt der Bewegung"* (Munich: Klinkhardt & Biermann, 1993).

Murphy, David T., The Heroic Earth: Geopolitical Thought in Weimar Germany 1918–1933 (Kent, Ohio: Kent State University, 1997).

Murray, Williamson, "The Collapse of Empire: British Strategy, 1919–1945," in Williamson Murray, MacGregor Knox, and Alvin Bernstein, *The Making of Strategy: Rulers, States and War* (Cambridge: Cambridge University Press, 1994), 399–425.

Murray, Williamson, Macgregor Knox, and Alvin Bernstein, *The Making of Strategy: Rulers, States and War* (New York: Cambridge University Press, 1994).

Neufeldt, Hans-Joachim, Jürgen Huck, Georg Tessin, *Zur Geschichte der Ordnungspolizei 1936–1945* (Koblenz, 1957).

Niven, Bill, *Facing the Nazi Past: United Germany and the Legacy of the Third Reich* (London: Routledge, 2002).

Overy, Richard, *Interrogations: Inside the Minds of the Nazi Elite* (London: Allen Lane, 2002).

———, *War and Economy in the Third Reich* (Oxford: Clarendon, 1994).

Padfield, Peter, *Himmler: Reichsführer-SS* (London: Heinemann, 1990).

Paret, Peter (ed.), *Makers of Modern Strategy: From Machiavelli to the Nuclear Age* (Princeton: Princeton University Press, 1986).

Pearson, Michael, *Tears of Glory* (London: Macmillan, 1978).

Perras, Arne, *Carl Peters and German Imperialism 1856–1918* (Oxford: Oxford University Press, 2004).

Peukert, Detlev, trans. Richard Deveson, *The Weimar Republic: The Crisis of Classical Modernity* (London: Penguin, 1991).

Phillips, C. E. Lucas, *The Greatest Raid of All* (London: Heinemann, 1958).

Piekalkiewicz, Janus, *Kampf um Warschau: Stalins Verrat an der polnischen Heimatarmee 1944* (Munich: F.A. Herbig, 1994).

Pierik, Perry, *Hungary 1944–1945: The Forgotten Tragedy* (Nieuwegein: Aspekt, 1996).

Pool, Gerhardus, *Samuel Maherero* (Windhoek: Gamsberg Macmillan, 1991).

Pottgiesser, Hans, *Die Deutsche Reichsbahn im Ostfeldzug 1939–1944* (Neckargemünd: Kurt Vowinckel, 1975)

Prusin, Alexander Victor, "'Fascist Criminals to the Gallows!': The Holocaust and Soviet War Crimes Trials, December 1945–February 1946," *Holocaust and Genocide Studies* 17 (2003), 1–30.

Reinke, Herbert, "'Armed as if for a War': The State, the Military and Professionalization of the Prussian Police in Imperial Germany," in Clive Emsley and

Barbara Weinberger (eds.), *Policing Western Europe: Politics, Professionalism and Public Order, 1850–1940* (Westport, Conn: Greenwood Press, 1991).

Reitlinger, Gerald, *The Final Solution: The Attempt to Exterminate the Jews of Europe* (New York: Perpetua Edition, 1961).

———, *The House Built on Sand* (New York: Viking, 1960).

———, *The SS: Alibi of a Nation 1922–1945* (London: Faber & Faber, 1956).

Reynolds, Michael, *Steel Inferno: 1st SS Panzer Corps in Normandy* (Staplehurst: Perseus, 1997).

Rossino, Alexander B., "Destructive Impulses: German Soldiers and the Conquest of Poland," *Holocaust and Genocide Studies* 2 (Winter 1997), 351–65.

———, *Hitler Strikes Poland: Blitzkrieg, Ideology and Atrocity* (Lawrence: University of Kansas, 2003).

Rothenberg, Gunther E., "Moltke, Schlieffen and the Doctrine of Strategic Envelopment," in Peter Paret (ed.), *Makers of Modern Strategy: From Machiavelli to the Nuclear Age* (Princeton: Princeton University Press, 1986).

Rudel, Hans-Ulrich, *Trotzdem* (Oldendorf, 1981).

Sawodny, Wolfgang, *Die Panzerzüge des Deutschen Reiches 1904–1945* (Freiburg: EK-Verlag, 1996).

Schellenberg, Walter, *The Schellenberg Memoirs* (London: Andre Deutsch, 1956).

Schreiber, Gerhard, "Partisanenkrieg und Kriegsverbrechen der Wehrmacht in Italien 1943 bis 1945," in *Beiträge zur Nationalsozialistichen Gesundheits- und Sozialpolitik, Band 14, Repression und Kriegsverbrechen: Die Bekämpfung von Widerstand und Partisanenbewegungen gegen die deutsche Besatzung in West- und Südeuropa* (Berlin: Schwarze Risse, 1997), 93–129.

Schulze-Kossens, Richard, *Militärischer Führernachswuchs der Waffen-SS: Die Junkerschulen* (Osnabrück: Munin, 1982).

Scotland, A. P., *The London Cage* (London: Evans Brothers, 1957).

Sereny, Gitta, *Into That Darkness: From Mercy Killing to Mass Murder* (London: Pimlico, 1995).

Shakespeare, William, *The Collected Works* (London: Cook & Wedderburn, 1982).

Shandley, Robert R., *Unwilling Germans? The Goldhagen Debate* (Minneapolis: University of Minnesota, 1998).

Shepherd, Ben, "Hawks, Doves and Tote Zonen; A Wehrmacht Security Division in Central Russia, 1943," *Journal of Contemporary History* 37(3) (2002), 349–369.

———, *War in the Wild East. The German Army and Soviet Partisans*, Cambridge, Harvard University Press, 2004.

Shepperd, G. A., "Ground to Air Liaison: Strategy and Tactics," *Purnell's History of Second World War* 8 (1975), 3217–20.

Shy, John, "Jomini," in Peter Paret (ed.), *Makers of Modern Strategy: From Machiavelli to the Nuclear Age* (Princeton: Princeton University Press, 1986).

Shy, John, and Thomas W. Collier, "Revolutionary War," in Peter Paret (ed.), *Makers of Modern Strategy: From Machiavelli to the Nuclear Age* (Princeton: Princeton University Press, 1986).

Sibley, J. R., *Tanganyikan Guerrilla: East African Campaign 1914–18* (New York: Ballentine, 1971).

Simpson, Keith, "The German Experience of Rear Area Security on the Eastern Front 1941–1945," *RUSI Journal*, December 1976, 39–46.

Skorzeny, Otto, trans. David Johnson, *My Commando Operations* (Atglen, Pa.: Schiffer Press, 1995).

Smith, Bradley F., and Elena Agarossi, *Operation Sunrise: The Secret Surrender* (London: Andre Deutsch, 1979).

Smith, Woodruff D., *The German Colonial Empire* (Chapel Hill: University of North Carolina, 1978).

———, *The Ideological Origins of Nazi Imperialism* (Oxford: Oxford University Press, 1986).

Soviet Embassy (London), *Soviet Government Statements on Nazi Atrocities* (London: Hutchinson, 1946).

Speer, Albert, *The Slave State* (London: Weidenfeld & Nicolson, 1981).

Speier, Hans, "Ludendorff: The German Concept of Total War," in Edward Mead Earle (ed.), *Makers of Modern Strategy: Military Thought from Machiavelli to Hitler* (Princeton: Princeton University Press, 1971).

Steenberg, Sven, *Vlasov* (New York, Alfred A. Knopf, 1970).

Stein, George H., *Waffen-SS: Hitler's Elite Guard at War, 1939–1945* (Ithaca and London: Cornell University Press, 1966).

Steiner, Felix, *Der Freiwillige: der Waffen-SS Idee und Opfergang* (Rosenheim: Deutsche Verlagsgesellschaft, 1958).

Stevens, E. H., *Trial of Nikolaus von Falkenhorst: Formerly Generaloberst in the German Army* (London: William Hodge, 1949).

Stone, Norman, *The Eastern Front 1914–1917* (London: Penguin, 1975).

Stoneman, Mark, "The Bavarian Army and French Civilians in the War of 1870–1871: A Cultural Interpretation," *War in History* 8 (2001), 271–93.

Strachen, Hew, "Total War in the Twentieth Century," in Arthur Marwick, Clive Emsley, and Wendy Simpson, *Total War and Historical Change: Europe 1914–1955* (Buckingham: Open University Press, 2001).

Streit, Christian, *Keine Kameraden: Die Wehrmacht und die sowjetischen Kriegsgefangenen 1941–1945* (Stuttgart: Deutsche Verlags-Anstalt, 1978).

———, "The German Army and the Policies of Genocide," in Gerhard Hirschfeld, *The Policies of Genocide: Jews and Soviet Prisoners of War in Nazi Germany* (London, 1986), 1–14.

Stroop, Jürgen, "Es gibt keinen jüdischen Wohnbezirk in Warschau mehr!" published as *The Stroop Report*, trans. Sybil Milton and intro. by Andrej Wirth, (London, 1980).

Sydnor, Charles, *Soldiers of Destruction: The SS Death's Head Division, 1933–1945* (Princeton: Princeton University Press, 1977).

Szöllösi-Janze, Margit, *Poison Gas, Lice and Mites: Fritz Haber (1868–1934) and the Uses and Abuses of Science* (Munich and St. Antony's: Oxford University Press).

Taylor, Telford, *The Anatomy of the Nuremberg Trials: A Personal Memoir* (London: Bloomsbury, 1993).

———, *Sword and Swastika: Generals and Nazis in the Third Reich* (New York: Barnes and Noble Books, 1995).

Terry, Nicholas, "Conflicting Signals: British Intelligence on the 'Final Solution' through Radio Intercepts and Other Sources, 1941–1942," *Yad Vashem Studies*, 2004.

Thomaneck, Jürgen, "Police and Public Order in the Federal Republic of Germany," in John Roach and Jürgen Thomaneck (eds.), *Police and Public Order in Europe* (London: Croom Helm, 1985).

Thomason, Frank, "Uniformed Police in the City of Berlin under the Empire," in Emilio C. Viano and Jeffrey H. Reiman (eds.), *The Police in Society* (Lexington, Mass: D.C. Heath, 1975).

Tolver, Raymond F., and Trevor J. Constable, *The Blond Knight of Germany* (Blue Ridge Summit, Pa.: Aero Pub., 1985).

Townsend, Charles, *The Oxford History of Modern War* (Oxford: Oxford University Press, 1997).

Trevor-Roper, Hugh R., *The Last Days of Hitler* (London: Pan, 1973).

Vagts, Alfred, *A History of Militarism: Civilian and Military* (Toronto: Meridian, 1959).

Vanneste, Alex, *Kroniek van Een Dorp in oorlog Neerpelt 1914–1918* (Antwerp, The Netherlands: Universitas, 1998).

Verhey, Jeffrey, *The Spirit of 1914: Militarism, Myth and Mobilisation in Germany* (Cambridge: Cambridge University Press, 2000).

Viano, Emilio C., and Jeffrey H. Reiman (eds.), *The Police in Society* (Lexington, Mass: D.C. Heath, 1975).

Vogt, Timothy R., *Denazification in Soviet-Occupied Germany: Brandenburg 1945– 1948* (Cambridge, Mass.: Harvard University Press, 2000).

Vopersal, Wolfgang, "Die SS-Ersatzbataillone in Breslau und das SS-Ersatzbataillon 'Ost,'" in *Der Freiwillige* 19, no. 5 (April 1973), 18–19.

Wade, D. A. L., "A Survey of the Trials of War Criminals," *The Royal Institute of International Affairs* 96 (1951), 66–70.

Warlimont, Walter, *Inside Hitler's Headquarters 1939–45* (Navato: Presidio Press, 1964).

Webster, Graham, *The Roman Imperial Army of the First and Second Centuries AD* (London: Grosvenor, 1969).

Wehler, Hans-Ulrich, *The German Empire 1871–1918* (Warwickshire: Berg, 1985).

Weidinger, Otto, *Comrades to the End: The 4th SS Panzer-Grenadier Regiment "Der Führer" 1938–1945* (Atglen: Schiffer, 1998).

Weigley, Russell, *The American Way of War: A History of United States Military Strategy and Policy* (Bloomington: Indiana University Press, 1973).

Weinberg, Gerhard L. "Airpower in Partisan Warfare," in John A. Armstrong (ed.), *Soviet Partisans in World War II* (Madison: University of Wisconsin Press, 1964), 361–88.

———, *Germany, Hitler and World War II: Essays in Modern German and World History* (Cambridge: Cambridge University Press, 1995).

Weiss, Hermann, *Biographisches Lexikon zum Dritten Reich* (Frankfurt am Main: Fischer Taschenbuch, 2002).

Weitz, John, *Hitler's Bankier: Hjalmar Schacht* (New York: St. Martin's Griffin, 1998).

Werth, Alexander, *Russia at War, 1941–1945* (London: Pan, 1965).

Westermann, Edward B., "'Friend and Helper': German Uniformed Police Operations in Poland and the General Government, 1939–1941," *Journal of Military History* 58 (October 1994), 643–61.

———, "Himmler's Uniformed Police on the Eastern Front: The Reich's Secret Soldiers, 1941–1942." *War in History* 3 (1996), 309–29.

———, *Hitler's Police Battalions: Enforcing Racial War in the East*, Modern War Studies (Lawrence: University Press of Kansas, 2005).

———, "'Ordinary Men' or 'Ideological Soldiers'?" Police Battalion 310 in Russia, 1942, *German Studies Review* 21 (February 1998), 41–68.

Whittlesey, Derwent, "Haushofer: The Geopoliticians," in Edward Mead Earle (ed.), *Makers of Modern Strategy: Military Thought from Machiavelli to Hitler* (Princeton: Princeton University Press, 1971), 388–411.

Wilson, Charles McMoran, *Winston Churchill: The Struggle for Survival, 1940- 1965: Taken from the Diaries of Lord Moran* (London: Constable, 1966).

Wisniewski, Tomasz, *Jewish Bialystok and Surroundings in Eastern Poland* (Ipswich, Mass.: Ipswich Press, 1998).

Wood, Derek, and Derek Dempster, *The Narrow Margin: The Battle of Britain and the Rise of Air Power, 1930–1940* (London: Hutchinson, 1961).

Wykes, Alan, *Himmler* (New York: Ballentine, 1972).

Yerger, Mark C., *Allgemeine-SS: The Commands, Units and Leaders of the General SS* (Winnepeg, Canada: J. J. Fedorowicz, 1997).

———, *Waffen SS Commanders: The Army, Corps and Division Leaders of a Legend-Augsberger to Kreutz* (Atglen, Pa.: Schiffer, 1997).

Young, Peter, *Commando* (New York: Ballentine, 1969).

Zarubinsky, O. A., "The 'Red' Partisan Movement in Ukraine During World War II: A Contemporary Assessment," *The Journal of Slavic Military Studies* 9 (June 1996), 399–416.

Zimmerer, Jürgen, *Deutsche Herrschaft Über Afrikaner: Staalicher Machtanspruch und Wirklichkeit im Kolonialen Namibia* (Münster: LIT, 2001).

Zirkel, Kirsten, "Military Power in German Colonial Policy: The Schutztruppen and Their Leaders in East and South-West Africa, 1888–1918," in David Killingray and David Omissi (eds.), *Guardians of Empire: The Armed Forces of the Colonial Powers c.1700–1964* (Manchester: Palgrave, 2000).

# INDEX

# ABOUT THE AUTHOR

**Philip W. Blood** has taught at the University of Aachen and is now the general editor of the "Wehrmacht in War" series for the Association of the U.S. Army. A British citizen, he lives in Aachen, Germany.